# Linux®
## ALL-IN-ONE
## FOR
# DUMMIES®
### 4TH EDITION

## by Emmett Dulaney

## Wiley Publishing, Inc.

**Linux® All-in-One For Dummies®, 4th Edition**

Published by
**Wiley Publishing, Inc.**
111 River Street
Hoboken, NJ 07030-5774

www.wiley.com

Copyright © 2010 by Wiley Publishing, Inc., Indianapolis, Indiana

Published by Wiley Publishing, Inc., Indianapolis, Indiana

Published simultaneously in Canada

005.432 OCLC 14/2/2010
DUL

WILEY

# Dedication

For Karen, Kristin, Evan, and Spencer.

# About the Author

**Emmett Dulaney** is the author of several books on operating systems and certifications, and an assistant professor at Anderson University. Other books he has written include *CompTIA A+ Complete Study Guide* (Sybex) and *Security + Study Guide* (Sybex).

Emmett is a columnist for *CertCities* and is a contributor to a number of other magazines.

# Author's Acknowledgments

I would like to thank Naba Barkakati, who wrote the first two editions and did a fantastic job of condensing a wealth of information into a small tome. Equal thanks go to Graham Brown for his assistance in doing a similar task with the 4th edition of this book and never saw a task that couldn't be tackled.

I would also like to thank Elizabeth Zinkann for being one of the best technical editors in the business and Susan Pink for keeping everything on track and on time.

## Publisher's Acknowledgments

We're proud of this book; please send us your comments at http://dummies.custhelp.com. For other comments, please contact our Customer Care Department within the U.S. at 877-762-2974, outside the U.S. at 317-572-3993, or fax 317-572-4002.

Some of the people who helped bring this book to market include the following:

### Acquisitions and Editorial

**Project Editor:** Susan Pink
   *(Previous Edition: Pat O'Brien)*

**Acquisitions Editor:** Kyle Looper

**Copy Editor:** Susan Pink
   *(Previous Edition: Jen Riggs)*

**Technical Editor:** Elizabeth Zinkann

**Editorial Manager:** Jodi Jensen

**Editorial Assistant:** Leslie Saxman

**Sr. Editorial Assistant:** Cherie Case

**Cartoons:** Rich Tennant
   (www.the5thwave.com)

### Composition Services

**Project Coordinator:** Sheree Montgomery

**Layout and Graphics:** Samantha Cherolis

**Proofreaders:** Melissa Cossell,
   The Well-Chosen Word

**Indexer:** Sherry Massey

---

**Publishing and Editorial for Technology Dummies**

   **Richard Swadley,** Vice President and Executive Group Publisher

   **Andy Cummings,** Vice President and Publisher

   **Mary Bednarek,** Executive Acquisitions Director

   **Mary C. Corder,** Editorial Director

**Publishing for Consumer Dummies**

   **Diane Graves Steele,** Vice President and Publisher

**Composition Services**

   **Debbie Stailey,** Director of Composition Services

# Contents at a Glance

*Introduction* ........................................................... *1*

*Book I: Linux Basics* ............................................. *7*

Chapter 1: Introducing Linux ..............................................9

Chapter 2: Installing Linux...............................................31

Chapter 3: Installing Linux on a Flash Drive....................41

Chapter 4: Troubleshooting and Configuring Linux............45

Chapter 5: Trying Out Linux..............................................65

*Book II: Linux Desktops* .................................... *75*

Chapter 1: The GNOME Desktop........................................77

Chapter 2: The KDE Desktop ............................................87

Chapter 3: Commanding the Shell ....................................99

Chapter 4: Navigating the Linux File System ..................119

Chapter 5: Introducing Linux Applications ......................137

Chapter 6: Using Text Editors .........................................161

*Book III: Networking* ....................................... *173*

Chapter 1: Connecting to the Internet ............................175

Chapter 2: Setting Up a Local Area Network....................195

Chapter 3: Going Wireless ..............................................207

Chapter 4: Managing the Network ...................................217

*Book IV: The Internet* ....................................... *231*

Chapter 1: E-Mailing and IMing in Linux .........................233

Chapter 2: Browsing the Web..........................................249

Chapter 3: Reading Newsgroups and RSS Feeds...............261

Chapter 4: Using FTP .......................................................277

*Book V: Administration* .................................... *289*

Chapter 1: Introducing Basic System Administration........291

Chapter 2: Managing Users and Groups ..........................331

Chapter 3: Managing File Systems ..................................343

Chapter 4: Installing and Updating Applications..............367

# Book VI: Security .................................................... 389

Chapter 1: Introducing Linux Security ........................................ 391
Chapter 2: Securing Linux .................................................... 407
Chapter 3: Performing Computer Security Audits ............................... 437

# Book VII: Linux Servers ........................................ 453

Chapter 1: Managing Internet Services ........................................ 455
Chapter 2: Managing Mail and News Servers .................................... 473
Chapter 3: Managing DNS ...................................................... 495
Chapter 4: Working with Samba and NFS ........................................ 515

# Book VIII: Programming ......................................... 525

Chapter 1: Programming in Linux .............................................. 527
Chapter 2: Introductory Shell Scripting ...................................... 553
Chapter 3: Advanced Shell Scripting .......................................... 565

# Appendix: About the DVD ....................................... 573

# Index ......................................................... 589

# Table of Contents

*Introduction* ................................................................. *1*

About This Book ...........................................................2
Conventions Used in This Book...................................2
What You Don't Have to Read.......................................3
Who Are You? ...............................................................3
How This Book Is Organized .......................................3
What's on the DVD?......................................................5
Icons Used in This Book ...............................................5
Where to Go from Here.................................................6

*Book 1: Linux Basics* ................................................ *7*

**Chapter 1: Introducing Linux** . . . . . . . . . . . . . . . . . . . . . . . . . . . . . . .9

What Is Linux?..............................................................9
Linux distributions .............................................11
Making sense of version numbers .....................14
Linux Standard Base (LSB) ...............................15
Contents of a Linux Distribution ...............................16
GNU software.....................................................17
GUIs and applications .......................................20
Networks ............................................................21
Internet servers..................................................22
Software development .......................................22
Online documentation.......................................23
Managing Your PC with Linux....................................24
Disks, CD-ROMs, and DVD-ROMs .....................25
Peripheral devices .............................................26
File systems and sharing....................................26
Network ..............................................................27
Getting Started ...........................................................27
Step 1: Install .....................................................27
Step 2: Configure ...............................................28
Step 3: Explore...................................................28
Step 4: Find out more ........................................29

### Chapter 2: Installing Linux . . . . . . . . . . . . . . . . . . . . . . . . . . . . . . . . . . . 31

Following the Installation Steps . . . . . . . . . . . . . . . . . . . . . . . . . . . . . . . 31
Checking Your PC's Hardware . . . . . . . . . . . . . . . . . . . . . . . . . . . . . . . . 35
Trying the Ubuntu Live CD . . . . . . . . . . . . . . . . . . . . . . . . . . . . . . . . . . 36
Burning CDs or DVDs from ISO Images . . . . . . . . . . . . . . . . . . . . . . . 37
Setting Aside Space for Linux . . . . . . . . . . . . . . . . . . . . . . . . . . . . . . . . 38
Installing Ubuntu . . . . . . . . . . . . . . . . . . . . . . . . . . . . . . . . . . . . . . . . . . 39

### Chapter 3: Installing Linux on a Flash Drive . . . . . . . . . . . . . . . . . . . . 41

Creating the Bootable Flash Drive . . . . . . . . . . . . . . . . . . . . . . . . . . . . 41
Troubleshooting the Workstation . . . . . . . . . . . . . . . . . . . . . . . . . . . . . 43
Working Daily with the New Drive . . . . . . . . . . . . . . . . . . . . . . . . . . . . 44

### Chapter 4: Troubleshooting and Configuring Linux . . . . . . . . . . . . . . 45

Using Text Mode Installation . . . . . . . . . . . . . . . . . . . . . . . . . . . . . . . . 46
Troubleshooting X . . . . . . . . . . . . . . . . . . . . . . . . . . . . . . . . . . . . . . . . . 46
Resolving Other Installation Problems . . . . . . . . . . . . . . . . . . . . . . . . 48
    Using Knoppix boot commands . . . . . . . . . . . . . . . . . . . . . . . . . . 48
    The fatal signal 11 error . . . . . . . . . . . . . . . . . . . . . . . . . . . . . . . . 51
    Getting around the PC reboot problem . . . . . . . . . . . . . . . . . . . . 51
    Using Linux kernel boot options . . . . . . . . . . . . . . . . . . . . . . . . . 51
Setting Up Printers . . . . . . . . . . . . . . . . . . . . . . . . . . . . . . . . . . . . . . . . 55
Managing DVDs and CD-ROMs . . . . . . . . . . . . . . . . . . . . . . . . . . . . . . 58
Installing Other Software . . . . . . . . . . . . . . . . . . . . . . . . . . . . . . . . . . . 58
    Installing software in Debian and Ubuntu . . . . . . . . . . . . . . . . . 58
    Installing software in Fedora . . . . . . . . . . . . . . . . . . . . . . . . . . . . 61
    Installing software in SUSE . . . . . . . . . . . . . . . . . . . . . . . . . . . . . 62
    Installing software in Xandros . . . . . . . . . . . . . . . . . . . . . . . . . . 62

### Chapter 5: Trying Out Linux . . . . . . . . . . . . . . . . . . . . . . . . . . . . . . . . . . 65

Starting Linux . . . . . . . . . . . . . . . . . . . . . . . . . . . . . . . . . . . . . . . . . . . . 65
Playing with the Shell . . . . . . . . . . . . . . . . . . . . . . . . . . . . . . . . . . . . . . 68
    Starting the bash shell . . . . . . . . . . . . . . . . . . . . . . . . . . . . . . . . . 69
    Understanding shell commands . . . . . . . . . . . . . . . . . . . . . . . . . 70
    Trying a few Linux commands . . . . . . . . . . . . . . . . . . . . . . . . . . . 70
Shutting Down . . . . . . . . . . . . . . . . . . . . . . . . . . . . . . . . . . . . . . . . . . . . 72

## *Book II: Linux Desktops* . . . . . . . . . . . . . . . . . . . . . . . . . . . . . . . . *75*

### Chapter 1: The GNOME Desktop . . . . . . . . . . . . . . . . . . . . . . . . . . . . . . . 77

Getting to Know the GNOME Desktop . . . . . . . . . . . . . . . . . . . . . . . . . 78
    Desktop context menus . . . . . . . . . . . . . . . . . . . . . . . . . . . . . . . . 78
    Icon context menus . . . . . . . . . . . . . . . . . . . . . . . . . . . . . . . . . . . . 79

Understanding the GNOME Panels.................................................................80
    The top panel ..................................................................................81
    The Main Menu button...................................................................81
    The Places Menu button .................................................................83
    The System Menu button.................................................................84
    Top panel icons................................................................................85
    The bottom panel ...........................................................................85

**Chapter 2: The KDE Desktop.....................................87**
    Getting to Know the KDE Desktop..............................................................87
        Desktop context menus ..................................................................88
        Icon context menus .........................................................................89
    Understanding the KDE Panel......................................................................90
        The Main Menu button...................................................................90
        Panel icons.......................................................................................93
    Configuring the KDE Bottom Panel ............................................................94
    Configuring the KDE Desktop......................................................................95

**Chapter 3: Commanding the Shell ............................99**
    Opening Terminal Windows and Virtual Consoles ....................................99
    Using the bash Shell....................................................................................100
        Understanding the syntax of shell commands............................100
        Combining shell commands .........................................................102
        Controlling command input and output .....................................102
        Typing less with automatic command completion .......................105
        Going wild with asterisks and question marks ...........................105
        Repeating previously typed commands .......................................107
    Discovering and Using Linux Commands..................................................108
        Becoming root (superuser) ..........................................................111
        Managing processes .....................................................................112
        Working with date and time .........................................................113
        Processing files .............................................................................114
    Writing Shell Scripts...................................................................................117

**Chapter 4: Navigating the Linux File System ...............119**
    Understanding the Linux File System .......................................................119
    Navigating the File System with Linux Commands .................................124
        Commands for directory navigation ...........................................124
        Commands for directory listings and permissions ......................126
        Commands for changing permissions and ownerships...............128
        Commands for working with files ................................................129
        Commands for working with directories .....................................130
        Commands for finding files ..........................................................131
        Commands for mounting and unmounting...................................132
        Commands for checking disk-space usage....................................133

**Chapter 5: Introducing Linux Applications** . . . . . . . . . . . . . . . . . . . . .**137**

Taking Stock of Linux Applications . . . . . . . . . . . . . . . . . . . . . . . . . . . . . . . . . . . . 137
Introducing Office Applications and Tools . . . . . . . . . . . . . . . . . . . . . . . . . . . . 143
    OpenOffice.org office suite . . . . . . . . . . . . . . . . . . . . . . . . . . . . . . . . . . . 143
    Calendars . . . . . . . . . . . . . . . . . . . . . . . . . . . . . . . . . . . . . . . . . . . . . . . . . . . . 147
    Calculators . . . . . . . . . . . . . . . . . . . . . . . . . . . . . . . . . . . . . . . . . . . . . . . . . . . 148
Checking out Multimedia Applications . . . . . . . . . . . . . . . . . . . . . . . . . . . . . . . 149
    Using a digital camera . . . . . . . . . . . . . . . . . . . . . . . . . . . . . . . . . . . . . . . 149
    Playing audio CDs . . . . . . . . . . . . . . . . . . . . . . . . . . . . . . . . . . . . . . . . . . . 150
    Playing sound files . . . . . . . . . . . . . . . . . . . . . . . . . . . . . . . . . . . . . . . . . . 151
    Burning a CD . . . . . . . . . . . . . . . . . . . . . . . . . . . . . . . . . . . . . . . . . . . . . . . . 151
Using Graphics and Imaging Apps . . . . . . . . . . . . . . . . . . . . . . . . . . . . . . . . . . . 152
    The GIMP . . . . . . . . . . . . . . . . . . . . . . . . . . . . . . . . . . . . . . . . . . . . . . . . . . . . 152
    GNOME Ghostview . . . . . . . . . . . . . . . . . . . . . . . . . . . . . . . . . . . . . . . . . . 154
Using GUI File Managers . . . . . . . . . . . . . . . . . . . . . . . . . . . . . . . . . . . . . . . . . . . . 154
    Using the Nautilus shell . . . . . . . . . . . . . . . . . . . . . . . . . . . . . . . . . . . . . 154
    Using Dolphin . . . . . . . . . . . . . . . . . . . . . . . . . . . . . . . . . . . . . . . . . . . . . . . 157

**Chapter 6: Using Text Editors** . . . . . . . . . . . . . . . . . . . . . . . . . . . . . . . . .**161**

Using GUI Text Editors . . . . . . . . . . . . . . . . . . . . . . . . . . . . . . . . . . . . . . . . . . . . . . 161
Text Editing with ed and vi . . . . . . . . . . . . . . . . . . . . . . . . . . . . . . . . . . . . . . . . . . 163
    Using ed . . . . . . . . . . . . . . . . . . . . . . . . . . . . . . . . . . . . . . . . . . . . . . . . . . . . . 163
    Using vi . . . . . . . . . . . . . . . . . . . . . . . . . . . . . . . . . . . . . . . . . . . . . . . . . . . . . 167

# *Book III: Networking* . . . . . . . . . . . . . . . . . . . . . . . . . . . . . . . . *173*

**Chapter 1: Connecting to the Internet** . . . . . . . . . . . . . . . . . . . . . . . . . . .**175**

Understanding the Internet . . . . . . . . . . . . . . . . . . . . . . . . . . . . . . . . . . . . . . . . . . 175
Deciding How to Connect to the Internet . . . . . . . . . . . . . . . . . . . . . . . . . . . . . 176
Connecting with DSL . . . . . . . . . . . . . . . . . . . . . . . . . . . . . . . . . . . . . . . . . . . . . . . . 178
    How DSL works . . . . . . . . . . . . . . . . . . . . . . . . . . . . . . . . . . . . . . . . . . . . . 179
    DSL alphabet soup: ADSL, IDSL, SDSL . . . . . . . . . . . . . . . . . . . . . . . 180
    Typical DSL setup . . . . . . . . . . . . . . . . . . . . . . . . . . . . . . . . . . . . . . . . . . . 180
Connecting with a Cable Modem . . . . . . . . . . . . . . . . . . . . . . . . . . . . . . . . . . . . 184
    How a cable modem works . . . . . . . . . . . . . . . . . . . . . . . . . . . . . . . . . . 184
    Typical cable modem setup . . . . . . . . . . . . . . . . . . . . . . . . . . . . . . . . . . 186
Setting Up Dial-up Networking . . . . . . . . . . . . . . . . . . . . . . . . . . . . . . . . . . . . . . 189
    Connecting the modem . . . . . . . . . . . . . . . . . . . . . . . . . . . . . . . . . . . . . . 191
    Setting up and activating a PPP connection . . . . . . . . . . . . . . . . . . . 192
    Configuring CHAP and PAP authentication . . . . . . . . . . . . . . . . . . . 193

## Chapter 2: Setting Up a Local Area Network .................... 195

Understanding TCP/IP .................................................. 195
    IP addresses ........................................................ 197
    Internet services and port numbers ............................ 198
Setting Up an Ethernet LAN ........................................ 199
    How Ethernet works ............................................. 200
    Ethernet cables .................................................... 201
Configuring TCP/IP Networking .................................... 203
Connecting Your LAN to the Internet ............................. 204

## Chapter 3: Going Wireless ................................... 207

Understanding Wireless Ethernet Networks ....................... 207
    Understanding infrastructure and ad hoc modes .............. 208
    Understanding Wired Equivalent Privacy (WEP) .............. 209
Setting Up Wireless Hardware ...................................... 211
Configuring the Wireless Access Point ............................. 212
Configuring Wireless Networking .................................. 213

## Chapter 4: Managing the Network ........................... 217

Discovering the TCP/IP Configuration Files ....................... 217
    /etc/hosts .......................................................... 218
    /etc/networks ...................................................... 219
    /etc/host.conf ..................................................... 219
    /etc/resolv.conf ................................................... 219
    /etc/hosts.allow ................................................... 220
    /etc/hosts.deny ................................................... 220
    /etc/nsswitch.conf ................................................ 221
Checking Out TCP/IP Networks .................................... 221
    Checking the network interfaces ............................... 222
    Checking the IP routing table ................................... 222
    Checking connectivity to a host ................................ 223
    Checking network status ......................................... 224
    Sniffing network packets ........................................ 225
    Using GUI Tools .................................................. 226
Configuring Networks at Boot Time ............................... 227

## Book IV: The Internet .................................... 231

## Chapter 1: E-Mailing and IMing in Linux .................... 233

Understanding Electronic Mail ..................................... 234
    How MUAs and MTAs work ..................................... 234
    Mail message enhancements .................................... 235

Taking Stock of Mail Readers and IM Clients in Linux..........................236
E-Mailing in Linux .......................................................................237
Introducing Evolution..........................................................237
Introducing Thunderbird.....................................................241
Introducing KMail ...............................................................244
Instant Messaging in Linux...........................................................246
Using Pidgin.........................................................................246
Using Kopete ......................................................................247

**Chapter 2: Browsing the Web . . . . . . . . . . . . . . . . . . . . . . . . . . . . . . .249**

Discovering the Web ....................................................................249
Like a giant spider's web......................................................250
Links and URLs.....................................................................251
Web servers and Web browsers .........................................253
Web Browsing in Linux .................................................................254
Checking out Web browsers for Linux................................255
Introducing Firefox's user interface ..................................255
Changing your home page ...................................................258
Surfing the Net with Firefox................................................259

**Chapter 3: Reading Newsgroups and RSS Feeds. . . . . . . . . . . . . . . .261**

Understanding Newsgroups..........................................................261
Newsgroup hierarchy...........................................................262
Top-level newsgroup categories .........................................263
Linux-related newsgroups ...................................................264
Reading Newsgroups from Your ISP .............................................266
Taking stock of newsreaders...............................................266
Reading newsgroups with Thunderbird .............................267
Newsgroup subscriptions....................................................269
Posting news.........................................................................270
Using KNode .........................................................................271
Reading and Searching Newsgroups at Web Sites ......................272
Reading RSS Feeds.........................................................................273
Examining an RSS Feed........................................................274
Reading RSS Feeds ..............................................................275

**Chapter 4: Using FTP . . . . . . . . . . . . . . . . . . . . . . . . . . . . . . . . . . . . . . .277**

Using Graphical FTP Clients.........................................................277
Using gFTP ...........................................................................278
Introducing KFTPGrabber.....................................................280
Using a Web browser as an FTP client................................281
Using the Command-Line FTP Client............................................283

# Book V: Administration .............................. 289

## Chapter 1: Introducing Basic System Administration ............291

Taking Stock of System Administration Tasks........................291
Introducing Some GUI Sysadmin Tools ...............................293
    GUI sysadmin tools in Debian ....................................293
    GUI sysadmin tools in Fedora ....................................293
    GUI sysadmin tools in Knoppix...................................294
    GUI sysadmin tools in SUSE.......................................295
    GUI sysadmin tools in Ubuntu....................................296
    GUI sysadmin tools in Xandros ..................................297
How to Become root ....................................................298
    Using the su - command...........................................299
    Becoming root for the GUI utilities.............................299
    Recovering from a forgotten root password...................299
Understanding How Linux Boots......................................301
    Understanding the init process...................................301
    Examining the /etc/inittab file....................................303
    Trying a new run level with the init command .............304
    Understanding the Linux startup scripts.....................305
    Manually starting and stopping servers .....................306
    Automatically starting servers at system startup .........306
Taking Stock of Linux System Configuration Files .............307
Monitoring System Performance....................................310
    Using the top utility...............................................310
    Using the uptime command.......................................312
    Using the vmstat utility...........................................313
    Checking disk performance and disk usage ................314
Viewing System Information with the /proc File System.......315
Understanding Linux Devices .........................................319
    Device files..........................................................319
    Persistent device naming with udev ..........................321
Managing Loadable Driver Modules ................................322
    Loading and unloading modules................................322
    Using the /etc/modprobe.conf file..............................323
Scheduling Jobs in Linux.............................................324
    Scheduling one-time jobs.........................................325
    Scheduling recurring jobs........................................327

## Chapter 2: Managing Users and Groups ......................331

Adding User Accounts ................................................331
    Managing user accounts by using a GUI user manager ...............332
    Managing user accounts by using commands ...............334

XX *Linux All-in-One For Dummies, 4th Edition*

Understanding the /etc/passwd File .......................................................335
Managing Groups..................................................................................337
Exploring the User Environment ...........................................................338
Changing User and Group Ownership of Files...................................340

## Chapter 3: Managing File Systems . . . . . . . . . . . . . . . . . . . . . . . . . . . .343

Exploring the Linux File System .........................................................343
    Understanding the file-system hierarchy ..................................344
    Mounting a device on the file system.........................................347
    Examining the /etc/fstab file.......................................................349
Sharing Files with NFS..........................................................................350
    Exporting a file system with NFS...............................................351
    Mounting an NFS file system .....................................................352
Backing Up and Restoring Files ...........................................................352
    Selecting a backup strategy and media......................................353
    Commercial backup utilities for Linux......................................354
    Using the tape archiver — tar ....................................................354
Accessing a DOS or Windows File System...........................................359
    Mounting a DOS or Windows disk partition .............................359
    Mounting those old DOS floppy disks .......................................360
    Mounting an NTFS partition .......................................................362
Using mtools...........................................................................................362
    Trying mtools ...............................................................................363
    Understanding the /etc/mtools.conf file....................................363
    Understanding the mtools commands ........................................364

## Chapter 4: Installing and Updating Applications . . . . . . . . . . . . . . . .367

Working with RPM Files.........................................................................367
    Using the RPM command..............................................................368
    Understanding RPM filenames ...................................................369
    Querying RPMs...............................................................................369
    Installing an RPM ..........................................................................371
    Removing an RPM ..........................................................................372
    Upgrading an RPM .........................................................................372
    Verifying an RPM............................................................................373
Working with DEB Files..........................................................................374
    Understanding DEB filenames ....................................................374
    Using the dpkg command ............................................................375
    Introducing dselect.......................................................................376
    Using APT to manage DEB packages ..........................................377
Building Software Packages from Source Files ...................................378
    Downloading and unpacking the software ................................378
    Building the software from source files .....................................380
    Installing SRPMs.............................................................................382

Updating Linux Applications Online .......................................382
  Keeping Debian and Ubuntu updated with APT ...........383
  Updating Fedora Applications....................................383
  Updating SUSE online ...............................................387
  Using Xandros Networks.............................................387

## *Book VI: Security* ................................. **389**

### Chapter 1: Introducing Linux Security . . . . . . . . . . . . . . . . . . . . . .391

Why Worry about Security? ...............................................391
Establishing a Security Framework...................................392
  Determining business requirements for security.........393
  Performing risk analysis ............................................394
  Establishing a security policy ....................................395
  Implementing security solutions (mitigation) ...........396
  Managing security......................................................397
Securing Linux.....................................................................397
  Understanding the host security issues .....................398
  Understanding network security issues .....................398
Delving into Computer Security Terminology .................399
Keeping Up with Security News and Updates..................404

### Chapter 2: Securing Linux. . . . . . . . . . . . . . . . . . . . . . . . . . . . . . . .407

Securing Passwords ...........................................................407
  Shadow passwords .....................................................408
  Pluggable authentication modules (PAMs) ...............409
Protecting Files and Directories .......................................410
  Viewing ownerships and permissions........................410
  Changing file ownerships ...........................................411
  Changing file permissions ..........................................411
  Setting default permission..........................................412
  Checking for set user ID permission ..........................413
Encrypting and Signing Files with GnuPG .......................414
  Understanding public key encryption........................414
  Understanding digital signatures................................415
  Using GPG ....................................................................417
Monitoring System Security .............................................421
Securing Internet Services.................................................421
  Turning off standalone services..................................422
  Configuring the Internet super server........................422
  Configuring TCP wrapper security .............................423
Using Secure Shell (SSH) for Remote Logins...................424

Setting Up Simple Firewalls ................................................... 426
    Using NAT ...................................................................... 430
    Enabling packet filtering on your Linux system............................ 430

## Chapter 3: Performing Computer Security Audits . . . . . . . . . . . . . . .437

Understanding Security Audits................................................. 437
    Nontechnical aspects of security audits............................ 438
    Technical aspects of security audits.................................... 439
Implementing a Security Test Methodology ........................ 439
    Some common computer vulnerabilities.......................... 440
    Host-security review............................................................ 442
    Network-security review ..................................................... 445
Exploring Security Testing Tools ........................................... 447
    nmap..................................................................................... 448
    Nessus .................................................................................. 449

# Book VII: Linux Servers ................................................. 453

## Chapter 1: Managing Internet Services . . . . . . . . . . . . . . . . . . . . . .455

Understanding Internet Services............................................ 455
    TCP/IP and sockets............................................................. 456
    Internet services and port numbers................................ 459
Using the Internet Super Server............................................ 461
    Using inetd ........................................................................... 461
    Using xinetd ........................................................................ 462
Running Standalone Servers .................................................. 464
    Starting and stopping servers manually ........................ 465
    Starting servers automatically at boot time.................. 466

## Chapter 2: Managing Mail and News Servers . . . . . . . . . . . . . . . . .473

Installing the Mail Server........................................................ 473
    Using sendmail .................................................................. 474
    A mail-delivery test........................................................... 474
    The mail-delivery mechanism ......................................... 475
    The sendmail configuration file ...................................... 476
    Syntax of the sendmail.cf file........................................... 481
    Other sendmail files........................................................... 483
    The .forward file................................................................. 485
    The sendmail alias file....................................................... 485
Installing the INN Server........................................................ 486
Configuring and Starting the INN Server ............................. 486
    InterNetNews components ............................................... 487
    The incoming.conf file....................................................... 491

The readers.conf file.........................................................492
InterNetNews startup .......................................................492
Setting Up Local Newsgroups .................................................493
Defining a newsgroup hierarchy ...........................................493
Updating configuration files ..............................................493
Adding the newsgroups ....................................................494
Testing your newsgroups ..................................................494

## Chapter 3: Managing DNS ....................................495

Understanding Domain Name System (DNS) ...........................................495
What is DNS?....................................................................495
Discovering hierarchical domain names .......................................497
Exploring Berkeley Internet Name Domain (BIND) .....................498
Configuring DNS................................................................501
Configuring the resolver ....................................................502
Configuring a caching name server ........................................503
Configuring a primary name server.........................................513

## Chapter 4: Working with Samba and NFS .....................515

Sharing Files with NFS...........................................................515
Exporting a file system with NFS..........................................516
Mounting an NFS file system ..............................................518
Setting Up a Windows Server Using Samba...............................519
Installing Samba ............................................................521
Configuring Samba...........................................................521
Trying out Samba...........................................................523

# *Book VIII: Programming............................ 525*

## Chapter 1: Programming in Linux ...........................527

An Overview of Programming................................................527
A simplified view of a computer ...........................................527
Role of the operating system..............................................529
Basics of computer programming .........................................530
Exploring the Software-Development Tools in Linux...........................531
GNU C and C++ compilers................................................532
The GNU make utility .....................................................537
The GNU debugger.........................................................543
Understanding the Implications of GNU Licenses...........................550
The GNU General Public License .........................................550
The GNU Lesser General Public License.................................551

**Chapter 2: Introductory Shell Scripting** . . . . . . . . . . . . . . . . . . . . . . .**553**

Trying Out Simple Shell Scripts . . . . . . . . . . . . . . . . . . . . . . . . . . . . . . . . 553
Exploring the Basics of Shell Scripting . . . . . . . . . . . . . . . . . . . . . . . . . . 555
    Storing stuff . . . . . . . . . . . . . . . . . . . . . . . . . . . . . . . . . . . . . . . . . . . . 556
    Calling shell functions . . . . . . . . . . . . . . . . . . . . . . . . . . . . . . . . . . . . 556
    Controlling the flow . . . . . . . . . . . . . . . . . . . . . . . . . . . . . . . . . . . . . . 557
    Exploring bash's built-in commands . . . . . . . . . . . . . . . . . . . . . . . . 560

**Chapter 3: Working with Advanced Shell Scripting** . . . . . . . . . . . . .**565**

Trying Out sed . . . . . . . . . . . . . . . . . . . . . . . . . . . . . . . . . . . . . . . . . . . . . . 565
Working with awk and sed . . . . . . . . . . . . . . . . . . . . . . . . . . . . . . . . . . . . . 567
    Step one: Pull out the ISBN . . . . . . . . . . . . . . . . . . . . . . . . . . . . . . . . 568
    Step two: Calculate the 13th digit . . . . . . . . . . . . . . . . . . . . . . . . . . 569
    Step three: Add the 13th digit to the other 12 . . . . . . . . . . . . . . . . 570
    Step four: Finish the process . . . . . . . . . . . . . . . . . . . . . . . . . . . . . . 571
Final Notes on Shell Scripting . . . . . . . . . . . . . . . . . . . . . . . . . . . . . . . . . 571

*Appendix: About the DVD* . . . . . . . . . . . . . . . . . . . . . . . . . . . . . *573*

System Requirements . . . . . . . . . . . . . . . . . . . . . . . . . . . . . . . . . . . . . . . . 573
DVD Installation Instructions . . . . . . . . . . . . . . . . . . . . . . . . . . . . . . . . . . 574
    Starting Linux . . . . . . . . . . . . . . . . . . . . . . . . . . . . . . . . . . . . . . . . . . 575
    Other options . . . . . . . . . . . . . . . . . . . . . . . . . . . . . . . . . . . . . . . . . . 576
What You'll Find on the DVD . . . . . . . . . . . . . . . . . . . . . . . . . . . . . . . . . . . 576
Troubleshooting . . . . . . . . . . . . . . . . . . . . . . . . . . . . . . . . . . . . . . . . . . . . . 578

*Index* . . . . . . . . . . . . . . . . . . . . . . . . . . . . . . . . . . . . . . . . . . . . . . . *589*

# Introduction

*L*inux is truly amazing when you consider how it originated and how it continues to evolve. From its modest beginning as the hobby of one person — Linus Torvalds of Finland — Linux has grown into a full-fledged operating system with features that rival those of any commercial UNIX operating system. To top it off, Linux — with all of its source code — is available free to anyone. All you have to do is download it from an Internet site or get it on CDs or a DVD for a nominal fee from one of many Linux CD vendors.

Linux certainly is an exception to the rule that "you get what you pay for." Even though Linux is free, it is no slouch when it comes to performance, features, and reliability. The robustness of Linux has to do with the way it is developed and updated. Developers around the world collaborate to add features. Incremental versions are continually downloaded by users and tested in a variety of system configurations. Linux revisions go through much more rigorous beta testing than any commercial software does.

Since the release of Linux kernel 1.0 on March 14, 1994, the number of Linux users around the world has grown exponentially. Many Linux distributions — combinations of the operating system with applications and installation tools — have been developed to simplify installation and use. Some Linux distributions are commercially sold and supported, while many continue to be freely available.

Linux, unlike many freely available software programs, comes with extensive online information on topics such as installing and configuring the operating system for a wide variety of PCs and peripherals. A small group of hard-core Linux users are expert enough to productively use Linux with the online documentation alone. A much larger number of users, however, move to Linux with some specific purpose in mind (such as setting up a Web server or learning Linux). Also, a large number of Linux users use their systems at home. For these new users, the online documentation is not easy to use and typically does not cover the specific uses of Linux that the user may have in mind.

If you're beginning to use Linux, what you need is a practical guide that not only gets you going with Linux installation and setup but also shows you how to use Linux for a specific task. You may also want to try out different Linux distributions before settling on one.

Accordingly, *Linux All-in-One For Dummies,* 4th Edition comes with a DVD that includes five Linux distributions — Debian GNU/Linux, Fedora, open-SUSE Linux, Ubuntu, and Xandros — and the instructions to install and use any of these distributions.

# About This Book

*Linux All-in-One For Dummies* gives you eight quick-reference guides in a single book. Taken together, these eight minibooks provide detailed information on installing, configuring, and using Linux.

What you'll like most about this book is that you don't have to sequentially read each chapter by chapter or even each section in a chapter. You can pretty much turn to the topic you want and quickly get the answer to your pressing questions about Linux, be it about using the OpenOffice.org word processor or setting up the Apache Web server.

Here are some of the things you can do with this book:

✦ Install and configure Linux — Debian, Fedora, openSUSE, Ubuntu, or Xandros — from the DVD-ROM included with the book

✦ Connect the Linux PC to the Internet through a DSL or cable modem as well as dial-up

✦ Add a wireless Ethernet to your existing network

✦ Get tips, techniques, and shortcuts for specific uses of Linux, such as

  • Setting up and using Internet services: Web, Mail, News, FTP, NFS, and DNS

  • Setting up a Windows server using Samba

  • Using Linux commands

  • Using shell programming

  • Using the OpenOffice.org office suite and other applications that come with Linux

✦ Understand the basics of system and network security

✦ Perform system administration tasks

# Conventions Used in This Book

I use a simple notational style in this book. All listings, filenames, function names, variable names, and keywords are typeset in a `monospace` font for ease of reading. I *italicize* the first occurrences of new terms and concepts and then provide a definition right there. I show typed commands in **boldface.** The output of commands and any listing of files are shown in a `monospace` font.

# What You Don't Have to Read

Each minibook zeros in on a specific task area — such as using the Internet or running Internet servers — and then provides hands-on instructions on how to perform a series of related tasks. You can jump right to a section and read about a specific task. You don't have to read anything but the few paragraphs or the list of steps that relate to your question. Use the Table of Contents or the Index to locate the pages relevant to your question.

You can safely ignore text next to the Technical Stuff icons as well as text in sidebars. However, if you're the kind of person who likes to know some of the hidden details of how Linux works, by all means, dig into the Technical Stuff icons and the sidebars.

# Who Are You?

I assume that you are familiar with a PC — you know how to turn it on and off and you have dabbled with Windows. Considering that most new PCs come preloaded with Windows, this assumption is safe, right? And you know how to use some Windows applications, such as Microsoft Office.

When installing Linux on your PC, you may want to retain your Windows installations. I assume that you don't mind shrinking the Windows partition to make room for Linux. For this you can invest in a good disk-partitioning tool or use one of the partitioning tools included with most Linux distributions.

I also assume that you're willing to accept the risk that when you try to install Linux, some things may not quite work. Problems can happen if you have some uncommon types of hardware. If you're afraid of ruining your system, try finding a slightly older, spare Pentium PC that you can sacrifice and then install Linux on that PC.

# How This Book Is Organized

*Linux All-in-One Desk Reference For Dummies* has eight minibooks, each of which focuses on a small set of related topics. If you're looking for information on a specific topic, check the minibook names on the spine or consult the Table of Contents.

This desk reference starts with a minibook that explains the basics of Linux and guides you through the installation process (a useful aspect of this book because you typically do not purchase a PC with Linux pre-installed). The second minibook serves as a user's guide to Linux — it focuses on exploring various aspects of a Linux workstation, including the GNOME and KDE GUIs and many of the applications that come bundled with Linux. The third minibook covers networking, and the fourth minibook goes into using the Internet. The fifth minibook introduces system administration. The sixth minibook turns to the important subject of securing a Linux system and its associated network. The seventh minibook shows you how to run a variety of Internet servers from mail to a Web server. The eighth and final minibook introduces you to programming.

Here's a quick overview of the eight books and what they contain:

✦ **Book I, Linux Basics:** What is Linux? Understanding what's new in the latest Linux kernel. Installing, configuring, and troubleshooting different Linux distributions. Taking Linux for a test drive.

✦ **Book II, Linux Desktops:** Exploring GNOME and KDE. Using the shell (what's a shell anyway?). Navigating the Linux file system. Exploring the applications such as multimedia software as well as the text editors (vi and ed).

✦ **Book III, Networking:** Connecting the Linux PC to the Internet through a dial-up connection or a high-speed, always-on connection such as DSL or cable modem. Configuring and managing TCP/IP networks, including wireless networks.

✦ **Book IV, The Internet:** Using various Internet services such as e-mail, Web surfing, and reading newsgroups. Transferring files with FTP.

✦ **Book V, Administration:** Performing basic system administration. Managing user accounts and the file system. Installing applications. Working with devices and printers. Using USB devices. Upgrading and customizing the Linux kernel.

✦ **Book VI, Security:** Understanding network and host security. Securing the host and the network. Performing security audits.

✦ **Book VII, Linux Servers:** Managing Internet services. Configuring the Apache Web server. Setting up the FTP server. Configuring the mail and news servers. Providing DNS. File sharing with NFS. Using Samba to set up a Windows server.

✦ **Book VIII, Programming:** Finding out the basics of programming. Exploring the software development tools in Linux. Writing shell scripts.

---

## Sidebars

Sometimes, I use sidebars to highlight interesting, but not critical, information. Sidebars explain concepts you may not have encountered before or give a little insight into a related topic. If you're in a hurry, you can safely skip the sidebars.

---

# What's on the DVD?

The DVD contains five Linux distributions — `dists` folders contain ISO image files for Debian, Fedora, openSUSE, Ubuntu, and Xandros, organized into individual folders. You may use the DVD in accordance with the license agreements accompanying the software.

# Icons Used in This Book

Following the time-honored tradition of the *All-in-One For Dummies* series, I use icons to help you quickly pinpoint useful information. The icons include the following:

The Distribution Specific icon points out information that applies to specific distributions that this book covers: Debian, Fedora, Knoppix, SUSE, Ubuntu, and Xandros.

The Remember icon marks a general, interesting fact — something that you want to know and remember. You might even find interesting trivia worth bringing up at an evening dinner party.

When you see the Tip icon, you're about to read about something you can do to make your job easier. Long after you've finished with the first reading of this book, you can skim the book, looking for only the tips.

I use the Warning icon to highlight potential pitfalls. With this icon, I'm telling you: "Watch out! Whatever is being discussed could hurt your system." They say that those who are forewarned are forearmed, so I hope these entities will save you some frustration.

The Technical Stuff icon marks technical information that could be of interest to an advanced user (or those aspiring to be advanced users).

## *Where to Go from Here*

It's time to get started on your Linux adventure. Take out the DVD and install Linux — choose a distribution, any distribution (as long as it's Debian, Fedora, openSUSE, Ubuntu, or Xandros). Then, turn to a relevant chapter and let the fun begin. Use the Table of Contents and the Index to figure out where you want to go. Before you know it, you'll become an expert at Linux!

I hope you enjoy consulting this book as much as I enjoyed writing it!

# Book I

# Linux Basics

"Drive carefully, remember your lunch, and always make a backup of your directory tree before modifying your hard disk partition file."

# Contents at a Glance

**Chapter 1: Introducing Linux** . . . . . . . . . . . . . . . . . . . . . . . . . . . . . .**9**

What Is Linux? . . . . . . . . . . . . . . . . . . . . . . . . . . . . . . . . . . . . . . . . . . . . . . . . . .9

Contents of a Linux Distribution . . . . . . . . . . . . . . . . . . . . . . . . . . . . . . 16

Managing Your PC with Linux . . . . . . . . . . . . . . . . . . . . . . . . . . . . . . . . . . 24

Getting Started . . . . . . . . . . . . . . . . . . . . . . . . . . . . . . . . . . . . . . . . . . . . . . . . 27

**Chapter 2: Installing Linux** . . . . . . . . . . . . . . . . . . . . . . . . . . . . . . .**31**

Following the Installation Steps . . . . . . . . . . . . . . . . . . . . . . . . . . . . . . . . 31

Checking Your PC's Hardware . . . . . . . . . . . . . . . . . . . . . . . . . . . . . . . . . . 35

Trying the Ubuntu Live CD . . . . . . . . . . . . . . . . . . . . . . . . . . . . . . . . . . . . . 36

Burning CDs or DVDs from ISO Images . . . . . . . . . . . . . . . . . . . . . . . . . 37

Setting Aside Space for Linux . . . . . . . . . . . . . . . . . . . . . . . . . . . . . . . . . . 38

Installing Ubuntu . . . . . . . . . . . . . . . . . . . . . . . . . . . . . . . . . . . . . . . . . . . . . . . 39

**Chapter 3: Installing Linux on a Flash Drive** . . . . . . . . . . . . . . . . .**41**

Creating the Bootable Flash Drive . . . . . . . . . . . . . . . . . . . . . . . . . . . . . . 41

Troubleshooting the Workstation . . . . . . . . . . . . . . . . . . . . . . . . . . . . . . . 43

Working Daily with the New Drive . . . . . . . . . . . . . . . . . . . . . . . . . . . . . . 44

**Chapter 4: Troubleshooting and Configuring Linux** . . . . . . . . . . . . . . .**45**

Using Text Mode Installation . . . . . . . . . . . . . . . . . . . . . . . . . . . . . . . . . . . 46

Troubleshooting X . . . . . . . . . . . . . . . . . . . . . . . . . . . . . . . . . . . . . . . . . . . . . 46

Resolving Other Installation Problems . . . . . . . . . . . . . . . . . . . . . . . . . . 48

Setting Up Printers . . . . . . . . . . . . . . . . . . . . . . . . . . . . . . . . . . . . . . . . . . . . 55

Managing DVDs and CD-ROMs . . . . . . . . . . . . . . . . . . . . . . . . . . . . . . . . . 58

Installing Other Software . . . . . . . . . . . . . . . . . . . . . . . . . . . . . . . . . . . . . . 58

**Chapter 5: Trying Out Linux** . . . . . . . . . . . . . . . . . . . . . . . . . . . . . .**65**

Starting Linux . . . . . . . . . . . . . . . . . . . . . . . . . . . . . . . . . . . . . . . . . . . . . . . . . 65

Playing with the Shell . . . . . . . . . . . . . . . . . . . . . . . . . . . . . . . . . . . . . . . . . . 68

Shutting Down . . . . . . . . . . . . . . . . . . . . . . . . . . . . . . . . . . . . . . . . . . . . . . . . . 72

# Chapter 1: Introducing Linux

## In This Chapter

✔ Explaining what Linux is

✔ Going over what Linux distributions typically include

✔ Discovering what Linux helps you manage

✔ Getting started with Linux

*B*y virtue of your holding this book in your hands, it's a safe bet that you've heard something about Linux. If you're wondering just exactly what Linux is, whether it's worth serious consideration, and what it can help you do, this chapter is for you. Here, I provide a broad picture of Linux and tell you how you can start using it right away.

Although Linux can run on many platforms, this book focuses on Linux for Intel 80x86 and Pentium processors (basically any PC that can run any flavor of Windows).

## What Is Linux?

A PC can be thought of as a combination of *hardware* — things you can touch, such as the system box, monitor, keyboard, and mouse. The system box contains the most important hardware of all — the *central processing unit* (CPU), the microchip that runs the *software* (any program that tells the computer how to do your bidding), which you can't actually touch. In a typical Pentium-based PC, the Pentium microprocessor is the CPU. Other important hardware in the system box includes the memory (RAM chips) and the hard drive.

The *operating system* is the program that has to interact with all the hardware and get it to play nice. The operating system software manages all that hardware and runs other software at your command. You, the user, provide those commands by choosing menus, clicking icons, or typing cryptic text. Linux is an operating system — as are UNIX, Windows XP, and Windows Vista. The Linux operating system is modeled after UNIX; in its most basic, no-frills form, the Linux operating system also goes by *Linux kernel*.

## Does Linux really run on any computer?

Linux has so many distributions that it does seem able to run on nearly any type of computer.

Linus Torvalds and other programmers developed Linux for the Intel 80x86 (and compatible) line of processors. This book covers Linux for Intel 80x86 and Pentium processors. (These are known as the IA32 architecture processors, or i386, because they support the instruction set of the 80386 processor.)

Nowadays, Linux is also available for systems based on other processors — such as the following:

✔ AMD's 64-bit AMD64 processors

✔ The Motorola 68000 family

✔ Alpha AXPs

✔ Sun SPARCs and UltraSPARCs

✔ Hewlett-Packard's HP PA-RISC

✔ The PowerPC and PowerPC64 processors

✔ The MIPS R4x00 and R5x00

IBM has released its own version of Linux for its S/390 and zSeries mainframes. And a number of popular Linux distributions, including Ubuntu and Fedora, can even be run on Sony's Playstation 3 video game system.

The operating system is what gives a computer — any computer — its personality. For example, you can run Windows XP or Windows Vista on a PC — and on that same PC, you can also install and run Linux. Then, depending on which operating system is installed and running at any particular time, the same PC can be a Windows XP system or a Linux system.

The primary job of an operating system is to load software (computer programs) from the hard drive (or other permanent storage) into the memory and get the CPU to run those programs. Everything you do with your computer is possible because of the operating system, so if the operating system somehow messes up, the entire system freezes. You may know how infuriating it can be when your favorite operating system — maybe even the one that came with your PC — suddenly calls it quits just as you were about to click the Send button after composing that long e-mail to your friend. You try a number of things frantically, but nothing happens. Then it's time for the Reset button (or pulling the cord from the back of the machine if your computer's builders weren't wise enough to include a Reset). Luckily, that sort of thing almost never happens with Linux — it has a reputation for being a very reliable operating system.

In technical mumbo jumbo, Linux is a *multiuser, multitasking operating system.* Those terms just mean that Linux enables multiple users to log in, and each of those users can run more than one program at the same time. Nearly all operating systems are multiuser and multitasking these days, but when Linux first started in 1993, *multiuser* and *multitasking* were big selling points.

## Linux distributions

A *Linux distribution* consists of the Linux *kernel* (the operating system) and a collection of applications, together with an easy-to-use installation program.

Most people just say *Linux* to refer to a specific Linux distribution.

You will find many Linux distributions, and each includes the standard Linux operating system and the following major packages:

+ **The X Window System:** It's the graphical user interface.

+ **One or more graphical desktops:** Among the most popular are GNOME and KDE.

+ **A selection of applications:** Linux programs come in the form of ready-to-run software, but the *source code* (the commands we humans use to tell the computer what to do) is included (or available), as is its documentation.

    Current Linux distributions include a huge selection of software — so much that some distributions usually require multiple CD-ROMs or a single DVD-ROM (which this book includes).

The development and maintenance of the Linux kernel, the software packages in a Linux distribution, and the Linux distributions themselves are organized as *open source* projects. In a nutshell, *open source* means access to the source code and the right to freely redistribute the software without any restrictions. There's a lot more to the definition than this succinct note. To find out the details of what open source means and the acceptable open source licenses, you can visit the Open Source Initiative Web site at www. opensource.org.

Table 1-1 lists a few major Linux distributions along with a brief description of each. Note, however, that there are many more Linux distributions than the ones shown in Table 1-1. To find out more about Linux distributions, visit DistroWatch.com at http://distrowatch.com. At that Web site, you can read up on specific distributions as well as find links for ordering CDs or DVDs for specific distributions.

| Table 1-1 | Major Linux Distributions |
| --- | --- |
| *Distribution* | *Description* |
| Debian GNU/Linux | This noncommercial distribution started in 1993 and continues to be a popular distribution, with many volunteer developers around the world contributing to the project. Debian is a huge distribution that takes some time to install. After you have installed the base Debian system, you can install and upgrade Debian packages easily with a package installer called `apt-get` (where *apt* stands for the Advanced Package Tool.) Debian is available free of charge from `www.debian.org`. Debian is the basis for several other recent distributions including Knoppix, MEPIS, Ubuntu, and Xandros. |
| Fedora | This distribution, once known as Fedora Core, is the successor to Red Hat Linux, which is the Linux distribution from Red Hat. Fedora Core 1, released in November 2003, was the successor to Red Hat Linux 9. The alpha release of Fedora 13 was March 2010. Fedora is freely available and uses the Red Hat Package Manager (RPM) format for its software packages. You can download Fedora Core from `http://fedoraproject.org`. |
| Gentoo Linux | This is a noncommercial, *source-based* (all software is provided in source code form) distribution that first appeared in 2002. The installer provides some binary packages to get the Linux going, but the idea is to compile all source packages on the user's computer. The requirement to install so much makes it time-consuming to build a full-fledged Gentoo system with the latest graphical desktops, multimedia, and development tools because all the packages have to be downloaded and compiled. Gentoo Linux is freely available from `www.gentoo.org`. |
| Knoppix | This Live CD distribution is based on Debian and named after its developer, Klaus Knopper of Germany. Knoppix can be used as a recovery tool (to fix problems with an already installed Linux system) because you can run Knoppix directly from the CD without having to first install it on the hard drive. (Although other distributions have this capability, Knoppix is ideally suited for the task.) The Knoppix CD stores software in compressed format, and Knoppix decompresses the programs on-the-fly. With this approach, Knoppix can pack up to 2GB of software on a CD. Knoppix uses the Debian package management. Knoppix 6.2 was released in November 2009. For information on downloading Knoppix free of charge, visit the Knoppix Web site at `www.knopper.net/knoppix/index-en.html`. |
| Linspire | This commercial distribution was first released in 2002 under the name LindowsOS. Linspire uses the Debian package format and offers software downloads for a fee through what it calls the Click-N-Run Web-based interface. You can download a Live CD version called LindowsLive! via BitTorrent. In 2008, Linspire was acquired by Xandros. For more information about Linspire, visit `www.linspire.com`. |

| Distribution | Description |
|---|---|
| Mandriva Linux One | This popular distribution began life as a 1998 release of Red Hat Linux with an easy-to-use installer and with KDE as the default desktop. Until recently, this distribution was called Mandrakelinux. Mandriva Linux One uses the Red Hat Package Manager (RPM) format for its software packages. You can download the latest version at `www.mandriva.com`. Click the Download link for more information. Mandriva also offers Mandriva Flash — an 8GB bootable flash drive that contains everything you need to get the operating system up and running without installing it on the hard drive. |
| MEPIS Linux | This Debian-based Live CD distribution was first released in July 2003. It includes a graphical installer that can be launched from the Live CD to install MEPIS on the hard drive. MEPIS has good hardware detection and comes with Java and multimedia software, which makes it popular. MEPIS uses the Debian package format. You can download the SimplyMEPIS Live CD free of charge from `www.mepis.org`. |
| Slackware Linux | This distribution is one of the oldest, having been first released in 1992. Slackware uses compressed `tar` files for its packages and provides a text-based installer with limited automatic detection of hardware. You do all software configurations by editing text files. Slackware is freely available from `www.slackware.com`. |
| SUSE Linux | This commercial distribution switched to a community development project called openSUSE in August 2005. SUSE Linux Open Source Software (OSS) is now freely available, and the retail SUSE Linux is based on the open source version. SUSE comes with the YaST installation and configuration tool, which is one of the best administration tools available. SUSE Linux uses RPM packages. The openSUSE project provides the ISO image files from various mirror sites (see `http://en.opensuse.org/Download`). Visit `www.opensuse.org` for more information. |
| Ubuntu Linux | This Debian-based, noncommercial Linux distribution has become very popular since its initial release in 2004. Ubuntu is available as both an install CD and a Live CD. Because it's Debian based, you can install the basic desktop system from the install CD and then use the `apt-get` tool to install other packages as well as keep the system up-to-date. You can download Ubuntu free of charge from `www.ubuntulinux.com`. |
| Xandros Desktop OS | This distribution is the successor to Corel Linux and is based on Debian. Xandros is aimed at first-time Linux users, with an installer that can repartition the hard drive. The versatile Xandros File Manager is a key selling point of this distribution. However, Xandros includes some proprietary components that prevent redistribution. A trial version of both Xandros Desktop and Server can be downloaded for evaluation. In 2008, Xandros acquired Linspire, developer of the Linspire and Freespire Linux desktop operating systems. Visit `www.xandros.com` for more information about Xandros. |

As you can see from the brief descriptions in Table 1-1, some Linux distributions, such as Knoppix and MEPIS, are in the form of Live CDs. A *Live CD* (or Live DVD) includes a Linux kernel that you can boot and run directly from the CD or DVD without having to first install it on your hard drive. Such Live CD distributions can be handy if you want to try out a distribution before you decide whether to install it.

Many Linux distributions, such as SUSE Linux and Xandros Desktop, are commercial products that you can buy online or in computer stores and bookstores. If you have heard about open source and the *GNU* (which stands for GNU's Not UNIX) license, you may think that no one can sell Linux for profit. Luckily for companies that sell Linux distributions, the GNU license — also called the GNU General Public License (GPL) — does allow commercial, for-profit distribution (but requires that the software be distributed in source-code form) and stipulates that anyone may copy and distribute the software in source-code form to anyone else. Several Linux distributions are available free of charge under the GPL, which means that the publisher may include these distributions on a DVD-ROM with this book and that you may make as many copies of the DVD as you like.

## Making sense of version numbers

The Linux kernel and each Linux distribution have their own version number. Additional software programs (such as GNOME and KDE) that come with the Linux distribution have their own version numbers as well. The version numbers for the Linux kernel and the Linux distributions are unrelated, but each has particular significance.

### Linux kernel version numbers

After Linux kernel version 1.0 was released on March 14, 1994, the loosely knit Linux development community adopted a version-numbering scheme. Version numbers such as 1.*x.y* and 2.*x.y*, where *x* is an even number, are considered the stable versions. The last number, *y*, is the patch level, which is incremented as problems are fixed. For example, 2.6.14 is a typical, stable version of the Linux kernel. Notice that these version numbers are in the form of three integers separated by periods — *major.minor.patch* — where *major* and *minor* are numbers denoting the major and minor version numbers, and *patch* is another number representing the patch level.

Version numbers of the form 2.*x.y* with an odd *x* number are beta releases for developers only; they may be unstable, so you shouldn't adopt such versions for day-to-day use. For example, if you were to find version 2.7.5 of the Linux kernel, the 7 in the minor version number tells you it's a beta release. Developers add new features to these odd-numbered versions of Linux.

You can find out about the latest version of the Linux kernel online at `www.kernel.org`.

### Distribution-specific version numbers

Each Linux distribution has a version number as well. These version numbers usually follow the format *x.y,* where *x* is the *major* version, and *y* is the *minor* version.

Unlike with the Linux kernel version numbers, no special meaning is associated with odd- and even-numbered minor versions. Each version of a Linux distribution includes specific versions of the Linux kernel and other major components, such as GNOME, KDE, and various applications.

The developers of active Linux distributions usually release new versions of their distribution on a regular basis — about every six to nine months. For example, Ubuntu 9.10 was released in October 2009; 10.04 was released in April 2010. Typically, each new major version of a Linux distribution provides significant new features.

Debian always has at least three releases at any time — *stable, unstable,* and *testing.*

✦ **Stable:** Most users prefer this type of release because it's the latest officially released distribution.

✦ **Unstable:** The developers are working on this release.

✦ **Testing:** The release contains packages that have gone through some testing but aren't ready for inclusion in the stable release yet.

## Linux Standard Base (LSB)

Linux has become important enough that there's a standard for Linux called the Linux Standard Base (or LSB, for short). *LSB* is a set of binary standards that should help reduce variations among the Linux distributions and promote portability of applications. The idea behind LSB is to provide an application binary interface (ABI) so that software applications can run on any Linux (or other UNIX) systems that conform to the LSB standard. The LSB specification references POSIX (Portable Operating System Interface) standards as well as many other standards, such as the C and C++ programming language standards, the X Window System version 11 release 6 (X11R6), and the Filesystem Hierarchy Standard (FHS). LSB version 1.2 (commonly referred to as *LSB 1.2*) was released on June 28, 2002. LSB 2.0 was released on August 30, 2004, and LSB 4.0, on November 11, 2008.

The LSB specification is organized into two parts — a common specification that remains the same across all types of processors and a set of hardware-specific specifications, one for each type of processor architecture. For example, LSB 1.2 has architecture-specific specifications for Intel 32-bit (IA32) and PowerPC 32-bit (PPC32) processors. LSB 1.3 adds a specification for the Intel 64-bit (IA64) architecture and IBM zSeries 31-bit (S390) and 64-bit (S390X) processors, in addition to the ones for IA32 and PPC32. LSB 2.0 added specification for the AMD 64-bit (AMD64 or X86_64) processors. The current LSB specification — LSB 4.0 — supports seven processor architectures: IA32, IA64, PPC32, PPC64 (64-bit PowerPC), S390, S390X, and X86_64.

An LSB certification program exists. By now, several Linux distributions are certified to be LSB 1.3 compliant, IA32 runtime environments. Several others are certified as LSB 2.0 compliant, IA32 runtime environments. Distributions currently LSB 3.1 certified include Red Hat Enterprise Linux Version 5, open-SUSE 10.2, and Xandros Server 1.0. LSB 4.0 certified distributions include Mandriva Enterprise Server 5, SUSE Linux Enterprise 11, and Ubuntu 9.04.

To discover more about LSB, visit `www.linuxbase.org`. The latest list of LSB-certified systems is available at `www.linux-foundation.org/en/LSB_Distribution_Status`.

## Contents of a Linux Distribution

A Linux distribution comes with the Linux kernel and a lot more software. These software packages include everything from graphical desktops to Internet servers to programming tools for creating new software. In this section, I briefly describe some major software packages that are bundled with typical Linux distributions. Without this bundled software, Linux wouldn't be as popular as it is today.

# What is the GNU Project?

*GNU* is a recursive acronym that stands for GNU's Not UNIX. The GNU Project was launched in 1984 by Richard Stallman to develop a complete UNIX-like operating system. The GNU Project developed nearly everything needed for a complete operating system except for the operating system kernel.

All GNU software was distributed under the GNU General Public License (GPL). GPL essentially requires that the software is distributed in source-code form and stipulates that any user may copy, modify, and distribute the software to anyone else in source-code form. Users may, however, have to pay for their individual copies of GNU software. (The GPL is printed in the back of this book.)

The Free Software Foundation (FSF) is a tax-exempt charity that raises funds for work on the GNU Project. To find out more about the GNU Project, visit its home page at `www.gnu.org`. The home page is also where you can find information about how to contact the Free Software Foundation and how to help the GNU Project.

## GNU software

At the heart of a Linux distribution is a collection of software that came from the GNU Project. You get to know these GNU utilities only if you use your Linux system through a *text terminal* — a basic command-line interface that doesn't use on-screen visuals but a prompt at which you type your commands. (Or you could use a graphical window that mimics a text terminal and still have use of GNU utilities.) The GNU software is one of the basic parts of any Linux distribution.

As a Linux user, you may not realize the extent to which all Linux distributions rely on GNU software. Nearly all the tasks you perform in a Linux system involve one or more GNU software packages. For example, the GNOME graphical user interface (GUI) and the command interpreter (that is, the bash) are both GNU software programs. By the way, the *shell* is the command-interpreter application that accepts the commands you type and then runs programs in response to those commands. If you rebuild the kernel or develop software, you do so with the GNU C and C++ *compiler* (which is part of the GNU software that accompanies Linux). If you edit text files with the ed or emacs editor, you're again using a GNU software package. The list goes on and on.

Table 1-2 lists some well-known GNU software packages that come with most Linux distributions. Depending on your interests, you may never need to use many of these packages, but knowing what they are there in case you ever do need them is a good idea.

| Table 1-2 | Well-Known GNU Software Packages |
|---|---|
| *Software Package* | *Description* |
| autoconf | Generates shell scripts that automatically configure source-code packages |
| automake | Generates Makefile.in files for use with autoconf |
| bash | The default shell (command interpreter) in Linux |
| bc | An interactive calculator with arbitrary precision numbers |
| Binutils | A package that includes several utilities for working with binary files: ar, as, gasp, gprof, ld, nm, objcopy, objdump, ranlib, readelf, size, strings, and strip |

*(continued)*

### Table 1-2 *(continued)*

| Software Package | Description |
|---|---|
| Coreutils | A package that combines three individual packages called Fileutils, Shellutils, and Textutils and implements utilities such as `chgrp, chmod, chown, cp, dd, df, dir, dircolors, du, install, ln, ls, mkdir, mkfifo, mknod, mv, rm, rmdir, sync, touch, vdir, basename, chroot, date, dirname, echo, env, expr, factor, false, groups, hostname, id, logname, nice, nohup, pathchk, printenv, printf, pwd, seq, sleep, stty, su, tee, test, true, tty, uname, uptime, users, who, whoami, yes, cut, join, nl, split, tail,` and `wc` |
| `cpio` | Copies file archives to and from disk or to another part of the file system |
| `diff` | Compares files, showing line-by-line changes in several different formats |
| `ed` | A line-oriented text editor |
| `emacs` | An extensible, customizable, full-screen text editor and computing environment |
| Findutils | A package that includes the `find, locate,` and `xargs` utilities |
| `finger` | A utility program designed to enable users on the Internet to get information about one another |
| `gawk` | The GNU Project's implementation of the `awk` programming language |
| `gcc` | Compilers for C, C++, Objective C, and other languages |
| `gdb` | Source-level debugger for C, C++, and Fortran |
| `gdbm` | A replacement for the traditional `dbm` and `ndbm` database libraries |
| `gettext` | A set of utilities that enables software maintainers to *internationalize* (make the software work with different languages such as English, French, and Spanish) a software package's user messages |
| `ghostscript` | An interpreter for the PostScript and Portable Document Format (PDF) languages |
| `ghostview` | An X Window System application that makes `ghostscript` accessible from the GUI, enabling users to view PostScript or PDF files in a window |
| The GIMP | The GNU Image Manipulation Program, an Adobe Photoshop–like image processing program |

| Software Package | Description |
| --- | --- |
| GNOME | Provides a graphical user interface (GUI) for a wide variety of tasks that a Linux user may perform |
| GNUchess | A chess game |
| GNU C Library | For use with all Linux programs |
| Gnumeric | A graphical spreadsheet (similar to Microsoft Excel) that works in GNOME |
| grep package | Includes the grep, egrep, and fgrep commands, which are used to find lines that match a specified text pattern |
| groff | A document formatting system similar to troff |
| gtk+ | A GUI toolkit for the X Window System (used to develop GNOME applications) |
| gzip | A GNU utility for compressing and decompressing files |
| indent | Formats C source code by indenting it in one of several different styles |
| less | A page-by-page display program similar to more but with additional capabilities |
| libpng | A library for image files in the Portable Network Graphics (PNG) format |
| m4 | An implementation of the traditional UNIX macro processor |
| make | A utility that determines which files of a large software package need to be recompiled, and issues the commands to recompile them |
| mtools | A set of programs that enables users to read, write, and manipulate files on a DOS file system (typically a floppy disk) |
| ncurses | A package for displaying and updating text on text-only terminals |
| patch | A GNU version of Larry Wall's program to take the output of diff and apply those differences to an original file to generate the modified version |
| rcs | Revision Control System; used for version control and management of source files in software projects |
| sed | A stream-oriented version of the ed text editor |
| Sharutils | A package that includes shar (used to make shell archives out of many files) and unshar (to unpack these shell archives) |

*(continued)*

**Table 1-2 *(continued)***

| Software Package | Description |
|---|---|
| tar | A tape archiving program that includes multivolume support — the capability to archive *sparse files* (files with big chunks of data that are all zeros), handle compression and decompression, and create remote archives — and other special features for incremental and full backups |
| texinfo | A set of utilities that generates printed manuals, plain ASCII text, and online hypertext documentation (called info), and enables users to view and read online info documents |
| time | A utility that reports the user, system, and actual time that a process uses |

## GUIs and applications

Face it — typing cryptic Linux commands on a terminal is boring. For average users, using the system through a *graphical user interface* (GUI, pronounced "GOO-ee") — one that gives you icons to click and windows to open — is much easier. This is where the X Window System, or *X,* comes to the rescue.

X is kind of like Microsoft Windows, but the underlying details of how X works are different from Windows. X provides the basic features of displaying windows on-screen, but (unlike Microsoft Windows) it doesn't come with any specific look or feel for graphical applications. That look and feel comes from GUIs, such as GNOME and KDE, which make use of the X Window System.

Most Linux distributions come with the X Window System in the form of XFree86 or X.Org X11 — implementations of the X Window System for 80x86 systems. XFree86 and X.Org X11 work with a wide variety of video cards available for today's PCs.

Until early 2004, XFree86 from the XFree86 Project (www.xfree86.org) was the most commonly used X Window System implementation for x86 systems. However, around version 4.4, some changes to the XFree86 licensing terms caused concerns to many Linux and UNIX vendors — they felt that the licensing terms were no longer compatible with the GNU General Public License (GPL). In January 2004, several vendors formed the X.Org Foundation (www.x.org) to promote continued development of an open source X Window System and graphical desktop. The first release of X.Org X11 uses the same code that was used by XFree86 4.4, up until the time when the XFree86 license changes precipitated the creation of X.Org Foundation.

As for the GUI, Linux distributions include one or both of two powerful GUI desktops: *KDE* (K Desktop Environment) and *GNOME* (GNU Object Model Environment). If both GNOME and KDE are installed on a PC, you can choose which desktop you want as the default — or switch between the two. KDE and GNOME provide desktops similar to those of Microsoft Windows and the Mac OS. GNOME also comes with the Nautilus graphical shell, which makes finding files, running applications, and configuring your Linux system easy. With GNOME or KDE, you can begin using your Linux workstation without having to know cryptic Linux commands. However, if you ever need to use those commands directly, all you have to do is open a terminal window and type the commands at the prompt.

Linux also comes with many graphical applications. One of the most note-worthy programs is *The GIMP* (The GNU Image Manipulation Program), a program for working with photos and other images. The GIMP's capabilities are on a par with Adobe Photoshop.

Although Linux used to lack in providing common productivity software — such as word processing, spreadsheet, and database applications — this situation has changed. Linux comes with the OpenOffice.org office produc-tivity applications. In addition, you may want to check out the following prominent, commercially available office productivity applications for Linux that are *not* included on this book's companion DVD-ROM:

+ **Applixware:** This office package is a good example of productivity soft-ware for Linux. You can find it at `www.vistasource.com`.

+ **Open Office:** From Oracle (`www.oracle.com/us/products/ applications/open-office/index.html`), Open Office is another well-known productivity software package.

+ **CrossOver Office:** From CodeWeavers (`www.codeweavers.com/ products/cxlinux`), CrossOver Office can be used to install your Microsoft Office applications (Office 2000 and Office XP, for example) as well as several other Windows applications in Linux.

As you can see, there's no shortage of Linux office applications that are compatible with Microsoft Office.

## Networks

Linux comes with everything you need to use the system in networks to exchange data with other systems. On networks, computers that exchange data must follow well-defined rules, or protocols. A *network protocol* is a method that the sender and receiver agree upon for exchanging data across a network. Such a protocol is similar to the rules you might follow when you're having a polite conversation with someone at a party. You typically start by saying hello, exchanging names, and then taking turns talking. That's about the same way network protocols work. The two computers use the same protocol to send bits and bytes back and forth across the network.

One of the most well-known and popular network protocols is Transmission Control Protocol/Internet Protocol (TCP/IP). TCP/IP is the protocol of choice on the Internet — the "network of networks" that now spans the globe. Linux sup-ports the TCP/IP protocol and any network applications that make use of TCP/IP.

## *Internet servers*

Some popular network applications are designed to deliver information from one system to another. When you send electronic mail (e-mail) or visit Web sites using a Web browser, you use these network applications (also called *Internet services*). Here are some common Internet services:

✦ **Electronic mail** (e-mail) that you use to send messages to any other person on the Internet using addresses like `joe@someplace.com`

✦ **World Wide Web** (or simply, Web) that you browse using a Web browser

✦ **News services**, where you can read newsgroups and post news items to newsgroups with names such as `comp.os.linux.networking` or `comp.os.linux.setup`

✦ **File transfer utilities** that you can use to upload and download files

✦ **Remote login** that you can use to connect to and work with another computer (the remote computer) on the Internet — assuming you have the required username and password to access that remote computer

Any Linux PC can offer these Internet services. To do so, the PC must be connected to the Internet, and it must run special server software called *Internet servers*. Each of the servers uses a specific protocol for transferring information. For example, here are some common Internet servers that you find in Linux:

✦ `sendmail` is the mail server for exchanging e-mail messages between systems using SMTP (Simple Mail Transfer Protocol).

✦ Apache `httpd` is the Web server for sending documents from one system to another using HTTP (HyperText Transfer Protocol).

✦ `vsftpd` is the server for transferring files between computers on the Internet using FTP (File Transfer Protocol).

✦ `innd` is the news server for distribution of news articles in a store-and-forward fashion across the Internet using NNTP (Network News Transfer Protocol).

✦ `in.telnetd` allows a user on one system to log in to another system on the Internet using the TELNET protocol.

✦ `sshd` allows a user on one system to securely log in to another system on the Internet using the SSH (Secure Shell) protocol.

## *Software development*

Linux is particularly well suited to software development. Straight out the box, it's chock-full of software-development tools, such as the compiler and libraries of code needed to build programs. If you happen to know UNIX and the C programming language, you'll feel right at home programming in Linux.

As far as the development environment goes, Linux has the same basic tools (such as an editor, a compiler, and a debugger) that you might use on other UNIX workstations, such as those from IBM, Sun Microsystems, and Hewlett-Packard (HP).

If you work by day on one of these UNIX workstations, you can use a Linux PC in the evening at home to duplicate that development environment at a fraction of the cost. Then you can either complete work projects at home or devote your time to software you write for fun and to share on the Internet.

## Online documentation

As you become more adept at using Linux, you may want to look up information quickly — without having to turn the pages of (ahem) this great book, for example. Luckily, Linux comes with enough online information to jog your memory in those situations when you vaguely recall a command's name but can't remember the exact syntax of what you're supposed to type.

If you use Linux commands, you can view the manual page — commonly referred to as the *man page* — for a command by using the man command. (You do have to remember that command to access online help.)

You can also get help from the GUI desktops. Both GNOME and KDE desktops come with help viewers to view online help information. Most distributions include a help option in the desktop menu or a help icon on the desktop that you can use to get online help. You can then browse the help information by clicking the links on the initial help window. Figure 1-1 shows a typical help window — this one from Ubuntu's desktop.

**Figure 1-1:**
Online help is available from the GUI desktop.

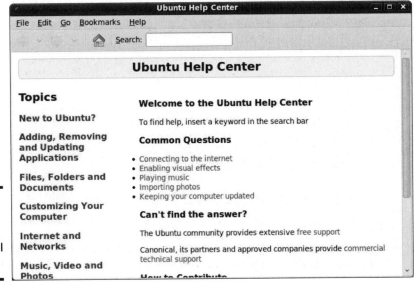

## Stuff programmers want to know about Linux

The following features make Linux a productive software-development environment:

- **GNU C compiler (gcc):** Compiles ANSI-standard C programs.

- **GNU C++ compiler (g++):** Supports ANSI-standard C++ features.

- **GNU compiler for Java (gcj):** Compiles programs written in the Java programming language.

- **GNU make utility:** Enables you to compile and link large programs.

- **GNU debugger (gdb):** Enables you to step through your program to find problems and to determine where and how a program failed. (The failed program's memory image is saved in the core file; gdb can examine this file.)

- **GNU profiling utility (gprof):** Enables you to determine the degree to which a piece of software uses your computer's processor time.

- **Subversion, Concurrent Versions System (CVS), and Revision Control System (RCS):**
Maintains version information and controls access to the source files so that two programmers don't inadvertently modify the same source file at the same time.

- **GNU emacs editor:** Prepares source files and even launches a compile-link process to build the program.

- **Perl:** Enables you to write scripts to accomplish a specific task, tying together many smaller programs with Linux commands.

- **Tool Command Language and its graphical toolkit (Tcl/Tk):** Enables you to build graphical applications rapidly.

- **Python:** Enables you to write code in an interpreted programming language comparable to Perl and Tcl. (For example, the Fedora Core installation program, called anaconda, is written in Python.)

- **Dynamically linked, shared libraries:** Allows your actual program files to be much smaller because all the library code that several programs may need is shared — with only one copy loaded in the system's memory.

## Managing Your PC with Linux

As an operating system, Linux acts as the intermediary through which you — as the "lord of the system" — manage all the hardware. The hardware includes the system box, the monitor, the keyboard, the mouse, and anything else connected to the system box. The catchall term *peripheral* refers to any equipment attached to the system. If you use a laptop computer, all your hardware is packaged into the laptop.

Inside that system box is the system's brain — the microprocessor (Intel Pentium 4, for example) or the CPU — that performs the instructions contained in a computer program. When the microprocessor runs a computer program, that program's instructions are stored in the memory, or *RAM* (random access memory). This means that any part of the memory can be accessed randomly — in arbitrary order.

The system box has another crucial component — the hard drive (or *hard disk,* as it is sometimes called). The hard drive is the permanent storage space for computer programs and data. It's permanent in the sense that the contents don't disappear when you power off the PC. The hard drive is organized into files, which are in turn organized in a hierarchical fashion into directories and subdirectories (somewhat like organizing papers in folders in the drawers of a file cabinet).

To keep a Linux system running properly, you or someone else has to make sure that the hardware is working properly and that the files are backed up regularly. There's also the matter of *security* — making sure that only legitimate people can access and use the system. These tasks are called *system administration.*

If you use Linux at a big facility with many computers, a full-time system administrator probably takes care of all system administration tasks. On the other hand, if you run Linux on a home PC, you're the system administrator. Don't let the thought frighten you. You don't have to know any magic incantations or prepare cryptic configuration files to be a system administrator. Most Linux distributions include many graphical tools that make system administration a point-and-click job, just like running any other application.

## Disks, CD-ROMs, and DVD-ROMs

Some Linux distributions come on a single DVD-ROM. After installation, the Linux kernel and all the applications are stored on your hard drive — which is where your PC looks first when you tell it to do something.

Typically, the hard drive is prepared to use Linux during the installation process. After that, you usually leave the hard drive alone except to back up the data stored there or (occasionally) to install and update applications.

Using CD-ROMs or DVD-ROMs in Linux is easy. While you're logged in at the GNOME or KDE desktop, just pop a CD or DVD in to the drive, and the system should automatically detect the DVD/CD-ROM. Depending on the Linux distribution, either a DVD/CD-ROM icon appears on the desktop or a file manager automatically opens and displays the contents of the DVD/CD-ROM. If all else fails, you can type a simple mount command to associate the DVD/CD-ROM with a directory on your system. This process of accessing the files on a CD or a DVD from Linux is called *mounting* the CD or the DVD.

Besides the hard drive and DVD/CD-ROM drive, of course, your PC may have other drives, such as a floppy disk drive, a Zip drive, or a USB flash drive. Using those disks in Linux is also simple: You insert a disk and double-click the icon that represents the disk drive on the GUI desktop. Doing so mounts the disk so that you can begin using it.

## Peripheral devices

Anything connected to your PC is a peripheral device, as are some components (such as sound cards) that are installed inside the system box. You can configure and manage these peripheral devices in Linux.

One of the common peripherals is a printer, typically hooked up to the USB (Universal Serial Bus) or parallel port of your PC. (Many distributions come with a graphical printer configuration tool that you can use to configure the printer.)

Another peripheral device that needs configuration is the sound card. Most Linux distributions detect and configure sound cards, just as Windows does. However, if Linux can't detect the sound card correctly, you may have to run a text mode or graphical tool to configure the sound card.

Linux configures other peripheral devices, such as the mouse and keyboard, at the time of installation. You can pretty much leave them alone after installation.

Nowadays, PCs come with the USB interface; many devices, including printers and scanners, plug into a PC's USB port.

One nice feature of USB devices is that you can plug them into the USB port and unplug them at any time — the device doesn't have to be connected when you power up the system. These devices are called *hot plug* because you can plug in a device when the system is *hot,* meaning while it's running. Linux supports many hot plug USB devices. When you plug a device into the USB port, Linux loads the correct driver and makes the device available to applications.

## File systems and sharing

The entire organization of directories and files is the *file system.* You can, of course, manage the file system using Linux. When you browse the files from the GNOME or KDE graphical desktop, you work with the familiar folder icons.

A key task in caring for a file system is to back up important files. In Linux, you can use the `tar` program to archive one or more directories on a floppy disk or a Zip drive. You can even back up files on a tape (if you have a tape drive). If you have a CD or DVD burner, you can also burn a CD or DVD with the files you want to back up or save for posterity.

Linux can also share parts of the file system with other systems on a network. For example, you can use the Network File System (NFS) to share files across the network. To a user on the system, the remote system's files appear to be in a directory on the local system.

Linux also comes with the Samba package, which supports file sharing with Microsoft Windows systems. Samba makes a Linux system work just like a Windows file or print server. You can also access shared folders on other Windows systems on your network.

## Network

Now that most PCs are either in a local area network (LAN) or connected to the Internet, you need to manage the network as well. Linux comes with a network configuration tool to set up the LAN. For connecting to the Internet with a modem, there's usually a GUI Internet dial-up tool.

If, like many users, you connect to the Internet with DSL or cable modem, you need a PC with an Ethernet card that connects to the cable or DSL modem. It also means that you have to set up a local area network and configure the Ethernet card. Fortunately, these steps are typically a part of Linux installation. If you want to do the configurations later, you can by using a GUI network configuration tool.

Linux also includes tools for configuring a *firewall,* which is a protective buffer that helps keep your system relatively secure from anyone trying to snoop over your Internet connection. You can configure the firewall by using `iptables` commands or by running a GUI firewall configuration tool.

# Getting Started

Based on personal experience in exploring new subjects, I prescribe a four-step process to get started with Linux (and *Linux All-in-One Desk Reference For Dummies*):

*1.* Install Linux on your PC (as shown in Book I).

*2.* Configure Linux so that everything works to your liking (as shown in Book I).

*3.* Explore the GUI desktops and the applications (as shown in Book II).

*4.* Find out the details of specific subjects, such as Internet servers (as shown in Book IV).

In the rest of this chapter, I explain this prescription a bit more.

## Step 1: Install

Microsoft Windows usually comes installed on your new PC, but Linux usually doesn't. So your first hurdle is to get Linux onto your PC. Although some vendors are now offering Linux pre-installed, this is still a rarity.

After you overcome that initial human fear of the unknown, I'll bet you find Linux fairly easy to install — but where do you *get* it in the first place? Well, the good news is that it's included on the DVD for this book. After you drop the DVD into your PC, Book I shows how to install Linux, step by step.

Because a typical complete Linux distribution is *huge* — it takes several CDs or at least a single DVD — your best bet is to buy or borrow a book (such as this one) that includes Linux on a CD or DVD. However, if you have a lot of patience and bandwidth, Linux is also free to download. For example, you can visit the Linux Online Web site at `www.linux.org` and click the Download button.

## Step 2: Configure

When you finish installing Linux, the next step is to configure individual system components (for example, the sound card and the printer) and tweak any needed settings. Book I shows how to configure the nooks and crannies of Linux.

If you aren't getting a graphical login screen, the X Window System may not have been configured correctly during installation. You have to fix the X configuration file for the GUI to work.

You may want to configure your GUI *desktop* of choice — GNOME or KDE (or both). Each has configuration tools. You can use these tools to adjust the look and feel of the desktop (background, title fonts, or even the entire color scheme). Book II shows how to make your desktop even more your own.

After you're through with configuration, all the hardware on your system and the applications should run to your liking.

## Step 3: Explore

With a properly configured Linux PC at your disposal, you're ready to explore Linux itself. You can begin the process from the GUI desktop — GNOME or KDE — that you see after logging in. Look at the GUI desktops and the folders and files that make up the Linux file system, as discussed in Book II. You can also try out the applications from the desktop. You find office and multimedia applications and Internet applications to explore.

Also try out the shell: Open a terminal window and type some Linux commands in that window. You can also explore the text editors that work in text mode, as covered in Book II. Knowing how to edit text files without the GUI, just in case the GUI isn't available, is a good idea. At least you won't be helpless.

## *Step 4: Find out more*

After you explore the Linux landscape and know what is what, you can dig deeper and find out more about specific subject areas. For example, you may be interested in setting up Internet servers. You can then learn the details of setting up individual servers, such as `sendmail` for e-mail, Apache for a Web server, and the INN server for news, as covered in Book IV.

You can find out about many more areas, such as security, programming, and system administration, as discussed in Books V, VI, VII, and VIII.

Of course, you can expect this step to go on and on, even after you have your system running the way you want it — for now. After all, learning is a lifelong journey.

*Bon voyage!*

# Chapter 2: Installing Linux

## In This Chapter

✔ **Understanding the installation steps**

✔ **Making a list of your PC's hardware**

✔ **Checking out the Ubuntu Live CD**

✔ **Burning CDs or DVDs for your distribution**

✔ **Setting aside hard drive space for Linux**

✔ **Installing Ubuntu**

Most PCs come with Microsoft Windows pre-installed; if you want to use Linux, you usually have to install it.

This book comes with a DVD-ROM that contains several Linux distributions — Ubuntu, Debian, Fedora, openSUSE, and Xandros. Some are full distributions, and a few are Live CDs that you can try without installing on the hard drive. (*Full distributions* include everything you need to install those distributions; *Live CDs* are CDs from which you can directly boot Linux.) All you have to do to install or try any of these distributions is follow the steps in this chapter.

You may feel a tad worried about installing a new operating system on your PC because it's a bit like brain surgery — or, rather, more like grafting a new brain because you can install Linux in addition to Microsoft Windows. When you install two operating systems like that, you can choose to start one or the other as you power up the PC. The biggest headache in adding Linux to a PC with Windows is creating a new *disk partition* — basically setting aside a part of the hard drive for Linux. The rest of the installation is routine — just a matter of following the instructions. If you want to try any of the Live CDs, you don't have to do any disk partitioning; just boot your PC from the Live CD. But first, take a deep breath and exhale slooowwwly. You have nothing to worry about.

## Following the Installation Steps

Installing any Linux distribution involves a number of steps, and I will walk through them briefly, without the details. Then you can follow the detailed steps for the specific distributions and install what you want from this book's companion DVD-ROM.

Some Linux distributions require that you have quite a bit of information about your PC's hardware on hand before installation. If you plan to install Debian, go ahead and gather information about your PC and its peripheral components before starting the installation. Luckily, most Linux installation programs can detect and work with most PC peripherals. Nevertheless, it's a good idea to figure out your PC's hardware so that you can troubleshoot in case something goes wrong with the installation.

The very first step is to burn the CD or DVD for your distribution. You can burn the CDs on any system that has a CD/DVD burner. (You must have a DVD burner if you want to burn a DVD, but a DVD burner can burn both CDs and DVDs.) Typically, if you already have a Windows PC with a CD/DVD burner, you can simply use that system to burn the CDs. Remember that you must have a DVD drive as well because you have to burn the CDs from this book's companion DVD-ROM. A PC with a DVD burner or a combination DVD-ROM and CD burner is adequate for this task.

The second step is to make sure that your PC can boot from the DVD/CD drive. Most new PCs can boot directly from the DVD/CD drive, but some PCs may require your intervention. Typically, the PC may be set to boot from the hard drive before the DVD/CD drive, and you have to get into Setup to change the order of boot devices.

To set up a PC to boot from the DVD drive, you have to go into Setup as the PC powers up. The exact steps for entering Setup and setting the boot device vary from one PC to the next, but typically they involve pressing a key, such as F2. When the PC powers up, a brief message tells you what key to press to enter Setup. When you're in Setup, you can designate the DVD/CD drive as the boot device. After your PC is set up to boot from the DVD/CD drive, simply put the DVD or CD in the DVD/CD drive and restart your PC.

If you plan to try a Live CD distribution, the third step is to boot your PC from the Live CD or DVD. Otherwise, the third step is to make room for Linux on your PC's hard drive. If you're running Microsoft Windows, this step can be easy or hard, depending on whether you want to replace Windows with Linux or keep both Windows and a Linux distribution.

If you want to install Linux without removing (or disturbing) Windows, remember that your existing operating system uses the entire hard drive. That means you have to *partition* (divide) the hard drive so that Windows can live in one part of it, and Linux can live in the other. Doing so can be a scary step because you run the risk of clearing the hard drive and wiping out whatever is on the drive. Therefore, *always* make a backup of your system before undertaking any significant changes.

To set aside space on your hard drive that the Linux installation program can use, you should use a partitioning program to help you create the partition. If your PC runs Windows 7, Vista, or XP (as well as the much older

NT or 2000), you might want to invest in a commercial hard drive partitioning product. On the other hand, you can repartition your PC's hard drive by using a GUI (graphical user interface) tool called *QTParted,* which comes with Knoppix and a number of other distributions.

Note that the installers for some Linux distributions, such as openSUSE and Xandros Desktop, can automatically create partitions for Linux by reducing the size of a Windows partition. In that case, you don't need to use a tool such as QTParted to shrink the size of the existing Windows partition on your hard drive.

After you set aside a hard drive partition for Linux, you can boot the PC from the selected distribution's CD and start the Linux installation. Quite a few steps occur during installation, and they vary from one distribution to another. When you've come this far, it should be smooth sailing. Just go through the installation screens, and you'll be finished in an hour or two. Most installers, such as the openSUSE interface in Figure 2-1, display a GUI and guide you through all the steps.

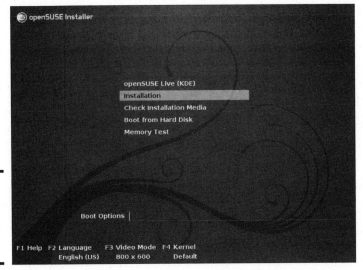

**Figure 2-1:**
The GUI walks you through the installation.

One key step during installation involves partitioning the hard drive again, but this time you simply use the extra partition you created previously. Figure 2-2 shows the actions recommended for this step by the openSUSE installation interface.

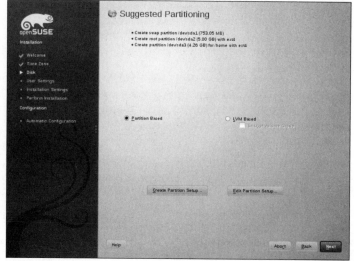

**Figure 2-2:**
The
system's
recommend-
ations
for the
partitions.

After a few configuration steps, such as setting up the network and the time zone, select the software packages to install and then let the installer complete the remaining installation chores. Some distributions make it even easier and do away with the software selection step and instead install a default set of software packages.

At the end of the installation, reboot the PC. Rebooting is sometimes required as a part of the installation process, as shown in Figure 2-3.

**Figure 2-3:**
A reboot
is needed
during this
openSUSE
installation
before the
automatic
configuration
can run.

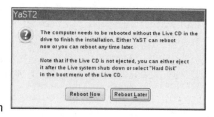

When Linux runs for the first time, you get a chance to perform some more configuration steps and install additional software packages.

# Checking Your PC's Hardware

If you're concerned that your PC may not be able to run Linux, here are some of the key components of your PC that you need to consider before you start the Linux installation:

✦ **DVD drive:** You must have a DVD drive (either DVD-ROM or DVD burner), and the PC must be able to boot from that drive.

The exact model doesn't matter. What does matters is how the DVD drive connects to the PC. Most new PCs have DVD drives that connect to the hard drive controller (*IDE,* for Integrated Drive Electronics, or *ATA,* for AT Attachment). If you add an external DVD drive, it most likely connects to the USB port. Any IDE/ATA or USB DVD drive works in Linux.

✦ **Hard drives:** Any IDE disk drive works in Linux. Another type of hard drive controller is SCSI (Small Computer System Interface), which Linux also supports. To comfortably install and play with Linux, you need about 5GB of hard drive space. On the other hand, to try the Live CD versions of Linux, you don't need any space on the hard drive.

✦ **Keyboard:** All keyboards work with Linux and the X Window System.

✦ **Modem:** If you plan to dial out to the Internet, you need a modem that Linux supports. For software-based modems, called *softmodems* or *Winmodems,* you may have to download a driver from the manufacturer or the Linux modem sites (such as www.linmoderm.org). A download may or may not be freely available.

✦ **Monitor:** The kind of monitor isn't particularly critical except that it must be capable of displaying the screen resolutions that the video card uses. The screen resolution is expressed in terms of the number of picture elements (*pixels*), horizontally and vertically (for example, 1024 x 768). The installer can detect most modern monitors. If it doesn't detect your monitor, you can select a generic monitor type with a specific resolution (such as 1024 x 768). You can also specify the monitor by its make and model (which you can find on the back of the monitor).

✦ **Mouse:** The installation program can detect the mouse. All types of mouse (such as PS/2 or USB) work with Linux and the X Window System.

✦ **Network card:** Not all PCs have network cards, but if yours does, the installer can probably detect and use it. If you have problems, try to find the make and model (such as Linksys LNE100TX Fast Ethernet Adapter) so that you can search for information on whether Linux supports that card.

✦ **Processor:** A 400 MHz Pentium II or better is best. The processor speed, expressed in *MHz* (megahertz) or *GHz* (gigahertz), isn't that important as long as it's over 400 MHz. But the faster the better. Linux can run on other Intel-compatible processors, such as AMD and VIA processors.

+ **RAM:** *RAM* is the amount of memory your system has. As with processing speed, the more RAM, the better. You need a minimum of 256MB to install both Linux and the X Window System. With some distributions, the minimum amount has climbed to 384MB, and you'll want still more memory to be able to comfortably run a GUI desktop.

+ **SCSI controller:** Some high-performance PCs have SCSI controllers that connect disk drives and other peripherals to a PC. If your PC happens to have a SCSI controller, you might want to find out the make and model of the controller.

+ **Sound card:** If your PC has a sound card and you want to have sound in Linux, you have to make sure it's compatible. You can configure the sound card after successfully installing Linux.

+ **Video card:** Linux works fine with all video cards (also known as *display adapters*) in text mode, but if you want the GUI, you need a video card that works with the X Window System. The installer can detect a supported video card and configure the X Window System correctly. However, if the installer can't detect the video card, it helps if you know the make and model of your video card.

+ **Printer:** In addition to this hardware, you also need to find out the make and model of any printer you plan to use in Linux.

Many distributions, such as Debian GNU/Linux, work on any hardware that's compatible with the Linux kernel. For information on Linux-compatible hardware, see `www.tldp.org/HOWTO/Hardware-HOWTO`.

To check whether your PC's hardware is compatible with individual distributions, visit that vendor's site and find their hardware compatibility list.

# Trying the Ubuntu Live CD

Before you install anything, you'll find it worthwhile to try out Ubuntu from the companion DVD. In addition to getting a feel for a Linux desktop, you can perform a few additional pre-installation chores from Ubuntu.

To start Ubuntu, boot your PC from this book's companion DVD. A menu will appear from which you can enter various options to control the boot process or check your system to see if it meets hardware requirements. You should choose the default option of booting Ubuntu (this option is automatically performed if you don't make a selection before the menu times out in 30 seconds).

A few minutes later, you see the GNOME GUI desktop, which Ubuntu uses. You can now start exploring Ubuntu. If you click the `Examples` folder, you'll find a number of things that Ubuntu can do. You can also choose GParted (the partition editor) from the System, Administration menu (System⇨Administration⇨GParted) to reconfigure the hard drive.

When you finish using Ubuntu, choose System⇨Quit. After Ubuntu shuts down, remove the DVD and press Enter. Should you decide you want to install Ubuntu, click the Install icon on the desktop to begin the process.

# *Burning CDs or DVDs from ISO Images*

This book's companion DVD has Debian, openSUSE, and Xandros distributions in the form of ISO images, organized into separate folders in the `dists` folder of the DVD. To install any of these distributions, you must first burn the selected distribution's ISO images onto CD or DVD. You can typically perform this step on a PC with a CD/DVD burner, most likely while using Microsoft Windows because most new PCs come with Windows pre-installed.

---

## Using a Windows CD burner application

In Microsoft Windows, you can use a CD burner application, such as Nero, to burn ISO images onto recordable CDs. If you don't have a CD burner application for Microsoft Windows, boot Ubuntu from the DVD and choose Places⇨CD/DVD Creator from the GUI desktop to start the CD/DVD burning application. The exact steps for burning a CD from an ISO image depend on the CD burner application that you use. The general steps follow. (Use the same instructions to burn a DVD, provided you have a DVD burner.)

1. **Place the companion DVD-ROM into the PC's DVD drive.**

   If your DVD drive is a combination DVD/CD burner, you have to first copy the ISO image files of the Linux distribution from the DVD to the PC's hard drive so that you can use the same drive to burn the CDs.

2. **Start the CD burner application.**

3. **From the CD burner application, open the image file.**

   The exact steps depend on the CD burner application.

4. **Place a blank, recordable CD in the CD burner.**

5. **Burn the ISO image to the recordable CD.**

   Typically, the CD burner application has a toolbar button that you can click to start burning the ISO image onto the blank CD.

6. **If the distribution has more ISO images, repeat Steps 3–5 for the remaining ISO images.**

   Live CD distributions come in a single ISO image that you can burn on a single CD. Other distributions typically come in multiple ISO images, and you have to burn each image file onto a separate CD.

# Setting Aside Space for Linux

In a typical Windows PC, Windows is sitting on one big partition, taking over the entire hard drive. You want to shrink that partition and create room for Linux. During Linux installation, the installation program uses the free space for the Linux partitions.

To try out any of the Live CD distributions — such as Ubuntu — you don't have to repartition your hard drive. Just boot your PC from the Live CD. The installers can nondestructively shrink a Windows partition, so you don't need to perform the repartitioning step beforehand. If you plan to install Fedora, Debian, or any other Linux distribution on the hard drive, you have to repartition your hard drive. If you want to resize the disk partition under Windows, you can use a commercial product, or boot Ubuntu from this book's companion DVD and then use GParted, the partition editor, to resize the Windows partitions. GParted can resize NTFS (NT File System) partitions, which are used by most newer versions of Windows.

When you resize the disk partition, you always risk losing all the data on the hard drive. Therefore, before you resize hard drive partitions with a disk partitioning tool, *back up your hard drive.* After making your backup — and before you do *anything* to the partitions — please make sure that you can restore your files from the backup.

After Ubuntu boots and the GUI desktop appears, follow these steps to reduce the size of the Windows partition:

*1.* **Choose System➪Administration➪GParted from the Ubuntu desktop.**

   The GParted window appears, and the tool displays the drives it finds on your PC. The first hard drive appears with a device name /dev/sda, the second one as /dev/sdb, and so on.

*2.* **Click the hard drive from the list of devices on the right side of the GParted window.**

*3.* **From the list of partitions, click the partition you want to resize.**

   This partition would normally be the largest partition. For Windows 7, Vista, or XP, the partition type is ntfs, as shown in the Type column in the list of partitions. In a typical new PC, you might see two partitions — a smaller fat16 partition and a large ntfs partition.

*4.* **Choose Resize/Move from the GParted menu.**

   The Resize partition dialog box appears.

*5.* **Set the setting for the new size for the partition and then click Resize/Move.**

You should choose a size such that you get 4GB or more free space after the partition. You'll see the size of the free space in the Free Space After field in the dialog box.

6. **Click Apply to begin the operation after you have specified all changes you want to make. When the warning appears, click Apply and all pending operations will be performed.**

   The partition is changed, and you have free space after the Windows partition.

After you create free space on the hard drive for Linux, you can proceed to install the Linux distribution of your choice using the CDs or DVD that you've burned from the ISO image files provided on the companion DVD.

# Installing Ubuntu

The companion DVD includes a single-CD ISO image for installing Ubuntu. First, burn that ISO image onto a CD-R by following the steps outlined in the "Burning CDs or DVDs from ISO Images" section, previously in this chapter. Ubuntu is based on Debian, so the installation steps are similar to those for Debian.

To install Ubuntu on your PC, follow these steps:

1. **Boot your PC from the Ubuntu installation CD.**

   The initial boot screen prompts you to press Enter to start installation or press F1 for more help. You can press F1 and then look at help information by pressing the specified function key. These options are similar to what you see on the Debian installer's boot screen because Ubuntu is based on Debian.

2. **Press Enter or type a boot command followed by any options and then press Enter.**

   For example, on a PC that doesn't support ACPI (Advanced Configuration and Power Interface), type `linux acpi=off` to start the Ubuntu installation. The installer prompts you to select the language. For most installations, just choose Install Ubuntu.

3. **Select the language and click Forward.**

   For most installations, just choose Install Ubuntu. The installer displays the location based on your language choice. If release notes are available, you see them here and can also choose to update the installer should a new one be available.

4. **Select the location, and then click Forward.**

The installer shows a map and attempts to guess your time zone location based on the current clock's time. You can also change the default time zone to the one correct for your location if the installer did not guess correctly.

5. **Select the keyboard layout, and then click Forward.**

   The installer detects hardware, including the hard drive configuration.

6. **(Optional) Choose how to prepare the disk space.**

   You can remove the existing operating system, install in another partition, and so on. If you've created space for Ubuntu on your hard drive (see the "Setting Aside Space for Linux" section), select that space.

7. **Click Forward.**

8. **Create your user account, type a host name for your system, and then click Forward.**

   Enter the primary user account information for this system (the superuser) and assign a computer name that you want this system to be known as across the network.

9. **Confirm the Installation, and then click Install.**

   All the variables you've entered or choices you've selected are displayed one last time. You can Quit, go back to change something, or Install (you can also click the Advanced button to configure less common settings). After you click Install, the installer installs the Ubuntu base system.

10. **Remove the CD and press Enter to reboot the PC.**

    After the PC reboots, Ubuntu downloads and installs many more packages from online repositories. (Your PC needs to be connected to the Internet for everything to work.)

The X Window System and the GNOME GUI are among the packages Ubuntu downloads and installs. After these packages are installed and configured, Ubuntu starts a GUI login screen, where you can log in using the user account that you defined previously.

Congratulations! You can now start using Ubuntu!

# Chapter 3: Installing Linux on a Flash Drive

## In This Chapter

✔ **Creating a drive**

✔ **Troubleshooting the workstation**

✔ **Using the flash drive on a daily basis**

*I*was a fan of Live CD versions of Linux distributions for a while — but no more. I liked Live CDs because I could create cheap media that I could distribute to students and users so they could enjoy the Linux experience on their own machines without installing the operating system, changing what they were comfortable with, or risking doing harm. In addition, this same user group could quickly change from Fedora to Ubuntu to openSUSE and more. My biggest dislikes of the Live CD were their incredibly slow speed and the inability to save configuration changes easily. Given these substantial issues, I've been seeking a better solution. Thankfully, I've found it: bootable USB distributions.

Bootable USB distributions have been around for some time but have all had weaknesses that prevented me from embracing them. Fedora's Live USB implementation, however, is the best I've encountered. It provides a simple method for creation that most users can walk through unescorted, the installation process is nondestructive — allowing you to keep existing files on the USB drive — and retaining changes (data persistence) is straightforward.

In this chapter, I show you how to create a bootable flash drive and use it in your own setting.

## Creating the Bootable Flash Drive

Although you can create a bootable flash drive using a number of command line methods in Linux, the simplest technique uses Windows. (I realize that it might sound like heresy to suggest making a Linux boot from Windows, but most users interested in a Live USB implementation of Linux probably run Windows.) Follow these steps to create a bootable flash drive:

1. Go to `http://fedorahosted.org/liveusb-creator` and download the `liveusb-creator` program.

2. Install the `liveusb-creator` program.

3. Open the folder where `liveusb-creator` was installed.

4. Double-click the `liveusb-creator` program to run it.

   You see the program shown in Figure 3-1.

**Figure 3-1:**
The Fedora
Live USB
Creator
simplifies
the creation
of the
bootable
flash drive.

5. Under Target Device, select the flash drive.

   For example, the flash drive in Figure 3-1 appears as TravelDrive.

6. Choose where the image (the ISO file) will come from.

   If you have a slow Internet connection, you can have one Live CD from which you pull the ISO file. If you have a faster Internet connection, use the download option to access a current ISO file.

7. Set the Persistent Storage amount.

   This is the amount of storage space allocated to the installation that will always be available. I suggest a value of at least 300MB for the average user. (I don't know why this defaults to 0MB.)

8. Click the Create Live USB button and sit back.

   You can watch the progress, as shown in Figure 3-2. Be prepared to wait ten minutes for the process to complete. Two folders are created on the drive: `syslinux` (less than 7MB and responsible for the booting) and `LiveOS` (the size depends on your storage setting).

9. Close the application and test the newly created bootable drive.

**Figure 3-2:**
The creation
process
takes about
ten minutes.

# Troubleshooting the Workstation

I experimented with a number of flash drives and failed to encounter a problem with any as long as 1GB of free space remained after the installation. Smaller drives (2GB or less) are often factory formatted with FAT (file allocation table) and larger ones are formatted with FAT32; this did not make any difference in installation or usability that I could ascertain.

You must be sure that the workstation settings will allow the machine to boot from USB, which typically requires reconfiguring the BIOS. To begin, reboot the workstation and press the key that takes you to the BIOS configuration (usually F12 or DEL or sometimes F1 or F2). Choose the Boot menu and enable the setting that reads Boot USB Devices First or something similar. On some computers, the flash drive is hidden under the hard drive section of the boot BIOS. In this case, you need to choose Boot⇨Hard Drives, change the primary hard drive to the storage media, and then make sure that the USB is the first choice listed under Boot Device. If the option to boot from USB is Enable/Disable, select Enable and then go to the order of boot devices and move the USB selection above the hard drive selection. Save your changes and exit the BIOS configuration. At this point, the workstation will continue with the reboot and — if your USB drive is plugged in — should boot Fedora. *Note:* If you get the single line entry `Boot Error` and nothing else happens, update the system BIOS per the manufacturer's instructions.

# Working Daily with the New Drive

When your system boots, the Fedora environment will load much more quickly than it does with Live CDs. As shown in Figure 3-3, the USB drive displays the new folders created on it, and other devices can be accessed as usual. The Install to Hard Drive icon remains on the desktop, allowing for a quick permanent transition to Fedora should you decide to do so.

To use the operating system, an Internet connection is not required on but is strongly recommended because most users will want to download additional programs that allow them to test the operating system's functionality further.

**Figure 3-3:**
Working
within the
Live USB
environment.

# Chapter 4: Troubleshooting and Configuring Linux

## In This Chapter

✔ **Troubleshooting the installation**

✔ **Configuring the X Window System**

✔ **Resolving installation problems**

✔ **Setting up your printers**

✔ **Managing your DVDs and CD-ROMs**

✔ **Installing additional software packages**

During the installation of Linux, the installer attempts to detect key hardware components, such as the SCSI controller and network card. According to what it detects, the installer takes you through a sequence of installation steps. For example, if the installer can't detect the network card, it skips the network configuration step. This is okay if you don't in fact have a network card, but if you do have one and the installer mistakenly insists that you don't, you have an installation problem on your hands.

Another installation problem occurs when you restart the PC and see not the graphical login screen but a text terminal. This error means that something is wrong with the X Window System configuration.

In addition, the Linux installation typically doesn't include configuration procedures for every piece of hardware on your PC system. For example, most installations don't set up printers during installation.

In this chapter, I show you some ways to troubleshoot installation problems. You find out how to configure X Window System to start with a GUI screen and how to configure a printer.

You may also have to install additional software packages from the companion DVD-ROM. I show you how to install packages in different formats, such as the Red Hat Package Manager (RPM) and Debian package — the two formats in which most Linux software is distributed.

# Using Text Mode Installation

Most Linux installers attempt to use the X Window System (X) to display the graphical installation screens. If, for instance, the installer fails to detect a video card, X does not start. If — for this reason or any other reason — the installer fails to start X, you can always fall back on a text mode installation. Then you can specify the video card manually or configure X later by using a separate configuration program. You can also configure X by editing its text configuration file.

Table 4-1 lists how you can get to the text mode installation from the initial installer screen for the Linux distributions included on this book's DVD. Typically, the text mode installation sequence is similar to that of the graphical installation that I outline in Chapter 2 of this minibook. You respond to the prompts and perform the installation.

| Table 4-1 | Text Mode Installation in Some Linux Distributions |
|---|---|
| *Distribution* | *How to Get to the Text Mode Installer* |
| Debian | Runs in text mode by default. |
| Fedora | Type **text** at the `boot:` prompt after you start the PC from the Fedora CD or DVD. |
| Knoppix | Start Knoppix in text mode by typing **knoppix 2** at the `boot:` prompt (because Knoppix is a Live CD distribution, you don't have to install it). |
| SUSE | At the first installation screen, press F3, use the arrow keys to select the text mode option, and then press Enter. |
| Ubuntu | Runs in text mode by default. |
| Xandros | Hold down the Shift key while booting the CD and select Rescue Console. When the `bash-3.00#` prompt appears, type **quick_install** and follow the instructions. |

# Troubleshooting X

Every time I installed Linux on an older PC, the GUI installation worked fine during installation, but then the graphical login screen didn't appear when I rebooted the PC for the first time after installation. Instead, I ended up with a text login screen or a black screen with a small X in the middle, or the boot process seemed to hang with a gray screen. If this problem happens to you, here's how you can troubleshoot it:

*1.* **Press Ctrl+Alt+Delete to reboot the PC.**

The PC starts to boot. You get to a screen where GRUB (GRand Unified Bootloader) prompts you for the operating system to boot. (If the distribution uses LILO as the boot loader, you get a text prompt.)

*2.* **For GRUB, press the A key to add an option that tells the Linux kernel to boot to a prompt. For LILO, skip this step.**

The GRUB boot loader then displays a command line for the Linux kernel and prompts you to add what you want.

*3.* **For GRUB, type a space followed by the word** single **and press Enter. For LILO, type** linux single **and press Enter.**

The Linux kernel boots in a single-user mode and displays a prompt that looks like the following:

```
sh-3.00#
```

Now you're ready to configure X.

X uses a configuration file (`XF86Config-4` or `xorg.conf`, depending on the distribution) to figure out your display card, your monitor, and the kind of screen resolution you want. The Linux installer prepares the configuration file, but sometimes the configuration isn't correct.

To quickly create a working configuration file, follow these steps:

*1.* **Type the following command:**

```
X -configure
```

The X server runs and creates a configuration file. The screen goes blank and then the X server exits after displaying some messages. In Fedora, the last line of the message says the following:

```
To test the server, run 'X -config ///etc/xorg.conf.new'
```

*2.* **Use a text editor, such as vi, to edit the ///etc/xorg.conf.new file and insert the following line after the line Section "Files":**

```
FontPath "unix/:7100"
```

In Fedora, you must also change /dev/mouse to /dev/input/mice.

*3.* **Type xfs & to start the X font server.**

*4.* **Try the new configuration file by typing** X -config ///etc/xorg.conf.new.

If you see a blank screen with an X-shaped cursor, the configuration file is working fine.

*5.* **Press Ctrl+Alt+Backspace to kill the X server.**

*6.* **Copy the new configuration file to the /etc/X11 directory with the following command:**

```
cp ///etc/xorg.conf.new /etc/X11/xorg.conf
```

**7. Reboot the PC by pressing Ctrl+Alt+Delete or typing** reboot.

If all goes well, you should get the graphical login screen.

The X configuration file created by using the `-configure` option of the X server does not display at the best resolution. To fine-tune the configuration file, you have to run a utility to adjust the display settings after you reboot the system. Which utility you use depends on the Linux distribution, but most distributions include a utility that enables you to configure the video card, monitor, and display settings through a graphical user interface.

# Resolving Other Installation Problems

I'm sure I haven't exhausted all the installation problems lurking out there. No one can. So many components in Intel x86 PCs exist that Murphy's Law practically requires that there be some combination of hardware that the installation program can't handle. In this section, I list a few known problems. For others, I advise you to go to Google Groups (`http://groups.google.com`) and type some of the symptoms of the trouble. Assuming that others are running into similar problems, you can get some indication of how to troubleshoot your way out of your particular predicament.

## Using Knoppix boot commands

The Knoppix Live CD can be a great troubleshooting tool because Knoppix is good at detecting hardware and can be run directly from the CD.

If you have trouble starting Knoppix, try entering Knoppix boot commands at the `boot:` prompt. For example, if Knoppix seems to hang when trying to detect a SCSI card, you can disable SCSI probing by typing **knoppix noscsi** at the `boot:` prompt. Or, if you want the X server to load the *nv module* (for graphics cards based on the NVIDIA chipset), you can type **knoppix xmodule=nv** at the `boot:` prompt.

Table 4-2 lists some commonly used Knoppix boot commands.

| Table 4-2 | Some Common Knoppix Boot Commands |
|---|---|
| *Boot Command* | *What It Does* |
| expert | Starts in *expert mode,* which enables the user to interactively set up and configure Knoppix. |
| failsafe | Boots without attempting to detect hardware (except for the bare minimum needed to start Linux). |

| Boot Command | What It Does |
|---|---|
| `fb1280x1024` | Uses fixed framebuffer graphics at the specified resolution (specify the resolution you want, such as 1024 x 768 or 800 x 600). |
| `knoppix 1` | Starts Knoppix in run level 1 (single-user mode), which you can use to perform rescue operations. |
| `knoppix 2` | Starts at run level 2, which provides a text mode shell prompt only. |
| `knoppix acpi=off` | Disables ACPI (Advanced Configuration and Power Interface) completely. |
| `knoppix atapicd` | Uses the ATAPI CD-ROM interface instead of emulating a SCSI interface for IDE CD-ROM drives. |
| `knoppix desktop=`*wmname* | Uses the specified Window Manager instead of the default KDE `desktop=`*wmname* (where *wmname* is `fluxbox`, `icewm`, `kde`, `larswm`, `twm`, `wmaker`, or `xfce`). |
| `knoppix dma` | Enables direct memory access (DMA) for all IDE drives. |
| `knoppix floppyconfig` | Runs the shell script named `knoppix.sh` from a floppy. (The shell script contains Linux commands that you want to run.) |
| `knoppix fromhd=/ dev/hda1` | Boots from a previously copied image of Live CD that's in the specified hard drive partition. |
| `knoppix hsync=80` | Uses an 80 kHz horizontal refresh rate for X (enter the horizontal refresh rate you want X to use). |
| `knoppix lang=`*xx* | Sets the keyboard language as specified by the two-letter code *xx* (where *xx* is `cn` = Simplified Chinese, `de` = German, `da` = Danish, `es` = Spanish, `fr` = French, `it` = Italian, `nl` = Dutch, `pl` = Polish, `ru` = Russian, `sk` = Slovak, `tr` = Turkish, `tw` = Traditional Chinese, or `us` = U.S. English). |
| `knoppix mem=256M` | Specifies that the PC has the stated amount of memory (in megabytes). |
| `knoppix myconf=/ dev/hda1` | Runs the shell script `knoppix.sh` from the `/ dev/hda1` partition (enter the partition name where you have the `knoppix.sh` file). |
| `knoppix myconf=scan` | Causes Knoppix to search for the file named `knoppix.sh`, scan, and execute the commands in that file, if it exists. |
| `knoppix noeject` | Does not eject the Live CD after you halt Knoppix. |

*(continued)*

**Table 4-2** *(continued)*

| Boot Command | What It Does |
|---|---|
| knoppix noprompt | Does not prompt to remove the Live CD after you halt Knoppix. |
| knoppix nowheel | Forces the PS/2 protocol for a PS/2 mouse or touchpad (as opposed to the mouse being detected automatically). |
| knoppix no*xxx* | Causes Knoppix to skip specific parts of the hardware detection (where *xxx* identifies the hardware or server that should not be probed: apic = Advanced Programmable Interrupt Controller, agp = Accelerated Graphics Port, apm = Advanced Power Management, audio = sound card, ddc = Display Data Channel, dhcp = Dynamic Host Configuration Protocol, fstab = file system table, firewire = IEEE 1394 high-speed serial bus, pcmcia = PC Card, scsi = Small Computer System Interface, swap = hard drive space used for virtual memory, usb = Universal Serial Bus). |
| knoppix pci=bios | Uses BIOS directly for bad PCI controllers. |
| knoppix pnpbios=off | Skips the Plug and Play (PnP) BIOS initialization. |
| knoppix screen=*resolution* | Sets the screen resolution in pixels (where *resolution* is the resolution you want, such as 1024x768, 800x600, 640x480, and so on). |
| knoppix testcd | Checks the data integrity of the Live CD by using the MD5 sum. |
| knoppix tohd=/dev/hda1 | Copies the Live CD to the specified hard drive partition and runs from there (requires 1GB of RAM). |
| knoppix toram | Copies the Live CD to RAM (memory) and runs from there (requires 1GB of RAM). |
| knoppix vga=ext | Uses a 50-line text mode display. |
| knoppix vsync=60 | Uses a vertical refresh rate of 60 Hz for X (enter the vertical refresh rate you want X to use). |
| knoppix wheelmouse | Enables the IMPS/2 protocol for wheel mice. |
| knoppix xmodule=*modname* | Causes the X server to load the module specified by *modname* so that X works on your video card (where *modname* is ati, fbdev, i810, mga, nv, radeon, savage, svga, or s3). |
| knoppix xserver=*progname* | Starts the X server specified by *progname* (where *progname* is XFree86 or XF86_SVGA). |

When you want to issue multiple Knoppix boot commands, simply combine them in a single line. For example, to specify that you want to skip the SCSI auto detection, turn off ACPI, use the U.S. keyboard, use a wheel mouse, and require the X server to load the nv module, enter the following at the boot: prompt:

```
knoppix noscsi acpi=off lang=us wheelmouse xmodule=nv
```

## The fatal signal 11 error

During installation, some people get a fatal signal 11 error message, which stops the process cold. This error usually happens past the initial boot screen as the installer is starting its GUI or text interface. The most likely cause of a signal 11 error during installation is a hardware error related to memory or the cache associated with the CPU (microprocessor).

A signal 11, or SIGSEGV (short for Segment Violation Signal), error can occur in Linux applications. A *segment violation* occurs when a process tries to access a memory location that it's not supposed to access. The operating system catches the problem before it happens and stops the offending process by sending it a signal 11. When that happens during installation, it means the installer made an error while accessing memory, and the most likely reason is a hardware problem. A commonly suggested cure for the signal 11 problem is to turn off the CPU cache in the BIOS. To do so, you have to enter Setup while the PC boots (by pressing a function key, such as F2) and turn off the CPU cache from the BIOS Setup menu.

If the problem is due to a hardware error in memory (in other words, the result of bad memory chips), you can try swapping the memory modules around in their slots. You may also consider replacing an existing memory module with another memory module if you have one handy.

You can read more about the signal 11 problem at www.bitwizard.nl/sig11.

## Getting around the PC reboot problem

On some PCs, when you press Enter at the boot prompt, the initial Linux kernel loads and immediately reboots the PC. This could be due to a bad implementation of ACPI in the PC's BIOS. To bypass the problem, type **linux acpi=off** at the boot prompt to turn off ACPI. If that doesn't work, consult Table 4-3 for other boot options that you might want to try.

## Using Linux kernel boot options

When you boot the PC for Linux installation, either from the DVD or the first CD-ROM, you get a text screen with the boot: prompt. Typically, you press Enter at that prompt or do nothing, and the installation begins shortly. You can, however, specify a variety of options at the `boot:` prompt. The options control various aspects of the Linux kernel startup, such as disabling support for troublesome hardware or starting the X server using a specific X driver module. Some of these boot options can be helpful in bypassing problems that you may encounter during installation.

To use these boot options, typically you type **linux** followed by the boot options. For example, to perform text mode installation and tell the kernel that your PC has 512MB of memory, you type the following at the `boot:` prompt:

```
linux text mem=512M
```

Consult Table 4-3 for a brief summary of some of the Linux boot options. You can use these commands to turn certain features on or off.

 Although I mention these Linux kernel boot commands in the context of troubleshooting installation problems, you can use many of these commands anytime you boot a PC with any Linux distribution and you want to turn specific features on or off.

| Table 4-3 | Some Linux Boot Options |
|---|---|
| *Boot Option* | *What It Does* |
| `allowcddma` | Enables DMA for CD/DVD drive. |
| `apic` | Works around a bug commonly encountered in the Intel 440GX chipset BIOS and only executes with the installation program kernel. |
| `acpi=off` | Disables ACPI in case there are problems with it. |
| `dd` | Prompts for a driver disk during the installation of Red Hat Linux. |
| `display=IP_ address:0` | Causes the installer GUI to appear on the remote system identified by the IP address. (Make sure that you run the command `xhost +`*hostname* on the remote system where *hostname* is the host where you run the installer.) |
| `driverdisk` | Prompts for a driver disk during the installation of Red Hat Linux. |
| `enforcing=0` | Turns off Security Enhanced Linux (SELinux) mandatory access control. |
| `expert` | Enables you to partition removable media and prompts for a driver disk. |

| Boot Option | What It Does |
|---|---|
| `ide=nodma` | Disables DMA on all IDE devices and can be useful when you're having IDE-related problems. |
| `ks` | Configures the Ethernet card using DHCP and runs a kickstart installation by using a kickstart file from an NFS server identified by the boot server parameters provided by the DHCP server. |
| `ks=kickstartfile` | Runs a kickstart installation by using the kickstart file, specified by `kickstartfile`. (The idea behind kickstart is to create a text file with all the installation options and then kickstart the installation by booting and providing the kickstart file as input.) |
| `lowres` | Forces the installer GUI to run at a lower resolution (640 x 480). |
| `mediacheck` | Prompts you to check the integrity of the CD image (also called the ISO image). The image is checked by computing the MD5 checksum and comparing that with the official Fedora value. Checking a CD-ROM can take a few minutes. |
| `mem=xxxM` | Overrides the amount of memory that the kernel detects on the PC. (Some older machines could detect only 16MB of memory, and on some new machines, the video card may use a portion of the main memory.) Make sure you replace *xxx* with the number representing the megabytes of memory on your PC. |
| `nmi_watchdog=1` | Enables the built-in kernel deadlock detector that makes use of Non-Maskable Interrupt (NMI). |
| `noapic` | Prevents the kernel from using the Advanced Programmable Interrupt Controller (APIC) chip. (You can use this command on motherboards known to have a bad APIC.) |
| `nofirewire` | Does not load support for FireWire. |
| `noht` | Disables *hyper-threading*, which is a feature that enables a single processor to act as multiple virtual processors at the hardware level. |
| `nomce` | Disables self-diagnosis checks performed on the CPU by using Machine Check Exception (MCE). On some machines, these checks are performed too often and need to be disabled. |
| `nomount` | Does not automatically mount any installed Linux partitions in rescue mode. |

*(continued)*

**Table 4-3** *(continued)*

| Boot Option | What It Does |
| --- | --- |
| nopass | Does not pass the keyboard and mouse information to stage 2 of the installation program. |
| nopcmcia | Ignores any PCMCIA controllers in system. |
| noprobe | Disables automatic hardware detection and instead prompts the user for information about SCSI and network hardware installed on the PC. You can pass parameters to modules by using this approach. |
| noshell | Disables shell access on virtual console 2 (the one you get by pressing Ctrl+Alt+F2) during installation. |
| nousb | Disables the loading of USB support during the installation. (Booting without USB support may be useful if the installation program hangs early in the process.) |
| nousbstorage | Disables the loading of the usbstorage module in the installation program's loader. This option may help with device ordering on SCSI systems. |
| reboot=b | Changes the way the kernel tries to reboot the PC so that it can reboot even if the kernel hangs during system shutdown. |
| pci=noacpi | Causes the kernel to not use ACPI to route interrupt requests. |
| pci=biosirq | Causes the kernel to use BIOS settings to route interrupt requests (IRQs). |
| rescue | Starts the kernel in rescue mode, where you get a shell prompt and can try to fix problems. |
| resolution=*HHH*x*VVV* | Causes the installer GUI to run in the specified video mode (where *HHH* and *VVV* are standard resolution numbers, such as 640x480, 800x600, or 1024x768). |
| selinux=0 | Disables the SELinux kernel extensions. |
| serial | Turns on serial console support during installation. |
| skipddc | Skips the Display Data Channel (DDC) probe of monitors. (This option is useful if probing causes problems.) |
| vnc | Starts a VNC (Virtual Network Computing) server so that you can control the GUI installer from another networked system that runs a VNC client. |

# Setting Up Printers

In most Linux distributions, you can set up printers only after you install the distribution. The following sections outline the printer configuration steps for Ubuntu and are similar for all distributions.

To set up a printer, follow these steps:

***1.*** **From the GNOME desktop, choose System⇨Administration⇨Printing.**

If you're not logged in as `root`, the printer configuration tool prompts you for the `root` password. The printer configuration tool, shown in Figure 4-1, is called `system-config-printer`.

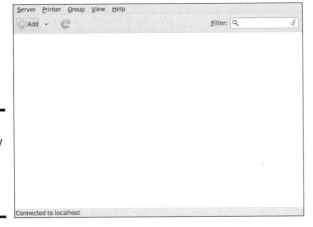

**Figure 4-1:**
The primary printer configuration interface.

***2.*** **Click the Add button to configure a new printer.**

If the device can be identified, it will appear in the list. If it can't be identified, you can still continue with the installation and manually add the drivers and configuration data needed. Figure 4-2 shows that the Epson Stylus printer has been identified as connected to the USB port.

**Figure 4-2:**
You can
install a
local printer
or a network
printer using
the same
interface.

**3. Click Forward to continue.**

The system will search for drivers and offer choices based on what it thinks you're installing.

In the following example, the host is connecting to a local printer.

**4. Select the appropriate driver (see Figure 4-3), and then click Forward.**

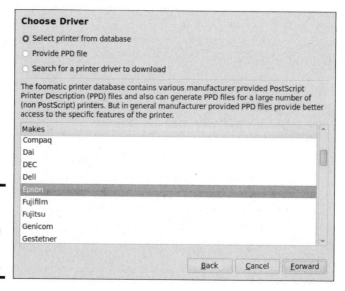

**Figure 4-3:**
Choose the
appropriate
drivers to
install.

5. **Enter the printer name and description variables (see Figure 4-4), and then click Apply.**

   Both the description and location variables are optional, but are helpful if you are configuring this for access by others across the network.

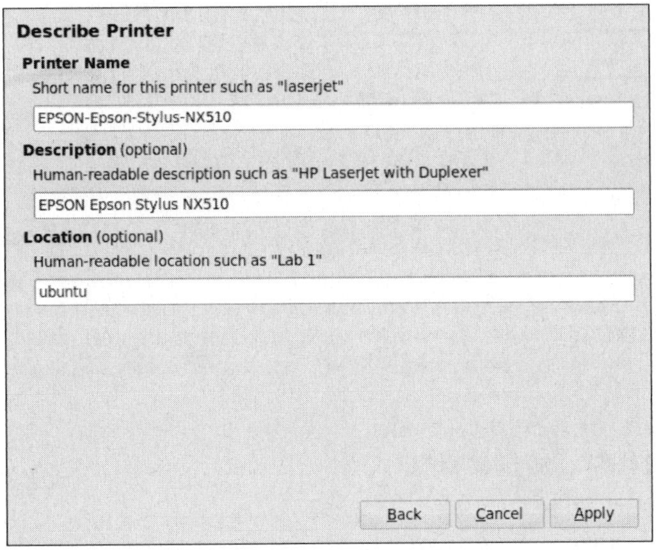

**Describe Printer**

**Printer Name**
Short name for this printer such as "laserjet"

EPSON-Epson-Stylus-NX510

**Description** (optional)
Human-readable description such as "HP LaserJet with Duplexer"

EPSON Epson Stylus NX510

**Location** (optional)
Human-readable location such as "Lab 1"

ubuntu

Back     Cancel     Apply

**Figure 4-4:**
The only required configuration value is the printer name.

6. **Print a test page to make sure all is working as it should.**

   Make any modifications to the settings as needed using the configuration options, which are shown in Figure 4-5.

7. **When the printer is configured as it should be, exit the printer configuration tool.**

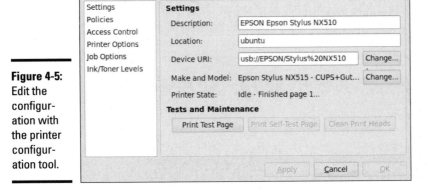

**Figure 4-5:**
Edit the configuration with the printer configuration tool.

# Managing DVDs and CD-ROMs

The GUI desktop makes using DVDs and CD-ROMs in Linux easy. Just place a DVD or a CD-ROM in the drive, and an icon appears on the desktop.

You can then access the CD or DVD by double-clicking the icon on the desktop. In some Linux distributions, the GUI automatically opens the contents of a CD or DVD in a file manager window soon after you insert the CD or DVD in the drive. To access the files and folders, you simply double-click the icons that appear in the GUI file manager window.

If you see a DVD/CD-ROM icon, right-click that icon for a context menu. From that menu, you can eject the CD or DVD when you're finished.

The Knoppix desktop displays icons for each detected drive. To open a CD or DVD, simply click the icon for that drive. In SUSE, click the My Computer icon and click the icon for the DVD/CD drive. Ubuntu and Fedora open the CD/DVD in a Nautilus window and also place an icon on the desktop. Xandros Desktop opens the CD/DVD in a Xandros File Manager window.

# Installing Other Software

The exact steps for installing software depend on the type of package in which the software is distributed. Most Linux software comes in either an RPM file or a Debian package file. The RPM files have an .rpm extension, and the Debian packages have a .deb extension.

Most distributions provide GUI installers to ease the process of installing new software packages. In this section, I provide a quick overview of adding software in Debian, Fedora, SUSE, and Xandros. You typically do not add software to Knoppix (or any other Live CD distribution) because Live CD distributions run from CD-ROM.

Fedora and SUSE use RPM packages. Debian, Ubuntu, and Xandros are all Debian-based distributions, and as expected, they typically use Debian packages (also called DEB files). However, both RPM and DEB packages can be installed in any Linux distribution.

## Installing software in Debian and Ubuntu

The best way to manage software packages in Debian and Debian-based distributions, such as Ubuntu, is to use *APT* — the Advanced Packaging Tool — which you usually control through the apt-get command.

When you install Debian, one of the last steps is to configure the sources for APT. The *APT sources* are the Internet servers (both FTP and Web) where APT looks for software packages to download and install on your system. Assuming that APT is properly configured and that your system has a high-speed Internet connection, you can begin installing any package by typing the following command in a terminal window:

```
apt-get install pkgname
```

where *pkgname* is the name of the package that you want to install. If you don't know the package name, start by typing the following command in the terminal window:

```
apt-cache search keyword
```

where *keyword* is related to the package you want to install. For example, to search for a package that has the word *screenshot* in its description and also contains the word *KDE,* I'd type the following. (I use grep to search the output for occurrences of the text *KDE.*)

```
apt-cache search screenshot | grep KDE
```

This command then prints the following line as the result:

```
ksnapshot - Screenshot application for KDE
```

This shows that the ksnapshot package is what I need. If this package was not yet installed, I could then install it by typing the following command:

```
apt-get install ksnapshot
```

That, in a nutshell, is how you can use the command-line tools to look for and install packages in Debian.

Debian and Ubuntu also come with a GUI package installer for APT called *Synaptic Package Manager,* whose use is intuitive:

✦ **Debian:** Depending upon your version, you will either choose Applications⇨System Tools⇨Synaptic Package Manager from the GNOME desktop or Desktop⇨Administration⇨Synaptic Package Manager.

✦ **Ubuntu:** Choose Select System⇨Administration⇨Synaptic Package Manager. When prompted for a password in Ubuntu, enter your normal user password because Ubuntu has no root user.

After Synaptic Package Manager starts, it displays a Quick Introduction dialog box that tells you, briefly, how to mark packages for installation, upgrade, or removal, and how to get to the menu to perform these actions. After reading the Introduction, click Close to get rid of that dialog box and access the Synaptic Package Manager (see Figure 4-6).

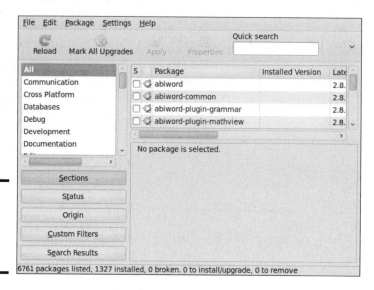

**Figure 4-6:**
The
Synaptic
Package
Manager.

If your package information is older than 48 hours, another dialog box prompts you to update the package information. Click Reload in that dialog box. Synaptic Package Manager then downloads the latest package information, closes the dialog box, and displays information about the packages in the main window.

By clicking the categories on the left side of the Synaptic Package Manager window, you can view lists of various categories of packages on the right side of the window. A box to the left of each package indicates whether the package is installed or not. If you click the package name, Synaptic Package Manager displays information about the selected package in the lower-right part of the window.

To select a package for installation or removal, click the box to the left of its name and choose Mark for Installation or Mark for Removal from the pop-up menu that appears. If selecting a package for installation requires other packages, Synaptic Package Manager displays a dialog box with that information, and you can click Mark to install the required packages also. Mark as many packages as you want and click Apply on the toolbar to perform all marked actions.

# *Installing software in Fedora*

Most Fedora software comes in the form of RPM files. An *RPM* (Red Hat Package Manager) file is basically a single package that contains everything — all the files and configuration information — needed to install a software product.

From the GNOME desktop, you use the Add or Remove Software utility — a graphical utility for installing and uninstalling RPMs. Follow these steps:

*1.* **Choose System➪Administration➪Add/Remove Software.**

If you're not logged in as root, a dialog box prompts you for the root password. The Add or Remove Packages utility starts and gathers information about the status of packages installed on your system. After it sorts through the information about all the installed packages, the utility displays the Package Manager dialog box, which contains a list of all the packages, as shown in Figure 4-7.

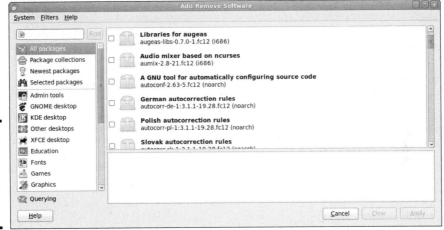

**Figure 4-7:**
Package
Manager
displays the
packages
available.

*2.* **To install an uninstalled package group, select the check box to the left of that package group's name.**

For partially uninstalled package groups, click the Details link (or the Optional Packages button) that appears in a column to the right of the package name.

A dialog box appears with details of the packages in the package group.

*3.* **In the dialog box, select the packages that you want to install or remove by clicking the names, and then click Close to exit the dialog box.**

You return to the Package Management dialog box, and if you added or removed any package, the Update (or Apply) button becomes active.

4. **Click the Update (or Apply) button to update the packages based on any additions or removals you made in the lists of packages.**

## Installing software in SUSE

In SUSE, follow these steps to install or remove software:

1. **From the main menu, choose YaST to start the YaST Control Center.**

   The YaST Control Center displays categories of tasks on the left side and specific tasks for that category on the right side.

2. **Click the Software category on the left side so that the right side shows the options for software.**

3. **Click the Software Management icon on the right side.**

   YaST displays a new window where you can search for software packages.

4. **Search for a package by name or select a package by browsing available packages.**

   To search for a package by name, type a keyword in the Search field in the upper-left corner of the window and then click Search. YaST displays the matching packages on the right side of the window. To browse for packages, click Filter in the upper-left corner, select Package Groups from the drop-down list, and click a group to see the list of individual packages in that group.

5. **Click the Accept button in the bottom-right corner to begin installing selected packages.**

   YaST checks for *dependencies* — if a package requires other packages to install correctly — before installing packages. If you want to view what changes would occur when you click Accept, click Filter and select Installation Summary.

## Installing software in Xandros

Xandros Desktop OS comes with Xandros Networks, which enables you to buy software online as well as install software from a CD or DVD. To start Xandros Networks, double-click the Xandros Networks icon on the Xandros desktop. Xandros Networks starts, connects to a Xandros server, and displays information about installed, updated, and new applications.

To look at the list of new applications, click the plus sign to the left of the New Applications label on the left side of the Xandros Networks window. You get a further list of application categories. If you click a category, the right side of the window displays the names of packages within that category. You can then select a package or an entire category for installation.

To install any selected software packages, choose File⇨Enter Administrator Mode. You're prompted for the administrator (root) password. After entering the root password, you can choose File⇨Install Selected Applications. Xandros Networks checks for dependencies, prompts you if any further information is needed, and downloads and installs the new software.

If you've downloaded a Debian package, you can install it by choosing File⇨ Install DEB File from the Xandros Networks menu. Similarly, the menu choice File⇨Install RPM File installs an RPM package.

# Chapter 5: Trying Out Linux

## In This Chapter

✔ **Starting Linux and logging in**

✔ **Getting familiar with the shell**

✔ **Shutting down the system**

**Y**ou're sitting in front of your PC about to turn it on. You know that the PC has Linux installed. (Maybe you did the installing yourself, but who's keeping track?) You're wondering what to expect when you turn it on and what you do afterward. Not to worry. If you're using Linux for the first time, this chapter shows you how to log in, check out the graphical desktops, try out some cryptic Linux commands, and finally, shut down the PC.

If you try out the Ubuntu Live CD, all you have to do is boot from the Ubuntu Live CD (as explained in Chapter 2 of this minibook), and you can try it just like any other Linux distribution.

For those of you who already know something about Linux, flip through this chapter to see if anything looks new. You never know what you may not know!

## Starting Linux

When you turn on the PC, it goes through the normal power-up sequence and loads the boot loader — GRUB or LILO, depending on your Linux distribution and what you select during installation. The *boot loader* (once known as the bootstrap loader) is a tiny computer program that loads the rest of the operating system from the hard drive into the computer's memory. The entire process of starting a computer is called *booting*.

For Live CDs, the boot loader is typically ISOLINUX, a boot loader designed to work from an ISO 9660 CD-ROM.

The LILO and GRUB boot loaders display a graphical screen with the names of the operating systems that the boot loader can load. For example, if your PC has Windows and Linux, you see both names listed. You can then use the up- and down-arrow keys to select the operating system you want to use. If the PC is set up to load Linux by default, wait a few seconds, and the boot loader starts Linux. To be more precise, the boot loader loads the *Linux kernel* — the core of the Linux operating system — into the PC's memory.

Other boot loaders, such as ISOLINUX, may display a text `boot:` prompt at which you can type boot commands to load specific operating systems and to pass options to that operating system.

While the Linux kernel starts, you see a long list of opening messages, often referred to as the *boot messages*. (You can see these messages at any time by typing the command **dmesg** in a terminal window.) These messages include the names of the devices that Linux detects. One of the first lines in the boot messages reads

```
Calibrating delay loop . . . 4997.12 BogoMIPS (lpj=2498560)
```

*BogoMIPS* is Linux jargon (explained in this chapter in a handy sidebar) for a measure of time. The number that precedes `BogoMIPS` depends on your PC's processor speed, whether it's an old 200 MHz Pentium or a new 4 GHz Pentium 4. The kernel uses the BogoMIPS measurement when it has to wait a small amount of time for some event to occur (such as getting a response back from a disk controller when it's ready).

After the boot messages display, some Linux distributions, such as Fedora, switch to a graphical boot screen that shows information about the progress of system startup. When you boot some Linux distributions, such as Fedora and Xandros Desktop OS, for the first time after installation, you get a configuration program that guides you through some configuration steps, such as setting the date and time and adding user accounts. To complete such first-time configuration steps, all you have to do is enter the requested information.

After Linux boots, you typically get a graphical login screen. For some distributions, such as Knoppix, you get the desktop without having to log in as a user. On other Live CDs, you have to log in.

Figure 5-1 shows the Ubuntu desktop after I booted a PC from the Ubuntu Live CD. For some distributions, you might be logged in automatically. For others, a graphical login screen will appear asking you to authenticate with the username and password given during (or at any time after) the installation.

Every distribution utilizes the `root` username, which happens to be the *superuser* (the administrator account). Whether you install Linux yourself or someone installs it for you, you need to know the `root` password. Without that, you can't do many of the tasks necessary to find out how Linux works.

**Figure 5-1:**
The Ubuntu
Live CD
desktop.

# What are BogoMIPS and LPJ?

When Linux boots, you get a message that says `Calibrating delay loop . . . 4997.12 BogoMIPS (lpj=2498560)`, with some number before the word *BogoMIPS*. BogoMIPS is one of those words that confounds new Linux users, but it's just jargon with a simple meaning.

BogoMIPS is Linus's invention (yes, the same Linus Torvalds who started Linux), and it means bogus MIPS. As you may know, *MIPS* is an acronym for millions of instructions per second — a measure of how fast your computer runs programs. Unfortunately, MIPS isn't a very good measure of performance; the MIPS measurements of different types of computers are difficult to compare accurately. BogoMIPS is

basically a way to measure the computer's speed that's independent of the exact processor type. Linux uses the BogoMIPS number to calibrate a *delay loop,* in which the computer keeps running some useless instructions until a specified amount of time passes. The reason for killing valuable processor time like this is to wait for some slowpoke device to get ready for work.

Oh . . . about LPJ — it's a recent term that stands for loops per jiffy, and it's another measure of time delay used by the kernel. The Linux kernel considers time in increments of jiffies, and a *jiffy* is defined as the time period that is equal to one second divided by the value of a kernel variable named HZ. In other words, HZ jiffies are in each second.

You shouldn't normally log in as root. When you log in as root, you could accidentally damage your system because you can do anything when you're root. Always log in as a normal user. When you need to perform any task as root, type **su –** in a terminal window and enter the root password.

In Ubuntu, you define only a normal user account; Ubuntu doesn't give you the opportunity to define a root user account. Whenever you want to perform any tasks that require you to be root, you have to use the sudo command (an abbreviation for "superuser do"). The default password for root is the one you gave during the installation of the operating system.

To log in as user spiderman, for example, type **spiderman** in the first text field and press Enter. (Move the cursor to the login dialog box before you begin typing.) Then type spiderman's password and press Enter. You then see the initial graphical user interface (GUI). What you get depends on your choice of GUI — GNOME or KDE. If someone made the choice for you, don't worry — GNOME and KDE are both quite good and versatile.

Chapters 1 and 2 in Book II explore the GUI desktops — first GNOME and then KDE. This section focuses on the command line — the only interface you'll have access to if you experience problems loading a graphical desktop.

## Playing with the Shell

Linux is basically UNIX, and UNIX just doesn't feel like UNIX unless you can type cryptic commands in a text terminal. Although GNOME and KDE do a lot to bring us into the world of windows, icons, mouse, and pointer — affectionately known as *WIMP* — sometimes you're stuck with nothing but a plain text screen with a prompt that looks something like this (when you log in as edulaney):

```
edulaney@linux:/etc>
```

You see the text screen most often when something is wrong with the X Window System, which is essentially the machinery that runs the windows and menus that you normally see. In those cases, you have to work with the shell and know some cryptic Linux commands.

You can prepare for unexpected encounters with the shell by trying some Linux commands in a terminal window while you're in the GNOME or KDE GUI. After you get the hang of using the terminal, you might even keep a terminal window open so you can use one of those cryptic commands — simply because it's faster than pointing and clicking. Those two-letter commands do pack some punch!

## *Starting the bash shell*

Simply put, the *shell* is the Linux *command interpreter* — a program that reads what you type, interprets that text as a command, and does what the command is supposed to do.

Before you start playing with the shell, open a terminal window. In either GNOME or KDE, the panel typically includes an icon that looks like a monitor. When you click that icon, what appears is a window with a prompt, like the one shown in Figure 5-2. That's a terminal window, and it works just like an old-fashioned terminal. A shell program is running and ready to accept any text that you type. You type text, press Enter, and something happens (depending on what you typed).

**Figure 5-2:**
The terminal window awaits your input.

If the GNOME or KDE panel on your desktop doesn't seem to have an icon that starts a terminal or shell window, search through the Main menu hierarchy and you should be able to find an item labeled Console or Terminal. Choosing that item should then open a terminal window.

The prompt that you see depends on the shell that runs in that terminal window. The default Linux shell is *bash* (which stands for Bourne-Again SHell).

bash understands a host of standard Linux commands, which you can use to look at files, go from one directory to another, see what programs are running (and who else is logged in), and a whole lot more.

In addition to the Linux commands, bash can run any program stored in an executable file. bash can also execute *shell scripts* — text files that contain Linux commands.

## Understanding shell commands

Because a shell interprets what you type, knowing how the shell figures out the text that you enter is important. All shell commands have this general format:

```
command option1 option2 . . . optionN
```

Such a single line of commands is commonly called a *command line.* On a command line, you enter a command followed by one or more optional parameters (or *arguments*). Such command-line options (or command-line arguments) help you specify what you want the command to do.

One basic rule is that you have to use a space or a tab to separate the command from the options. You also must separate options with a space or a tab. If you want to use an option that contains embedded spaces, you have to put that option within quotation marks. For example, to search for two words of text in the password file, I enter the following grep command. (grep is one of those cryptic commands used to search for text in files.)

```
grep "WWW daemon" /etc/passwd
```

When grep prints the line with those words, it looks like the following. (What you see on your system may differ from what I show.)

```
wwwrun:x:30:8:WWW daemon apache:/var/lib/wwwrun:/bin/false
```

If you created a user account in your name, go ahead and type the grep command with your name as an argument but remember to enclose the name in quotes.

## Trying a few Linux commands

While you have the terminal window open, try a few Linux commands just for fun. I will guide you through some examples to give you a feel for what you can do at the shell prompt.

To see how long the Linux PC has been up since you last powered it up, type the following. (*Note:* I show the typed command in bold, followed by the output from that command.)

```
uptime
12:06:34 up 59 days, 16:23, 4 users, load average: 0.56, 0.55, 0.37
```

The part up 59 days, 16:23 tells you that this particular PC has been up for nearly two months. Hmmm . . . can Windows do that?

To see what version of Linux kernel your system is running, use the uname command like this:

```
uname -srv
```

This runs the uname command with three options: -s, -r, and -v (which can be combined as -srv, as this example shows). The -s option causes uname to print the name of the kernel, -r prints the kernel release number, and -v prints the kernel version number. The command generates the following output on one of my Linux systems:

```
Linux 2.6.31.5-127.fc12.i686 #1 SMP Sat Nov 7 21:41:45 EST 2009
```

In this case, the system is running Linux kernel version 2.6.31.

To read a file, use the more command. For example, type **more /etc/passwd** to read the /etc/passwd file. The resulting output looks similar to the following:

```
root:x:0:0:root:/root:/bin/bash
bin:x:1:1:bin:/bin:/bin/bash
daemon:x:2:2:Daemon:/sbin:/bin/bash
lp:x:4:7:Printing daemon:/var/spool/lpd:/bin/bash
mail:x:8:12:Mailer daemon:/var/spool/clientmqueue:/bin/false
news:x:9:13:News system:/etc/news:/bin/bash
uucp:x:10:14:Unix-to-Unix Copy system:/etc/uucp:/bin/bash
. . . lines deleted . . .
```

To see a list of all the programs currently running on the system, use the ps command, like this:

```
ps ax
```

The ps command takes many options, and you can provide these options without the usual dash prefix. This example uses the a and x options. The a option lists all processes that you're running, and the x option displays the rest of the processes. The result is that ps ax prints a list of all processes running on the system, as shown in the following sample output of the ps ax command:

```
PID TTY STAT TIME COMMAND
1 ? S 0:01 init [5]
2 ? SN 0:00 [ksoftirqd/0]
3 ? S< 0:00 [events/0]
4 ? S< 0:00 [khelper]
9 ? S< 0:00 [kthread]
22 ? S< 0:00 [kblockd/0]
58 ? S 0:00 [kapmd]
79 ? S 0:00 [pdflush]
80 ? S 0:00 [pdflush]
82 ? S< 0:00 [aio/0]
. . . lines deleted . . .
5325 ? Ss 0:00 /opt/kde3/bin/kdm
5502 ? S 0:12 /usr/X11R6/bin/X -br -nolisten tcp :0 vt7 -auth /var/lib/xdm/
     authdir/authfiles/A:0-p1AOrt
5503 ? S 0:00 -:0
6187 ? Ss 0:00 /sbin/portmap
6358 ? Ss 0:00 /bin/sh /usr/X11R6/bin/kde
6566 ? Ss 0:00 /usr/sbin/cupsd
6577 ? Ssl 0:00 /usr/sbin/nscd
. . . lines deleted . . .
```

Amazing how many programs can run on a system even when only you are logged in as a user, isn't it?

As you can guess, you can do everything from a shell prompt, but it does take some getting used to.

# Shutting Down

When you're ready to shut down Linux, you must do so in an orderly manner. Even if you're the sole user of a Linux PC, several other programs usually run in the background. Also, operating systems, such as Linux, try to optimize the way that they write data to the hard drive. Because hard drive access is relatively slow (compared with the time needed to access memory locations), data generally is held in memory and written to the hard drive in large chunks. Therefore, if you simply turn off the power, you run the risk that some files aren't updated properly.

Any user (you don't even have to be logged in) can shut down the system from the desktop or from the graphical login screen, although some distributions, such as Debian, prompt you for the `root` password. Choose Main Menu⇨Log Out (or look for a Log Out option in the menus). A Log Out dialog box appears, such as the one shown in Figure 5-3, providing options for rebooting, halting the system, or simply logging out. To shut down the system, simply select Shutdown and click OK. The system then shuts down in an orderly manner.

**Figure 5-3:**
The Log Out
dialog box.

If the logout menu doesn't have an option to shut down, first log out and then select Shutdown from the graphical login screen. You can also shut down a Linux computer from a terminal with the command `init 0`. This method is sometimes required if you are running the operating system within a virtual software manager such as VMWare.

While the system shuts down, you see messages about processes shutting down. You may be surprised at how many processes there are even when no one is explicitly running any programs on the system. If your system doesn't automatically power off on shutdown, you can manually turn off the power.

Shutting down or rebooting the system may *not* require `root` access. This is why it's important to make sure that physical access to the console is protected adequately so that anyone who wants to can't simply walk up to the console and shut down your system.

You don't always need to shut down when you're finished with a session; instead, you may choose to simply log out. To log out of KDE, choose Main Menu⇨Logout. You can also right-click an empty area of the desktop and choose Logout from the context menu that appears. To log out from GNOME, choose System⇨Log Out. Click OK when a dialog box asks if you really want to log out. (In some GNOME desktop distributions, the menu option to log out is the second or third menu button from the left in the top panel.)

# Book II

# Linux Desktops

The 5th Wave          By Rich Tennant

"It's called Linux Poker. Everyone gets to see everyone else's cards, everything's wild, you can play off your opponents' hands, and everyone wins except Bill Gates, whose face appears on the jokers."

# Contents at a Glance

**Chapter 1: The GNOME Desktop** . . . . . . . . . . . . . . . . . . . . . . . . . . . . . . .**77**

Getting to Know the GNOME Desktop . . . . . . . . . . . . . . . . . . . . . . . . . . . . . 78
Understanding the GNOME Panels . . . . . . . . . . . . . . . . . . . . . . . . . . . . . . . . . . 80

**Chapter 2: The KDE Desktop** . . . . . . . . . . . . . . . . . . . . . . . . . . . . . . . . .**87**

Getting to Know the KDE Desktop . . . . . . . . . . . . . . . . . . . . . . . . . . . . . . . . . 87
Understanding the KDE Panel . . . . . . . . . . . . . . . . . . . . . . . . . . . . . . . . . . . . . . 90
Configuring the KDE Bottom Panel . . . . . . . . . . . . . . . . . . . . . . . . . . . . . . . 94
Configuring the KDE Desktop . . . . . . . . . . . . . . . . . . . . . . . . . . . . . . . . . . . . . . 95

**Chapter 3: Commanding the Shell** . . . . . . . . . . . . . . . . . . . . . . . . . . . .**99**

Opening Terminal Windows and Virtual Consoles . . . . . . . . . . . . . . . . . 99
Using the bash Shell . . . . . . . . . . . . . . . . . . . . . . . . . . . . . . . . . . . . . . . . . . . . . . 100
Discovering and Using Linux Commands . . . . . . . . . . . . . . . . . . . . . . . . . 108
Writing Shell Scripts . . . . . . . . . . . . . . . . . . . . . . . . . . . . . . . . . . . . . . . . . . . . . . 117

**Chapter 4: Navigating the Linux File System** . . . . . . . . . . . . . . . . .**119**

Understanding the Linux File System . . . . . . . . . . . . . . . . . . . . . . . . . . . . . 119
Navigating the File System with Linux Commands . . . . . . . . . . . . . . . 124

**Chapter 5: Introducing Linux Applications** . . . . . . . . . . . . . . . . . . . .**137**

Taking Stock of Linux Applications . . . . . . . . . . . . . . . . . . . . . . . . . . . . . . . 137
Introducing Office Applications and Tools . . . . . . . . . . . . . . . . . . . . . . . . 143
Checking out Multimedia Applications . . . . . . . . . . . . . . . . . . . . . . . . . . . 149
Using Graphics and Imaging Apps . . . . . . . . . . . . . . . . . . . . . . . . . . . . . . . . 152
Using GUI File Managers . . . . . . . . . . . . . . . . . . . . . . . . . . . . . . . . . . . . . . . . . 154

**Chapter 6: Using Text Editors** . . . . . . . . . . . . . . . . . . . . . . . . . . . . . . . .**161**

Using GUI Text Editors . . . . . . . . . . . . . . . . . . . . . . . . . . . . . . . . . . . . . . . . . . . 161
Text Editing with ed and vi . . . . . . . . . . . . . . . . . . . . . . . . . . . . . . . . . . . . . . . 163

# Chapter 1: The GNOME Desktop

## In This Chapter

✓ **Discovering GNOME's common features**

✓ **Presenting the Main Menu**

✓ **Introducing the Places Menu**

✓ **Examining the System Menu**

✓ **Introducing the bottom panel**

*L*inux distributions come with one or both of two popular graphical user interfaces (GUIs): GNOME and KDE. GNOME and KDE are similar to Microsoft Windows but unique in one respect. Unlike Microsoft Windows, you can choose your GUI in Linux. If you don't like GNOME, you can use KDE; and if you don't like KDE, you can use GNOME. With both installed, you can switch between the two in a matter of seconds. Try doing that with Microsoft Windows!

GNOME and KDE were developed independently of Linux and run on other UNIX operating systems besides Linux. You also have the option to install other GUIs, such as FVWM and Xfce, in Linux. Visit `www.freedesktop.org/wiki/Desktops` to see a list of other X desktops (desktops that run on X Window System).

This chapter explores the major features of GNOME, and Chapter 2 in this minibook does a similar comparison of KDE. You can best figure out these GUIs by simply starting to use them. No matter which GUI you decide to use, all GUI applications — whether they're based on GNOME or KDE — run on all GUI desktops. In other words, you can run KDE applications under GNOME and vice versa. The only hurdle is that sometimes both GNOME and KDE applications may not be installed by default.

Each Linux distribution typically installs one of the GUIs by default. Each distribution also customizes GNOME or KDE to create a desktop that's unique to the distribution. Because of this, there may be subtle, minor differences between what you see in your distribution and what is described here.

# Getting to Know the GNOME Desktop

The initial desktop for GNOME looks like any other popular GUI, such as Microsoft Windows or the Mac OS X desktop. Figure 1-1, for example, shows the typical GNOME desktop.

**Figure 1-1:**
A clean
GNOME
desktop in
Ubuntu.

Running the Live CD, a number of icons that would be present if the operating system were installed will not be there. When the system is installed, the desktop initially shows icons for your computer, your home folder, and the trash can for deleted files. (Unlike other distributions, Ubuntu strives for a minimum of desktop icons and has a clean look. Some Ubuntu versions feature no desktop icons.)

## Desktop context menus

The GNOME desktop displays a context menu when you right-click a clear area on the desktop. The menu offers the following menu options:

✦ Create a new folder

✦ Create a shortcut to a command (Create Launcher)

✦ Create a new document

✦ Clean up the desktop, or align icons

✦ Configure the desktop background

Figure 1-2 shows the desktop context menus in a typical GNOME desktop. Desktop menu options with a right-pointing arrow have other menus that appear when you put the mouse pointer over the arrow.

Book II
Chapter 1

The GNOME Desktop

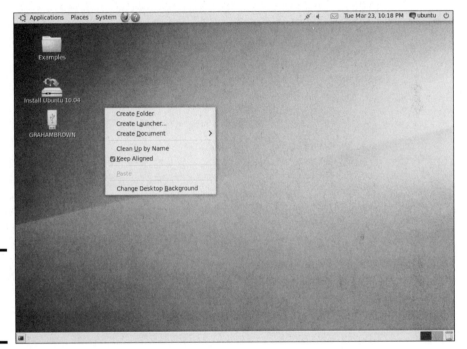

**Figure 1-2:**
Standard
menu
choices in
GNOME.

## *Icon context menus*

Right-clicking any desktop icon in GNOME displays another menu, as shown in Figure 1-3.

Many items on this context menu are the same no matter what icon you click, but right-clicking certain icons (for example, the Trash icon) produces a somewhat different menu. You can perform the following typical tasks from icon context menus:

✦ Open a folder in a file manager

✦ Open a file with an application that you choose

✦ Rename the icon

✦ Move the icon to trash

✦ View the properties of that icon

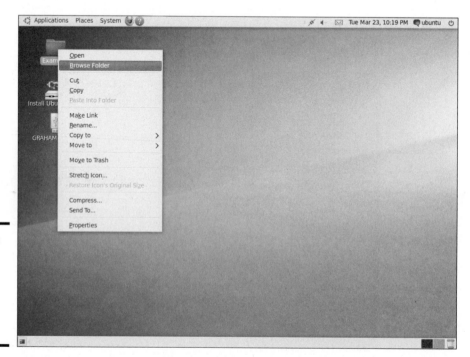

**Figure 1-3:**
The menu
choices
for the
Examples
icon in
GNOME.

For the Trash icon, the icon context menu typically provides an option to permanently delete the items in the trash. (You get a chance to say Yes or No.)

I bet you see a pattern here: the right-click. No matter where you are in a GUI desktop, *always right-click before you pick.* You're bound to find something useful when you right-click!

## Understanding the GNOME Panels

The GNOME desktop has two *panels* — the top and bottom bars. (The KDE desktop has only one panel.) Each panel is similar to the Windows taskbar. The top panel has buttons on the left (shortcuts to various programs) and a time display to the right. The middle part of the panel shows buttons for any applications you've started (or that were automatically started for you).

Move the mouse over any icon on the panel, and a small pop-up window displays the name of that icon. The pop-up window also gives a hint about what you can do with that icon.

## The top panel

The top panel is the long bar that stretches across the top of the GNOME desktop. Figure 1-4 shows a typical view of the GNOME top panel.

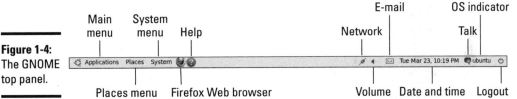

Figure 1-4:
The GNOME
top panel.

The panel is a parking place for icons. Some icons start programs when you click them. Some show status (for example, what programs are currently running) as well as information such as date and time.

## The Main Menu button

The leftmost icon on the GNOME top panel is the *Main Menu* button. The Main Menu button, like the Start button in Microsoft Windows, is where you typically find all your applications, organized into submenus. The term Main Menu is generic; in GNOME, the button is typically labeled Applications.

Click the Main Menu button to bring up the first-level menu. Then mouse over any menu item containing an arrow to bring up the next-level menu, and so on. You can go through a menu hierarchy and make selections from the final menu. Figure 1-5 shows the main menu hierarchy in the typical GNOME desktop.

I use the notation Applications⇨Internet⇨Firefox Web Browser to refer to the menu sequence highlighted in Figure 1-5. This style of notation is used throughout this book.

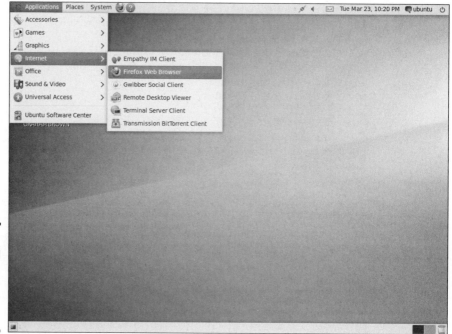

**Figure 1-5:**
The standard menu hierarchy on the GNOME desktop.

In most desktops, the top-level main menu has the following types of menu categories:

+ **Accessories:** Lots of utility programs, such as a scientific calculator, a character selector, a floppy formatter, a dictionary, and a Palm Pilot or Handspring syncing software

+ **Games:** A menu of games (and a whole lot of them at that), such as Solitaire, Mahjongg, Mines, and Reversi

+ **Graphics:** Programs such as *The GIMP* (an Adobe Photoshop–like program), a digital camera interface, a scanner interface, a screen-capture program, and an Adobe Acrobat viewer

+ **Internet:** Internet applications, such as a Web browser, e-mail reader, and instant messenger

+ **Office:** Office applications such as the OpenOffice.org office suite (which includes the Writer word processor, Calc spreadsheet, Impress slide presentation program, and Draw drawing program)

+ **Sound & Video:** Multimedia applications such as a CD player, a sound mixer, a sound recorder, and volume control

The main menu typically also has a few submenu items for some commonly performed tasks, such as Add/Remove Applications.

In each distribution, the main menu has different categories but a similar organization, so you can usually find what you need.

## The Places Menu button

The second menu choice from the left on the GNOME top panel is the *Places Menu.* That's where you typically find an easy way to get to all the locations you may need to visit, as well as access the network, search for files, and perform other common functions. Figure 1-6 shows an example of this menu.

**Book II**
**Chapter 1**

**The GNOME Desktop**

**Figure 1-6:**
The GNOME
Places
menu
choices.

Of particular help is the Search for Files option, which displays the dialog box shown in Figure 1-7. You can use this option to find files based on almost any criteria — date created, changed, name, containing certain phrases, and so on. It's worth your time to experiment with this tool and get to know it well.

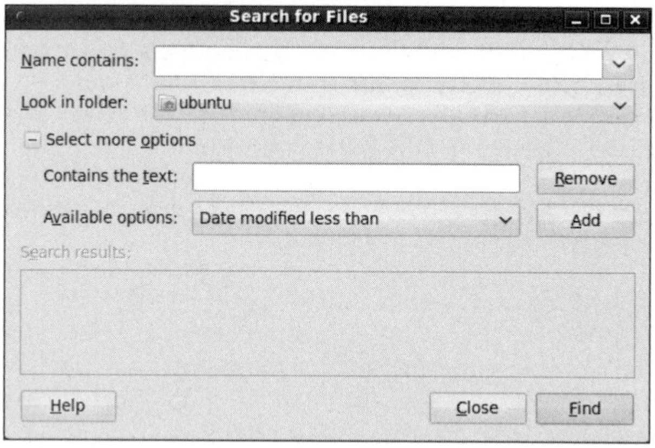

**Figure 1-7:**
The default search options can be changed through the dialog box.

## The System Menu button

The third menu choice from the left on the GNOME top panel is the *System Menu.* This is where you typically turn to for administrative tasks. Figure 1-8 shows an example of this menu.

**Figure 1-8:**
The standard System menu in GNOME.

The Preferences options allow you to perform such tasks as choosing your default printer, configuring power management on a laptop, and tweaking sound settings. The Administration options let you run the administrative utilities needed to see what's going on with the system and make changes (administration is covered in detail in Book V).

Other options on this menu allow you to get information about the distribution, as well as access help and support.

## Top panel icons

In addition to the menu choices in the top panel, a number of icons are commonly present (refer to Figure 1-4). You can identify each of these icons by moving the cursor over them and reading the pop-up descriptions that appear. The most common ones (in the order they typically appear from left to right) are

+ **Firefox Web browser:** Start the popular browser and access the Internet.

+ **Evolution Mail:** Start the Evolution e-mail and calendar software.

+ **Help:** Display online help information in a documentation viewer for GNOME.

+ **Network:** Display information about current wired or wireless connections.

+ **Volume:** Display a volume control bar that you can use to change the sound's volume by dragging a slider.

+ **E-mail:** Open your preferred e-mail reader.

+ **Date and time:** Display the current date and time; clicking displays a calendar showing the current date.

+ **Talk:** Allow instant messaging with fellow workers.

+ **OS indicator:** Signify which operating system you are running.

+ **Logout:** Change users, lock the desktop, or shut down the system.

## The bottom panel

In addition to the top panel, GNOME also includes a bottom panel. Figure 1-9 shows an example of this menu. The items that appear here are

**Figure 1-9:**
The bottom
panel in
GNOME.

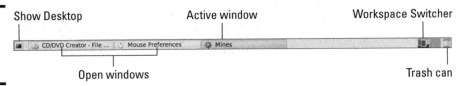

Show Desktop                    Active window                    Workspace Switcher

Open windows                                                      Trash can

✦ **Show Desktop:** Hide (but do not close) all windows and display the desktop.

✦ **Open windows:** Display all currently open windows.

✦ **Active window:** Switch to another running application or window.

✦ **Workspace Switcher:** Display a different workspace by clicking a square. This has the same function as the Desktop Pager in KDE desktops. Explore the three menus (Applications, Places, and System) to see the categories of tasks you can perform from the selections in these menus.

✦ **Trash can:** View or empty the contents of the trash can.

# Chapter 2: The KDE Desktop

## In This Chapter

✓ **Discovering KDE's common features**

✓ **Introducing the Main Menu**

✓ **Configuring the panel and the desktop**

**A**s mentioned in Chapter 1 of this minibook, Linux distributions come with one (or both) of two popular graphical user interfaces (GUIs) — GNOME and KDE. With both installed, you can switch between the two in a matter of seconds. If you don't like GNOME, you can use KDE; or if you don't like KDE, you can use GNOME.

This chapter explores the major features of KDE, just as Chapter 1 of this minibook examined GNOME. I strongly encourage you to try both GUIs before you decide which one you're most comfortable using. Remember, you can run KDE applications under GNOME and vice versa. Several installations, including Fedora and openSUSE, allow you to choose to install KDE or GNOME. Installing only one by default allows for a quicker and easier setup and installation; you can always go back and install the other interface later.

Each distribution customizes the desktop, so there may be subtle, minor differences between what you see in your distribution and what's described here.

## Getting to Know the KDE Desktop

The initial desktop for KDE looks like any other popular GUI, such as Microsoft Windows desktop or the Mac OS X desktop. Figure 2-1 shows a typical KDE desktop.

*KDE* stands for the *K Desktop Environment*. The KDE project started in October 1996 with the intent to develop a common GUI for UNIX systems that use the X Window System. The first beta version of KDE was released a year later, in October 1997. KDE version 1.0 was released in July 1998.

Figure 2-1 is from Fedora 12, which strives for a minimum of desktop icons. Along the bottom of the desktop is the *panel* — which is similar to the top and bottom bars in GNOME and the Windows taskbar. The panel has buttons on the left (shortcuts to various programs), a set of buttons to the available desktops, a task area, and a time display and icons for volume control and access to the KDE's Clipboard manager, Klipper, to the right. In the middle part of the panel are buttons for any applications that you started (or that were automatically started for you).

**Figure 2-1:**
A clean KDE desktop.

## Desktop context menus

The KDE desktop displays a context menu when you right-click a clear area on the desktop. The context menu offers a menu that includes the following options (with slight variations between distributions):

✦ Konsole (access to a terminal window)

✦ Run Command

✦ Lock Screen

✦ Leave (exit the desktop)

✦ Desktop Activity Settings (set such things as the wallpaper)

Figure 2-2 shows the desktop context menu in a typical KDE desktop.

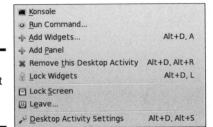

**Figure 2-2:**
The context
menu in
KDE.

## Icon context menus

Right-clicking any desktop icon in KDE displays another menu, as shown in
Figure 2-3. Many items on this context menu are the same no matter what
icon you click, but right-clicking certain icons (for example, the CD-ROM
device icon) produces a somewhat different menu. Desktop menu options
with a right-pointing arrow have other menus that appear when you put the
mouse pointer over the arrow. You can perform the following typical tasks
from icon context menus:

**Figure 2-3:**
The pop-up
menu for an
icon in KDE.

✦ Open a folder in a file manager

✦ Open a file with an application that you choose

✦ Cut or copy

✦ Rename the icon

✦ Move the icon to the trash

✦ View the properties of that icon

For the CD-ROM device icon and similar devices, the icon context menu typically provides an option to eject the media.

No matter where you are in a GUI desktop, *always right-click before you pick.*
You're bound to find something useful when you right-click!

# Understanding the KDE Panel

The *panel* is the long bar that stretches across the bottom of the desktop. KDE, as opposed to GNOME, has only one panel by default. Figure 2-4 shows a typical view of the KDE panel.

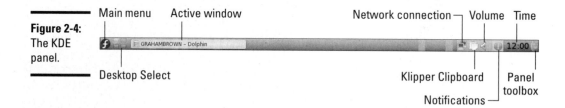

Main menu    Active window          Network connection ─┐ Volume   Time

**Figure 2-4:**
The KDE
panel.

Desktop Select                     Klipper Clipboard   Panel
                                                   toolbox
                                           Notifications ─┘

The panel is a parking place for icons. Some icons start programs when you click them. Some show status (for example, what programs are currently running) as well as information such as the date and time.

If you move the mouse pointer on top of an icon, a Help balloon pops up and gives you a helpful hint about the icon.

## The Main Menu button

The leftmost icon on the KDE panel is the *Main Menu* button. (KDE documentation calls the Main Menu button the *Application Starter*). Like the Start button in Microsoft Windows, the Main Menu button is where you typically find all your applications, organized into submenus. The Main Menu button is often labeled K, although the letter can be changed by the distribution.

Click the Main Menu button to see the first-level menu. Then mouse over any menu item with an arrow to bring up the next-level menu and so on. You can go through a menu hierarchy and make selections from the final menu. Figure 2-5 shows the Main Menu hierarchy in a typical KDE desktop.

I use the notation Applications⇨Internet to refer to the menu sequence highlighted in Figure 2-5. This style of notation is used throughout this book.

The most recent versions of KDE feature the KickOff application launcher as their main menu. KickOff allows you to access frequently used applications more quickly than navigating through the traditional menu hierarchy. In most desktops, clicking the Main Menu button to open KickOff presents the following top-level categories:

✦ **Favorites:** Easy access to frequently used applications and documents. To quickly add a file to your Favorites, right-click it and choose Add to Favorites.

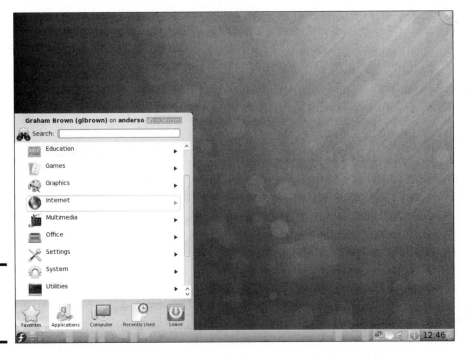

Book II
Chapter 2

The KDE Desktop

**Figure 2-5:**
The KDE
menu
hierarchy.

✦ **Applications:** The applications and tools installed on your system. Click a subcategory with a right-pointing arrow to open more options.

✦ **Computer:** Access to hard drives and removable memory devices, as well as the trash.

✦ **Recently Used:** A chronological display of recently opened documents and applications.

✦ **Leave:** Options to log out, restart, shut down the computer, and more.

In the Applications tab, you will find the following menu subcategories (and probably a few more depending on which distribution you are using):

✦ **Administration:** Access to the utility programs you need to manage the system, such as managing the firewall and adding users and groups. Figure 2-6 shows an example of the Administration menu.

✦ **Games:** A menu of games (and a lot of them at that) such as arcade games, board games, and card games.

✦ **Graphics:** Programs such as Flickr, KolourPaint, and KSnapshot (used to take the screenshots in this chapter).

✦ **Internet:** Internet applications, such as a Web browser, an e-mail reader, and instant messenger.

**Figure 2-6:**
The Admin-
istration
menu
choices.

✦ **Multimedia:** Multimedia applications such as a CD player, a sound mixer, a sound recorder, and volume control.

✦ **Office:** Office applications such as the OpenOffice.org Office suite (includes the Writer word processor, the Calc spreadsheet, the Impress slide presentation program, and the Draw drawing program).

✦ **Settings:** Access to configuration settings and the utilities needed to make changes. An example of the Settings menu is shown in Figure 2-7.

**Figure 2-7:**
The Settings
menu
choices.

✦ **System:** The utilities needed for system configuration. An example of the System menu is shown in Figure 2-8.

**Figure 2-8:**
The System menu choices.

✦ **Utilities:** Additional miscellaneous utilities that can be utilized by KDE, including text-to-speech tools, a personal alarm scheduler, and a screen magnifier.

Three KDE menu choices — Administration, Settings, and System — will help you configure almost anything you need.

In each distribution, the main menu and KickOff have different categories but the same menu organization, so you should usually be able to find what you need.

## Panel icons

In addition to the Main Menu button, the KDE panel has several icons (labeled in Figure 2-4). You can identify any icon by moving your cursor over it and reading the pop-up description that appears. The most common ones (in the order they typically appear from left to right) are as follows:

✦ **Desktop Pager:** Navigate between workspaces or "virtual desktops."

✦ **Open windows:** Display all currently open windows.

✦ **Active window:** Switch to another running application or window.

✦ **Network connection:** Display information about current wired or wireless connections.

✦ **Klipper Clipboard:** Configure and edit contents of your clipboard.

✦ **Volume:** Display a volume control bar that you can use to change the sound's volume by dragging a slider.

✦ **Notifications and Jobs:** Mouse over to see the progress of current jobs such as file transfers or printing documents.

✦ **Time:** Display the time; clicking displays a calendar showing the current date.

✦ **Panel toolbox:** Adjust size, location, and controls for the panel.

## Configuring the KDE Bottom Panel

For all the power inherent in the KDE panel, it also has a great deal of flexibility. If you right-click a blank spot on the panel, the menu shown in Figure 2-9 appears. You use this menu to add and remove items from the panel and even create an additional panel (allowing you to configure your desktop as much like GNOME as you want it to be).

**Figure 2-9:**
You have
a lot of
flexibility
when
configuring
the panel.

The most powerful menu choice is Panel Settings. Choosing Panel Settings⇨ More Settings displays the utility shown in Figure 2-10. From here, you can place the panel in a location other than its default location along the bottom, adjust the alignment of the panel, automatically hide the panel, select whether windows will appear in front of or behind the panel, and more.

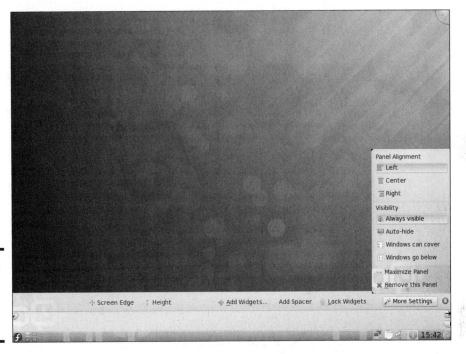

**Figure 2-10:**
Configuring the KDE panel is easy.

# Configuring the KDE Desktop

After right-clicking an empty spot on the desktop, you can choose Configure Desktop from the pop-up menu. Doing so displays the configuration tool shown in Figure 2-11. You can configure such items as the background and special mouse controls to perform helpful functions on the desktop.

For more thorough desktop configurations, choose Desktop from the System Settings menu (which I discuss more in a few moments) to display the configuration options shown in Figure 2-12. You can set the screen size, adjust settings for multiple desktops, change the screen saver, and play around with desktop effects (a new addition to KDE version 4).

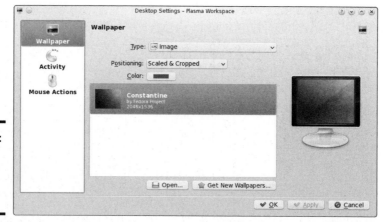

**Figure 2-11:**
You can
change the
desktop
settings.

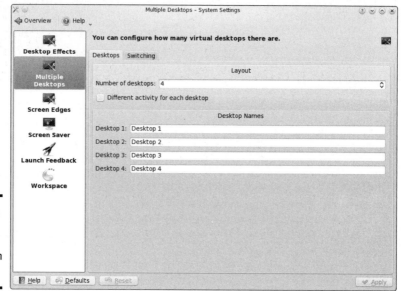

**Figure 2-12:**
More
desktop
configuration
options.

If you're using an older version of KDE, you have the choice to set a desktop menu bar at the top of the screen — an example of which is shown in Figure 2-13. However, the ability to add a desktop menu is no longer available in KDE 4.

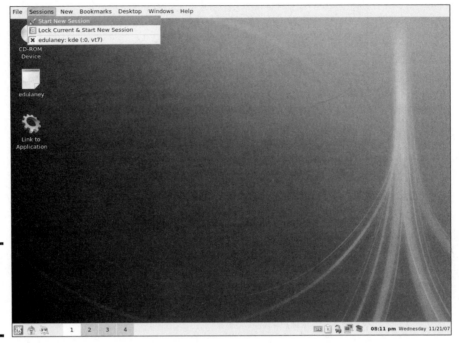

**Figure 2-13:**
A desktop
menu
adds more
flexibility.

Another tool to experiment with is System Settings, KDE's control center
interface (shown in Figure 2-14). To get to System Settings, choose
Applications➪Settings➪System Settings. The System Settings menu is
organized into categories, such as Look and Feel, Personal, Network
Connectivity, and Computer Administration. Click an item to view the subcategories for that item. Click one of the subcategory items to change it.
After making any changes you want, click the Apply button to enact the
change. If you don't like the result, you can often click Reset to go back to
the original setting.

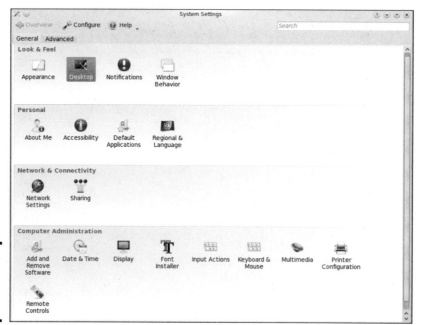

**Figure 2-14:**
The System
Settings
menu.

Depending upon your distribution, you may also want to use downloadable programs such as SAX2 or YAST (in openSUSE) for desktop configuration. SAX2 is an open source program that simplifies configuration.

# Chapter 3: Commanding the Shell

## In This Chapter

✔ Opening a terminal window or a virtual console

✔ Discovering the bash shell

✔ Using Linux commands

✔ Writing a shell script

Sometimes, things just don't work. What do you do if the GUI desktop stops responding to your mouse clicks? What if the GUI doesn't start at all? You can still tell your Linux system what to do, but you have to do it by typing commands into a text screen. In these situations, you work with the shell — the Linux command interpreter. This chapter introduces the bash shell, the default shell in most Linux distributions.

After you figure out how to work with the shell, you may even begin to like the simplicity and power of the Linux commands. And then, even if you're a GUI aficionado, someday soon you may find yourself firing up a terminal window and making the system sing and dance with two- or three-letter commands strung together by strange punctuation characters. (Hey, I can dream, can't I?)

## Opening Terminal Windows and Virtual Consoles

First things first. If you're working in a GUI desktop, such as GNOME or KDE, where do you type commands for the shell? Good question.

The easiest way to get to the shell is to open a *terminal* (also called *console*) window. The GNOME and KDE GUIs in most distributions include an icon (or a Main Menu option) to open a terminal window. Click that icon or choose the menu option to get a terminal window. If you don't see such an icon in GNOME, choose Applications➪Accessories➪Terminal. Now you can type commands to your heart's content.

If, for some reason, the GUI seems to be *hung* (you click and type but nothing happens), you can turn to the *virtual consoles*. (The *physical console* is the monitor-and-keyboard combination.) The idea of virtual consoles is to give you the ability to switch between several text consoles even though you have only one physical console. Whether you're running a GUI or not, you can then use different text consoles to type different commands.

To get to the first virtual console from the GNOME or KDE desktop, press Ctrl+Alt+F1. Press Ctrl+Alt+F2 for the second virtual console, and so on. Each of these virtual consoles is a text screen where you can log in and type Linux commands to perform various tasks. When you're finished, type **exit** to log out.

You can use up to six virtual consoles. In most distributions, the seventh one is used for the GUI desktop. To get back to the GUI desktop, press Ctrl+Alt+F7.

## Using the bash Shell

If you've used MS-DOS, you may be familiar with COMMAND.COM, the DOS command interpreter. That program displays the infamous C:\> prompt. In Windows, you can see this prompt if you open a command window. (To open a command window in Microsoft Windows, choose Start⇨Run, type **command** in the text box, and then click OK.)

Linux comes with a command interpreter that resembles COMMAND.COM in DOS, but it can do a whole lot more. The Linux command interpreter is called a *shell*.

The default shell in many Linux distributions is bash. When you open a terminal window or log in at a text console, the bash shell is what prompts you for commands. Then, when you type a command, the shell executes your command.

Just as there are multiple GUIs (GNOME or KDE) for Linux, you have a choice of shells besides bash. For example, some people prefer the C shell. You can easily change your default shell by using the chsh command.

In addition to the standard Linux commands, bash can execute any computer program. So you can type the name of an application (the name is usually more cryptic than what you see in GNOME or KDE menus) at the shell prompt, and the shell starts that application.

### Understanding the syntax of shell commands

Because a shell interprets what you type, knowing how the shell processes the text you enter is important. All shell commands have the following general format. (Some commands have no options.)

*command [option1] [option2] . . . [optionN]*

Issuing such a command is commonly referred to as a *command line*. On a command line, you enter a command, followed by zero or more options (or *arguments*). These strings of options — the *command-line options* (or command-line arguments) — modify the way the command works so that you can get it to do specific tasks.

The shell uses a blank space or a tab to distinguish between the command and options. This means you must use a space or a tab to separate the command from the options and the options from one another.

If an option contains spaces, you put that option inside quotation marks. For example, to search for my name in the password file, I enter the following `grep` command (`grep` is used for searching for text in files):

```
grep "Emmett Dulaney" /etc/passwd
```

Book II
Chapter 3

When `grep` prints the line with my name, it looks like this:

```
edulaney:x:1000:100:Emmett Dulaney:/home/edulaney:/bin/bash
```

Commanding
the Shell

If you create a user account with your username, type the `grep` command with your username as an argument to look for that username in the `/etc/passwd` file.

In the output from the `grep` command, you can see the name of the shell (`/bin/bash`) following the last colon (`:`). Because the `bash` shell is an executable file, it resides in the `/bin` directory; you must provide the full path to it.

The number of command-line options and their format depend on the actual command. Typically, these options look like `-X`, where `X` is a single character. For example, you can use the `-l` option with the `ls` command. The command lists the contents of a directory, and the option provides additional details. Here is a result of typing **`ls -l`** in a user's home directory:

```
total 0
drwxr-xr-x 2 edulaney users 48 2010-09-08 21:11 bin
drwx------ 2 edulaney users 320 2010-09-08 21:16 Desktop
drwx------ 2 edulaney users 80 2010-09-08 21:11 Documents
drwxr-xr-x 2 edulaney users 80 2010-09-08 21:11 public_
    html
drwxr-xr-x 2 edulaney users 464 2010-09-17 18:21 sdump
```

If a command is too long to fit on a single line, you can press the backslash key (`\`) followed by Enter. Then, continue typing the command on the next line. For example, type the following command. (Press Enter after each line.)

```
cat \
/etc/passwd
```

The `cat` command then displays the contents of the `/etc/passwd` file.

You can *concatenate* (that is, string together) several shorter commands on a single line by separating the commands by semicolons ( ; ). For example, the following command

```
cd; ls -l; pwd
```

changes the current directory to your home directory, lists the contents of that directory, and then shows the name of that directory.

## Combining shell commands

You can combine simple shell commands to create a more sophisticated command. For example, suppose that you want to find out whether a device file named sbpcd resides in your system's /dev directory because some documentation says you need that device file for your CD-ROM drive. You can use the ls /dev command to get a directory listing of the /dev directory and then browse through it to see whether that listing contains sbpcd.

Unfortunately, the /dev directory has a great many entries, so you may find it hard to find any item that has sbpcd in its name. You can, however, combine the ls command with grep and come up with a command line that does exactly what you want. Here's that command line:

```
ls /dev | grep sbpcd
```

The shell sends the output of the ls command (the directory listing) to the grep command, which searches for the string sbpcd. That vertical bar ( | ) is known as a *pipe* because it acts as a conduit (think of a water pipe) between the two programs — the output of the first command is fed into the input of the second one.

## Controlling command input and output

Most Linux commands have a common feature — they always read from the *standard input* (usually, the keyboard) and write to the *standard output* (usually, the screen). Error messages are sent to the *standard error* (usually to the screen as well). These three devices often are referred to as stdin, stdout, and stderr.

You can make a command get its input from a file and then send its output to another file. Just so you know, the highfalutin term for this feature is *input and output redirection or I/O redirection.*

Table 3-1 shows the syntax of common I/O redirection commands, and the next few sections explain how to use some of these commands.

### Table 3-1        Common Standard I/O Redirections

| *Task* | *Command Syntax* |
|---|---|
| Send stdout to a file | `command > file` |
| Send stderr to file | `command 2> file` |
| Send stdout and stderr to file | `command > file 2>&1` |
| Read stdin from a file | `command < file` |
| Read stdin from file.in and send stdout to file.out | `command < file.in > file.out` |
| Append stdout to the end of a file | `command >> file` |
| Append stderr to the end of a file | `command 2>> file` |
| Append stdout and stderr to the end of a file | `command >> file 2>&1` |
| Read stdin from the keyboard until the character c | `command <<c` |
| Pipe stdout to command2 | `command | command2` |
| Pipe stdout and stderr to command2 | `command 2>&1 | command2` |

### Getting command input from a file

If you want a command to read from a file, you can redirect the standard input to come from that file instead of from the keyboard. For example, type the following command:

```
sort < /etc/passwd
```

This command displays a sorted list of the lines in the /etc/passwd file. In this case, the less-than sign (<) redirects stdin so that the sort command reads its input from the /etc/passwd file.

### Saving command output in a file

To save the output of a command in a file, redirect the standard output to a file. For example, type **cd** to change to your home directory and then type the following command:

```
grep typedef /usr/include/* > typedef.out
```

This command searches through all files in the /usr/include directory for the occurrence of the text typedef — and then saves the output in a file called typedef.out. The greater-than sign (>) redirects stdout to a file. This command also illustrates another feature of bash: When you use an asterisk (*), bash replaces the asterisk with a list of all filenames in the specified directory. Thus, `/usr/include/*` means *all the files in the* `/usr/include` *directory*.

If you want to append a command's output to the end of an existing file instead of saving the output in a new file, use two greater-than signs (>>) like this:

```
command >> filename
```

Another interesting use of sending `stdout` to a file is the use of the `cat` command to quickly prepare small text files. For example, suppose that you want to create a new text file to store lines of text you type until you type **ZZ** and press Enter. Here is how you can accomplish that task:

```
cat <<ZZ > input.txt
```

After you type this command, you can keep typing lines and then type **ZZ** on a line when you are finished. Everything you type is saved in the file `input.txt`.

### Saving error messages in a file

Sometimes you type a command, and it generates a lot of error messages that scroll by so fast you can't tell what's going on. One way to see all the error messages is to save them in a file so that you can see what the heck happened. You can do that by redirecting `stderr` to a file.

For example, type the following command:

```
find / -name COPYING -print 2> finderr
```

This command looks through the file system for files named `COPYING` and saves all the error messages (if there are any) in the `finderr` file. The number 2 followed by the greater-than sign (`2>`) redirects `stderr` to a file.

If you want to simply discard the error messages instead of saving them in a file, use `/dev/null` as the filename, like this:

```
find / -name COPYING -print 2> /dev/null
```

That `/dev/null` is a special file — often called the bit bucket and sometimes glorified as the *Great Bit Bucket in the Sky* — that simply discards whatever it receives. So now you know what they mean when you hear phrases, such as "Your mail probably ended up in the bit bucket."

## Typing less with automatic command completion

Many commands take a filename as an argument. To view the contents of the /etc/modprobe.conf text file, for example, type the following command:

```
cat /etc/modprobe.conf
```

The cat command displays the /etc/modprobe.conf file. For any command that takes a filename as an argument, you can use a bash feature to avoid having to type the entire filename. All you have to type enough characters to uniquely identify the file in its directory.

To see an example, type **cat /etc/mod** but don't press Enter; press Tab instead. bash automatically completes the filename, so the command becomes cat /etc/modprobe.conf. Now press Enter to run the command.

**Book II
Chapter 3**

Commanding
the Shell

Whenever you type a filename, press Tab after the first few characters of the filename. bash probably can complete the filename so that you don't have to type the entire name. If you don't enter enough characters to uniquely identify the file, bash beeps. Just type a few more characters and press Tab again.

## Going wild with asterisks and question marks

You can avoid typing long filenames another way. (After all, making less work for users is why we use computers, isn't it?)

This particular trick involves using the asterisk (*) and question mark (?). These special characters are *wildcards* because they match zero or more characters in a line of text.

If you know MS-DOS, you may have used commands such as COPY *.* A: to copy all files from the current directory to the A: drive. bash accepts similar wildcards in filenames. As you expect, bash provides many more wildcard options than the MS-DOS command interpreter does. Of course, newer computers (particularly notebook computers and especially netbooks) don't have A and B drives anymore. That deprives an entire generation of the fun of trying to copy a large file onto floppy disks!

You can use three types of wildcards in bash:

✦ **Asterisk (*):** Matches zero or more characters in a filename. That means * denotes all files in a directory.

✦ **Question mark (?):** Matches any single character. If you type test?, that matches any five-character text that begins with *test*.

✦ **Set of characters in brackets:** Matches any single character from that set. The string [aB], for example, matches only files named a or B, The string [aB]*, though, matches any filename that starts with a or B.

Wildcards are handy when you want to do something to many files. For example, to copy all the files from the /media/cdrom directory to the current directory, type the following:

```
cp /media/cdrom/* .
```

bash replaces the wildcard character * with the names of all the files in the /media/cdrom directory. The period at the end of the command represents the current directory.

You can use the asterisk with other parts of a filename to select a more specific group of files. Suppose you want to use the grep command to search for the text typedef struct in all files of the /usr/include directory that meet the following criteria:

✦ The filename starts with s

✦ The filename ends with .h

The wildcard specification s*.h denotes all filenames that meet these criteria. Thus you can perform the search with the following command:

```
grep "typedef struct" /usr/include/s*.h
```

The string contains a space that you want the grep command to find, so you have to enclose that string in quotation marks. That way, bash doesn't try to interpret each word in that text as a separate command-line argument.

The question mark (?) matches a single character. Suppose that you have four files — image1.pcx, image2.pcx, image3.pcx, and image4.pcx — in the current directory. To copy these files to the /media/floppy directory, use the following command:

```
cp image?.pcx /media/floppy
```

bash replaces the single question mark with any single character and copies the four files to /media.

The third wildcard format — [ . . . ] — matches a single character from a specific set of characters enclosed in square brackets. You may want to combine this format with other wildcards to narrow the matching filenames to a smaller set. To see a list of all filenames in the /etc/X11/xdm directory that start with x or X, type the following command:

```
ls /etc/X11/xdm/[xX]*
```

## Repeating previously typed commands

To make repeating long commands easy for you, bash stores up to 500 old commands as part of a *command history* (basically just a list of old commands). To see the command history, type **history**. bash displays a numbered list of the old commands, including those that you entered during previous logins.

If the command list is too long, you can limit the number of old commands that you want to see. For example, to see only the 10 most recent commands, type this command:

```
history 10
```

To repeat a command from the list that the history command shows, simply type an exclamation point (!), followed by that command's number. To repeat command number 3, type **!3**.

You can repeat a command without knowing its command number. Suppose you typed more /usr/lib/X11/xdm/xdm-config a few minutes ago and now you want to look at that file again. To repeat the previous more command, type the following:

```
!more
```

Often, you may want to repeat the last command that you just typed, perhaps with a slight change. For example, you may have displayed the contents of the directory by using the ls -l command. To repeat that command, type two exclamation points as follows:

```
!!
```

Sometimes, you may want to repeat the previous command but add extra arguments to it. Suppose that ls -l shows too many files. Simply repeat that command but pipe the output through the more command as follows:

```
!! | more
```

bash replaces the two exclamation points with the previous command and then appends | more to that command.

Here's the easiest way to recall previous commands: Just press the up-arrow key, and bash keeps going backward through the history of commands you previously typed. To move forward in the command history, press the down-arrow key.

# Discovering and Using Linux Commands

You type Linux commands at the shell prompt. By *Linux commands,* I mean some of the commands that the bash shell understands as well as the command-line utilities that come with Linux. In this section, I introduce you to a few major categories of Linux commands.

I can't cover every single Linux command in this chapter, but I want to give you a feel for the breadth of the commands by showing you common Linux commands. Table 3-2 lists common Linux commands by category. Before you start memorizing any Linux commands, browse this table.

| Table 3-2 | Essential Linux Commands |
|---|---|
| *Command Name* | *Action* |
| **Help and Abbreviations** | |
| apropos | Find online manual pages for a specified keyword |
| info | Display online help information about a specified command |
| man | Display online help information |
| whatis | Search for complete words only and find the online manual pages |
| alias | Define an abbreviation for a long command |
| type | Show the type and location of a command |
| unalias | Delete an abbreviation defined using alias |
| **Managing Files and Directories** | |
| cd | Change the current directory |
| chmod | Change file permissions |
| chown | Change the file owner and group |
| cp | Copy files |
| ln | Create symbolic links to files and directories |
| ls | Display the contents of a directory |
| mkdir | Create a directory |
| mv | Rename a file and move the file from one directory to another |
| rm | Delete files |
| rmdir | Delete directories |
| pwd | Display the current directory |
| touch | Update a file's timestamp |

| Command Name | Action |
|---|---|
| **Finding Files** | |
| find | Find files based on specified criteria, such as name and size |
| locate | Find files using a periodically updated filename database (the database is created by the updatedb program.) |
| whereis | Finds files based in the typical directories where *executable* (also known as *binary*) files are located |
| which | Find files in the directories listed in the PATH environment variable |
| **Processing Files** | |
| cat | Display a file on standard output (can be used to concatenate several files into one big file) |
| cut | Extract specified sections from each line of text in a file |
| dd | Copy blocks of data from one file to another (used to copy data from devices) |
| diff | Compare two text files and find any differences |
| expand | Convert all tabs to spaces |
| file | Display the type of data in a file |
| fold | Wrap each line of text to fit a specified width |
| grep | Search for regular expressions in a text file |
| less | Display a text file one page at a time (go backward by pressing **b**) |
| lpr | Print files |
| more | Display a text file, one page at a time (goes forward only) |
| nl | Number all nonblank lines in a text file and print the lines to standard output |
| paste | Concatenate corresponding lines from several files |
| patch | Update a text file using the differences between the original and revised copy of the file |
| sed | Copy a file to standard output while applying specified editing commands |
| sort | Sort lines in a text file |
| split | Break up a file into several smaller files with specified size |
| tac | Reverse a file (last line first and so on) |
| tail | Display the last few lines of a file |
| tr | Substitute one group of characters for another throughout a file |

**Book II Chapter 3**

Commanding the Shell

*(continued)*

### Table 3-2 *(continued)*

| Command Name | Action |
|---|---|
| **Processing Files** | |
| uniq | Eliminate duplicate lines from a text file |
| wc | Count the number of lines, words, and characters in a text file |
| zcat | Display a compressed file (after decompressing) |
| zless | Display a compressed file one page at a time (go backward by pressing **b**) |
| zmore | Display a compressed file one page at a time |
| **Archiving and Compressing Files** | |
| compress | Compress files |
| cpio | Copy files to and from an archive |
| gunzip | Decompress files compressed with GNU Zip (gzip) |
| gzip | Compress files using GNU Zip |
| tar | Create an archive of files in one or more directories (originally meant for archiving on tape) |
| uncompress | Decompress files compressed with compress |
| **Managing Files** | |
| bg | Run an interrupted process in the background |
| fg | Run a process in the foreground |
| free | Display the amount of free and used memory in the system |
| halt | Shut down Linux and halt the computer |
| kill | Send a signal to a process (usually used to terminate a process) |
| ldd | Display the shared libraries needed to run a program |
| nice | Run a process with a lower priority (referred to as nice mode) |
| ps | Display a list of currently running processes |
| printenv | Display the current environment variables |
| pstree | Show parent-child process relationships |
| reboot | Stop Linux and then restart the computer |
| shutdown | Shut down Linux |
| top | Display a list of most processor- and memory-intensive processes |
| uname | Display information about the system and the Linux kernel |

| Command Name | Action |
|---|---|
| **Managing Users** | |
| chsh | Change the shell (command interpreter) |
| groups | Print the list of groups that include a specified user |
| id | Display the user and group ID for a specified username |
| passwd | Change the password |
| su | Start a new shell as another user (the other user is assumed to be root when the command is invoked without any argument) |
| **Managing the File System** | |
| df | Summarize free and available space in all mounted storage devices |
| du | Display disk usage information |
| fdformat | Format a floppy disk |
| fdisk | Partition a hard drive |
| fsck | Check and repair a file system |
| mkfs | Create a new file system |
| mknod | Create a device file |
| mkswap | Create a swap space for Linux in a file or a hard drive partition |
| mount | Mount a device (for example, the CD-ROM) on a directory in the file system |
| swapoff | Deactivate a swap space |
| swapon | Activate a swap space |
| sync | Writes *buffered* (saved in memory) data to files |
| tty | Display the device name for the current terminal |
| umount | Unmount a device from the file system |
| **Dates and Times** | |
| cal | Display a calendar for a specified month or year |
| date | Display the current date and time or set a new date and time |

**Book II
Chapter 3**

**Commanding
the Shell**

# Becoming root (superuser)

When you want to do anything that requires a high privilege level (for example, administering your system), you have to become root. Normally, you log in as a regular user with your everyday username. When you need the privileges of the superuser, though, use the following command to become root:

su -

That's su followed by a space and the minus sign (or hyphen). The shell then prompts you for the root password. Type the password and press Enter.

After you've finished with whatever you want to do as root (and you have the privilege to do anything as root), type **exit** to return to your normal username.

Instead of becoming root by using the su - command, you can also type **sudo** followed by the command that you want to run as root. In Ubuntu, you must use the sudo command because you don't get to set up a root user when you install Ubuntu. If you're listed as an authorized user in the /etc/sudoers file, sudo executes the command as if you were logged in as root. Type **man sudoers** to read more about the /etc/sudoers file.

## Managing processes

Every time the shell executes a command that you type, it starts a process. The shell itself is a process as are any scripts or programs that the shell runs.

Use the ps ax command to see a list of processes. When you type **ps ax**, bash shows you the current set of processes. Here are a few lines of output when I type **ps ax --cols 132**. (I included the --cols 132 option to ensure that you can see each command in its entirety.)

```
PID TTY STAT TIME COMMAND
1 ? S 0:01 init [5]
2 ? SN 0:00 [ksoftirqd/0]
3 ? S< 0:00 [events/0]
4 ? S< 0:00 [khelper]
9 ? S< 0:00 [kthread]
19 ? S< 0:00 [kacpid]
75 ? S< 0:00 [kblockd/0]
115 ? S 0:00 [pdflush]
116 ? S 0:01 [pdflush]
118 ? S< 0:00 [aio/0]
117 ? S 0:00 [kswapd0]
711 ? S 0:00 [kseriod]
1075 ? S< 0:00 [reiserfs/0]
2086 ? S 0:00 [kjournald]
2239 ? S<s 0:00 /sbin/udevd -d
. . . lines deleted . . .
6374 ? S 1:51 /usr/X11R6/bin/X :0 -audit 0 -auth /var/lib/gdm/:0.Xauth
    -nolisten tcp vt7
6460 ? Ss 0:02 /opt/gnome/bin/gdmgreeter
6671 ? Ss 0:00 sshd: edulaney [priv]
6675 ? S 0:00 sshd: edulaney@pts/0
6676 pts/0 Ss 0:00 -bash
```

```
6712 pts/0 S 0:00 vsftpd
14702 ? S 0:00 pickup -l -t fifo -u
14752 pts/0 R+ 0:00 ps ax --cols 132
```

In this listing, the first column has the heading PID and shows a number for each process. PID stands for *process ID* (identification), which is a sequential number assigned by the Linux kernel. If you look through the output of the ps ax command, you see that the init command is the first process and has a PID of 1. That's why init is referred to as the *mother of all processes.*

The COMMAND column shows the command that created each process, and the TIME column shows the cumulative CPU time used by the process. The STAT column shows the state of a process — S means the process is sleeping, and R means it's running. The symbols following the status letter have further meanings; for example < indicates a high-priority process, and + means that the process is running in the foreground. The TTY column shows the terminal, if any, associated with the process.

The process ID, or process number, is useful when you have to forcibly stop an errant process. Look at the output of the ps ax command and note the PID of the offending process. Then, use the kill command with that process number to stop the process. For example, to stop process number 8550, start by typing the following command:

```
kill 8550
```

If the process doesn't stop after five seconds, repeat the command. The next step in stopping a stubborn process is to type **kill -INT *pid***, where *pid* is the process number. If that doesn't work, try the following command as a last resort:

```
kill -9 8550
```

The -9 option means send signal number 9 to the process. Signal number 9 is the KILL signal, which should cause the process to exit. You could also type this command as **kill -KILL *pid***, where *pid* is the process ID.

## Working with date and time

You can use the date command to display the current date and time or set a new date and time. Type **date** at the shell prompt and you get a result similar to the following:

```
Fri Mar 14 15:10:07 EST 2010
```

As you can see, the date command alone displays the current date and time.

To set the date, log in as root and then type **date** followed by the date and time in the MMDDhhmmYYYY format, where each character is a digit. For example, to set the date and time to December 31, 2010 and 9:30 p.m., you type

```
date 123121302010
```

The MMDDhhmmYYYY date and time format is similar to the 24-hour military clock and has the following meaning:

+ MM is a two-digit number for the month (01 through 12).

+ DD is a two-digit number for the day of the month (01 through 31).

+ hh is a two-digit hour in 24-hour format (00 is midnight and 23 is 11 p.m.).

+ mm is a two-digit number for the minute (00 through 59).

+ YYYY is the four-digit year (such as 2010).

The other interesting date-related command is cal. If you type cal without any options, it prints a calendar for the current month. If you type cal followed by a number, cal treats the number as the year and prints the calendar for that year. To view the calendar for a specific month in a specific year, provide the month number (1 = January, 2 = February, and so on) followed by the year. Thus, type **cal 8 2010** and you get the calendar for August 2010, as follows:

```
August 2010
Su Mo Tu We Th Fr Sa
 1  2  3  4  5  6  7
 8  9 10 11 12 13 14
15 16 17 18 19 20 21
22 23 24 25 26 27 28
29 30 31
```

## Processing files

You can search through a text file with grep and view a text file, a screen at a time, with more. For example, to search for my username in the /etc/passwd file, I use

```
grep edulaney /etc/passwd
```

To view the /etc/inittab file a screen at a time, I type

```
more /etc/inittab
```

As each screen pauses, I press the spacebar to go to the next page.

Many more Linux commands work on files — mostly on text files, but some commands also work on any file. The sections that follow describe a few of the file-processing tools.

## Counting words and lines in a text file

I am always curious about the size of files. For text files, the number of characters is basically the size of the file in bytes (because each character takes up a byte of storage space). What about words and the number of lines, though?

The Linux wc command comes to the rescue. The wc command displays the total number of lines, words, and characters in a text file. For example, type **wc /etc/inittab** and you see output similar to the following:

**Book II
Chapter 3**

**Commanding
the Shell**

```
97 395 2926 /etc/inittab
```

In this case, wc reports that 97 lines, 395 words, and 2,926 characters are in the /etc/inittab file. If you simply want to see the number of lines in a file, use the –1 option and type **wc -1 /etc/inittab**. The resulting output should be similar to the following:

```
97 /etc/inittab
```

As you can see, with the –1 option, wc simply displays the line count.

If you don't specify a filename, the wc command expects input from the standard input. You can use the pipe feature ( | ) of the shell to feed the output of another command to wc, which can be handy sometimes.

Suppose you want a rough count of the processes running on your system. You can get a list of all processes with the ps ax command, but instead of counting lines manually, just pipe the output of ps to wc and you get a rough count automatically:

```
ps ax | wc -1
86
```

Here the ps command produces 86 lines of output. Because the first line simply shows the headings for the tabular columns, you can estimate that about 85 processes are running on your system. (This count probably includes the processes used to run the ps and wc commands as well.)

## Sorting text files

You can sort the lines in a text file by using the sort command. To see how the sort command works, first type **more /etc/passwd** to see the current contents of the /etc/passwd file. Now type **sort /etc/passwd** to see the lines sorted alphabetically. If you want to sort a file and save the sorted version in another file, you have to use the `bash` shell's output redirection feature, like this:

```
sort /etc/passwd > ~/sorted.text
```

This command sorts the lines in the `/etc/passwd` file and saves the output in a file named `sorted.text` in your home directory.

### Substituting or deleting characters from a file

Another interesting command is `tr`, which substitutes one group of characters for another (or deletes a selected character) throughout a file. Suppose that you have to occasionally use MS-DOS text files on your Linux system. Although you may expect to use a text file on any system without any problems, you find one catch: DOS uses a carriage return followed by a line feed to mark the end of each line whereas Linux uses only a line feed.

On your Linux system, you can get rid of the extra carriage returns in the DOS text file by using the `tr` command with the `-d` option. Essentially, to convert the DOS text file named `filename.dos` to a Linux text file named `filename.linux`, type the following:

```
tr -d '\015' < filename.dos > filename.linux
```

In this command, `'\015'` denotes the code for the carriage-return character in octal notation.

### Splitting a file into several smaller files

The `split` command is handy for those times when you want to copy a file but the file is too large to fit on a single floppy or send as one e-mail attachment. You can then use the `split` command to break up the file into multiple smaller files.

By default, `split` puts 1,000 lines into each file. The new, split files are named by groups of letters such as aa, ab, ac, and so on. You can specify a prefix for the filenames. For example, to split a large file called `hugefile.tar` into smaller files, use `split` as follows:

```
split -b 1440k hugefile.tar part.
```

This command splits the `hugefile.tar` file into 1440K chunks. The command creates files named `part.aa`, `part.ab`, `part.ac`, and so on.

To combine the split files back into a single file, use the `cat` command as follows:

```
cat part.?? > hugefile.tar
```

In this case, the two question marks (??) match any two-character extension in the filename. In other words, the filename part.?? matches all filenames such as part.12, part.aa, part.ab, and part.2b.

# Writing Shell Scripts

If you've ever used MS-DOS, you may remember MS-DOS *batch files,* which are text files with MS-DOS commands. Similarly, *shell scripts* are also text files with a bunch of shell commands.

If you aren't a programmer, you may feel apprehensive about programming, but shell programming can be as simple as storing a few commands in a file. Right now, you might not be up to writing complex shell scripts, but you can certainly try out a simple shell script.

**Book II**
**Chapter 3**

Commanding the Shell

To try your hand at a little shell programming, type the following text at the shell prompt exactly as shown and then press Ctrl+D when you're finished:

```
cd
cat > simple
#!/bin/sh
echo "This script's name is: $0"
echo Argument 1: $1
echo Argument 2: $2
```

Press Ctrl+D. The cd command changes the current directory to your home directory. Then the cat command displays the next line and any other lines you type before pressing Ctrl+D. In this case, I use > simple to send the output to a file named simple. After you press Ctrl+D, the cat command ends, and you see the shell prompt again. You created a file named simple that contains the following shell script:

```
#!/bin/sh
echo "This script's name is: $0"
echo Argument 1: $1
echo Argument 2: $2
```

The first line causes Linux to run the bash shell program (of the name / bin/bash). The shell then reads the rest of the lines in the script.

Just as most Linux commands accept command line options, a bash script also accepts command-line options. Inside the script, you can refer to the options as $1, $2, and so on. The special name $0 refers to the name of the script itself.

To run this shell script, first you have to make the file executable (that is, turn it into a program) with the following command:

```
chmod +x simple
```

Now type ./simple one two to run the script, and it displays the following output:

```
This script's name is: ./simple
Argument 1: one
Argument 2: two
```

The ./ prefix to the script's name indicates that the simple file is in the current directory.

This script simply prints the script's name and the first two command-line options that the user types after the script's name.

Next, try running the script with a few arguments, as follows:

```
./simple "This is one argument" second-argument third
This script's name is: ./simple
Argument 1: This is one argument
Argument 2: second-argument
```

The shell treats the entire string in the double quotation marks as a single argument. Otherwise, the shell uses spaces as separators between arguments on the command line.

Most useful shell scripts are more complicated than this simple script, but this easy exercise gives you a rough idea of how to write shell scripts.

Place Linux commands in a file and use the chmod command to make the file executable. Voilà! You created a shell script!

# Chapter 4: Navigating the Linux File System

## In This Chapter

✔ Finding out about the Linux file system

✔ Navigating the system with Linux commands

✔ Understanding file permissions

✔ Manipulating files and directories with Linux commands

To use files and directories well, you need to understand the concept of a hierarchical file system. Even if you use the GUI file managers (addressed in the next chapter) to access files and folders (folders are also called *directories*), you can benefit from a lay of the land of the file system.

This chapter introduces the Linux file system and shows you how to work with files and directories using several Linux commands.

## Understanding the Linux File System

Like any other operating system, Linux organizes information in files and directories. A *directory* is a special file that can contain other files and directories. Because a directory can contain other directories, this method of organizing files gives rise to a hierarchical structure. This hierarchical organization of files is the *file system*.

The Linux file system gives you a unified view of all storage on your PC. The file system has a single `root` directory, indicated by a forward slash (/). Within the `root` directory is a hierarchy of files and directories. Parts of the file system can reside in different physical media, such as a hard drive, a floppy disk, and a CD-ROM. Figure 4-1 illustrates the concept of the Linux file system (which is the same in any Linux system) and how it spans multiple physical devices.

If you're familiar with MS-DOS or Windows, you may find something missing in the Linux file system: You don't find drive letters in Linux. All disk drives and CD-ROM drives are part of a single file system.

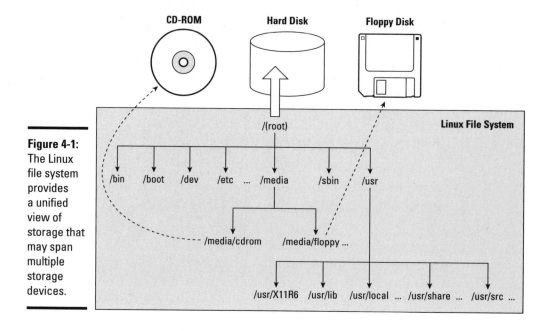

**Figure 4-1:**
The Linux file system provides a unified view of storage that may span multiple storage devices.

In Linux, you can have long filenames (up to 256 characters), and filenames are case-sensitive. Often these filenames have multiple extensions, such as `sample.tar.Z`. UNIX filenames can take many forms, such as the following: `index.html`, `Makefile`, `binutils-2.15.92.0.2-5.i386.rpm`, `vsftpd_2.0.3-1_i386.deb`, `.bash_profile`, and `httpd_src.tar.gz`.

To locate a file, you need more than just the filename. You also need information about the directory hierarchy. The extended filename, showing the full hierarchy of directories leading to the file, is the *pathname*. As the name implies, it's the path to the file through the maze of the file system. Figure 4-2 shows a typical pathname for a file in Linux.

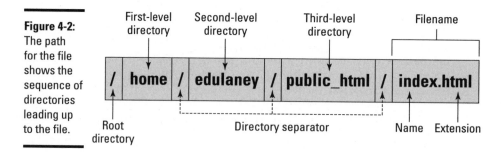

**Figure 4-2:**
The path for the file shows the sequence of directories leading up to the file.

As Figure 4-2 shows, the pathname has the following parts:

✦ **The root directory,** indicated by a forward slash (/) character.

✦ **The directory hierarchy,** with each directory name separated from the previous one by a forward slash (/) character. A / appears after the last directory name.

✦ **The filename,** with a name and one or more optional extensions. (A period appears before each extension.)

The Linux file system has a well-defined set of top-level directories, and some of these directories have specific purposes. Finding your way around the file system is easier if you know the purpose of these directories. You also become adept at guessing where to look for specific types of files when you face a new situation. Table 4-1 briefly describes the top-level directories in the Linux file system.

**Book II
Chapter 4**

Navigating the
Linux File System

**Table 4-1    Top-Level Directories in the Linux File System**

| *Directory* | *Contains* |
| --- | --- |
| / | Base of the file system. All files and directories are contained logically in the root, or /, directory, regardless of their physical locations. |
| /bin | Executable programs that are part of the Linux operating system. Many Linux commands, such as cat, cp, ls, more, and tar, are located in /bin. |
| /boot | Linux kernel and other files that the LILO and GRUB boot managers need. (The kernel and other files can be anywhere, but placing them in the /boot directory is customary.) |
| /dev | Special files that represent devices attached to the system. |
| /etc | Most system configuration files and the initialization scripts (in the /etc/rc.d subdirectory). |
| /home | Home directories of all users. User edulaney's home directory, for example, is /home/edulaney. |
| /lib | Library files for all programs stored in /sbin and /bin directories (including the loadable driver modules) needed to start Linux. |
| /lost+found | Lost files. Every disk partition has a lost+found directory. |

*(continued)*

### Table 4-1 *(continued)*

| Directory | Contains |
| --- | --- |
| /media | The /media/floppy directory for mounting floppy disks and the /media/cdrom or /media/cdrom0 directory for mounting the CD/DVD-ROM drive. If you have a CD/DVD recorder, you find a /media/cdrecorder directory instead of /media/cdrom and may also find /media/DVD. Used for mounting file systems on removable media, such as CD/DVD-ROM drives, flash drives, external drives, floppy disks, and Zip drives. |
| /mnt | Temporarily mounted file systems |
| /opt | Storage for large application software packages. For example, some distributions install the OpenOffice.org Office suite in the /opt directory. |
| /proc | Various information about the processes running in the Linux system. |
| /root | Home directory for the root user. |
| /sbin | Executable files representing commands typically used for system administration tasks and used by the root user. Commands such as halt and shutdown reside in the /sbin directory. |
| /srv | Data for services (such as Web and FTP) offered by this system. |
| /sys | Information about the devices, as seen by the Linux kernel. |
| /tmp | Temporary directory that any user can use as a *scratch* directory, meaning that the contents of this directory are considered unimportant and usually are deleted every time the system boots. |
| /usr | Subdirectories for many important programs, such as the X Window System (in the /usr/X11R6 directory) and the online manual. (Table 4-2 shows some of the standard subdirectories in /usr.) |
| /var | Various system files (such as logs), as well as directories for holding other information, such as files for the Web server and anonymous FTP server. |

The /usr and /var directories also contain a number of standard subdirectories. Table 4-2 lists the important subdirectories in /usr. Table 4-3 shows a similar breakdown for the /var directory.

**Table 4-2**       **Important /usr Subdirectories**

| Subdirectory | Description |
|---|---|
| /usr/bin | Executable files for many more Linux commands, including utility programs that are commonly available in Linux but aren't part of the core Linux operating system. |
| /usr/games | Some old Linux games. |
| /usr/include | Header files (filenames ending in .h) for the C and C++ programming languages and the X11 header files in the /usr/include/X11 directory and the Linux kernel header files in the /usr/include/linux directory. |
| /usr/lib | Libraries for C and C++ programming languages and many other libraries, such as database libraries and graphical toolkit libraries. |
| /usr/local | Local files. The /usr/local/bin directory, for example, is supposed to be the location for any executable program developed on your system. |
| /usr/sbin | Many administrative commands, such as commands for e-mail and networking. |
| /usr/share | Shared data, such as default configuration files and images for many applications. For example, /usr/share/gnome contains various shared files for the GNOME desktop, and /usr/share/doc has the documentation files for many Linux applications (such as the bash shell, the Sawfish window manager, and The GIMP image processing program). |
| /usr/share/man | Online manual (which you can read by using the man command). |
| /usr/src | Source code for the Linux kernel (the core operating system). |

**Table 4-3**       **Important /var Subdirectories**

| Subdirectory | Contains |
|---|---|
| /var/cache | Storage area for cached data for applications. |
| /var/lib | Information relating to the current state of applications. |
| /var/lock | Locked files to ensure that a resource is used by one application only. |

*(continued)*

## Table 4-3 *(continued)*

| Subdirectory | Contains |
|---|---|
| /var/log | Log files organized into subdirectories. The syslogd server stores its log files in /var/log, with the exact content of the files depending on the syslogd configuration file /etc /syslog.conf. For example, /var/log/messages is the main system log file; /var/log/secure contains log messages from secure services (such as sshd and xinetd); and /var/log/maillog contains the log of mail messages. |
| /var/mail | User mailbox files. |
| /var/opt | Variable data for packages stored in /opt directory. |
| /var/run | Data describing the system since it was booted. |
| /var/spool | Data that's waiting for some kind of processing. |
| /var/tmp | Temporary files preserved between system reboots. |
| /var/yp | Network Information Service (NIS) database files. |

# Navigating the File System with Linux Commands

Although GUI file managers such as Nautilus (in GNOME) or Konqueror (in KDE) are easy to use, you can use them only if you have a working GUI desktop. Sometimes, you may not have a graphical environment to run a graphical file manager. For example, you may be logged in through a text terminal, or X may not be working on your system. In those situations, you have to rely on Linux commands to work with files and directories. You can always use Linux commands, even in the graphical environment — all you have to do is open a terminal window and type the Linux commands.

In this section, I briefly describe some Linux commands for moving around the Linux file system.

## Commands for directory navigation

In Linux, when you log in as root, your home directory is /root. For other users, the home directory is usually in the /home directory. My home directory (when I log in as edulaney) is /home/edulaney. This information is stored in the /etc/passwd file. By default, only you have permission to save files in your home directory, and only you can create subdirectories in your home directory to further organize your files.

Linux supports the concept of a *current* directory, which is the directory on which all file and directory commands operate. After you log in, for example, your current directory is the home directory. To see the current directory, type the pwd command.

To change the current directory, use the `cd` command. To change the current directory to `/usr/lib`, type the following:

`cd /usr/lib`

Then, to change the directory to the `cups` subdirectory in `/usr/lib`, type this command:

`cd cups`

Now, if you use the `pwd` command, that command shows `/usr/lib/cups` as the current directory.

**Book II**
**Chapter 4**

Navigating the
Linux File System

These two examples show that you can refer to a directory's name in two ways:

✦ **Absolute pathname:** An example is `/usr/lib`, which is an exact directory in the directory tree. Think of the absolute pathname as the complete mailing address for a package that the postal service will deliver to your next-door neighbor.

✦ **Relative directory name:** An example is `cups`, which represents the `cups` subdirectory of the current directory, whatever that may be. Think of the relative directory name as giving the postal carrier directions from your house to the one next door so the carrier can deliver the package.

If I type `cd cups` in `/usr/lib`, the current directory changes to `/usr/lib/cups`. However, if I type the same command in `/home/edulaney`, the shell tries to change the current directory to `/home/edulaney/cups`.

Use the `cd` command without any arguments to change the current directory back to your home directory. No matter where you are, typing **cd** at the shell prompt brings you back home!

The tilde character (~) refers to your home directory. Thus, you can change the current directory to your home directory also by using the command `cd ~`. You can refer to another user's home directory by appending that user's name to the tilde. Thus, `cd ~superman` changes the current directory to the home directory of superman.

Wait, there's more. A single dot (.) and two dots (. .) — often cleverly referred to as *dot-dot* — also have special meanings. A single dot (.) indicates the current directory, whereas two dots (. .) indicate the parent directory. For example, if the current directory is `/usr/share`, you go one level up to `/usr` by typing the following:

`cd . .`

## Commands for directory listings and permissions

You can get a directory listing by using the ls command. By default, the ls command — without options — displays the contents of the current directory in a compact, multicolumn format. For example, type the next two commands to see the contents of the /etc/X11 directory:

```
cd /etc/X11
ls
```

The output looks like this. (On the console, you see some items in different colors.)

```
X Xsession.d cursors rgb.txt xkb
XF86Config-4 Xsession.options default-display-manager rstart xserver
Xresources Xwrapper.config fonts sysconfig xsm
Xsession app-defaults gdm xinit
```

From this listing (without the colors), you can't tell whether an entry is a file or a directory. To tell the directories and files apart, use the -F option with ls, like this:

```
ls -F
```

This time, the output gives you some more clues about the file types:

```
X@ Xsession.d/ cursors/ rgb.txt xkb/
XF86Config-4 Xsession.options default-display-manager rstart/ xserver/
Xresources Xwrapper.config fonts/ sysconfig/ xsm/
Xsession* app-defaults/ gdm@ xinit/
```

The output from ls -F shows the directory names with a slash (/) appended to them. Plain filenames appear as is. The at sign (@) appended to a filename (for example, notice the file named X) indicates that this file is a link to another file. (In other words, this filename simply refers to another file; it's a shortcut.) An asterisk (*) is appended to executable files. (Xsession, for example, is an executable file.) The shell can run any executable file.

You can see even more detailed information about the files and directories with the -l option:

```
ls -l
```

For the /etc/X11 directory, a typical output from ls -l looks like the following:

```
total 84
lrwxrwxrwx 1 root root 20 Jul 15 20:32 X -> /usr/bin/X11/XFree86
-rw-r--r-- 1 root root 2878 Jul 16 14:50 XF86Config-4
drwxr-xr-x 2 root root 4096 Jul 15 20:32 Xresources
```

```
-rwxr-xr-x 1 root root 3456 Jun 1 01:59 Xsession
drwxr-xr-x 2 root root 4096 Jul 15 20:34 Xsession.d
-rw-r--r-- 1 root root 217 Jun 1 01:59 Xsession.options
-rw------- 1 root root 771 Jul 15 20:32 Xwrapper.config
drwxr-xr-x 2 root root 4096 Jul 15 20:35 app-defaults
. . . lines deleted . . .
```

This listing shows considerable information about every directory entry — each of which can be a file or another directory. Looking at a line from the right column to the left, you see that the rightmost column shows the name of the directory entry. The date and time before the name show when the last modifications to that file were made. To the left of the date and time is the size of the file in bytes.

The file's group and owner appear to the left of the column that shows the file size. The next number to the left indicates the number of links to the file. (A *link* is like a shortcut in Windows.) Finally, the leftmost column shows the file's permission settings, which determine who can read, write, or execute the file.

The first letter has a special meaning, as the following list shows:

✦ **l:** The file is a *symbolic link* to another file. In other words, it's a short-cut to something else.

✦ **d:** The file is a directory. It will appear as a folder in a GUI.

✦ **– (hyphen):** The file is normal. By *normal,* I mean that it isn't a directory, a link, or anything else odd. Most of the items on your system are just normal files.

✦ **b:** The file represents a block device, such as a disk drive.

✦ **c:** The file represents a character device, such as a serial port or a terminal.

After that first letter, the leftmost column shows a sequence of nine charac-ters, which appear as `rwxrwxrwx` when each letter is present. Each letter indicates a specific permission. A hyphen (–) in place of a letter indicates no permission for a specific operation on the file. Think of these nine letters as three groups of three letters (`rwx`), interpreted as follows:

✦ **Leftmost `rwx` group:** Controls the read, write, and execute permission of the file's owner. In other words, if you see `rwx` in this position, the file's owner can read (`r`), write (`w`), and execute (`x`) the file. A hyphen in the place of a letter indicates no permission. Thus, the string `rw-` means the owner has read and write permission but not execute permission. Although executable programs (including shell programs) typically have execute permission, directories treat execute permission as equivalent to *use* permission: A user must have execute permission on a directory before he or she can open and read the contents of the directory.

✦ **Middle rwx group:** Controls the read, write, and execute permission of any user belonging to that file's group.

✦ **Rightmost rwx group:** Controls the read, write, and execute permission of all other users (collectively thought of as *the world*).

Thus, a file with the permission setting rwx------ is accessible only to the file's owner, whereas the permission setting rwxr--r-- makes the file readable by the world.

An interesting feature of the ls command is that it doesn't list any file whose name begins with a period. To see these files, you must use the ls command with the -a option, as follows:

ls -a

Try this command in your home directory and then compare the result with what you see when you don't use the -a option:

1. **Type cd to change to your home directory.**
2. **Type ls -F to see the files and directories in your home directory.**
3. **Type ls -aF to see everything, including hidden files.**

Most Linux commands take single-character options, each with a hyphen as a prefix. When you want to use several options, type a hyphen and *concatenate* (string together) the option letters, one after another. Thus, ls -al is equivalent to ls -a -l as well as ls -l -a.

## Commands for changing permissions and ownerships

You may need to change a file's permission settings to protect it from others. Use the chmod command to change the permission settings of a file or a directory.

To use chmod effectively, you have to specify the permission settings. A good way is to concatenate letters from the columns of Table 4-4 in the order shown (Who/Action/Permission).

| Table 4-4 | Letter Codes for File Permissions | |
|---|---|---|
| *Who* | *Action* | *Permission* |
| u (user) | + (add) | r (read) |
| g (group) | − (remove) | w (write) |
| o (others) | = (assign) | x (execute) |
| a (all) | s (set user ID) | |

You use only the single character from each column — the text in parentheses is for explanation only.

For example, to give everyone read access to all files in a directory, pick a (for *all*) from the first column, + (for *add*) from the second column, and r (for *read*) from the third column to come up with the permission setting a+r. Then use the set of options with chmod, like this:

```
chmod a+r *.
```

On the other hand, to permit everyone to execute one specific file, type

```
chmod a+x filename
```

Suppose you have a file named mystuff that you want to protect. You can make it accessible to no one but you if you type the following commands, in this order:

```
chmod a-rwx mystuff
chmod u+rw mystuff
```

The first command turns off all permissions for everyone, and the second command turns on the read and write permissions for the owner (you). Type **ls -l** to verify that the change took place. (You see a permission setting of -rw-------.)

Sometimes you have to change a file's user or group ownership for everything to work correctly. For example, suppose you're instructed (by a manual, what else?) to create a directory named cups and give it the ownership of user ID lp and group ID sys. How do you it?

Well, you can log in as root and create the cups directory with the command mkdir:

```
mkdir cups
```

If you check the file's details with the ls -l command, you see that the user and group ownership is root root.

To change the owner, use the chown command. For example, to change the ownership of the cups directory to user ID lp and group ID sys, type

```
chown lp.sys cups
```

## Commands for working with files

To copy files from one directory to another, use the cp command. If you want to copy a file to the current directory but retain the original name, use a period (.) as the second argument of the cp command. Thus, the following command copies the Xresources file from the /etc/X11 directory to the current directory (denoted by a single period):

```
cp /etc/X11/Xresources .
```

The cp command makes a new copy of a file and leaves the original intact.

If you want to copy the entire contents of a directory — including all sub-directories and their contents — to another directory, use the command cp -ar sourcedir destdir. (This command copies everything in the sourcedir directory to destdir.) For example, to copy all files from the /etc/X11 directory to the current directory, type the following command:

```
cp -ar /etc/X11 .
```

To move a file to a new location, use the mv command. The original copy is gone, and a new copy appears at the destination. You can use mv to rename a file. If you want to change the name of today.list to old.list, use the mv command, as follows:

```
mv today.list old.list
```

On the other hand, if you want to move the today.list file to a subdirectory named saved, use this command:

```
mv today.list saved
```

An interesting feature of mv is that you can use it to move entire directories (with all their subdirectories and files) to a new location. If you have a directory named data that contains many files and subdirectories, you can move that entire directory structure to old_data by using the following command:

```
mv data old_data
```

To delete files, use the rm command. For example, to delete a file named old.list, type the following command:

```
rm old.list
```

Be careful with the rm command — especially when you log in as root. You can inadvertently delete important files with rm.

## Commands for working with directories

To organize files in your home directory, you have to create new directories. Use the mkdir command to create a directory. For example, to create a directory named images in the current directory, type the following:

```
mkdir images
```

After you create the directory, you can use the `cd images` command to change to that directory.

You can create an entire directory tree by using the -p option with the `mkdir` command. For example, suppose your system has a `/usr/src` directory and you want to create the directory tree `/usr/src/book/java/examples/applets`. To create this directory hierarchy, type the following command:

```
mkdir -p /usr/src/book/java/examples/applets
```

When you no longer need a directory, use the `rmdir` command to delete it.

You can delete a directory only when the directory is empty.

To remove an empty directory tree, you can use the -p option, like this:

```
rmdir -p /usr/src/book/java/examples/applets
```

This command removes the empty parent directories of `applets`. The command stops when it encounters a directory that's not empty.

Book II
Chapter 4

Navigating the
Linux File System

## Commands for finding files

The `find` command is useful for locating files (and directories) that meet your search criteria.

When I began using UNIX many years ago (Berkeley UNIX in the early 1980s), I was confounded by the `find` command. I stayed with one basic syntax of `find` for a long time before graduating to more complex forms. The basic syntax that I discovered first was for finding a file anywhere in the file system. Here's how it goes: Suppose you want to find any file or directory with a name that starts with `gnome`. Type the following `find` command to find these files:

```
find / -name "gnome*" -print
```

If you're not logged in as `root`, you may get a bunch of error messages. If these error messages annoy you, just modify the command as follows and the error messages are history. (Or, as Unix aficionados say, "Send 'em to the bit bucket.")

```
find / -name "gnome*" -print 2> /dev/null
```

This command tells `find` to start looking at the `root` directory (`/`) to look for filenames that match `gnome*` and to display the full pathname of any matching file. The last part (`2> /dev/null`) simply sends the error messages to a special file that's the equivalent of simply ignoring them.

You can use variations of this simple form of `find` to locate a file in any directory (as well as any subdirectories contained in the directory). If you forget where in your home directory you've stored all files named `report*` (names that start with *report*), you can search for the files by using the following command:

```
find ~ -name "report*" -print
```

When you become comfortable with this syntax of `find`, you can use other options of `find`. For example, to find only specific types of files (such as directories), use the `type` option. The following command displays all top-level directory names in your Linux system:

```
find / -type d -maxdepth 1 -print
```

You probably don't have to use the complex forms of `find` in a typical Linux system. But if you ever need to, you can look up the rest of the `find` options by using the following command:

```
man find
```

An easy way to find all files that match a name is to use the `locate` command, which searches a periodically updated database of files on your system. For example, here's a typical output I get when I type **locate Xresources** on a Debian system (the output may differ based on your distribution):

```
/etc/X11/Xresources
/etc/X11/Xresources/xbase-clients
/etc/X11/Xresources/xfree86-common
```

The `locate` command isn't installed by default in some Linux distributions. To install it, open the Add/Remove Software application for your distribution and search for `locate`. Then select the package from the search results and click Accept to install it.

## Commands for mounting and unmounting

Suppose you want to access the files on this book's companion DVD-ROM when you're logged in at a text console (with no GUI to help you). To do so, you have to first mount the DVD-ROM drive's file system on a specific directory in the Linux file system.

Start by looking at the `/etc/fstab` file for clues to the name of the CD-ROM device. For example, some Linux distributions use the device name `/dev/cdrom` to refer to CD/DVD-ROM drives, whereas others may use device names such as `/dev/hdc`, `/dev/cdroms/cdrom0`, or `/dev/cdrecorder` (for a DVD/CD-R drive). The entry in `/etc/fstab` file also tells you the directory where that distribution expects the CD/DVD to be mounted. Some distributions use /media/cdrom as the mount point, whereas others use /media/cdrom0, or /media/cdrecorder.

It is customary to use the cdrom term to mean both CD-ROM and DVD-ROM.

Log in as root (or type **su** - to become root), insert the DVD-ROM in the DVD drive, and then type the following command:

```
mount /dev/hdc /media/cdrom0
```

This command mounts the file system on the device named /dev/hdc (an IDE DVD/CD-ROM drive) on the /media/cdrom0 directory (which is also called the *mount point*) in the Linux file system.

**Book II**
**Chapter 4**

After the mount command successfully completes its task, you can access the files on the DVD-ROM by referring to the /media/cdrom0 directory as the top-level directory of the disc. In other words, to see the contents of the DVD-ROM, type

**Navigating the
Linux File System**

```
ls -F /media/cdrom0
```

When you've finished using the DVD-ROM — and before you eject it from the drive — you have to unmount the disc drive with the following umount command:

```
umount /dev/hdc
```

You can mount devices on any empty directory on the file system. However, each distribution has customary locations with directories meant for mounting devices. For example, some distributions use directories in /mnt whereas others use the /media directory for the mount points.

## Commands for checking disk-space usage

You can use two simple commands — df and du — to check the disk-space usage on your system. The df command shows you a summary of disk-space usage for all mounted devices. For example, when I type **df** on a PC with many mounted storage devices, here's what I get as output:

```
Filesystem 1K-blocks Used Available Use% Mounted on
/dev/hdb6 28249372 2377292 25872080 9% /
tmpfs 383968 12 383956 1% /dev/shm
/dev/hda5 5766924 1422232 4051744 26% /ubuntu/boot
/dev/hda7 6258100 2989200 2951004 51% /debian/boot
/dev/hda9 5766924 1422232 4051744 26% /ubuntu
/dev/hda10 5766924 1872992 3600984 35% /mepis
/dev/hda11 6258100 2989200 2951004 51% /debian
/dev/hdb3 19558500 1370172 18188328 8% /xandros
/dev/hda2 16087676 10593364 5494312 66% /windows/C
/dev/hdb1 107426620 9613028 97813592 9% /windows/D
```

This table lists the device, the total kilobytes of storage, how much of that memory is in use, how much is available, the percentage being used, and the mount point.

To see the output of df in a more readable format, type df -h. The output follows:

```
Filesystem Size Used Avail Use% Mounted on
/dev/hdb6 27G 2.3G 25G 9% /
tmpfs 375M 12K 375M 1% /dev/shm
/dev/hda5 5.5G 1.4G 3.9G 26% /ubuntu/boot
/dev/hda7 6.0G 2.9G 2.9G 51% /debian/boot
/dev/hda9 5.5G 1.4G 3.9G 26% /ubuntu
/dev/hda10 5.5G 1.8G 3.5G 35% /mepis
/dev/hda11 6.0G 2.9G 2.9G 51% /debian
/dev/hdb3 19G 1.4G 18G 8% /xandros
/dev/hda2 16G 11G 5.3G 66% /windows/C
/dev/hdb1 103G 9.2G 94G 9% /windows/D
```

If you compare this output with the output of the plain df (the preceding listing), you see that df -h prints the sizes with terms like M for megabytes and G for gigabytes. These are easier to understand than 1K-blocks.

The other command, du, is useful for finding out how much space a directory takes up. For example, type **du /etc/X11** to view the contents of all the directories in the /etc/X11 directory. (This directory contains X Window System configuration files.) You see the following:

```
12 /etc/X11/Xresources
36 /etc/X11/Xsession.d
272 /etc/X11/app-defaults
20 /etc/X11/cursors
12 /etc/X11/xinit
. . . lines deleted . . .
12 /etc/X11/fonts/misc
8 /etc/X11/fonts/100dpi
8 /etc/X11/fonts/75dpi
8 /etc/X11/fonts/Speedo
8 /etc/X11/fonts/Type1
48 /etc/X11/fonts
2896 /etc/X11
```

Each directory name is preceded by a number — which tells you the number of kilobytes of disk space used by that directory. Thus, the /etc/X11 directory uses 2896KB (or about 2.9MB) disk space. If you simply want the total disk space used by a directory (including all the files and subdirectories contained in that directory), use the -s option, as follows:

```
du -s /etc/X11
2896 /etc/X11
```

The -s option causes du to print just the summary information for the entire directory.

Just as df -h prints the disk-space information in megabytes and gigabytes, you can use the du -h command to view the output of du in more readable form. For example, here's how I combine it with the -s option to see the space that I'm using in my home directory (/home/edulaney):

```
du -sh /home/edulaney
645M /home/edulaney
```

Book II
Chapter 4

Navigating the
Linux File System

# Chapter 5: Introducing Linux Applications

## In This Chapter

✔ Taking stock of typical Linux applications

✔ Trying out the office applications

✔ Playing with multimedia

✔ Working with images

✔ Trying out GUI file managers

*E*ach Linux distribution comes with plenty of applications for all your diverse computing needs, as you can see by simply looking at the menus in the GUI desktops. Often, more than one application of the same type exists. Most distributions come with the OpenOffice.org office application suite with a word processor, spreadsheet, presentation software, and more. You'll find many choices for CD players and multimedia players, plus games, utility programs, and other useful tools, such as a scanner and digital camera applications. Some commercial distributions come with commercial office suites such as StarOffice from Sun Microsystems.

When it comes to playing *multimedia* (audio and video in various formats, such as MP3, MPEG, and QuickTime), freely available Linux distributions rarely come with the appropriate decoders because of licensing restrictions; the multimedia application runs but cannot play the MP3 file or the DVD movie because it lacks a decoder. Commercial distributions, such as Xandros and SUSE, usually come with some of these decoders.

This chapter offers an overview of some Linux applications. After you read about these applications, you can explore them further and have them at your disposal when needed. This chapter also provides an introduction to the GUI file managers, which allow you to browse and manipulate individual files.

## Taking Stock of Linux Applications

Table 5-1 shows a sampling of major Linux applications, organized by category. For the major applications, there is also a relevant Web site where you can get more information about that application. This list is by no means comprehensive. Each Linux distribution comes with many more applications and utilities than the ones shown in this table. If your system has both GNOME and KDE installed, most of these applications are already available from either GUI desktop.

| Table 5-1 | A Sampling of Linux Applications |
|---|---|
| *Application* | *Description* |
| **Office Applications** | |
| OpenOffice.org | Free open source office suite (compatible with Microsoft Office) that includes the Writer word processor, Calc spreadsheet, Impress presentation application, Draw drawing program, and Math equation editor (`www.open office.org`) |
| StarOffice | Commercial office suite from which OpenOffice.org was derived (`www.sun.com/staroffice`) |
| CrossOver Office | Commercial office suite that enables you to install and run Microsoft Office software on Linux (`www.codeweavers. com/products/office`) |
| AbiWord | Free word processing program similar to Microsoft Word (`www.abisource.com`) |
| Dia | Diagram drawing program, designed to be like Visio, the Windows application (`http://live.gnome. org/dia`) |
| **Office Tools** | |
| GNOME Calculator | Simple calculator for GNOME |
| KCalc | Calculator for KDE |
| KOrganizer | Calendar and scheduling program for KDE (`http:// userbase.kde.org/KOrganizer`) |
| Kontact | Personal information management suite for KDE, includes applications for e-mail, scheduling, contacts, and time tracking (`http://userbase.kde.org/Kontact`) |
| Aspell | Text mode spell checker (`http://aspell.net`) |
| Dictionary | Provides definitions through a graphical client for the dict. org dictionary server |
| **Text Editors** | |
| emacs | Well-known text editor with both text and graphical interfaces (`www.gnu.org/software/emacs`) |
| gedit | Text editor for GNOME (`http://projects.gnome. org/gedit/`) |

| Application | Description |
|---|---|
| **Office Applications** | |
| KWrite | Text editor for KDE |
| Kate | Advanced text editor for KDE (`http://kate-editor.org`) |
| vim | Text editor with text mode interface and compatible with the well-known UNIX editor `vi` (`www.vim.org`) |
| **Database** | |
| PostgreSQL | Sophisticated object-relational database-management system (`www.postgresql.org`) that supports Structured Query Language (SQL) |
| MySQL | Popular relational database-management system that supports SQL (`www.mysql.com`) |
| **Multimedia** | |
| GNOME CD Player | Audio CD player (needs a working sound card) |
| KsCD | Audio CD player from KDE (needs a working sound card) |
| amaroK | Multimedia audio player (`http://amarok.kde.org`) that can play several sound formats, including MP3 files if the MP3 decoders are installed |
| Rhythmbox | Multimedia audio player (`http://projects.gnome.org/rhythmbox`) designed for the GNOME desktop that can play several sound formats, including MP3 files if the proper plug-ins have been downloaded |
| XMMS | X Multimedia System: a multimedia audio player (`www.xmms.org`) that can play many different sound formats, including MP3 files. (For some distributions, you have to download a plug-in to play MP3.) |
| xine | Free multimedia player (`http://xine-project.org`) that can play CDs, DVDs, and video CDs (VCDs) and also decode multimedia files such as AVI, MOV, WMV, and MP3, provided you have the appropriate decoders |
| Kaffeine | KDE media player based on xine; Kaffeine's capabilities are similar to those of xine (`http://kaffeine.kde.org`) |
| Totem | GNOME movie player that is based on xine; Totem's capabilities are similar to those of xine (`http://projects.gnome.org/totem`) |
| Pitivi | Video editor for GNOME that allows for video clip manipulation, audio editing, and more (`www.pitivi.org`) |

*(continued)*

**Book II
Chapter 5**

Introducing Linux
Applications

## Table 5-1 *(continued)*

| Application | Description |
| --- | --- |
| **Multimedia** | |
| cdrdao | Command-line application that can burn audio or data CD-Rs in disk-at-once (DAO) mode based on the descriptions of the CD's content in a text file (`http://cdrdao.sourceforge.net`) |
| cdrecord | Command-line application that can burn audio and data CD-Rs as well as DVD-Rs (`http://cdrecord.berlios.de/old/private/cdrecord.html`) |
| growisofs | Command-line application that uses the `mkisofs` command to append data to an ISO 9660 file system used in CD-Rs and DVD-Rs (`http://fy.chalmers.se/~appro/linux/DVD+RW`) |
| X-CD-Roast | GUI front-end for cdrecord and cdrdao that makes burning data and audio CD-Rs easy (`www.xcdroast.org`) |
| K3b | KDE-based GUI front-end for cdrecord, cdrdao, and growisofs for burning CD-Rs and DVD-Rs (`www.k3b.org`) |
| digiKam | Digital camera and photo management application that supports all the digital cameras supported by gPhoto2 (`www.digikam.org`) |
| **Graphics and Imaging** | |
| The GIMP | The GNU Image Manipulation Program: an application suitable for tasks such as photo retouching, image composition, and image authoring (`www.gimp.org`) |
| GQview | Powerful image viewer (`http://gqview.sourceforge.net`) |
| KFax | Fax viewer for KDE |
| KView | Simple image viewer for KDE |
| GGv | Gnome Ghostview (GGv): a PostScript document viewer (`www.directory.fsf.org/project/ggv/`) |
| Xpdf | Adobe PDF document viewer (`www.foolabs.com/xpdf/`) |
| XSane | Graphical front-end for accessing scanners with the SANE (Scanner Access Now Easy) library (`www.xsane.org`) |
| KSnapshot | Screen-capture program |
| Kooka | Scanner program for KDE that uses the SANE library (`http://kooka.kde.org`) |
| xscanimage | Graphical front-end for controlling a scanner |

| Application | Description |
|---|---|
| **Internet** | |
| Evolution | Personal information management application that integrates e-mail, calendar, contact management, and online task lists (`http://projects.gnome.org/evolution/`) |
| gFTP | Graphical FTP client for downloading files from the Internet |
| Pidgin | Instant messenger client compatible with multiple GUIs (`www.pidgin.im`) |
| Kopete | KDE instant messenger client (`http://kopete.kde.org`) |
| Empathy | Instant-messaging program that supports text, voice, and video chat over multiple protocols (`http://live.gnome.org/Empathy`) |
| Gwibber | Microblogging client for GNOME (`http://launchpad.net/gwibber`) |
| Mozilla | Well-known open source Web browser that started with source code from Netscape (`www.mozilla.org`) |
| Firefox | New and improved Web browser from the Mozilla Project (`www.mozilla.org/products/firefox`) |
| Thunderbird | E-mail client from the Mozilla Project (`www.mozillamessaging.com`) |
| Epiphany | Mozilla-based open source Web browser for GNOME (`http://projects.gnome.org/epiphany/`) |
| Lynx | Text mode Web browser (`http://lynx.browser.org`) |
| KNode | GUI newsreader for KDE (`http://userbase.kde.org/KNode`) |
| Pan | GUI newsreader for GNOME (`http://pan.rebelbase.com`) |
| Akregator | RSS feed aggregator and reader for KDE (`http://akregator.kde.org`) |
| KPhone | Internet telephony application that supports the Session Initiation Protocol (SIP) (`http://sourceforge.net/projects/kphone`) |
| Linphone | Internet telephony application that supports the Session Initiation Protocol (SIP) and Real-time Transport Protocol (RTP) (`www.linphone.org`) |

**Book II
Chapter 5**

**Introducing Linux Applications**

*(continued)*

**Table 5-1** *(continued)*

| Application | Description |
|---|---|
| **Internet** | |
| Skype | Internet telephony application for using voice over IP (VOIP) to make voice phone calls (`www.skype.com`) |
| XChat | Internet Relay Chat (IRC) client (`www.xchat.org`) |
| Konqueror | Web browser and file manager in KDE (`www.konqueror.org`) |
| KMail | E-mail client for KDE (`http://userbase.kde.org/Kmail`) |
| **Games** | |
| Kapman | New version of an old classic; eat delicious pills while avoiding pesky ghosts |
| Kolf | Virtual minigolf game |
| Konquest Battle | Game of intergalactic takeover |
| Mines | Safer than crossing a real minefield but still nerve wracking |
| Solitaire | Classic prescription for chronic boredom |
| Sudoku | Puzzles with different levels |

Later sections of this chapter include some of the applications from Table 5-1, selecting one or two from each category. Internet applications are discussed in Book IV.

Not all Linux distributions come with all the applications shown in Table 5-1, although you can often download and install all these applications in any distribution.

You typically must select specific groups of applications to install as you install a Linux distribution. The exact list of applications on your Linux system depends on the choices you make during the installation.

It's easy to install missing applications in Debian (and Debian-based distributions, such as Ubuntu) as long as you have a broadband (cable or DSL) connection to the Internet. For example, to see whether the K3b CD/DVD burner exists for Debian, type **apt-cache search k3b**. You get output similar to the following:

```
k3b - A sophisticated KDE cd burning application
k3b-i18n - Internationalized (i18n) files for k3b
k3blibs - The KDE cd burning application library - runtime files
k3blibs-dev - The KDE cd burning application library - development files
```

Next, type **apt-get install k3b** and a few moments later you'll have K3b installed on your Debian system. This ease of installing (or upgrading) software is why Debian users swear by `apt-get` (even though it's a command-line tool).

# Introducing Office Applications and Tools

Word processor, spreadsheet, presentation software, calendar, calculator — these are some office staples. Most Linux distributions come with the OpenOffice.org (often shortened as *OO.o* or *Ooo*) suite of office applications and tools. You can try all of them one by one and see which one takes your fancy. Each application is fairly intuitive to use. Although some nuances of the user interface may be new to you, you'll become comfortable with the interface after using it a few times. This section briefly introduces the following applications, as well as some other commercially available office applications for Linux:

✦ **OpenOffice.org Office Suite:** A Microsoft Office–like office suite with the Writer word processor, the Calc spreadsheet program, the Impress presentation program, the Draw drawing and illustration application, and Math, a mathematical formula editor

✦ **Kontact:** A personal information management application in KDE

✦ **Calculators:** A GNOME calculator and KDE calculator

✦ **Aspell:** A spelling checker

## OpenOffice.org office suite

OpenOffice.org is an office suite developed by the OpenOffice.org project (`www.openoffice.org`). OpenOffice.org is similar to major office suites such as Microsoft Office. Its main components are the Writer word processor, the Calc spreadsheet, and the Impress presentation program.

You can easily start OpenOffice.org — either the overall suite or an individual application — from most GUI desktops by clicking a panel icon or by making a choice from the main menu. For example, in SUSE, you can click a desktop icon to open the initial window of the OpenOffice.org suite. You can create new Open Office documents or open existing documents (which can be Microsoft Office files as well) from the main window of the OpenOffice.org.

### Writer

Choosing File➪New➪Text Document from any OpenOffice.org window starts OpenOffice.org Writer with a blank document in its main window. Using Writer is simple — if you're familiar with Microsoft Word, you should have no trouble finding your way around Writer. You can type text into the blank document, format text, and save text.

You can also open documents that you have prepared with Microsoft Word on a Windows machine. Figure 5-1 shows a Microsoft Word document opened in OpenOffice.org Writer.

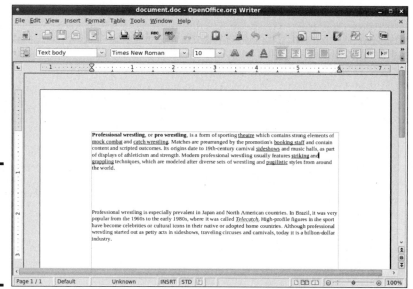

**Figure 5-1:**
You can prepare documents in OpenOffice. org Writer.

When you save a document, by default, Writer saves it in OpenDocument text format in a file with the `.odt` extension.

OpenOffice.org version 2.0 and later uses the standard OASIS OpenDocument XML format as the default file format (the file extension is `.odt`). The OASIS OpenDocument format is not tied to any vendor or any specific office suite software. For more information on OpenDocument format, see

```
http://www.oasis-open.org/committees/tc_home.php?wg_abbrev=office
```

If you need to share OpenOffice.org Writer documents with Microsoft Word, you can save the documents in several formats, including Microsoft Word 97/2000/XP and Rich Text Format (`.rtf`). For exchanging files with users of OpenOffice.org versions before 2.0, save the file in StarOffice text document format with an `.odt` extension.

Writer is simple and intuitive to use. If you need help, online help is available by choosing Help➪OpenOffice.org Help from the Writer menu (or pressing

F1 in newer versions). This brings up the OpenOffice.org Help window with help information on Writer. You can then click the links to view specific help information.

## Calc

Calc is the spreadsheet program in the OpenOffice.org application suite. To start Calc, choose Spreadsheet from the Office category in the main menu or choose File⇨New⇨Spreadsheet from any OpenOffice.org window. Calc displays its main window, which looks similar to Windows-based spreadsheets, such as Microsoft Excel. (Calc can read and write Microsoft Excel format spreadsheet files.)

Use Calc in the same way you use Microsoft Excel. You can type entries in cells, use formulas, and format the cells. (For example, you can specify the type of value and the number of digits after the decimal point.) Figure 5-2 shows a typical spreadsheet in Calc.

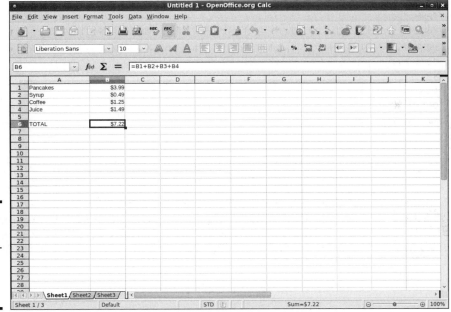

**Figure 5-2:**
Prepare
your spread-
sheets with
OpenOffice.
org Calc.

When preparing the spreadsheet, use formulas in the same format that you would in Microsoft Excel. For example, use the formula **SUM(D2:D6)** to add the entries from cell D2 to D6. To set cell D2 as the product of the entries A2 and C2, type **=A2*C2** in cell D2. To find out more about the functions available in OpenOffice.org Calc, choose Help⇨OpenOffice.org Help from the menu (or press F1 in newer versions). This opens the OpenOffice.org Help window, from which you can browse the functions by category and click a function to read more about it.

To save the spreadsheet, choose File⇨Save As. A dialog box appears, from which you can specify the file format, the directory location, and the name of the file. When you save a document, Calc saves it in OpenDocument spreadsheet format in a file with the .ods extension by default.

OpenOffice.org Calc can save the file in several other formats, including Microsoft Excel 5.0/95/97/2000/XP, as well as text file with comma-separated values (CSV).

If you want to exchange files with Microsoft Excel, save the spreadsheet in Microsoft Excel format (choose an appropriate version of Excel). Then you can transfer that file to a Windows system and open it in Microsoft Excel.

### Impress

Impress is similar to Microsoft PowerPoint, in that it allows you to create unique and creative slide presentations for a variety of purposes. To run Impress, choose Presentation from the Office category in the main menu or choose File⇨New⇨Presentation from any OpenOffice.org window.

When you first open Impress, the program prompts you for the presentation style and template. To begin working, select Empty presentation and click Create. To open an existing document, select the appropriate option from the Presentation Wizard and click Open. Then select the presentation file you want to open. You can open Microsoft PowerPoint files in Impress. Figure 5-3 shows a typical slide presentation in Impress.

The Impress window shows the first slide together with an outline view of the slides along the left side. The exact appearance depends on the document type and template you select. You can begin adding text and other graphic objects such as images, text, and lines to the slide.

To insert a new slide, choose Insert⇨Slide from the menu. A blank slide appears. You can then add text and graphics to that new slide.

To save a presentation, choose File⇨Save. For new documents, you have to provide a filename and select the directory where you want to save the file.

If you want to share the slides with someone who uses Microsoft PowerPoint, save the presentation in Microsoft PowerPoint 97/2000/XP format.

**Figure 5-3:**
You can
prepare
presen-
tations in
OpenOffice.
org Impress.

## Calendars

KDE comes with Kontact — an application that integrates existing KDE applications such as KMail mail reader and KOrganizer calendar program in a single graphical personal information manager. You can start Kontact from panel icons or the main menu. (The location of the menu entry depends on the Linux distribution.)

When Kontact starts, it usually displays a summary window with information about new e-mail messages, upcoming scheduled events, and more. You can explore each application individually by clicking the icons in the left pane of the Kontact window. For example, Figure 5-4 shows the Kontact window after you click the Calendar icon. In this case, Kontact displays the output of KOrganizer. The KOrganizer program displays a calendar view, in which you can click a date to set or view that day's schedule.

To add events or appointments for a specific date and time, select the date from the calendar, double-click the time, and type a brief description of the appointment in the New Event dialog box that appears. Click OK when you're finished.

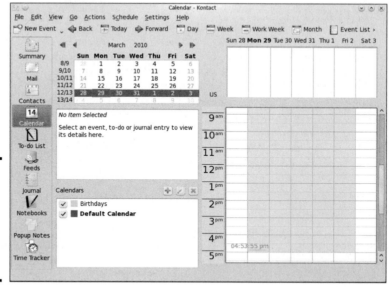

**Figure 5-4:**
Store your appointments and view your calendar in KOrganizer.

## Calculators

You have a choice of the GNOME calculator or the KDE calculator. Both are scientific calculators, and you can do the typical scientific calculations, such as square root and inverse, as well as trigonometric functions, such as sine, cosine, and tangent.

To use the calculator, look for it in the Utilities or Accessories category of the main menu. Figure 5-5 shows the KDE calculator in SUSE.

**Figure 5-5:**
Do your calculations in the KDE calculator.

You can display additional buttons by selecting options from the Settings menu. For example, choose Settings⇨Statistic Buttons to show buttons that enable you to perform statistical calculations with the calculator.

# Checking out Multimedia Applications

Most Linux distributions include quite a few multimedia applications — mostly multimedia audio players and CD players but also applications for using digital cameras and burning CD-ROMs. To play some other multimedia files (such as MPEG video), you may have to download and install additional software on your Linux system. Here's a quick sketch of a few typical multimedia tasks and the applications you can use to perform these tasks:

✦ **Using digital cameras:** Use a digital camera tool to download photos from your digital camera in Linux (or simply access the camera as a USB mass storage device).

✦ **Playing audio CDs:** Use one of many audio CD players that come with Linux.

✦ **Playing sound files:** Use Rhythmbox or XMMS multimedia audio players. (You have to download some additional software to play MP3 files with Rhythmbox or XMMS.) You can also download other players from the Internet.

✦ **Burning a CD:** Use a CD burner, such as K3b, to burn audio and data CDs.

**Book II
Chapter 5**

**Introducing Linux Applications**

## Using a digital camera

Most Linux distributions come with a digital camera application that you can use to download pictures from digital cameras. For example, SUSE and Xandros come with digiKam, which works with many makes and models of digital cameras. Depending on the model, the cameras can connect to the serial port or the Universal Serial Bus (USB) port.

To use digiKam with your digital camera, follow these steps:

*1.* **Connect your digital camera to the serial port or USB port (whichever interface the camera supports) and turn on the camera.**

*2.* **Start digiKam.**

Look for digiKam in the main menu under the Graphics or Images submenu. The first time you open digiKam, you will be asked to specify a default location to store images and choose a number of other configuration preferences.

*3.* **From the digiKam menu, choose Settings⇨Configure digiKam.**

A configuration dialog box appears.

*4.* **Click the Cameras tab in the dialog box, and then click Auto Detect.**

If your camera is supported and the camera is configured to be in PTP (Picture Transfer Protocol) mode, the camera is detected. If not, you can get the photos from your camera by using an alternate method described after these steps.

5. **Choose your camera model from the Camera menu.**

   A new window appears and, after a short while, displays the photos in the camera.

6. **Click the thumbnails to select the images you want to download; then choose Camera⇨Download to download the images.**

   digiKam downloads the images. You can save these files in a folder and edit the photos in The GIMP or your favorite photo editor.

Don't despair if digiKam doesn't recognize your digital camera. You can still access the digital camera's storage media (compact flash card, for example) as a USB mass storage device, provided your camera supports USB mass storage. To access the images on your USB digital camera, use the following steps.

1. **Read the camera manual and use the menu options of the camera to set the USB mode to Mass Storage.**

   If the camera doesn't support USB mass storage, you can't use this procedure to access the photos. If the camera supports the Picture Transfer Protocol mode, you can use digiKam to download the pictures.

2. **Connect your digital camera to the USB port by using the cable that came with the camera. Then turn on the camera.**

   Linux detects the camera and opens the contents of the camera in a file manager window.

3. **Click to select photos and copy them to your hard drive by dragging and dropping them into a selected folder.**

4. **Close the file manager window, disconnect the USB cable from the PC, and turn off the camera.**

Whether you are using a digital camera tool such as digiKam or accessing your camera like any other storage device, Linux makes it easy to get your pictures onto your computer!

## Playing audio CDs

All Linux distributions come with either the GNOME or KDE CD player applications. To play an audio CD, you need a sound card, and that sound card must be configured to work in Linux.

In some distributions, you can insert an audio CD into the drive, and a dialog box appears and asks whether you want to play the CD with the CD player. If this dialog box doesn't appear, locate an audio CD player by choosing Applications⇨Sound and Video from the main menu.

The KDE CD player displays the title of the CD and the name of the current track. The CD player gets the song titles from `http://freedb.org` — a free, open source CD database on the Internet (freedb.freedb.org at port 888). You need an active Internet connection for the CD player to download song information from the CD database. After the CD player downloads information about a particular CD, it caches that information in a local database for future use. The CD player user interface is intuitive, and you can figure it out easily. One nice feature is that you can select a track by title.

## Playing sound files

You can use Rhythmbox or XMMS to open and play sound files (for example, MP3 files). Users with large MP3 music libraries usually like Rhythmbox because it can help organize their music files. You can start Rhythmbox by choosing the music player application from the main menu in several distributions, including Debian and Fedora. When you first start Rhythmbox, it displays an assistant that prompts you for the location of your music files so that Rhythmbox can manage your music library.

After you identify the locations of music files, Rhythmbox starts and displays the library in an organized manner. You can then select music and play it.

XMMS is another music player that can play many types of sound files, including Ogg Vorbis, FLAC (Free Lossless Audio Codec, an audio file format similar to MP3), and Windows WAV.

You can start XMMS by choosing the audio player application from the main menu (look under Multimedia or Sound & Video). After XMMS starts, you can open a sound file (such as an MP3 file) by choosing Window Menu➪Play File or by pressing L. Then select one or more music files from the Load File dialog box. Click the Play button, and XMMS starts playing the sound file.

In some free Linux distributions, you may not be able to play MP3 files because the MP3 decoder is not included. However, MP3 playing works fine in Debian, Knoppix, SUSE, and Xandros. Because of legal reasons, the versions of Rhythmbox and XMMS in Fedora don't include the code needed to play MP3 files, so you have to translate MP3s into a supported format, such as WAV, before you can play them. You can, however, download the source code for Rhythmbox and XMMS and build the applications with MP3 support. You can also use the Ogg Vorbis format for compressed audio files because Ogg Vorbis is a patent- and royalty-free format.

## Burning a CD

Nowadays, most GUI file managers have the capability to burn CDs. For example, Nautilus File Manager and Xandros File Manager have built-in features to burn CDs. Linux distributions also come with standalone GUI programs that enable you to easily burn CDs and DVDs. For example, K3b is a popular CD/DVD burning application for KDE that's available in Knoppix and SUSE.

Most CD burning applications are simple to use. You basically gather the files that you want to burn to the CD or DVD and then start the burning process. Of course, for this to work, your PC must have a CD or DVD burner installed.

The upper part of the K3b window is for browsing the file system to select what you want to burn onto a CD or DVD. The upper-left corner shows the CD writer device installed.

To burn a CD, you start with one of the projects shown in the lower part of the K3b window — New Audio CD Project, for example, or New Data DVD Project. Then you have to add files and, finally, burn the project to the CD or DVD by choosing Project⇨Burn or pressing Ctrl+B. For an audio CD, you can drag and drop MP3 files as well as audio tracks.

K3b needs the external command-line programs cdrecord and cdrdao to burn CDs. K3b also needs the growisofs program to burn DVDs.

If you get an error about missing cdrdao in Debian, make sure that your Debian system is connected to the Internet and then type **apt-get install cdrdao** to install it.

# Using Graphics and Imaging Apps

You can use graphics and imaging applications to work with images and graphics (line drawings and shapes). Two of the most popular of these applications are

✦ **The GIMP (GNU Image Manipulation Program):** A program for viewing and performing image manipulation tasks, such as photo retouching, image composition, and image creation.

✦ **Gnome Ghostview (GGv):** A graphical application capable of displaying PostScript files.

## The GIMP

The GIMP is an image manipulation program written by Peter Mattis and Spencer Kimball and released under the GNU General Public License (GPL). Most Linux distributions come with this program, although you may have to specifically select a package to install it. The GIMP is comparable to other image manipulation programs, such as Adobe Photoshop and Corel PHOTO-PAINT.

To try out The GIMP, look for it under the Graphics category in the main menu. When you start The GIMP, it displays a window with copyright and license information. Click the Continue button to proceed with the installation. The next screen shows the directories to be created when you proceed with a personal installation of The GIMP.

If you can't find The GIMP under the Graphics category, choose Add/Remove Software from the System Settings menu and install it from there.

The GIMP installation involves creating a directory in your home directory and placing a number of files there. This directory essentially holds information about any changes to user preferences you may make to The GIMP. Go ahead and click the Continue button at the bottom of the window. The GIMP creates the necessary directories, copies the necessary files to those directories, and guides you through a series of dialog boxes to complete the installation.

When the installation is finished, click the Continue button. The GIMP then loads any *plug-ins* — external modules that enhance its functionality. It displays a startup window that shows a message about each plug-in as it loads. After finishing the startup, The GIMP displays a tip of the day in a window. You can browse the tips and click the Close button to close the Tip window. At the same time, The GIMP displays a number of other windows, including a main navigation window titled The GIMP, a Toolbox window (usually on the left side), a Brush Selection window, and a Layers, Channels, Paths window. The center navigation window gives you access to new images to work with, image editing functions, and a number of effect filters that you can apply to the image. The Toolbox window lets you quickly select a number of important image manipulation tools.

To open an image file in The GIMP, choose File➪Open. The Load Image dialog box appears. You can change directories and select the image file that you want to open. The GIMP can read all common image file formats, such as GIF, JPEG, TIFF, PCX, BMP, PNG, and PostScript. After you select the file and click OK, The GIMP loads the image into a new window.

The Toolbox window has many buttons that represent the tools you use to edit the image and apply special effects. You can get pop-up help on each tool button by placing the mouse pointer over the button. You can select a tool by clicking the tool button, and you can apply that tool's effects to the image to see what it does.

When you right-click the image window, The GIMP displays a pop-up menu that has most of the options from the GIMP's top toolbar.

You can do much more than just load and view images with The GIMP, but a complete discussion of all its features is beyond the scope of this book. If you want to try the other features of The GIMP, consult *The GIMP User*

*Manual* (GUM), available online at `http://manual.gimp.org`. You can also choose Help⇨GIMP Online⇨User Manual Website to access the online documentation for The GIMP. (You need an Internet connection for this command to work.)

Visit The GIMP home page at `www.gimp.org` to find the latest news about The GIMP as well as links to other resources.

### GNOME Ghostview

GNOME Ghostview is a graphical application ideal for viewing and printing PostScript or PDF documents. For a long document, you can view and print selected pages. You can also view the document at various levels of magnification by zooming in or out.

To run GNOME Ghostview in Fedora, choose Graphics⇨PostScript Viewer from GUI desktop. The GNOME Ghostview application window appears. In addition to the menu bar and toolbar along the top edge, a vertical divide splits the main display area of the window into two parts.

To load and view a PostScript document in GNOME Ghostview, choose File⇨Open, or click the Open icon on the toolbar. GNOME Ghostview displays a File-Selection dialog box. Use this dialog box to navigate the file system and select a PostScript file. For example, select the file `tiger.ps` in the `/usr/share/ghostscript-8.64/examples` directory. (Use your system's version number of Ghostscript in place of `8.64`).

To open the selected file, click the Open File button in the File-Selection dialog box. GNOME Ghostview opens the selected file, processes its contents, and displays the output in its window.

GNOME Ghostview is useful for viewing various kinds of documents that come in PostScript format. (These files typically have the `.ps` extension.) You can also open PDF files — which typically have `.pdf` extensions — in GNOME Ghostview.

## Using GUI File Managers

Both GNOME and KDE desktops come with GUI file managers that enable you to easily browse the file system and perform tasks such as copying or moving files. The GNOME file manager is Nautilus, and the KDE file manager is Dolphin. I briefly describe these GUI file managers in this section.

### Using the Nautilus shell

The Nautilus file manager (more accurately called a *graphical shell*) comes with GNOME. Nautilus is intuitive to use; it's similar to the Windows Active

Desktop. You can manage files and folders as well as your system with Nautilus. When you double-click any object on the desktop, Nautilus opens an object window that shows that object's contents.

### Viewing files and folders in object windows

When you double-click a file or a folder, Nautilus opens that object in what it calls an *object window*. If you then double-click an object inside that window, Nautilus opens another object window where that object's contents appear. You can use the Back button to return to the original folder. Alternatively, you can right-click a folder and choose to open it in a new window from the pop-up menu. Figure 5-6 shows the contents of a folder in Nautilus.

**Book II**
**Chapter 5**

**Introducing Linux
Applications**

**Figure 5-6:**
How
Nautilus
displays
folder
contents.

### Burning data CDs and DVDs

If you have a CD or DVD recorder attached to your system (it can be a built-in recorder or an external one attached to the USB port), you can use Nautilus to burn data CDs and DVDs. Just follow these simple steps:

### 1. In any Nautilus object window, choose Go⇨CD/DVD Creator.

Nautilus opens the CD/DVD Creator object window. You can open the Nautilus CD/DVD Creator also from the menu that appears automatically when you insert a blank disc.

If you don't have a Nautilus object window open, just double-click the Computer icon on the desktop.

2. **From other Nautilus windows, drag and drop into the CD/DVD Creator window the files and folders you want to put on the media.**

   To get to files on your computer, double-click the Computer icon to open the Nautilus window and find the files you want. Then drag and drop those file or folder icons into the CD/DVD Creator window.

3. **From the CD/DVD Creator window, choose File⇨Write to Disc.**

   Nautilus displays a dialog box where you can select the CD or DVD recorder, the write speed, and several other options, such as whether to eject the media when you are finished. You can also specify the title.

4. **(Optional) Make your selections in the dialog box that appears.**

5. **Click the Write button.**

   Nautilus burns the CD/DVD.

### Changing the view

If you prefer to view the contents of a folder in a tree view instead of as icons, you can change what you're seeing simply enough:

1. **Choose View from the Nautilus menu.**

2. **Click List (as opposed to Icons).**

   Nautilus displays the contents of the selected directory by using smaller icons in a list format, along with detailed information, such as the size of each file or directory and the time when each was last modified, as shown in Figure 5-7.

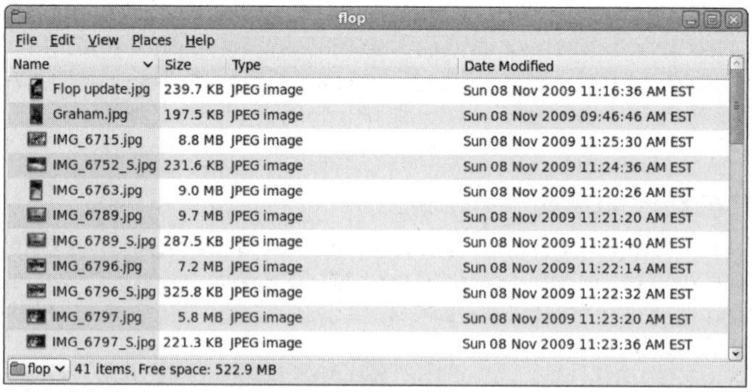

**Figure 5-7:**
The Nautilus navigation window with a list of the directory contents.

| | | flop | |
| --- | --- | --- | --- |
| File Edit View Places Help | | | |
| Name | ∨ Size | Type | Date Modified |
| Flop update.jpg | 239.7 KB | JPEG image | Sun 08 Nov 2009 11:16:36 AM EST |
| Graham.jpg | 197.5 KB | JPEG image | Sun 08 Nov 2009 09:46:46 AM EST |
| IMG_6715.jpg | 8.8 MB | JPEG image | Sun 08 Nov 2009 11:25:30 AM EST |
| IMG_6752_S.jpg | 231.6 KB | JPEG image | Sun 08 Nov 2009 11:24:36 AM EST |
| IMG_6763.jpg | 9.0 MB | JPEG image | Sun 08 Nov 2009 11:20:26 AM EST |
| IMG_6789.jpg | 9.7 MB | JPEG image | Sun 08 Nov 2009 11:21:20 AM EST |
| IMG_6789_S.jpg | 287.5 KB | JPEG image | Sun 08 Nov 2009 11:21:40 AM EST |
| IMG_6796.jpg | 7.2 MB | JPEG image | Sun 08 Nov 2009 11:22:14 AM EST |
| IMG_6796_S.jpg | 325.8 KB | JPEG image | Sun 08 Nov 2009 11:22:32 AM EST |
| IMG_6797.jpg | 5.8 MB | JPEG image | Sun 08 Nov 2009 11:23:20 AM EST |
| IMG_6797_S.jpg | 221.3 KB | JPEG image | Sun 08 Nov 2009 11:23:36 AM EST |
| flop ∨ | 41 items, Free space: 522.9 MB | | |

If you click a column heading along the top of the list view (such as Name, Size, Type, or Date Modified), Nautilus sorts the list according to that column. For example, go ahead and click the Date Modified column heading. Nautilus now displays the list of files and directories sorted according to the time they were last modified. Clicking the Name column heading sorts the files and folders alphabetically.

Not only can you move around different folders by using the Nautilus navigation window, you can also move a file from one folder to another, delete a file, and more, as in the following. (I don't outline each step because the steps are intuitive and similar to what you do in any GUI, such as Windows or Mac.)

+ **To move a file to a different folder:** Drag and drop the file's icon on the folder where you want the file.

+ **To copy a file to a new location:** Select the file's icon and choose Edit⇨ Copy from the Nautilus menu. (Or you can right-click the file's icon and choose Copy from the context menu.) Then move to the folder where you want to copy the file and choose Edit⇨Paste.

+ **To delete a file or directory:** Right-click the icon and choose Move to Trash from the context menu. (You can do this only if you have permission to delete the file.) To permanently delete the file, right-click the Trash icon on the desktop and choose Empty Trash from the context menu. Do this only if you really want to delete the file because you won't see the file again after you empty the trash. If you haven't emptied the trash and want to retrieve a file, double-click the Trash icon and then drag the file's icon back to the folder where you want to save it.

+ **To rename a file or a directory:** Right-click the icon for the file or directory and choose Rename from the context menu. Then type the new name (or edit the name) in the text box that appears.

+ **To create a new folder:** Right-click an empty area of the window on the right and choose Create Folder from the context menu. After the new folder icon appears, you can rename it by right-clicking the icon and choosing Rename from the context menu. If you don't have permission to create a folder, that menu item appears dimmed.

## Using Dolphin

Dolphin is one of the most popular file managers that come with KDE. It's intuitive to use — somewhat similar to the Windows Active Desktop. You can manage files and folders with Dolphin (use F9 to toggle the Navigational bar on the left side).

When you double-click a folder icon on the KDE desktop, Dolphin starts automatically and opens that folder. Click the Home Folder icon on the vertical toolbar on the left side of the Dolphin window. Dolphin now displays the contents of your home directory in its main window. From here you can navigate to other directories, folders, and files. Figure 5-8 shows a typical folder display in Dolphin.

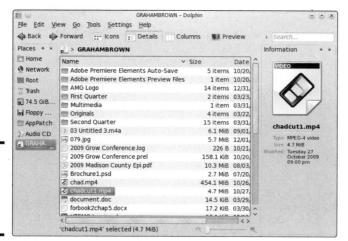

**Figure 5-8:**
You can
view files
and folders
in Dolphin.

You can use Dolphin in a similar manner to using Windows Explorer. The Dolphin window is vertically divided into three parts:

✦ A narrow left pane: Displays icons for various places on your system (including Home, Trash, and any removable hard drives).

✦ The main middle pane: Uses icons to show the files and folders in the current folder.

✦ The right pane: Displays additional information about the selected file or folder, as well as providing a thumbnail preview of image files.

Dolphin uses different types of icons for different files and shows a preview of each file's contents. Each directory appears as a folder, with the name of the directory below the folder icon. Ordinary files appear as a sheet of paper. For image files, the preview is a thumbnail version of the image.

The Dolphin window's title bar shows the name of the currently selected directory. The Location text box (along the top of the window) shows the full name of the directory — Figure 5-9 shows the contents of the user's /home directory. If you don't see the Location text box, choose View⇨Location Bar⇨Editable Location to toggle its display on or off.

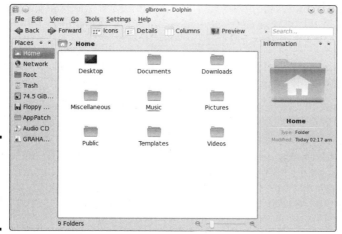

**Figure 5-9:**
The /home
directory as
it appears in
Dolphin.

The Dolphin window has the usual menu bar and a toolbar. You can view the
files and folders in other formats as well. For example, choose View⇨View
Mode⇨Details to see the folder's contents with smaller icons in a list format
(see Figure 5-10). To view more detailed information (such as the size of
each file or directory and at what time each was last modified), choose View⇨
Additional Information and select which information you would like to display.

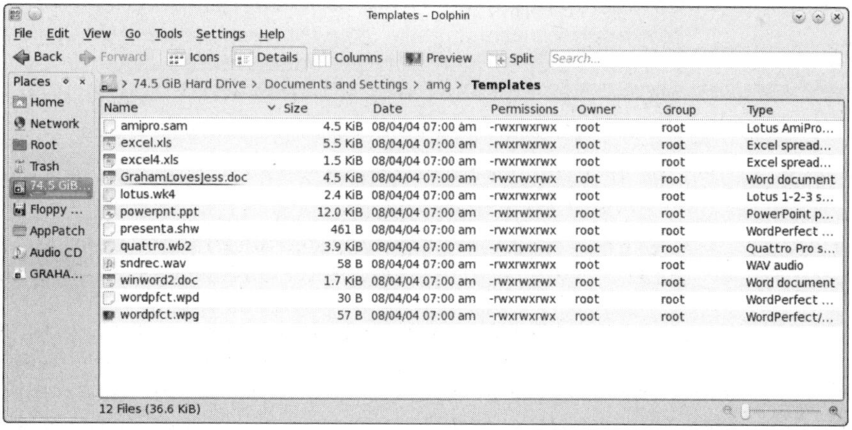

**Figure 5-10:**
Dolphin
shows a
detailed list
view of the
directory.

If you click a column heading along the top of the list view (such as Name,
Size, Type, or Date), Dolphin sorts the list according to that column. For
example, if you click the Date column heading, Dolphin displays a list of files
and folders sorted according to the time they were last modified. Clicking the
Name column heading sorts the files and directories alphabetically by name.

You can do several other tasks in Dolphin, such as the following. (I don't outline each step because the steps are intuitive and similar to what you do in any GUI, such as Windows or the Mac interface.)

+ **View a text file:** Click the filename, and Dolphin runs the default word processor, displaying the file in a new window.

+ **Copy or move a file to a different folder:** Drag and drop the file's icon on the folder where you want the file to go. A menu pops up and asks you whether you want to copy, move, or link the file to that directory.

+ **Delete a file or directory:** Right-click the icon for the file or directory and choose Move to Trash from the context menu. To permanently delete the file, right-click the Trash icon on the desktop and choose Empty Trash from the context menu. Do this only if you want to delete the file, because after you empty the trash, any deleted files are gone forever. If you haven't emptied the trash and want to recover a file from the trash, double-click the Trash icon on the desktop; from the window that appears, drag and drop the file icon into the folder where you want to save the file. On some distributions, you will be asked whether you want to copy or move; select Move.

+ **Rename a file or a directory:** Right-click the corresponding icon and choose Rename from the context menu. Then you can type the new name (or edit the old name) in the text box that appears.

+ **Create a new folder:** Choose View⇨View Mode⇨Icons. Then right-click an empty area of the middle pane and choose Create New⇨Folder from the context menu. Finally, type the name of the new directory and click OK. (If you don't have permission to create a directory, you get an error message.)

# Chapter 6: Using Text Editors

## In This Chapter

✔ **Checking out different GUI text editors**

✔ **Working with the ed text editor**

✔ **Getting to know the vi text editor**

Although the desktop provides a beautiful graphical interface that's a pleasure to work in, much goes on outside that interface. Most Linux system configuration files are text files. Additionally, Linux gives you the ability to create shell scripts and interact with the operation of a number of programs — all by using text files.

When all is working as it should, you can edit (and even create) those files with graphical tools, but it's highly recommended that you also know how to edit them outside that interface, should a problem exist that keeps the X Window System from loading. Whether in the interface or not, you'll be using *text editors,* programs designed to interact with text files.

In this chapter, you're introduced to a few text editors — both GUI editors and text mode editors.

## Using GUI Text Editors

Each of the GUI desktops — GNOME and KDE — comes with GUI text editors (text editors that have graphical user interfaces).

To use a GUI text editor, look in the main menu and search for text editors in an appropriate category. For example, in the GNOME desktop, choose Applications➪Accessories➪gedit Text Editor. After you have a text editor up and running, you can open a file by clicking the Open button on the toolbar to display the Open File dialog box. You can change directories and then select the file to edit by clicking the OK button.

The GNOME text editor loads the file in its window. You can open more than one file at a time and move among them as you edit the files. Figure 6-1 shows a typical editing session with the editor.

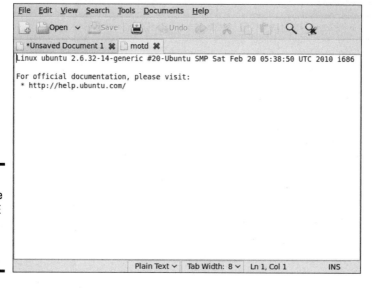

**Figure 6-1:**
You can use
the GNOME
text editor
to edit text
files.

In this case, the editor has two files — a new file being written, and `motd` (from the `/etc` directory) — open for editing. The filenames appear as tabs below the toolbar of the editor's window. You can switch between the files by clicking the tabs. The current filename appears in the last line of the window.

If you open a file for which you have only read permission, the text `[Read Only]` is appended to the filename shown in the window title to indicate that the file is read-only and the location of the file is displayed at the top (such as `/etc`). The indication that the file is read-only often appears when a regular user is opening system files that only the `root` can modify.

The rest of the text editing steps are intuitive. To enter new text, click to position the cursor and begin typing. You can select text, copy, cut, and paste by using the buttons on the toolbar above the text editing area.

From the KDE desktop, you can start the KDE text editor (KWrite) by choosing Applications➪Accessories➪Text Editor. To open a text file, choose File➪ Open to display a dialog box. From this dialog box, you can go to the directory of your choice, select the file to open, and click OK. KWrite opens the file and displays its contents in the window, and you can then edit the file as shown in Figure 6-2.

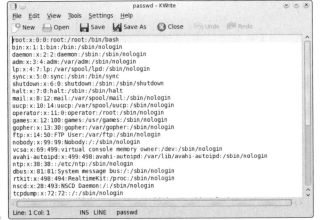

**Book II
Chapter 6**

**Using Text Editors**

**Figure 6-2:**
You can
use the KDE
KWrite text
editor to edit
files.

# Text Editing with ed and vi

GUI text editors enable you to edit text files using the mouse and keyboard
much the same way as you use any word processor. Text mode editors are
a different beast — you work using only the keyboard and you have to type
cryptic commands to perform editing tasks, such as cutting and pasting text
or entering and deleting text. Linux comes with two text mode text editors:

✦ ed: A line-oriented text editor

✦ vi: A full-screen text editor that supports the command set of an earlier
editor named ex

The ed and vi editors are cryptic compared to the graphical text editors.
However, you should still get to know the basic editing commands of ed
and vi because sometimes these two may be the only editors available. For
example, if Linux refuses to boot from the hard drive, you may have to boot
from a CD, DVD, or flash drive. In that case, you have to edit system files
with the ed editor because that editor is small enough to fit on the floppy. I
walk you through the basic text editing commands of ed and vi — they're
not that hard.

## Using ed

Typically, you have to use ed only when you boot a minimal version of Linux
(for example, from a floppy you've set up as a boot disk), and the system
doesn't support full-screen mode. In all other situations, you can use the vi
editor, which works in full-screen text mode.

When you use ed, you work in command mode or text input mode:

+ **Command mode:** This mode is the default. In this mode, anything that you type is interpreted as a command. The ed text editor has a simple command set in which each command consists of one or more characters.

+ **Text input mode:** This mode is for typing text. You can enter text input mode with the commands a (append), c (change), or i (insert). After entering lines of text, you can leave text input mode by entering a period (.) on a line by itself.

To practice editing a file, copy the /etc/fstab file to your home directory by issuing the following commands:

```
cd
cp /etc/fstab .
```

Now you have a file named fstab in your home directory. Type **ed -p: fstab** to begin editing a file in ed. The editor responds:

```
878
:
```

This example uses the -p option to set the prompt to the colon character (:) and opens the fstab file (in the current directory, which is your home directory) for editing. The ed editor opens the file, reports the number of characters in the file (878), displays the prompt (:), and waits for a command.

When you're editing with ed, make sure that you always turn on a prompt character (use the -p option). Without the prompt, distinguishing whether ed is in text input mode or command mode is difficult.

After ed opens a file for editing, the current line is the last line of the file. To see the current line number (the current line is the line to which ed applies your command), use the . = command, like this:

```
:.=
9
```

This output tells you that the fstab file has nine lines. (Your system's /etc/fstab file may have a different number of lines, in which case ed shows a different number.)

You can use the 1, $p command to see all lines in a file, as the following example shows:

```
:1,$p
# This file is edited by fstab-sync - see 'man fstab-sync' for details
/dev/VolGroup00/LogVol00 / ext3 defaults 1 1
LABEL=/boot /boot ext3 defaults 1 2
/dev/devpts /dev/pts devpts gid=5,mode=620 0 0
/dev/shm /dev/shm tmpfs defaults 0 0
/dev/proc /proc proc defaults 0 0
/dev/sys /sys sysfs defaults 0 0
/dev/VolGroup00/LogVol01 swap swap defaults 0 0
/dev/scd0 /media/cdrecorder auto pamconsole,exec,noauto,managed 0 0
/dev/fd0 /media/floppy auto pamconsole,exec,noauto,managed 0 0
/dev/hdc /media/cdrom auto pamconsole,exec,noauto,managed 0 0
:
```

To go to a specific line, type the line number:

```
:2
```

The editor responds by displaying that line:

```
/dev/VolGroup00/LogVol00 / ext3 defaults 1 1
:
```

Suppose you want to delete the line that contains cdrom. To search for a string, type a slash (/) followed by the string that you want to locate:

```
:/cdrom
/dev/hdc /media/cdrom auto pamconsole,exec,noauto,managed 0 0
:
```

The editor locates the line that contains the string and then displays it. That line becomes the current line.

To delete the current line, use the d command as follows:

```
:d
:
```

To replace a string with another, use the s command. To replace cdrom with the string cd, for example, use this command:

```
:s/cdrom/cd/
:
```

To insert a line in front of the current line, use the i command:

```
:i
(type the line you want to insert)
. (type a single period to indicate you're done)
:
```

You can enter as many lines as you want. After the last line, enter a period (.) on a line by itself. That period marks the end of text input mode, and the editor switches to command mode. In this case, you can tell that ed switches to command mode because you see the prompt (:).

When you're happy with the changes, you can write them to the file with the w command. If you want to save the changes and exit, type **wq** to perform both steps at the same time:

```
:wq
857
```

The ed editor saves the changes in the file, displays the number of saved characters, and exits. If you want to quit the editor without saving any changes, use the Q command.

These examples give you an idea of how to use ed commands to perform the basic tasks of editing a text file. Table 6-1 lists some of the commonly used ed commands.

| Table 6-1 | Common ed Commands |
|---|---|
| *Command* | *Does the Following* |
| !command | Executes a shell command. (For example, !pwd displays the current directory.) |
| $ | Goes to the last line in the buffer. |
| % | Applies a command that follows to all lines in the buffer. (For example, %p prints all lines.) |
| + | Goes to the next line |
| +n | Goes to the *n*th next line (where *n* is a number you designate). |
| , | Applies a command that follows to all lines in the buffer. (For example, ,p prints all lines.) This command is similar to %. |
| – | Goes to the preceding line. |
| -n | Goes to the *n*th previous line (where *n* is a number you designate). |
| . | Refers to the current line in the buffer. |
| /text/ | Searches forward for the specified text. |
| ; | Refers to a range of lines — the current line through the last line in the buffer. |
| = | Prints the line number. |
| ?text? | Searches backward for the specified text. |

| Command | Does the Following |
|---|---|
| ^ | Goes to the preceding line. (See also the – command.) |
| ^n | Goes to the *n*th previous line (where *n* is a number you designate). (See also the –n command.) |
| a | Appends the current line. |
| c | Changes the specified lines. |
| d | Deletes the specified lines. |
| i | Inserts text before the current line. |
| n | Goes to line number *n* (where *n* is a number you designate). |
| Press Enter | Displays the next line and makes that line current. |
| q | Quits the editor. |
| Q | Quits the editor without saving changes. |
| r *file* | Reads and inserts the contents of the file after the current line. |
| s/old/ new/ | Replaces an old string with a new one. |
| u | Undoes the last command. |
| W *file* | Appends the contents of the buffer to the end of the specified file. |
| w *file* | Saves the buffer in the specified file. (If no file is named, it saves in the default file — the file whose contents ed is currently editing.) |

## Using vi

After you dabble with ed, you'll find vi is a dream come true, even though it's still a command-line editor. The vi editor is a full-screen text editor, so you can view several lines at the same time. Most UNIX systems, including Linux, come with vi. Therefore, if you know the basic features of vi, you can edit text files on almost any UNIX-based system.

When vi edits a file, it reads the file into a *buffer* — a block of memory — so you can change the text in the buffer. The vi editor also uses temporary files during editing, but the original file isn't altered until you save the changes.

To start the editor, type **vi** and follow it with the name of the file you want to edit, like this:

```
vi /etc/fstab
```

The vi editor then loads the file into memory and displays the first few lines in a text screen and positions the cursor on the first line, as shown in Figure 6-3.

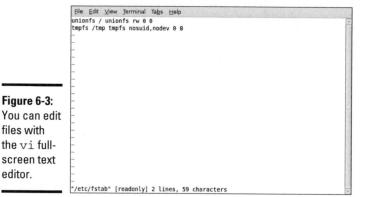

```
File  Edit  View  Terminal  Tabs  Help
unionfs / unionfs rw 0 0
tmpfs /tmp tmpfs nosuid,nodev 0 0
~
~
~
~
~
~
~
~
~
~
~
~
~
~
~
~
~
"/etc/fstab" [readonly] 2 lines, 59 characters
```

**Figure 6-3:** You can edit files with the vi full-screen text editor.

The last line shows the pathname of the file as well as the number of lines (2) and the number of characters (59) in the file. In this case, the text [readonly] appears after the filename because I'm opening the /etc/fstab file while I'm logged in as a normal user (which means I don't have permission to modify the file). Later, the last line in the vi display functions as a command entry area. The rest of the lines display the file. If the file contains fewer lines than the screen, vi displays the empty lines with a tilde (~) in the first column.

The current line is marked by the cursor, which appears as a small black rectangle. The cursor appears on top of a character.

When using vi, you work in one of three modes:

✦ **Visual command mode:** This mode is the default. In this mode, anything that you type is interpreted as a command that applies to the line containing the cursor. The vi commands are similar to the ed commands.

✦ **Colon command mode:** You use this mode for reading or writing files, setting vi options, and quitting vi. All colon commands start with a colon (:). When you type the colon, vi positions the cursor on the last line and waits for you to type a command. The command takes effect when you press Enter.

✦ **Text input mode:** This mode is for typing text. You can enter text input mode with the command a (insert after cursor), A (append at end of line), or i (insert after cursor). After entering lines of text, you have to press Esc to leave text input mode and re-enter visual command mode.

One problem with all these modes is that you can't easily tell the current mode that vi is in. You may begin typing only to realize that vi isn't in text input mode, which can be frustrating.

If you want to make sure that vi is in command mode, just press Esc a few times. (Pressing Esc more than once doesn't hurt.)

To view online help in vi, type **:help** while in colon command mode. When you're finished with help, type **:q** to exit the Help screen and return to the file you're editing.

The vi editor initially positions the cursor on the first character of the first line, and one of the handiest things you can know is how to move the cursor around. To get a bit of practice, try the commands shown in Table 6-2.

| Table 6-2 | Cursor Movement Commands in vi |
|---|---|
| *Key* | *Moves the Cursor* |
| ↓ | One line down |
| ↑ | One line up |
| ← | One character to the left |
| → | One character to the right |
| W | One word forward |
| B | One word backward |
| Ctrl+D | Half a screen down |
| Ctrl+U | Half a screen up |

You can go to a specific line number at any time by using the handy colon command. To go to line 6, for example, type the following and then press Enter:

```
:6
```

When you type the colon, vi displays the colon on the last line of the screen. From then on, vi uses any text you type as a command. You have to press Enter to submit the command to vi. In colon command mode, vi accepts all commands that the ed editor accepts — and then some.

To search for a string, first type a slash (/). The vi editor displays the slash on the last line of the screen. Type the search string and then press Enter. The vi editor locates the string and positions the cursor at the beginning of that string. Thus, to locate the string cdrom in the file /etc/fstab, type

```
/cdrom
```

To delete the line that contains the cursor, type **dd**. The vi editor deletes that line of text and makes the next line the current one.

To begin entering text in front of the cursor, type **i**. The vi editor switches to text input mode. Now you can enter text. When you finish entering text, press Esc to return to visual command mode.

After you finish editing the file, you can save the changes in the file with the :w command. To quit the editor without saving any changes, use the :q! command. If you want to save the changes and exit, you can use the :wq command to perform both steps at the same time. The vi editor saves the changes in the file and exits. You can also save the changes and exit the editor by pressing Shift+ZZ (hold Shift down and press Z twice).

vi accepts a large number of commands in addition to the commands I just mentioned. Table 6-3 lists some commonly used vi commands, organized by task.

| Table 6-3 | Common vi Commands |
|---|---|
| *Command* | *Does the Following* |
| **Insert Text** | |
| a | Inserts text after the cursor |
| A | Inserts text at the end of the current line |
| I | Inserts text at the beginning of the current line |
| i | Inserts text before the cursor |
| **Delete Text** | |
| D | Deletes up to the end of the current line |
| dd | Deletes the current line |
| dG | Deletes from the current line to the end of the file |
| dw | Deletes from the cursor to the end of the following word |
| x | Deletes the character on which the cursor rests |
| **Change Text** | |
| C | Changes up to the end of the current line |
| cc | Changes the current line |
| J | Joins the current line with the next one |
| rx | Replaces the character under the cursor with $x$ (where x is any character) |

| Command | Does the Following |
|---|---|
| **Move Cursor** | |
| h or ← | Moves one character to the left |
| j or ↓ | Moves one line down |
| k or ↑ | Moves one line up |
| L | Moves to the end of the screen |
| l or → | Moves one character to the right |
| w | Moves to the beginning of the following word |
| b | Moves to the beginning of the previous word |
| **Scroll Text** | |
| Ctrl+D | Scrolls forward by half a screen |
| Ctrl+U | Scrolls backward by half a screen |
| **Refresh Screen** | |
| Ctrl+L | Redraws screen |
| **Cut and Paste Text** | |
| yy | Yanks (copies) current line to an unnamed buffer |
| P | Puts the yanked line above the current line |
| p | Puts the yanked line below the current line |
| **Colon Commands** | |
| :!command | Executes a shell command |
| :q | Quits the editor |
| :q! | Quits without saving changes |
| :r filename | Reads the file and inserts it after the current line |
| :w filename | Writes a buffer to the file |
| :wq | Saves changes and exits |
| **Search Text** | |
| /string | Searches forward for a string |
| ?string | Searches backward for a string |
| **Miscellaneous** | |
| u | Undoes the last command |
| Esc | Ends input mode and enters visual command mode |
| U | Undoes recent changes to the current line |

# Book III

# Networking

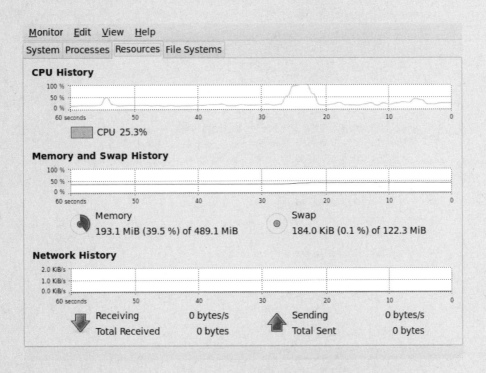

Check the status of your network with the System Monitor

# Contents at a Glance

**Chapter 1: Connecting to the Internet . . . . . . . . . . . . . . . . . . . . . . . . .175**

Understanding the Internet ........................................................................ 175
Deciding How to Connect to the Internet ............................................... 176
Connecting with DSL ................................................................................. 178
Connecting with a Cable Modem .............................................................. 184
Setting Up Dial-up Networking .................................................................. 189

**Chapter 2: Setting Up a Local Area Network . . . . . . . . . . . . . . . . . . .195**

Understanding TCP/IP ................................................................................ 195
Setting Up an Ethernet LAN ...................................................................... 199
Configuring TCP/IP Networking ............................................................... 203
Connecting Your LAN to the Internet ...................................................... 204

**Chapter 3: Going Wireless . . . . . . . . . . . . . . . . . . . . . . . . . . . . . . . . . .207**

Understanding Wireless Ethernet Networks ........................................... 207
Setting Up Wireless Hardware .................................................................. 211
Configuring the Wireless Access Point .................................................... 212
Configuring Wireless Networking ............................................................ 213

**Chapter 4: Managing the Network . . . . . . . . . . . . . . . . . . . . . . . . . . . .217**

Discovering the TCP/IP Configuration Files ........................................... 217
Checking Out TCP/IP Networks ............................................................... 221
Configuring Networks at Boot Time ......................................................... 227

# Chapter 1: Connecting to the Internet

## In This Chapter

✓ **Understanding the Internet**

✓ **Deciding how to connect to the Internet**

✓ **Connecting to the Internet with DSL**

✓ **Connecting to the Internet with a cable modem**

✓ **Setting up a dial-up PPP link**

*G*iven the prevalence and popularity of the Internet, it's a safe bet to assume that you want to connect your Linux system to the Internet. In this chapter, I show you how to connect to the Internet in several ways — depending on whether you have a DSL, cable modem, or dial-up network connection.

Two of the options for connecting to the Internet — DSL and cable modem — involve attaching a special modem to an Ethernet card on your Linux system. In these cases, you have to set up Ethernet networking on your Linux system. (I explain networking in Chapter 2 of this minibook.)

The other option — dial-up networking — involves dialing up an Internet service provider (ISP) from your Linux system.

## Understanding the Internet

How you view the Internet depends on your perspective. Most people see the Internet in terms of the services they use. For example, as a user, you might think of the Internet as an information-exchange medium with features such as

✦ **E-mail:** Send e-mail to any other user on the Internet, using addresses such as mom@home.net.

✦ **Web:** Download and view documents from millions of servers throughout the Internet.

✦ **Newsgroups:** Read newsgroups and post news items to newsgroups with names such as `comp.os.linux.networking` or `comp.os.linux.setup`.

✦ **Information sharing:** Download software, music files, videos, and so on. Reciprocally, you may provide files that users on other systems can download.

✦ **Remote access:** Log in to another computer on the Internet, assuming that you have access to that remote computer.

The techies say that the Internet is a worldwide *network of networks*. The term *internet* (without capitalization) is a shortened form of *internetworking* — the interconnection of networks. The Internet Protocol (IP) was designed with the idea of connecting many separate networks.

In terms of physical connections, the Internet is similar to a network of highways and roads. This similarity is what has prompted the popular press to dub the Internet "the Information Superhighway." Just as the network of highways and roads includes some interstate highways, many state roads, and many more residential streets, the Internet has some very high-capacity networks (for example, a 10 Gbps backbone can handle 10 billion bits per second) and a large number of lower-capacity networks ranging from 56 Kbps dial-up connections to 45 Mbps T3 links. (*Kbps* is thousand-bits-per-second, and *Mbps* is million-bits-per-second.) The high-capacity network is the backbone of the Internet.

In terms of management, the Internet isn't run by a single organization, nor is it managed by any central computer. You can view the physical Internet as a *network of networks* managed collectively by thousands of cooperating organizations. Yes, a collection of networks managed by *thousands* of organizations — sounds amazing, but it works!

# Deciding How to Connect to the Internet

So you want to connect your Linux workstation to the Internet, but you don't know how? Let me count the ways. Nowadays you have three popular options for connecting homes and small offices to the Internet (huge corporations and governments have many other ways to connect):

✦ **Digital Subscriber Line (DSL):** Your local telephone company as well as other telecommunications companies may offer DSL. DSL provides a way to send high-speed digital data over a regular phone line. Typically, DSL offers data transfer rates of between 128 Kbps and 3.0 Mbps (usually, the higher the speed, the more you pay). You can often download from the Internet at much higher rates than when you send data from your PC to the Internet *(upload)*. One caveat with DSL is that your home must be between 15,000 and 20,000 feet from your local central office (the DSL provider's facility where your phone lines end up). The distance limitation varies from provider to provider. In the United States, you can check out the distance limits for many providers at www.dsl reports.com/distance.

✦ **Cable modem:** If the cable television company in your area offers Internet access over cable, you can use that service to hook up your Linux system to the Internet. Typically, cable modems offer higher data-transfer rates than DSL — for about the same cost. Downloading data from the Internet via cable modem is much faster than sending data from your PC to the Internet. You can expect routine download speeds of 12 Mbps and upload speeds of around 2 Mbps, but sometimes you may get even higher speeds than these.

✦ **Dial-up networking:** Although its popularity is certainly waning, a dial-up connection is what most folks were using before DSL and cable modems came along. You hook up your PC to a modem that's connected to the phone line. Then you dial up an ISP to connect to the Internet. That's why it's called *dial-up networking* — establishing a network connection between your Linux PC and another network (the Internet) through a dial-up modem. In this case, the maximum data-transfer rate is 56 Kbps.

**Book III**
**Chapter 1**

**Connecting to the Internet**

DSL and cable modem services connect you to the Internet and also act as your Internet service provider (ISP); in addition to improved speed, what you're paying for is an IP address and your e-mail accounts. If you use a dial-up modem to connect to the Internet, first you have to connect to the phone line (for which you pay the phone company) and then select and pay a separate ISP — which gives you a phone number to dial and all the other necessary goodies (such as an IP address and e-mail accounts).

Table 1-1 summarizes these options. You can consult that table and select the type of connection that's available to you and that best suits your needs.

Besides the three options shown in Table 1-1, a few other less common options may be available to you. These include fiber-to-the-home (FTTH), broadband over power lines (BPL), fixed wireless broadband (called FWB or WiMAX), and satellite Internet access (for example, DIRECWAY and StarBand). If one or more of these options are available in your geographic area and you want to use one of them for Internet access, follow the specific service provider's instructions on setting up the Internet connection. Typically, satellite Internet access is available across large geographical regions (even places that don't have phone or cable), but the initial equipment cost and monthly fees are higher than DSL and cable.

| Table 1-1 | Comparison of Dial-up, DSL, and Cable | | |
|---|---|---|---|
| *Feature* | *Dial-up* | *DSL* | *Cable* |
| **Equipment** | Modem | DSL modem, Ethernet card | Cable modem, Ethernet card |
| **Also requires** | Phone service and an Internet service provider (ISP) | Phone service and location within 15,000 to 20,000 feet of central office | Cable TV connection |
| **Connection type** | Dial to connect | Always on, dedicated | Always on, shared |
| **Typical speed** | 56 Kbps maximum | 12 Mbps download, 2 Mbps upload (higher speeds cost more) | 1.5 Mbps download, 128 Kbps upload |
| **One-time costs (estimate)*** | None | Installation is $100–200 (none for self install); equipment costs $50–100 (may be leased and may require activation cost) | Installation is $100–200 (none for self install); equipment costs $50–100 (may be leased) |
| **Typical monthly cost (2010)*** | Phone charges are $20 per month; ISP charges are $15–30 per month | $40–50 per month; may require monthly modem lease | $40–50 per month; may require monthly modem lease |

*Costs vary by region and provider. Costs shown are typical for U.S. metropolitan areas.*

# Connecting with DSL

DSL stands for Digital Subscriber Line. DSL uses your existing phone line to send digital data in addition to the normal analog voice signals (*analog* means continuously varying, whereas digital data is represented by 1s and 0s). The phone line goes from your home to a central office, where the line connects to the DSL provider's network. By the way, the connection from your home to the central office is called the *local loop*.

When you sign up for DSL service, the DSL provider hooks up your phone line to some special equipment at the central office. That equipment can separate the digital data from voice. From then on, your phone line can carry digital data that is then directly sent to an Internet connection at the central office.

## How DSL works

A special box called a *DSL modem* takes care of sending digital data from your PC to the DSL provider's central office over your phone line. Your PC can connect to the Internet with the same phone line that you use for your normal telephone calls — you can make voice calls even as the line is being used for DSL. Figure 1-1 shows a typical DSL connection to the Internet.

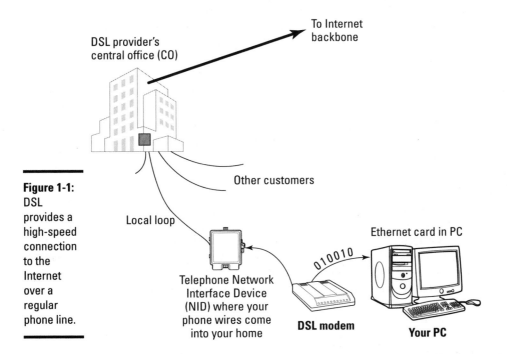

**Figure 1-1:**
DSL
provides a
high-speed
connection
to the
Internet
over a
regular
phone line.

Your PC talks to the DSL modem through an Ethernet connection, which means that you need an Ethernet card in your Linux system.

Your PC sends digital data over the Ethernet connection to the DSL modem. The DSL modem sends the digital data at different frequencies than those used by the analog voice signals. The voice signals occupy a small portion of all the frequencies that the phone line can carry. DSL uses the higher frequencies to transfer digital data, so both voice and data can travel on the same phone line.

# DSL alphabet soup: ADSL, IDSL, SDSL

I have been using the term *DSL* as if there were only one kind of DSL, but DSL has three variants of DSL, each with different features. Take a look:

✦ **ADSL:** Asymmetric DSL is the most common form of DSL and has much higher download speeds (from the Internet to your PC) than upload speeds (from your PC to the Internet). ADSL can have download speeds of up to 8 Mbps and upload speeds of up to 1 Mbps. ADSL works best when your location is within about two to two-and-a-half miles (12,000 feet) of the central office. ADSL service is priced according to the download and upload speeds you want. A popular form of ADSL, called G.lite, has a maximum download speed of 1.5 Mbps and a maximum upload speed of 512 Kbps.

✦ **IDSL:** ISDN DSL (ISDN is an older technology called *Integrated Services Digital Network*) is a special type of DSL that works at distances of up to five miles between your phone and the central office. The downside is that IDSL averages *downstream* (from the Internet to your PC) and *upstream* (from your PC to the Internet) speeds of around 144 Kbps.

✦ **SDSL:** Symmetric DSL provides equal download and upload speeds of up to 2.0 Mbps. SDSL is priced according to the speed you want, with the higher speeds costing more. The closer your location is to the central office, the faster the connection you can get.

DSL (and cable modem) speeds are typically specified by two numbers separated by a slash, such as 1500/384. The numbers refer to data-transfer speeds in kilobits per second (that is, thousands of bits per second, abbreviated Kbps). The first number is the download speed; the second, the upload. Thus, 1500/384 means you can expect to download from the Internet at a maximum rate of 1,500 Kbps (or 1.5 Mbps) and upload to the Internet at 384 Kbps. If your phone line's condition isn't perfect, you may not get these maximum rates — both ADSL and SDSL adjust the speeds to suit existing line conditions.

The price of DSL service depends on which variant — ADSL, IDSL, or SDSL — you select. For most home users, the primary choice is ADSL (or, more accurately, the G.lite form of ADSL) with transfer speed ratings of up to 9000/640.

## Typical DSL setup

To get DSL for your home or business, you have to contact a DSL provider. You can find many other DSL providers in addition to your phone company. No matter who provides the DSL service, some work has to be done at the central office — the place where your phone lines connect to the rest of the phone network. The work involves connecting your phone line to equipment that can work with the DSL modem at your home or office. The central office equipment and the DSL modem at your location can then do whatever magic is needed to send and receive digital data over your phone line.

The distance between your home and the central office — the *loop length* — is a factor in DSL's performance. Unfortunately, the phone line can reliably carry the DSL signals over only a limited distance — typically three miles or less, which means that you can get DSL service only if your home (or office) is located within about three miles of the central office. Contact your DSL provider to verify. You may be able to check this availability on the Web. Try typing into Google (www.google.com) the words **DSL availability** and then your provider's name. The search results will probably include a Web site where you can type in your phone number to find out if DSL is available for your home or office.

If DSL is available, you can look for the types of service — ADSL versus SDSL — and the pricing. The price depends on what download and upload speeds you want. Sometimes, phone companies offer a simple residential DSL (basically the G.lite form of ADSL) with a 1500/128 speed rating — meaning you can download at up to 1,500 Kbps and upload at 128 Kbps. Of course, these are the *maximums,* and your mileage may vary.

After selecting the type of DSL service and provider you want, you can place an order and have the provider install the necessary equipment at your home or office. Figure 1-2 shows a sample connection diagram for typical residential DSL service.

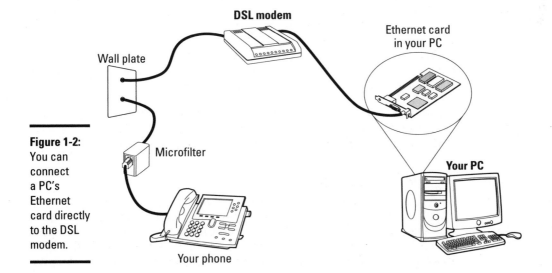

**Figure 1-2:**
You can connect a PC's Ethernet card directly to the DSL modem.

Here are some key points to note in Figure 1-2:

✦ Connect your DSL modem's data connection to the phone jack on a wall plate.

✦ Connect the DSL modem's Ethernet connection to the Ethernet card on your PC.

✦ When you connect other telephones or fax machines on the same phone line, install a microfilter between the wall plate and each of these devices.

Because the same phone line carries both voice signals and DSL data, you need the microfilter to protect the DSL data from possible interference. You can buy them at electronics stores or from the DSL provider.

When you connect your Linux PC to the Internet using DSL, the connection is always on, which means a greater potential for outsiders to break into the PC.

You can protect your Linux system from intruders and, as a bonus, share the high-speed connection with other PCs in a local area network (LAN) by using a router that can perform Network Address Translation (NAT). A NAT router translates multiple private Internet Protocol (IP) addresses from an internal LAN into a single public IP address, which allows all the internal PCs to access the Internet. The NAT router acts as a gateway between your LAN and the Internet, and it isolates your LAN from the Internet — this makes it harder for intruders to reach the systems on your LAN.

If you also want to set up a local area network, you need an Ethernet hub or switch to connect the other PCs to the network. Figure 1-3 shows a typical setup that connects a LAN to the Internet through a NAT router and a DSL modem.

Here are the points to note when setting up a connection like the one shown in Figure 1-3:

✦ You need a NAT router with two 100BaseT or 10BaseT Ethernet ports (the 100BaseT and 10BaseT ports look like a large phone jack, also known as an *RJ-45 jack*). Typically, one Ethernet port is labeled *Internet* (or *External* or *WAN,* for wide area network), and the other one is labeled *Local* or *LAN* (for local area network).

✦ You also need an Ethernet hub/switch. For a small home network, you can buy a 4- or 8-port Ethernet hub. Basically, you want a hub with as many ports as the number of PCs you intend to connect to your local area network. For a business, you'll want to replace the hub with a switch.

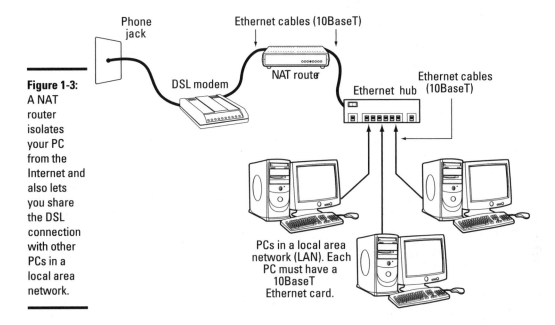

**Figure 1-3:**
A NAT router isolates your PC from the Internet and also lets you share the DSL connection with other PCs in a local area network.

Phone jack

Ethernet cables (10BaseT)

DSL modem

NAT route

Ethernet hub

Ethernet cables (10BaseT)

PCs in a local area network (LAN). Each PC must have a 10BaseT Ethernet card.

**Book III
Chapter 1**

Connecting to
the Internet

+ Connect the Ethernet port of the DSL modem to the Internet port of the NAT router, using a 100BaseT Ethernet cable. (These look like phone wires with bigger RJ-45 jacks and are often labeled *Category 5* or *Cat 5* wire.)

+ Connect the Local Ethernet port of the NAT router to one of the ports on the Ethernet hub/switch, using a 100BaseT Ethernet cable.

+ Now connect each of the PCs to the Ethernet hub/switch. (To do so, you must first have an Ethernet card installed and configured in each PC.)

You can also buy a NAT router with a built-in 4-port or 8-port Ethernet hub. With such a combined router and hub, you need only one box to set up a LAN and connect it to the Internet via a DSL modem. These boxes are typically sold under the name Cable/DSL router because they work with both DSL and a cable modem.

Consult Chapter 2 of this minibook for information on how to configure networking on the Linux system so that your system can access the Internet.

DSL providers typically use a protocol known as PPP over Ethernet (PPPoE) to establish a connection between your PC and the equipment at the provider's central office. PPPoE requires you to provide a username and password to establish the network connection over Ethernet. To set up your system for a PPPoE DSL connection, all you have to do is run a utility program that configures the system for PPPoE. You can find the utility by searching in the Main menu in the GUI desktop.

In Ubuntu, you can set up a PPPoE DSL connection by choosing System⇨ Administration⇨Network Tools, clicking the modem connection, and choosing Properties. Then go through the successive screens and provide the requested account information, such as username and password.

# Connecting with a Cable Modem

Cable TV companies also offer high-speed Internet access over the same coaxial cable that carries television signals to your home. After the cable company installs the necessary equipment at its facility to send and receive digital data over the coaxial cables, customers can sign up for cable Internet service. You can then get high-speed Internet access over the same line that delivers cable TV signals to your home.

## How a cable modem works

A box called a *cable modem* is at the heart of Internet access over the cable TV network. (See Figure 1-4.) The cable modem takes digital data from your PC's Ethernet card and puts it in an unused block of frequency. (Think of this frequency as another TV channel, but instead of pictures and sound, this channel carries digital data.)

The cable modem places *upstream data* — data that's being sent from your PC to the Internet — in a different channel than the *downstream* data that's coming from the Internet to your PC. By design, the speed of downstream data transfers is much higher than that of upstream transfers. The assumption is that people download far more stuff from the Internet than they upload (which is probably true for most of us).

The coaxial cable that carries all those hundreds of cable TV channels to your home is a very capable signal carrier. In particular, the coaxial cable can carry signals covering a huge range of frequencies — hundreds of megahertz (MHz). Each TV channel requires 6 MHz — and the coaxial cable can carry hundreds of such channels. The cable modem places the upstream data in a small frequency band and expects to receive the downstream data in another frequency band.

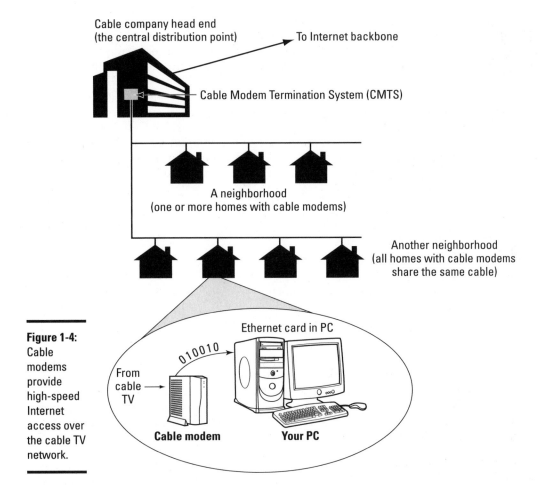

**Figure 1-4:**
Cable modems provide high-speed Internet access over the cable TV network.

At the other end of your cable connection to the Internet is the *Cable Modem Termination System* (CMTS) — also known as the *head end* — that your cable company installs at its central facility. (Refer to Figure 1-4.) The CMTS connects the cable TV network to the Internet. It also extracts the upstream digital data sent by your cable modem (and by those of your neighbors as well) and sends it to the Internet. The CMTS also puts digital data into the upstream channels so that your cable modem can extract that data and provide it to your PC via the Ethernet card.

Cable modems can receive downstream data at the rate of about 50 Mbps and send data upstream at around 10 Mbps. However, all the cable modems in a neighborhood share the same downstream capacity. Each cable modem filters out — separates — the data it needs from the stream of data that the CMTS sends out. Cable modems follow a modem standard called DOCSIS, which stands for Data Over Cable Service Interface. You can buy any DOCSIS-compliant modem and use it with your cable Internet service; all you have to do is call the cable company and give them the modem's identifying information so that the CMTS can recognize and initialize the modem.

In practice, with a cable modem, you will most likely get downstream transfer rates of around 12 Mbps and upstream rates of 2 Mbps. These are maximum rates, and your transfer rate is typically lower, depending on how many people in your neighborhood are using cable modems at the same time.

If you want to check your downstream transfer speed, go to `http://band widthplace.com/speedtest` and click the link to start the test. For my cable modem connection, for example, a recent test reported a downstream transfer rate of about 2.2 Mbps, but at other times the rate has been as high as 5.2 Mbps.

## Typical cable modem setup

To set up cable modem access, your cable TV provider must offer high-speed Internet access. If the service is available, you can call to sign up. The cable companies often have promotional offers, such as no installation fee or a reduced rate for three months. If you're lucky, a local cable company may have a promotion going on just when you want to sign up.

The installation is typically performed by a technician, who splits your incoming cable into two — one side goes to the TV and the other to the cable modem. The technician provides information about the cable modem to the cable company's head end for setup at its end. When that work is completed, you can plug in your PC's Ethernet card to the cable modem, and you'll be all set to enjoy high-speed Internet access. Figure 1-5 shows a typical cable modem hookup.

The cable modem connects to an Ethernet card in your PC. If you don't have an Ethernet card in your PC, the cable company technician often provides one.

Here are some key points to note about the cable modem setup in Figure 1-5:

✦ Split the incoming cable TV signal into two parts by using a two-way splitter. (The cable company technician installs the splitter.)

The two-way splitter needs to be rated for 1 GHz; otherwise, it may not let the frequencies that contain the downstream data from the Internet pass through.

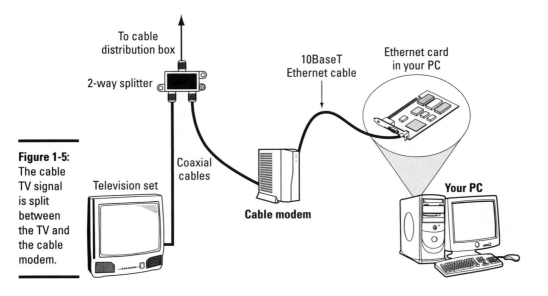

**Figure 1-5:**
The cable
TV signal
is split
between
the TV and
the cable
modem.

+ Connect one of the video outputs from the splitter to your cable modem's F-type video connector using a coaxial cable.

+ Connect the cable modem's 100BaseT Ethernet connection to the Ethernet card on your PC.

+ Connect your TV to the other video output from the two-way splitter.

When you use cable modem to directly connect your Linux PC to the Internet, the connection is always on, so you have more of a chance that someone may try to break into the PC. Linux includes the `iptables` packet filtering capability, which you may want to use to protect your PC from unwanted Internet connections.

In Ubuntu, you can install the `firestarter` package (from the Universe repository). After installed, configure settings by choosing System⇨ Administration⇨Firestarter. This kicks off the Firewall Wizard and walks you through the steps of configuration.

To isolate your Linux PC or local area network from the public Internet, you may want to add a NAT router between your PC and the cable modem. One of the NAT router's network interfaces connects to the Internet, and the other connects to your LAN; the router then acts as a gateway between your LAN and the Internet. As a bonus, you can even share a cable modem connection with all the PCs in your own local area network (LAN) by adding an Ethernet hub. Better yet, buy a combination NAT router and hub so you have only box to do the entire job.

**Book III
Chapter 1**

**Connecting to
the Internet**

The NAT router and hubs are typically sold under the name *cable/DSL router* because they work with both DSL and cable modem.

The NAT router translates private IP addresses into a public IP address. When connected through a NAT router, any PC in the internal LAN can access the Internet as if it had its own unique IP address. As a result, you can share a single Internet connection among many PCs — an ideal solution for a family of Net surfers!

Figure 1-6 shows a typical setup with a cable modem connection being shared by a number of PCs in a LAN.

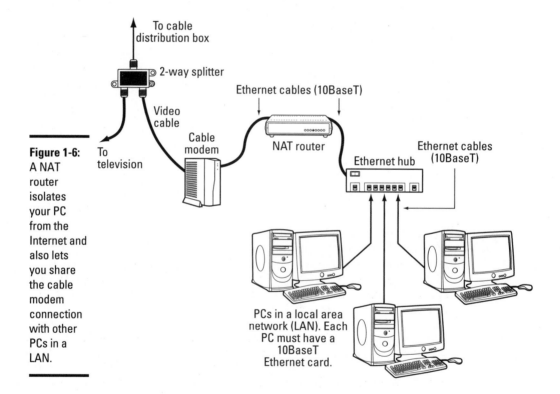

**Figure 1-6:** A NAT router isolates your PC from the Internet and also lets you share the cable modem connection with other PCs in a LAN.

Here are the points to note when setting up a connection like the one shown in Figure 1-6:

✦ You need a cable/DSL NAT router with two 100BaseT Ethernet ports (the 100BaseT port — also known as an *RJ-45 jack,* which looks like a large phone jack). Typically, one Ethernet port is labeled *Internet* (or *External* or *WAN,* for wide area network), and the other one is labeled *Local.*

✦ If you plan to set up a LAN, you also need an Ethernet hub/switch. For a small home network, you can buy a 4- or 8-port Ethernet hub. Basically, you want a hub with as many ports as the number of PCs you intend to connect to your local area network.

✦ Consider buying a single box that acts as both a NAT router and a hub with a number of Ethernet ports.

✦ Connect the video cable to the video input port of the cable modem.

✦ Connect the Ethernet port of the cable modem to the Internet port of the NAT router using a 100BaseT Ethernet cable. (The cable looks like a phone wire except that the Ethernet cable has bigger RJ-45 jacks and is often labeled *Category 5* or *Cat 5 wire.*)

✦ Connect the Local Ethernet port of the NAT router to one of the ports on the Ethernet hub using a 100BaseT Ethernet cable.

✦ Now connect each of the PCs to the Ethernet hub. Each PC must have an Ethernet card.

In Chapter 2 of this minibook, I explain how to configure the PCs in a LAN so that they can all access the Internet through the router.

**Book III
Chapter 1**

Connecting to
the Internet

# Setting Up Dial-up Networking

With the rise in popularity of both DSL and cable networks, dial-up networking is becoming a thing of the past. That said, this section outlines the important features to know about dial-up for those who live in areas where DSL or cable are not available.

*Dial-up networking* refers to connecting a PC to a remote network through a dial-up modem. If you're ancient enough to remember the days of dialing up with Procomm or some serial communications software, realize that there's a significant difference between dial-up networking and the old days of serial communication. Both approaches use a modem to dial up a remote computer and to establish a communication path, but the serial communication software makes your computer behave like a dumb terminal connected to the remote computer. The serial communication software exclusively uses a dial-up connection. You can't run another copy of the communication software and use the same modem connection, for example.

In dial-up networking, both your PC and the remote system run network protocol (called TCP/IP) software. When your PC dials up and sets up a communication path, the network protocols exchange data packets over that dial-up connection. The neat part is that any number of applications can use the same dial-up connection to send and receive data packets. So your PC becomes a part of the network to which the remote computer belongs. (If the remote computer isn't on a network, dial-up networking creates a network that consists of the remote computer and your PC.)

In Chapter 2 of this minibook, I describe TCP/IP protocol some more, but I have to use the term as well as a few concepts such as *Internet Protocol* (IP) address and *Domain Name System* (DNS) when describing how to set up dial-up networking.

Setting up a TCP/IP network over a dial-up link involves specifying the protocol — the convention — for packaging a data packet over the communication link. *Point-to-Point Protocol* (PPP) is such a protocol for establishing a TCP/IP connection over any point-to-point link, including dial-up phone lines. Linux supports PPP, and it comes with the configuration tools you can use to set up PPP so that your system can establish a PPP connection with your ISP.

Here's what you have to do to set up dial-up networking in Linux:

1. Install an internal or external modem in your PC. If your PC didn't already come with an internal modem, you can buy an external modem and connect it to the PC's serial or USB port.

2. Connect the modem to the phone line and power up the modem and the computer.

3. Get an account with an ISP. Every ISP provides you a phone number to dial, a username, and a password. Additionally, the ISP gives you the full names of servers for e-mail and news. Typically, your system automatically gets an IP address.

4. Run a GUI tool (if available) to set up a PPP connection. If you can't find a GUI tool, type **wvdialconf /etc/wvdial.conf** at the shell prompt. (If this program isn't installed yet, use your distribution's installation tools or type **apt-get install wvdial** in the shell prompt of Ubuntu, Debian, or Xandros.) The wvdialconf program automatically detects the modem and sets up the configuration file /etc/wvdial.conf. Now use a text editor to edit the file /etc/wvdial.conf and enter the ISP's phone number as well as the username and password of your Internet account with the ISP. (Look for fields labeled Username, Password, and Phone.)

5. Use a GUI tool (if available) to activate the PPP connection to connect to the Internet. If no GUI tool is available, log in as root and type **wvdial** to establish the PPP connection.

I briefly go over these steps in the following sections.

## Connecting the modem

The word *modem* is a contraction of modulator/demodulator — a device that converts digital signals (strings of 1s and 0s) into continuously varying analog signals that transmit over telephone lines and radio waves. Thus, the modem is the intermediary between the digital world of the PC and the analog world of telephones. Figure 1-7 illustrates the concept of a modem.

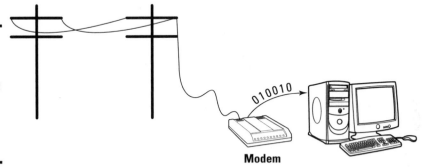

**Figure 1-7:** A modem bridges the digital world of PCs and the analog world of telephones.

**Modem**

Inside the PC, 1s and 0s are represented with voltage levels, but signals carried over telephone lines are usually tones of different frequencies. The modem sits between the PC and the telephone lines and makes data communication possible over the phone lines. The modem converts information back and forth between the voltage/no voltage representation of digital circuits and different frequency tones that are appropriate for transmission over phone lines.

Before you can dial out using an external modem, you have to make sure that the modem is properly connected to one of the serial or USB ports of your PC.

---

# Winmodems: They do *only* Windows

A quick word of caution about the *Winmodems* that come with many new PCs and laptops: Winmodems are software-based internal modems — different from the traditional hardware modems. Also known as *Windows modems* or *software modems* (*softmodem* for short), they work only with special driver software (which in turn works only with Microsoft Windows). With Winmodems and Linux, you're pretty much on your own, but you can find some useful guidance online at the Linux Winmodem Support home page at www.linmodems.org.

If you have an external modem, make sure that your modem is properly connected to the power supply and that the modem is connected to the telephone line. Buy the right type of cable to connect the modem to the PC. You need a straight-through serial cable to connect the modem to the PC. The connectors at the ends of the cable depend on the type of serial connector on your PC. The modem end of the cable needs a male 25-pin connector. The PC end of the cable often is a female 9-pin connector. You can buy modem cables at most computer stores. Often, you can find 9-pin-female-to-25-pin-male modem cables sold under the label *AT modem cable.* Connect USB modems by using a USB cable.

If your PC has an internal modem, all you have to do is connect the phone line to the phone jack at the back of the internal modem card. If your PC has a Winmodem, you still connect the phone line, but you also have to do a bit of research on the Internet and download a driver that makes the Winmodem work in Linux. After you install a working Linux driver for a Winmodem, it works just like the older serial port modems. See the sidebar, "Winmodems: They do *only* Windows," for more information.

## Setting up and activating a PPP connection

Most ISPs provide PPP dial-up access to the Internet through one or more systems that the ISP maintains. If you sign up for such a service, the ISP provides you the information that you need to make a PPP connection to the ISP's system. Typically, this information includes the following:

+ The phone number to dial to connect to the remote system.

+ The username and password that you must use to log in to the remote system.

+ The names of the ISP's mail and news servers.

+ The IP address for your PPP connection. Your ISP doesn't provide this address if the IP address is assigned *dynamically* (which means the IP address may change every time that your system establishes a connection).

+ IP addresses of the ISP's DNS. The ISP doesn't provide these addresses if it assigns the IP address dynamically.

Of this information, the first two items are what you need to set up a PPP connection. The exact steps for setting up and using a PPP connection depend on the distribution. For distributions with a GUI Internet connection tool, you can easily figure out where to enter your ISP account information — the phone number, username, and password. I point out a few distribution-specific approaches for configuring PPP next.

Debian has a GUI tool to set up a PPP connection, and the tool uses `wvdial`, which isn't installed by default. Type **apt-get install wvdial** to install it. Then you can use the GUI tool to configure and activate the dial-up PPP connection.

The most recent versions of Ubuntu do not support dial-up modems, but drivers can be installed that can enable the use of these modems. For more information, consult Ubuntu's Help menu.

## Configuring CHAP and PAP authentication

The PPP server on your system has to authenticate itself to the ISP's PPP server before the PPP connection can get fully up and running. *Authentication* requires proving that you have a valid account with the ISP, essentially providing a username and a *secret* (that is, a password). PPP specifies two ways of exchanging the authentication information between the two ends of the connection:

✦ **Challenge Handshake Authentication Protocol (CHAP)** requires the remote end to send a randomly generated challenge string along with the remote server's name. The local system looks up the secret, using the server's name; then it sends back a response that includes its name and a value that combines the secret and the challenge, using a one-way hash function. The remote system then checks that value against its own calculation of the expected hash value. If the values match, the authentication succeeds; otherwise, the remote system terminates the connection. In this case, the name and secret are stored in the /etc/ppp/ chap-secrets file.

The remote system can repeat the CHAP authentication any time while the PPP link is up.

✦ **Password Authentication Protocol (PAP)** is like the normal login process. When using PAP, the local system repeatedly sends a username (name) and password (secret) until the remote system acknowledges the authentication or ends the connection. The name and secret are stored in the /etc/ppp/pap-secrets file.

The username and password are sent in the clear (unencrypted).

The Linux PPP server supports both types of authentication. For PAP and CHAP, the information that the PPP server needs is a name and a secret — a username and password pair. This authentication information is stored in the following configuration files:

✦ /etc/ppp/chap-secrets stores the information for CHAP. Here's what a typical chap-secrets file looks like:

```
# Secrets for authentication using CHAP
# client server secret IP addresses
"edulaney" * "mypassword"
```

✦ /etc/ppp/pap-secrets stores the information for PAP. Here's a typical pap-secrets file:

```
# Secrets for authentication using PAP
# client server secret IP addresses
"edulaney" * "mypassword"
```

As you can see, the formats of the entries are the same for both chap-
secrets and pap-secrets. Four fields are in each line, in the following
order:

✦ client: This field contains the name that's used during authentication.
You get this name from the ISP.

✦ server: This field contains the name of the remote system to which
you're authenticating the local system. If you don't know the server's
name, type an asterisk to indicate any server.

✦ secret: This field is the secret that your system's PPP server has to
send to the remote system to authenticate itself. You receive this password from the ISP.

✦ IP addresses: This optional field can contain a list of the IP addresses
that the local system may use when connecting to the specified server.
Typically, this field is left blank because the local system usually gets a
dynamic IP address from the server and (therefore) doesn't know what
IP address it uses.

# Chapter 2: Setting Up a Local Area Network

## In This Chapter

✔ Understanding TCP/IP networks

✔ Setting up an Ethernet local area network

✔ Discovering how to configure TCP/IP networking

✔ Connecting a LAN for the Internet

*L*inux comes with built-in support for Transmission Control Protocol/ Internet Protocol (TCP/IP) networking, as do most modern operating systems from Windows to Mac OS. You can have TCP/IP networking over many different physical interfaces, such as Ethernet cards, serial ports, and parallel ports.

Typically, you use an Ethernet network for your local area network (LAN) — at your office or even your home (if you happen to have two or more systems at home) — with wireless (the subject of the next chapter) gaining in popularity.

This chapter describes how to set up an Ethernet network. Even if you have a single PC, you may need to set up an Ethernet network interface so that you can connect your PC to high-speed Internet access that uses a DSL or cable modem. (I cover DSL and cable modems in Chapter 1 of this minibook.)

## Understanding TCP/IP

You can understand TCP/IP networking best if you think in terms of a four-layer model, with each layer responsible for performing a particular task. The layered model describes the flow of data between the physical connection to the network and the end-user application. Figure 2-1 shows the four-layer network model for TCP/IP.

In this four-layer model, information always moves from one layer to the next. For example, when an application sends data to another application, the data goes through the layers in this order: application⇨transport⇨ network⇨physical. At the receiving end, the data goes up from physical⇨ network⇨transport⇨application.

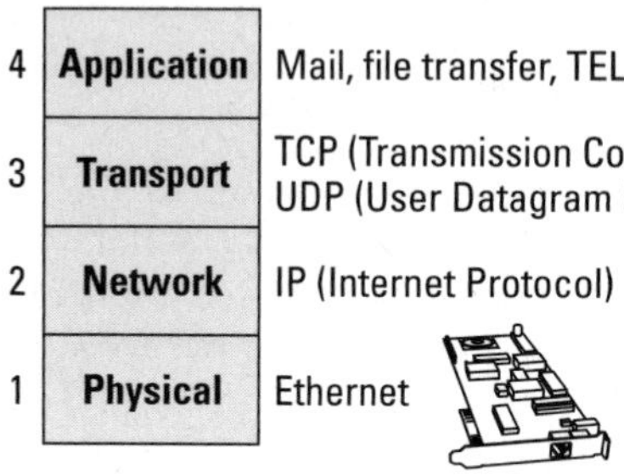

**Figure 2-1:**
You can
understand
TCP/IP
using the
four-layer
network
model.

| | | |
|---|---|---|
| 4 | **Application** | Mail, file transfer, TELNET |
| 3 | **Transport** | TCP (Transmission Control Protocol)<br>UDP (User Datagram Protocol) |
| 2 | **Network** | IP (Internet Protocol) |
| 1 | **Physical** | Ethernet |

Each layer has its own set of *protocols* — conventions — for handling and formatting the data. If you think of sending data as something akin to sending letters through the postal service, a typical protocol is a preferred sequence of actions for a task, such as addressing an envelope (first the name, then the street address, and then the city, state, and zip or other postal code).

These four layers, depending on what reference you look at, might have different names. For example, if you look at the old DOD model, the transport is called host-to-host, network is called internetwork or Internet, application is process/application, and physical is network access.

Here's what each of the four layers does, top to bottom:

+ **Application:** Runs the applications that users use, such as e-mail readers, file transfers, and Web browsers. Application-level protocols are Simple Mail Transfer Protocol (SMTP) and Post Office Protocol (POP) for e-mail, HyperText Transfer Protocol (HTTP) for the Web, and File Transfer Protocol (FTP) for file transfers. Application-level protocols also have a *port number* that you can think of as an identifier for a specific application. For example, port 80 is associated with HTTP or the Web server.

+ **Transport:** Sends data from one application to another. The two most important protocols in this layer are Transmission Control Protocol (TCP) and User Datagram Protocol (UDP). TCP guarantees delivery of data; UDP just sends the data without ensuring that it actually reaches the destination.

+ **Network:** This layer is responsible for getting data packets from one network to another. If the networks are far apart, the data packets are routed from one network to the next until they reach their destination. The primary protocol in this layer is the Internet Protocol (IP).

+ **Physical:** Refers to the physical networking hardware (such as an Ethernet card or token ring card) that carries the data packets in a network.

---

# TCP/IP and the Internet

TCP/IP has become the protocol of choice on the Internet — *the network of networks* that evolved from ARPANET. The U.S. Government's Advanced Research Projects Agency (ARPA) initiated research in the 1970s on a new way of sending information, using packets of data sent over a network. The result was ARPANET: a national network of linked computers. Subsequently, ARPA acquired a Defense prefix

and became DARPA. Under the auspices of DARPA, the TCP/IP protocols emerged as a popular collection of protocols for *internetworking* — communication among networks.

TCP/IP has flourished because the protocol is *open.* That means the technical descriptions of the protocol appear in public documents, so anyone can implement TCP/IP on specific hardware and software.

---

The beauty of the layered model is that each layer takes care of only its specific task, leaving the rest to the other layers. The layers can mix and match — you can have TCP/IP network over any type of physical network medium, from Ethernet to radio waves (in a wireless network). The software is modular as well because each layer can be implemented in different modules. For example, typically the transport and network layers already exist as part of the operating system, and any application can make use of these layers.

TCP/IP also made great inroads because stable, working software was available. Instead of a paper description of network architecture and protocols, the TCP/IP protocols started out as working software — and who can argue with what's already working? These days, as a result, TCP/IP rules the Internet.

## IP addresses

When you have many computers on a network, you need a way to identify each one uniquely. In TCP/IP networking, the address of a computer is the IP address. Because TCP/IP deals with internetworking, the address is based on the concepts of a network address and a host address. You may think of the idea of a network address and a host address as having to provide two addresses to identify a computer uniquely:

+ **Network address** indicates the network on which the computer is located.
+ **Host address** indicates a specific computer on that network.

The network and host addresses together constitute an *IP address,* and it's a 4-byte (32-bit) value. The convention is to write each byte as a decimal value and to put a dot (.) after each number. Thus, you see network addresses such as 132.250.112.52. This way of writing IP addresses is known as *dotted-decimal* or *dotted-quad* notation.

## Next-generation IP (IPv6)

When the 4-byte IP address was created, the number of available addresses seemed adequate. Now, however, the 4-byte addresses are running out. The Internet Engineering Task Force (IETF) recognized the potential for running out of IP addresses in 1991 and began work on the next-generation IP addressing scheme. They called it IPng (for Internet Protocol Next Generation) and intended for it to eventually replace the old 4-byte addressing scheme (called IPv4, for IP version 4).

Several alternative addressing schemes for IPng were proposed and debated. The final contender, with a 128-bit (16-byte) address, was dubbed IPv6 (for IP version 6). On September 18, 1995, the IETF declared the core set of IPv6 addressing protocols to be an IETF Proposed Standard. By now, there are many RFCs (Request for Comments) dealing with various aspects of IPv6, from IPv6 over PPP for the transmission of IPv6 packets over Ethernet.

IPv6 is designed to be an evolutionary step from IPv4. The proposed standard provides direct interoperability between hosts using the older IPv4 addresses and any new IPv6 hosts. The idea is that users can upgrade their systems to use IPv6 when they want and that network operators are free to upgrade their network hardware to use IPv6 without affecting current users of IPv4. Sample implementations of IPv6 are being developed for many operating systems, including Linux. For more information about IPv6 in Linux, consult the Linux IPv6 HOWTO at `www.tldp.org/HOWTO/Linux+IPv6-HOWTO`. For information about IPv6 in general, visit the IPv6 home page at `www.ipv6.org`.

The IPv6 128-bit addressing scheme allows for a total of $2^{128}$ or 340,282,366,920,938,463,463,374,607,431,768,211,456 theoretically assignable addresses. That should last us for a while!

In decimal notation, a byte (which has 8 bits) can have a value between 0 and 255. Thus, a valid IP address can use only the numbers between 0 and 255 in the dotted-decimal notation.

## *Internet services and port numbers*

The TCP/IP protocol suite has become the lingua franca of the Internet because many standard services are available on any system that supports TCP/IP. These services make the Internet tick by facilitating the transfer of mail, news, and Web pages. These services go by well-known names such as the following:

✦ **DHCP** (Dynamic Host Configuration Protocol) is for dynamically configuring TCP/IP network parameters on a computer. DHCP is primarily used to assign dynamic IP addresses and other networking information (such as name server, default gateway, and domain names) needed to configure TCP/IP networks. The DHCP server listens on port 67.

✦ **FTP** (File Transfer Protocol) is used to transfer files between computers on the Internet. FTP uses two ports — data is transferred on port 20, and control information is exchanged on port 21.

✦ **HTTP** (HyperText Transfer Protocol) is a protocol for sending documents from one system to another. HTTP is the underlying protocol of the Web. By default, the Web server and client communicate on port 80.

✦ **SMTP** (Simple Mail Transfer Protocol) is for exchanging e-mail messages between systems. SMTP uses port 25 for information exchange.

✦ **NNTP** (Network News Transfer Protocol) is for distribution of news articles in a store-and-forward fashion across the Internet. NNTP uses port 119.

✦ **SSH** (Secure Shell) is a protocol for secure remote login and other secure network services over an insecure network. SSH uses port 22.

✦ **TELNET** is used when a user on one system logs in to another system on the Internet. (The user must provide a valid user ID and password to log in to the remote system.) TELNET uses port 23 by default, but the TELNET client can connect to any port.

✦ **SNMP** (Simple Network Management Protocol) is for managing all types of network devices on the Internet. Like FTP, SNMP uses two ports: 161 and 162.

✦ **TFTP** (Trivial File Transfer Protocol) is for transferring files from one system to another. (It's typically used by X terminals and diskless workstations to download boot files from another host on the network.) TFTP data transfer takes place on port 69.

✦ **NFS** (Network File System) is for sharing files among computers. NFS uses Sun's Remote Procedure Call (RPC) facility, which exchanges information through port 111.

A well-known port is associated with each of these services. The TCP protocol uses each such port to locate a service on any system. (A *server process* — a special computer program running on a system — provides each service.)

# Setting Up an Ethernet LAN

Ethernet is a standard way to move packets of data between two or more computers connected to a single hub, router, or switch. (You can create larger networks by connecting multiple Ethernet segments with gateways.) To set up an Ethernet LAN, you need an Ethernet card for each PC. Linux supports a wide variety of Ethernet cards for the PC.

Ethernet is a good choice for the physical data-transport mechanism for the following reasons:

+ Ethernet is a proven technology that has been in use since the early 1980s.

+ Ethernet provides good data-transfer rates: typically 10 million bits per second (10 Mbps), although 100-Mbps Ethernet and Gigabit Ethernet (1,000 Mbps) are now common.

+ Ethernet hardware is often built into the PC or can be installed at a relatively low cost. (PC Ethernet cards cost about $10–20.)

+ With wireless Ethernet, you can easily connect laptop PCs to your Ethernet LAN without having to run wires all over the place. (Go to Chapter 3 of this minibook for more information on wireless Ethernet.)

## How Ethernet works

So what makes Ethernet tick? In essence, it's the same thing that makes any conversation work: listening and taking turns.

In an Ethernet network, all systems in a segment are connected to the same wire. A protocol is used for sending and receiving data because only one data packet can exist on the single wire at any time. An Ethernet LAN uses a data-transmission protocol known as *Carrier-Sense Multiple Access/Collision Detection* (CSMA/CD) to share the single transmission cable among all the computers. Ethernet cards in the computers follow the CSMA/CD protocol to transmit and receive Ethernet packets.

The idea behind the CSMA/CD protocol is similar to the way in which you have a conversation at a party. You listen for a pause (that's sensing the carrier) and talk when no one else is speaking. If you and another person begin talking at the same time, both of you realize the problem (that's collision detection) and pause for a moment; then one of you starts speaking again. As you know from experience, everything works out.

In an Ethernet LAN, each Ethernet card checks the cable for signals — that's the carrier-sense part. If the signal level is low, the Ethernet card sends its packets on the cable; the packet contains information about the sender and the intended recipient. All Ethernet cards on the LAN listen to the signal, and the recipient receives the packet. If two cards send out a packet simultaneously, the signal level in the cable rises above a threshold, and the cards know a collision has occurred. (Two packets have been sent out at the same time.) Both cards wait for a random amount of time before sending their packets again.

Ethernet was invented in the early 1970s at the Xerox Palo Alto Research Center (PARC) by Robert M. Metcalfe. In the 1980s, Ethernet was standardized by the cooperative effort of three companies: Digital Equipment Corporation (DEC), Intel, and Xerox. Using the first initials of the company names, that Ethernet standard became known as the DIX standard. Later, the DIX standard was included in the 802-series standards developed by the Institute of Electrical and Electronics Engineers (IEEE). The final Ethernet specification is formally known as IEEE 802.3 CSMA/CD, but people continue to call it *Ethernet*.

Ethernet sends data in *packets* (discrete chunks also known as *frames*). You don't have to hassle much with the innards of Ethernet packets, except to note the 6-byte source and destination addresses. Each Ethernet controller has a unique 6-byte (48-bit) address at the physical layer; every packet must have one.

## Ethernet cables

Any time you hear experts talking about Ethernet, you'll also hear some bewildering terms used for the cables that carry the data. Here's a quick rundown.

The original Ethernet standard used a thick coaxial cable, nearly half an inch in diameter. This wiring is called *thicknet, thickwire,* or just *thick Ethernet* although the IEEE 802.3 standard calls it *10Base5.* That designation means several things: The data-transmission rate is 10 megabits per second (10 Mbps); the transmission is *baseband* (which simply means that the cable's signal-carrying capacity is devoted to transmitting Ethernet packets only), and the total length of the cable can be no more than 500 meters. Thickwire was expensive, and the cable was rather unwieldy. Unless you're a technology history buff, you don't have to care one whit about 10Base5 cables.

Nowadays, several other forms of Ethernet cabling are more popular. An alternative to thick Ethernet cable is *thinwire,* or 10Base2, which uses a thin, flexible coaxial cable. A thinwire Ethernet segment can be, at most, 185 meters long. The other, more recent, alternative is Ethernet over unshielded twisted-pair cable (UTP), known as 10BaseT. More recent Ethernet cabling options that support higher transmission rates include 100BaseT4, 100BaseT2, and 100BaseTX for 100 Mbps Ethernet and 1000BaseT for Gigabit Ethernet. The Electronic Industries Association/Telecommunications Industries Association (EIA/TIA) defines the following five categories of shielded and unshielded twisted-pair cables:

✦ **Category 1 (Cat 1):** Traditional telephone cable.

✦ **Category 2 (Cat 2):** Cable certified for data transmissions up to 4 Mbps.

✦ **Category 3 (Cat 3):** Cable that can carry signals up to a frequency of 16 MHz. Cat 3 is the most common type of wiring in old corporate networks, and it normally contains four pairs of wire. Now considered obsolete.

✦ **Category 4 (Cat 4):** Cable that can carry signals up to a frequency of 20 MHz. Cat 4 wires aren't common. Now considered obsolete.

✦ **Category 5 (Cat 5):** Cable that can carry signals up to a frequency of 100 MHz. Cat 5 cables normally have four pairs of copper wire. Cat 5 UTP is the most popular cable used in new installations today. This category of cable is being superseded by Category 5e (enhanced Cat 5).

✦ **Category 5e (Cat 5e):** Similar to Cat 5 but with improved technical parameters, such as near-end cross talk and attenuation. Cat 5e cables support 10BaseT, 100BaseT4, 100BaseT2, and 100BaseTX and 1000BaseT Ethernet. Nowadays, Cat 5e is the minimum acceptable wiring.

✦ **Category 6 (Cat 6):** Similar to Cat 5e but capable of carrying signals up to a frequency of 250 MHz. Cat 6 cables can support all existing Ethernet standards and also support Gigabit Ethernet standard 1000BaseTX, which uses two pairs of wires in each direction as opposed to all four pairs for 1000BaseT Ethernet over Cat 5e cables.

To set up a 10BaseT or 100BaseT Ethernet network, you need an Ethernet hub — a hardware box with RJ-45 jacks. (This type of jack looks like a big telephone jack.) You build the network by running twisted-pair wires (usually Category 5 cables) from each PC's Ethernet card to this hub. You can get a 4-port 10BaseT/100BaseT hub for about $40. Figure 2-2 shows a typical small 10BaseT/100BaseT Ethernet LAN that you may set up at a small office or your home.

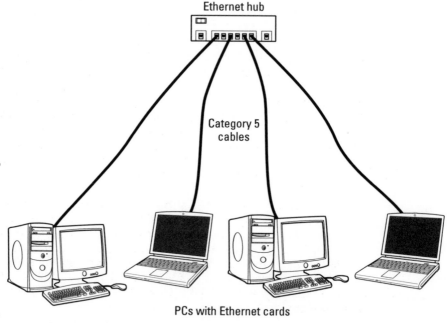

Ethernet hub

Category 5 cables

**Figure 2-2:**
You can use an Ethernet hub to set up a 10BaseT or 100BaseT Ethernet LAN.

PCs with Ethernet cards

When you install any of the Linux distributions from this book's companion DVD-ROM on a PC connected with an Ethernet card, the Linux kernel automatically detects the Ethernet card and installs the appropriate drivers. The installer also lets you set up TCP/IP networking.

The Linux kernel loads the driver for the Ethernet card every time it boots. To verify that the Ethernet driver is loaded, type the following command in a terminal window:

```
dmesg | grep eth0
```

On one of my Linux PCs, I get the following output when I type that command:

```
eth0: RealTek RTL8139 at 0xf0e20000, 00:0c:76:f4:38:b3, IRQ 161
eth0: Identified 8139 chip type 'RTL-8101'
eth0: link up, 100Mbps, full-duplex, lpa 0x45E1
eth0: no IPv6 routers present
```

You should see something similar, showing the name of your Ethernet card and other related information.

# Configuring TCP/IP Networking

When you set up TCP/IP networking during Linux installation, the installation program prepares all appropriate configuration files using the information you provide. This means that you typically never have to manually configure the network. However, most Linux distributions come with GUI tools to configure the network devices, just in case something needs changing. For all distributions, the steps are similar.

In Ubuntu, for example, you can use the graphical network configuration tool. To start the GUI network configuration tool, choose System⇨Preferences⇨ Network Connections. The network configuration tool displays a tabbed dialog box, as shown in Figure 2-3. You can then configure your network through the tabs that appear along the top of the dialog box. Clicking the Add button displays a dialog box similar to the one shown in Figure 2-4.

In most cases, you can set the network card so that it can automatically obtain an IP address (which is the case when the Ethernet card is connected to DSL or cable modem) by using DHCP. If your network doesn't have a DHCP server (which is typically built into routers), you have to specify an IP address for the network card. If you are running a private network, you may use IP addresses in the 192.168.0.0 to 192.168.255.255 range. (Other ranges of addresses are reserved for private networks, but this range suffices for most needs.)

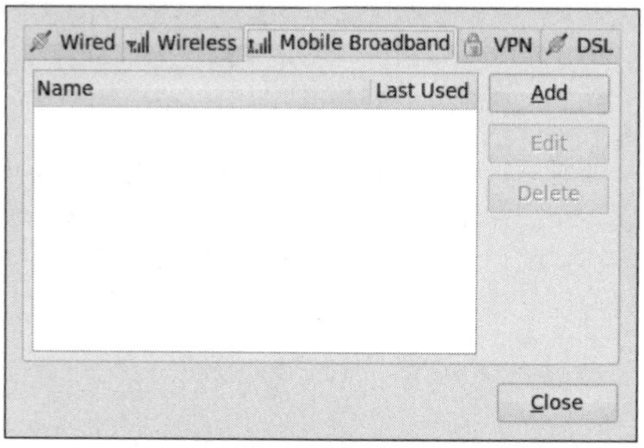

**Figure 2-3:**
Move
through
the tabbed
dialog boxes
to configure
the
connection.

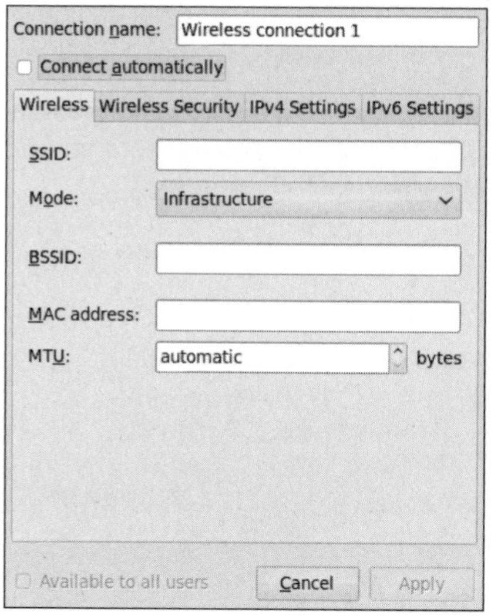

Wired | Wireless | Mobile Broadband | VPN | DSL

| Name | Last Used | Add |
| --- | --- | --- |
| | | Edit |
| | | Delete |

Close

Connection name:  Wireless connection 1

☐ Connect automatically

Wireless | Wireless Security | IPv4 Settings | IPv6 Settings

SSID:

Mode:  Infrastructure

BSSID:

MAC address:

MTU:  automatic  bytes

**Figure 2-4:**
The Add
option
allows you
add new
connections.

☐ Available to all users   Cancel   Apply

# Connecting Your LAN to the Internet

If you have a LAN with several PCs, you can connect the entire LAN to the Internet by using DSL or a cable modem. Basically, you can share the high-speed DSL or cable modem connection with all the PCs in the LAN.

Chapter 1 of this minibook explains how to set up a DSL or cable modem. In this section, I briefly explain how to connect a LAN to the Internet so that all the PCs can access the Internet.

The most convenient way to connect a LAN to the Internet via DSL or a cable modem is to buy a hardware device called *DSL/cable modem NAT router* with a 4- or 8-port Ethernet hub. NAT stands for Network Address Translation, and the NAT router can translate many private IP addresses into a single, externally known IP address. The Ethernet hub part appears to you as a number of RJ-45 Ethernet ports where you can connect the PCs to set up a LAN. In other words, you need only one extra box besides the DSL or cable modem.

Figure 2-5 shows how you might connect your LAN to the Internet through a NAT router with a built-in Ethernet hub. You need a DSL or cable modem hookup for this scenario to work, and you have to sign up with a DSL provider (for DSL service) or with a cable provider for cable Internet service.

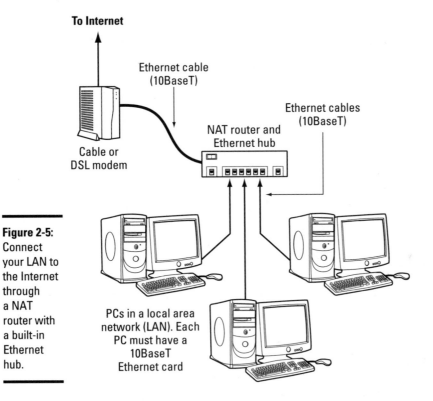

**To Internet**

Ethernet cable
(10BaseT)

Ethernet cables
(10BaseT)

NAT router and
Ethernet hub

Cable or
DSL modem

**Figure 2-5:**
Connect your LAN to the Internet through a NAT router with a built-in Ethernet hub.

PCs in a local area network (LAN). Each PC must have a 10BaseT Ethernet card

When you connect a LAN to the Internet, the NAT router acts as a gateway for your LAN. The NAT router also dynamically provides IP addresses to the PCs in your LAN. Therefore, on each PC, you have to set up the networking options to obtain the IP address dynamically.

If you are using DSL and incurring speeds slower than you should (2 Mbps when it should be 5 Mbps, for example), try a different phone cord. Make sure that the phone cord that runs from the modem to the wall jack is no longer than 10 feet and does not go through a filter, surge protector, or splitter (which can attenuate the signal). All other phone devices (fax machines, for example) should go through a filter or surge protector.

Your LAN can mix and match all kinds of computers: Some may be running Linux, and some may be running Microsoft Windows or any other operating system that supports TCP/IP. When configuring the network settings, remember to select the option that enables Linux to automatically obtain IP address settings and DNS information with DHCP.

# Chapter 3: Going Wireless

## In This Chapter

✔ **Understanding the wireless Ethernet network**

✔ **Setting up your wireless hardware**

✔ **Finding out how to configure a wireless access point**

✔ **Configuring a wireless network**

*I*f you have laptop computers on your LAN — or if you don't want to run a rat's nest of wires to connect a PC to the LAN — you have the option of using a wireless Ethernet network. In a typical scenario, you have a cable modem or DSL connection to the Internet, and you want to connect one or more laptops with wireless network cards to access the Internet through the cable or DSL modem. This chapter shows you how to set up wireless networking for connecting to an Ethernet LAN and accessing the Internet.

## Understanding Wireless Ethernet Networks

You've probably heard about Wi-Fi. Wi-Fi stands for *Wireless Fidelity* — a short-range wireless network similar to wired Ethernet networks. A number of standards from an organization known as *IEEE* (the Institute of Electrical and Electronics Engineers) define the technical details of how Wi-Fi networks work. Manufacturers use these standards to build the components that you can buy to set up a wireless network, also known as WLAN for short.

Until mid-2003, two popular IEEE standards — 802.11a and 802.11b — were for wireless Ethernet networks. These two standards were finalized in 1999. A third standard — 802.11g — was finalized by the IEEE in the summer of 2003, and the latest amendment, 802.11n, was published in October 2009. All these standards specify how the wireless Ethernet network works at the physical layer. You don't have to fret all the details of all those standards to set up a wireless network, but knowing some pertinent details is good so that you can buy the right kind of equipment for your wireless network.

The three wireless Ethernet standards you'll commonly encounter today have the following key characteristics:

✦ **802.11b:** Operates in the 2.4 GHz radio band (2.4 GHz to 2.4835 GHz) in up to three nonoverlapping frequency bands or channels. Supports a maximum bit rate of 11 Mbps per channel. One disadvantage of 802.11b is that the 2.4 GHz frequency band is crowded — many devices (such as microwave ovens, cordless phones, medical and scientific equipment, as well as Bluetooth devices), all work within the 2.4 GHz frequency band. Nevertheless, 802.11b is popular in corporate and home networks.

✦ **802.11a:** Operates in the 5 GHz radio band (5.725 GHz to 5.850 GHz) in up to eight nonoverlapping channels. Supports a maximum bit rate of 54 Mbps per channel. The 5 GHz band isn't as crowded as the 2.4 GHz band, but the 5 GHz band isn't approved for use in Europe. Products conforming to 802.11a standard are on the market, and some wireless access points are designed to handle both 802.11a and 802.11b connections.

✦ **802.11g:** Supports up to 54 Mbps data rate in the 2.4 GHz band (the same band that 802.11b uses). 802.11g achieves the higher bit rate by using a technology called *OFDM* (orthogonal frequency-division multiplexing), which is also used by 802.11a. Equipment that complies with 802.11g is on the market. 802.11g has generated excitement by working in the same band as 802.11b but promising much higher data rates and by being backward compatible with 802.11b devices. Vendors currently offer access points that can support both the 802.11b and 802.11g connection standards.

In all cases, the maximum data throughput that a user sees is much less than the channel's total capacity because all users of that radio channel share this capacity. Also, the data transfer rate decreases as the distance between the user's PC and the wireless access point increases.

The 802.11n standard is garnering increased usage and supports data rates with five times the existing throughput and double the range of previous standards.

An 802.11g access point can also communicate with older (and slower) 802.11b devices. You can also consider a MIMO (multiple input multiple output) access point, which supports multiple 802.11 standards and implements techniques for getting higher throughputs and better range.

To find out more about wireless Ethernet, visit www.wi-fi.org, the home page of the Wi-Fi Alliance, which is the nonprofit international association formed in 1999 to certify interoperability of wireless LAN products based on IEEE 802.11 standards.

## Understanding infrastructure and ad hoc modes

The 802.11 standard defines two modes of operation for wireless Ethernet networks: ad hoc and infrastructure. *Ad hoc mode* is simply two or more wireless Ethernet cards communicating with each other without an access point.

*Infrastructure mode* refers to the approach in which all the wireless Ethernet cards communicate with each other and with the wired LAN through an access point. For the discussions in this chapter, I assume that you set your wireless Ethernet card to infrastructure mode. In the configuration files, this mode is referred to as *managed mode*.

## Understanding Wired Equivalent Privacy (WEP)

The 802.11 standard includes Wired Equivalent Privacy (WEP) for protecting wireless communications from eavesdropping. WEP relies on a 40-bit or 104-bit secret key that's shared between a mobile station (such as a laptop with a wireless Ethernet card) and an access point (also called a *base station*). The secret key is used to encrypt data packets before they are transmitted, and an integrity check is performed to ensure that packets aren't modified in transit. The 802.11 standard doesn't explain how the shared key is established. In practice, most wireless LANs use a single key that's shared between all mobile stations and access points. Such an approach, however, doesn't scale very well to an environment such as a college campus because the keys are shared with all users — and you know how it is if you share a *secret* with hundreds of people. That's why WEP typically isn't used on large wireless networks, such as the ones at universities. In such wireless networks, you have to use other security approaches, such as SSH (Secure Shell), to log in to remote systems. WEP, however, is good to use on a home wireless network.

WEP has its weaknesses, but it's better than nothing. You can use it in smaller wireless LANs where sharing the same key among all wireless stations isn't an onerous task.

In 2003, the Wi-Fi Alliance published a specification called *Wi-Fi Protected Access* (WPA) that replaced the existing WEP standard and improved security by making some changes. For example, unlike WEP, which uses fixed keys, the WPA standard uses Temporal Key Integrity Protocol (TKIP), which generates new keys for every 10K of data transmitted over the network. This makes WPA more difficult to break. In 2004, the Wi-Fi Alliance introduced a follow-on to WPA called *Wi-Fi Protected Access 2* (WPA2 — the second generation of WPA security). WPA2 is based on the final IEEE 802.11i standard, which uses public key encryption with digital certificates and an authentication, authorization, and accounting RADIUS (Remote Authentication Dial-In User Service) server to provide better security for wireless Ethernet networks. WPA2 uses the Advanced Encryption Standard (AES) for data encryption.

**Book III
Chapter 3**

**Going Wireless**

# Is the WEP stream cipher good enough?

WEP uses the RC4 encryption algorithm, which is known as a *stream cipher*. Such an algorithm works by taking a short secret key and generating an infinite stream of pseudorandom bits. Before sending the data, the sending station performs an exclusive-OR operation between the pseudorandom bits and the bits representing the data packet, which results in a *1* when two bits are different and *0* if they are the same. The receiver has a copy of the same secret key and generates an identical stream of pseudorandom bits — and performs an identical exclusive-OR operation between this pseudorandom stream and the received bits. Doing so regenerates the original, unencrypted data packet.

This stream cipher method has a few problems. If a bit is flipped (from a *0* to *1* or vice versa) in the encrypted data stream, the corresponding bit is flipped in the decrypted output, which can help an attacker derive the encryption key. Also, an eavesdropper who intercepts two encoded messages that were encoded with the same stream can generate the exclusive-OR of the original messages. That knowledge is enough to mount attacks that can eventually break the encryption.

To counter these weaknesses, WEP uses some defenses:

- **Integrity check (IC) field:** To make sure that data packets aren't modified in transit, WEP uses an integrity check field in each packet.

- **Initialization vector (IV):** To avoid encrypting two messages with the same key stream, WEP uses a 24-bit IV that augments the shared secret key to produce a different RC4 key for each packet. The IV itself is also included in the packet.

Experts say that both these defenses are poorly implemented, making WEP ineffective. IC and IV have two main problems:

- The integrity check field is implemented by using a checksum algorithm called 32-bit cyclic redundancy code (CRC-32); that checksum is then included as part of the data packet. Unfortunately, an attacker can flip arbitrary bits in an encrypted message and correctly adjust the checksum so that the resulting message appears valid.

- The 24-bit IV is sent in the clear (unencrypted). There are only $2^{24}$ possible initialization vectors (no big challenge for a fast machine), and they have to be reused after running through them all. In other words, the IV is repeated after sending $2^{24}$, or 16,777,216, packets. The number may sound like a lot, but consider the case of a busy access point that sends 1,500-byte packets at a rate of 11 Mbps. Each packet has 12,000 bits (8 x 1,500). That means each second the access point sends 916 packets (11,000,000/12,000). At that rate, the access point sends 16,777,216 packets in 5 hours (16,777,216/916 = 18,315 seconds = 5 hours). That means the IV is reused after 5 hours or less because many messages are smaller than 1,500 bytes. Thus, an attacker has ample opportunities to collect two messages encrypted with the same key stream — and perform *statistical attacks* (which amount to trying the possible *combinations* really fast) to decrypt the message.

# Setting Up Wireless Hardware

To set up the wireless connection, you need a wireless access point and a wireless network card in each PC. You can also set up an ad hoc wireless network among two or more PCs with wireless network cards, but that is a standalone wireless LAN among those PCs only. In this section, I focus on the scenario in which you want to set up a wireless connection to an established LAN that has a wired Internet connection through a cable modem or DSL.

In addition to the wireless access point, you also need a cable modem or DSL connection to the Internet, along with a NAT router and hub, as described in the Chapters 1 and 2 of this minibook. Figure 3-1 shows a typical setup for wireless Internet access through an existing cable modem or DSL connection.

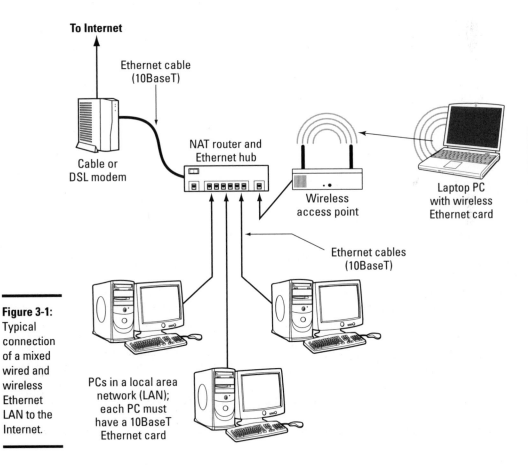

**To Internet**

Ethernet cable
(10BaseT)

Cable or
DSL modem

NAT router and
Ethernet hub

Wireless
access point

Laptop PC
with wireless
Ethernet card

Ethernet cables
(10BaseT)

**Figure 3-1:**
Typical
connection
of a mixed
wired and
wireless
Ethernet
LAN to the
Internet.

PCs in a local area
network (LAN);
each PC must
have a 10BaseT
Ethernet card

As Figure 3-1 shows, the LAN has both wired and wireless PCs. In this example, either a cable or DSL modem connects the LAN to the Internet through a NAT router and hub. Laptops with wireless network cards connect to the LAN through a wireless access point attached to one of the RJ-45 ports on the hub. To connect desktop PCs to this wireless network, you can use a USB wireless network card (which connects to a USB port).

If you haven't yet purchased a NAT router and hub for your cable or DSL connection, consider buying a router and hub that has a built-in wireless access point.

## Configuring the Wireless Access Point

Configuring the wireless access point involves the following tasks:

✦ **Setting a name for the wireless network.** (The technical term for this name is the ESSID.)

✦ **Setting the frequency or channel on which the wireless access point communicates with the wireless network cards.** The access point and the cards must use the same channel.

✦ **Deciding whether to use encryption.**

✦ **If encryption is to be used, setting the number of bits in the encryption key and the value of the encryption key.** For the encryption key, 24 bits are internal to the access point; you specify only the remaining bits. Thus, for 64-bit encryption, you have to specify a 40-bit key, which comes to 10 hexadecimal digits. (A *hexadecimal digit* is an integer from 0–9 or a letter from A–F.) For a 128-bit encryption key, you specify 104 bits, or 26 hexadecimal digits.

✦ **Setting the access method that wireless network cards must use when connecting to the access point.** You can opt for either open access or shared key. The open-access method is typical (even when using encryption).

✦ **Setting the wireless access point to operate in infrastructure (managed) mode** You use this mode to connect wireless network cards to an existing Ethernet LAN.

The exact method of configuring a wireless access point depends on the device's make and model; the vendor provides instructions to configure the wireless access point. You typically work through a graphical client application on a Windows PC to do the configuration. If you enable encryption, make note of the encryption key; you have to specify that same key for each wireless network card on your laptops or desktops.

# Configuring Wireless Networking

On your Linux laptop, the PCMCIA or PC Card manager recognizes the wireless network card and loads the appropriate driver for the card. Linux treats the wireless network card like another Ethernet device and assigns it a device name such as `eth0` or `eth1`. If you already have an Ethernet card in the laptop, that card gets the `eth0` device name and the wireless PC Card becomes the `eth1` device.

You do have to configure certain parameters to enable the wireless network card to communicate with the wireless access point. For example, you have to specify the wireless network name assigned to the access point, and the encryption settings must match those on the access point. You can usually configure everything using a graphical network configuration tool that's available for your Linux distribution — just select the Wireless Network option and fill in the requested information.

For example, in Fedora, choose System➪Preferences➪Network Connections from the GNOME desktop. Then select the Wireless tab and click Add to add a new wireless device (see Figure 3-2). You can then select the wireless device and get to a window where you can configure the wireless connection. In particular, set the Mode to Infrastructure, specify the name of the wireless network (the one you want to connect to), and set the encryption key, if any. You can set the option for getting the IP address to DHCP (a protocol for obtaining network configuration parameters, including IP addresses from a server on the network). When you're finished and return to the Network Configuration tool's main window, select the new wireless device and click the Activate button. If all goes well, the wireless network will be up and running after a few moments.

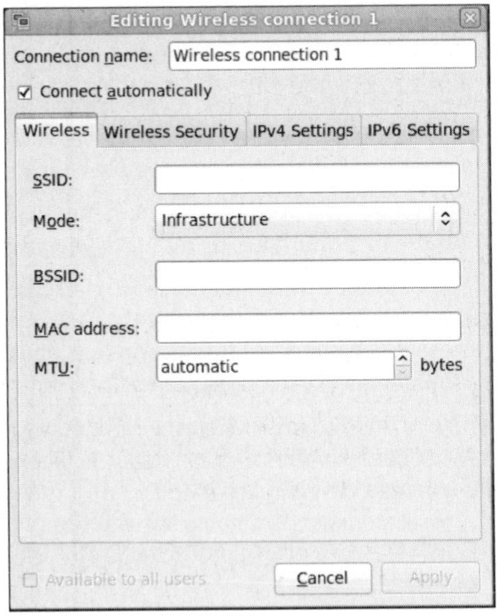

**Book III
Chapter 3**

**Going Wireless**

**Figure 3-2:**
Configure
a new
wireless
connection
in Fedora.

Editing Wireless connection 1

Connection name: Wireless connection 1

☑ Connect automatically

| Wireless | Wireless Security | IPv4 Settings | IPv6 Settings |

SSID:

Mode: Infrastructure

BSSID:

MAC address:

MTU: automatic    bytes

☐ Available to all users    Cancel    Apply

In Fedora, the Network Configuration tool saves your wireless network settings in a text file. The name of the text file depends on the wireless network device name. If the wireless network device name is eth0, the configuration is stored in the text file /etc/sysconfig/network-scripts/ifcfg-eth0. If the wireless device name is eth1, the file is /etc/sysconfig/network-scripts/ifcfg-eth1. This configuration file contains various settings for the wireless network card. Table 3-1 explains the meaning of the settings. Here is a slightly edited version of the /etc/sysconfig/network-scripts/ifcfg-eth1 file from my laptop PC running Fedora:

```
IPV6INIT=no
USERCTL=no
PEERDNS=yes
TYPE=Wireless
DEVICE=eth1
HWADDR=00:02:2d:8c:f9:c4
BOOTPROTO=dhcp
ONBOOT=no
DHCP_HOSTNAME=
NAME=
ESSID='HOME'
CHANNEL=6
MODE=Managed
RATE=auto
```

| Table 3-1 | Settings in Configuration File for a Wireless Ethernet Network Interface in Fedora |
|---|---|
| *This Parameter* | *Means the Following* |
| BOOTPROTO | The name of the protocol to use to get the IP address for the interface. The protocol used is either dhcp or bootp for an Ethernet interface. |
| CHANNEL | Channel number (between 1 and 14 in United States and Canada). Must be the same as that set for the wireless access point. In managed mode, you don't need to specify the channel. |
| DEVICE | The device name for the wireless Ethernet network interface (eth0 for the first interface, eth1 for the second, and so on). |
| ESSID | Extended Service Set (ESS) Identifier (ID), also known as the wireless network name. It is case-sensitive and must be the same as the name specified for the wireless access point. Provide the name within single quotes (for example, 'HOME'). |
| HWADDR | The hardware address (also called the MAC address) of the wireless network card (six pairs of colon-separated hexadecimal numbers; for example, 00:02:2d:8c:f9:c4). The wireless card's device driver automatically detects this address. |

| This Parameter | Means the Following |
|---|---|
| IPV6INIT | When set to `yes`, this parameter initializes IPv6 configuration for the wireless interface. Set it to `no` if you're not using IPv6. |
| MODE | The mode of operation of the wireless network card. Set to `Managed` for a typical network that connects through a wireless access point. |
| NAME | A nickname for your wireless network. If you don't specify it, the host name is used as the nickname. |
| ONBOOT | Set to `yes` to activate the wireless interface at boot time; otherwise, set to `no`. |
| PEERDNS | Set to `yes` to enable the interface to modify your system's `/etc/resolv.conf` file to use the DNS servers obtained from the DHCP server (the same server that provides the IP address for the interface). If you set this parameter to `no`, the `/etc/resolv.conf` file is left unchanged. |
| RATE | Bit rate for the wireless connection (set to one of the following options: `1M`, `2M`, `5.5M`, `11M`, or `auto`). The *M* means Mbps, or a million bits per second. Set to `auto` to use the maximum possible transmission rate. |
| TYPE | Set to `Wireless` for wireless network interface. |
| USERCTL | When set to `yes`, a user who isn't logged in as `root` can control the device. Set it to `no` so that only `root` can control the device. |

In Fedora, the encryption key is stored separately. For a wireless Ethernet card whose device name is `eth1`, the encryption key is stored in the `/etc/sysconfig/network-scripts/keys-eth1` file. For example, here is what this file contains for my example:

```
KEY=1fdf3fdefe
```

The key has 10 hexadecimal digits for a 40-bit key (for example, `1fdf-3fde-fe`) or 26 hexadecimal digits for a 104-bit key. The keys are 64-bit and 128-bit, respectively, but the encryption algorithm automatically generates 24 bits of the key, so you need to specify only the remaining bits. The longer the key, the more secure the encryption.

If you ever manually edit the parameters in the wireless Ethernet configuration file in Fedora, type the following command to reactivate the wireless network interface after editing the configuration file:

```
/etc/init.d/network restart
```

In SUSE Linux, use YaST to configure the wireless network. SUSE stores the wireless configuration parameters in a file whose name begins with `ifcfg-wlan`, followed by a number such as 0 or 1, depending on the sequence number of the wireless network interface. The configuration file is stored in the `/etc/sysconfig/network` directory. Here's a typical list of wireless configuration parameters from a configuration file in SUSE Linux:

```
WIRELESS_MODE='Managed'
WIRELESS_ESSID='HOME'
WIRELESS_NICK=''
WIRELESS_RATE='auto'
WIRELESS_AUTH_MODE='open'
WIRELESS_KEY_0='0123-4567-89'
```

To check the status of the wireless network interface, type the following command:

```
iwconfig
```

Here's a typical output from a Fedora laptop with a wireless Ethernet PC card. (The output should be similar in other Linux distributions.)

```
lo no wireless extensions.
eth0 no wireless extensions.
sit0 no wireless extensions.
eth1 IEEE 802.11b ESSID:"HOME" Nickname:"localhost.localdomain"
Mode:Managed Frequency:2.437 GHz Access Point: 00:30:AB:06:E2:5D
Bit Rate=11 Mb/s Sensitivity:1/3
Retry limit:4 RTS thr:off Fragment thr:off
Encryption key:1FDF-3FDE-FE Security mode:open
Power Management:off
Link Quality=51/92 Signal level=-40 dBm Noise level=-91 dBm
Rx invalid nwid:0 Rx invalid crypt:0 Rx invalid frag:27
Tx excessive retries:0 Invalid misc:0 Missed beacon:0
```

Here, the `eth1` interface refers to the wireless network card. I edited the encryption key and some other parameters to hide those details, but the sample output shows you what you'd typically see when the wireless link is working.

# Chapter 4: Managing the Network

## In This Chapter

✔ Finding out about the TCP/IP configuration files

✔ Checking TCP/IP networks

✔ Configuring networks at boot time

*L*ike almost everything else in Linux, TCP/IP setup is a matter of preparing numerous configuration files (text files you can edit with any text editor). Most of these configuration files are in the /etc directory. The Linux installer tries to be helpful by hiding the details of the TCP/IP configuration files. Nevertheless, if you know the names of the files and their purposes, editing the files manually, if necessary, is easier.

## Discovering the TCP/IP Configuration Files

You can configure TCP/IP networking when you install Linux. However, if you want to effectively manage the network, you need to become familiar with the TCP/IP configuration files so that you can edit the files, if necessary. (For example, if you want to check whether the name servers are specified correctly, you have to know about the /etc/resolv.conf file, which stores the IP addresses of name servers.)

Table 4-1 summarizes the basic TCP/IP configuration files. I describe these configuration files in the next few sections.

| Table 4-1 | Basic TCP/IP Network Configuration Files |
|---|---|
| *This File* | *Contains the Following* |
| /etc/hosts | IP addresses and host names for your local network as well as any other systems that you access often |
| /etc/networks | Names and IP addresses of networks |
| /etc/host.conf | Instructions on how to translate host names into IP addresses |
| /etc/resolv.conf | IP addresses of name servers |
| /etc/hosts.allow | Instructions on which systems can access Internet services on your system |
| /etc/hosts.deny | Instructions on which systems must be denied access to Internet services on your system |
| /etc/nsswitch.conf | Instructions on how to translate host names into IP addresses |

A pound sign (#) in a text file indicates a comment.

## /etc/hosts

The /etc/hosts text file contains a list of IP addresses and host names for your local network. In the absence of a name server, any network program on your system consults this file to determine the IP address that corresponds to a host name. Think of /etc/hosts as the local phone directory where you can look up the IP address (instead of a phone number) for a local host.

Here is the /etc/hosts file from a system, showing the IP addresses and names of other hosts on a typical LAN:

```
127.0.0.1 localhost localhost.localdomain
# Other hosts on the LAN
192.168.0.100 lnbp933
192.168.0.50 lnbp600
192.168.0.200 lnbp200
192.168.0.233 lnbp233
192.168.0.40 lnbp400
```

As the example shows, each line in the file starts with an IP address followed by the host name for that IP address. (You can have more than one host name for any given IP address.) In some distributions, such as openSUSE 10.3, the /etc/hosts file has the following: IP-Address, Fully-Qualified-Hostname, Short-Hostname. In all cases, anything after the host name (such as the Short-Hostname) is taken as an alias.

## /etc/networks

`/etc/networks` is another text file that contains the names and IP addresses of networks. These network names are commonly used in the routing command (`/sbin/route`) to specify a network by name instead of by its IP address.

Don't be alarmed if your Linux PC doesn't have the `/etc/networks` file. Your TCP/IP network works fine without this file. In fact, the Linux installer doesn't create a `/etc/networks` file.

## /etc/host.conf

Linux uses a special *library* (that is, a collection of computer code) called the *resolver* to obtain the IP address that corresponds to a host name. The `/etc/host.conf` file specifies how names are *resolved* (that is, how the name gets converted to a numeric IP address). A typical `/etc/host.conf` file might contain the following lines:

```
order hosts, bind
multi on
```

The entries in the `/etc/host.conf` file tell the resolver what services to use (and in which order) to resolve names.

The `order` option indicates the order of services (in recent distributions, the `nsswitch.conf` file, discussed in a later section, performs this function). The sample entry tells the resolver to first consult the `/etc/hosts` file and then check the name server to resolve a name.

Use the `multi` option to indicate whether a host in the `/etc/hosts` file can have multiple IP addresses. Hosts that have more than one IP address are called *multihomed* because the presence of multiple IP addresses implies that the host has several network interfaces. (In effect, the host *lives* in several networks simultaneously.)

## /etc/resolv.conf

The `/etc/resolv.conf` file is another text file used by the resolver — the library that determines the IP address for a host name. Here is a sample `/etc/resolv.conf` file:

```
nameserver 192.168.0.1 # dhcp: eth0
search nrockv01.md.comcast.net
```

The `nameserver` line provides the IP addresses of name servers for your domain. If you have multiple name servers, list them on separate lines. They're queried in the order in which they appear in the file.

**Book III
Chapter 4**

Managing the
Network

The search line tells the resolver how to search for a host name. For example, when trying to locate a host name myhost, the search directive in the example causes the resolver to try myhost.nrockv01.md.comcast.net first, then myhost.md.comcast.net, and finally myhost.comcast.net.

If you don't have a name server for your network, you can safely ignore this file. TCP/IP still works, even though you may not be able to refer to hosts by name (other than those listed in the /etc/hosts file).

## /etc/hosts.allow

The /etc/hosts.allow file specifies which hosts are allowed to use the Internet services (such as TELNET and FTP) running on your system. This file is consulted before certain Internet services start. The services start only if the entries in the hosts.allow file imply that the requesting host is allowed to use the services.

The entries in /etc/hosts.allow are in the form of a *server:IP address* format, where *server* refers to the name of the program providing a specific Internet service and *IP address* identifies the host allowed to use that service. For example, if you want all hosts in your local network (which has the network address 192.168.0.0) to access the TELNET service (provided by the in.telnetd program), add the following line in the /etc/hosts.allow file (the last octet is left off to signify all possibilities within that range):

```
in.telnetd:192.168.0.
```

If you want to let all local hosts have access to all Internet services, you can use the ALL keyword and rewrite the line as follows:

```
ALL:192.168.0.
```

Finally, to open all Internet services to all hosts, you can replace the IP address with ALL, as follows:

```
ALL:ALL
```

You can also use host names in place of IP addresses.

To find out the detailed syntax of the entries in the /etc/hosts.allow file, type **man hosts.allow** at the shell prompt in a terminal window.

## /etc/hosts.deny

The /etc/hosts.deny file is just the opposite of /etc/hosts.allow. Whereas hosts.allow specifies which hosts may access Internet services (such as TELNET and TFTP) on your system, the hosts.deny file identifies the hosts that must be denied services. The /etc/hosts.deny file is consulted if no rules are in the /etc/hosts.allow file that apply to the requesting host. Service is denied if the hosts.deny file has a rule that applies to the host.

The entries in /etc/hosts.deny file have the same format as those in the /etc/hosts.allow file; they're in the form of a *server: IP address* format, where *server* refers to the name of the program providing a specific Internet service and *IP address* identifies the host that must not be allowed to use that service.

If you already set up entries in the /etc/hosts.allow file to allow access to specific hosts, you can place the following line in /etc/hosts.deny to deny all other hosts access to any service on your system:

```
ALL:ALL
```

To find out the detailed syntax of the entries in the /etc/hosts.deny file, type **man hosts.deny** at the shell prompt in a terminal window.

## /etc/nsswitch.conf

The /etc/nsswitch.conf file, known as the *name service switch* (NSS) file, specifies how services such as the resolver library, NIS, NIS+, and local configuration files (such as /etc/hosts and /etc/shadow) interact.

NIS and NIS+ are *network information systems* — another type of name-lookup service. Newer versions of the Linux kernel use the /etc/nsswitch.conf file to determine what takes precedence: a local configuration file, a service such as DNS (Domain Name System), or NIS.

As an example, the following hosts entry in the /etc/nsswitch.conf file says that the resolver library first tries the /etc/hosts file, then tries NIS+, and finally tries DNS:

```
hosts: files nisplus dns
```

You can find out more about the /etc/nsswitch.conf file by typing **man nsswitch.conf** in a terminal window.

# Checking Out TCP/IP Networks

After you configure Ethernet and TCP/IP (whether during Linux installation or by running a network configuration tool or command later), you can use various networking applications without much problem. On the off chance that you do run into trouble, Linux includes several tools to help you monitor and diagnose problems.

## Checking the network interfaces

Use the `/sbin/ifconfig` command to view the currently configured network interfaces. The `ifconfig` command is used to configure a network interface (that is, to associate an IP address with a network device). If you run `ifconfig` without any command-line arguments, the command displays information about current network interfaces. The following is a typical output when you type **/sbin/ifconfig**:

```
eth0 Link encap:Ethernet HWaddr 00:08:74:E5:C1:60
inet addr:192.168.0.7 Bcast:192.168.0.255 Mask:255.255.255.0
inet6 addr: fe80::208:74ff:fee5:c160/64 Scope:Link
UP BROADCAST RUNNING MULTICAST MTU:1500 Metric:1
RX packets:612851 errors:0 dropped:0 overruns:0 frame:0
TX packets:574187 errors:0 dropped:0 overruns:0 carrier:0
collisions:0 txqueuelen:1000
RX bytes:99834031 (95.2 MiB) TX bytes:76034821 (72.5 MiB)
Interrupt:10 Base address:0x3000
eth1 Link encap:Ethernet HWaddr 00:02:2D:8C:F8:C5
inet addr:192.168.0.9 Bcast:192.168.0.255 Mask:255.255.255.0
inet6 addr: fe80::202:2dff:fe8c:f8c5/64 Scope:Link
UP BROADCAST RUNNING MULTICAST MTU:1500 Metric:1
RX packets:3833 errors:0 dropped:0 overruns:0 frame:0
TX packets:1242 errors:0 dropped:0 overruns:0 carrier:0
collisions:0 txqueuelen:1000
RX bytes:560194 (547.0 KiB) TX bytes:250287 (244.4 KiB)
Interrupt:3 Base address:0x100
lo Link encap:Local Loopback
inet addr:127.0.0.1 Mask:255.0.0.0
inet6 addr: ::1/128 Scope:Host
UP LOOPBACK RUNNING MTU:16436 Metric:1
RX packets:2456 errors:0 dropped:0 overruns:0 frame:0
TX packets:2456 errors:0 dropped:0 overruns:0 carrier:0
collisions:0 txqueuelen:0
RX bytes:2891581 (2.7 MiB) TX bytes:2891581 (2.7 MiB)
```

This output shows that three network interfaces — the loopback interface (`lo`) and two Ethernet cards (`eth0` and `eth1`) — are currently active on this system. For each interface, you can see the IP address, as well as statistics on packets delivered and sent. If the Linux system has a dial-up PPP link up and running, you also see an item for the `ppp0` interface in the output.

## Checking the IP routing table

The other network configuration command, `/sbin/route`, also provides status information when you run it without a command-line argument. If you're having trouble checking a connection to another host (that you specify with an IP address), check the IP routing table to see whether a default gateway is specified. Then check the gateway's routing table to ensure that paths to an outside network appear in that routing table.

A typical output from the `/sbin/route` command looks like the following:

```
Kernel IP routing table
Destination Gateway Genmask Flags Metric Ref Use Iface
```

```
192.168.0.0  *  255.255.255.0 U 0 0 0 eth0
192.168.0.0  *  255.255.255.0 U 0 0 0 eth1
169.254.0.0  *  255.255.0.0 U 0 0 0 eth1
default 192.168.0.1 0.0.0.0 UG 0 0 0 eth0
```

As this routing table shows, the local network uses the eth0 and eth1 Ethernet interfaces, and the default gateway is the eth0 Ethernet interface. The default gateway is a routing device that handles packets addressed to any network other than the one in which the Linux system resides. In this example, packets addressed to any network address other than those beginning with 192.168.0 are sent to the gateway — 192.168.0.1. The gateway forwards those packets to other networks (assuming, of course, that the gateway is connected to another network, preferably the Internet).

## Checking connectivity to a host

To check for a network connection to a specific host, use the ping command. ping is a widely used TCP/IP tool that uses a series of Internet Control Message Protocol (ICMP, pronounced *EYE-comp*) messages. ICMP provides for an echo message to which every host responds. Using the ICMP messages and replies, ping can determine whether the other system is alive and can compute the round-trip delay in communicating with that system.

The following example shows how I run ping to see whether a system on my network is alive:

```
ping 192.168.0.1
```

Here is what this command displays on my home network:

```
PING 192.168.0.1 (192.168.0.1) 56(84) bytes of data.
64 bytes from 192.168.0.1: icmp_seq=1 ttl=63 time=0.256 ms
64 bytes from 192.168.0.1: icmp_seq=2 ttl=63 time=0.267 ms
64 bytes from 192.168.0.1: icmp_seq=3 ttl=63 time=0.272 ms
64 bytes from 192.168.0.1: icmp_seq=4 ttl=63 time=0.267 ms
64 bytes from 192.168.0.1: icmp_seq=5 ttl=63 time=0.275 ms
--- 192.168.0.1 ping statistics ---
5 packets transmitted, 5 received, 0% packet loss, time 3999ms
rtt min/avg/max/mdev = 0.256/0.267/0.275/0.016 ms
```

In Linux, ping continues to run until you press Ctrl+C to stop it; then it displays summary statistics showing the typical time it takes to send a packet between the two systems. On some systems, ping simply reports that a remote host is alive. However, you can still get the timing information by using appropriate command-line arguments.

The ping command relies on ICMP messages that many firewalls are configured to block. Therefore, ping may not always work and is no longer a reliable way to test network connectivity. If ping fails for a specific host, don't assume that the host is down or not connected to the network. You can typically use ping to successfully check connectivity within your local area network.

## *Checking network status*

To check the status of the network, use the `netstat` command. This command displays the status of network connections of various types (such as TCP and UDP connections). You can view the status of the interfaces quickly by typing **netstat -i**, which results in an output similar to the following:

```
Kernel Interface table
Iface MTU Met RX-OK RX-ERR RX-DRP RX-OVR TX-OK TX-ERR TX-DRP TX-OVR Flg
eth0 1500 0 613175 0 0 1 574695 0 0 0 BMRU
eth1 1500 0 4298 0 0 0 1375 1 0 0 BMRU
lo 16436 0 3255 0 0 0 3255 0 0 0 LRU
```

In this case, the output shows the current status of the loopback and Ethernet interfaces. Table 4-2 describes the meanings of the columns.

| Table 4-2 | Meaning of Columns in the Kernel Interface Table |
|---|---|
| *Column* | *Meaning* |
| Iface | Name of the interface |
| MTU | Maximum Transmission Unit — the maximum number of bytes that a packet can contain |
| Met | Metric value for the interface — a number indicating distance (in terms of number of hops) that routing software uses when deciding which interface to send packets through |
| RX-OK, TX-OK | Number of error-free packets received (RX) or transmitted (TX) |
| RX-ERR, TX-ERR | Number of packets with errors |
| RX-DRP, TX-DRP | Number of dropped packets |
| RX-OVR, TX-OVR | Number of packets lost due to overflow |
| Flg | A = receive multicast; B = broadcast allowed; D = debugging turned on; L = loopback interface (notice the flag on lo), M = all packets received, N = trailers avoided; O = no ARP on this interface; P = point-to-point interface; R = interface is running; and U = interface is up |

Another useful form of `netstat` option is `-t`, which shows all active TCP connections. Following is a typical result of typing **netstat -t** on one Linux PC:

```
Active Internet connections (w/o servers)
Proto Recv-Q Send-Q Local Address Foreign Address State
tcp 0 0 localhost:2654 localhost:1024 ESTABLISHED
tcp 0 0 localhost:1024 localhost:2654 ESTABLISHED
tcp 0 0 LNBNECXAN.nrockv01.:ssh 192.168.0.6:1577 ESTABLISHED
```

In this case, the output columns show the protocol (`Proto`), the number of bytes in the receive and transmit queues (`Recv-Q`, `Send-Q`), the local TCP port in `hostname:service` format (`Local Address`), the remote port (`Foreign Address`), and the state of the connection.

Type **netstat -ta** to see all TCP connections — both active and the ones your Linux system is listening to (with no connection established yet). For example, here's a typical output from the `netstat -ta` command:

```
Active Internet connections (servers and established)
Proto Recv-Q Send-Q Local Address Foreign Address State
tcp 0 0 *:32769 *:* LISTEN
tcp 0 0 *:mysql *:* LISTEN
tcp 0 0 *:sunrpc *:* LISTEN
tcp 0 0 *:ftp *:* LISTEN
tcp 0 0 localhost.localdomain:ipp *:* LISTEN
tcp 0 0 *:telnet *:* LISTEN
tcp 0 0 localhost.localdomain:5335 *:* LISTEN
tcp 0 0 localhost.localdomain:smtp *:* LISTEN
tcp 0 0 192.168.0.9:45876 www.redhat.com:http ESTABLISHED
tcp 0 0 192.168.0.9:45877 www.redhat.com:http ESTABLISHED
tcp 0 0 192.168.0.9:45875 www.redhat.com:http ESTABLISHED
tcp 0 0 *:ssh *:* LISTEN
tcp 0 0 ::ffff:192.168.0.7:ssh ::ffff:192.168.0.3:4932 ESTABLISHED
```

## Sniffing network packets

Sniffing network packets — sounds like something illegal, doesn't it? Nothing like that. *Sniffing* simply refers to viewing the TCP/IP network data packets. The concept is to capture all the network packets so that you can examine them later.

If you feel like sniffing TCP/IP packets, you can use `tcpdump`, a command-line utility that comes with Linux. As its name implies, it *dumps* (prints) the headers of TCP/IP network packets.

To use `tcpdump`, log in as `root` and type the `tcpdump` command in a terminal window. Typically, you want to save the output in a file and examine that file later. Otherwise, `tcpdump` starts spewing results that just flash by on the window. For example, to capture 1,000 packets in a file named `tdout` and attempt to convert the IP addresses to names, type the following command:

```
tcpdump -a -c 1000 > tdout
```

After capturing 1,000 packets, `tcpdump` quits. Then you can examine the output file, `tdout`. It's a text file, so you can simply open it in a text editor or type **more tdout** to view the captured packets.

Just to whet your curiosity, here are some lines from a typical output from `tcpdump`:

```
20:05:57.723621 arp who-has 192.168.0.1 tell LNBNECXAN.nrockv01.md.comcast.net
20:05:57.723843 arp reply 192.168.0.1 is-at 0:9:5b:44:78:fc
20:06:01.733633 LNBNECXAN.nrockv01.md.comcast.net.1038 > 192.168.0.6.auth:
    S 536321100:536321100(0) win 5840 <mss 1460,sackOK,timestamp 7030060
    0,nop,wscale 0> (DF)
20:06:02.737022 LNBNECXAN.nrockv01.md.comcast.net.ftp > 192.168.0.6.1596: P 1:72
    (71) ack 1 win 5840 (DF)
20:06:02.935335 192.168.0.6.1596 > LNBNECXAN.nrockv01.md.comcast.net.ftp: . ack
    72 win 65464 (DF)
20:06:05.462481 192.168.0.6.1596 > LNBNECXAN.nrockv01.md.comcast.net.ftp: P 1:12
    (11) ack 72 win 65464 (DF)
20:06:05.462595 LNBNECXAN.nrockv01.md.comcast.net.ftp > 192.168.0.6.1596: . ack
    12 win 5840 (DF)
20:06:05.465344 LNBNECXAN.nrockv01.md.comcast.net.ftp > 192.168.0.6.1596: P
    72:105(33) ack 12 win 5840 (DF)
. . . lines deleted . . .
```

The output offers some clues to what's going on, with each line showing information about one network packet. Every line starts with a timestamp followed by details of the packet (information such as where it originates and where it is going). I don't try to explain the details here, but you can type **man tcpdump** to find out more about some of the details (and more importantly, see what other ways you can use `tcpdump`).

If `tcpdump` isn't installed in Debian, type **apt-get install tcpdump** to install it.

You can use another packet sniffer called Ethereal in Linux. To find out more about Ethereal, visit `www.ethereal.com`.

## Using GUI Tools

You can check the status of your network through the graphical interfaces a number of ways. One of those is to use the System Monitor (in GNOME, choose System⇨ Administration⇨System Monitor), as shown in Figure 4-1. In addition to seeing the network load, you can click the Processes tab to see the status of various processes.

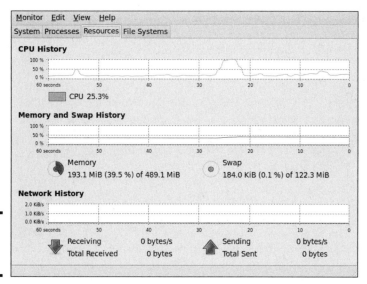

**Figure 4-1:**
The System
Monitor.

# Configuring Networks at Boot Time

It makes sense to start your network automatically every time you boot the
system. For that to happen, various startup scripts must contain appropriate commands. You don't have to do anything special other than configure
your network (either during installation or by using the network configuration tool at a later time). If the network balks at startup, however, you can
troubleshoot by checking the files I mention in this section.

In Debian, Ubuntu, and Xandros, the `/etc/network/interfaces` file
describes the network interfaces available in your system, and the `/sbin/`
`ifup` command activates the interfaces when you boot the system. Here
is the content of a typical `/etc/network/interfaces` file from a Debian
system:

```
# This file describes the network interfaces available on your system
# and how to activate them. For more information, see interfaces(5).
# The loopback network interface
auto lo
iface lo inet loopback
# The primary network interface
auto eth0
iface eth0 inet dhcp
```

The `auto eth0` line indicates that you can bring up the Ethernet interface at initialization by using the command `ifup -a` invoked by a system startup script. The line `ifup eth0 inet dhcp` identifies Ethernet as a TCP/IP network interface that is configured by Dynamic Host Configuration Protocol (DHCP).

In Fedora, the network-activation script uses a set of text files in the `/etc/sysconfig` directory to activate the network interfaces. For example, the script checks the variables defined in the `/etc/sysconfig/network` file to decide whether to activate the network. In `/etc/sysconfig/network`, you see a line with the `NETWORKING` variable as follows:

```
NETWORKING=yes
```

The network activates only if the `NETWORKING` variable is set to `yes`. A number of scripts in the `/etc/sysconfig/network-scripts` directory activate specific network interfaces. For example, the configuration file for activating the Ethernet interface `eth0` is the file `/etc/sysconfig/network-scripts/ifcfg-eth0`. Here's what a typical `/etc/sysconfig/network-scripts/ifcfg-eth0` file contains:

```
DEVICE=eth0
BOOTPROTO=dhcp
HWADDR=00:08:74:E5:C1:06
ONBOOT=yes
TYPE=Ethernet
```

The `DEVICE` line provides the network device name. The `BOOTPROTO` variable is set to `dhcp`, indicating that the IP address is obtained dynamically by using DHCP. The `ONBOOT` variable states whether this network interface activates when Linux boots. If your PC has an Ethernet card and you want to activate the `eth0` interface at boot time, `ONBOOT` must be set to `yes`. The configuration file `ifcfg-eth0` in the `/etc/sysconfig/network-scripts` directory works only if your PC has an Ethernet card and the Linux kernel has detected and loaded the specific driver for that card.

In SUSE, the network information is kept in the `/etc/sysconfig/network` directory in files with names beginning with `ifcfg`. For Ethernet interfaces, the configuration filename begins with `ifcfg-eth-id-` followed by the unique hardware address of the Ethernet card. Here are the key lines in a typical Ethernet configuration file:

```
BOOTPROTO='dhcp'
STARTMODE='auto'
```

The `BOOTPROTO='dhcp'` line indicates that the interface is set up using DHCP, and `STARTMODE='auto'` means that the interface is initialized when the system boots.

Within KDE, you can start the Control Center by typing **Session Manager** in the Search box and configuring the default operations for the system, as shown in Figure 4-2.

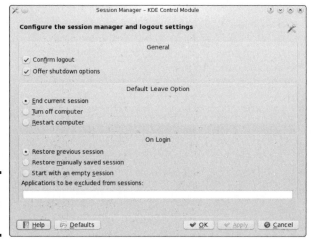

**Figure 4-2:**
The Session
Manager.

Within KDE and GNOME, you can run the Login Manager utility to choose the default operations for the system. Figure 4-3 shows an example of the Login Manager dialog box as it appears in Fedora (based upon your version, the Login Manager may not be installed by default). If a boot manager was installed to handle multiple operating systems, the Boot Manager option in Figure 4-3 would be enabled.

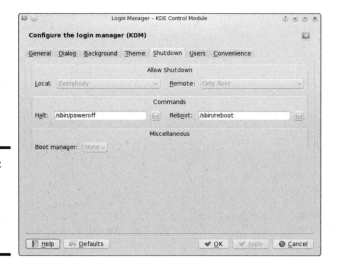

**Figure 4-3:**
The Login
Manager
offers
several
options.

# Book IV

# The Internet

# Contents at a Glance

## Chapter 1: E-Mailing and IMing in Linux . . . . . . . . . . . . . . . . . . . . . . .233

Understanding Electronic Mail ....................................................................234
Taking Stock of Mail Readers and IM Clients in Linux...........................236
E-Mailing in Linux ........................................................................................237
Instant Messaging in Linux.........................................................................246

## Chapter 2: Browsing the Web . . . . . . . . . . . . . . . . . . . . . . . . . . . . . .249

Discovering the Web.....................................................................................249
Web Browsing in Linux ................................................................................254

## Chapter 3: Reading Newsgroups and RSS Feeds. . . . . . . . . . . . . . . .261

Understanding Newsgroups.........................................................................261
Reading Newsgroups from Your ISP ..........................................................266
Reading and Searching Newsgroups at Web Sites ...................................272
Reading RSS Feeds........................................................................................273

## Chapter 4: Using FTP . . . . . . . . . . . . . . . . . . . . . . . . . . . . . . . . . . . .277

Using Graphical FTP Clients........................................................................277
Using the Command-Line FTP Client.........................................................283

# Chapter 1: E-Mailing and IMing in Linux

## In This Chapter

✔ **Understanding e-mail**

✔ **Looking at mail readers and IM (instant messaging) clients**

✔ **Introducing Evolution, Thunderbird, and KMail**

✔ **Instant messaging with Pidgin and Kopete**

**E**lectronic mail (e-mail) is the killer app of the Internet. With e-mail, you can exchange messages and documents with anyone on the Internet: friends, acquaintances, loved ones, and complete strangers. Under normal conditions, you can send messages anywhere in the world from any Internet host, and that message typically makes its way to its destination within minutes — something you can't do with paper mail (also known as *snail mail,* and appropriately so).

E-mail eliminates the hassles of trying to arrange schedules and availability to communicate over the phone. When I send an e-mail message, it waits in the recipient's mailbox to be read at the recipient's convenience. Likewise, when people send me e-mail, I can read and reply at *my* convenience.

Linux comes with several mail clients — also called *mail readers* — that you can use to download mail from your Internet service provider (ISP) or from a number of Web sites. After installed, you can read and send e-mail using these mail clients. In this chapter, I mention several mail clients available in Linux and briefly introduce you to a few of them. Because of the similarities among them, generally when you know one, you can easily use any of the mail readers.

Yet another type of keeping in touch is more in line with today's generation. I'm talking about *IM* — instant messaging. IM is basically one-to-one chat, and most Linux implementations include IM clients for AOL Instant Messenger (or AIM), as well as other instant messaging protocols such as Jabber, ICQ, MSN Messenger, Yahoo!, Gadu-Gadu, IRC (Internet Relay Chat), and SMS (Short Message Service, or text messaging). I briefly describe a few IM clients in this chapter.

# Understanding Electronic Mail

E-mail messages are addressed to a username at an e-mail domain, with the two values separated by an @ sign. That means if John Doe logs in with the username `jdoe`, the first half of his e-mail address is `jdoe`. The only other piece of information needed to identify the recipient uniquely is the e-mail domain (also known as the fully qualified domain name of the recipient's system). Thus, if John Doe's system is named `someplace.com`, his complete e-mail address becomes `jdoe@someplace.com`. Given that address, anyone on the Internet can send e-mail to John Doe.

## How MUAs and MTAs work

The two types of mail software are as follows:

✦ **Mail user agent (MUA)** is the fancy name for a *mail reader* — a client that you use to read your mail messages, write replies, and compose new messages. Typically, the mail user agent retrieves messages from the mail server by using the POP3 or IMAP4 protocol. POP3 is the *Post Office Protocol version 3,* and IMAP4 is the *Internet Message Access Protocol version 4.* Most Linux implementations come with mail user agents such as Balsa, Thunderbird, KMail, and Evolution.

✦ **Mail transport agent (MTA)** is the fancy name for a *mail server,* which sends and receives mail message text. The method used for mail transport depends on the underlying network. In TCP/IP networks, the mail transport agent delivers mail using the *Simple Mail Transfer Protocol* (SMTP). Just about every Linux distribution includes `sendmail`, a powerful and popular mail transport agent for TCP/IP networks.

Figure 1-1 shows how the MUAs and MTAs work with one another when Alice sends an e-mail message to Bob. (Using *Alice* and *Bob* to explain e-mail and cryptography is customary — just pick up any book on cryptography and you'll see what I mean.) The Internet is always diagrammed as a cloud — the boundaries of the Internet are so fuzzy that a cloud seems just right to represent it. (Or is it because no one knows where the Internet starts and where it ends?)

The scenario in Figure 1-1 is typical. Alice and Bob both connect to the Internet through an ISP, which they use to get and send their e-mail. When Alice types a message and sends it, her mail user agent (MUA) sends the message to her ISP's mail transfer agent (MTA) using the Simple Mail Transfer Protocol (SMTP). The sending MTA then sends that message to the receiving MTA — Bob's ISP's MTA — using SMTP. When Bob connects to the Internet, his MUA downloads the message from his ISP's MTA using the POP3 (or IMAP4) protocol. That's the way mail moves around the Internet — from sending MUA to sending MTA to receiving MTA to receiving MUA.

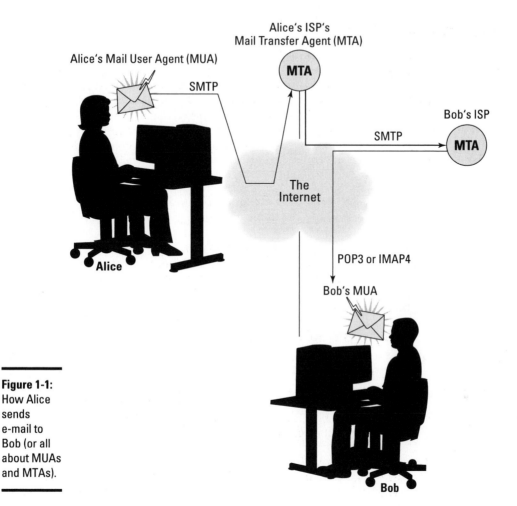

**Figure 1-1:**
How Alice
sends
e-mail to
Bob (or all
about MUAs
and MTAs).

## Mail message enhancements

Mail messages used to be plain text (and most still are), but many messages today have much more than text. Two typical features of today's mail are

+ **Attachments:** Many messages today include attached files, which can be anything from documents to images. The recipient can save the attachment on disk or open it directly from the mail reader. Unfortunately, one of the ways hackers try to get viruses and worms into your PC is by placing them in attachments. (If it's any consolation, most Windows-based viruses and worms don't work in Linux.)

+ **HTML messages:** Mail messages can be in *HTML* (HyperText Markup Language), the language used to lay out Web pages. When you read an

HTML message on a capable mail reader, the message appears in its full glory with fancy fonts and embedded graphics.

Although HTML messages are nice, they don't appear correctly when you use a text-based mail reader. In a text mail reader, HTML messages appear as a bunch of gobbledygook (which is just the HTML code).

If you have an ISP account, all you need is a mail client to access your e-mail. In this case, your e-mail resides on your ISP's server, and the mail reader downloads mail when you run it. You have to do some setup before you can start reading mail from your ISP's mail server. The setup essentially requires you to enter information that you get from your ISP — the mail server's name, server type (POP3, for example), your username, and your password.

# Taking Stock of Mail Readers and IM Clients in Linux

There was a time when most mail readers were text programs, but those times have changed. Now mail readers are graphical applications capable of displaying HTML messages and handling attachments with ease. They're easy to use; if you can work with one, it's a pretty sure bet that you can use any of the graphical mail readers out there. (As mentioned, most Linux distributions come with several mail readers; feel free to try a few out to see which one fits your needs best.)

IM (instant messaging) is a more recent phenomenon, but Linux tries to stay on top of things, so most implementations come with two IM clients that can work with various IM protocols. Table 1-1 gives you an overview of the major mail readers and IM clients in Linux.

| Table 1-1 | Linux Mail Readers and IM Clients |
|---|---|
| *Software* | *Description* |
| KMail | The KDE e-mail client that supports both POP3 and IMAP4. |
| Thunderbird | A redesign of the Mozilla Mail client, which was a part of the Mozilla Web browser (open source incarnation of Netscape Communicator). |
| Evolution | A personal information manager (PIM) that includes e-mail, calendar, contact management, and an online task list. |
| Pidgin | An IM client for GNOME that supports a number of instant-messaging protocols such as AIM, ICQ, Yahoo!, MSN, Gadu-Gadu, and Jabber. This software was formerly known as Gaim. |
| Kopete | An IM client for KDE that supports a number of messaging protocols, such as Jabber, ICQ, AIM, MSN, Yahoo!, IRC, Gadu-Gadu, and SMS. |

If you don't see a specific mail or IM client in your distribution, chances are that you can easily download and install it from the Internet.

# E-Mailing in Linux

Each Linux distribution's GUI desktop has one or two default e-mail clients. GNOME desktops typically offer Evolution, whereas KDE desktops go with KMail. Both GNOME and KDE desktops often come with Mozilla as the Web browser, and Mozilla includes a mail client as well.

Debian and Fedora include KMail and Evolution (for the KDE and GNOME interfaces, respectively). Ubuntu offers Evolution as the default mail client. SUSE uses KMail as the default mail reader, and Xandros provides both KMail and Thunderbird mail.

In the following sections, I briefly introduce you to Evolution, Thunderbird mail, and KMail. All mail clients are intuitive, so you don't need much more than an introduction to start using them effectively.

## Introducing Evolution

Evolution is one of Linux's most popular e-mail clients, so I want to start with it. What better way than to just jump right in!

In Fedora, you can start Evolution by choosing Application⇨Office⇨Evolution Mail and Calendar from the GNOME desktop or Applications⇨Internet⇨Mail Client from the KDE desktop. With open-SUSE, choose Main Menu⇨Internet⇨ E-mail⇨ Evolution Email. (In Debian, I had to choose Applications⇨Debian Menu⇨Apps⇨Net⇨Evolution.)

When you start Evolution for the first time, the Evolution Setup Assistant window appears, as shown in Figure 1-2.

Click Forward in the Welcome screen, and the Setup Assistant guides you through the following steps:

1.  **Enter your name and e-mail address in the Identity screen, and then click the Forward button.**

    For example, if your e-mail address is `jdoe@someplace.com`, that's what you enter. You may also have the option of choosing to make this your default account and adding additional information such as your organization's name.

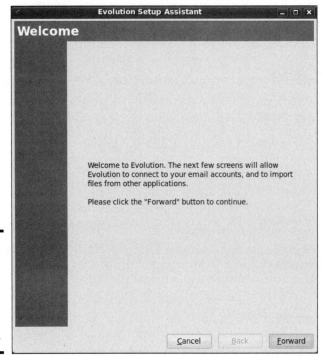

**Figure 1-2:**
Evolution
Setup
Assistant
guides you
through the
initial setup.

2. **Set up the options for receiving e-mail, and then click Forward.**

   Select the type of mail download protocol — POP or IMAP. Then provide the name of the mail server (for example, `mail.comcast.net`). You're prompted for the password when Evolution connects to the mail server for the first time.

3. **Provide further information about receiving e-mail — how often to check for mail, whether to leave messages on the server, and more — and then click Forward.**

   Typically, you want to download the messages and delete them from the server (otherwise the ISP complains when your mail piles up).

4. **Set up the following options for sending e-mail and click Forward when you're finished:**

   a. **Select the server type as SMTP.**

   b. **Enter the name of the server, such as smtp.comcast.net.**

   c. **If the server requires you to log in, select the Server Requires Authentication check box.**

d. **Enter your username — the same username you use to log in to your ISP's mail server.**

Often, you don't have to log in to send mail; you only log in when receiving — downloading — mail messages.

5. **(Optional) Give this e-mail account a descriptive name, such as Work or Personal.**

6. **Click Forward.**

7. **Click Apply to complete the Evolution setup.**

After you complete the one-time setup, Evolution opens its main window, as shown in Figure 1-3.

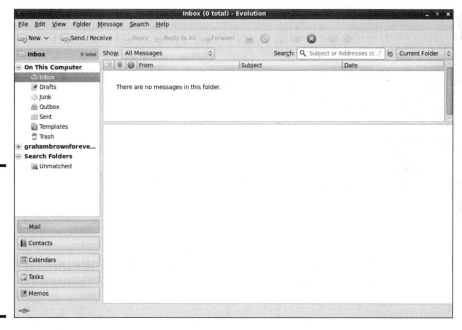

**Figure 1-3:** Evolution takes care of mail, calendar, contact management, and to-do lists.

Evolution's main display area is vertically divided into two windows: a narrow pane on the left with a number of shortcut buttons — Mail, Contacts, Calendars, Tasks, Memos — arranged in a column and a bigger right pane where Evolution displays information relevant to the currently selected shortcut icon. In Figure 1-3, Evolution displays the Inbox for mail.

You can click the shortcut buttons in the left window to switch to different views. These buttons provide access to all the necessary components of a PIM — e-mail, contacts, calendar, task list, and memos. You'll find all these tasks intuitive to perform in Evolution.

To access your e-mail, click the Inbox icon. Evolution opens your Inbox, as shown in Figure 1-4. If you turn on the feature to automatically check for mail every so often, Evolution prompts you for your mail password, gives you the option of having Evolution remember your password in the future, and downloads your mail. The e-mail Inbox looks very much like any other mail reader's inbox, such as the Outlook Express Inbox.

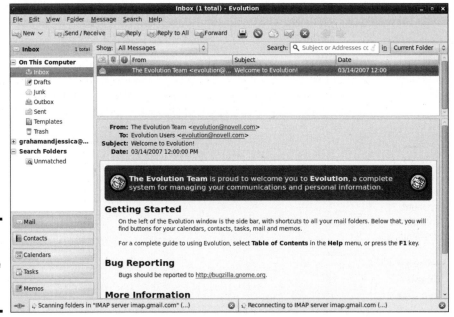

**Figure 1-4:**
Read your
e-mail in the
Evolution
Inbox.

To read a message, click the message in the upper window of the Inbox, and the message text appears in the lower window. Figure 1-4 shows a welcome e-mail message from the Evolution team.

To reply to the current message, click the Reply button on the toolbar. A message composition window pops up. You can write your reply and then click the Send button on the toolbar to send the reply. Simple, isn't it?

To send a new e-mail, choose New⇨Mail Message on the Evolution toolbar or simply click the New icon. A new message composition window appears. You can type your message in that window; when you're finished composing the message, click the Send icon.

Evolution comes with extensive online help. Choose Help⇨Contents from the Evolution menu and your version of Evolution's user's guide appears in a window. You can then read the user's guide in that window.

## Introducing Thunderbird

Mozilla Thunderbird 3 is a redesign of *Mozilla Mail,* the mail and newsreader that comes with the Mozilla Web browser — the open source successor to Netscape Communicator. As this reader increases in popularity, more and more distributions are including it and even making it the default primary reader. Thunderbird works well as a complement to the Firefox Web browser and runs faster than Evolution and even Mozilla Mail. A bonus is that it runs not only on Linux but also on a number of other operating systems, including Microsoft Windows and Mac OS X, making it a reader that your organization can standardize on.

After installing Thunderbird, you can start it by choosing Applications↔ Debian Menu↔Apps↔Net↔Mozilla Thunderbird from the GNOME desktop in Debian. When Thunderbird runs, it starts the Account Wizard (as shown in Figure 1-5) and prompts you for information about your e-mail account.

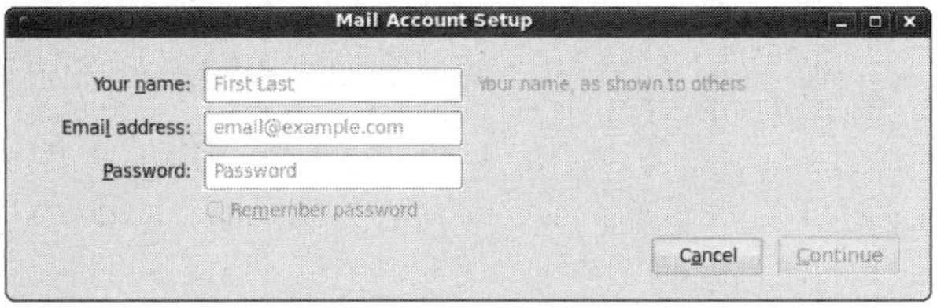

**Figure 1-5:**
Enter your e-mail account information in Thunderbird's Account Wizard.

The Account Wizard takes you through the following steps:

1. **Enter your identity information — your name, your full e-mail address, such as** `jdoe@someplace.com`, **and your e-mail password — and click Next.**

2. **In most situations, Thunderbird will automatically locate information about your ISP's mail server — the protocol type (POP or IMAP) as well as the incoming and outgoing server names. Click Next if they are correct.**

   The incoming server is the POP or IMAP server, whereas the outgoing server is the one through which you send mail out. If the information Thunderbird automatically displays is not correct, choose Manual Setup to enter the information yourself.

3. **Verify all information. If it's correct, click Create Account. Otherwise, click Back and fix the errors.**

**Book IV
Chapter 1**

**E-Mailing and
IMing in Linux**

After you set up the e-mail account, Thunderbird's main window appears and displays the contents of your Inbox. Thunderbird downloads your messages and displays them in a familiar format. To read a message, click that message, and the full text appears in the lower window, as shown in Figure 1-6.

**Figure 1-6:**
You can read and send e-mail messages from Thunderbird.

Thunderbird's intuitive to use. Most of the time, you can click the toolbar buttons to do most anything you want with the e-mail messages. Here's what each toolbar button does:

✦ **Get Mail:** Downloads messages from your e-mail accounts. (You can set up as many accounts as you want.)

✦ **Write:** Opens a window where you can compose and send a message.

✦ **Address Book:** Opens the Address Book window where you can maintain a list of your contacts.

✦ **Tag:** Assigns various tags to the selected e-mail message, such as Important, Personal, and To-Do.

✦ **Reply:** Opens a window where you can send a reply to the person who sent you the message you're reading now. You can also reply to all recipients of the message.

✦ **Forward:** Displays the current message in a window so that you can forward it to someone else.

✦ **Archive:** Sends e-mail messages from the default folder to an archive folder. To designate a location for archived messages to be sent, choose Tools➪Account Settings➪Copies and Folders and select a location under Keep Message Archives In.

✦ **Junk:** Marks the selected messages as junk. (You can mark selected messages as junk and choose Tools➪Junk Mail Controls to block similar messages.)

✦ **Delete:** Deletes the selected message.

If you use any GUI mail reader — from Microsoft Outlook Express to Novell GroupWise — you find a similar set of toolbar buttons. In the following sections, I describe how to perform a few common e-mail-related tasks.

### Managing your Inbox

Thunderbird downloads your incoming mail and stores it in the Inbox folder. You can see the folders organized along the narrow window on the left side. (Refer to Figure 1-6.) Each e-mail account you have set up has a set of folders. You have the following folders by default:

✦ **Inbox:** Holds all your incoming messages for this e-mail account.

✦ **Trash:** Contains the messages you delete. (To empty the Trash folder, choose File➪Empty Trash from the Thunderbird Mail menu.)

✦ **Outbox:** Contains the messages that haven't yet been sent to the mail server.

✦ **Drafts:** Contains the messages that you save as a draft. (Click the Save button on the message composition window to save something as a draft.)

✦ **Sent:** Holds all the messages you've successfully sent.

✦ **Spam:** Contains any messages identified as spam.

You can create other folders to better organize your mail. To create a folder, do the following:

*1.* **Right-click the Local Folder label on the left side of the Thunderbird window and choose New Folder from the menu that appears.**

The New Folder dialog box appears.

*2.* **Fill in the folder name, select where you want to put the folder, and click OK.**

The new folder appears in the left window of Thunderbird. You can then drag and drop messages into the folder.

When you select a folder from the left window, Thunderbird displays the contents of that folder in the upper window on the right side. The list is normally sorted by date, with the latest messages shown at the end of the list. If you want to sort the list any other way — say, by sender or by subject — simply click that column heading and Thunderbird sorts the list according to that column.

### Composing and sending messages

To send an e-mail message, you either write a new message or reply to a message you're reading. The general steps for sending an e-mail message are as follows:

*1.* **To reply to a message, click the Reply or Reply All button on the toolbar while you're reading the message. To write a new message, click the Write button on the toolbar. To forward a message, click the Forward button.**

A message composition window appears.

*2.* **In the message composition window, fill in the subject line and type your message.**

The message can include images as well as links to Web sites. To insert any of these items, choose Insert⇨Image or Insert⇨Link from the menu.

*3.* **If you're creating a new message or forwarding a message, type the e-mail addresses of the recipients.**

To select addressees from the Address Book, click the Address button on the toolbar. Your Address Book opens, from which you can select the addressees.

*4.* **When you've finished composing the message, click the Send button.**

If you want to complete a message later, click Save in the message composition window and then close the window. Thunderbird saves the message in the Drafts folder. When you're ready to work on that message again, go to the Drafts folder and then double-click the saved message to open it.

## Introducing KMail

*KMail* is a mail reader for KDE. When you first run KMail, you get its main window (see Figure 1-7), but you can't start using it to send and receive e-mail until you've configured the mail accounts in KMail.

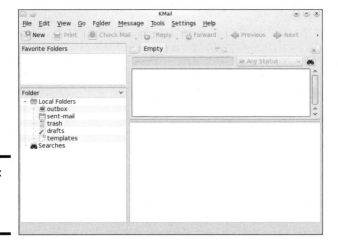

**Figure 1-7:**
The initial
KMail
window.

To configure KMail, choose Settings⇨Configure KMail. In the Configure
KMail window (see Figure 1-8), click Accounts on the left side of the window
and set up the information about your e-mail accounts. KMail uses this information to send and receive mail.

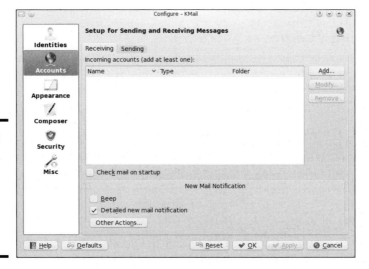

**Figure 1-8:**
Configure
e-mail
accounts
in the
Configure
KMail
window.

For outgoing mail, click the Add button on the Sending tab (see Figure 1-8) and then select the mail transport agent. Typically, for an ISP-provided mail account, you should select SMTP and enter the mail server's name (for example, `smtp.comcast.net`) that your ISP provided you.

To set up the incoming mail information, click Add on the Receiving tab and select the mail protocol, such as POP3 or IMAP. Your ISP can tell you what protocol to use. (Typically, it's POP3 or IMAP.) Then enter the mail server's name (for example, `mail.comcast.net`) as well as the username and password of your ISP account.

After the e-mail account information is set up, you can start using KMail. The user interface is intuitive and similar to other mail readers, such as Thunderbird and Evolution. KMail periodically checks and downloads messages from your incoming mail accounts. You can view messages when they arrive in your Inbox.

# Instant Messaging in Linux

Two major IM clients are in Linux. In GNOME desktops, you can use Pidgin (formerly known as Gaim), whereas Kopete is designed to work well on KDE desktops. I briefly describe both IM clients in the following sections.

## Using Pidgin

You can use Pidgin to keep in touch with all your contacts on many different IM services, such as AIM, ICQ, Yahoo!, MSN, Gadu-Gadu, and Jabber. If you use any of the IM services, you'll be right at home with Pidgin.

In Fedora, start Pidgin by choosing Applications⇨Internet⇨Pidgin from the GNOME desktop. You can start Pidgin in a similar manner from GNOME desktops in other distributions.

Start by setting up your messaging accounts in the Accounts window. Click the Add button and fill in the requested information in the Add Account window. You have to select the protocol for your IM service. For example, the protocol for AIM is AIM/ICQ. Other protocol choices include Gadu-Gadu, Jabber, Yahoo!, and MSN.

After you enter account information, the Accounts window displays all currently defined accounts. You can then select an account from the Pidgin main window and click Sign On.

After Pidgin logs you in, it opens the standard Buddy List window. To add buddies, choose Buddies⇨Add Buddy. In the Add Buddy window that appears, enter the screen name of the buddy and click Add. To create a new group, choose Buddies⇨Add Group. Type the name of the new group in the Add Group window that appears, and then click Add.

If any of your buddies are online, their names show up in the Buddy List window. To send a message to a buddy, double-click the name and a message window pops up. If someone sends you a message, a message window pops up with the message and you can begin conversing in that window.

## Using Kopete

Kopete — the KDE IM client — enables you to connect to many messaging services including AIM, IRC, MSN Messenger, Yahoo!, Gadu-Gadu, and SMS.

You can start Kopete by choosing Chat or Instant Messaging in the applications menu in Debian, SUSE, and Xandros.

When you first run Kopete, choose Settings⇨Configure to get the Configure Kopete window, where you can enter information about your IM and other messaging service accounts.

For example, to add your AIM account information, click Add Account and then answer and respond to the prompts from the Account Wizard. The first step is to select your messaging service. Select the appropriate messaging service, such as AIM if you use AOL's instant messaging service. Then provide the AIM screen name and the password.

After you set up your messaging service accounts, the Account Wizard closes and you get the regular Kopete window. To sign on with your messaging services and begin using Kopete, choose File⇨Set Status⇨Online.

Click the magnifying-glass icon to see your buddies. You see a solid smiley face icon for buddies who are online. Right-click an online buddy and choose Start Chat from the menu to start chatting. Choose File⇨Add Contact to add more contacts.

Well, if you know AIM, you know what to do: Have fun IMing with Kopete!

# Chapter 2: Browsing the Web

## In This Chapter

- ✔ Discovering the Web
- ✔ Understanding a URL
- ✔ Checking out Web servers and Web browsers
- ✔ Taking stock of Web browsers for Linux
- ✔ Web browsing with Mozilla Firefox

*I* suspect you already know about the Web or have been living under a rock for a number of years. However, did you know that the Web (or more formally, the World Wide Web) made the Internet what it is today? The Internet's been around for quite a while, but it didn't reach the masses until the Web came along in 1993.

Before the Web was created, you had to use arcane UNIX commands to download and use files, which was simply too complicated for most of us. With the Web, however, anyone can enjoy the benefits of the Internet by using a *Web browser* — a graphical application that downloads and displays Web documents. A click of the mouse is all you need to go from reading a document from your company Web site to downloading a video clip from across the country.

In this chapter, I briefly describe the Web and introduce Mozilla Firefox — the primary Web browser (and, for that matter, mail and newsreader, too) in most Linux distributions.

KDE desktops often use Konqueror as the Web browser, but after you've used one Web browser, you can easily use any other Web browser.

## Discovering the Web

If you've used a file server at work, you know the convenience of sharing files. You can use the word processor on your desktop to get to any document on the shared server.

Now imagine a word processor that enables you to open and view a document that resides on any computer on the Internet. You can view the document in its full glory, with formatted text and graphics. If the document makes a reference to another document (possibly residing on yet another computer), you can open that linked document simply by clicking the reference. That kind of easy access to distributed documents is essentially what the Web provides.

Of course, the documents have to be in a standard format so that any computer (with the appropriate Web browser software) can access and interpret the document. And a standard protocol is necessary for transferring Web documents from one system to another.

 The standard Web document format is *HyperText Markup Language* (HTML), and the standard protocol for exchanging Web documents is *HyperText Transfer Protocol* (HTTP). HTML documents are text files and don't depend on any specific operating system, so they work on any system from Windows and Mac to any type of UNIX and Linux.

 A *Web server* is software that provides HTML documents to any client that makes the appropriate HTTP requests. A *Web browser* is the client software that actually downloads an HTML document from a Web server and displays the contents graphically.

## Like a giant spider's web

The Web is the combination of the Web servers and the HTML documents that the servers offer. When you look at the Web in this way, the Web is like a giant book whose pages are scattered throughout the Internet. You use a Web browser running on your computer to view the pages — the pages are connected like a giant spider's web, with the documents everywhere, as illustrated in Figure 2-1.

**Figure 2-1:** The Web is like billions of pages, scattered across the network, that you can read from your computer by using a Web browser.

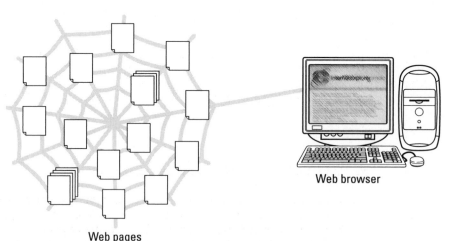

Web browser

Web pages

Imagine that the Web pages — HTML documents — are linked by network connections that resemble a giant spider's web, so you can see why the Web is called *the Web*. The *World Wide* part comes from the fact that the Web pages are scattered around the world.

## Links and URLs

Like the pages of printed books, Web pages contain text and graphics. Unlike printed books, however, Web pages can include multimedia, such as video clips, sound, and links to other Web pages.

The *links* in a Web page are references to other Web pages that you can follow to go from one page to another. The Web browser typically displays these links as underlined text (in a different color) or as images. Each link is like an instruction to you — something such as, "For more information, please consult Chapter 4," that you might find in a book. In a Web page, all you have to do is click the link; the Web browser brings up the referenced page, even though that document may actually reside on a far-away computer somewhere on the Internet.

The links in a Web page are referred to as *hypertext links* because when you click a link, the Web browser jumps to the Web page referenced by that link.

This arrangement brings up a question. In a printed book, you might ask the reader to go to a specific chapter or page in the book. How does a hypertext link indicate the location of the referenced Web page? In the Web, each Web page has a special name, called a *Uniform Resource Locator* (URL). A URL uniquely specifies the location of a file on a computer. Figure 2-2 shows the parts of a URL.

**Figure 2-2:**
The parts of a Uniform Resource Locator (URL).

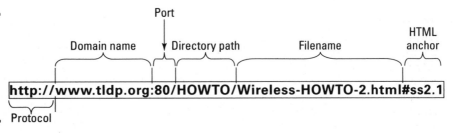

As Figure 2-2 shows, a URL has the following parts:

✦ **Protocol:** Name of the protocol that the Web browser uses to access the data from the file the URL specifies. In Figure 2-2, the protocol is `http://`, which means that the URL specifies the location of a Web page. Here are some of the common protocol types and their meanings:

`file://` means the URL points to a local file. You can use this URL to view HTML files without having to connect to the Internet. For example, `file:///var/www/html/index.html` opens the file `/var/www/html/index.html` from your Linux system.

`ftp://` means that you can download a file using the File Transfer Protocol (FTP). For example, `ftp://ftp.purdue.edu/pub/uns/NASA/nasa.jpg` refers to the image file `nasa.jpg` from the `/pub/uns/NASA` directory of the FTP server `ftp.purdue.edu`. If you want to access a specific user account via FTP, use a URL in the following form:

> `ftp://username:password@ftp.somesite.com/`

with *username* and *password* embedded in the URL.

The password is in plain text and not secure.

`http://` means that you download the file using the HyperText Transfer Protocol (HTTP). This protocol is the well-known format of URLs for all Web sites, such as `http://fedoraproject.org` for the Fedora Project's home page. If the URL doesn't have a filename, the Web server sends a default HTML file named `index.html`. (That's the default filename for the popular UNIX-based Apache Web servers; Microsoft Windows Web servers use a different default filename.)

`https://` specifies that you access the file through a *Secure Sockets Layer* (SSL) connection — a protocol designed by Netscape Communications for encrypted data transfers across the Internet. Typically, this form of URL is used when the Web browser sends sensitive information (such as credit card number, username, and password) to a Web server. For example, a URL such as

> `https://some.site.com/secure/takeorder.html`

may display an HTML form that requests credit card information and other personal information (such as name, address, and phone number).

`mailto:` specifies an e-mail address that you can use to send an e-mail message. This URL opens your e-mail program, from which you can send the message. For example, `mailto:webmaster@someplace.com` refers to the Webmaster at the host `someplace.com`.

`news://` specifies a newsgroup that you can read by means of the Network News Transfer Protocol (NNTP). For example:

> `news://news.md.comcast.giganews.com/comp.os.linux.setup`

accesses the `comp.os.linux.setup` newsgroup at the news server `news.md.comcast.giganews.com`. If you have a default news server configured for the Web browser, you can omit the news server's name and use the URL `news:comp.os.linux.setup` to access the newsgroup.

✦ **Domain name:** Contains the fully qualified domain name of the computer that has the file this URL specifies. You can also provide an IP address in this field. The domain name is not case-sensitive.

✦ **Port:** Port number that is used by the protocol listed in the first part of the URL. This part of the URL is optional; all protocols have default ports. The default port for HTTP, for example, is 80. If a site configures the Web server to listen to a different port, the URL has to include the port number.

✦ **Directory path:** Directory path of the file referred to in the URL. For Web pages, this field is the directory path of the HTML file. The directory path is case-sensitive.

✦ **Filename:** Name of the file. For Web pages, the filename typically ends with `.htm` or `.html`. If you omit the filename, the Web server returns a default file (often named `index.html`). The filename is case-sensitive.

✦ **HTML anchor:** Optional part of the URL that makes the Web browser jump to a specific location in the file. If this part starts with a question mark (?) instead of a pound sign(#), the browser takes the text following the question mark to be a query. The Web server returns information based on such queries.

## Web servers and Web browsers

The Web server serves up the Web pages, and the Web browser downloads them and displays them to the user. That's pretty much the story with these two cooperating software packages that make the Web work.

In a typical scenario, the user sits in front of a computer that's connected to the Internet and runs a Web browser. When the user clicks a link or types a URL into the Web browser, the browser connects to the Web server and requests a document from the server. The Web server sends the document (usually in HTML format) and ends the connection. The Web browser interprets and displays the HTML document with text, graphics, and multimedia (if applicable). Figure 2-3 illustrates this typical scenario of a user browsing the Web.

**Book IV
Chapter 2**

**Browsing the Web**

**Web server**

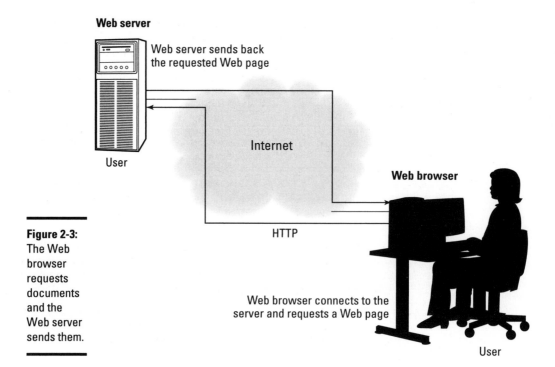

**Figure 2-3:**
The Web browser requests documents and the Web server sends them.

The Web browser's connection to the Web server ends after the server sends the document. When the user browses through the downloaded document and clicks another hypertext link, the Web browser again connects to the Web server named in the hypertext link, downloads the document, ends the connection, and displays the new document. That's how the user can move from one document to another with ease.

A Web browser can do more than simply "talk" HTTP with the Web server; Web browsers can also download documents and files using FTP, and many have integrated mail and newsreaders as well.

## Web Browsing in Linux

As Web pages become more interactive and complex, Web browsing turned into a stimulating, engaging experience. Also, there's always the element of surprise: You can click a link and end up at unexpected Web pages. Links are the most curious (and useful) aspect of the Web. You can start at a page that shows today's weather, and a click later, you can be reading this week's issue of *Time* magazine.

To browse the Web, all you need is a Web browser and an Internet connection. I assume that you've already taken care of the Internet connection (see Book III, Chapter 1 if you haven't yet set up your Internet connection), so all you need to know are the Web browsers in Linux.

## Checking out Web browsers for Linux

Many Linux distributions come with the Mozilla Firefox Web browser. Firefox is Mozilla's improvement on their original browser, an open source version of the venerable Netscape Communicator.

Several other Web browsers are available for Linux. I briefly mention the other browsers, but I focus on Firefox in the rest of the discussions. Here are the major Web browsers for Linux:

✦ **Mozilla Navigator:** Mozilla's first browser, a reincarnation of that old workhorse Netscape Communicator — only better. Since 2005, however, development of Navigator has stopped as Mozilla shifted focus to newer Web applications such as Firefox and Thunderbird.

✦ **Epiphany:** The GNOME Web browser that uses parts of the Mozilla code to draw the Web pages but has a simpler user interface than Mozilla. If Epiphany isn't installed, you can download it from `www.projects.gnome.org/epiphany`.

✦ **Firefox:** Mozilla's next-generation browser that blocks pop-up ads, provides tabs for easily viewing multiple Web pages in a single window, and includes a set of privacy tools. You can download Firefox from `www.mozilla.com/firefox`.

✦ **Konqueror:** The KDE Web browser that can also double as a file manager and a universal viewer.

In addition to these, many other applications are capable of downloading and displaying Web pages.

Nowadays most distributions include the Mozilla Firefox Web browser. I briefly introduce the Firefox Web browser in the next section. All other Web browsers have similarly intuitive user interfaces.

If your distribution doesn't install Firefox by default, you can easily install it by typing **su -** to become `root` and then typing **apt-get install mozilla-firefox**.

## Introducing Firefox's user interface

You can typically start Firefox by clicking an icon on the panel or by choosing Firefox from the GUI desktop's menu.

When Firefox starts, it displays a browser window with a default home page. (The main Web page on a Web server is the *home page.*) You can configure Firefox to use a different Web page as the default home page.

Figure 2-4 shows a Web page from a U.S. government Web site (`www.irs.gov`), as well as the main elements of the Firefox browser window.

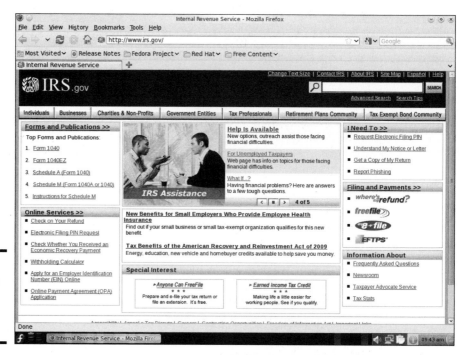

**Figure 2-4:**
The Firefox Web browser in action.

Firefox supports *tabbed browsing,* which means that you can open a new tab (by pressing Ctrl+T or clicking the plus sign to the right of the last open tab) and view a Web page in that tab. That way, you can view multiple Web pages in a single window.

The Firefox Web browser includes lots of features in its user interface, but you can master it easily. You can start with just the basics to get going with Firefox and then gradually expand to areas that you haven't yet explored.

### Firefox toolbars

Starting from the top of the window, you see a menu bar with the standard menus (File, Edit, and so forth) followed by the two toolbars — first the Navigation toolbar and then the Bookmarks toolbar. The area below the Bookmarks toolbar is where any open tabs and the current Web page appears.

Here's what you can do with the buttons and text boxes on the Navigation toolbar, from left to right:

✦ **Back:** Move to the previous Web page.

✦ **Forward:** Move to the page from which you have gone backward.

✦ **Recent Pages:** Open a drop-down list of recently visited Web pages.

✦ **Reload:** Reload the current Web page.

✦ **Stop:** Stop loading the current page.

✦ **Home:** Go to the home page.

✦ **Location:** Show the URL of the current Web page. (Type a URL in this box and press Enter to view that Web page.)

✦ **Bookmark:** Bookmark the page you are currently viewing. (Click the star icon at the end of the location bar.)

✦ **Google Search:** Search various Web sites such as Google, Yahoo!, Amazon.com, Dictionary.com, and eBay. (Type text and press Enter to search the currently selected Web site; the default is Google.)

Immediately below the Navigation toolbar comes the Bookmarks toolbar with buttons that take you to specific Web pages.

### Status bar

You can think of the bar along the bottom edge of the Firefox window as the status bar because the middle part of that area displays status information while Firefox loads a Web page.

In the right corner of Firefox's status bar, a security padlock icon appears when you access a secure Web site. Firefox supports a secure version of HTTP that uses SSL to transfer encrypted data between the browser and the Web server. When Firefox connects to a Web server that supports secure HTTP, a locked security padlock icon appears on the right edge of the status bar. Otherwise there's no security padlock icon, signifying an insecure connection. The URL for secure HTTP transfers begins with `https://` instead of the usual `http://` (note the extra s in `https`). You can click the padlock icon for more security information about the page.

Firefox displays status messages in the left part of the status bar. You can watch the messages in this area to see what's going on. If you mouse over a link on the Web page, the status bar displays the URL for that link.

### Firefox menus

I haven't mentioned the Firefox menus much. That's because you can usually get by without having to go to them. Nevertheless, taking a quick look through the Firefox menus is worthwhile so you know what each one offers. Table 2-1 gives you an overview of the Firefox menus.

| Table 2-1 | Firefox Menus |
|---|---|
| *Menu* | *Enables You to Do the Following* |
| File | Open a file or Web location, open or close a tab, send a Web page or link by e-mail, edit a Web page, print the current page, import settings and data, and quit Firefox. |
| Edit | Copy and paste selections, find text in the current page, and edit your preferences. |
| View | Show or hide various toolbars, reload the current page, make the text larger or smaller, and view the HTML code for the page. |
| History | Go backward and forward in the list of pages you've visited, or jump to other recently visited Web pages. |
| Bookmarks | Bookmark a page, organize the bookmarks, and add links to the Bookmarks toolbar folder. (These links appear in the Bookmarks toolbar.) |
| Tools | Search the Web and manage various aspects of the Web page, such as themes; view information about the current page; and clear browsing history |
| Help | Get online help on Firefox. |

## Changing your home page

Your home page is the page that Firefox loads when you start it. The default home page depends on the distribution. Often the home page is a file from your system's hard drive. Changing the home page is easy.

First, locate the page on the Web that you want to be the home page. You can get to that page any way you want. You can search with a search engine to find the page you want, you can type in the URL in the Location text box, or you may even accidentally end up on a page that you want to make your home page. It doesn't matter.

When you're viewing the Web page that you want to make your home page in Firefox, choose Edit⇨Preferences from the Firefox menu. The Preferences dialog box appears, as shown in Figure 2-5.

**Figure 2-5:**
Configure
the Firefox
browser to
suit your
preferences.

In Figure 2-5, notice the Home Page text box. Below the text box is a Use
Current Page button. Click that button to make the current page your home
page. If you select this option while multiple tabs are open, the browser will
open each tab with every new session.

You can set a lot of other options using the Preferences dialog box. Although
I don't explain all the options here, you can click around to explore everything that you can do from this window. For example, you can click the Use
Bookmark button to select a saved URL bookmark as the home page. (You
have to select the bookmark from a dialog box.)

## Surfing the Net with Firefox

Where you go from the home page depends on you. All you have to do is
click and see where you end up. Move your mouse around. You know when
you're on a link because the mouse pointer changes to a hand with an
extended index finger. Click the link, and Firefox downloads the Web page
referenced by that link.

How you use the Web depends on what you want to do. When you first get
started, you may explore a lot — browsing through Web sites and following
links without any specific goal in mind (what you may call Web window-
shopping).

The other, more purposeful, use of the Web is to find specific information from the Net. For example, you might want to locate all the Web sites that contain documents with a specified keyword. For such searches, you can use one of many Web search tools available on the Net. Firefox's Search text-box takes you to the Google Web Search page (www.google.com).

A third type of use is a visit to a specific site with a known URL. For example, when reading about a particular topic in this book, you may come across a specific URL. In that case, you want to go directly to that Web page.

If you want to surf the Net with Firefox, all you need is a starting Web page — then you can click whatever catches your fancy. For example, select the text in the Location text box in Firefox's Navigation toolbar, type **www.yahoo. com**, and then press Enter. You get to the Yahoo! home page that shows the Yahoo! Web directory — organized by subject. There's your starting point. All you have to do is click and you're on your way.

# Chapter 3: Reading Newsgroups and RSS Feeds

## In This Chapter

✔ **Finding out about newsgroups**

✔ **Reading a newsgroup from your ISP**

✔ **Reading and searching newsgroups**

✔ **Reading an RSS feed**

*N*ewsgroups provide a distributed conferencing system that spans the globe. You can post articles — essentially e-mail messages to an entire group of people — and respond to articles others have posted.

Think of an Internet newsgroup as a gathering place — a virtual meeting place where you can ask questions and discuss various issues. (And best of all, everything you discuss is archived for posterity.) Internet newsgroups are similar to the bulletin board systems (BBSs) of the pre-Web age or the forums offered on online systems such as AOL and MSN.

To participate in newsgroups, you need access to a news server — your Internet service provider (ISP) can give you this access. You also need a newsreader. Luckily, Linux comes with software that you can use to read newsgroups. In this chapter, I introduce you to newsgroups and show you how to read newsgroups with a few of the newsreaders. I also briefly explain how you can read and search newsgroups for free from a few Web sites.

Nowadays another popular way to read summaries of Web sites and weblogs is to use a program that can accept RSS feeds. At the end of this chapter, I briefly describe what an RSS feed is and how you can use a program such as KDE Akregator to subscribe to RSS feeds and read them on your Linux system.

## Understanding Newsgroups

Newsgroups originated in *Usenet* — a store-and-forward messaging network that was widely used for exchanging e-mail and news items. Usenet works like a telegraph in that news and mail are relayed from one system to another. In Usenet, the systems aren't on any network; the systems simply dial up one another and use the UNIX-to-UNIX Copy Protocol (UUCP) to transfer text messages.

Although it's a loosely connected collection of computers, Usenet works well and continues to be used because little expense is involved in connecting to it. All you need is a modem and a site willing to store and forward your mail and news. You have to set up UUCP on your system, but you don't need a sustained network connection; just a few phone calls are all you need to keep the e-mail and news flowing. The downside of Usenet is that you can't use TCP/IP services such as the Web, TELNET, or FTP with UUCP.

From their Usenet origins, newsgroups have now migrated to the Internet (even though the newsgroups are still called *Usenet newsgroups*). Instead of UUCP, the Network News Transfer Protocol (NNTP) now transports the news.

Although (for most of the online world) the news transport protocol has changed from UUCP to NNTP, the store-and-forward concept of news transfer remains. Thus, if you want to get news on your Linux system, you have to find a news server from which your system can download news. Typically, you can use your ISP's news server.

## Newsgroup hierarchy

The Internet newsgroups are organized in a hierarchy for ease of maintenance as well as ease of use. The newsgroup names help keep things straight by displaying this hierarchy.

Admittedly, these newsgroup names are written in Internet-speak, which can seem obscure at first. But the language is easy to pick up after a little bit of explanation. For example, a typical newsgroup name looks like this:

```
comp.os.linux.announce
```

This is a newsgroup for announcements (`announce`) about the Linux operating system (`os.linux`), and these subjects fall under the broad category of computers (`comp`). As you can see, the format of a newsgroup name is a sequence of words separated by periods. These words denote the hierarchy of the newsgroup. Figure 3-1 illustrates the concept of the hierarchical organization of newsgroups.

To understand the newsgroup hierarchy, compare the newsgroup name with the pathname of a file (for example, `/usr/lib/X11/xinit/Xclients`) in Linux. Just as a file's pathname shows the directory hierarchy of the file, the newsgroup name shows the newsgroup hierarchy. In filenames, a slash (/) separates the names of directories; in a newsgroup's name, a period (.) separates the different levels in the newsgroup hierarchy.

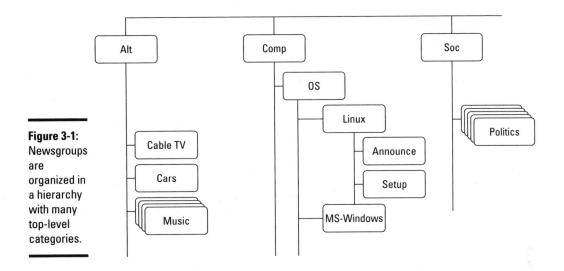

**Figure 3-1:**
Newsgroups
are
organized in
a hierarchy
with many
top-level
categories.

In a newsgroup name, the first word represents the newsgroup *category*. The
comp.os.linux.announce newsgroup, as mentioned, is in the comp category, whereas alt.books.technical is in the alt category.

## Top-level newsgroup categories

Table 3-1 lists some of the major newsgroup categories. You find a wide variety of newsgroups covering subjects ranging from politics to computers. The
Linux-related newsgroups are in the comp.os.linux hierarchy.

| Table 3-1 | Some Major Newsgroup Categories |
|-----------|----------------------------------|
| *Category* | *Subject* |
| alt | *Alternative* newsgroups (not subject to any rules), ranging from the mundane to the bizarre |
| bionet | Biology newsgroups |
| bit | Bitnet newsgroups |
| biz | Business newsgroups |
| clari | Clarinet news service (daily news) |
| comp | Computer hardware and software newsgroups (includes operating systems such as Linux and Microsoft Windows) |
| ieee | Newsgroups for the Institute of Electrical and Electronics Engineers (IEEE) |

*(continued)*

**Book IV
Chapter 3**

**Reading
Newsgroups
and RSS Feeds**

**Table 3-1** *(continued)*

| Category | Subject |
|----------|---------|
| k12 | Newsgroups devoted to elementary and secondary education |
| linux | Newsgroups devoted to Linux (includes a linux.redhat hierarchy) |
| misc | Miscellaneous newsgroups |
| news | Newsgroups about Internet news administration |
| rec | Recreational and art newsgroups |
| sci | Science and engineering newsgroups |
| soc | Newsgroups for discussing social issues and various cultures |
| talk | Discussions of current issues (think talk radio) |

This short list of categories is deceptive because it doesn't tell you about the wide-ranging variety of newsgroups available in each category. The top-level categories alone number more than a thousand, but many top-level categories are distributed only in specific regions of the world. Because each newsgroup category contains several levels of subcategories, the overall count of newsgroups is close to 100,000! The comp category alone has close to 1,200 newsgroups.

Unfortunately, many newsgroups are flooded with spam, like your e-mail Inbox only worse because anyone can post anything on a newsgroup. Moderated newsgroups offer some relief. Anyone who wants to post on a *moderated newsgroup* must first submit the article to a moderator — a human being — who then decides whether to post or reject the article. You can reduce the spam overload by browsing moderated newsgroups whenever possible.

To browse newsgroup categories and get a feel for the breadth of topics covered by the newsgroups, visit the Google Groups Web site at http://groups.google.com and click the Browse All of Usenet link. (You will need to click the Browse Group Categories link on the first page.)

## Linux-related newsgroups

Typically, you have to narrow your choice of newsgroups according to your interests. If you want to know more about Linux, for example, you can choose one or more of these newsgroups:

✦ comp.os.linux.admin: Linux system administration (inactive).

✦ comp.os.linux.advocacy: Linux promotion.

✦ `comp.os.linux.announce`: Important announcements about Linux. This newsgroup is moderated, which means you must mail the article to a moderator, who then posts it to the newsgroup if the article is appropriate for the newsgroup.

✦ `comp.os.linux.answers`: Questions and answers about Linux. All the Linux HOWTOs are posted in this moderated newsgroup.

✦ `comp.os.linux.development`: Current Linux development work.

✦ `comp.os.linux.development.apps`: Linux application development.

✦ `comp.os.linux.development.system`: Linux operating system development.

✦ `comp.os.linux.embedded`: Running the Linux operating system on embedded hardware.

✦ `comp.os.linux.hardware`: Linux and various types of hardware.

✦ `comp.os.linux.help`: Help with various aspects of Linux (inactive).

✦ `comp.os.linux.misc`: Miscellaneous Linux-related topics.

✦ `comp.os.linux.networking`: Networking under Linux.

✦ `comp.os.linux.portable`: Running the Linux operating system on laptop computers and portable PCs.

✦ `comp.os.linux.powerpc`: Running the Linux operating system on PowerPC microprocessors.

✦ `comp.os.linux.redhat`: Red Hat Linux-related topics (inactive).

✦ `comp.os.linux.setup`: Linux setup and installation.

✦ `comp.os.linux.x`: Setting up and running the X Window System under Linux.

✦ `comp.os.linux.xbox`: Running Linux on the Xbox video game console.

✦ `linux.debian`: Moderated newsgroup about Debian GNU/Linux (inactive).

✦ `linux.debian.news`: Moderated newsgroup for news items about Debian GNU/Linux.

✦ `linux.redhat`: Red Hat Linux discussions.

You have to be selective about what newsgroups you read because keeping up with all the news is impossible, even in a specific area such as Linux. When you first install and set up Linux, you might read newsgroups such as `comp.os.linux.answers`, `comp.os.linux.setup`, `comp.os.linux.hardware`, and `comp.os.linux.x` (especially if you have problems with X). After you have Linux up and running, you may want to find out about only new things happening in Linux. For such information, read the `comp.os.linux.announce` newsgroup.

Although a number of newsgroups are currently inactive and not being added to, these groups can still be referenced and searched for help with specific questions.

# Reading Newsgroups from Your ISP

If you sign up with an ISP for Internet access, it can provide you with access to a news server. Such Internet news servers communicate by using the Network News Transfer Protocol (NNTP). You can use an NNTP-capable newsreader, such as KNode, to access the news server and read selected newsgroups. You can also read news by using Thunderbird. Using a newsreader is the easiest way to access news from your ISP's news server.

My discussion of reading newsgroups assumes that you obtained access to a news server from your ISP. The ISP provides you with the name of the news server and any username and password needed to set up your news account on the newsreader you use.

To read news, you need a *newsreader* — a program that enables you to select a newsgroup and view the items in that newsgroup. You also have to understand the newsgroup hierarchy and naming conventions (which I describe in the "Newsgroup hierarchy" section, earlier in this chapter). In this section, I show you how to read news from a news server.

If you don't have access to newsgroups through your ISP, you can try using one of the many public news servers that are out there. For a list of public news servers, visit Newzbot at www.newzbot.com. At this Web site, you can search for news servers that carry specific newsgroups.

## Taking stock of newsreaders

You can use one of several software packages to download and read newsgroups in Linux. Here are a few major newsreaders:

✦ **Thunderbird:** Thunderbird includes the ability to download news from an NNTP server. You can read newsgroups and post items to newsgroups. Xandros uses Thunderbird for mail and news.

✦ **KNode:** This is a newsreader for KDE that you can download from knode.sourceforge.net. Debian and SUSE provide KNode as the newsreader.

✦ **Pan:** Pan is a GUI newsreader that, according to the developer's Web site (http://pan.rebelbase.com), "attempts to be pleasing to both new and experienced users." You can download Pan for various Linux distributions from http://pan.rebelbase.com/download.

If you don't find a newsreader in your Linux system, you can download and install any of these newsreaders easily in any of the Linux distributions. Often, you can locate the download site by a simple search at a search engine — just search for the word *download* followed by the name of the newsreader.

## Reading newsgroups with Thunderbird

You can browse newsgroups and post articles from Thunderbird, a mail and newsreader from the Mozilla project.

In many Linux distributions, the mail and news component of Thunderbird may not be installed. In that case, you have to download and install the Thunderbird mail and news component or use another newsreader. To download Thunderbird, visit www.mozillamessaging.com/thunderbird/.

When you're starting to read newsgroups with Thunderbird for the first time, follow these steps to set up the news account:

1. **Choose Edit⇨Account Settings from the Thunderbird menu.**

   A dialog box appears.

2. **Select the Account Actions option and then click Add Other Account.**

   The Account Wizard appears, as shown in Figure 3-2.

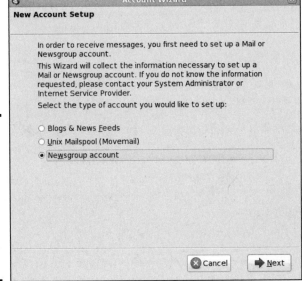

**Figure 3-2:** Thunderbird's Account Wizard guides you through the newsgroup account setup.

**Book IV Chapter 3**

Reading Newsgroups and RSS Feeds

3. **Select the Newsgroup Account option and click Next.**

4. **In the new screen that appears, fill in your identity information —
   name and e-mail address. Then click Next to move to the next screen.**

5. **Enter your news server name and click Next.**

6. **Enter a descriptive name of the newsgroup account and click Next.**

7. **Click Finish to complete the newsgroup account setup.**

The new newsgroup account now appears in the list of accounts on the left
side of the Thunderbird window. Click the newsgroup account name, and
the right side of the window displays the options for the newsgroup account.

Click the Manage Newsgroup Subscriptions option. Thunderbird starts to
download the list of newsgroups from the news server. Don't be surprised if
this process takes considerable time — the number of newsgroups is vast,
and the speed of your connection can slow the downloading of the list to a
point where you begin to get frustrated.

If your ISP's news server requires a username and password, you're
prompted for that information. After that, Thunderbird downloads the list of
newsgroups and displays them in the Subscribe dialog box. (You can enter a
search string in a text box to narrow the list.) When you find the newsgroups
you want, click the check box to the right of their names and then click the
Subscribe button to subscribe to these newsgroups, as shown in Figure 3-3.
Then click OK to close the dialog box.

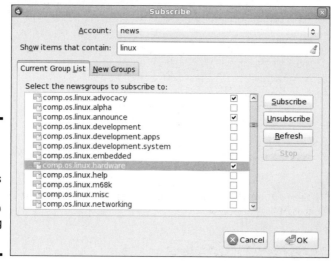

**Figure 3-3:**
Indicate
which
newsgroups
you want to
subscribe to
in this dialog
box.

After you subscribe to newsgroups, these newsgroups appear under the newsgroup account name on the left side of the Thunderbird window. You can then read a newsgroup using these steps:

*1.* **Click a newsgroup name (for example, `comp.os.linux.announce`).**

*2.* **If prompted, enter your username and password.**

   Some news servers require a username and password.

*3.* **Specify the number of headers (for example, 500) you want to down-load and click Download to proceed.**

   Thunderbird downloads the headers from the newsgroup and displays a list in the upper-right area of the window.

*4.* **From the list of headers, click an item to read that article, as shown in Figure 3-4.**

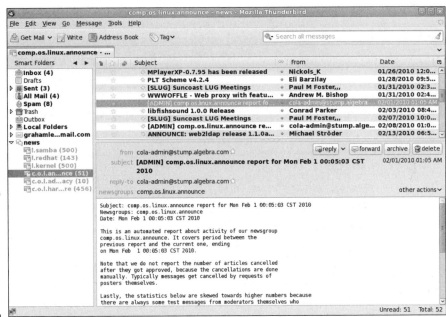

**Figure 3-4:** Click an article to read it in the lower-right part of the window.

Book IV
Chapter 3

Reading Newsgroups and RSS Feeds

To select other subscribed newsgroups, simply click the newsgroup's name in the left side of the window.

## Newsgroup subscriptions

Unlike magazines or newspapers, newsgroups don't require that you sub-scribe to them; you can read any available newsgroup on the news server.

The news server's administrator may decide to exclude certain newsgroups, however; if they aren't included, you can't read them.

The only thing that can be called *subscribing* is indicating the newsgroups you routinely want to read. The news server doesn't receive any of this subscription information — the information is used only by the newsreader to determine what to download from the news server.

## Posting news

You can use any newsreader to post a news article (a new item or a reply to an old posting) to one or more newsgroups. The command for posting a news item depends on the newsreader. For example, in the Thunderbird newsreader, you follow these steps to post an article:

*1.* **Click the Reply button on the toolbar to post a follow-up to a news item you're reading. To post a new news article, click the Write button.**

A window appears where you can compose the message.

*2.* **Type the names of the newsgroups, just as you'd type the addresses of recipients when sending e-mail. Enter the subject and your message.**

For this test posting, type `ignore` as the subject line and enter `misc.test` as the name of the newsgroup. Otherwise, any site that receives your article replies by mail to tell you the article has reached the site; that's in keeping with the purpose of the `misc.test` newsgroup.

*3.* **After you finish composing the message, click Send on the toolbar.**

Thunderbird sends the message to the news server, which in turn sends it to other news servers, and soon it's all over the world!

*4.* **To verify that the test message reaches the newsgroup, choose File⇨Subscribe. Then subscribe to `misc.test` newsgroup (that's where you recently posted the new article).**

To subscribe, click the check box to the right of the group name and then click the Subscribe button.

*5.* **Look at the latest article or one of the most recent ones in `misc.test` to find the article you recently posted.**

If you post an article and read the newsgroup immediately, you see the new article, but that doesn't mean the article has reached other sites on the Internet. After all, your posting shows up on your news server immediately because that's where you posted the article. Because of the store-and-forward model of news distribution, the news article gradually propagates from your news server to others around the world.

The `misc.test` newsgroup provides a way to see whether your news posting is getting around. If you post to that newsgroup and don't include the word *ignore* in the subject, news servers acknowledge receipt of the article by sending an e-mail message to the address listed in the Reply To field of the article's header.

## Using KNode

Debian and SUSE provide KNode as the default newsreader. Typically, you can start KNode by selecting Newsreader from the menu (look in the Internet applications); or choose Applications⇨Internet⇨KNode. If you don't see a choice for Newsreader or KNode in the menus, type **knode** in a terminal window to start KNode.

When KNode runs for the first time, it displays the Configure KNode dialog box, as shown in Figure 3-5, through which you can configure everything you need to read newsgroups and post items to newsgroups.

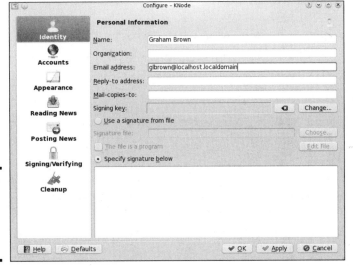

**Figure 3-5:**
Configure
KNode from
this dialog
box.

**Book IV
Chapter 3**

**Reading
Newsgroups
and RSS Feeds**

The left side of the dialog box displays all the items that you can configure, and the right side is where you enter the information for the item that you've selected on the left.

When the Configure KNode dialog box first opens, it prompts for your personal information. Enter your identification information, such as name, e-mail address, and organization — this information is used when you post a new item to a newsgroup.

Then, click Accounts on the left side (refer to Figure 3-5) and then click the Newsgroup Servers tab on the right side to set up information about the news server from which you'll be reading news. Click Add in the Newsgroup Servers tab to display the dialog box shown in Figure 3-6, where you can enter the information about the news server. Your ISP should have provided you with the information needed to access the news server. If the news server requires a login name and a password, you must enter that information as well.

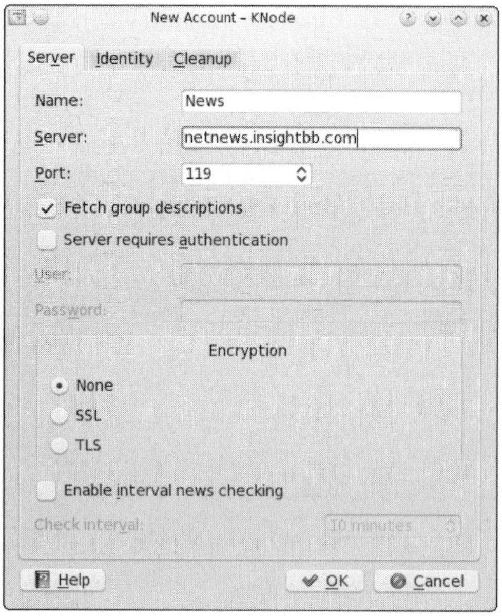

**Figure 3-6:**
Enter
information
about the
news server
in this dialog
box.

After you set up the news account, the KNode window shows the name of the news server on the left. Right-click the server's name and choose Subscribe to Newsgroups from the pop-up menu. A dialog box appears where you can subscribe to selected newsgroups (such as `comp.os.linux.announce`). The first time you access this menu, the list of newsgroups must be fetched. The KNode user interface is similar to many other mail and newsreaders, including Thunderbird.

# Reading and Searching Newsgroups at Web Sites

If you don't have access to newsgroups through your ISP, you can still read newsgroups and post articles to newsgroups at a number of Web sites. Some of them archive old news articles and provide good search capabilities, so you can search these sites for articles related to some question you may have.

The best parts about reading newsgroups through a Web site is that you don't even need access to a news server and you can read news from your Web browser.

Table 3-2 lists Web sites that offer free access to Usenet newsgroups. To get a list of all Web sites that offer newsgroup access (including the ones that charge a fee), use Google (`www.google.com`) and type the search words **usenet newsgroup access**.

| Table 3-2 | Web Sites with Free Access to Usenet Newsgroups |
|---|---|
| **Web Site** | **URL** |
| Google Groups | `http://groups.google.com` |
| mail2web | `http://usenet.mail2web.com` |
| InterBulletin | `http://news.interbulletin.com` |
| Usenet Replayer | `www.usenet-replayer.com` |

One of the best places to read newsgroups, post articles, and search old newsgroup archives is Google Groups (Google's Usenet discussion forums) on the Web at `http://groups.google.com`. At that Web site, you can select a newsgroup to browse and post replies to articles posted on various newsgroups.

The best part of Google Groups is the search capability. You already know how good Google's Web search is; you get that same comprehensive search capability to locate newsgroup postings that relate to your search words. To search newsgroups, fill in the search form at `http://groups.google.com` and press Enter.

To browse newsgroups in Google Groups, ignore the search box and look at the list of high-level newsgroup categories such as `alt`, `comp`, and `soc`. Click the category, and you can gradually drill down to specific newsgroups. When viewing an article in Google Groups, you can click a link that enables you to post a follow-up to that article.

# Reading RSS Feeds

RSS stands for Really Simple Syndication. RSS is a format for *syndicating* — gathering and making available — the content of Web sites, primarily news-oriented sites and blogs. The term *blog* is short for weblog — a frequently updated journal with thoughts, comments, and opinions of the blog's creator. RSS can be used to provide any kind of information that can be broken down into discrete items and put into RSS format. Such RSS-formatted content is an *RSS feed,* and an RSS-aware program can check the feed periodically for changes, download new items, and make them available to the user.

The RSS format is a dialect of XML (eXtensible Markup Language). All RSS files conform to XML 1.0 specification.

Many versions of RSS are available, but three versions — 0.91, 1.0, and 2.0 — are in widespread use. Netscape designed RSS version 0.90 for gathering and displaying headlines from news sites. A simpler version, 0.91, was proposed, and UserLand Software picked up that version for use in its blogging product. At the same time, another noncommercial group had evolved RSS 0.90 into RSS 1.0, which is based on resource description format, or RDF (see www.w3.org/rdf). UserLand didn't accept RSS 1.0 but instead continued evolving RSS 0.91 through versions 0.92, 0.93, and 0.94 and finally settled on RSS 2.0 (skipping 1.0 because that version number was already taken). Currently, many blogs and Web sites use RSS 0.91 for basic syndication (title, URL, and description), RSS 1.0 for readers that use RDF, and RSS 2.0 for advanced syndication with more metadata. (Think of metadata as *data about data,* which is what the RSS format provides: It provides data about other information, such as blogs and news.) RSS 1.0 files have an .rdf extension, whereas RSS 0.91 and 2.0 files have an .xml extension. However, all RSS files are text files that use XML tags.

## Examining an RSS Feed

An RSS feed is a text file with XML tags that describe a Web site's content. You typically use an automated program to periodically generate the RSS feed file, but you can prepare the RSS feed file using a text editor. It's good to know what an RSS feed looks like, just so you can debug problems with the feed.

The specific details of an RSS feed depend on the version of RSS. The simplest feed is RSS 0.91, and here's a typical RSS 0.91 feed:

```
<?xml version="1.0" ?>
<!-- A comment line --->
<rss version="0.91">

<channel> <!--- This tag specifies general information about
    the feed--->
<title>Title of this feed</title>
<link>URL of this feed, for example, http://edulaney.typepad.
    com/</link>
```

```
<description>Brief description of feed</description>
<language>en-us</language>
<item>
<title>Title of this item</title>
<link>URL for this item</link>
<description>Description of this item</description>
</item>
. . . more items . . .
</channel>
</rss>
```

As you can see from that listing, an RSS feed includes a channel with a title, link, description, and language followed by a series of items, each of which has a title, link, and description.

The format is more verbose for RSS 1.0, which uses the RDF format. RSS 1.0 essentially provides the basic information that's in RSS 0.91 and adds more details such as item-level authors, subject, and publishing dates, which RSS 0.91 doesn't support.

## Reading RSS Feeds

Many GUI programs are available for subscribing to RSS feeds and reading items from a feed. These programs are RSS *aggregators* because they can gather information from many RSS feeds and make everything available in a single place.

The two types of RSS aggregators are Web browser plug-ins and standalone programs. Browser plug-ins, such as NewsMonster (www.newsmonster. org), run in a Web browser so that the feeds appear in the Web browser. Standalone programs such as GNOME Straw (http://projects.gnome. org/straw) and KDE Akregator (http://akregator.kde.org) are complete GUI applications and usually look similar to other mail and newsreader programs.

Fedora and SUSE come equipped with the Akregator program, a standalone RSS feed aggregator. To run it, look for a link in the GUI desktop's applications menu (choose Application➪Internet➪Akregator). If you don't see Akregator listed, type **akregator** in a terminal window. In Debian, you can install Akregator by typing **apt-get install akregator** (after typing **su -** to become `root`).

When Akregator first runs, it displays its main window without any RSS feeds. To subscribe to a feed, choose Feed➪Add Feed from the menu or right-click All Feeds in the left pane of the window (see Figure 3-7) and select Add Feed from the pop-up menu. Then type the URL for the feed in the Add Feed dialog box and click OK. For example, to read Slashdot's RSS feed, type

**http://slashdot.org/index.rss**. The feed's title appears in the left pane of the window. Click the feed title to view the items in this feed. Then you can click an item in the upper-right pane, and that item appears in the lower-right pane, as shown in Figure 3-7. You can add many different RSS feeds, organize them into folders, and browse them in Akregator.

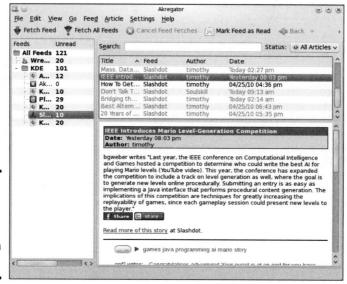

**Figure 3-7:** You can organize and read RSS feeds in Akregator.

# Chapter 4: Using FTP

## In This Chapter

✔ Using the GNOME FTP client

✔ Using any Web browser as an FTP client

✔ Getting to know the FTP commands

*J*ust as the name implies, *File Transfer Protocol* (FTP) is used to transfer files between computers. For example, if your Internet service provider (ISP) gives you space for a personal Web site, you may have already used FTP to upload the files making up the Web site. Using an FTP client on your computer, you log in to your ISP account, provide your password, and then copy the files from your home system to the ISP's server.

You can also use FTP to download other files anonymously, such as open source software from other computers on the Internet — in which case, you don't need an account on the remote system to download files. You can simply log in using anonymous as the username and provide your e-mail address as the password. (In fact, your Web browser can do this on your behalf, so you may not even know this process is happening.) This type of anonymous FTP is great for distributing files to anyone who wants them. For example, a hardware vendor might use anonymous FTP to provide updated device drivers to anyone who needs them.

Linux comes with several FTP clients, both command-line ones and GUI (graphical user interface) ones. This chapter introduces you to a few GUI FTP clients and a command-line FTP client. It also describes the commands you use to work with remote directories.

Based upon your distribution, and version, you may need to install the FTP clients discussed in this chapter.

## Using Graphical FTP Clients

You can use one of the following GUI FTP clients in Linux:

✦ **gFTP:** A graphical FTP client for GNOME at (http://gftp.seul.org)

✦ **KFTPGrabber:** A graphical FTP client for KDE (K Desktop Environment) at www.kftp.org

✦ **Web browser:** A browser such as Firefox, for anonymous FTP downloads

For uploading files, you may want to use gFTP because you typically have to provide a username and password for such transfers. Web browsers work fine for anonymous downloads, which is how you typically download software from the Internet.

All three GUI FTP clients are discussed in the next three sections.

## Using gFTP

GNOME comes with gFTP, a graphical FTP client. gFTP isn't installed by default, but you can download it from `http://gftp.seul.org` and install it easily. In some distributions, gFTP may be included in a package already, and you just have to install that package.

In Debian, type **su -** in a terminal window, enter the `root` password, and then type **apt-get install gftp**.

In Fedora, log in as `root`, choose Add/Remove Software from the System Settings menu, and search for gFTP. Choose the package that appears in the search list (`gftp-1:2.0.18-7.fc8`, as of this writing), click Apply, and the software will be installed.

In Fedora, start gFTP by choosing Applications➪Internet➪gFTP. (If you don't see gFTP, log in as `root` and type **yum install gftp**, and then look for it in the menu again.) In other distributions, you can find gFTP in the main menu. The gFTP window appears, as shown in Figure 4-1.

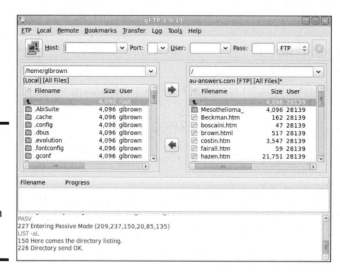

**Figure 4-1:** The gFTP window just after opening a connection to an FTP server.

The gFTP window has a menu bar with menus for performing various tasks. Just below the menu bar is a toolbar with a number of buttons and text fields. Here you can type the name or IP address of the remote host, and the username and password needed to log in to the remote host. Figure 4-1 shows the gFTP window after you fill in this information and establish a connection with the remote host by clicking the button with the icon showing two computers (the leftmost one on the toolbar).

To upload or download files with gFTP, follow these steps:

*1.* **Fill in the hostname or the IP address of the remote system in the Host field.**

If you've used that host before, you can select it from the drop-down list that appears when you click the downward-pointing arrow next to the Host field.

*2.* **Provide the username in the User field and the password in the Pass field, and then click the button with the icon showing two computers (to the left of the Host field).**

This operation causes gFTP to connect to your chosen host and to log in with the username and password you provided. The lower part of the gFTP window shows the FTP protocol messages exchanged between the two systems.

*3.* **Observe the lower part of the screen for any indication of error messages.**

The directory listing of the remote system appears in the right half of the gFTP window. The left half shows the current local directory.

*4.* **To upload one or more files from the current system to the remote system, select the files in the list on the left and then click the right-pointing arrow button.**

*5.* **To download files from the remote system, select the filenames in the list on the right and click the left-pointing arrow button.**

*6.* **When you have finished transferring files, choose FTP⇨Quit.**

As these steps show, transferring files with a GUI FTP client, such as gFTP, is simple.

Believe it or not, gFTP isn't for FTP transfers alone. It can also transfer files using the HTTP (HyperText Transfer Protocol) and secure file transfers using the Secure Shell (SSH) protocol.

**Book IV**
**Chapter 4**

**Using FTP**

## Introducing KFTPGrabber

KFTPGrabber is a GUI FTP client for KDE. You find it in the main menu (in the Internet category) on KDE desktops. In Debian, type **apt-get install kftpgrabber** to install KFTPGrabber (after you type **su -** to become `root`).

In Fedora, log in as `root`, choose System Settings➪Add/Remove Software, and search for KFTPGrabber. Choose the package that appears in the search list (`kftpgrabber`) and then click Apply. Click Continue at the prompt, and the software will be installed.

When the main KFTPGrabber window appears, it displays your home folder in a view similar to that in Windows Explorer. To connect to an FTP server, choose File➪Quick Connect. A dialog box like the one shown in Figure 4-2 prompts you for the hostname of the FTP server as well as the username and password.

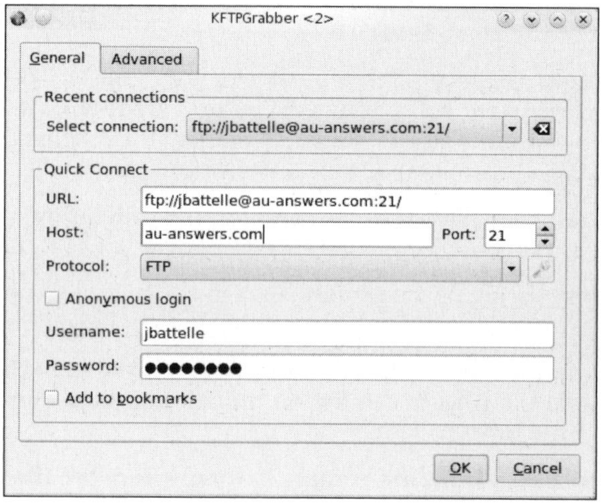

**Figure 4-2:**
Enter information about the remote FTP server and click OK.

After entering the requested information, click OK. KFTPGrabber establishes a connection to the remote FTP server. In the KFTPGrabber main window, shown in Figure 4-3, you see both the local and remote directories side by side.

FTP transfers become just normal drag-and-drop file copying: Transfer files by simply dragging them from one system's folder and dropping them on the other system's folder.

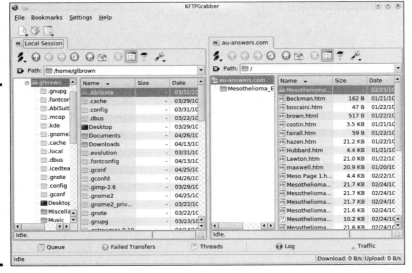

**Figure 4-3:**
KFTP-
Grabber
window
displays
the local
directory
and the
remote FTP
server's
directory.

When you finish using KFTPGrabber, choose File⇨Quit.

## Using a Web browser as an FTP client

Any Web browser can act as an FTP client, but such programs are best for anonymous FTP downloads, where the Web browser can log in using the `anonymous` username and any password.

For example, you can use the Firefox Web browser as an FTP client. All you have to know is how to write the URL so that the Web browser can tell that you want to download a file using FTP. The syntax of the FTP URL is

```
ftp://hostname/pathname
```

The first part (`ftp://`) indicates that you want an FTP transfer. The *host name* part is the name of the FTP server (the name often starts with `ftp` — for example, `ftp.wiley.com`). The *pathname* is the full directory path and filename of the file that you want to download.

If you simply provide the hostname for the FTP server, the Web browser displays the contents of the anonymous FTP directory. If you want to access anonymous FTP on your Linux system, start Firefox (click the Web browser icon on the GNOME panel), type the FTP URL in the Location text box, and press Enter.

Figure 4-4 shows a typical appearance of an FTP directory in Firefox. You can click folders to see their contents and download any files. You can access your local system by using Firefox's FTP capabilities; for example, type **ftp://localhost/pub/** to access the pub directory. (You won't get a response from your system if you're not running an FTP server or if you've set up your firewall so that no FTP connections are allowed.)

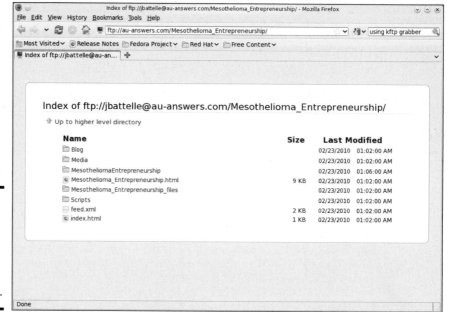

**Figure 4-4:** You can use a Web browser to download files from FTP servers.

In Debian and Fedora, log in as root and type **/etc/init.d/vsftpd start** (in a terminal window) to start the FTP server. In SUSE, the xinetd super server controls the FTP server vsftpd. The /etc/xinetd.d/vsftpd configuration file specifies how vsftpd is started. See Book VII, Chapter 1 for more information about xinetd configuration files.

The same approach of accessing anonymous FTP sites works if you type the hostname of some other anonymous FTP server. For example, try typing the following URL:

```
ftp://ftp.netscape.com/
```

You get the directory of the ftp.netscape.com server.

# Using the Command-Line FTP Client

Knowing how to use FTP from the command line is a good idea. For example, if your GUI desktop isn't working, you may need to download some files to fix the problem; you can do so if you know how to use the command-line FTP client. The command-line ftp client is available in all Linux distributions and using it is not difficult.

The best way to figure out the command-line FTP client is to try it out. The command is ftp, and you can try out the ftp commands from your Linux system. You don't even need an Internet connection because you can use the ftp command to connect to your own system.

Note that the output from the ftp command might be different because some distributions, such as Debian, use a text mode version of gFTP as the command-line FTP client.

In the following sample FTP session, the command-line FTP client was used to log in and browse the directories on a Linux system. Here's the listing illustrating interaction with a typical command-line FTP client:

```
ftp localhost
Connected to localhost.localdomain.
220 (vsFTPd 2.0.3)
Name (localhost:jdoe): (press Enter.)
331 Please specify the password.
Password: (enter the password for the user.)
230 Login successful.
Remote system type is UNIX.
Using binary mode to transfer files.
ftp> help
Commands may be abbreviated. Commands are:
! debug mdir qc send
$ dir mget sendport site
account disconnect mkdir put size
append exit mls pwd status
ascii form mode quit struct
bell get modtime quote system
binary glob mput recv sunique
bye hash newer reget tenex
case help nmap rstatus tick
cd idle nlist rhelp trace
cdup image ntrans rename type
chmod lcd open reset user
close ls prompt restart umask
cr macdef passive rmdir verbose
delete mdelete proxy runique ?
```

```
ftp> help mget (to get help on a specific command.)
mget get multiple files
ftp> cd /var (This changes directory to /var.)
250 Directory successfully changed.
ftp> ls (This command lists the contents of the directory.)
227 Entering Passive Mode (127,0,0,1,38,142)
150 Here comes the directory listing.
. . . lines deleted . . .
226 Directory send OK.
ftp> bye (This command ends the session.)
```

As the listing shows, you can start the command-line FTP client by typing the command **ftp** *hostname*, where *hostname* is the name of the system you want to access. When the FTP client establishes a connection with the FTP server at the remote system, the FTP server prompts you for a username and password. After you supply the information, the FTP client displays the ftp> prompt, and you can begin typing commands to perform specific tasks. If you can't remember a specific FTP command, type **help** to view a list of them. You can get additional help for a specific command by typing **help** *command*, where *command* is the command for which you want help.

Many FTP commands are similar to the Linux commands for navigating the file system. For example, cd changes directory, pwd prints the name of the current working directory, and ls lists the contents of the current directory. Two other common commands are get and put: get is what downloads a file from the remote system to your system, and put uploads (sends) a file from your system to the remote host.

Table 4-1 describes some commonly used FTP commands. You don't have to type the entire FTP command. For a long command, you have to type only the first few characters — enough to identify the command uniquely. For example, to delete a file, you can type **dele**, and to change the file transfer mode to binary, you can type **bin**.

| Table 4-1 | Common FTP Commands |
|-----------|---------------------|
| *Command* | *Description* |
| ! | Executes a shell command on the local system. For example, !ls lists the contents of the current directory on the local system. |
| ? | Displays a list of commands (same as help). |
| append | Appends a local file to a remote file. |

| Command | Description |
|---|---|
| ascii | Sets the file transfer type to ASCII (or plain text). This command is the default file transfer type. |
| binary | Sets the file transfer type to binary. |
| bye | Ends the FTP session with the remote FTP server and quits the FTP client. |
| cd | Changes the directory on the remote system. For example, `cd /pub/Linux` changes the remote directory to `/pub/Linux`. |
| chmod | Changes the permission settings of a remote file. For example, `chmod 644 index.html` changes the permission settings of the `index.html` file on the remote system. |
| close | Ends the FTP session with the FTP server and returns to the FTP client's prompt. |
| delete | Deletes a remote file. For example, `delete bigimage.jpg` deletes that file on the remote system. |
| dir | Lists the contents of the current directory on the remote system. |
| disconnect | Ends the FTP session and returns to the FTP client's prompt. (This command is the same as `close`.) |
| get | Downloads a remote file. For example, `get junk.tar.gz junk.tgz` downloads the file `junk.tar.gz` from the remote system and saves it as the file `junk.tgz` on the local system. |
| hash | Turns on or off the hash mark (#) printing that shows the progress of the file transfer. When this feature is turned on, a hash mark prints on-screen for every 1,024 bytes transferred from the remote system. (It's the command-line version of a progress bar.) |
| help | Displays a list of commands. |
| image | Same as `binary`. |
| lcd | Changes the current directory on the local system. For example, `lcd /var/ftp/pub` changes the current local directory to `/var/ftp/pub`. |
| ls | Lists the contents of the current remote directory. |
| mdelete | Deletes multiple files on a remote system. For example, `mdelete *.jpg` deletes all remote files with names ending in `.jpg` in the current directory. |
| mdir | Lists multiple remote files and saves the listing in a specified local file. For example, `mdir /usr/share/doc/w* wlist` saves the listing in the local file named `wlist`. |

*(continued)*

**Book IV
Chapter 4**

**Using FTP**

## Table 4-1 *(continued)*

| Command | Description |
|---------|-------------|
| mget | Downloads multiple files. For example, `mget *.jpg` downloads all files with names ending in `.jpg`. If the prompt is turned on, the FTP client asks for confirmation before downloading each file. |
| mkdir | Creates a directory on the remote system. `mkdir images` creates a directory named `images` in the current directory on the remote system. |
| mls | Same as `mdir`. |
| mput | Uploads multiple files. For example, `mput *.jpg` sends all files with names ending in `.jpg` to the remote system. If the prompt is turned on, the FTP client asks for confirmation before sending each file. |
| open | Opens a connection to the FTP server on the specified host. For example, `open ftp.netscape.com` connects to the FTP server on the host `ftp.netscape.com`. |
| prompt | Turns the prompt on or off. When the prompt is on, the FTP client prompts you for confirmation before downloading or uploading each file during a multiple-file transfer. |
| put | Sends a file to the remote system. For example, `put index.html` sends the `index.html` file from the local system to the remote system. |
| pwd | Displays the full path name of the current directory on the remote system. When you log in as a user, the initial current working directory is your home directory. |
| quit | Same as `bye`. |
| recv | Same as `get`. |
| rename | Renames a file on the remote system. For example, `rename old.html new.html` renames the file `old.html` to `new.html` on the remote system. |
| rmdir | Deletes a directory on the remote system. For example, `rmdir images` deletes the `images` directory in the current directory of the remote system. |
| send | Same as `put`. |
| size | Shows the size of a remote file. For example, `size bigfile.tar.gz` shows the size of that remote file. |
| status | Shows the current status of the FTP client. |
| user | Sends new user information to the FTP server. For example, user `jdoe` sends the username `jdoe`; the FTP server then prompts for the password for that username. |

When downloading files from the Internet, you almost always want to transfer the files in binary mode because the software is usually archived and compressed in a binary form. (Its files aren't plain text files.) So always use the binary command to set the mode to binary. Then use the get command to download the files.

When transferring multiple files with similar names (such as image1.jpg, image2.jpg, and so on), type **prompt** to turn off prompting. (Otherwise the FTP client will ask you after each file transfer whether you want to transfer the next file.) Then type **mget** followed by the filename with a wildcard. For example, to download all files with names starting with image and ending with the .jpg extension, type **mget image*.jpg**.

# Book V

# Administration

The 5th Wave                    By Rich Tennant

"A centralized security management system
sounds fine, but then what would we do
with all the dogs?"

# Contents at a Glance

## Chapter 1: Introducing Basic System Administration . . . . . . . . . . . . .291

Taking Stock of System Administration Tasks.........................................291
Introducing Some GUI Sysadmin Tools ....................................................293
How to Become root ................................................................................298
Understanding How Linux Boots................................................................301
Taking Stock of Linux System Configuration Files ..................................307
Monitoring System Performance..............................................................310
Viewing System Information with the /proc File System........................315
Understanding Linux Devices ..................................................................319
Managing Loadable Driver Modules ........................................................322
Scheduling Jobs in Linux ........................................................................324

## Chapter 2: Managing Users and Groups . . . . . . . . . . . . . . . . . . . . . . .331

Adding User Accounts ..............................................................................331
Understanding the /etc/passwd File ........................................................335
Managing Groups......................................................................................337
Exploring the User Environment ..............................................................338
Changing User and Group Ownership of Files ........................................340

## Chapter 3: Managing File Systems . . . . . . . . . . . . . . . . . . . . . . . . . . .343

Exploring the Linux File System ..............................................................343
Sharing Files with NFS..............................................................................350
Backing Up and Restoring Files ..............................................................352
Accessing a DOS or Windows File System................................................359
Using mtools..............................................................................................362

## Chapter 4: Installing and Updating Applications . . . . . . . . . . . . . . . .367

Working with RPM Files............................................................................367
Working with DEB Files............................................................................374
Building Software Packages from Source Files ........................................378
Updating Linux Applications Online ........................................................382

# Chapter 1: Introducing Basic System Administration

## In This Chapter

✔ **Introducing the GUI sysadmin tools**

✔ **Becoming root**

✔ **Understanding the system startup process**

✔ **Taking stock of the system configuration files**

✔ **Viewing system information through the /proc file system**

✔ **Monitoring system performance**

✔ **Managing devices**

✔ **Scheduling jobs**

*S*ystem administration, or *sysadmin,* refers to whatever has to be done to keep a computer system up and running. The *system administrator* (the *sysadmin*) is whoever is in charge of taking care of these tasks.

If you're running Linux at home or in a small office, you're most likely the system administrator for your systems. Or maybe you're the system administrator for an entire LAN full of Linux systems. Regardless of your position or title, this chapter will introduce you to basic system administration procedures and show you how to perform some common tasks.

## Taking Stock of System Administration Tasks

So what are system administration tasks? An off-the-cuff reply is *anything you have to do to keep the system running well.* More accurately, though, a system administrator's duties include

+ **Adding and removing user accounts:** You have to add new user accounts and remove unnecessary user accounts. If a user forgets the password, you have to change the password.

+ **Managing the printing system:** You have to turn the print queue on or off, check the print queue's status, and delete print jobs if necessary.

✦ **Installing, configuring, and upgrading the operating system and various utilities:** You have to install or upgrade parts of the Linux operating system and other software that are part of the operating system.

✦ **Installing new software:** You have to install software that comes in various package formats, such as RPM or DEB. You also have to download and unpack software that comes in source-code form — and then build executable programs from the source code.

✦ **Managing hardware:** Sometimes, you have to add new hardware and install drivers so the devices work properly.

✦ **Making backups:** You have to back up files, to a DVD drive, a USB memory stick, an external hard drive, or on tape.

✦ **Mounting and unmounting file systems:** When you want to access the files on a CD-ROM, for example, you have to mount that CD-ROM's file system on one of the directories in your Linux file system. You may also have to mount floppy disks, in both Linux format and DOS format.

✦ **Automating tasks:** You have to schedule Linux tasks to take place automatically (at specific times) or periodically (at regular intervals).

✦ **Monitoring the system's performance:** You may want to keep an eye on system performance to see where the processor is spending most of its time and to see the amount of free and used memory in the system.

✦ **Starting and shutting down the system:** Although starting the system typically involves nothing more than powering up the PC, you do have to take some care when you shut down your Linux system. If your system is set up for a graphical login screen, you can perform the shutdown operation by choosing a menu item from the login screen. Otherwise, use the `shutdown` command to stop all programs before turning off your PC's power switch.

✦ **Monitoring network status:** If you have a network presence (whether a LAN, a DSL line, or a cable modem connection), you may want to check the status of various network interfaces and make sure your network connection is up and running.

✦ **Setting up host and network security:** You have to make sure that system files are protected and that your system can defend itself against attacks over the network.

✦ **Monitoring security:** You have to keep an eye on any intrusions, usually by checking the log files.

That's a long list of tasks! Not all these items are covered in this chapter, but the rest of this minibook describes most of these tasks. The focus in this chapter is on some of the basics, such as using the GUI tools, explaining how to become `root` (the superuser), describing the system configuration files, and showing you how to monitor system performance, manage devices, and set up periodic jobs.

# Introducing Some GUI Sysadmin Tools

Each Linux distribution comes with GUI tools for performing system administration tasks. The GUI tools prompt you for input and then run the necessary Linux commands to perform the task. The following sections briefly introduce the GUI sysadmin tools in Debian, Fedora, Knoppix, SUSE, Ubuntu, and Xandros.

## GUI sysadmin tools in Debian

Debian uses the GNOME desktop by default and provides some GUI tools for performing sysadmin tasks. These tools are available by choosing Applications➪System Tools. Table 1-1 lists some common tasks and the menu choices you use to start the GUI tool that enables you to perform that task.

**Table 1-1    Performing Sysadmin Tasks with GUI Tools in Debian**

| To Do This | Choose the Following from the Debian GNOME Desktop |
|---|---|
| Add or remove software packages | Applications➪System Tools➪Synaptic Package Manager |
| Change the date or time | Applications➪System Tools➪Time and Date |
| Change a password | Main Menu➪Settings➪Change Password |
| Configure a desktop | Applications➪Desktop Preferences |
| Configure a network | Applications➪Networking |
| Format a floppy | Applications➪System Tools➪Floppy Formatter |
| Manage printers | Applications➪System Tools➪Printers |
| Manage user accounts | Applications➪System Tools➪Users and Groups |
| Monitor system performance | Applications➪System Tools➪System Monitor |
| View system logs | Applications➪System Tools➪System Log |

## GUI sysadmin tools in Fedora

Fedora comes with a set of GUI system configuration tools that can ease the burden of performing typical sysadmin chores. Table 1-2 briefly summarizes the menu choices you use to start a GUI tool for a specific task.

| Table 1-2 | Starting GUI Sysadmin Tools in Fedora |
|---|---|
| *To Configure or Manage This* | *Start GUI Tool by Choosing This* |
| Date and time | System➪Administration➪Date & Time |
| Disks and DVD/CD-ROM | Applications➪System Tools➪Disk Utility |
| Display settings | System➪Preference➪Display |
| Firewall settings | System➪Administration➪Firewall |
| Internet connection | System➪Preferences➪Network Connectivity |
| Network | System➪Preferences➪Network Connectivity |
| Preferences such as desktop and password | System➪Preferences |
| Printer | System➪Administration➪Printing |
| Software | System➪Administration➪Add/Remove Software |
| System performance | Applications➪System Tools➪System Monitor |
| User accounts | System➪Administration➪Users and Groups |

## GUI sysadmin tools in Knoppix

Knoppix is a Live CD distribution that you can use either to try out Linux or to fix problems in an existing Linux system. As such, Knoppix comes with several GUI tools that you can use for system administration tasks. Table 1-3 summarizes some of the GUI tools in Knoppix.

| Table 1-3 | Using GUI tools for Sysadmin Tasks in Knoppix |
|---|---|
| *To Do This* | *Choose This from the Knoppix GUI Desktop* |
| Configure a desktop | Main Menu➪Preferences➪Appearances |
| | Main Menu➪Preferences➪Openbook Configuration Manager |
| Configure KDE | Main Menu➪System Tools➪Configuration Editor |
| Configure a network | Main Menu➪Preferences➪ISDN Connection |
| Configure a printer | Main Menu➪Preferences➪KNOPPIX➪Printer Configuration |
| Manage disk partitions (for troubleshooting existing Linux installations) | Main Menu➪Preferences➪GParted |

| To Do This | Choose This from the Knoppix GUI Desktop |
|---|---|
| Change the root password | Main Menu⇨Preferences⇨KNOPPIX⇨Set password for root |
| See disk usage | Main Menu⇨System Tools⇨Disk usage analyzer |
| Configure software | Main Menu⇨Preferences⇨KNOPPIX⇨ Synaptic Package Manager |
| View log files | Main Menu⇨System Tools⇨Log file viewer |

## GUI sysadmin tools in SUSE

In SUSE, from the main menu, choose YaST to start your system administration tasks in the YaST Control Center. Figure 1-1 shows the YaST Control Center window.

**Figure 1-1:** YaST Control Center is your starting point for many sysadmin tasks in SUSE.

The left side of the YaST Control Center shows icons for the categories of tasks you can perform. The right side shows icons for specific tasks in the currently selected category. When you click an icon on the right side of the YaST Control Center, a new YaST window appears and enables you to perform that task.

Table 1-4 summarizes the tasks for each of the category icons on the left side of the YaST Control Center. As you can see from the entries in the second column of Table 1-4, YaST Control Center is truly one-stop shopping for all of your sysadmin chores.

| Table 1-4 | Tasks by Category in the YaST Control Center |
|---|---|
| *This Category* | *Enables You to Configure or Manage the Following* |
| Software | Online Update, Installation Source, Installation in Xen Environment, Installation into Directory, Media Check, Patch CD Update, Software Management, System Update |
| Hardware | Bluetooth, CD-ROM Drives, Disk Controller, Graphics Card and Monitor, Hardware Information, IDE DMA Mode, Infrared Device, Joystick, Keyboard Layout, Mouse Model, Printer, Scanner, Sound, TV Card |
| System | `/etc/sysconfig` Editor, Boot Loader Configuration, Boot or Rescue Floppy, Date and Time, LVM, Language, PCI Device Drivers, Partitioner, Power Management, Powertweak, Profile Manager, System Backup, System Restoration, System Services (run level) |
| Network Devices | DSL, Fax, ISDN, Modem, Network Card, Phone Answering Machine |
| Network Services | DHCP Server, DNS Server, DNS Host and Name, HTTP Server, Host Names, Kerberos Client, LDAP Client, Mail Transfer Agent, NFS Client, NFS Server, NIS Client, NIS Server, NTP Client, Network Services (xinetd), Proxy, Remote Administration, Routing, SLP Browser, Samba Client, Samba Server, TFTP Server |
| Security and Users | Firewall, Group Management, Local Security, User Management |
| Miscellaneous | Autoinstallation, Post a Support Query, Vendor Driver CD, View Start-up Log, View System Log |

## GUI sysadmin tools in Ubuntu

Ubuntu uses the GNOME desktop, and its menu organization is similar to that of Fedora's GNOME desktop. You can find Ubuntu's GUI system administration tools in the following menus: Applications⇨System Tools, System⇨Administration, and System⇨Preferences. Table 1-5 lists the menu choices for starting some of the GUI tools.

| Table 1-5 | Starting GUI Sysadmin Tools in Ubuntu |
|---|---|
| *To Configure or Manage This* | *Start GUI Tool by Choosing This* |
| Date and time | System⇨Administration⇨Time and Date |
| Display settings | System⇨Preferences⇨Display |

| To Configure or Manage This | Start GUI Tool by Choosing This |
|---|---|
| Hardware | System⇨Administration⇨Hardware Drivers |
| Internet connection | System⇨Administration⇨Network Tools |
| Network | System⇨Administration⇨Network Tools |
| Preferences such as desk-top and default applications | System⇨Preferences |
| Printer | System⇨Administration⇨Printing |
| Software | System⇨Administration⇨Software Sources Manager |
| System logs | Applications⇨System Tools⇨System Log |
| System performance | System⇨Administration⇨System Monitor |
| Updates | System⇨Administration⇨Ubuntu Update Manager |
| User accounts | System⇨Administration⇨Users and Groups |

## GUI sysadmin tools in Xandros

Xandros is designed to be a desktop operating system, and as such, you can access everything easily from the desktop. For most sysadmin tasks, you start at the Xandros Control Center — choose Main Menu⇨Control Center to get there. (Figure 1-2 shows you what you find when you do get there.)

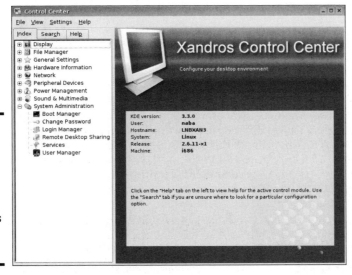

**Figure 1-2:**
You can perform many sysadmin tasks from the Xandros Control Center.

The left side of the window shows a tree menu of task categories. Click the plus sign next to a category to view the subcategories. When you click a specific task, the right side of the window displays the GUI through which you can perform that task.

For some tasks, such as mounting file systems or adding printers, you can open the Xandros File Manager as a system administrator by choosing Main Menu⇨Applications⇨System⇨Administrator Tools⇨Xandros File Manager (Administrator). You're prompted for the `root` password. Figure 1-3 shows the Xandros File Manager window from which you can perform some sysadmin tasks.

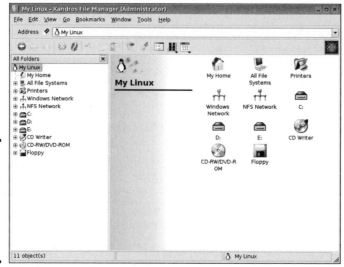

**Figure 1-3:** For some sysadmin tasks, use the Xandros File Manager.

# How to Become root

You have to log in as `root` to perform system administration tasks. The `root` user is the superuser and the only account with all the privileges needed to do anything in the system.

Common wisdom says you should *not* normally log in as `root`. When you're `root`, you can easily delete all the files with one misstep — especially when you're typing commands. For example, you type the command `rm *.html` to delete all files that have the `.html` extension. But what if you accidentally press the spacebar after the asterisk (*)? The shell takes the command to be `rm * .html` and — because * matches any filename — deletes everything in the current directory. Seems implausible until it happens to you!

## Using the su - command

If you're logged in as a normal user, how do you do any system administration chores? Well, you become `root` for the time being. If you're working at a terminal window or console, type

```
su -
```

Then enter the `root` password in response to the prompt. From this point, you're `root`. Do whatever you have to do. To return to your usual self, type

```
exit
```

That's it! It's that easy.

By the way, Knoppix has a `root` user but doesn't have a `root` password, so you can become `root` by simply typing **su** – at the shell prompt in a terminal window. Also, Ubuntu doesn't have a `root` user. To perform any task that requires `root` privileges in Ubuntu, you must type **sudo** followed by the command and then provide your normal user password when prompted.

## Becoming root for the GUI utilities

Most Linux distributions include GUI utilities to perform system administration chores. If you use any of these GUI utilities to perform a task that requires you to be `root`, the utility typically pops up a dialog box that prompts you for the `root` password, as shown in Figure 1-4 (except in Ubuntu, where the GUI tools prompt for your normal user password). Just type the password and press Enter. If you don't want to use the utility, click Cancel.

**Figure 1-4:**
Type
the root
password
and press
Enter to
gain root
privileges.

## Recovering from a forgotten root password

To perform system administration tasks, you have to know the `root` password. What happens if you forget the `root` password? Not to worry. You can reset the `root` password by following these steps:

1. **Reboot the PC (select Reboot as you log out of the GUI screen) or power up as usual.**

   As soon you see the graphical GRUB boot loader screen that shows the names of the operating systems, you can boot. If your system runs the LILO boot loader, press Ctrl+X, type **linux single** at the boot: prompt, and press Enter. Then proceed to Step 4. If you don't see the graphical loader screen on reboot, it might not be installed (which can occasionally occur when choosing to install from a Live CD). If this is the case, it is recommended that you reinstall from the CD.

2. **If you have more than one operating system installed, use the arrow key to select Linux as your operating system and then press the A key.**

   GRUB prompts you for commands to add to its default boot command.

3. **Press the spacebar, and then type** single **and press Enter.**

   Linux starts as usual but runs in a single-user mode that doesn't require you to log in. After Linux starts, you see the following command-line prompt similar to the following:

   ```
   sh-3.00#
   ```

4. **Type the** passwd **command to change the** root **password as follows:**

   ```
   sh-3.00# passwd
   Changing password for user root.
   New password:
   ```

5. **Type the new root password that you want to use (it doesn't appear on-screen) and then press Enter.**

   Linux asks for the password again, like this:

   ```
   Retype new password:
   ```

6. **Type the password again and press Enter.**

   If you enter the same password both times, the passwd command changes the root password.

7. **Now type** reboot **to reboot the PC.**

   After Linux starts, it displays the familiar login screen. Now you can log in as root with the new password.

In SUSE Linux, in Step 3, type **single init=/bin/sh** (instead of **single**) and before proceeding to Step 4, at the command-line prompt, type **mount / -n -0 remount,rw**. Then perform Steps 4 through 6 to change the root password. After changing the password, type **mount / -n -o remount,ro**. Then continue to Step 7 and reboot the PC.

Make sure that your Linux PC is *physically* secure. As these steps show, anyone who can physically access your Linux PC can simply reboot, set a new `root` password, and do whatever he or she wants with the system. Another way to protect against resetting the password is to set a GRUB password, which causes GRUB to require a valid password before it boots Linux. Of course, you must then remember to enter the GRUB password every time you boot your system!

# Understanding How Linux Boots

Knowing the sequence in which Linux starts processes as it boots is important. You can use this knowledge to start and stop services, such as the Web server and Network File System (NFS). The next few sections provide you with an overview of how Linux boots and starts the initial set of processes. These sections also familiarize you with the shell scripts that start various services on a Linux system.

## Understanding the init process

When Linux boots, it loads and runs the core operating system program from the hard drive. The core operating system is designed to run other programs. A process named `init` starts the initial set of processes on your Linux system.

To see the processes currently running on the system, type

```
ps ax | more
```

You get an output listing that starts like this:

```
PID TTY STAT TIME COMMAND
1 ? S 0:22 init [2]
```

The first column, with the heading PID, shows a number for each process. *PID* stands for process ID (identification) — a sequential number assigned by the Linux kernel. The first entry in the process list, with a PID of 1, is the `init` process. It's the first process, and it starts all other processes in your Linux system. That's why `init` is sometimes referred to as the *mother of all processes.*

What the `init` process starts depends on

✦ **The run level,** an identifier that identifies a system configuration in which only a selected group of processes can exist.

✦ **The contents of the `/etc/inittab` file,** a text file that specifies which processes to start at different run levels.

✦ **A number of shell scripts that are executed at specific run levels.** (The scripts are located in the `/etc/init.d` directory and a number of subdirectories in `/etc` — these subdirectories have names that begin with `rc`.)

Most Linux distributions use seven run levels — 0 through 6. The meaning of the run levels differs from one distribution to another. Table 1-6 shows the meanings of the run levels and points out some of the actions specific to Fedora, Debian, SUSE, Ubuntu, and Xandros.

| **Table 1-6** | **Run Levels in Linux** |
|---|---|
| *Run Level* | *Meaning* |
| 0 | Shut down the system |
| 1 | Run in single-user standalone mode (no one else can log in; you work at the text console) |
| 2 | Run in multiuser mode (Debian, Ubuntu, and Xandros use run level 2 as the default run level) |
| 3 | Run in full multiuser mode (used for text mode login in Fedora and SUSE) |
| 4 | Run in full multiuser mode (unused in Fedora and SUSE) |
| 5 | Run in full multiuser mode (used as the default run level with graphical login in Fedora and SUSE) |
| 6 | Reboot the system |

The current run level together with the contents of the `/etc/inittab` file control which processes `init` starts in Linux. The default run level is 2 in Debian, Ubuntu, and Xandros. In Fedora and SUSE, run level 3 is used for text mode login screens and 5 for the graphical login screen. You can change the default run level by editing a line in the `/etc/inittab` file.

To check the current run level, type the following command in a terminal window:

```
/sbin/runlevel
```

In Debian, the `runlevel` command prints an output like this:

```
N 2
```

The first character of the output shows the previous run level (N means no previous run level), and the second character shows the current run level (2). In this case, the system started at run level 2. If you're in a GUI desktop in Fedora, the `runlevel` command should show 5 as the current run level.

## Examining the /etc/inittab file

The `/etc/inittab` file is the key to understanding the processes that `init` starts at various run levels. You can look at the contents of the file by using the `more` command, as follows:

```
more /etc/inittab
```

To see the contents of the `/etc/inittab` file with the `more` command, you don't have to log in as `root`.

To interpret the contents of the `/etc/inittab` file, follow these steps:

*1.* **Look for the line that contains the phrase initdefault.**

Here's that line from the `/etc/inittab` file from a Debian system:

```
id:2:initdefault:
```

That line shows the default run level. In this case, it's 2.

*2.* **Find all the lines that specify what init runs at run level 2.**

Look for a line that has a 2 between the first two colons (:). Here's a relevant line in Debian:

```
l2:2:wait:/etc/init.d/rc 2
```

This line specifies that `init` executes the file `/etc/init.d/rc` with 2 as an argument.

If you look at the file `/etc/init.d/rc` in a Debian system, you find it's a shell script. You can study this file to see how it starts various processes for run levels 1 through 5.

Each entry in the `/etc/inittab` file tells `init` what to do at one or more run levels — you simply list all run levels at which the process runs. Each `inittab` entry has four fields — separated by colons — in the following format:

```
id:runlevels:action:process
```

Table 1-7 shows what each field means.

| Table 1-7 | Fields in Each inittab Entry |
|---|---|
| *Field* | *Meaning* |
| id | A unique one- or two-character identifier. The init process uses this field internally. You can use any identifier you want, as long as you don't use the same identifier on more than one line. |
| runlevels | A sequence of zero or more characters, each denoting a run level. For example, if the runlevels field is 12345, that entry applies to each of the run levels 1 through 5. This field is ignored if the action field is set to sysinit, boot, or bootwait. |
| action | What the init process will do with this entry. If this field is initdefault, for example, init interprets the run levels field as the default run level. If this field is set to wait, init starts the program or script specified in the process field and waits until that process exits. |
| process | Name of the script or program that init starts. Some settings of the action field require no process field. For example, when the action field is initdefault, there's no need for a process field. |

## *Trying a new run level with the init command*

To try a new run level, you don't have to change the default run level in the /etc/inittab file. If you log in as root, you can change the run level (and, consequently, the processes that run in Linux) by typing **init** followed by the run level.

For example, to put the system in single-user mode, type the following:

```
init 1
```

Thus, if you want to try run level 3 without changing the default run level in /etc/inittab file, enter the following command at the shell prompt:

```
init 3
```

The system ends all current processes and enters run level 3. By default, the init command waits 20 seconds before stopping all current processes and starting the new processes for run level 3.

To switch to run level 3 immediately, type the command **init -t0 3**. The number after the -t option indicates the number of seconds init waits before changing the run level.

You can also use the `telinit` command, which is simply a symbolic link (a shortcut) to `init`. If you make changes to the `/etc/inittab` file and want `init` to reload its configuration file, use the command `telinit q`.

## Understanding the Linux startup scripts

The `init` process runs a number of scripts at system startup. In the following discussions, a Debian system is used as an example, but the basic sequence is similar in other distributions — only the names and locations of the scripts may vary.

If you look at the `/etc/inittab` file in a Debian system, you find the following lines near the beginning of the file:

```
# Boot-time system configuration/initialization script.
si::sysinit:/etc/init.d/rcS
```

The first line is a comment line. The second line causes `init` to run the `/etc/init.d/rcS` script — the first Linux startup script that `init` runs in a Debian system. The `rcS` script performs many initialization tasks, such as mounting the file systems, setting the clock, configuring the keyboard layout, starting the network, and loading many other driver modules. The `rcS` script performs these initialization tasks by calling many other scripts and reading configuration files located in the `/etc/rcS.d` directory.

After executing the `/etc/init.d/rcS` script, the `init` process runs the `/etc/init.d/rc` script with the run level as an argument. For example, for run level 2, the following line in `/etc/inittab` specifies what `init` executes:

```
l2:2:wait:/etc/init.d/rc 2
```

This example says `init` executes the command `/etc/init.d/rc 2` and waits until that command completes.

The `/etc/init.d/rc` script is somewhat complicated. Here's how it works:

✦ It executes scripts in a directory corresponding to the run level. For example, for run level 2, the `/etc/init.d/rc` script runs the scripts in the `/etc/rc2.d` directory.

✦ In the directory that corresponds with the run level, `/etc/init.d/rc` looks for all files that begin with `K` and executes each of them with the `stop` argument. This argument kills any currently running processes. Then it locates all files that begin with `S` and executes each file with a `start` argument. This argument starts the processes needed for the specified run level.

To see it executed at run level 2, type the following command:

```
ls -l /etc/rc2.d
```

In the resulting listing, the K scripts — the files whose names begin with K — stop (or *kill*) servers, whereas the S scripts start servers. The /etc/init.d/rc script executes these files in the order in which they appear in the directory listing.

## Manually starting and stopping servers

In Linux, the server startup scripts reside in the /etc/init.d directory. You can manually invoke scripts in this directory to start, stop, or restart specific processes — usually servers. For example, to stop the FTP server (the server program is vsftpd), type the following command:

```
/etc/init.d/vsftpd stop
```

If vsftpd is already running and you want to restart it, type the following command:

```
/etc/init.d/vsftpd restart
```

You can enhance your system administration skills by familiarizing yourself with the scripts in the /etc/init.d directory. To see its listing, type the following command:

```
ls /etc/init.d
```

The script names give you some clue about which server the script can start and stop. For example, the samba script starts and stops the processes required for Samba Windows networking services. At your leisure, you may want to study some of these scripts to see what each one does. You don't have to understand all the shell programming; the comments help you discover the purpose of each script.

## Automatically starting servers at system startup

You want some servers to start automatically every time you boot the system. The exact commands to configure the servers vary from one distribution to another.

In Fedora and SUSE, use the chkconfig command to set up a server to start whenever the system boots into a specific run level. For example, if you start the SSH server, you want the sshd server to start whenever the system starts. You can make that happen by using the chkconfig command. To set sshd to start whenever the system boots into run level 3, 4, or 5, type the following command (while logged in as root):

```
chkconfig --level 345 sshd on
```

In Fedora and SUSE, you can also use the `chkconfig` command to check which servers are turned on or off. For example, to see the complete list of all servers for all run levels, type the following command:

```
chkconfig --list
```

In Debian, Ubuntu, and Xandros, you can use the `update-rc.d` command to enable a server to start automatically at system startup. For example, to set `sshd` to start automatically at the default run levels, type **update-rc.d sshd defaults** in a terminal window while logged in as `root`. You can also specify the exact run levels and the sequence number (the order in which each server starts). To find out more about the `update-rc.d` command, type **man update-rc.d** in a terminal window.

# Taking Stock of Linux System Configuration Files

Linux includes a host of configuration files. All these files share text files that you can edit with any text editor. To edit these configuration files, you must log in as `root`. A selection of the most popular configuration files appears in Table 1-8, along with a brief description of each. This table gives you an idea of what types of configuration files a system administrator has to work with. In many cases, Linux includes GUI utility programs to set up many of these configuration files.

| Table 1-8 | Some Linux Configuration Files |
|---|---|
| *Configuration File* | *Description* |
| `/boot/grub` | Location of files for the GRUB boot loader. |
| `/boot/grub/menu.lst` | Configuration file for the boot menu that GRUB displays before it boots your system. |
| `/boot/System.map` | Map of the Linux kernel (maps kernel addresses into names of functions and variables). |
| `/boot/vmlinuz` | The Linux kernel (the operating system's core). |
| `/etc/apache2/httpd.conf` | Configuration file for the Apache Web server (Debian). |
| `/etc/apt/sources.list` | Configuration file that lists the sources — FTP or Web sites or CD-ROM — from which the Advanced Packaging Tool (APT) obtains packages (Debian, Ubuntu, and Xandros). |

*(continued)*

### Table 1-8 *(continued)*

| Configuration File | Description |
|---|---|
| /etc/at.allow | Usernames of users allowed to use the at command to schedule jobs for later execution. |
| /etc/at.deny | Usernames of users forbidden to use the at command. |
| /etc/bashrc | System-wide functions and aliases for the bash shell (Fedora). |
| /etc/bash.bashrc | System-wide functions and aliases for the bash shell (Debian, SUSE, Ubuntu, and Xandros). |
| /etc/cups/cupsd.conf | Printer configuration file for the Common UNIX Printing System (CUPS) scheduler. |
| /etc/fonts | Directory with font configuration files. (In particular, you can put local font configuration settings in the file /etc/fonts/local.conf.) |
| /etc/fstab | Information about file systems available for mounting and where each file system is to be mounted. |
| /etc/group | Information about groups. |
| /etc/grub.conf | The configuration for the GRUB boot loader in Fedora and SUSE. |
| /etc/hosts | List of IP numbers and their corresponding hostnames. |
| /etc/hosts.allow | Hosts allowed to access Internet services on this system. |
| /etc/hosts.deny | Hosts forbidden to access Internet services on this system. |
| /etc/httpd/conf/httpd.conf | Configuration file for the Apache Web server (Fedora). |
| /etc/init.d | Directory with scripts to start and stop various servers. |
| /etc/inittab | Configuration file used by the init process that starts all the other processes. |
| /etc/issue | File containing a message to be printed before displaying the text mode login prompt (usually the distribution name and the version number). |
| /etc/lilo.conf | The configuration for the Linux Loader (LILO) — one of the boot loaders that can load the operating system from disk (present only if you use the LILO boot loader). |

| Configuration File | Description |
|---|---|
| /etc/login.defs | Default information for creating user accounts, used by the useradd command. |
| /etc/modprobe.conf | Configuration file for loadable kernel modules, used by the modprobe command (Fedora and SUSE). |
| /etc/modules.conf | Configuration file for loadable modules (Debian and Xandros). |
| /etc/mtab | Information about currently mounted file systems. |
| /etc/passwd | Information about all user accounts. (Actual passwords are stored in /etc/shadow.) |
| /etc/profile | System-wide environment and startup file for the bash shell. |
| /etc/profile.d | Directory containing script files (with names that end in .sh) that the /etc/profile script executes. |
| /etc/init.d/rcS | Linux initialization script in Debian, SUSE, Ubuntu, and Xandros. |
| /etc/rc.d/ rc.sysinit | Linux initialization script in Fedora. |
| /etc/shadow | Secure file with encrypted passwords for all user accounts (can be read by only root). |
| /etc/shells | List of all the shells on the system that the user can use. |
| /etc/skel | Directory that holds initial versions of files such as .bash_profile that copy to a new user's home directory. |
| /etc/sysconfig | Linux configuration files (Fedora and SUSE). |
| /etc/sysctl.conf | Configuration file with kernel parameters that are read in and set by sysctl at system startup. |
| /etc/termcap | Database of terminal capabilities and options (Fedora and SUSE). |
| /etc/udev | Directory containing configuration files for udev — the program that provides the ability to dynamically name hot-pluggable devices and create device files in the /dev directory. |
| /etc/X11 | Directory with configuration files for the X Window System (X11) and various display managers such as gdm and xdm. |

*(continued)*

**Table 1-8** *(continued)*

| Configuration File | Description |
|---|---|
| /etc/X11/xorg.conf | Configuration file for X.org X11 — the X Window System (Fedora, Ubuntu, and SUSE). |
| /etc/xinetd.conf | Configuration for the xinetd daemon that starts a number of Internet services on demand. |
| /etc/yum.conf | Configuration for the yum package updater and installer (Fedora). |
| /var/log/apache2 | Web server access and error logs (Debian). |
| /var/log/cron | Log file with messages from the cron process that runs scheduled jobs. |
| /var/log/boot.msg | File with boot messages (SUSE). |
| /var/log/dmesg | File with boot messages (Debian, Fedora, Ubuntu, and Xandros). |
| /var/log/httpd | Web server access and error logs (Fedora). |
| /var/log/messages | System log. |

# Monitoring System Performance

When you're the system administrator, you must keep an eye on how well your Linux system is performing. You can monitor the overall performance of your system by looking at information such as

+ Central processing unit (CPU) usage

+ Physical memory usage

+ Virtual memory (swap-space) usage

+ Hard drive usage

Linux comes with a number of utilities that you can use to monitor one or more of these performance parameters. The following sections introduce a few of these utilities and show you how to understand the information presented by said utilities.

## Using the top utility

To view the top CPU processes — the ones that use most of the CPU time — you can use the text mode top utility. To start that utility, type **top** in a terminal window (or text console). The top utility then displays a text screen listing the current processes, arranged in the order of CPU usage, along with various other information, such as memory and swap-space usage. Figure 1-5 shows a typical output from the `top` utility.

**Figure 1-5:**
You can see the top CPU processes by using the top utility.

```
naba@linux:~ - Shell - Konsole                                          [_][□][x]
Session  Edit  View  Bookmarks  Settings  Help
top - 21:54:33 up 2 min,  3 users,  load average: 1.44, 0.81, 0.31
Tasks:  76 total,   2 running,  74 sleeping,   0 stopped,   0 zombie
Cpu(s):  0.0% us,   0.3% sy,   0.0% ni,  99.7% id,   0.0% wa,   0.0% hi,   0.0% si
Mem:    767692k total,    381276k used,    386416k free,    37984k buffers
Swap:  1543104k total,         0k used,  1543104k free,   219760k cached

  PID USER      PR  NI  VIRT  RES  SHR S %CPU %MEM    TIME+  COMMAND
 4479 root      15   0  153m  20m 3096 S  0.3  2.8  0:05.93 X
    1 root      16   0   688  264  224 S  0.0  0.0  0:01.30 init
    2 root      34  19     0    0    0 S  0.0  0.0  0:00.00 ksoftirqd/0
    3 root      10  -5     0    0    0 S  0.0  0.0  0:00.06 events/0
    4 root      10  -5     0    0    0 S  0.0  0.0  0:00.00 khelper
    5 root      10  -5     0    0    0 S  0.0  0.0  0:00.00 kthread
    7 root      10  -5     0    0    0 S  0.0  0.0  0:00.00 kblockd/0
   39 root      15   0     0    0    0 S  0.0  0.0  0:00.00 kapmd
   60 root      20   0     0    0    0 S  0.0  0.0  0:00.00 pdflush
   61 root      15   0     0    0    0 S  0.0  0.0  0:00.01 pdflush
   63 root      20  -5     0    0    0 S  0.0  0.0  0:00.00 aio/0
   62 root      25   0     0    0    0 S  0.0  0.0  0:00.03 kswapd0
  653 root      10  -5     0    0    0 S  0.0  0.0  0:00.01 reiserfs/0
  959 root      10  -5     0    0    0 S  0.0  0.0  0:00.95 udevd
 1893 root      13  -4  1840  904  600 S  0.0  0.1  0:00.95 udevd
 2225 root      10  -5     0    0    0 S  0.0  0.0  0:00.00 khubd
 2433 messageb  16   0  3520 1544 1312 S  0.0  0.2  0:00.06 dbus-daemon
  Shell
```

The `top` utility updates the display every five seconds. If you keep `top` running in a window, you can continually monitor the status of your Linux system. To quit `top`, press Q or Ctrl+C or close the terminal window.

The first five lines of the output screen (see Figure 1-5) provide summary information about the system, as follows:

✦ The first line shows the current time, how long the system has been up, how many users are logged in, and three *load averages* — the average number of processes ready to run during the last 1, 5, and 15 minutes.

✦ The second line lists the total number of processes and the status of these processes.

✦ The third line shows CPU usage — what percentage of CPU time is used by user processes, what percentage by system (kernel) processes, and during what percentage of time the CPU is idle.

✦ The fourth line shows how the physical memory is being used — the total amount, how much is used, how much is free, and how much is allocated to buffers (for reading from the hard drive, for example).

✦ The fifth line shows how the virtual memory (or swap space) is being used — the total amount of swap space, how much is used, how much is free, and how much is being cached.

The table that appears below the summary information (refer to Figure 1-5) lists information about the current processes, arranged in decreasing order by amount of CPU time used. Table 1-9 summarizes the meanings of the column headings in the table that `top` displays.

| Table 1-9 | Column Headings in top Utility's Output |
|-----------|------------------------------------------|
| *Heading* | *Meaning* |
| PID | Process ID of the process. |
| USER | Username under which the process is running. |
| PR | Priority of the process. |
| NI | Nice value of the process — the value ranges from –20 (highest priority) to 19 (lowest priority) and the default is 0. (The *nice value* represents the relative priority of the process: The higher the value, the lower the priority and the nicer the process because it yields to other processes.) |
| VIRT | Total amount of virtual memory used by the process, in kilobytes. |
| RES | Total physical memory used by a task (typically shown in kilobytes, but an m suffix indicates megabytes). |
| SHR | Amount of shared memory used by process. |
| S | State of the process (S for sleeping, D for uninterruptible sleep, R for running, Z for zombies — processes that should be dead but are still running — or T for stopped). |
| %CPU | Percentage of CPU time used since last screen update. |
| %MEM | Percentage of physical memory used by the process. |
| TIME+ | Total CPU time the process has used since it started. |
| COMMAND | Shortened form of the command that started the process. |

## Using the uptime command

You can use the `uptime` command to get a summary of the system's state. Just type the command like this:

```
uptime
```

It displays output similar to the following:

```
15:03:21 up 32 days, 57 min, 3 users, load average: 0.13, 0.23, 0.27
```

This output shows the current time, how long the system has been up, the number of users, and (finally) the three load averages — the average number of processes that were ready to run in the past 1, 5, and 15 minutes.

Load averages greater than 1 imply that many processes are competing for CPU time simultaneously.

The load averages give you an indication of how busy the system is.

## Using the vmstat utility

You can get summary information about the overall system usage with the vmstat utility. To view system usage information averaged over 5-second intervals, type the following command (the second argument indicates the total number of lines of output vmstat displays):

```
vmstat 5 8
```

You see output similar to the following listing:

```
procs -----------memory---------- ---swap-- -----io---- --system-- ----cpu----
 r  b  swpd  free buff cache   si so  bi  bo  in  cs  us sy id wa
 0  0 31324 4016 18568 136004 1  1  17  16  8  110  33  4 61  1
 0  1 31324 2520 15348 139692 0  0 7798 199 1157 377  8  8  6 78
 1  0 31324 1584 12936 141480 0 19 5784 105 1099 437 12  5  0 82
 2  0 31324 1928 13004 137136 7  0 1586 138 1104 561 43  6  0 51
 3  1 31324 1484 13148 132064 0  0 1260  51 1080 427 50  5  0 46
 0  0 31324 1804 13240 127976 0  0 1126  46 1082 782 19  5 47 30
 0  0 31324 1900 13240 127976 0  0    0   0 1010 211  3  1 96  0
 0  0 31324 1916 13248 127976 0  0    0  10 1015 224  3  2 95  0
```

The first line of output shows the averages since the last reboot. After that, vmstat displays the 5-second average data seven more times, covering the next 35 seconds. The tabular output is grouped as six categories of information, indicated by the fields in the first line of output. The second line shows further details for each of the six major fields. You can interpret these fields by using Table 1-10.

| Table 1-10 | Meaning of Fields in the vmstat Utility's Output |
|---|---|
| *Field Name* | *Description* |
| procs | Number of processes and their types: r = processes waiting to run, b = processes in uninterruptible sleep, w = processes swapped out but ready to run. |
| memory | Information about physical memory and swap-space usage (all numbers in kilobytes): swpd = virtual memory used, free = free physical memory, buff = memory used as buffers, cache = virtual memory that's cached. |
| swap | Amount of swapping (the numbers are in kilobytes per second): si = amount of memory swapped in from disk, so = amount of memory swapped to disk. |

*(continued)*

**Table 1-10** *(continued)*

| Field Name | Description |
|---|---|
| io | Information about input and output. (The numbers are in blocks per second, where the block size depends on the disk device.) bi = rate of blocks sent to disk, bo = rate of blocks received from disk. |
| system | Information about the system: in = number of interrupts per second (including clock interrupts), cs = number of context switches per second — how many times the kernel changed which process was running. |
| cpu | Percentages of CPU time used: us = percentage of CPU time used by user processes, sy = percentage of CPU time used by system processes, id = percentage of time CPU is idle, wa = time spent waiting for input or output (I/O). |

In the vmstat utility's output, high values in the si and so fields indicate too much swapping. (*Swapping* refers to the copying of information between physical memory and the virtual memory on the hard drive.) High numbers in the bi and bo fields indicate too much disk activity.

## Checking disk performance and disk usage

Linux comes with the /sbin/hdparm program to control IDE or ATAPI hard drives, which are common on most PCs. One feature of the hdparm program is that you can use the -t option to determine the rate at which data is read from the disk into a buffer in memory. For example, here's the result of typing **/sbin/hdparm -t /dev/hda** on one system:

```
/dev/hda:
Timing buffered disk reads: 178 MB in 3.03 seconds = 58.81 MB/sec
```

The command requires the IDE drive's device name (/dev/hda for the first hard drive and /dev/hdb for the second hard drive) as an argument. If you have an IDE hard drive, you can try this command to see how fast data is read from your system's disk drive.

To display the space available in the currently mounted file systems, use the df command. If you want a more readable output from df, type the following command:

```
df -h
```

Here's a typical output from this command:

*Viewing System Information with the /proc File System* **315**

Book V
Chapter 1

Introducing
Basic System
Administration

```
Filesystem Size Used Avail Use% Mounted on
/dev/hda5 7.1G 3.9G 2.9G 59% /
/dev/hda3 99M 18M 77M 19% /boot
none 125M 0 125M 0% /dev/shm
/dev/scd0 2.6G 2.6G 0 100% /media/cdrecorder
```

As this example shows, the –h option causes the df command to display the sizes in gigabytes (G) and megabytes (M).

To check the disk space being used by a specific directory, use the du command — you can specify the –h option to view the output in kilobytes (K) and megabytes (M), as shown in the following example:

```
du -h /var/log
```

Here's a typical output of that command:

```
152K /var/log/cups
4.0K /var/log/vbox
4.0K /var/log/httpd
508K /var/log/gdm
4.0K /var/log/samba
8.0K /var/log/mail
4.0K /var/log/news/OLD
8.0K /var/log/news
4.0K /var/log/squid
2.2M /var/log
```

The du command displays the disk space used by each directory, and the last line shows the total disk space used by that directory. If you want to see only the total space used by a directory, use the -s option. For example, type **du -sh /home** to see the space used by the /home directory. The command produces output that looks like this:

```
89M /home
```

# Viewing System Information with the /proc File System

Your Linux system has a special /proc file system. You can find out many things about your system from this file system. In fact, you can even change kernel parameters through the /proc file system (just by writing to a file in that file system), thereby modifying the system's behavior.

The /proc file system isn't a real directory on the hard drive but a collection of data structures in memory, managed by the Linux kernel, that appears to you as a set of directories and files. The purpose of /proc (also called the *process file system*) is to give you access to information about the Linux kernel as well as to help you find out about all processes currently running on your system.

You can access the /proc file system just as you access any other directory, but you have to know the meaning of various files to interpret the information. Typically, you can use the cat or more commands to view the contents of a file in /proc. The file's contents provide information about some aspect of the system.

As with any directory, start by looking at a detailed directory listing of /proc. To do so, log in as root and type **ls -l /proc** in a terminal window. In the output, the first set of directories (indicated by the letter d at the beginning of the line) represents the processes currently running on your system. Each directory that corresponds to a process has the process ID (a number) as its name.

Notice also a very large file named /proc/kcore; that file represents the *entire* physical memory of your system. Although /proc/kcore appears in the listing as a huge file, no single physical file occupies that much space on your hard drive — so don't try to remove the file to reclaim disk space.

Several files and directories in /proc contain interesting information about your Linux PC. The /proc/cpuinfo file, for example, lists the key characteristics of your system, such as processor type and floating-point processor information. You can view the processor information by typing **cat /proc/cpuinfo**. For example, here's what appears when **cat /proc/cpuinfo** is run on a sample system:

```
processor : 0
vendor_id : GenuineIntel
cpu family : 15
model : 3
model name : Intel(R) Celeron(R) CPU 2.53GHz
stepping : 3
cpu MHz : 2533.129
cache size : 256 KB
fdiv_bug : no
hlt_bug : no
f00f_bug : no
coma_bug : no
fpu : yes
fpu_exception : yes
cpuid level : 5
wp : yes
flags : fpu vme de pse tsc msr pae mce cx8 apic sep mtrr pge
    mca cmov pat pse36 clflush dts acpi mmx fxsr sse sse2 ss
    ht tm pbe pni monitor ds_cpl cid
bogomips : 4997.12
```

This output is from a 2.5 GHz Celeron system. The listing shows many interesting characteristics of the processor. Note the line that starts with `fdiv_bug`. Remember the infamous Pentium floating-point division bug? The bug is in an instruction called `fdiv` (for *floating-point division*). Thus, the `fdiv_bug` line indicates whether this particular Pentium has the bug.

The last line in the `/proc/cpuinfo` file shows the BogoMIPS for the processor, as computed by the Linux kernel when it boots. BogoMIPS is something that Linux uses internally to time-delay loops.

Table 1-11 summarizes some of the files in the `/proc` file system that provide information about your Linux system. You can view some of these files on your system to see what they contain, but note that not all files shown in Table 1-11 are present on your system. The specific contents of the `/proc` file system depend on the kernel configuration and the driver modules that are loaded (which, in turn, depend on your PC's hardware configuration).

| Table 1-11 | Some Files and Directories in /proc |
|---|---|
| *File Name* | *Content* |
| `/proc/acpi` | Information about Advanced Configuration and Power Interface (ACPI) — an industry-standard interface for configuration and power management on laptops, desktops, and servers. |
| `/proc/bus` | Directory with bus-specific information for each bus type, such as PCI. |
| `/proc/cmdline` | The command line used to start the Linux kernel (for example, `ro root=LABEL=/ rhgb`). |
| `/proc/cpuinfo` | Information about the CPU (the microprocessor). |
| `/proc/devices` | Available block and character devices in your system. |
| `/proc/dma` | Information about DMA (direct memory access) channels that are used. |
| `/proc/driver/rtc` | Information about the PC's real-time clock (RTC). |
| `/proc/filesystems` | List of supported file systems. |
| `/proc/ide` | Directory containing information about IDE devices. |
| `/proc/interrupts` | Information about interrupt request (IRQ) numbers and how they are used. |
| `/proc/ioports` | Information about input/output (I/O) port addresses and how they're used. |

*(continued)*

### Table 1-11 *(continued)*

| File Name | Content |
|---|---|
| /proc/kcore | Image of the physical memory. |
| /proc/kmsg | Kernel messages. |
| /proc/loadavg | Load average (average number of processes waiting to run in the last 1, 5, and 15 minutes). |
| /proc/locks | Current kernel locks (used to ensure that multiple processes don't write to a file at the same time). |
| /proc/meminfo | Information about physical memory and swap-space usage. |
| /proc/misc | Miscellaneous information. |
| /proc/modules | List of loaded driver modules. |
| /proc/mounts | List of mounted file systems. |
| /proc/net | Directory with many subdirectories that contain information about networking. |
| /proc/partitions | List of partitions known to the Linux kernel. |
| /proc/pci | Information about PCI devices found on the system. |
| /proc/scsi | Directory with information about SCSI devices found on the system (present only if you have a SCSI device). |
| /proc/stat | Overall statistics about the system. |
| /proc/swaps | Information about the swap space and how much is used. |
| /proc/sys | Directory with information about the system. You can change kernel parameters by writing to files in this directory. (Using this method to tune system performance requires expertise to do properly.) |
| /proc/uptime | Information about how long the system has been up. |
| /proc/version | Kernel version number. |

You can navigate the /proc file system just as you'd work with any other directories and files in Linux. Use the more or cat commands to view the contents of a file.

# Understanding Linux Devices

Linux treats all devices as files and uses a device just as it uses a file —
opens it, writes data to it, reads data from it, and closes it when finished.
This ability to treat every device as a file is possible because of *device drivers,* which are special programs that control a particular type of hardware.
When the kernel writes data to the device, the device driver does whatever
is appropriate for that device. For example, when the kernel writes data to
the floppy drive, the floppy device driver puts that data onto the physical
medium of the floppy disk. On the other hand, if the kernel writes data to
the parallel port device, the parallel port driver sends the data to the printer
connected to the parallel port.

Thus, the device driver isolates the device-specific code from the rest of
the kernel and makes a device look like a file. Any application can access a
device by opening the file specific to that device. Figure 1-6 illustrates this
concept of a Linux device driver.

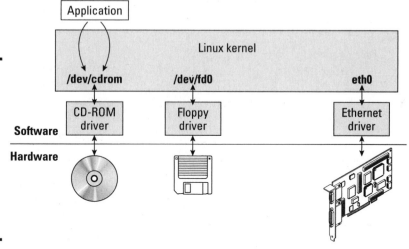

**Figure 1-6:**
An
application
can access
a device
through
a special
file that, in
turn, uses
a device
driver.

## Device files

As Figure 1-6 shows, applications can access a device as if it were a file.
These files, called device files, appear in the /dev directory in the Linux file
system.

If you use the `ls` command to look at the list of files in the `/dev` directory, you see several thousand files. These files don't mean that your system has several thousand devices. The `/dev` directory has files for all possible types of devices — that's why the number of device files is so large.

So how does the kernel know which device driver to use when an application opens a specific device file? The answer is in two numbers called the *major* and *minor device numbers.* Each device file is mapped to a specific device driver through these numbers.

To see an example of the major and minor device numbers, type the following command in a terminal window:

```
ls -l /dev/hda
```

You see a line of output similar to the following:

```
brw-rw---- 1 root disk 3, 0 Aug 16 14:50 /dev/hda
```

In this line, the major and minor device numbers appear just before the date. In this case, the major device number is 3 and the minor device number is 0. The kernel selects the device driver for this device file by using the major device number.

You don't have to know much about device files and device numbers, except to be aware of their existence.

In case you're curious, all the major and minor numbers for devices are assigned according to device type. The Linux Assigned Names And Numbers Authority (LANANA) assigns these numbers. You can see the current device list at `www.lanana.org/docs/device-list/devices.txt`.

### Block devices

The first letter in the listing of a device file also provides an important clue. For the `/dev/hda` device, the first letter is b, which indicates that `/dev/hda` is a *block device* — one that can accept or provide data in chunks (typically 512 bytes or 1K). By the way, `/dev/hda` refers to the first IDE hard drive on your system (the C: drive in Windows). Hard drives, floppy drives, and CD-ROM drives are all examples of block devices.

### Character devices

If the first letter in the listing of a device file is c, the device is a *character device* — one that can receive and send data one character (one byte) at a time. For example, the serial port and parallel ports are character devices. To see the specific listing of a character device, type the following command in a terminal window:

```
ls -l /dev/ttyS0
```

The listing of this device is similar to the following:

```
crw-rw---- 1 root uucp 4, 64 Aug 16 14:50 /dev/ttyS0
```

Note that the very first letter is c because /dev/ttyS0 — the first serial port — is a character device.

### Network devices

Network devices that enable your system to interact with a network — for example, Ethernet and dial-up *Point-to-Point Protocol* (PPP) connections — are special because they need no file to correspond to the device. Instead, the kernel uses a special name for the device. For example, Ethernet devices are named eth0 for the first Ethernet card, eth1 for the second one, and so on. PPP connections are named ppp0, ppp1, and so on.

Because network devices aren't mapped to device files, no files corresponding to these devices are in the /dev directory.

## Persistent device naming with udev

Linux kernel 2.6 introduces a new approach for handling devices, based on the following features:

✦ **sysfs:** Kernel 2.6 provides the sysfs file system, which is mounted on the /sys directory of the file system. The sysfs file system displays all the devices in the system as well as lots of information about each device, including the location of the device on the bus, attributes such as name and serial number, and the major and minor numbers of the device.

✦ **/sbin/hotplug:** This program is called whenever a device is added or removed. It can then do whatever is necessary to handle the device.

✦ **/sbin/udev:** This program takes care of dynamically named devices based on device characteristics such as serial number, device number on a bus, or a user-assigned name based on a set of rules that are set through the text file /etc/udev/udev.rules.

The udev program's configuration file is /etc/udev/udev.conf. Based on settings in that configuration file, udev creates device nodes automatically in the directory specified by the udev_root parameter. For example, to manage the device nodes in the /dev directory, udev_root should be defined in /etc/udev/udev.conf as follows:

```
udev_root="/dev/"
```

# Managing Loadable Driver Modules

To use any device, the Linux kernel must contain the driver. If the driver code is linked into the kernel as a *monolithic* program (a program in the form of a single, large file), adding a new driver means rebuilding the kernel with the new driver code. Rebuilding the kernel means you have to reboot the PC with the new kernel before you can use the new device driver. Luckily, the Linux kernel uses a modular design that does away with rebooting hassles. Linux device drivers can be created in the form of modules that the kernel can load and unload without having to restart the PC.

Driver modules are one type of a broader category of software modules called *loadable kernel modules.* Other types of kernel modules include code that can support new types of file systems, modules for network protocols, and modules that interpret different formats of executable files.

## Loading and unloading modules

You can manage the loadable device driver modules by using a set of commands. You have to log in as `root` to use some of these commands. Table 1-12 summarizes a few commonly used module commands.

| Table 1-12 | Commands to Manage Kernel Modules |
|---|---|
| *This Command* | *Does the Following* |
| `insmod` | Inserts a module into the kernel. |
| `rmmod` | Removes a module from the kernel. |
| `depmod` | Determines interdependencies between modules. |
| `ksyms` | Displays a list of symbols along with the name of the module that defines the symbol. |
| `lsmod` | Lists all currently loaded modules. |
| `modinfo` | Displays information about a kernel module. |
| `modprobe` | Inserts or removes a module or a set of modules intelligently. (For example, if module A requires B, `modprobe` automatically loads B when asked to load A.) |

If you have to use any of these commands, log in as `root` or type **su** – in a terminal window to become `root`.

To see what modules are currently loaded, type

```
lsmod
```

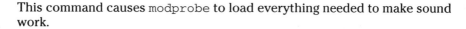

You see a long list of modules. The list that you see will depend on the types of devices installed on your system.

The list displayed by `lsmod` includes all types of Linux kernel modules, not just device drivers. For example, if you use the Ext3 file system, you typically find two modules — `jbd` and `ext3` — that are part of the Ext3 file system (the latest file system for Linux).

Besides `lsmod`, one commonly used module command is `modprobe`. Use `modprobe` when you need to manually load or remove one or more modules. The best thing about `modprobe` is that you don't need to worry if a module requires other modules to work. The `modprobe` command automatically loads any other module needed by a module. For example, to manually load the sound driver, use the command

```
modprobe snd-card-0
```

This command causes `modprobe` to load everything needed to make sound work.

You can use `modprobe` with the `-r` option to remove modules. For example, to remove the sound modules, use the following command:

```
modprobe -r snd-card-0
```

This command gets rid of all the modules that the `modprobe snd-card-0` command had loaded.

## Using the /etc/modprobe.conf file

How does the `modprobe` command know that it needs to load the `snd-intel8x0` driver module? The answer's in the `/etc/modprobe.conf` configuration file. That file contains a line that tells `modprobe` what it should load when it sees the module name `snd-card-0`.

To view the contents of `/etc/modprobe.conf`, type

```
cat /etc/modprobe.conf
```

For example, consider a `/etc/modprobe.conf` file that contains the following lines:

```
alias eth0 3c59x
alias snd-card-0 snd-intel8x0
alias usb-controller uhci-hcd
```

Each line that begins with the keyword `alias` defines a standard name for an actual driver module. For example, the first line defines `3c59x` as the actual driver name for the alias `eth0`, which stands for the first Ethernet card. Similarly, the third line defines `snd-intel8x0` as the module to load when the user uses the name `snd-card-0`.

The `modprobe` command consults the `/etc/modprobe.conf` file to convert an alias to the real name of a driver module. It also consults the `/etc/modprobe.conf` file for other tasks, such as obtaining parameters for driver modules. For example, you can insert lines that begin with the `options` keyword to provide values of parameters that a driver may need.

For example, to set the debug level parameter for the Ethernet driver to 5 (this parameter generates lots of information in `/var/log/messages`), add the following line to the `/etc/modprobe.conf` file:

```
options 3c59x debug=5
```

This line specifies 5 as the value of the `debug` parameter in the `3c59x` module.

If you want to know the names of the parameters that a module accepts, use the `modinfo` command. For example, to view information about the `3c59x` driver module, type

```
modinfo 3c59x | more
```

From the resulting output, it's possible to tell that `debug` is the name of the parameter for setting the debug level.

Unfortunately, the information displayed by the `modinfo` command can be cryptic. The only saving grace is that you may not have to do much more than use a graphical utility to configure the device, and the utility takes care of adding whatever is needed to configuration files, such as `/etc/modprobe.conf`.

# Scheduling Jobs in Linux

As a system administrator, you may have to run some programs automatically at regular intervals or execute one or more commands at a specified time in the future. Your Linux system includes the facilities to schedule jobs to run at any future date or time you want. You can also set up the system to perform a task periodically or just once. Here are some typical tasks you can perform by scheduling jobs on your Linux system:

+ Back up the files in the middle of the night

+ Download large files in the early morning when the system isn't busy

✦ Send yourself messages as reminders of meetings

✦ Analyze system logs periodically and look for any abnormal activities

You can set up these jobs by using the `at` command or the `crontab` facility of Linux. The next few sections introduce these job-scheduling features of Linux.

## Scheduling one-time jobs

If you want to run one or more commands at a later time, you can use the `at` command. The `atd` *daemon* — a program designed to process jobs submitted using `at` — runs your commands at the specified time and mails the output to you.

Before you try the `at` command, you need to know that the following configuration files control which users can schedule tasks using the `at` command:

✦ `/etc/at.allow` contains the names of the users who may submit jobs using the `at` command.

✦ `/etc/at.deny` contains the names of users not allowed to submit jobs using the `at` command.

If these files aren't present or if you find an empty `/etc/at.deny` file, any user can submit jobs by using the `at` command. The default in Linux is an empty `/etc/at.deny` file; with this default in place, anyone can use the `at` command. If you don't want some users to use `at`, simply list their usernames in the `/etc/at.deny` file.

To use `at` to schedule a one-time job for execution at a later time, follow these steps:

**1. Run the `at` command with the date or time when you want your commands executed.**

When you press Enter, the `at>` prompt appears, as follows:

```
at 21:30
at>
```

This method is the simplest way to indicate the time when you want to execute one or more commands — simply specify the time in a 24-hour format. In this case, you want to execute the commands at 9:30 p.m. tonight (or tomorrow, if it's already past 9:30 p.m.). You can, however, specify the execution time in many different ways. (See Table 1-13 for examples.)

**2. At the `at>` prompt, type the commands you want to execute as if you were typing at the shell prompt. After each command, press Enter and**

**continue with the next command. When you finish entering the commands you want to execute, press Ctrl+D to indicate the end.**

Here's an example that shows how to execute the `ps` command at a future time:

```
at> ps
at> <EOT>
job 1 at 2006-12-28 21:30
```

After you press Ctrl+D, the `at` command responds with the `<EOT>` message, a job number, and the date and time when the job will execute.

### Table 1-13  Formats for the at Command for the Time of Execution

| Command | When the Job Will Run |
| --- | --- |
| `at now` | Immediately |
| `at now + 15 minutes` | 15 minutes from the current time |
| `at now + 4 hours` | 4 hours from the current time |
| `at now + 7 days` | 7 days from the current time |
| `at noon` | At noontime today (or tomorrow, if already past noon) |
| `at now next hour` | Exactly 60 minutes from now |
| `at now next day` | At the same time tomorrow |
| `at 17:00 tomorrow` | At 5 p.m. tomorrow |
| `at 4:45pm` | At 4:45 p.m. today (or tomorrow, if it's already past 4:45 p.m.) |
| `at 3:00 Dec 28, 2011` | At 3:00 a.m. on December 28, 2011 |

After you enter one or more jobs, you can view the current list of scheduled jobs with the `atq` command:

```
atq
```

The output looks similar to the following:

```
4 2010-12-28 03:00 a root
5 2010-10-26 21:57 a root
6 2011-10-26 16:45 a root
```

The first field on each line shows the job number — the same number that the `at` command displays when you submit the job. The next field shows the year, month, day, and time of execution. The last field shows the jobs pending in the `a` queue.

If you want to cancel a job, use the `atrm` command to remove that job from the queue. When removing a job with the `atrm` command, refer to the job by its number, as follows:

```
atrm 4
```

This command deletes job 4 scheduled for 3:00 a.m. December 28, 2010.

When a job executes, the output is mailed to you. Type **mail** at a terminal window to read your mail and to view the output from your jobs.

## Scheduling recurring jobs

Although `at` is good for running commands at a specific time, it's not useful for running a program automatically at repeated intervals. You have to use `crontab` to schedule such recurring jobs — for example, if you want to back up your files to tape at midnight every evening.

You schedule recurring jobs by placing job information in a file with a specific format and submitting this file with the `crontab` command. The `cron` daemon — `crond` — checks the job information every minute and executes the recurring jobs at the specified times. Because the `cron` daemon processes recurring jobs, such jobs are also referred to as *cron jobs.*

Any output from a `cron` job is mailed to the user who submits the job. (In the submitted job-information file, you can specify a different recipient for the mailed output.)

Two configuration files control who can schedule `cron` jobs using `crontab`:

✦ `/etc/cron.allow` contains the names of the users who may submit jobs using the `crontab` command.

✦ `/etc/cron.deny` contains the names of users not allowed to submit jobs using the `crontab` command.

If the `/etc/cron.allow` file exists, only users listed in this file can schedule `cron` jobs. If only the `/etc/cron.deny` file exists, users listed in this file can't schedule `cron` jobs. If neither file exists, the default Linux setup enables any user to submit `cron` jobs.

To submit a `cron` job, follow these steps:

*1.* **Prepare a shell script (or an executable program in any programming language) that can perform the recurring task you want to perform.**

You can skip this step if you want to execute an existing program periodically.

2. **Prepare a text file with information about the times when you want the shell script or program (from Step 1) to execute and then submit this file by using `crontab`.**

   You can submit several recurring jobs with a single file. Each line with timing information about a job has a standard format, with six fields — the first five specify when the job runs, and the sixth and subsequent fields constitute the command that runs. For example, here's a line that executes the `myjob` shell script in a user's home directory at five minutes past midnight each day:

   ```
   5 0 * * * $HOME/myjob
   ```

   Table 1-14 shows the meaning of the first five fields. ***Note:*** An asterisk (*) means all possible values for that field. Also, an entry in any of the first five fields can be a single number, a comma-separated list of numbers, a pair of numbers separated by a hyphen (indicating a range of numbers), or an asterisk.

3. **Suppose the text file `jobinfo` (in the current directory) contains the job information. Submit this information to `crontab` with the following command:**

   ```
   crontab jobinfo
   ```

That's it! You're set with the `cron` job. From now on, the `cron` job runs at regular intervals (as specified in the job information file), and you receive mail messages with the output from the job.

To verify that the job is indeed scheduled, type the following command:

```
crontab -l
```

The output of the `crontab -l` command shows the `cron` jobs currently installed in your name. To remove your `cron` jobs, type **`crontab -r`**.

### Table 1-14     Format for the Time of Execution in crontab Files

| Field Number | Meaning of Field | Acceptable Range of Values* |
|---|---|---|
| 1 | Minute | 0–59 |
| 2 | Hour of the day | 0–23 |
| 3 | Day of the month | 0–31 |

| Field Number | Meaning of Field | Acceptable Range of Values* |
|---|---|---|
| 4 | Month | 1–12 (1 means January, 2 means February, and so on) or the names of months using the first three letters — Jan, Feb, Mar, Apr, May, Jun, Jul, Aug, Sep, Oct, Nov, Dec |
| 5 | Day of the week | 0–6 (0 means Sunday, 1 means Monday, and so on) or the three-letter abbreviations of weekdays — Sun, Mon, Tue, Wed, Thu, Fri, Sat |

*An asterisk in a field means all possible values for that field. For example, if an asterisk is in the third field, the job is executed every day.

If you log in as `root`, you can also set up, examine, and remove `cron` jobs for any user. To set up `cron` jobs for a user, use this command:

```
crontab -u username filename
```

Here, *username* is the user for whom you install the `cron` jobs, and *file name* is the file that contains information about the jobs.

Use the following form of `crontab` command to view the `cron` jobs for a user:

```
crontab -u username -l
```

To remove a user's `cron` jobs, use the following command:

```
crontab -u username -r
```

***Note:*** The cron daemon also executes the `cron` jobs listed in the system-wide `cron` job file `/etc/crontab`. Here's a typical `/etc/crontab` file from a Linux system (type **cat /etc/crontab** to view the file):

```
SHELL=/bin/bash
PATH=/sbin:/bin:/usr/sbin:/usr/bin
MAILTO=root
HOME=/
# run-parts
01 * * * * root run-parts /etc/cron.hourly
02 4 * * * root run-parts /etc/cron.daily
22 4 * * 0 root run-parts /etc/cron.weekly
42 4 1 * * root run-parts /etc/cron.monthly
```

The first four lines set up several environment variables for the jobs listed in this file. The MAILTO environment variable specifies the user who receives the mail message with the output from the cron jobs in this file.

The line that begins with # is a comment line. The four lines following the run-parts comment execute the run-parts shell script (located in the /usr/bin directory) at various times with the name of a specific directory as argument. Each of the arguments to run-parts — /etc/cron.hourly, /etc/cron.daily, /etc/cron.weekly, and /etc/cron.monthly — are directories. Essentially, run-parts executes all scripts located in the directory that you provide as an argument.

Table 1-15 lists the directories where you can find these scripts and when they execute. You have to look at the scripts in these directories to know what executes at these periodic intervals.

| Table 1-15 | Script Directories for cron Jobs |
|---|---|
| *Directory Name* | *Script Executes* |
| /etc/cron.hourly | Every hour |
| /etc/cron.daily | Each day |
| /etc/cron.weekly | Weekly |
| /etc/cron.monthly | Once each month |

# Chapter 2: Managing Users and Groups

## In This Chapter

✔ Managing a user account with a GUI user manager and commands

✔ Understanding the password file

✔ Managing your groups

✔ Working in the user environment

✔ Changing user and group ownerships of files and directories

*L*inux is a multiuser system, so it has many user accounts. Even if you're the only user on your system, many servers require a unique username and group name. For example, the FTP server runs under the username ftp. A whole host of system user accounts aren't for people but just for running specific programs.

Also, user accounts can belong to one or more groups. Typically, each username has a corresponding private group name. By default, each user belongs to that corresponding private group. However, you can define other groups for the purpose of providing access to specific files and directories based on group membership.

User and group ownerships of files are a way to make sure that only the right people (or the right process) can access the right files and directories. Managing the user and group accounts is a typical system administration job. It's not hard to do this part of the job, given the tools that come with Linux, as you discover in this chapter.

## Adding User Accounts

You get the chance to add user accounts when you boot your system for the first time after installing Linux. The root account is the only one that you must set up during installation. If you don't add other user accounts when you start the system for the first time, you can add new users later on, using a GUI user account manager or the useradd command.

Creating other user accounts besides `root` is a good idea. Even if you're the only user of the system, logging in as a less privileged user is good practice because that way you can't damage any important system files inadvertently. If necessary, you can type **su** – to log in as `root` and then perform any system administration tasks.

## Managing user accounts by using a GUI user manager

Most Linux distributions come with a GUI tool to manage user accounts. You can use that GUI tool to add new user accounts. The tool displays a list of current user accounts and has an Add button for adding new users, as shown in Figure 2-1.

**Figure 2-1:**
In Ubuntu, you can manage user and group accounts from the Users and Groups interface.

The basic steps, regardless of the specific GUI tool, are as follows:

*1.* **Click the Add User button.**

A dialog box prompts you for information about the password for the new user account, as shown in Figure 2-2.

*2.* **Enter the requested information.**

The GUI tool takes care of adding the new user account.

*3.* **(Optional) Click Advanced Settings for the user (refer to Figure 2-1) to configure additional information.**

The Advanced tab (shown in Figure 2-3) allows you to override the defaults for the home directory, shell, and ID information.

**Figure 2-2:**
You can assign a password for the new user account in Ubuntu in several ways.

**Figure 2-3:**
Use Advanced Settings to configure settings other than the defined defaults for user accounts.

For example, in SUSE, select the Security and Users category from the left side of the YaST Control Center, and then click the User Management icon in the right side of the window. YaST displays the User and Group Administration pane, where you can define new user accounts.

Note that the pane has two types of accounts it can configure: Users and Groups. Selecting Manage Groups displays the names of groups from the /etc/group, as shown in Figure 2-4.

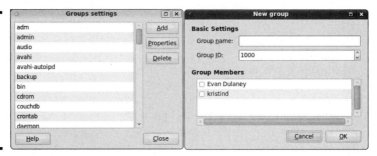

**Figure 2-4:**
Groups
can be
created and
managed
in Ubuntu
similar to
users.

Initially, the User and Group Administration tool filters out any system users and groups. However, you can view the system users by choosing Edit⇨Preferences and setting the filter to System Users from the drop-down list or check box, depending on your distribution. (*System Users* refers to user accounts that aren't assigned to human users; rather, these user accounts are used to run various services.) You need to be the `root` user to access the features of this utility.

To add a new user account, click the Add button and enter the information requested in the New Local User window.

Fill in the requested information in the window and then click the Accept button. The new user now appears in the list of users in the User and Group Administration pane.

You can add more user accounts, if you like. When you finish, click the Finish button in the User and Group Administration pane to create the new user accounts.

By default, YaST places all local users in a group named `users`. Sometimes you want a user to be in another group as well so that the user can access the files owned by that group. Adding a user to another group is easy. For example, to add the username `kdulaney` to the group called `wheel`, type the following command in a terminal window:

```
usermod -G wheel kdulaney
```

To remove a user account, click the username in the list of user accounts and then click the Delete button.

## Managing user accounts by using commands

If you're working from a text console, you can create a new user account by using the `useradd` command. Follow these steps to add an account for a new user:

*1.* **Log in as root.**

If you're not already logged in as root, type **su** **-** to become root.

*2.* **Type the following useradd command with the -c option to create the account:**

```
/usr/sbin/useradd -c "Kristin Dulaney" kdulaney
```

*3.* **Set the password by using the passwd command, as follows:**

```
passwd kdulaney
```

You're prompted for the password twice. If you type a password that someone can easily guess, the passwd program will scold you and suggest that you use a more difficult password.

The useradd command consults the following configuration files to obtain default information about various parameters for the new user account:

✦ **/etc/default/useradd:** Specifies the default shell (/bin/bash) and the default home directory location (/home)

✦ **/etc/login.defs:** Provides system-wide defaults for automatic group and user IDs, as well as password-expiration parameters

✦ **/etc/skel:** Contains the default files that useradd creates in the user's home directory

Examine these files with the cat or more commands to see what they contain.

You can delete a user account by using the userdel command. Simply type **/usr/sbin/userdel** *username* at the command prompt where *username* is the name of the user you want to remove. To wipe out that user's home directory as well, type **/usr/sbin/userdel -r** *username*.

To modify any information in a user account, use the usermod command. For example, for user kdulaney to have root as the primary group, type the following:

```
usermod -g root kdulaney
```

To find out more about the useradd, userdel, and usermod commands, type **man useradd**, **man userdel**, or **man usermod**, respectively, in a terminal window.

# Understanding the /etc/passwd File

The /etc/passwd file is a list of all user accounts. It's a text file and any user can read it — no special privileges needed. Each line in /etc/passwd has seven fields, separated by colons (:).

Here's a typical entry from the `/etc/passwd` file:

```
kdulaney:x:1000:1000:Kristin Dulaney,,,,:/home/kdulaney:/bin/bash
```

As the example shows, the format of each line in `/etc/passwd` looks like this:

```
username:password:UID:GID:GECOS:homedir:shell
```

Table 2-1 explains the meaning of the seven fields in each `/etc/passwd` entry.

| Table 2-1 | Fields in the /etc/passwd File |
|---|---|
| *This Field* | *Contains* |
| username | An alphanumeric username, usually 8 characters long and unique. (Linux allows usernames to be longer than 8 characters, but some other operating systems do not.) |
| password | When present, a 13-character encrypted password. (An *empty field* means that no password is required to access the account. An x means the password is stored in the /etc/shadow file, which is more secure.) |
| UID | A unique number that serves as the user identifier. (root has a UID of 0, and usually UIDs from 1 to 100 are reserved for nonhuman users such as servers; keeping the UID less than 32,767 is best.) |
| GID | The default group ID of the group to which the user belongs (GID 0 is for group root, other groups are defined in /etc/group, and users can be, and usually are, in more than one group at a time). |
| GECOS | Optional personal information about the user. (The finger command uses this field and *GECOS* stands for General Electric Comprehensive Operating System, a long-forgotten operating system that's immortalized by the name of this field in /etc/passwd.) |
| homedir | The name of the user's home directory. |
| shell | The command interpreter (shell), such as bash (/bin/bash), which executes when this user logs in. |

# Managing Groups

A *group* is something to which users belong. A group has a name and an identification number (ID). After a group is defined, users can belong to one or more of these groups.

You can find all the existing groups listed in /etc/group. For example, here's the line that defines the group named wheel:

wheel:x:10:root,kdulaney

As this example shows, each line in /etc/group has the following format, with four fields separated by colons:

*groupname*:*password*:*GID*:*membership*

Table 2-2 explains the meaning of the four fields in a group definition.

| Table 2-2 | Meaning of Fields in /etc/group File |
|---|---|
| *Field Name* | *Meaning* |
| *groupname* | The name of the group (for example, wheel) |
| *password* | The group password (an x means that the password is stored in the /etc/shadow file) |
| *GID* | The numerical group ID (for example, 10) |
| *membership* | A comma-separated list of usernames that belong to this group (for example, root,kdulaney) |

If you want to create a new group, you can simply use the groupadd command. For example, to add a new group called class with an automatically selected group ID, type the following command in a terminal window (you have to be logged in as root):

groupadd class

Then you can add users to this group with the usermod command. For example, to add the user kdulaney to the group named class, type the following commands:

usermod -G class kdulaney

If you want to remove a group, use the `groupdel` command. For example, to remove a group named `class`, type

```
groupdel class
```

# Exploring the User Environment

When you log in as a user, you get a set of environment variables that control many aspects of what you see and do on your Linux system. If you want to see your current environment, type the following command in a terminal window:

```
env
```

(By the way, the `printenv` command also displays the environment, but `env` is shorter.)

The `env` command prints a long list of lines. The collection of lines is the current environment, and each line defines an environment variable. For example, the `env` command displays this typical line:

```
HOSTNAME=localhost.localdomain
```

This line defines the environment variable `HOSTNAME` as `localhost.localdomain`.

An *environment variable* is nothing more than a name associated with a string. For example, the environment variable named `PATH` is typically defined as follows for a normal user:

```
PATH=/usr/local/bin:/bin:/usr/bin:/usr/local/sbin:/usr/
   sbin:/sbin
```

The string to the right of the equal sign (=) is the value of the `PATH` environment variable. By convention, the `PATH` environment variable is a sequence of directory names, each name separated by a colon (`:`).

Each environment variable has a specific purpose. For example, when the shell has to search for a file, it simply searches the directories listed in the `PATH` environment variable in the order of their appearance. Therefore, if two programs have the same name, the shell executes the one it finds first.

In a fashion similar to the shell's use of the `PATH` environment variable, an editor such as `vi` uses the value of the `TERM` environment variable to figure out how to display the file you edit with `vi`. To see the current setting of `TERM`, type the following command at the shell prompt:

```
echo $TERM
```

If you type this command in a terminal window, the output is as follows:

```
xterm
```

To define an environment variable in bash, use the following syntax:

```
export NAME=Value
```

Here, NAME denotes the name of the environment variable, and Value is the string representing its value. Therefore, you set TERM to the value xterm by using the following command:

```
export TERM=xterm
```

After you define an environment variable, you can change its value by simply specifying the new value with the syntax NAME=*new-value*. For example, to change the definition of TERM to vt100, type **TERM=vt100** at the shell prompt.

With an environment variable, such as PATH, you typically want to append a new directory name to the existing definition rather than define the PATH from scratch. For example, if you download and install the Java 5 Development Kit (available from http://java.sun.com/javase/downloads/index_jdk5.jsp), you have to add the location of the Java binaries to PATH. Here's how you accomplish that task:

```
export PATH=$PATH:/usr/java/jdk1.5.0/bin
```

This command appends the string :/usr/java/jdk1.5.0/bin to the current definition of the PATH environment variable. The net effect is to add /usr/java/jdk1.5.0/bin to the list of directories in PATH.

*Note:* You also can write this export command as follows:

```
export PATH=${PATH}:/usr/java/jdk1.5.0/bin
```

After you type that command, you can access programs in the /usr/java/jdk1.5.0/bin directory, such as javac, the Java compiler that converts Java source code into a form that the Java interpreter can execute.

PATH and TERM are only two of a handful of common environment variables. Table 2-3 lists some of the environment variables for a typical Linux user.

| Table 2-3 | Typical Environment Variables in Linux |
|---|---|
| *Environment Variable* | *Contents* |
| DISPLAY | The name of the display on which the X Window System displays output (typically set to :0.0) |
| HOME | Your home directory |
| HOSTNAME | The host name of your system |
| LOGNAME | Your login name |
| MAIL | The location of your mail directory |
| PATH | The list of directories in which the shell looks for programs |
| SHELL | Your shell (SHELL=/bin/bash for bash) |
| TERM | The type of terminal |

## Changing User and Group Ownership of Files

In Linux, each file or directory has two types of owners: a user and a group. In other words, a user and group own each file and directory. The user and group ownerships can control who can access a file or directory.

To view the owner of a file or directory, use the ls -l command to see the detailed listing of a directory. For example, here's a typical file's information:

```
-rw-rw-r-- 1 kdulaney kdulaney 40909 Aug 16 20:37 composer.
    txt
```

In this example, the first set of characters shows the file's permission setting — who can read, write, or execute the file. The third and fourth fields (in this example, kdulaney kdulaney) indicate the user and group owner of the file. Each user has a private group that has the same name as the username. So most files' user and group ownership appear to show the username twice.

As a system administrator, you may decide to change the group ownership of a file to a common group. For example, suppose you want to change the group ownership of the composer.txt file to the class group. To do that, log in as root and type the following command:

```
chgrp class composer.txt
```

This `chgrp` command changes the group ownership of `composer.txt` to `class`.

You can use the `chown` command to change the user owner. The command has the following format:

```
chown username filename
```

For example, to change the user ownership of a file named `sample.jpg` to `kdulaney`, type

```
chown kdulaney sample.jpg
```

The `chown` command can change both the user and group owner at the same time. For example, to change the user owner to `kdulaney` and the group owner to `class`, type

```
chown kdulaney.class composer.txt
```

In other words, you simply append the group name to the username with a period in between and then use that as the name of the owner.

# Chapter 3: Managing File Systems

## In This Chapter

✔ **Navigating the Linux file system**

✔ **Sharing files with NFS**

✔ **Backing up and restoring files**

✔ **Mounting the NTFS file system**

✔ **Accessing MS-DOS files**

*A* *file system* refers to the organization of files and directories. As a system administrator, you have to perform certain operations to manage file systems on various storage media. For example, you have to know how to *mount* — add a file system on a storage medium by attaching it to the overall Linux file system. You also have to back up important data and restore files from a backup. Other file-system operations include sharing files with the Network File System (NFS) and accessing MS-DOS files. This chapter shows you how to perform all file-system management tasks.

## Exploring the Linux File System

The files and directories in your PC store information in an organized manner, just like paper filing systems. When you store information on paper, you typically put several pages in a folder and then store the folder in a file cabinet. If you have many folders, you probably have some sort of filing system. For example, you may label each folder's tab and then arrange them alphabetically in the file cabinet. You might have several file cabinets, each with lots of drawers, which, in turn, contain folders full of pages.

Operating systems, such as Linux, organize information in your computer in a manner similar to your paper filing system. Linux uses a file system to organize all information in your computer. Of course, the storage medium isn't a metal file cabinet and paper. Instead, Linux stores information on devices such as hard drives, USB drives, and DVD drives.

To draw an analogy between your computer's file system and a paper filing system, think of a disk drive as the file cabinet. The drawers in the file cabinet correspond to the directories in the file system. The folders in each drawer are also directories — because a directory in a computer file system can contain other directories. You can think of files as the pages inside the folder — and that's where the actual information is stored. Figure 3-1 illustrates the analogy between a file cabinet and the Linux file system.

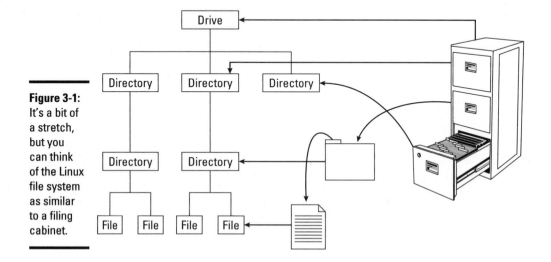

The Linux file system has a *hierarchical* structure — directories can contain other directories, which in turn contain individual files.

Everything in your Linux system is organized in files and directories. To access and use documents and programs on your system, you have to be familiar with the file system.

## Understanding the file-system hierarchy

The Linux file system is organized like a tree, with a root directory from which all other directories branch out. When you write a complete path-name, the root directory is represented by a single slash (/). Then there's a hierarchy of files and directories. Parts of the file system can be in different physical drives or different hard drive partitions.

Linux uses a standard directory hierarchy. Figure 3-2 shows some of the standard parts of the Linux file system. You can create new directories anywhere in this structure.

**Figure 3-2:**
The Linux
file system
uses a
standard
directory
hierarchy
similar to
this one.

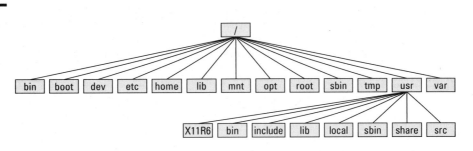

Write the name of any file or directory by concatenating the names of directories that identify where that file or directory is and by using the forward slash (/) as a separator. For example, in Figure 3-2, the usr directory at the top level is written as /usr because the root directory (/) contains usr. On the other hand, the X11R6 directory is inside the usr directory, which is inside the root directory (/). Therefore, the X11R6 directory is uniquely identified by the name /usr/X11R6. This type of full name is a *pathname* because the name identifies the path you take from the root directory to reach a file. Thus, /usr/X11R6 is a pathname.

The *Filesystem Hierarchy Standard (FHS)* specifies the organization of files and directories in UNIX-like operating systems, such as Linux. FHS defines a standard set of directories and their intended use. The FHS, if faithfully adopted by all Linux distributions, should help improve the interoperability of applications, system administration tools, development tools, and scripts across all Linux distributions. FHS even helps the system documentation as well as books like this one because the same description of the file system applies to all Linux distributions. Version 2.3 of FHS was announced on January 29, 2004. FHS 2.3 is part of the Linux Standard Base version 3.x (LSB 3.0), which was released on July 1, 2005. The standard was updated with 3.1 on October 25, 2005, and 3.2 on January 28, 2008. LSB 3.x (see www.linux base.org) is a set of binary standards aimed at reducing variations among the Linux distributions and promoting portability of applications. As of this writing, the most current Base is 4.0.3 (April 2010). To find out more about FHS, check out the FHS home page at www.pathname.com/fhs.

Each of the standard directories in the Linux file system has a specific purpose. Table 3-1, Table 3-2, and Table 3-3 summarize these directories.

| Table 3-1 | Standard Directories in Linux File System |
|---|---|
| *Directory* | *Used to Store* |
| /bin | Executable files for user commands (for use by all users) |
| /boot | Files needed by the boot loader to load the Linux kernel |
| /dev | Device files |
| /etc | Host-specific system configuration files |
| /home | User home directories |
| /lib | Shared libraries and kernel modules |
| /media | Mount point for removable media |
| /mnt | Mount point for a temporarily mounted file system |
| /opt | Add-on application software packages |
| /root | Home directory for the root user |
| /sbin | Utilities for system administration |
| /srv | Data for services (such as Web and FTP) offered by this system |
| /tmp | Temporary files |

| Table 3-2 | The /usr Directory Hierarchy |
|---|---|
| *Directory* | *Secondary Directory Hierarchy* |
| /usr/bin | Most user commands |
| /usr/include | Directory for *include files* — files that are inserted into source code of applications by using various directives — used in developing Linux applications |
| /usr/lib | Libraries used by software packages and for programming |
| /usr/libexec | Libraries for applications |
| /usr/local | Any local software |
| /usr/sbin | Nonessential system administrator utilities |
| /usr/share | Shared data that doesn't depend on the system architecture (whether the system is an Intel PC or a Sun SPARC workstation) |
| /usr/src | Source code |

| Table 3-3 | The /var Directory Hierarchy |
|---|---|
| *Directory* | *Variable Data* |
| /var/cache | Cached data for applications |
| /var/lib | Information relating to the current state of applications |
| /var/lock | Lock files to ensure that a resource is used by one application only |
| /var/log | Log files organized into subdirectories |
| /var/mail | User mailbox files |
| /var/opt | Variable data for packages stored in the /opt directory |
| /var/run | Data describing the system since it was booted |
| /var/spool | Data that's waiting for some kind of processing |
| /var/tmp | Temporary files preserved between system reboots |
| /var/yp | Network Information Service (NIS) database files |

## Mounting a device on the file system

The storage devices that you use in Linux contain Linux file systems. Each device has its own local file system consisting of a hierarchy of directories. Before you can access the files on a device, you have to attach the device's directory hierarchy to the tree that represents the overall Linux file system.

*Mounting* is the operation you perform to cause the file system on a physical storage device (a hard drive partition or a CD-ROM) to appear as part of the Linux file system. Figure 3-3 illustrates the concept of mounting.

Figure 3-3 shows each device with a name that begins with /dev. For example, /dev/cdrom is the first DVD/CD-ROM drive. Physical devices are mounted at specific mount points on the Linux file system. For example, the DVD/CD-ROM drive, /dev/cdrom, is mounted on /media/cdrom in the file system. After mounting the CD-ROM in this way, the Fedora directory on a CD-ROM or DVD-ROM appears as /media/cdrom/Fedora in the Linux file system.

You can use the mount command to manually mount a device on the Linux file system at a specified directory. That directory is the *mount point*. For example, to mount the DVD/CD-ROM drive at the /media/cdrom directory, type the following command (after logging in as root):

```
mount /dev/cdrom /media/cdrom
```

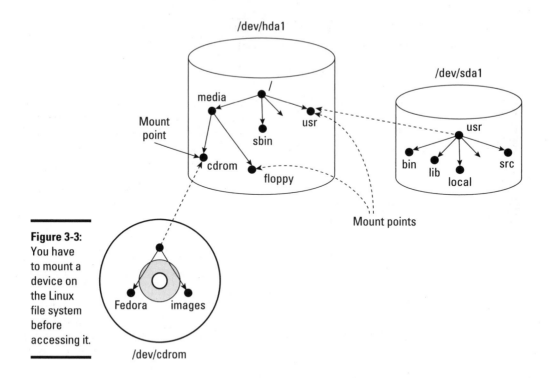

**Figure 3-3:**
You have
to mount a
device on
the Linux
file system
before
accessing it.

The mount command reports an error if the DVD/CD-ROM device is mounted already or if no CD or DVD media is in the drive. Otherwise, the mount operation succeeds, and you can access the contents of the DVD or CD through the /media/cdrom directory.

You can use any directory as the mount point. If you mount a device on a nonempty directory, however, you can't access the files in that directory until you unmount the device by using the umount command. Therefore, always use an empty directory as the mount point.

To unmount a device when you no longer need it, use the umount command. For example, for a DVD/CD-ROM device with the device name /dev/cdrom, type the following command to unmount the device:

```
umount /dev/cdrom
```

The umount command succeeds as long as no one is using the DVD/CD-ROM. If you get an error when trying to unmount the DVD/CD-ROM, check to see if the current working directory is on the DVD or CD. If you're currently working in one of the DVD/CD-ROM's directories, that also qualifies as a use of the DVD/CD-ROM.

## Examining the /etc/fstab file

The mount command has the following general format:

```
mount device-name mount-point
```

However, you can mount by specifying only the CD-ROM device name or the *mount-point* name, provided there's an entry in the /etc/fstab file for the CD-ROM mount point. That entry specifies the CD-ROM device name and the file-system type. That's why you can mount the CD-ROM with a shorter mount command.

For example, in Debian, you can mount the CD-ROM by typing one of the following commands:

```
mount /dev/cdrom
mount /media/cdrom
```

The /etc/fstab file is a *configuration file* — a text file containing information that the mount and umount commands use. Each line in the /etc/fstab file provides information about a device and its mount point in the Linux file system. Essentially, the /etc/fstab file associates various mount points within the file system with specific devices, which enables the mount command to work from the command line with only the mount point or the device as argument.

Here's a /etc/fstab file from a SUSE system. (The file has a similar format in other Linux distributions.)

```
/dev/hda11 / reiserfs acl,user_xattr 1 1
/dev/hda7 /boot ext3 acl,user_xattr 1 2
/dev/hda6 /data1 auto noauto,user 0 0
/dev/hda9 /data2 auto noauto,user 0 0
/dev/hda10 /data3 auto noauto,user 0 0
/dev/hda5 /data4 auto noauto,user 0 0
/dev/hda2 /windows/C ntfs ro,users,gid=users,umask=0002,nls=utf8 0 0
/dev/hda8 swap swap pri=42 0 0
devpts /dev/pts devpts mode=0620,gid=5 0 0
proc /proc proc defaults 0 0
usbfs /proc/bus/usb usbfs noauto 0 0
sysfs /sys sysfs noauto 0 0
/dev/cdrecorder /media/cdrecorder subfs fs=cdfss,ro,procuid,nosuid,nodev,exec,ioc
    harset=utf8 0 0
```

The first field on each line shows a device name, such as a hard drive partition. The second field is the mount point, and the third field indicates the type of file system on the device. You can ignore the last three fields for now.

This /etc/fstab file shows that the /dev/hda8 device functions as a swap device for virtual memory, which is why both the mount point and the file-system type are set to swap.

The Linux operating system uses the contents of the /etc/fstab file to mount various file systems automatically. During Linux startup, the init process executes a shell script that runs the mount -a command. That command reads the /etc/fstab file and mounts all listed file systems (except those with the noauto option). The third field on each line of /etc/fstab specifies the type of file system on that device, and the fourth field shows a comma-separated list of options that the mount command uses when mounting that device on the file system. Typically, you find the defaults option in this field. The defaults option implies — among other things — that the device mounts at boot time, that only the root user can mount the device, and that the device mounts for both reading and writing. If the options include noauto, the device doesn't mount automatically when the system boots.

In Fedora, you often find the managed option in the fourth field of /etc/fstab entries. The managed option indicates that the line was added to the fstab file by the HAL (hardware abstraction layer) daemon, which runs the fstab-sync command to add entries in the /etc/fstab file for each removable drive that it detects. You typically find that the entries for DVD/CD-ROM drive(s) (/dev/hdc in most systems) have the managed option in the fourth field.

## Sharing Files with NFS

Sharing files through the NFS is simple and involves two basic steps:

✦ On the NFS server, export one or more directories by listing them in the /etc/exports file and by running the /usr/sbin/exportfs command. In addition, you must run the NFS server.

✦ On each client system, use the mount command to mount the directories the server has exported.

How you start the NFS server depends on the Linux distribution. If a GUI sysadmin tool is available, you can start the NFS server from the GUI tool. Otherwise, you can type a command in a terminal window to start the NFS server. For example, in Debian, you can type **invoke-rc.d nfs-kernel-server start** and **invoke-rc.d nfs-common start** to start the NFS server. In Fedora, type **service nfs start**. To start the NFS server in SUSE, you can use the YaST Control Center: From the main menu, choose System⇨YaST⇨System⇨System Services (Runlevel). In Xandros, you can start the NFS server from the Xandros Control Center (Main Menu⇨Control Center) or by typing **invoke-rc.d nfs-user-server start** in a terminal window.

The only problem in using NFS is that each client system must support it. Most PCs don't come with NFS — that means you have to buy NFS software separately if you want to share files by using NFS. If, however, all systems on your LAN run Linux (or other variants of UNIX with built-in NFS support), using NFS makes sense.

NFS has security vulnerabilities. Therefore, don't set up NFS on systems directly connected to the Internet.

The upcoming section walks you through an NFS setup, using an example of two Linux PCs on a LAN.

## Exporting a file system with NFS

To export a file system with NFS, start with the server system that *exports* — makes available to the client systems — the contents of a directory. On the server, you must run the NFS service and also designate one or more file systems to be exported to the client systems.

You have to add an appropriate entry to the /etc/exports file. For example, suppose you want to export the /home directory and you want to enable the hostname LNBP75 to mount this file system for read and write operations. (You can use a host's IP address in place of the hostname.) You can do so by adding the following entry to the /etc/exports file:

```
/home LNBP75(rw)
```

If you use the IP address of a host, the entry might look like this:

```
/home 192.168.1.200(rw)
```

This specifies that 192.168.1.200 is the IP address of the host that's allowed full access to the /home directory.

After adding the entry in the /etc/exports file, start the NFS server using a method appropriate for your Linux distribution. For example, in Fedora, log in as root and type the following command in a terminal window:

```
service nfs start
```

When the NFS service is up, the server side of NFS is ready. Now you can try to mount the exported file system from a client system and access the exported file system.

If you ever make any changes to the exported file systems listed in the /etc/exports file, remember to restart the NFS service. For example, in Fedora, type **service nfs restart** in a terminal window. In Xandros, type **invoke-rc.d nfs-user-server restart**.

## Mounting an NFS file system

To access an exported NFS file system on a client system, you have to mount that file system on a *mount point* — which is, in practical terms, nothing more than a local directory. For example, suppose you want to access the /home/public directory exported from the server named LNBP200 at the local directory /mnt/lnbp200 on the client system. To do so, follow these steps:

1. **Log in as root and create the directory with the following command:**

    mkdir /mnt/lnbp200

2. **Type the following command to perform the mount operation:**

    mount lnbp200:/home/public /mnt/lnbp200

    If you know only the IP address of the server, replace the hostname (in this case, lnbp200) with the IP address.

3. **Change the directory to /mnt/lnbp200 with the command cd /mnt/lnbp200.**

    Now you can view and access exported files from this directory.

To confirm that the NFS file system is indeed mounted, log in as root on the client system and type **mount** in a terminal window. You see a line similar to the following about the NFS file system:

lnbp200:/home/public on /mnt/lnbp200 type nfs (rw,addr=192.168.1.200)

# Backing Up and Restoring Files

Backing up and restoring files is a crucial system administration task. If something happens to your system's hard drive, you have to rely on the backups to recover important files. The following discussion presents some backup strategies, describes several backup media, and explains how to back up and restore files by using the tape archiver (tar) program that comes with Linux. Also, you find out how to perform incremental and automatic backups on tapes.

If you have a CD burner, you can back up files also by recording them on a CD-R. Consult Book II, Chapter 4, for information on what application you can use to burn a data CD.

## Selecting a backup strategy and media

Your Linux system's hard drive contains everything you need to keep the system running — as well as other files (such as documents and databases) that keep your business running. You have to back up these files so you can recover quickly and bring the system back to normal in case the hard drive crashes. Typically, you have to follow a strict regimen of regular backups because you can never tell when the hard drive may fail or the file system may get corrupted. To implement such a regimen, first decide which files you want to back up, how often, and what backup storage media to use. This process is what is meant by selecting a backup strategy and backup media.

Your choice of backup strategy and backup media depends on your assessment of the risk of business disruption due to hard drive failure. Depending on how you use your Linux system, a disk failure may or may not have much effect on you.

For example, if you use your Linux system as a learning tool (to find out more about Linux or programming), all you may need are backup copies of some system files required to configure Linux. In this case, your backup strategy can be to save important system configuration files on one or more floppies every time you change any system configuration.

On the other hand, if you use your Linux system as an office server that provides shared file storage for many users, the risk of business disruption due to disk failure is much higher. In this case, you have to back up all the files every week and back up any new or changed files every day. You can perform these backups in an automated manner (with the job-scheduling features described in Chapter 1 of this minibook). Also, you probably need a backup storage medium that can store many gigabytes of data. In other words, for high-risk situations, your backup strategy is more elaborate and requires additional equipment (such as a tape drive).

Your choice of backup media depends on the amount of data you have to back up. For a small amount of data (such as system configuration files), you can use USB flash drives as the backup media. If your PC has a Zip drive, you can use Zip disks as backup media; these are good for backing up a single-user directory. To back up entire servers, use an external hard drive (which could be attached to the computer or the network) or a tape drive (typically a 4mm or 8mm tape drive that connects to a SCSI controller). Such tape drives can store several gigabytes of data per tape, and you can use them to back up an entire file system on a single tape.

When backing up files to these media, you have to refer to the backup device by name. Table 3-4 lists device names for some common backup devices.

| Table 3-4 | Device Names for Common Backup Devices |
|-----------|----------------------------------------|
| *Backup Device* | *Linux Device Name* |
| Floppy disk (where they still exist) | /dev/fd0 |
| IDE Zip drive | /dev/hdc4 or /dev/hdd4 |
| SCSI Zip drive | /dev/sda (assuming it's the first SCSI drive — otherwise, the device name depends on the SCSI ID) |
| SCSI tape drive | /dev/st0 or /dev/nst0 (the n prefix means that the tape isn't rewound after files are copied to the tape) |

## Commercial backup utilities for Linux

The next section explains how to back up and restore files using the tape archiver (tar) program that comes with Linux. Although you can manage backups with tar, a number of commercial backup utilities come with graphical user interfaces and other features to simplify backups. Here are some well-known commercial backup utilities for Linux:

✦ **BRU:** A backup and restore utility from the TOLIS Group, Inc. (www.tolisgroup.com)

✦ **LONE-TAR:** Tape backup software package from Lone Star Software Corp. (www.cactus.com)

✦ **Arkeia:** Backup and recovery software for heterogeneous networks from Arkeia (www.arkeia.com)

✦ **CA ARCserve Backup for Linux:** Data-protection technology for Linux systems from Computer Associates (http://www.arcserve.com/us/products/product.aspx?id=5282)

## Using the tape archiver — tar

You can use the tar command to archive files to a device, such as a floppy disk or tape. The tar program creates an archive file that can contain other directories and files and (optionally) compress the archive for efficient storage. The archive is then written to a specified device or another file. Many software packages are distributed in the form of a compressed tar file.

The command syntax of the tar program is as follows:

```
tar options destination source
```

Here, *options* are usually specified by a sequence of single letters, with each letter specifying what tar does. The *destination* is the device name of the backup device. And *source* is a list of file or directory names denoting the files to back up.

### Backing up and restoring a single-volume archive

Suppose you want to back up the contents of the /etc/X11 directory on a floppy disk. Log in as root, place a disk in the floppy drive, and type the following command:

```
tar zcvf /dev/fd0 /etc/X11
```

The tar program displays a list of filenames as each file is copied to the compressed tar archive on the floppy disk. In this case, the options are zcvf, the destination is /dev/fd0 (the floppy disk), and the source is the /etc/X11 directory (which implies all its subdirectories and their contents). You can use a similar tar command to back up files to a tape — simply replace /dev/fd0 with the tape device — such as /dev/st0 for a SCSI tape drive.

Table 3-5 defines a few common tar options.

| Table 3-5 | Common tar Options |
| --- | --- |
| *Option* | *Does the Following* |
| c | Creates a new archive. |
| f | Specifies the name of the archive file or device on the next field in the command line. |
| M | Specifies a multivolume archive. (The next section describes multivolume archives.) |
| t | Lists the contents of the archive. |
| v | Displays verbose messages. |
| x | Extracts files from the archive. |
| z | Compresses the tar archive using gzip. |

To view the contents of the tar archive you create on the floppy disk, type the following command:

```
tar ztf /dev/fd0
```

You see a list of filenames (each begins with /etc/X11) indicating what's in the backup. In this tar command, the t option lists the contents of the tar archive.

To extract the files from a tar backup, follow these steps while logged in as root:

**1. Change the directory to /tmp by typing this command:**

```
cd /tmp
```

This step is where you can practice extracting the files from the tar backup. For a real backup, change the directory to an appropriate location (typically, you type **cd /**).

**2. Type the following command:**

```
tar zxvf /dev/fd0
```

This tar command uses the x option to extract the files from the archive stored on /dev/fd0 (the floppy disk).

Now if you check the contents of the /tmp directory, you notice that the tar command creates an etc/X11 directory tree in /tmp and restores all the files from the tar archive into that directory. The tar command strips the leading / from the filenames in the archive and restores the files in the current directory. If you want to restore the /etc/X11 directory from the archive on the floppy, use this command:

```
tar zxvf /dev/fd0 -C /
```

The −C does a cd to the directory specified (in this case, the root directory of /) before doing the tar; the / at the end of the command denotes the directory where you want to restore the backup files.

You can use the tar command to create, view, and restore an archive. You can store the archive in a file or in any device you specify with a device name.

### Backing up and restoring a multivolume archive

Sometimes the capacity of a single storage medium is less than the total storage space needed to store the archive. In this case, you can use the M option for a multivolume archive — meaning the archive can span multiple tapes or floppies (if you happen to be using an older machine that still has them). Note, however, that you can't create a compressed, multivolume archive. That means you have to drop the z option. To see how multivolume archives work, log in as root, place one disk in the floppy drive, and type the following tar command:

```
tar cvfM /dev/fd0 /usr/share/doc/ghostscript*
```

*Note:* The M tells `tar` to create a multivolume archive. The `tar` command prompts you for a second floppy when the first one is filled. Take out the first floppy and insert another floppy when you see the following prompt:

```
Prepare volume #2 for '/dev/fd0' and hit return:
```

When you press Enter, the `tar` program continues with the second floppy. In this example, you need only two floppies to store the archive; for larger archives, the `tar` program continues to prompt for floppies as needed.

To restore from this multivolume archive, type **cd /tmp** to change the directory to /tmp. (I use the /tmp directory for illustrative purposes, but you have to use a real directory when you restore files from archive.) Then type

```
tar xvfM /dev/fd0
```

The `tar` program prompts you to feed the floppies as necessary.

Use the `du -s` command to determine the amount of storage you need for archiving a directory. For example, type **du -s /etc** to see the total size of the /etc directory in kilobytes. Here's a typical output of that command:

```
35724 /etc
```

The resulting output shows that the /etc directory requires at least 35,724K of storage space to back up.

## Backing up on tapes

Although backing up on tapes is as simple as using the right device name in the `tar` command, you do have to know some nuances of the tape device to use it well. When you use `tar` to back up to the device named /dev/st0 (the first SCSI tape drive), the tape device automatically rewinds the tape after the `tar` program finishes copying the archive to the tape. The /dev/st0 device is called a *rewinding tape device* because it rewinds tapes by default.

If your tape can hold several gigabytes of data, you may want to write several `tar` archives — one after another — to the same tape (otherwise much of the tape may be left empty). If you plan to do so, your tape device can't rewind the tape after the `tar` program finishes. To help you with scenarios like this one, several Linux tape devices are nonrewinding. The nonrewinding SCSI tape device is called /dev/nst0. Use this device name if you want to write one archive after another on a tape.

After each archive, the nonrewinding tape device writes an end-of-file (EOF) marker to separate one archive from the next. Use the `mt` command to control the tape — you can move from one marker to the next or rewind the tape. For example, after you finish writing several archives to a tape using the /dev/nst0 device name, you can force the tape to rewind with the following command:

```
mt -f /dev/nst0 rewind
```

After rewinding the tape, you can use the following command to extract files from the first archive to the current disk directory:

```
tar xvf /dev/nst0
```

After that, you must move past the EOF marker to the next archive. To do so, use the following mt command:

```
mt -f /dev/nst0 fsf 1
```

This positions the tape at the beginning of the next archive. Now use the tar xvf command again to read this archive.

If you save multiple archives on a tape, you have to keep track of the archives yourself. The order of the archives can be hard to remember, so you may be better off simply saving one archive per tape.

### Performing incremental backups

Suppose you use tar to back up your system's hard drive on a tape. Because such a full backup can take quite some time, you don't want to repeat this task every night. (Besides, only a small number of files may have changed during the day.) To locate the files that need backing up, you can use the find command to list all files that have changed in the past 24 hours:

```
find / -mtime -1 -type f -print
```

This command prints a list of files that have changed within the last day. The -mtime -1 option means you want the files that were last modified less than one day ago. You can now combine this find command with the tar command to back up only those files that have changed within the last day:

```
tar cvf /dev/st0 `find / -mtime -1 -type f -print`
```

When you place a command between single back quotes, the shell executes that command and places the output at that point in the command line. The result is that the tar program saves only the changed files in the archive. This process gives you an incremental backup of only the files that have changed since the previous day.

### Performing automated backups

Chapter 1 of this minibook shows how to use crontab to set up recurring jobs (called *cron jobs*). The Linux system performs these tasks at regular intervals. Backing up your system is a good use of the `crontab` facility. Suppose your backup strategy is as follows:

✦ Every Sunday at 1:15 a.m., your system backs up the entire hard drive on the tape.

✦ Monday through Saturday, your system performs an incremental backup at 3:10 a.m. by saving only those files that have changed during the past 24 hours.

To set up this automated backup schedule, log in as `root` and type the following lines in a file named `backups` (this example assumes that you are using a SCSI tape drive):

```
15 1 * * 0 tar zcvf /dev/st0 /
10 3 * * 1-6 tar zcvf /dev/st0 `find / -mtime -1 -type f -print`
```

Next, submit this job schedule by using the following `crontab` command:

```
crontab backups
```

Now you're set for an automated backup. All you need to do is to place a new tape in the tape drive every day. Remember also to give each tape an appropriate label.

# Accessing a DOS or Windows File System

If you're using a legacy machine that you just don't want to throw out and have Microsoft Windows 95, 98, or Me installed on your hard drive, you've probably already mounted the DOS or Windows partition under Linux. If not, you can easily mount DOS or Windows partitions in Linux. Mounting makes the DOS or Windows directory hierarchy appear as part of the Linux file system.

## Mounting a DOS or Windows disk partition

To mount a DOS or Windows hard drive partition or floppy in Linux, use the `mount` command but include the option `-t vfat` to indicate the file-system type as DOS. For example, if your DOS partition happens to be the first partition on your IDE (Integrated Drive Electronics) drive and you want to mount it on `/dosc`, use the following `mount` command:

```
mount -t vfat /dev/hda1 /dosc
```

The `-t vfat` part of the `mount` command specifies that the device you mount — `/dev/hda1` — has an MS-DOS file system. Figure 3-4 illustrates the effect of this `mount` command.

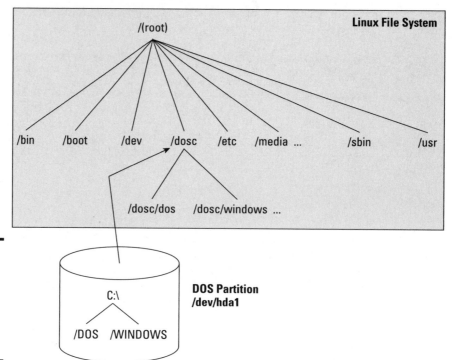

**Figure 3-4:**
Here's how you mount a DOS partition on the /dosc directory.

Figure 3-4 shows how directories in your DOS partition map to the Linux file system. What was the C:\DOS directory under DOS becomes /dosc/dos under Linux. Similarly, C:\WINDOWS now is /dosc/windows. You probably can see the pattern. To convert a DOS filename to Linux (when you mount the DOS partition on /dosc), perform the following steps:

1. **Change the DOS names to lowercase.**

2. **Change C:\ to /dosc/.**

3. **Change all backslashes (\) to slashes (/).**

## Mounting those old DOS floppy disks

Just as you mount a DOS hard drive partition on the Linux file system, you can also mount a DOS floppy disk on a legacy machine. You must log in as root to mount a floppy, but you can set up your system so that any user can mount a DOS floppy disk. You also have to know the device name for the floppy drive. By default, Linux defines the following two generic floppy device names:

✦ `/dev/fd0` is the A drive (the first floppy drive)

✦ `/dev/fd1` is the B drive (the second floppy drive, if you have one)

You can use any empty directory in the file system as the mount point, but the Linux system comes with a directory, `/media/floppy`, specifically for mounting a floppy disk.

To mount a DOS floppy disk on the `/media/floppy` directory, put the floppy in the drive and type the following command:

```
mount -t vfat /dev/fd0 /media/floppy
```

After you mount the floppy, you can copy files to and from the floppy by using the Linux copy command (`cp`). To copy the file `gnome1.pcx` from the current directory to the floppy, type the following:

```
cp gnome1.pcx /media/floppy
```

Similarly, to see the contents of the floppy disk, type the following:

```
ls /media/floppy
```

If you want to remove the floppy disk from the drive, first unmount the floppy drive. *Unmounting* removes the association between the floppy disk's file system and the mount point on the Linux file system. Use the `umount` command to unmount the floppy disk like this:

```
umount /dev/fd0
```

You can set up your Linux system so that any user can mount a DOS floppy. To enable any user to mount a DOS floppy in the A drive on the `/a` directory, for example, perform the following steps:

*1.* **Log in as root.**

*2.* **Create the** `/a` **directory (the mount point) by typing the following command in a terminal window:**

```
mkdir /a
```

*3.* **Edit the `/etc/fstab` file in a text editor (such as vi or emacs) by inserting the following line, and then save the file and quit the editor:**

```
/dev/fd0 /a vfat noauto,user 0 0
```

The first field in that line is the device name of the floppy drive (`/dev/fd0`); the second field is the mount directory (`/a`); the third field shows the type of file system (`vfat`). The user option (which appears next to `noauto`) enables all users to mount DOS floppy disks.

4. **Log out and then log back in as a normal user.**

5. **To confirm that you can mount a DOS floppy as a normal user and not just as root, insert a DOS floppy in the A drive and type the following command:**

```
mount /a
```

The `mount` operation succeeds, and you see a listing of the DOS floppy when you type the command **ls /a**.

6. **To unmount the DOS floppy, type umount /a.**

## Mounting an NTFS partition

Nowadays, most PCs come with Windows Vista or Windows 7 pre-installed on the hard drive. Both Windows Vista and Windows 7, as well as Windows XP, typically use the NT File System (NTFS). Linux supports read-only access to NTFS partitions, and many distributions come with the `ntfs.ko` kernel module, which is needed to access an NTFS partition.

If you've installed Linux on a Windows XP system and want to access files on the NTFS partition but your distribution doesn't include the `ntfs.ko` module, you can build the kernel after enabling an NTFS module during the kernel configuration step.

After rebuilding and booting from the new kernel, log in as `root` and type the following command to create a mount point for the NTFS partition. (In this case, I'm creating a mount point in the `/mnt` directory.)

```
mkdir /mnt/xp
```

Now, you can mount the NTFS partition with the following command:

```
mount /dev/hda2 /mnt/xp -t ntfs -r -o umask=0222
```

If necessary, replace `/dev/hda2` with the device name for the NTFS partition on your system. On most PCs that come with Windows XP pre-installed, the NTFS partition is the second one (`/dev/hda2`) — the first partition (`/dev/hda1`) is usually a hidden partition used to hold files used for Windows XP installation.

## Using mtools

One way to access the MS-DOS file system is to first mount the DOS hard drive or floppy disk by using the `mount` command and then use regular Linux commands, such as `ls` and `cp`, to work with the mounted DOS file system. This approach of mounting a DOS file system is fine for hard drives.

Linux can mount the DOS partition automatically at startup, and you can access the DOS directories on the hard drive at any time.

If you want a quick directory listing of a DOS floppy disk, however, mounting can soon become tedious. First, you have to mount the floppy drive. Then you must use the ls command. Finally, you must use the umount command before ejecting the floppy out of the drive.

This situation is where the mtools package comes to the rescue. The mtools package implements most common DOS commands; the commands use the same names as in DOS except you add an m prefix to each command. Thus, the mdir command lists the directory listing and mcopy copies files. The best part of mtools is the fact that you don't have to mount the floppy disk to use the mtools commands.

Because the mtools commands write to and read from the physical device (floppy disk), you must log in as root to perform these commands. If you want any user to access the mtools commands, you must alter the permission settings for the floppy drive devices. Use the following command to permit anyone to read from and write to the first floppy drive:

```
chmod o+rw /dev/fd0
```

## Trying mtools

To try out mtools, follow these steps:

*1.* **Place an MS-DOS floppy disk in your system's A drive.**

*2.* **Type** mdir.

You see the directory of the floppy disk (in the standard DOS directory listing format).

Typically, you use the mtools utilities to access floppy disks. The default configuration file, /etc/mtools.conf, is set up to access the floppy drive as the A drive. Although you can edit that file to define C and D drives for your DOS hard drive partitions, you can access the hard drive partitions also by using the Linux mount command to mount them. Because you can mount the hard drive partitions automatically at startup, accessing them through the Linux commands is normally just as easy.

## Understanding the /etc/mtools.conf file

The mtools package works with the default setup, but if you get any errors, check the /etc/mtools.conf file. That file contains the definitions of the drives (such as A, B, and C) that the mtools utilities see. Following are a few lines from a typical /etc/mtools.conf file:

```
drive a: file="/dev/fd0" exclusive mformat_only
drive b: file="/dev/fd1" exclusive mformat_only
# First SCSI hard disk partition
#drive c: file="/dev/sda1"
# First IDE hard disk partition on a Windows 98 PC
drive c: file="/dev/hda1"
# Internal IDE Zip drive
drive e: file="/dev/hdd4" exclusive
```

The pound sign (#) indicates the start of a comment. Each line defines a drive letter, the associated Linux device name, and some keywords that indicate how to access the device. In this example, the first two lines define drives A and B. The third noncomment line defines drive C as the first partition on the first IDE drive (/dev/hda1). If you have other DOS drives (D, for example), you can add another line that defines drive D as the appropriate disk partition.

If your system's A drive is a high-density, 3.5-inch drive, you don't need to change anything in the default /etc/mtools.conf file to access the floppy drive. If you also want to access any DOS partition in the hard drive, uncomment and edit an appropriate line for the C drive.

You also can access Iomega Zip drives through mtools. Simply specify a drive letter and the appropriate device's filename. For built-in IDE (ATAPI) Zip drives, try /dev/hdd4 as the device file and add the following line in the /etc/mtools.conf file:

```
drive e: file="/dev/hdd4"
```

After you have made this change, you can use mtools commands to access the Zip drive (refer to it as the E drive). For example, to see the directory listing, place the Zip disk in the Zip drive and type:

```
mdir e:
```

## Understanding the mtools commands

The mtools package is a collection of utilities. The discussion so far has included mdir — the mtools counterpart of the DIR command in DOS. The other mtools commands are fairly easy to use.

If you know MS-DOS commands, using the mtools commands is simple. Type the DOS command in lowercase letters and remember to add m in front of each command. Because the Linux commands and filenames are case-sensitive, you must use all lowercase letters when you type mtools commands.

Table 3-6 summarizes the commands available in mtools.

| Table 3-6 | | The mtools Commands |
|---|---|---|
| *mtools Utility* | *MS-DOS Command* | *The mtools Utility Does the Following (If Any)* |
| mattrib | ATTRIB | Changes MS-DOS file-attribute flags |
| mbadblocks | | Tests a floppy disk and marks the bad blocks in the file allocation table (FAT) |
| mcd | CD | Changes an MS-DOS directory |
| mcopy | COPY | Copies files between MS-DOS and Linux |
| mdel | DEL or ERASE | Deletes an MS-DOS file |
| mdeltree | DELTREE | Recursively deletes an MS-DOS directory |
| mdir | DIR | Displays an MS-DOS directory listing |
| mdu | | Lists space that a directory and its contents occupy |
| mformat | FORMAT | Places an MS-DOS file system on a low-level-formatted floppy disk (use fdformat to low-level-format a floppy disk in Linux). |
| minfo | | Gets information about an MS-DOS file system |
| mkmanifest | | Makes a list of short name equivalents |
| mlabel | LABEL | Initializes an MS-DOS volume label |
| mmd | MD or MKDIR | Creates an MS-DOS directory |
| mmove | | Moves or renames an MS-DOS file or subdirectory |
| mmount | | Mounts an MS-DOS disk |
| mpartition | | Creates an MS-DOS file system as a partition |
| mrd | RD or RMDIR | Deletes an MS-DOS directory |
| mren | REN or RENAME | Renames an existing MS-DOS file |
| mshowfat | | Shows FAT entries for an MS-DOS file |
| mtoolstest | | Tests and displays the current mtools configuration |
| mtype | TYPE | Displays the contents of an MS-DOS file |
| mwrite | COPY | Copies a Linux file to MS-DOS |
| mzip | | Performs certain operations on SCSI Zip disks |

You can use the `mtools` commands just as you use the corresponding DOS commands. The `mdir` command, for example, works the same as the `DIR` command in DOS. The same goes for all the other `mtools` commands shown in Table 3-6.

You can use wildcard characters (such as *) with `mtools` commands, but you must remember that the Linux shell is the first program to see your command. If you don't want the shell to expand the wildcard character all over the place, use quotation marks around filenames that contain any wildcard characters. For example, to copy all `*.txt` files from the A drive to your current directory, use the following command:

```
mcopy "a:*.txt" .
```

If you omit the quotation marks, the shell tries to expand the string `a:*.txt` with filenames from the current Linux directory. It also tries to copy those files (if any) from the DOS floppy disk.

On the other hand, if you want to copy files from the Linux directory to the DOS floppy disk, you do want the shell to expand any wildcard characters. To copy all `*.jpg` files from the current Linux directory to the DOS floppy disk, for example, use `mcopy` like this:

```
mcopy *.jpg a:
```

With the `mtools` utilities, you can use the backslash character (\) as the directory separator, just as you do in DOS. However, when you type a filename that contains the backslash character, you must enclose the name in double quotation marks (" "). For example, here's a command that copies a file from a subdirectory on the A drive to the current Linux directory:

```
mcopy "a:\test\sample.dat" .
```

# Chapter 4: Installing and Updating Applications

## In This Chapter

✔ Working with RPM files with the rpm command

✔ Working with DEB files with dpkg, dselect, and APT

✔ Building applications from source files

✔ Online updating of Linux applications

*M*ost software packages for Linux are distributed in one of two special file formats: Red Hat Package Manager (RPM) files or Debian (DEB) files. That's why you have to know how to install or remove software packages that come in the form of RPM or DEB files. This chapter illustrates how to work with both types of files.

You can install RPM and DEB files in all Linux distributions, but each distribution has its favored distribution format. Fedora, with its Red Hat Linux heritage, favors RPM files, whereas most Debian-based distributions, such as Knoppix, Ubuntu, and Xandros, use DEB files for distributing software. SUSE Linux uses RPM format.

Many other open source software packages come in source-code form, usually in compressed archives. You have to unpack, build, and install the software to use it. The following sections describe the steps you typically follow when downloading, building, and installing source-based software packages. There is also a brief description of how to update your Linux system online. As you'll find out, each distribution has its own tools for online updates.

## Working with RPM Files

RPM is a system for packaging all the necessary files for a software product in a single file — called an *RPM file,* or simply, an *RPM.* In fact, the Fedora and SUSE distributions are a whole lot of RPMs. The best way to work with RPMs is through the RPM commands. You have to type these commands at the shell prompt in a terminal window or a text console.

In Fedora, the RPM commands are suitable only if you have to install just a handful of RPM files. To install a large number of RPM files, you should choose Applications⇨Add/Remove Software from the desktop. If you install RPM files from a CD or DVD, first mount the CD/DVD and then type **system-cdinstall-helper /media/cdrom**. (If your CD/DVD is mounted at some other directory, replace /media/cdrom with that directory name.) You'll see a Package Management window from which you can select and install groups of packages.

## Using the RPM command

When you install an RPM-based distribution such as Fedora, the installer uses the rpm command to unpack the packages (RPM files) and to copy the contents to your hard drive.

You don't have to understand the internal structure of an RPM file, but you need to know how to use the rpm command to work with RPM files. Here are some of the things you can do with the rpm command:

✦ Find out the version numbers and other information about the RPMs installed on your system.

✦ Install a new software package from an RPM. For example, you may install a package you skipped during the initial installation.

✦ Remove (uninstall) unneeded software you previously installed from an RPM. You may uninstall a package to reclaim the disk space, if you find that you rarely (or never) use the package.

✦ Upgrade an older version of an RPM with a new one. For example, in Fedora, you may upgrade after you download a new version of a package from Fedora download sites (listed online at http://mirrors.fedora project.org). You must upgrade an RPM to benefit from the fixes in the new version.

✦ Verify that an RPM is in working order. You can verify a package to check that all necessary files are in the correct locations.

As you can see, the rpm command is versatile — it can do a lot of different things, depending on the options you use.

If you ever forget the rpm options, type the following command to see a list:

```
rpm --help | more
```

The number of rpm options will amaze you!

## Understanding RPM filenames

An RPM contains a number of files, but it appears as a single file on your Fedora system. By convention, the RPM filenames have a specific format. A typical RPM filename looks like this:

```
openoffice.org-writer-1.9.104-2.i386.rpm
```

This filename has the following parts, the first three of which are separated by hyphens (–):

+ **Package name:** openoffice.org-writer
+ **Version number:** 1.9.104
+ **Release number:** 2
+ **Architecture:** i386 (this package is for Intel 80x86 or Pentium-compatible processors)

Usually, the package name is descriptive enough for you to guess what the RPM may contain. The version number is the same as that of the software package's current version number (even when it's distributed in some other form, such as a `tar` file). Developers assign the release number to keep track of changes. The architecture is i386, or noarch, for the RPMs you want to install on a PC with an Intel x86-compatible processor.

## Querying RPMs

As the `rpm` command installs packages, it builds a database of installed RPMs. You can use the `rpm -q` command to query this database to find information about packages installed on your system.

For example, to find out the version number of the Linux kernel installed on your system, type the following `rpm -q` command:

```
rpm -q cups
```

You see a response similar to the following:

```
cups-1.4.1-15
```

The response is the name of the RPM for the kernel. (This version is the executable version of the kernel, not the source files.) The name is the same as the RPM filename, except that the last part — `.i386.rpm` — isn't shown. In this case, the version part of the RPM tells you that you have CUPS (the Common UNIX Printing System) version 1.4.1 installed.

You can see a list of all installed RPMs by using the following command:

```
rpm -qa
```

You see a long list of RPMs scroll by your screen. To view the list one screen at a time, type

```
rpm -qa | more
```

If you want to search for a specific package, feed the output of rpm -qa to the grep command. For example, to see all packages with *kernel* in their names, type

```
rpm -qa | grep kernel
```

The result depends on what parts of the kernel RPMs are installed on a system.

You can query much more than a package's version number with the rpm -q command. By adding single-letter options, you can find out other useful information. For example, try the following command to see the files in the CUPS package:

```
rpm -ql cups
```

Here are a few more useful forms of the rpm -q commands to query information about a package. (To use any of these rpm -q commands, type the command, followed by the package name.)

+ rpm -qc: Lists all configuration files in a package.

+ rpm -qd: Lists all documentation files in a package. These are usually the online manual pages (also known as *man pages*).

+ rpm -qf: Displays the name of the package (if any) to which a specified file belongs.

+ rpm -qi: Displays detailed information about a package ( version number, size, installation date, and a brief description).

+ rpm -ql: Lists all the files in a package. For some packages, you see a very long list.

+ rpm -qs: Lists the state of all files in a package. (The state of a file can be one of the following: normal, not installed, or replaced.)

These rpm commands provide information about installed packages only. If you want to find information about an uninstalled RPM file, add p to the command-line option of each command. For example, to view the list of files in the RPM file named rdist-6.1.5-792.i586.rpm, go to the directory where that file is located and type the following command:

```
rpm -qpl rdist-*.rpm
```

This command works only if the current directory contains that RPM file.

Two handy `rpm -q` commands enable you to find out which RPM file provides a specific file and which RPMs need a specified package. To find out the name of the RPM that provides a file, use the following command:

```
rpm -q --whatprovides filename
```

For example, to see which RPM provides the file `/etc/vsftpd.conf`, type

```
rpm -q --whatprovides /etc/vsftpd.conf
```

RPM then prints the name of the package that provides the file, like this:

```
vsftpd-2.0.3-1
```

If you provide the name of a package instead of a filename, RPM displays the name of the RPM package that contains the specified package. On the other hand, to find the names of RPMs that need a specific package, use the following command:

```
rpm -q --whatrequires packagename
```

For example, to see which packages need the `openssl` package, type

```
rpm -q --whatrequires openssl
```

The output from this command shows all the RPM packages that need the `openssl` package.

## Installing an RPM

To install an RPM, use the `rpm -i` command. You have to provide the name of the RPM file as the argument. If you want to view the progress of the RPM installation, use `rpm -ivh`. A series of pound signs (#) displays as the package is unpacked.

For example, to install the `kernel-devel` RPM (which contains the header files for the Linux operating system) for Fedora from the companion DVD-ROM, insert the DVD, and after it's mounted, type the following commands:

```
cd /media/cdrom/Fedora/RPMS
rpm -ivh kernel-devel*
```

You don't have to type the full RPM filename — you can use a few characters from the beginning of the name followed by an asterisk (*). Make sure you type enough of the name to identify the RPM file uniquely.

If you try to install an RPM that's already installed, the `rpm -i` command displays an error message. To force the `rpm` command to install a package even if errors are present, add `--force` to the `rpm -i` command, like this:

```
rpm -i --force man-2*
```

## Removing an RPM

You may want to remove — uninstall — a package if you realize that you don't need the software. For example, if you have installed the X Window System development package but discover you're not interested in writing X applications, you can easily remove the package by using the `rpm -e` command.

For example, to remove the package named `qt3-devel`, type

```
rpm -e qt3-devel
```

You have to know the name of the package before you can remove it. One good way to find the name is to use `rpm -qa` with `grep` to search for the appropriate RPM file.

To remove an RPM, you don't need the full RPM filename; all you need is the package name — the first part of the filename up to the hyphen (–) before the version number.

The `rpm -e` command does not remove a package that other packages need.

## Upgrading an RPM

Use the `rpm -U` command to upgrade an RPM. You must provide the name of the RPM file that contains the new software. For example, if you have version 1.1.20 of CUPS (printing system) installed but want to upgrade to version 1.1.23, download the RPM file `cups-1.1.23-15.i386.rpm` from a repository and use the following command:

```
rpm -U cups-1.1.23-15.i386.rpm
```

The `rpm` command performs the upgrade by removing the old version of the CUPS package and installing the new RPM.

Whenever possible, upgrade rather than remove the old package and install a new one. Upgrading automatically saves your old configuration files, so you don't have to reconfigure the software after a fresh installation.

When you're upgrading the kernel packages that contain a ready-to-run Linux kernel, install it by using the `rpm -i` command (instead of the `rpm -U` command). That way, you won't overwrite the current kernel.

## Verifying an RPM

If you suspect that a software package isn't properly installed, use the `rpm -V` command to verify it. For example, to verify the kernel package, type the following:

```
rpm -V kernel
```

`rpm` compares the size and other attributes of each file in the package against those of the original files. If everything verifies correctly, the `rpm -V` command does not print anything. If it finds any discrepancies, you see a report of them. For example, the command to type to verify the `httpd` package is

```
rpm -V httpd
```

The result may resemble the following:

```
S.5. . . . T c /etc/httpd/conf/httpd.conf
```

In this case, the output from `rpm -V` shows that a configuration file has changed. Each line of this command's output has three parts:

✦ The line starts with eight characters: Each character indicates the type of discrepancy found. For example, `S` means the size is different, and `T` means the time of last modification is different. Table 4-1 shows each character and its meaning. A period means that that specific attribute matches the original.

✦ For configuration files, a `c` appears next; otherwise, this field is blank. That's how you can tell whether a file is a configuration file. Typically, you don't worry if a configuration file has changed; you probably made the changes yourself.

✦ The last part of the line is the full pathname of the file. From this part, you can tell exactly where the file is located.

| Table 4-1 | Characters Used in RPM Verification Reports |
|-----------|---------------------------------------------|
| *Character* | *Meaning* |
| S | Size has changed |
| M | Permissions and file type are different |
| 5 | Checksum computed with the MD5 algorithm is different |

*(continued)*

**Table 4-1 *(continued)***

| Character | Meaning |
| --- | --- |
| D | Device type is different |
| L | Symbolic link is different |
| U | File's user is different |
| G | File's group is different |
| T | File's modification time is different |

# Working with DEB Files

Debian packages with .deb file extensions store executable files together with configuration files, online documentation, and other information. You can unpack and manipulate these DEB files using the Debian utility dpkg, which is a command-line program that takes many options. A text mode, menu-driven program called dselect is also available for you to manage the packages without having to type dpkg commands.

You typically use a higher-level utility called APT (Advanced Packaging Tool) to work with packages in Debian. For example, instead of downloading a DEB file and installing it with the dpkg command, you can simply use the apt-get command to install the package. The apt-get command can even download the package from an online Debian repository and install it on your system. The dpkg command is still useful when you want to look at the contents of a DEB file that you have manually downloaded from a repository or that might be in the apt cache directory (/var/cache/apt/archives in Debian).

dpkg, dselect, and apt are described in the following sections.

## Understanding DEB filenames

A typical DEB package has a filename like the following:

```
mozilla-firefox_1.0.4-2_i386.deb
```

The filename has three parts separated by underscores (_):

✦ **Package name:** mozilla-firefox

✦ **Version and revision:** 1.0.4-2 (the first part is the package maintainer's version number; the second part is the Debian revision number)

✦ **Architecture:** i386 (the package is for Intel x86-compatible systems)

The filename has a .deb extension, which indicates that this is a DEB file.

## Using the dpkg command

To get a feel for the dpkg command, type **dpkg --help | more**. The output shows the large number of options that dpkg accepts. You can also type **man dpkg** to read the online man page for dpkg.

You can use dpkg to perform many operations on packages, but you have to work at a shell prompt in a terminal window or a text console. The format of a dpkg command is

```
dpkg [options] action package
```

The command has zero or more options, an *action* indicating what dpkg has to do, and the name of a package, a DEB file, or a directory (depending on the *action* argument). Sometimes the dpkg command does not need any name of package or file, just an action.

Here are some examples of actions you can perform with dpkg:

✦ **Install** a package from a DEB file with the command dpkg -i *package file*, where *packagefile* is the name of the DEB file (for example, vsftpd-*.deb).

✦ **Remove** a package but retain the configuration files with the command dpkg -r *packagename*, where *packagename* is the name of the package (for example, vsftpd)

✦ **Configure** a package with the command dpkg --configure *package name*, where *packagename* is the name of a package (for example, vsftpd)

✦ **Purge** — remove everything including the configuration files — with the command dpkg -P *packagename*, where *packagename* is the name of a package (for example, vsftpd)

✦ **Audit** packages (and find the ones that are partially installed on your system) with the command dpkg -C (does not need a file or package name)

✦ **List contents** of a DEB file with the command dpkg -c *package file*, where *packagefile* is the name of the DEB file (for example, vsftpd-*.deb)

✦ **View information** about a DEB file with the command dpkg -I *package file*, where *packagefile* is the name of the DEB file (for example, vsftpd-*.deb)

✦ **List packages matching pattern** with the command dpkg -l *pattern*, where *pattern* is the package name pattern — usually with wildcard characters — that you want to match (for example, kernel*)

✦ **Find packages that contain files** with the command `dpkg -S pattern`, where *pattern* is the filename pattern — usually with wildcard characters — that the package contains (for example, `stdio*`)

✦ **List files installed from a package** with the command `dpkg -L package name`, where *packagename* is the name of a package (for example, `vsftpd`)

You can try these commands on a Debian system or any system that uses DEB packages. For example, to look for all packages matching names that begin with `mozilla`, type **dpkg -l mozilla*** in a terminal window. Here is the relevant portion of this command's output on a Debian system:

```
||/ Name Version Description
+++-==============-==========-==============================================
un mozilla <none> (no description available)
un mozilla-bonobo <none> (no description available)
ii mozilla-browse 1.7.8-1 The Mozilla Internet application suite - cor
ii mozilla-firefox 1.0.4-2 lightweight web browser based on Mozilla
```

The `ii` in the first column indicates that the package is installed; `un` means the package is not installed.

Another common use of `dpkg -l` is to list all packages and use `grep` to find lines that match a search string. For example, to find anything containing `kernel`, type **dpkg -l | grep kernel**. If the package names (in the second column of the `dpkg -l` output) are truncated, adjust the width of the output lines with a command like this:

```
COLUMNS=132 dpkg -l | grep kernel
```

The `dpkg -S` command is a handy way to locate which package provided a specific file in the system. For example, if you want to figure out what package includes the `/etc/host.conf` file, type **dpkg -S /etc/host.conf** and the output shows that the `base-files` package contains `/etc/host.conf`:

```
base-files: /etc/host.conf
```

## Introducing dselect

The `dselect` is meant to be a front-end to the `dpkg` utility. To try out `dselect`, log in as `root` and type **dselect** in a terminal window (or a text console). When `dselect` starts, you get `dselect`'s text mode menu.

`dselect` is not described in detail, but here are some of the tasks you can perform from the `dselect` main menu:

✦ Specify an access method — how to find the DEB packages

✦ Update the list of available packages

+ View the status of installed and available packages

+ Select packages and manage dependencies among packages

+ Install new packages or upgrade existing ones to newer versions

+ Configure packages that are not yet configured

+ Remove packages

One common sequence in `dselect` is to update the list of available packages and then upgrade all packages for which updates are available. You can, of course, perform that same task with a simple `apt` command as well.

## Using APT to manage DEB packages

APT is truly an advanced utility for keeping your Debian system up-to-date. You can use a number of APT utilities to manage DEB packages. The two commonly used commands are `apt-get` and `apt-cache`.

To install a package with `apt-get`, simply type **apt-get install** *package name*, where *packagename* is the name of the package that you want to install. For example, to install the `vsftpd` package, type **apt-get install vsftpd**.

Removing a package is equally simple. Type **apt-get remove** *package name*, where *packagename* is the name of the package you want to remove.

If you want to find the name of a package and you know some terms associated with the package, you can look for it with the `apt-cache` utility. For example, to look for a CD/DVD burner package, type **apt-cache search burn | more** to search through the APT's package cache (which is the list of Debian packages that APT downloads from the servers listed in the `/etc/apt/sources.list` file). Here are some lines of output from that command:

```
arson - KDE frontend for burning CDs
burn - Command line Data-CD, Audio-CD, ISO-CD, Copy-CD writing tool
caca-utils - text mode graphics utilities
cdcontrol - A parallel burner that allow you to write to one or more CD-Writers
at once
cdlabelgen - generates front cards and tray cards for CDs and DVDs
cdrtoaster - Tcl/Tk front-end for burning cdrom
cdw - Tool for burning CD's - console version
cdw-common - Tool for burning CD's - common files
cpuburn - a collection of programs to put heavy load on CPU
cwcdr - Chez Wam CD Ripper
dvd+rw-tools - DVD+-RW/R tools
dvdbackup - tool to rip DVD's from the command line
edenmath.app - Scientific calculator for GNUstep
gcdw - Tool for burning CD's - graphical version
gcombust - GTK+ based CD mastering and burning program
. . . lines deleted . . .
```

The output shows several potential CD/DVD burning programs that could be installed. To discover more about any of the packages, type **apt-cache show *packagename***, where ***packagename*** is the name of the package for which you want information. For example, to find out more about the dvd+rw-tools package, type **apt-cache show dvd+rw-tools** and the output shows a description of the package. You can then install the package with **apt-get install**.

To search for a keyword that appears in the package's name only, use the --names-only option like this: **apt-cache search - -names-only *keyword***, where ***keyword*** is something that appears in the package's name. For example, if you want to find packages that contain selinux in their names, type **apt-cache search - -names-only selinux**.

Run apt-get clean periodically to clean out the local repository (in the /var/cache/apt/archives directory) of DEB files that have already been installed. You can free up some disk space by removing these DEB files.

# Building Software Packages from Source Files

Many open source software packages are distributed in source-code form, without executable binaries. Before you can use such software, you have to compile the source files to build the executable binary files and then follow some instructions to install the package. This section shows you how to build software packages from source files.

## Downloading and unpacking the software

Typically, open source software source files are distributed in compressed tar archives. These archives are created by the tar program and compressed with the gzip program. The distribution is in the form of a single large file with the .tar.gz or .tar.Z extension — often referred to as a *compressed tarball*. If you want the software, you have to download the compressed tarball and unpack it.

Download the compressed tar file by using anonymous FTP or going through your Web browser. Typically, this process involves no effort on your part beyond clicking a link and saving the file in an appropriate directory on your system.

To try your hand at downloading and building a software package, you can practice on the X Multimedia System (XMMS) — a graphical X application for playing MP3 and other multimedia files. XMMS is bundled with Fedora and already installed on your system. However, you do no harm in downloading and rebuilding the XMMS package again.

Download the source files for XMMS from www.xmms.org/download.php. The files are packed in the form of a compressed tar archive. Click the http link for the source files and save them in the /usr/local/src directory in your Linux system. (Be sure to log in as root; otherwise you cannot save in the /usr/local/src directory.)

After downloading the compressed tar file, examine the contents with the following tar command:

```
tar ztf xmms*.gz | more
```

You see a listing similar to the following:

```
xmms-1.2.10/
xmms-1.2.10/intl/
xmms-1.2.10/intl/ChangeLog
xmms-1.2.10/intl/Makefile.in
xmms-1.2.10/intl/config.charset
xmms-1.2.10/intl/locale.alias
xmms-1.2.10/intl/ref-add.sin
xmms-1.2.10/intl/ref-del.sin
xmms-1.2.10/intl/gmo.h
xmms-1.2.10/intl/gettextP.h
xmms-1.2.10/intl/hash-string.h
xmms-1.2.10/intl/loadinfo.h
. . . lines deleted . . .
```

The output of this tar command shows you what's in the archive and gives you an idea of the directories that are created after you unpack the archive. In this case, a directory named xmms-1.2.10 is created in the current directory, which, in this case, is /usr/local/src. From the listing, you also figure out the programming language used to write the package. If you see .c and .h files, the source files are in the C programming language, which is used to write many open source software packages.

To extract the contents of the compressed tar archive, type the following tar command:

```
tar zxvf xmms*.gz
```

You again see a long list of files as they are extracted from the archive and copied to the appropriate directories on your hard drive.

Now you're ready to build the software.

## Building the software from source files

After you unpack the compressed `tar` archive, all source files are in a directory whose name is usually that of the software package with a version number suffix. For example, the XMMS version 1.2.10 source files extract to the `xmms-1.2.10` directory. To start building the software, change directories with the following command:

```
cd xmms*
```

You don't have to type the entire name — the shell can expand the directory name and change to the `xmms-1.2.10` directory.

Nearly all software packages come with a README or INSTALL file — a text file that tells you how to build and install the package. XMMS is no exception; it comes with a README file you can peruse by typing **more README**. An INSTALL file contains instructions for building and installing XMMS.

Most open source software packages, including XMMS, also come with a file named COPYING. This file contains the full text of the *GNU General Public License* (GPL), which spells out the conditions under which you can use and redistribute the software. If you're not familiar with the GNU GPL, read this file and show the license to your legal counsel for a full interpretation and an assessment of applicability to your business.

To build the software package, follow the instructions in the README or INSTALL file. For the XMMS package, the README file lists some of the prerequisites (such as libraries) and tells you what commands to type to build and install the package. In the case of XMMS, the instructions tell you to use the following steps:

*1.* **Type** ./configure **to check your system's configuration.**

This command also runs a shell script that creates a file named Makefile — a file the make command uses to build and install the package. (You can type **./configure --help** to see a list of options that configure accepts.)

If you get any errors about missing packages, you have to install those missing packages. Use your distribution's software installation tools to add the missing packages. For example, in Debian use the `apt-get install` command. In Fedora, choose Applications⇨Add/Remove Software. In SUSE, use the YaST GUI tool.

*2.* **Type** make **to build the software.**

This step compiles the source files in all the subdirectories. (Compiling source code converts each source file into an *object file* — a file containing binary instructions that your PC's processor can understand.)

3. **Type** make install **to install the software.**

   This step copies libraries and executable binary files to appropriate directories on your system.

Although the preceding list is specific to XMMS, most other packages follow these steps: configure, make, and make install. The configure shell script guesses system-dependent variables and creates a Makefile with commands needed to build and install the software.

> **WARNING!**
>
> To use these simple commands to build software packages, you must first install the software-development tools on your system. In Fedora, you must install the Development Tools and the GNOME Software Development packages. In Debian, to build and run XMMS, you must also install the X Software Development package because XMMS is an X application.

After you've installed XMMS, try running it from the GNOME or KDE desktop by typing **xmms** in a terminal window. From the XMMS window, press L to get the Load File dialog box. Select an MP3 file to play. Your PC must have a sound card, and the sound card must be configured correctly for XMMS to work.

To summarize, here's an overview of the steps you follow to download, unpack, build, and install a typical software package:

1. Use a Web browser to download the source code, usually in the form of a .tar.gz file, from the anonymous FTP site or Web site.

2. Unpack the file with a tar zxvf *filename* command. (If the compressed tar file has a .bz2 extension, that means the file is compressed with bzip2 and you can unpack that file with a tar jxvf *filename* command.)

3. Change the directory to the new subdirectory where the software is unpacked, with a command such as cd software_dir.

4. Read any README or INSTALL files to get a handle on any specific instructions you must follow to build and install the software.

5. The details of building the software may differ slightly from one software package to another, but typically you type the following commands to build and install the software:

   ```
   ./configure
   make
   make install
   ```

6. Read any other documentation that comes with the software to find out how to use the software and whether you must configure the software further before using it.

## Installing SRPMs

If you have the source CDs for Fedora (you can download the source CD images from one of the sites listed at http://mirrors.fedoraproject. org), you can install the source files and build various applications directly from the source files. Fedora source-code files, like the executable binary files, also come in RPMs, and these source-code RPM files are generally known as SRPMs (source RPMs).

To install a specific source RPM and build the application, follow these steps:

1. **Mount the DVD-ROM by typing** mount /media/cdrom **or wait for the GNOME desktop to mount the DVD.**

2. **Typically, source RPMs are in the SRPMs directory. Change to that directory by typing the following command:**

   ```
   cd /media/cdrom/SRPMS
   ```

3. **Install the source RPM file by using the rpm -i command. For example, to install the Web server (httpd) source, type**

   ```
   rpm -ivh httpd*.src.rpm
   ```

   The files are installed in the /usr/src/packages/SOURCES directory. A spec file with the .spec extension is placed in the /usr/src/ packages/SPECS directory. The *spec file* describes the software and contains information used to build and install the software.

4. **Use the rpmbuild command with the spec file to build the software and install the binary files.**

   You perform different tasks, from unpacking the source files to building and installing the binaries by using different options with the rpmbuild command. For example, to process the entire spec file, type:

   ```
   rpmbuild -ba packagename.spec
   ```

   where *packagename* is the name of the SRPM. This command builds the software and installs the binary files.

# Updating Linux Applications Online

Each Linux distribution comes with utilities that enable you to update the software online. The following sections provide an overview of the update methods in Debian, Fedora, SUSE, Ubuntu, and Xandros.

You need a fast Internet connection (such as a DSL or cable modem) to easily update your Linux applications or download new software packages. Make sure that your Internet connection is up and running before you attempt to update your Linux system online.

## *Keeping Debian and Ubuntu updated with APT*

The best way to keep your Debian system updated is to use APT. More specifically, you use the `apt-get` command-line utility with appropriate options. Because Ubuntu is Debian-based, you can use APT to update Ubuntu as well.

In a nutshell, assuming the APT sources were configured during Debian installation, you can keep the current collection of software updated with the following two commands, typed in this order:

```
apt-get update
apt-get upgrade
```

The `apt-get` update command checks the current list of packages against the ones available from the locations specified in `/etc/apt/sources.list` file and gathers information about new versions of installed packages.

The `apt-get` upgrade command installs any available new versions of the packages installed in your Debian system. You must perform `apt-get` `upgrade` to install any available upgrades.

To install a new package in Debian, use `apt-cache search` to find the package name in APT's package cache and then use `apt-get install` to install the package.

## *Updating Fedora Applications*

Fedora comes with a graphical Update Agent that can download any new RPM files your system requires and install those files for you.

To update Fedora software packages using the Software Update agent, follow these steps:

*1.* **Log in as root, and choose System➪Administration➪Software Update.**

The Update Agent starts and displays a list of updates that are available (see Figure 4-1).

*2.* **Click Install Updates to continue.**

The updater resolves dependencies for the updates. You may be asked to confirm the downloading of additional software needed to resolve these dependencies. If so, Software Update downloads the packages. Then Software Update updates the software. A progress bar is displayed during all steps of the operation.

Finally, Software Update displays a message about the package(s) it installs successfully (see Figure 4-2).

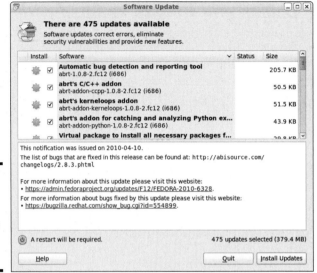

**Figure 4-1:**
Software
Update
displays the
available
updates.

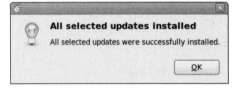

**Figure 4-2:**
Software
Update tells
you the
update was
successful.

3. **Click the OK button to exit Software Update.**

Ideally, you want to keep your system up-to-date and receive messages when you open Software Update like those shown in Figure 4-3.

**Figure 4-3:**
Software
Update
informs
you that all
packages
are up-to-
date.

In Fedora, you can also use Yum (which, by the way, stands for Yellow dog Updater, Modified) to keep your packages up-to-date. Yum is a command-line utility for updating as well as installing and removing RPM packages. Yum downloads RPM package headers from a specified Web site and uses the `rpm` utility to figure out any interdependencies among packages and what needs to be installed on your system. Then it downloads and uses `rpm` to install the necessary packages. Because Yum downloads just the headers, which are much smaller than the complete RPM packages, Yum is much faster than the alternative, where you manually download the complete RPM packages using the `rpm` command.

Typically, you keep your system up-to-date with the graphical Package Updater because it's easy to use. However, knowing how to run Yum from the command line is good, just in case you have problems with the GUI.

You can read more about Yum and keep up with Yum news by visiting the Yum Web page at `http://yum.baseurl.org`.

The command line for Yum has the following syntax:

```
yum [options] command [packagenames]
```

*options* is a list of Yum options, *command* specifies what you want Yum to do, and *packagenames* are the names of a packages on which Yum performs that action. You must provide *command*, but *options* and *package names* are optional (which is why they are shown in square brackets in the syntax). Table 4-2 summarizes the Yum commands and Table 4-3 lists some common Yum options.

| Table 4-2 | Yum Commands |
|---|---|
| **Command** | **Yum Will** |
| check-update | Check for available updates for your system |
| clean | Clean up the cache directory |
| info | Display summary information about the specified packages |
| install | Install latest versions of specified packages, making sure that all dependencies are satisfied |
| list | List information about available packages |
| list installed | List packages already installed on your machine |

*(continued)*

### Table 4-2 *(continued)*

| Command | Yum Will |
|---|---|
| list updates | List installed packages that have updates available |
| provides | Provide information on which package provides a file |
| remove | Remove specified packages as well as any packages that depend on the packages being removed |
| search | Find packages whose header contains what you specify as the package name |
| update | Update specified packages, making sure that all dependencies are satisfied |

### Table 4-3          Some Common Yum Options

| Option | Yum Will |
|---|---|
| --download-only | Download but not install the packages. |
| --exclude=*pkgname* | Exclude the specified package. (You can use this option more than once on the command line.) |
| --help | Display a help message and quit |
| --installroot=*path* | Use the specified pathname as the directory under which all packages are installed. |
| -y | Assume that your answer to any question is yes. |

If you simply want Yum to update your system, type the following. (You have to be logged in as `root`.)

```
yum update
```

Yum consults its configuration file, `/etc/yum.conf`, and does everything needed to update the packages installed on your system.

If you want to update only certain packages, you can specify the package names. For example, to update the `kernel` and `xorg-x11` packages, use the following Yum command:

```
yum update kernel* xorg-x11*
```

This command updates all packages whose names begin with `kernel` and `xorg-x11`.

You may use the options to further instruct Yum what to do. For example, if you want to download but not install the updated packages, type

```
yum --download-only update
```

Another typical option is `--exclude`, which enables you to exclude one or more packages from the update process. Suppose you want to update everything except the GNOME packages (whose names begin with `gnome`) and the `rhythmbox` package. You would type the following Yum command:

```
yum --exclude=gnome* --exclude=rhythmbox update
```

## Updating SUSE online

SUSE comes with YOU — YaST Online Update — for online software updates. To access YOU, choose System➪YaST from the main menu. Then, from the YaST Control Center's Software category, click Online Update. This brings up the YaST Online Update window.

To set up YOU automatic updates, click the Configure Fully Automatic Update button. You can then specify a time of the day when you want YOU to download any available patches and install them. You can instead specify that YOU download but not install the patches.

To update your SUSE system online, select the installation source and click Next. YOU then downloads the list of patches and displays them.

Select the patches (some are recommended and preselected for you) and then click Accept. YOU then downloads the required packages and installs them on your SUSE system.

## Using Xandros Networks

In Xandros, use Xandros Networks to update applications or install new ones. From the main menu, choose Xandros Networks (or double-click the Xandros Networks icon on the desktop) to open the Xandros Networks window.

To install the latest updates from Xandros, choose File➪Install All Latest Updates from Xandros or click the Update button. Xandros Networks then downloads information about the available updates and shows a summary of the packages to be downloaded and the disk space needed to install them.

Click OK. Xandros Networks prompts you for the `root` password. After you enter the `root` password, it downloads and installs the software updates.

Behind the scenes, Xandros Networks uses Debian's `apt-get` command to download and install the software updates.

The Xandros Networks window also offers options to install new software. You can even shop for new applications through Xandros Networks. If you have to install RPM or DEB files, you can do so in Xandros Networks by choosing File⇨Install RPM File or File⇨Install DEB File.

# Book VI

# Security

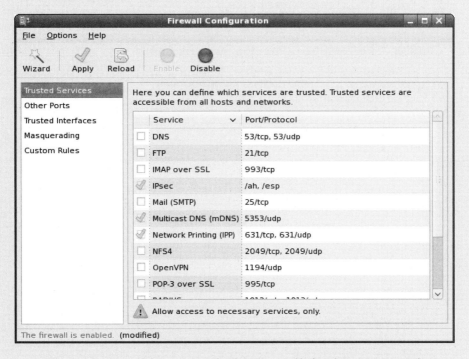

Set up packet filtering with the Firewall Configuration tool

# Contents at a Glance

## Chapter 1: Introducing Linux Security . . . . . . . . . . . . . . . . . . . . . . . .391

Why Worry about Security? . . . . . . . . . . . . . . . . . . . . . . . . . . . . . . . . . . . . . . . . . . . . . . . . . . . 391
Establishing a Security Framework . . . . . . . . . . . . . . . . . . . . . . . . . . . . . . . . . . . . . . . 392
Securing Linux . . . . . . . . . . . . . . . . . . . . . . . . . . . . . . . . . . . . . . . . . . . . . . . . . . . . . . . . . . . . . . . . . . . 397
Delving into Computer Security Terminology . . . . . . . . . . . . . . . . . . . . . . . . 399
Keeping Up with Security News and Updates . . . . . . . . . . . . . . . . . . . . . . . . 404

## Chapter 2: Securing Linux . . . . . . . . . . . . . . . . . . . . . . . . . . . . . . . . . . . . .407

Securing Passwords . . . . . . . . . . . . . . . . . . . . . . . . . . . . . . . . . . . . . . . . . . . . . . . . . . . . . . . . . 407
Protecting Files and Directories . . . . . . . . . . . . . . . . . . . . . . . . . . . . . . . . . . . . . . . . . 410
Encrypting and Signing Files with GnuPG . . . . . . . . . . . . . . . . . . . . . . . . . . . . 414
Monitoring System Security . . . . . . . . . . . . . . . . . . . . . . . . . . . . . . . . . . . . . . . . . . . . . . 421
Securing Internet Services . . . . . . . . . . . . . . . . . . . . . . . . . . . . . . . . . . . . . . . . . . . . . . . . 421
Using Secure Shell (SSH) for Remote Logins . . . . . . . . . . . . . . . . . . . . . . . . 424
Setting Up Simple Firewalls . . . . . . . . . . . . . . . . . . . . . . . . . . . . . . . . . . . . . . . . . . . . . . 426

## Chapter 3: Performing Computer Security Audits . . . . . . . . . . . . . . .437

Understanding Security Audits . . . . . . . . . . . . . . . . . . . . . . . . . . . . . . . . . . . . . . . . . . . 437
Implementing a Security Test Methodology . . . . . . . . . . . . . . . . . . . . . . . . . 439
Exploring Security Testing Tools . . . . . . . . . . . . . . . . . . . . . . . . . . . . . . . . . . . . . . . . 447

# Chapter 1: Introducing Linux Security

## In This Chapter

✓ **Establishing a security policy and framework**

✓ **Understanding host security issues**

✓ **Understanding network security issues**

✓ **Translating computer security terminology**

✓ **Keeping up with security news and updates**

This chapter explains why you need to worry about security and offers a high-level view of how to get a handle on security. The idea of an overall security framework is explained and the two key aspects of security — host security and network security — are discussed. This chapter ends by introducing you to the terminology used in discussing computer security.

## Why Worry about Security?

In today's networked world, you have to worry about your Linux system's security. For a standalone system or a system used in an isolated local area network (LAN), you have to focus on protecting the system from the users and the users from one another. In other words, you don't want a user to modify or delete system files, whether intentionally or unintentionally, and you don't want a user destroying another user's files.

If your Linux system is connected to the Internet, you have to secure the system from unwanted accesses over the Internet. These intruders — or *crackers,* as they're commonly known — typically impersonate a user, steal or destroy information, and even deny you access to your own system (known as a *Denial of Service,* or *DoS,* attack).

By its very nature, an Internet connection makes your system accessible to any other system on the Internet. After all, the Internet connects a huge number of networks across the globe. In fact, the client/server architecture of Internet services, such as HTTP (Web) and FTP, rely on the wide-open network access the Internet provides. Unfortunately, the easy accessibility to Internet services running on your system also means that anyone on the Net can easily access your system.

If you operate an Internet host that provides information to others, you certainly want everyone to access your system's Internet services, such as FTP and Web servers. However, these servers often have vulnerabilities that crackers may exploit to harm your system. You need to know about the potential security risks of Internet services — and the precautions you can take to minimize the risk of someone exploiting the weaknesses of your FTP or Web server.

You also want to protect your company's internal network from outsiders, even though your goal is to provide information to the outside world through your Web or FTP server. You can protect your internal network by setting up an Internet *firewall* — a controlled access point to the internal network — and placing the Web and FTP servers on a host outside the firewall.

# Establishing a Security Framework

The first step in securing your Linux system is to set up a *security policy* — a set of guidelines that state what you enable users (as well as visitors over the Internet) to do on your Linux system. The level of security you establish depends on how you use the Linux system — and on how much is at risk if someone gains unauthorized access to your system.

If you're a system administrator for one or more Linux systems at an organization, you probably want to involve company management, as well as the users, in setting up the security policy. Obviously, you can't create a draconian policy that blocks all access. (That would prevent anyone from effectively working on the system.) On the other hand, if the users are creating or using data valuable to the organization, you have to set up a policy that protects the data from disclosure to outsiders. In other words, the security policy should strike a balance between the users' needs and the need to protect the system.

For a standalone Linux system or a home system that you occasionally connect to the Internet, the security policy can be just a listing of the Internet services that you want to run on the system and the user accounts that you plan to set up on the system. For any larger organization, you probably have one or more Linux systems on a LAN connected to the Internet — preferably through a firewall. (To reiterate, a *firewall* is a device that controls the flow of Internet Protocol — IP — packets between the LAN and the Internet.) In such cases, thinking of computer security across the entire organization systematically is best. Figure 1-1 shows the key elements of an organization-wide framework for computer security.

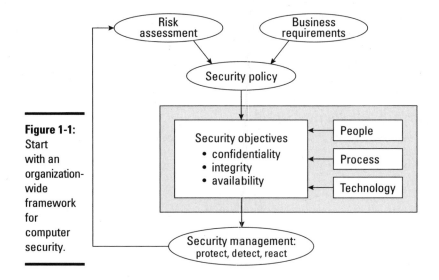

**Figure 1-1:**
Start
with an
organization-
wide
framework
for
computer
security.

The security framework outlined in Figure 1-1 focuses on

✦ Determining the business requirements for security

✦ Performing risk assessments

✦ Establishing a security policy

✦ Implementing a cybersecurity solution that includes people, process, and technology to mitigate identified security risks

✦ Continuously monitoring and managing security

The following sections discuss some of the key elements of the security framework.

## Determining business requirements for security

The business requirements for security identify the computer resources and information you have to protect (including any requirements imposed by applicable laws, such as the requirement to protect the privacy of some types of data). Typical security requirements may include items such as the following:

✦ Enabling access to information by authorized users

✦ Implementing business rules that specify who has access to what information

✦ Employing a strong user-authentication system

✦ Denying malicious or destructive actions on data

✦ Protecting data from end to end as it moves across networks

✦ Implementing all security and privacy requirements that applicable laws impose

## Performing risk analysis

Risk analysis is all about identifying and assessing risks — potential events that can harm your Linux system. The analysis involves determining the following and performing some analysis to establish the priority for handling the risks:

✦ **Threats:** What you're protecting against

✦ **Vulnerabilities:** Weaknesses that may be exploited by threats (these are the risks)

✦ **Probability:** The likelihood that a threat will exploit the vulnerability

✦ **Impact:** The effect of exploiting a specific vulnerability

✦ **Mitigation:** What to do to reduce vulnerabilities

### Typical threats

Some typical threats to your Linux system include the following:

✦ **Denial of Service:** The computer and network are tied up so legitimate users can't make use of the systems. For businesses, Denial of Service (DoS) can mean a loss of revenue.

✦ **Unauthorized access:** Use of the computer and network by someone who isn't an authorized user. The unauthorized user can steal information or maliciously corrupt or destroy data. Some businesses may be hurt by the negative publicity from the mere act of an unauthorized user gaining access to the system, even if the data shows no sign of explicit damage.

✦ **Disclosure of information to the public:** The unauthorized release of information to the public. For example, the disclosure of a password file enables potential attackers to figure out username and password combinations for accessing a system. Exposure of other sensitive information, such as financial and medical data, may be a potential liability for a business.

### Typical vulnerabilities

The threats to your system and network come from exploitation of vulnerabilities in your organization's resources –– both computer and people. Some common vulnerabilities follow:

✦ People's foibles (divulging passwords, losing security cards, and so on)

✦ Internal network connections (routers, switches)

✦ Interconnection points (gateways — routers and firewalls — between the Internet and the internal network)

✦ Third-party network providers (ISPs, long-distance carriers) with looser security

✦ Operating system security holes (potential holes in Internet servers, such as those associated with `sendmail`, `named`, and `bind`)

✦ Application security holes (known weaknesses in specific applications)

### The 1-2-3 of risk analysis (probability and effect)

To perform risk analysis, assign a numeric value to the probability and effect of each potential vulnerability. To develop a workable risk analysis, do the following for each vulnerability or risk:

1. Assign subjective ratings of low, medium, and high to the probability. As the ratings suggest, low probability means a lesser chance that the vulnerability will be exploited; high probability means a greater chance.

2. Assign similar ratings to the effect. What you consider the effect is up to you. If the exploitation of a vulnerability will affect your business greatly, assign it a high effect.

3. Assign a numeric value to the three levels — low = 1, medium = 2, and high = 3 — for both probability and effect.

4. Multiply the probability by the effect — you can think of this product as the risk level. Then make a decision to develop protections for vulnerabilities that exceed a specific threshold for the product of probability and effect. For example, you may choose to handle all vulnerabilities with a probability-times-effect greater than 6.

If you want to characterize the probability and effect with finer gradations, use a scale of 1 through 5 (for example) instead of 1 through 3, and follow the same steps as before.

## Establishing a security policy

Using risk analysis and any business requirements that you may have to address (regardless of risk level) as a foundation, you can craft a security policy for the organization. Such a security policy typically addresses high-level objectives such as ensuring the confidentiality, integrity, and availability of data and systems.

The security policy typically addresses the following areas:

+ **Authentication:** What method is used to ensure that a user is the real user? Who gets access to the system? What is the minimum length and complexity of passwords? How often do users change passwords? How long can a user be idle before that user is logged out automatically?

+ **Authorization:** What can different classes of users do on the system? Who can have the `root` password?

+ **Data protection:** What data must be protected? Who has access to the data? Is encryption necessary for some data?

+ **Internet access:** What are the restrictions on users (from the LAN) accessing the Internet? What Internet services (such as Web, Internet Relay Chat, and so on) can users access? Are incoming e-mails and attachments scanned for viruses? Is there a network firewall? Are virtual private networks (VPNs) used to connect private networks across the Internet?

+ **Internet services:** What Internet services are allowed on each Linux system? Are there any file servers, mail servers, or Web servers? What services run on each type of server? What services, if any, run on Linux systems used as desktop workstations?

+ **Security audits:** Who tests whether the security is adequate? How often is the security tested? How are problems found during security testing handled?

+ **Incident handling:** What are the procedures for handling any computer security incidents? Who must be informed? What information must be gathered to help with the investigation of incidents?

+ **Responsibilities:** Who is responsible for maintaining security? Who monitors log files and audit trails for signs of unauthorized access? Who maintains the security policy?

## *Implementing security solutions (mitigation)*

After you analyze the risks — vulnerabilities — and develop a security policy, you have to select the *mitigation approach:* how to protect against specific vulnerabilities. This is where you develop an overall security solution based on security policy, business requirements, and available technology — a solution that makes use of people, process, and technology and includes the following:

+ Services (authentication, access control, encryption)

+ Mechanisms (username and password, firewalls)

+ Objects (hardware, software)

Because it is impossible to protect computer systems from all attacks, solutions identified through the risk management process must support three integral concepts of a holistic security program:

✦ **Protection:** Provides countermeasures such as policies, procedures, and technical solutions to defend against attacks on the assets being protected.

✦ **Detection:** Monitors for potential breakdowns in the protective measures that could result in security breaches.

✦ **Reaction** or **Response:** Responds to detected breaches to thwart attacks before damage occurs; often requires human involvement

Because absolute protection from attacks is impossible to achieve, a security program that doesn't incorporate detection and reaction is incomplete.

## Managing security

In addition to implementing security solutions, you have to install security management that continually monitors, detects, and responds to any security incidents.

The combination of the risk analysis, security policy, security solutions, and security management provides the overall security framework. Such a framework helps establish a common level of understanding of security concerns — and a common basis for the design and implementation of security solutions.

# Securing Linux

After you define a security policy, you can proceed to secure the system according to the policy. The exact steps depend on what you want to do with the system, whether the system is a server or workstation, and how many users must access the system.

To secure the Linux system, you have to handle two broad categories of security issues:

✦ **Host security issues:** These issues relate to securing the operating system and the files and directories on the system.

✦ **Network security issues:** These issues refer to the threat of attacks over the network connection.

If your host is connecting to a large network, Directory Services can become a significant issue. Directory Services security is outside the scope of this book, but you can find a number of sources addressing the issue with a Google search.

## Understanding the host security issues

Here are some high-level guidelines to address host security. (I cover some of these topics in detail in Chapter 2 of this minibook.)

✦ When installing Linux, select only the package groups that you need for your system. Don't install unnecessary software. For example, if your system is used as a workstation, you don't have to install most of the servers (Web server, news server, and so on).

✦ Create initial user accounts and make sure that all passwords are strong enough that password-cracking programs can't guess them. Linux includes tools to enforce strong passwords.

✦ Set file ownerships and permissions to protect important files and directories.

✦ If available, enable mandatory access control capabilities provided by Security Enhanced Linux (SELinux). Linux kernel 2.6 supports SELinux.

✦ Use the GNU Privacy Guard (GnuPG) to encrypt or decrypt files with sensitive information and to authenticate files that you download from the Internet. GnuPG comes with Linux, and you can use the gpg command to perform tasks such as encrypting or decrypting a file and digitally signing a file. (See Chapter 2 of this minibook for an explanation of digital signatures.)

✦ Use file-integrity checking tools, such as Tripwire, to monitor any changes to crucial system files and directories. Visit www.tripwire. com for the commercial version.

✦ Periodically check various log files for signs of any break-ins or attempted break-ins. These log files are in the /var/log directory of your system.

✦ Install security updates as soon as they are available and tested. These security updates fix known vulnerabilities in Linux. Be sure to test the update on nonproduction machines before rolling it out to your production servers.

## Understanding network security issues

The issue of security comes up as soon as you connect your organization's internal network to the Internet. You need to think of security even if you connect a single computer to the Internet, but security concerns are more pressing when an entire internal network is opened to the world.

If you're an experienced system administrator, you already know that the cost of managing an Internet presence doesn't worry corporate management; their main concern is security. To get your management's backing for the Web site, you have to lay out a plan to keep the corporate network secure from intruders.

You may think that you can avoid jeopardizing the internal network by connecting only external servers, such as Web and FTP servers, to the Internet. However, employing this simplistic approach isn't wise. It's like deciding not to drive because you may have an accident. Not having a network connection between your Web server and your internal network also has the following drawbacks:

**Book VI Chapter 1**

Introducing Linux Security

+ You can't use network file transfers, such as FTP, to copy documents and data from your internal network to the Web server.

+ Users on the internal network can't access the corporate Web server.

+ Users on the internal network don't have access to Web servers on the Internet. Such a restriction makes a valuable resource — the Web — inaccessible to the users in your organization.

A practical solution to this problem is to set up an Internet firewall and to put the Web server on a highly secured host outside the firewall.

In addition to using a firewall, here are some other steps to take to address network security. (I explain these further in Chapter 2 of this minibook.)

+ Enable only those Internet services you need on a system. In particular, don't enable services that aren't properly configured.

+ Use Secure Shell (`ssh`) for remote logins. Don't use the `r` commands, such as `rlogin` and `rsh`.

+ Secure any Internet services, such as FTP or TELNET, that you want to run on your system. You can use the TCP wrapper access control files — `/etc/hosts.allow` and `/etc/hosts.deny` — to secure some of these services. (See Chapter 3 of this minibook for more on the TCP wrapper.)

+ Promptly fix any known vulnerabilities of Internet services that you choose to run. Typically, you can download and install the latest security updates from your Linux distribution's online update sites.

# Delving into Computer Security Terminology

Computer books, magazine articles, and experts on computer security use a number of terms that you need to know to understand discussions about computer security (and to communicate effectively with security vendors). Table 1-1 describes some of the commonly used computer security terms.

| Table 1-1 | Common Computer Security Terminology |
|---|---|
| *Term* | *Description* |
| Application gateway | A proxy service that acts as a gateway for application-level protocols, such as FTP, HTTP, NNTP, and SSH. |
| Authentication | The process of confirming that a user is indeed who he or she claims to be. The typical authentication method is a challenge-response method wherein the user enters a user-name and secret password to confirm his or her identity. |
| Backdoor | A security weakness a cracker places on a host to bypass security features. |
| Bastion host | A highly secured computer that serves as an organization's main point of presence on the Internet. A bastion host typi-cally resides on the perimeter network, but a dual-homed host (with one network interface connected to the Internet and the other to the internal network) is also a bastion host. |
| Buffer overflow | A security flaw in a program that enables a cracker to send an excessive amount of data to that program and to overwrite parts of the running program with code in the data being sent. The result is that the cracker can execute arbitrary code on the system and possibly gain access to the system as a privileged user. The new `exec-shield` fea-ture of the Linux kernel protects against buffer overflows. |
| Certificate | An electronic document that identifies an entity (such as an individual, an organization, or a computer) and associates a public key with that identity. A certificate contains the cer-tificate holder's name, a serial number, an expiration date, a copy of the certificate holder's public key, and the digital signature of the certificate authority so a recipient can verify that the certificate is real. |
| Certificate authority (CA) | An organization that validates identities and issues certificates. |
| Confidentiality | Of data, a state of being accessible to no one but you (usu-ally achieved by encryption). |
| Cracker | A person who breaks into (or attempts to break into) a host, often with malicious intent. |
| Decryption | The process of transforming encrypted information into its original, intelligible form. |

| Term | Description |
|------|-------------|
| Denial of Service (DoS) | An attack that uses so many of the resources on your computer and network that legitimate users can't access and use the system. From a single source, the attack overwhelms the target computer with messages and blocks legitimate traffic. It can prevent one system from being able to exchange data with other systems or prevent the system from using the Internet. |
| Digital signature | A one-way MD5 (Message Digest algorithm 5) or SHA-1 (Secure Hash Algorithm-1) hash of a message encrypted with the private key of the message originator, used to verify the integrity of a message and ensure nonrepudiation. |
| Distributed Denial of Service (DDoS) | A variant of the Denial of Service attack that uses a coordinated attack from a distributed system of computers rather than a single source. It often makes use of worms to spread to multiple computers that can then attack the target. |
| DMZ | Another name for the perimeter network. (DMZ originally stood for *demilitarized zone,* the buffer zone separating the warring North and South in Korea and Vietnam.) |
| Dual-homed host | A computer with two network interfaces (think of each network as a home). |
| Encryption | The process of transforming information so it's unintelligible to anyone but the intended recipient. The transformation is performed by a mathematical operation between a key and the information. |
| Exploit tools | Publicly available and sophisticated tools that intruders of various skill levels can use to determine vulnerabilities and gain entry into targeted systems. |
| Firewall | A controlled-access gateway between an organization's internal network and the Internet. A dual-homed host can be configured as a firewall. |
| Hash | The result when a mathematical function converts a message into a fixed-size numeric value known as a *message digest* (or *hash*). The MD5 algorithm, for example, produces a 128-bit message digest; SHA-1 generates a 160-bit message digest. The hash of a message is encrypted with the private key of the sender to produce the digital signature. |
| Host | A computer on a network that's configured to offer services to other computers on the network. |

*(continued)*

Book VI
Chapter 1

Introducing Linux Security

## Table 1-1 *(continued)*

| Term | Description |
|---|---|
| Integrity | Of received data, a state of being the same as originally sent (that is, unaltered in transit). |
| IP spoofing | An attack in which a cracker figures out the IP address of a trusted host and then sends packets that appear to come from the trusted host. The attacker can send packets but can't see responses. However, the attacker can predict the sequence of packets and essentially send commands that set up a backdoor for future break-ins. |
| IPSec (IP Security Protocol) | A security protocol for the network layer of the OSI networking model, designed to provide cryptographic security services for IP packets. IPSec provides encryption-based authentication, integrity, access control, and confidentiality. (For information on IPSec for Linux, visit www.ipsec-howto.org.) |
| Logic bombs | A form of sabotage in which a programmer inserts code that causes the program to perform a destructive action when some triggering event occurs, such as terminating the programmer's employment. |
| Nonrepudiation | A security feature that prevents the sender of data from being able to deny ever having sent the data. |
| Packet | A collection of bytes, assembled according to a specific protocol, that serves as the basic unit of communication on a network. On TCP/IP networks, for example, the packet may be referred to as an *IP packet* or a *TCP/IP packet.* |
| Packet filtering | Selective blocking of packets according to type of packet (as specified by the source and destination IP address or port). |
| Perimeter network | A network between the Internet and the protected internal network. The perimeter network (also known as DMZ) is where the bastion host resides. |
| Port scanning | A method of discovering which ports are open (in other words, which Internet services are enabled) on a system, performed by sending connection requests to the ports, one by one. This procedure is usually a precursor to further attacks. |
| Proxy server | A server on the bastion host that enables internal clients to access external servers (and enables external clients to access servers inside the protected network). There are proxy servers for various Internet services, such as FTP and HTTP. |

| Term | Description |
|---|---|
| Public key cryptography | An encryption method that uses a pair of keys — a private key and a public key — to encrypt and decrypt the information. Anything encrypted with the public key is decrypted only with the corresponding private key, and vice versa. |
| Public Key Infrastructure (PKI) | A set of standards and services that enables the use of public key cryptography and certificates in a networked environment. PKI facilitates tasks such as issuing, renewing, and revoking certificates, and generating and distributing public and private key pairs. |
| Screening router | An Internet router that filters packets. |
| Setuid program | A program that runs with the permissions of the owner regardless of who runs the program. For example, if `root` owns a `setuid` program, that program has `root` privileges regardless of who started the program. Crackers often exploit vulnerabilities in `setuid` programs to gain privileged access to a system. |
| Sniffer | Synonymous with *packet sniffer* — a program that intercepts routed data and examines each packet in search of specified information, such as passwords transmitted in clear text. |
| Spyware | Any software that covertly gathers user information through the user's Internet connection and usually transmits that information in the background to someone else. Spyware can also gather information about e-mail addresses and even passwords and credit card numbers. Spyware is similar to a Trojan horse in that users are tricked into installing spyware when they install something else. |
| Symmetric key encryption | An encryption method wherein the same key is used to encrypt and decrypt the information. |
| Threat | An event or activity, deliberate or unintentional, with the potential for causing harm to a system or network. |
| Trojan horse | A program that masquerades as a benign program but is a backdoor used for attacking a system. Attackers often install a collection of Trojan horse programs that enable the attacker to freely access the system with `root` privileges, yet hide that fact from the system administrator. Such collections of Trojan horse programs are *rootkits*. |
| Virus | A self-replicating program that spreads from one computer to another by attaching itself to other programs. |
| Vulnerability | A flaw or weakness that may cause harm to a system or network. |

*(continued)*

**Table 1-1** *(continued)*

| Term | Description |
|------|-------------|
| War-dialing | Simple programs that dial consecutive phone numbers looking for modems. |
| War-driving | A method of gaining entry into wireless computer networks that uses a laptop, antennas, and a wireless network card and involves patrolling locations to gain unauthorized access. |
| Worm | A self-replicating program that copies itself from one computer to another over a network. |

# Keeping Up with Security News and Updates

To keep up with the latest security alerts, you may want to visit one or both of the following sites on a daily basis:

✦ CERT Coordination Center (CERT/CC) at `www.cert.org`

✦ United States Computer Emergency Readiness Team (US-CERT) at `www.us-cert.gov`

If you have access to Internet newsgroups, you can periodically browse the following:

✦ `comp.security.announce`: A moderated newsgroup that includes announcements from CERT about security

✦ `comp.security.linux`: A newsgroup that includes discussions of Linux security issues

✦ `comp.security.unix`: A newsgroup that includes discussions of UNIX security issues, including items related to Linux

If you prefer to receive regular security updates through e-mail, you can also sign up for (subscribe to) various mailing lists:

✦ **FOCUS-LINUX:** Fill out the form at `www.securityfocus.com/archive` to subscribe to this mailing list focused on Linux security issues.

✦ **US-CERT National Cyber Alert System:** Follow the directions at `www.us-cert.gov` to subscribe to this mailing list. The Cyber Alert System features four categories of security information through its mailing lists:

- Technical Cyber Security Alerts: Alerts that provide technical information about vulnerabilities in various common software products.

- Cyber Security Alerts: Alerts sent when vulnerabilities affect the general public. They outline the steps and actions that nontechnical home and corporate computer users can take to protect themselves from attacks.

- Cyber Security Bulletins: Biweekly summaries of security issues and new vulnerabilities along with patches, workarounds, and other actions that users can take to help reduce risks.

- Cyber Security Tips: Advice on common security issues for nontechnical computer users.

**Book VI
Chapter 1**

Introducing Linux
Security

Finally, check your distribution's Web site for updates that may fix any known security problems with that distribution. In Debian and Ubuntu, you can update the system with the commands `apt-get update` followed by `apt-get upgrade`. For Fedora, the Web site is `http://fedoraproject.org`. In SUSE, use YaST Online Update to keep your system up-to-date. In Xandros, obtain the latest updates from Xandros Networks.

# Chapter 2: Securing Linux

## In This Chapter

✔ Securing passwords on your Linux system

✔ Protecting the system's files and directories

✔ Using GnuPG to encrypt and sign files

✔ Monitoring the security of your system

✔ Hardening Internet services

✔ Using Secure Shell for secure remote logins

✔ Setting up simple firewalls and enabling packet filtering

To secure your Linux system, you have to pay attention to both host security and network security. The distinction between the two types of security is somewhat arbitrary because securing the network involves securing the applications on the host that relate to what Internet services your system offers.

This chapter first examines host security and then explains how you can secure network services (mostly by not offering unnecessary services), how you can use a firewall to stop unwanted network packets from reaching your network, and how to use Secure Shell for secure remote logins.

*Host* is the techie term for your Linux system — especially when you use it to provide services on a network. But the term makes sense even when you think of the computer by itself; it's the host for everything that runs on it: the operating system and all applications. A key aspect of computer security is to secure the host.

## Securing Passwords

Historically, UNIX passwords are stored in the /etc/passwd file, which any user can read. For example, a typical old-style /etc/passwd file entry for the root user looks like this:

```
root:t6Z7NWDK1K8sU:0:0:root:/root:/bin/bash
```

The fields are separated by colons (:), and the second field contains the password in encrypted form. To check whether a password is valid, the login program encrypts the plain-text password the user enters and compares the password with the contents of the /etc/passwd file. If they match, the user is allowed to log in.

Password-cracking programs work just like the login program, except that these programs choose one word at a time from a dictionary, encrypt the word, and compare the encrypted word with the encrypted passwords in the /etc/passwd file for a match. To crack the passwords, the intruder needs the /etc/passwd file. Often, crackers use weaknesses of various Internet servers (such as mail and FTP) to get a copy of the /etc/passwd file.

Passwords have become more secure in Linux due to several improvements, including shadow passwords and pluggable authentication modules, or PAMs (described in the next two sections). You can install shadow passwords or a PAM easily while you install Linux. During Linux installation, you typically get a chance to configure the authentication. If you enable MD5 security and enable shadow passwords, you automatically enable more secure passwords in Linux.

## Shadow passwords

Obviously, leaving passwords lying around where anyone can get at them — even if the passwords are encrypted — is bad security. So instead of storing passwords in the /etc/passwd file (which any user can read), Linux now stores them in a shadow password file, /etc/shadow. Only the superuser (root) can read this file. For example, here's the entry for root in the new-style /etc/passwd file:

```
root:x:0:0:root:/root:/bin/bash
```

In this case, note that the second field contains an x instead of an encrypted password. The x is the *shadow password;* the actual encrypted password is now stored in the /etc/shadow file, where the entry for root is like this:

```
root:$1$AAAni/yN$uESHbzUpy9Cgfoo1Bf0tS0:11077:0:99999:7:-1:-1:134540356
```

The format of the /etc/shadow entries with colon-separated fields resembles the entries in the /etc/passwd file, but the meanings of most of the fields differ. The first field is still the username, and the second one is the encrypted password.

The remaining fields in each /etc/shadow entry control when the password expires. You don't have to interpret or change these entries in the /etc/shadow file. Instead, use the chage command to change the password expiration information. For starters, you can check a user's password expiration information by using the `chage` command with the `-l` option, as follows. (In this case, you have to be logged in as `root`.)

```
chage -l root
```

This command displays expiration information, including how long the password lasts and how often you can change the password.

If you want to ensure that the user is forced to change a password at regular intervals, you can use the `-M` option to set the maximum number of days that a password stays valid. For example, to make sure that user `kdulaney` is prompted to change the password in 90 days, log in as `root` and type the following command:

```
chage -M 90 kdulaney
```

You can use the command for each user account to ensure that all passwords expire when appropriate and that all users must choose new passwords.

## Pluggable authentication modules (PAMs)

In addition to improving the password file's security by using shadow passwords, Linux also improves the encryption of the passwords stored in the `/etc/shadow` file by using the MD5 message-digest algorithm described in RFC 1321 (www.ietf.org/rfc/rfc1321.txt or www.cse.ohio-state.edu/cgi-bin/rfc/rfc1321.html). MD5 reduces a message of any length to a 128-bit message digest (or *fingerprint*) of a document so that you can digitally sign it by encrypting it with your private key. MD5 works quite well for password encryption, too.

Another advantage of MD5 over older-style password encryption is that the older passwords were limited to a maximum of eight characters; new passwords (encrypted with MD5) can be much longer. Longer passwords are harder to guess, even if the `/etc/shadow` file falls into the wrong hands.

You can tell that MD5 encryption is in effect in the `/etc/shadow` file. The encrypted passwords are longer and they all sport the `$1$` prefix, as in the second field of the following sample entry:

```
root:$1$AAAni/yN$uESHbzUpy9Cgfoo1Bf0tS0:11077:0:99999:7:-1:-1:134540356
```

An add-on program module called a *pluggable authentication module* (PAM) performs the MD5 encryption. Linux PAMs provide a flexible method for authenticating users. By setting the PAM's configuration files, you can change your authentication method on-the-fly, without modifying vital programs that verify a user's identity (such as `login` and `passwd`).

Linux uses PAM capabilities extensively. The PAMs reside in many different modules (more on this momentarily); their configuration files are in the `/etc/pam.d` directory of your system. Check out the contents of this directory on your system by typing the following command:

```
ls /etc/pam.d
```

Each configuration file in this directory specifies how users are authenticated for a specific utility.

# Protecting Files and Directories

One important aspect of securing the host is to protect important system files — and the directories that contain these files. You can protect the files through file ownership and the permission settings that control who can read, write, or (in the case of executable programs) execute the file.

The default Linux file security is controlled through the following settings for each file or directory:

+ User ownership
+ Group ownership
+ Read, write, execute permissions for the owner
+ Read, write, execute permissions for the group
+ Read, write, execute permissions for others (everyone else)

## Viewing ownerships and permissions

You can see settings related to ownership and permissions for a file when you look at a detailed listing with the `ls -l` command. For example, type the following command to see the detailed listing of the `/etc/inittab` file:

```
ls -l /etc/inittab
```

The resulting listing looks something like this:

```
-rw-r--r-- 1 root root 1666 Feb 16 07:57 /etc/inittab
```

The first set of characters describes the file permissions for user, group, and others. The third and fourth fields show the user and group that own this file. In this case, both user and group names are the same: `root`.

## Changing file ownerships

You can set the user and group ownerships with the `chown` command. For example, if the file `/dev/hda` should be owned by the user `root` and the group `disk`, you type the following command as `root` to set up this ownership:

```
chown root.disk /dev/hda
```

To change the group ownership alone, use the `chgrp` command. For example, here's how you can change the group ownership of a file from whatever it was earlier to the group named `accounting`:

```
chgrp accounting ledger.out
```

## Changing file permissions

Use the `chmod` command to set the file permissions. To use `chmod` effectively, you have to specify the permission settings. One way is to concatenate one or more letters from each column of Table 2-1, in the order shown (Who/Action/Permission).

**Book VI Chapter 2**

**Securing Linux**

| Table 2-1 | File Permission Codes | |
|---|---|---|
| *Who* | *Action* | *Permission* |
| u (user) | + (add) | r (read) |
| g (group) | – (remove) | w (write) |
| o (others) | = (assign) | x (execute) |
| a (all) | s (set user ID) | |

To give everyone read and write access to all files in a directory, type **chmod a+rw \***. On the other hand, to permit everyone to execute a specific file, type **chmod a+x *filename***.

Another way to specify a permission setting is to use a three-digit sequence of numbers. In a detailed listing, the read, write, and execute permission settings for the user, group, and others appear as the sequence

```
rwxrwxrwx
```

with dashes in place of letters for disallowed operations. Think of `rwxrwxrwx` as three occurrences of the string `rwx`. Now assign the values r=4, w=2, and x=1. To get the value of the sequence `rwx`, simply add the values of r, w, and x.

Thus, `rwx = 7`. With this formula, you can assign a three-digit value to any permission setting. For example, if the user can read and write the file but everyone else can only read the file, the permission setting is `rw-r--r--` (that's how it appears in the listing), and the value is 644. Thus, if you want all files in a directory to be readable by everyone but writable only by the user, use the following command:

```
chmod 644 *
```

## Setting default permission

What permission setting does a file get when you (or a program) create a new file? The answer is in what is known as the *user file-creation mask*, which you can see and set by using the `umask` command.

Type **umask**, and the command prints a number showing the current file-creation mask. For the `root` user, the mask is set to `022`, whereas the mask for other users is `002`. To see the effect of this file-creation mask and to interpret the meaning of the mask, follow these steps:

1. **Log in as root and type the following command:**

   ```
   touch junkfile
   ```

   This command creates a file named `junkfile` with nothing in it.

2. **Type** ls -l junkfile **to see that file's permissions.**

   You see a line similar to the following:

   ```
   -rw-r--r-- 1 root root 0 Aug 24 10:56 junkfile
   ```

   Interpret the numerical value of the permission setting by converting each three-letter permission in the first field (excluding the very first letter) to a number between 0 and 7. For each letter that's present, the first letter gets a value of 4, the second letter is 2, and the third is 1. For example, `rw-` translates to 4+2+0 (because the third letter is missing), or 6. Similarly, `r--` is 4+0+0 = 4. Thus the permission string `-rw-r--r--` becomes 644.

3. **Subtract the numerical permission setting from 666 and what you get is the umask setting.**

   In this case, 666 – 644 results in a `umask` of 022.

Thus, a `umask` of 022 results in a default permission setting of 666 – 022 = 644. When you rewrite 644 in terms of a permission string, it becomes `rw-r--r--`.

To set a new `umask`, type **umask** followed by the numerical value of the mask. Here is how you go about it:

1. **Figure out what permission settings you want for new files.**

   For example, if you want new files that can be read and written only by the owner and no one else, the permission setting looks like this:

   ```
   rw-------
   ```

2. **Convert the permissions into a numerical value by using the conversion method that assigns 4 to the first field, 2 to the second, and 1 to the third.**

   Thus, for files that are readable and writable only by their owner, the permission setting is 600.

3. **Subtract the desired permission setting from 666 to get the value of the mask.**

   For a permission setting of 600, the mask becomes 666 – 600 = 066.

4. **Use the `umask` command to set the file-creation mask by typing**

   ```
   umask 066
   ```

A default `umask` of 022 is good for system security because it translates to files that have read and write permission for the owner and read permissions for everyone else. The bottom line is that you don't want a default `umask` that results in files that are writable by the whole world.

## Checking for set user ID permission

Another permission setting can be a security hazard. This permission setting, called the *set user ID* (or `setuid` for short), applies to executable files. When the `setuid` permission is enabled, the file executes under the user ID of the file's owner. In other words, if an executable program is owned by `root` and the `setuid` permission is set, the program runs as if `root` is executing it — no matter who executed the program. The `setuid` permission means that the program can do a lot more (for example, read all files, create new files, and delete files) than what a normal user program can do. Another risk is that if a `setuid` program file has a security hole, crackers can do a lot more damage through such programs than through other vulnerabilities.

You can find all `setuid` programs with a simple `find` command:

```
find / -type f -perm +4000 -print
```

You see a list of files such as the following:

```
/bin/su
/bin/ping
/bin/eject
/bin/mount
```

```
/bin/ping6
/bin/umount
/opt/kde3/bin/fileshareset
/opt/kde3/bin/artswrapper
/opt/kde3/bin/kcheckpass
. . . lines deleted . . .
```

Many of the programs have the setuid permission because they need it, but check the complete list and make sure that there are no strange setuid programs (for example, setuid programs in a user's home directory).

For example, if you type **ls -l /bin/su**, you see the following permission settings:

```
-rwsr-xr-x 1 root root 25756 Aug 19 17:06 /bin/su
```

The s in the owner's permission setting (-rws) tells you that the setuid permission is set for the /bin/su file, which is the executable file for the su command that you can use to become root or another user.

# Encrypting and Signing Files with GnuPG

Linux comes with the *GNU Privacy Guard* (GnuPG, or simply GPG) encryption and authentication utility. With GPG, you can create your public and private key pair, encrypt files using your key, and also digitally sign a message to authenticate that it's really from you. If you send a digitally signed message to someone who has your public key, the recipient can verify that it was you who signed the message.

## Understanding public key encryption

The basic idea behind public key encryption is to use a pair of keys — one private and the other public — that are related but can't be used to guess one from the other. Anything encrypted with the private key can be decrypted only with the corresponding public key, and vice versa. The public key is for distribution to other people while you keep the private key in a safe place.

You can use public key encryption to communicate securely with others; Figure 2-1 illustrates the basic idea. Suppose Alice wants to send secure messages to Bob. Each of them generates public key and private key pairs, after which they exchange their public keys. Then, when Alice wants to send a message to Bob, she simply encrypts the message using Bob's public key and sends the encrypted message to him. Now the message is secure from eavesdropping because only Bob's private key can decrypt the message — and only Bob has that key. When Bob receives the message, he uses his private key to decrypt the message and read it.

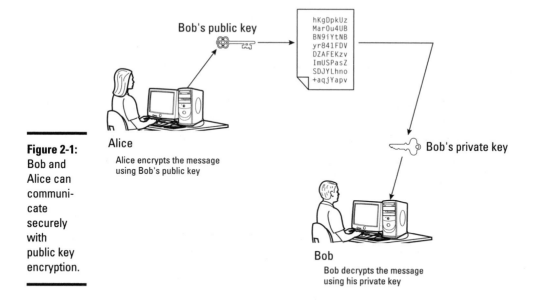

**Figure 2-1:**
Bob and
Alice can
communi-
cate
securely
with
public key
encryption.

At this point, you need to stop and think and say, "Wait a minute! How does
Bob know the message really came from Alice? What if someone else uses
Bob's public key and sends a message as if it came from Alice?" This situa-
tion is where digital signatures come in.

## Understanding digital signatures

The purpose of digital, or electronic, signatures is the same as pen-and-ink
signatures, but how you sign digitally is different. Unlike a pen-and-ink signature, your digital signature depends on the message you're signing. The first
step in creating a digital signature is to apply a mathematical function to the
message and reduce it to a fixed-size message digest (also called a *hash* or a
*fingerprint*). No matter how big your message, the message digest is usually
128 or 160 bits, depending on the hashing function.

The next step is to apply public key encryption. Simply encrypt the message
digest with your private key, and you get the digital signature for the message. Typically, the digital signature is added to the end of the message, and
voilà — you get an electronically signed message.

What good does the digital signature do? Well, anyone who wants to verify
that the message is indeed signed by you takes your public key and decrypts
the digital signature. What that person gets is the message digest (the
encrypted hash) of the message. Then he or she applies the same hash function to the message and compares the computed hash with the decrypted
value. If the two match, no one has tampered with the message. Because

your public key was used to verify the signature, the message must have been signed with the private key known only to you. So the message must be from you!

In the theoretical scenario of Alice sending private messages to Bob, Alice can digitally sign her message to make sure that Bob can tell that the message is really from her. Figure 2-2 illustrates the use of digital signatures along with normal public key encryption.

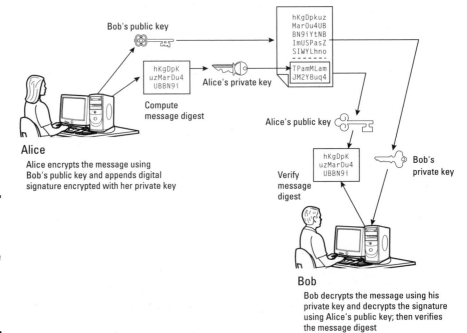

**Figure 2-2:**
Alice can digitally sign her message so that Bob can tell it's really from her.

Here's how Alice sends her private message to Bob with the assurance that Bob can really tell it's from her:

1. Alice uses software to compute the message digest of the message and then encrypts the digest by using her private key. This is her digital signature for the message.

2. Alice encrypts the message (again, using some convenient software *and* Bob's public key).

3. She sends both the encrypted message and the digital signature to Bob.

4. Bob decrypts the message, using his private key.

5. Bob decrypts the digital signature, using Alice's public key. This gives him the message digest.

6. Bob computes the message digest of the message and compares it with what he got by decrypting the digital signature.

7. If the two message digests match, Bob can be sure that the message really came from Alice.

# Using GPG

GPG includes the tools you need to use public key encryption and digital signatures. You can figure out how to use GPG gradually as you begin using encryption. The following shows you some of the typical tasks you can perform with GPG.

### Generating the key pair

The steps for generating the key pairs are as follows:

1. **Type** gpg --gen-key.

   If you're using gpg for the first time, it creates a .gnupg directory in your home directory and a file named gpg.conf in that directory. Then GPG asks what kind of keys you want:

   ```
   Please select what kind of key you want:
   (1) DSA and ElGamal (default)
   (2) DSA (sign only)
   (4) RSA (sign only)
   Your selection?
   ```

2. **Press Enter for the default choice because it's good enough.**

   GPG then prompts you for the key size (the number of bits).

3. **Press Enter again to accept the default value of 2,048 bits.**

   GPG asks you when the keys expire. The default is to never expire.

4. **If the default is what you want (and why not?), press Enter.**

5. **When GPG asks if you really want the keys to never expire, press the Y key to confirm.**

   GPG prompts you for your name, your e-mail address, and finally a comment to make it easier to associate the key pair with your name.

6. **Type each piece of requested information and press Enter.**

7. **When GPG gives you a chance to change the information or confirm it as is, confirm by typing o and pressing Enter.**

   GPG next prompts you for a passphrase that protects your private key.

8. **Type a long phrase that includes lowercase and uppercase letters, numbers, and punctuation marks — the longer the better — and then press Enter.**

Be careful to choose a passphrase that you can easily remember.

GPG generates the keys. It may ask you to perform some work on the PC so that the random-number generator can generate enough random numbers for the key-generation process.

### Exchanging keys

To communicate with others, you have to give them your public key. You also have to get public keys from those who may send you a message (or someone who might sign a file and you want to verify the signature). GPG keeps the public keys in your key ring. (The *key ring* is simply the public keys stored in a file, but it sounds nice to call it a key ring because everyone has a key ring in the real world, and these are keys of a sort, right?) To list the keys in your key ring, type

```
gpg --list-keys
```

To send your public key to someone or to place it on a Web site, you have to export the key to a file. The best way is to put the key in what GPG documentation calls an *ASCII-armored* format, with a command like this:

```
gpg --armor --export kdualney@insightbb.com > kdulaneykey.asc
```

This command saves the public key in an ASCII-armored format (it basically looks like garbled text) in the file named `kdulaneykey.asc`. You would replace the e-mail address with your e-mail address (the one you used when you created the key) and replace the output filename to something different.

After you export the public key to a file, you can mail that file to others or place it on a Web site for use by others.

When you import a key from someone, you typically get it in an ASCII-armored format as well. For example, if you have a `us-cert@us-cert.gov` GPG public key in a file named `uscertkey.asc` (obtained from the link at `www.us-cert.gov/pgp/email.html`), you then import it into the key ring with the following command:

```
gpg --import uscertkey.asc
```

Use the `gpg --list-keys` command to verify that the key is in your key ring. For example, here's what you might see when typing **gpg --list-keys** on the system:

```
/home/kdulaney/.gnupg/pubring.gpg
---------------------------
pub 1024D/7B38A728 2010-08-28
uid Kristin Dulaney <kdulaney@insightbb.com>
sub 2048g/3BD6D418 2005-08-28
pub 2048R/F0E187D0 2004-09-08 [expires: 2010-10-01]
uid US-CERT Operations Key <us-cert@us-cert.gov>
```

The next step is to check the fingerprint of the new key. Type the following command to get the fingerprint of the US-CERT key:

```
gpg --fingerprint us-cert@us-cert.gov
```

GPG prints the fingerprint:

```
pub 2048R/F0E187D0 2009-09-08 [expires: 2010-10-01]
Key fingerprint = 049F E3BA 240B 4CF1 3A76 06DC 1868 49EC F0E1 87D0
uid US-CERT Operations Key <us-cert@us-cert.gov>
```

At this point, you need to verify the key fingerprint with someone at the US-CERT organization. For a large organization such as US-CERT, you can verify the fingerprint on the US-CERT Web page (www.us-cert.gov/pgp/encryptmail.html).

If you think the key fingerprint is good, you can sign the key and validate it. Here's the command you use to sign the key:

```
gpg --sign-key us-cert@us-cert.gov
```

GPG asks for confirmation and then prompts you for your passphrase. After that, GPG signs the key.

Because key verification and signing is a potential weak link in GPG, be careful about what keys you sign. By signing a key, you basically say that you trust the key to be from that person or organization.

### Signing a file

You may find signing files useful if you send a file to someone and want to assure the recipient that no one tampered with the file and that you did, in fact, send the file. GPG makes signing a file easy. You can compress and sign a file named message with the following command:

```
gpg -o message.sig -s message
```

To verify the signature, type

```
gpg --verify message.sig
```

To get back the original document, simply type

```
gpg -o message --decrypt message.sig
```

Sometimes you don't care about keeping a message secret, but you simply want to sign it to indicate that the message is from you. In such a case, you can generate and append a clear-text signature with the following command:

```
gpg -o message.asc --clearsign message
```

This command basically appends a clear-text signature to the text message. Here's a typical clear-text signature block:

```
-----BEGIN PGP SIGNATURE-----
Version: GnuPG v1.4.2 (GNU/Linux)
iD8DBQFDEhAtaHWlHHs4pygRAhiqAJ9Qj0pPMgKVBuokDyUZaEYVsp6RIQCfaoBm
9zCwrSAG9mo2DXJvbKS3ri8=
=2uc/
-----END PGP SIGNATURE-----
```

When a message has a clear-text signature appended, you can use GPG to verify the signature with the following command:

```
gpg --verify message.asc
```

If you had indeed signed the message, the last line of the output says that it's a good signature.

### Encrypting and decrypting documents

To encrypt a message meant for a recipient, you can use the `--encrypt` (or `-e`) GPG command. Here's how you might encrypt a message for US-CERT using its GPG key:

```
gpg -o message.gpg -e -r us-cert@us-cert.gov message
```

The message is encrypted using the US-CERT public key (without a signature, but you can add the signature with the `-s` command).

When US-CERT receives the `message.gpg` file, the recipient has to decrypt it using US-CERT's private key. Here's the command someone at US-CERT can use:

```
gpg -o message --decrypt message.gpg
```

GPG then prompts for the passphrase to unlock the US-CERT private key, decrypts the message, and saves the output in the file named `message`.

If you simply want to encrypt a file and no one else has to decrypt the file, you can use GPG to perform *symmetric encryption.* In this case, you provide a passphrase to encrypt the file with the following GPG command:

```
gpg -o secret.gpg -c somefile
```

GPG prompts you for the passphrase and asks you to repeat the passphrase (to make sure that you didn't mistype anything). Then GPG encrypts the file using a key generated from the passphrase.

To decrypt a file encrypted with a symmetric key, type

```
gpg -o myfile --decrypt secret.gpg
```

GPG prompts you for the passphrase. If you enter the correct passphrase, GPG decrypts the file and saves the output (in this example) in the file named `myfile`.

# Monitoring System Security

Even if you secure your system, you have to monitor the log files periodically for signs of intrusion. You may want to use Tripwire (a good tool for detecting any changes made to the system files) so that you can monitor the integrity of critical system files and directories. Your Linux system probably doesn't come with the Tripwire package. To use Tripwire, you have to buy it from `www.tripwire.com`. After you purchase and install Tripwire, you can configure it to monitor any changes to specified system files and directories on your system.

Periodically examine the log files in the `/var/log` directory and its subdirectories. Many Linux applications, including some servers, write log information by using the logging capabilities of `syslogd` or `rsyslogd`. On Linux systems, the log files written by `syslogd` and `rsyslogd` reside in the `/var/log` directory. Make sure that only the `root` user can read and write these files.

Book VI
Chapter 2

Securing Linux

The `syslogd` configuration file is `/etc/syslog.conf`, and the `rsyslogd` configuration file (existing on many newer systems) is `/etc/rsyslog.conf`. The default configuration of `syslogd` generates the necessary log files; however, if you want to examine and understand the configuration file, type **man syslog.conf** for more information.

# Securing Internet Services

For an Internet-connected Linux system (or even one on a TCP/IP LAN that's not connected to the Internet), a significant threat is that someone could use one of many Internet services to gain access to your system. Each service — such as mail, Web, or FTP — requires running a server program that responds to client requests arriving over the TCP/IP network. Some of these server programs have weaknesses that can allow an outsider to log in to your system — maybe with `root` privileges. Luckily, Linux comes with some facilities that you can use to make the Internet services more secure.

Potential intruders can employ a *port-scanning tool* — a program that attempts to establish a TCP/IP connection at a port and then looks for a response — to check which Internet servers are running on your system. Then, to gain access to your system, the intruders can potentially exploit any known weaknesses of one or more services.

## Turning off standalone services

To provide Internet services, such as Web, e-mail, and FTP, your Linux system has to run server programs that listen to incoming TCP/IP network requests. Some of these servers start when your system boots, and they run all the time. Such servers are *standalone servers.* The Web server and mail server are examples of standalone servers.

Another server, xinetd, starts other servers that are configured to work under xinetd. Some Linux systems use the inetd server instead of xinetd to start other servers.

Some servers can be configured to run standalone or under a super server such as xinetd. For example, the vsftpd FTP server can be configured to run standalone or to run under the control of xinetd.

In Debian, Ubuntu, and Xandros, use the update-rc.d command to turn off standalone servers and use the invoke-rc.d command to start or stop servers interactively. To get a clue about the available services, type **ls /etc/init.d** and look at all the script files designed to turn services on or off. You have to use these filenames when you want to turn a service on or off. For example, to turn off Samba service, type **update-rc.d -f samba remove**. If the service was already running, type **invoke-rc.d samba stop** to stop the service. You can use the invoke-rc.d command to stop any service in a similar manner.

In Fedora and SUSE, you can turn standalone servers on or off by using the chkconfig command. You can get the names of the service scripts by typing **ls /etc/init.d**. Then you can turn off a service (for example, Samba) by typing **chkconfig --del smb**. If the service was already running, type **/etc/init.d/smb stop** to stop the service. You can run scripts from the /etc/init.d directory with the stop argument to stop any service in a similar manner.

## Configuring the Internet super server

In addition to standalone servers such as a Web server or mail server, other servers — inetd or xinetd — have to be configured separately. These servers are *Internet super servers* because they can start other servers on demand.

Type **ps ax | grep inetd** to see which Internet super server — inetd or xinetd — your system runs.

Debian, Ubuntu, and Xandros use inetd, and Fedora and SUSE use xinetd.

The inetd server is configured through the /etc/inetd.conf file. You can disable a service by locating the appropriate line in that file and commenting it out by placing a pound sign (#) at the beginning of the line. After saving the configuration file, type **/etc/init.d/inetd restart** to restart the inetd server.

Configuring the xinetd server is a bit more complicated. The xinetd server reads a configuration file named /etc/xinetd.conf at startup. This file, in turn, refers to configuration files stored in the /etc/xinetd.d directory. The configuration files in /etc/xinetd.d tell xinetd which ports to listen to and which server to start for each port. Type **ls /etc/xinetd.d** to see a list of the files in the /etc/xinetd.d directory on your system. Each file represents a service that xinetd can start. To turn off any of these services, edit the file in a text editor and add a disable = yes line in the file. After you make any changes to the xinetd configuration files, you must restart the xinetd server; otherwise, the changes don't take effect. To restart the xinetd server, type **/etc/init.d/xinetd restart**. This command stops the xinetd server and then starts it again. When it restarts, it reads the configuration files, and the changes take effect.

## Configuring TCP wrapper security

A security feature of both inetd and xinetd is their use of the TCP wrapper to start various services. The *TCP wrapper* is a block of code that provides an access-control facility for Internet services, acting like a protective package for your message. The TCP wrapper can start other services, such as FTP and TELNET; but before starting a service, it consults the /etc/hosts.allow file to see whether the host requesting the service is allowed to use that service. If nothing appears in /etc/hosts.allow about that host, the TCP wrapper checks the /etc/hosts.deny file to see if it denies the service. If both files are empty, the TCP wrapper provides access to the requested service.

Here are the steps to follow to tighten access to the services that inetd or xinetd are configured to start:

*1.* **Use a text editor to edit the /etc/hosts.deny file, adding the following line into that file:**

```
ALL:ALL
```

This setting denies all hosts access to any Internet services on your system.

2. **Edit the /etc/hosts.allow file and add to it the names of hosts that can access services on your system.**

   For example, to enable only hosts from the 192.168.1.0 network and the localhost (IP address 127.0.0.1) to access the services on your system, place the following line in the /etc/hosts.allow file:

   ```
   ALL: 192.168.1.0/255.255.255.0 127.0.0.1
   ```

3. **If you want to permit a specific remote host access to a specific Internet service, use the following syntax for a line in /etc/hosts. allow:**

   ```
   server_program_name: hosts
   ```

   Here, *server_program_name* is the name of the server program, and *hosts* is a comma-separated list of hosts that can access the service. You may also write *hosts* as a network address or an entire domain name, such as .mycompany.com.

# Using Secure Shell (SSH) for Remote Logins

Linux comes with the *Open Secure Shell* (OpenSSH) software, a suite of programs that provides a secure replacement for the Berkeley r commands: rlogin (remote login), rsh (remote shell), and rcp (remote copy). OpenSSH uses public key cryptography to authenticate users and to encrypt the communication between two hosts, so users can securely log in from remote systems and copy files securely.

This section briefly describes how to use the OpenSSH software in Linux. To find out more about OpenSSH and read the latest news about it, visit www. openssh.com or www.openssh.org.

The OpenSSH software is installed during Linux installation. Table 2-2 lists the main components of the OpenSSH software.

| Table 2-2 | Components of the OpenSSH Software |
|---|---|
| *Component* | *Description* |
| /usr/sbin/ sshd | This Secure Shell daemon must run on a host if you want users on remote systems to use the ssh client to log in securely. When a connection from the ssh client arrives, sshd performs authentication using public key cryptography and establishes an encrypted communication link with the ssh client. |
| /usr/bin/ssh | Users can run this Secure Shell client to log in to a host that is running sshd. Users can also use ssh to execute a command on another host. |

| Component | Description |
|---|---|
| `/usr/bin/ slogin` | This component is a symbolic link to `/usr/bin/ssh` |
| `/usr/bin/scp` | This secure-copy program works like `rcp` but securely. The `scp` program uses `ssh` for data transfer and provides the same authentication and security as `ssh`. |
| `/usr/bin/ ssh-keygen` | You use this program to generate the public and private key pairs you need for the public key cryptography used in OpenSSH. The `ssh-keygen` program can generate key pairs for both RSA and DSA (Digital Signature Algorithm) authentication. (RSA comes from the initial of the last name of Ron Rivest, Adi Shamir, and Leonard Adleman — the developers of the RSA algorithm.) |
| `/etc/ssh/ sshd_config` | This configuration file for the `sshd` server specifies many parameters for `sshd`, including the port to listen to, the protocol to use, and the location of other files. (There are two versions of SSH protocols: SSH1 and SSH2, both supported by OpenSSH.) |
| `/etc/ssh/ ssh_config` | This configuration file is for the `ssh` client. Each user can also have an `ssh` configuration file named `config` in the `.ssh` subdirectory of the user's home directory. |

**Book VI
Chapter 2**

**Securing Linux**

OpenSSH uses public key encryption, in which the sender and receiver both have a pair of keys — a public key and a private key. The public keys are freely distributed, and each party knows the other's public key. The sender encrypts data by using the recipient's public key. Only the recipient's private key can then decrypt the data.

To use OpenSSH, you first need to start the `sshd` server and then generate the host keys. Here's how:

✦ If you want to support SSH-based remote logins on a host, start the `sshd` server on your system. Type **ps ax | grep sshd** to see if the server is already running. If not, log in as `root` and turn on the SSH service.

In Fedora and SUSE, type **chkconfig --level 35 sshd on**. In Debian and Xandros, type **update-rc.d ssh defaults**. To start the `sshd` server immediately, type **/etc/init.d/ssh start** in Debian and Xandros, or type **/etc/init.d/sshd start** in Fedora and SUSE.

✦ Generate the host keys with the following command:

```
ssh-keygen -d -f /etc/ssh/ssh_host_key -N ''
```

The `-d` flag causes the `ssh-keygen` program to generate DSA keys, which the SSH2 protocol uses. If you see a message saying that the file `/etc/ssh/ssh_host_key` already exists, that means that the key pairs were generated during Linux installation. You can use the existing file without having to regenerate the keys.

A user who wants to log in using SSH can simply use the `ssh` command. For example:

```
ssh 192.168.0.4 -l kdulaney
```

where 192.168.0.4 is the IP address of the other Linux system. SSH then displays a message:

```
The authenticity of host '192.168.0.4 (192.168.0.4)' can't be established.
RSA key fingerprint is 7b:79:f2:dd:8c:54:00:a6:94:ec:fa:8e:7f:c9:ad:66.
Are you sure you want to continue connecting (yes/no)?
```

Type **yes** and press Enter. SSH then adds the host to its list of known hosts and prompts you for a password on the other Linux system:

```
kdulaney@192.168.0.4's password:
```

After entering the password, you have a secure login session with that system. You can also log in to this account with the following equivalent command:

```
ssh kdulaney@192.168.0.4
```

If you simply want to copy a file securely from another system on the LAN (identified by its IP address, 192.168.0.4), you can use `scp` like this:

```
scp 192.168.0.4:/etc/X11/xorg.conf
```

This command prompts for a password and securely copies the `/etc/X11/xorg.conf` file from the 192.168.0.4 host to the system from which the `scp` command was typed, as follows:

```
kdulaney@192.168.0.4's password: (type the password.)
xorg.conf 100% 2814 2.8KB/s 00:00
```

# Setting Up Simple Firewalls

A *firewall* is a network device or host with two or more network interfaces — one connected to the protected internal network and the other connected to unprotected networks, such as the Internet. The firewall controls access to and from the protected internal network.

If you connect an internal network directly to the Internet, you have to make sure that every system on the internal network is properly secured — which can be nearly impossible because a single careless user can render the entire internal network vulnerable. A firewall is a single point of connection to the Internet: You can direct all your efforts toward making that firewall system a daunting barrier to unauthorized external users. Essentially, a firewall is like a protective fence that keeps unwanted external data and software out and sensitive internal data and software in. (See Figure 2-3.)

**Figure 2-3:** A firewall protects hosts on a private network from the Internet.

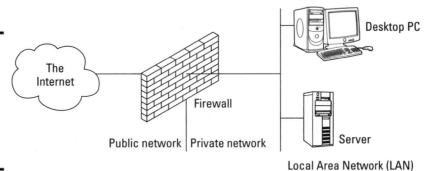

The firewall runs software that examines the network packets arriving at its network interfaces and takes appropriate action based on a set of rules. The idea is to define these rules so that they allow only authorized network traffic to flow between the two interfaces. Configuring the firewall involves setting up the rules properly. A configuration strategy is to reject all network traffic and then enable only a limited set of network packets to go through the firewall. The authorized network traffic would include the connections necessary to enable internal users to do things such as visit Web sites and receive electronic mail.

To be useful, a firewall has the following general characteristics:

✦ It must control the flow of packets between the Internet and the internal network.

✦ It must *not* provide dynamic routing because dynamic routing tables are subject to route *spoofing* — the use of fake routes by intruders. Instead, the firewall uses static routing tables (which you can set up with the `route` command on Linux systems).

✦ It must not allow any external user to log in as `root`. That way, even if the firewall system is compromised, the intruder is blocked from using `root` privileges from a remote login.

✦ It must be kept in a physically secure location.

✦ It must distinguish between packets that come from the Internet and packets that come from the internal protected network. This feature allows the firewall to reject packets that come from the Internet but have the IP address of a trusted system on the internal network.

✦ It acts as the SMTP mail gateway for the internal network. Set up the `sendmail` software so that all outgoing mail appears to come from the firewall system.

✦ Its user accounts are limited to a few user accounts for those internal users who need access to external systems. External users who need access to the internal network should use SSH for remote login (see "Using Secure Shell (SSH) for Remote Logins," earlier in this chapter).

✦ It keeps a log of all system activities, such as successful and unsuccessful login attempts.

✦ It provides DNS name-lookup service to the outside world to resolve any hostnames that are known to the outside world.

✦ It provides good performance so that it doesn't hinder the internal users' access to specific Internet services (such as HTTP and FTP).

A firewall can take many different forms. Here are three common forms of a firewall:

✦ **Packet filter firewall:** This simple firewall uses a router capable of filtering (blocking or allowing) packets according to a number of their characteristics, including the source and destination IP addresses, the network protocol (TCP or UDP), and the source and destination port numbers. Packet filter firewalls are usually placed at the outermost boundary with an untrusted network, and they form the first line of defense. An example of a packet filter firewall is a network router that employs filter rules to screen network traffic.

Packet filter firewalls are fast and flexible, but they can't prevent attacks that exploit application-specific vulnerabilities or functions. They can log only a minimal amount of information, such as source IP address, destination IP address, and traffic type. Also, they're vulnerable to attacks and exploits that take advantage of flaws within the TCP/IP protocol, such as IP address spoofing, which involves altering the address information in network packets to make them appear to come from a trusted IP address.

✦ **Stateful inspection firewall:** This type of firewall keeps track of the network connections that network applications are using. When an application on an internal system uses a network connection to create a session with a remote system, a port is also opened on the internal system. This port receives network traffic from the remote system. For successful connections, packet filter firewalls must permit incoming packets from the remote system. Opening up many ports to incoming traffic creates a risk of intrusion by unauthorized users who abuse the expected conventions of network protocols such as TCP. Stateful inspection firewalls solve this problem by creating a table of outbound network connections, along with each session's corresponding internal port. This "state table" is then used to validate any inbound packets. This stateful inspection is more secure than a packet filter because it tracks internal ports individually rather than opening all internal ports for external access.

✦ **Application-proxy gateway firewall:** This firewall acts as an intermediary between internal applications that attempt to communicate with external servers such as a Web server. For example, a Web proxy receives requests for external Web pages from Web browser clients running inside the firewall and relays them to the exterior Web server as though the firewall was the requesting Web client. The external Web server responds to the firewall, and the firewall forwards the response to the inside client as though the firewall was the Web server. No direct network connection is ever made from the inside client host to the external Web server.

Application-proxy gateway firewalls have some advantages over packet filter firewalls and stateful inspection firewalls. First, application-proxy gateway firewalls examine the entire network packet rather than only the network addresses and ports. This enables these firewalls to provide more extensive logging capabilities than packet filters or stateful inspection firewalls. Another advantage is that application-proxy gateway firewalls can authenticate users directly whereas packet filter firewalls and stateful inspection firewalls normally authenticate users based on the IP address of the system (that is, source, destination, and protocol type). Given that network addresses can be easily spoofed, the authentication capabilities of application-proxy gateway firewalls are superior to those found in packet filter and stateful inspection firewalls.

The advanced functionality of application-proxy gateway firewalls, however, results in some disadvantages when compared with packet filter or stateful inspection firewalls. First, because of the *full packet awareness* found in application-proxy gateways, the firewall is forced to spend significant time reading and interpreting each packet. Therefore, application-proxy gateway firewalls are generally not well suited to high-bandwidth or real-time applications. To reduce the load on the firewall, a dedicated proxy server can be used to secure less time-sensitive services, such as e-mail and most Web traffic. Another disadvantage is that application-proxy gateway firewalls are often limited in terms of support for new network applications and protocols. An individual application-specific proxy agent is required for each type of network traffic that needs to go through the firewall. Most vendors of application-proxy gateways provide generic proxy agents to support undefined network protocols or applications. However, those generic agents tend to negate many of the strengths of the application-proxy gateway architecture, and they simply allow traffic to *tunnel* through the firewall.

Most firewalls implement a combination of these firewall functionalities. For example, many vendors of packet filter firewalls or stateful inspection firewalls have also implemented basic application-proxy functionality to offset some of the weaknesses associated with their firewalls. In most cases, these vendors implement application proxies to provide better logging of network traffic and stronger user authentication. Nearly all major firewall vendors have introduced multiple firewall functions into their products in some manner.

In a large organization, you may also have to isolate smaller internal networks from the corporate network. You can set up such internal firewalls the same way that you set up Internet firewalls.

## Using NAT

Network Address Translation (NAT) is an effective tool that enables you to *hide* the network addresses of an internal network behind a firewall. In essence, NAT allows an organization to use private network addresses behind a firewall while maintaining the ability to connect to external systems through the firewall.

Here are the three methods for implementing NAT:

✦ **Static:** In static NAT, each internal system on the private network has a corresponding external, routable IP address associated with it. This particular technique is seldom used because unique IP addresses are in short supply.

✦ **Hiding:** With hiding NAT, all systems behind a firewall share the same external, routable IP address, while the internal systems use private IP addresses. Thus, with a hiding NAT, a number of systems behind a firewall still appear to be a single system.

✦ **Port address translation:** With port address translation, you can place hosts behind a firewall system and still make them selectively accessible to external users.

In terms of strengths and weaknesses, each type of NAT — static, hiding, or port address translation — is applicable in certain situations; the variable is the amount of design flexibility offered by each type. Static NAT offers the most flexibility, but it's not always practical because of the shortage of IP addresses. Hiding NAT technology is seldom used because port address translation offers additional features. Port address translation is often the most convenient and secure solution.

## Enabling packet filtering on your Linux system

The Linux kernel has built-in packet filtering software in the form of something called `netfilter`. You use the `iptables` command to set up the rules for what happens to the packets based on the IP addresses in their header and the network connection type.

To find out more about netfilter and iptables, visit the documentation section of the netfilter Web site at www.netfilter.org/documentation.

The built-in packet filtering capability is handy when you don't have a dedicated firewall between your Linux system and the Internet. This is the case, for example, when you connect your Linux system to the Internet through a DSL or cable modem. Essentially, you can have a packet filtering firewall inside your Linux system, sitting between the kernel and the applications.

### Using the security level configuration tool

Some Linux distributions, such as Fedora and SUSE, include GUI tools to turn on a packet filtering firewall.

In Fedora, you can turn on different levels of packet filtering through the graphical Firewall Configuration tool. To run the tool, log in as root and choose System⇨Administration⇨Firewall. The Firewall Configuration window appears (see Figure 2-4) along with an authentication window.

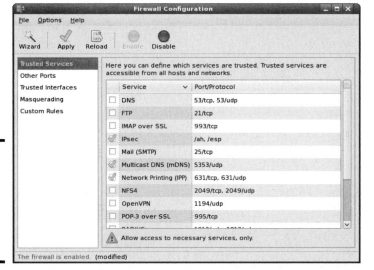

**Figure 2-4:** In Fedora, you can configure the firewall with this tool.

From the Firewall Configuration dialog box, you can select two predefined levels of simple firewalling (more precisely, packet filtering):

+ **Disabled:** This option doesn't perform any filtering and allows all connections. (You can still turn off Internet services by not running the servers or disabling them in the xinetd configuration files.) This security level is fine if your Linux system is inside a protected local area network or if you have a separate firewall device.

◆ **Enabled:** This option turns on packet filtering. You can then select the services that you want to allow and the network devices that you trust.

You can allow incoming packets meant for specific Internet services such as SSH, TELNET, and FTP. If you select a network interface such as eth0 (the first Ethernet card) as trusted, all network traffic over that interface is allowed without any filtering.

In SUSE, to set up a firewall, choose Main Menu⇨System⇨YaST. In the YaST Control Center window that appears, click Security and Users on the left side of the window and then click Firewall on the right side. YaST opens a window that you can use to configure the firewall.

You can designate network interfaces (by device name, such as eth0, ppp0, and so on) to one of three zones: internal, external, or demilitarized zone. Then for that zone, you can specify what services (such as HTTP, FTP, and SSH) are allowed. If you have two or more network interfaces and you use the Linux system as a gateway (a router), you can enable forwarding packets between network interfaces (a feature called *masquerading*). You can also turn on different levels of logging (for example, logging all dropped packets that attempt connection at specific ports). If you make changes to firewall settings, click the Startup category and click Save Settings and Restart Firewall Now.

### Using the iptables command

The GUI firewall configuration tools use the iptables command to implement the firewall. If your Linux system doesn't have a GUI tool, you can use iptables directly to configure firewalling on your Linux system.

Using the iptables command is somewhat complex. The iptables command uses the concept of a *chain,* which is a sequence of rules. Each rule says what to do with a packet if the header contains certain information (such as the source or destination IP address). If a rule doesn't apply, iptables consults the next rule in the chain. By default, there are three chains:

◆ **INPUT chain:** The first set of rules against which packets are tested. The packets continue to the next chain only if the INPUT chain doesn't specify DROP or REJECT.

◆ **FORWARD chain:** Contains the rules that apply to packets attempting to pass through this system to another system (when you use your Linux system as a router between your LAN and the Internet, for example).

◆ **OUTPUT chain:** Includes the rules applied to packets before they are sent out (either to another network or to an application).

When an incoming packet arrives, the kernel uses iptables to make a routing decision based on the destination IP address of the packet. If the packet is for this server, the kernel passes the packet to the INPUT chain. If the packet satisfies all the rules in the INPUT chain, the packet is processed by local processes such as an Internet server that is listening for packets of this type.

If the kernel has IP forwarding enabled and the packet has a destination IP address of a different network, the kernel passes the packet to the FORWARD chain. If the packet satisfies the rules in the FORWARD chain, it's sent out to the other network. If the kernel doesn't have IP forwarding enabled and the packet's destination address isn't for this server, the packet is dropped.

If the local processing programs that receive the input packets want to send network packets out, those packets pass through the OUTPUT chain. If the OUTPUT chain accepts those packets, they're sent out to the specified destination network.

**Book VI
Chapter 2**

Securing Linux

You can view the current chains, add rules to the existing chains, or create new chains of rules by using the iptables command. When you view the current chains, you can also save them to a file. For example, if you had configured nothing else and your system has no firewall configured, typing **iptables -L** should show the following:

```
Chain INPUT (policy ACCEPT)
target prot opt source destination
Chain FORWARD (policy ACCEPT)
target prot opt source destination
Chain OUTPUT (policy ACCEPT)
target prot opt source destination
```

In this case, all three chains — INPUT, FORWARD, and OUTPUT — show the same ACCEPT policy, which means everything is wide open.

If you're setting up a packet filter, the first thing you do is specify the packets that you want to accept. For example, to accept packets from the 192.168.0.0 network address, add the following rule to the INPUT chain:

```
iptables -A INPUT -s 192.168.0.0/24 -j ACCEPT
```

Now add a rule to drop everything except local loopback (the lo network interface) traffic and stop all forwarding with the following commands:

```
iptables -A INPUT -i ! lo -j REJECT
iptables -A FORWARD -j REJECT
```

The first iptables command, for example, appends to the INPUT chain (-A INPUT) the rule that if the packet does not come from the lo interface (-i ! lo), iptables rejects the packet (-j REJECT).

Before rejecting all other packets, you may also add more rules to each INPUT chain to allow specific packets in. You can select packets to accept or reject based on many parameters, such as IP addresses, protocol types (TCP, UDP), network interface, and port numbers.

You can do all sorts of specialized packet filtering with iptables. For example, suppose you set up a Web server and want to accept packets meant for only HTTP (port 80) and secure shell (SSH) services. The secure shell service (port 22) is for you to securely log in and administer the server. Suppose the server's IP address is 192.168.0.10. Here is how you might set up the rules for this server:

```
iptables -P INPUT DROP
iptables -A INPUT -s 0/0 -d 192.168.0.10 -p tcp --dport 80 -j ACCEPT
iptables -A INPUT -s 0/0 -d 192.168.0.10 -p tcp --dport 22 -j ACCEPT
```

In this case, the first rule sets up the default policy of the INPUT chain to DROP, which means that if none of the specific rules match, the packet will be dropped. The next two rules say that packets addressed to 192.168.0.10 and meant for ports 80 and 22 are accepted.

Don't type iptables commands from a remote login session. A rule that begins denying packets from all addresses can also stop what you type from reaching the system; if that happens, you may have no way of accessing the system over the network. To avoid unpleasant surprises, always type iptables rules at the console — the keyboard and monitor connected directly to your Linux PC that is running the packet filter. If you want to delete all filtering rules in a hurry, type **iptables -F** to flush them. To change the default policy for the INPUT chain to ACCEPT, type **iptables -t filter -P INPUT ACCEPT**. This causes iptables to accept all incoming packets by default.

Not every iptables command is discussed in this section. You can type **man iptables** to read a summary of the commands. You can also read about netfilter and iptables at www.iptables.org.

After you define the rules by using the iptables command, they're in memory and are gone when you reboot the system. Use the iptables-save command to store the rules in a file. For example, you can save the rules in a file named iptables.rules by using the following command:

```
iptables-save > iptables.rules
```

Here's a listing of the iptables.rules file generated on a Fedora system:

```
# Generated by iptables-save v1.3.0 on Sun Aug 28 16:10:12 2010
*filter
:FORWARD ACCEPT [0:0]
:INPUT ACCEPT [0:0]
:OUTPUT ACCEPT [6:636]
```

```
-A FORWARD -j REJECT --reject-with icmp-port-unreachable
-A INPUT -s 192.168.0.0/255.255.255.0 -j ACCEPT
-A INPUT -i ! lo -j REJECT --reject-with icmp-port-unreachable
COMMIT
# Completed on Sun Aug 28 16:10:12 2010
```

These rules correspond to the following `iptables` commands used to configure the filter:

```
iptables -A INPUT -s 192.168.0.0/24 -j ACCEPT
iptables -A INPUT -i ! lo -j REJECT
iptables -A FORWARD -j REJECT
```

If you want to load these saved rules into `iptables`, use the following command:

```
iptables-restore < iptables.rules
```

# Chapter 3: Performing Computer Security Audits

---

## In This Chapter

✔ Understanding computer security audits

✔ Learning a security test methodology

✔ Reviewing host and network security

✔ Exploring different security testing tools

*Y*ou see the term *audit* and think tax audit, right? Well, many types of audits exist, and one of them is a *computer security audit*. The purpose of a computer security audit, basically, is to test your system and network security. For larger organizations, an independent auditor (much like with the auditing of financial statements) can do the security audit. If you have only a few Linux systems or a small network, you can do the security audit as a self-assessment, just to figure out if you're doing everything okay.

This chapter explains how to perform computer security audits and shows you a number of free tools and resources to help you test your system's security.

## Understanding Security Audits

An *audit* is simply an independent assessment of whatever it is you're auditing. So a *computer security audit* is an independent assessment of computer security. If someone conducts a computer security audit of your organization, he or she focuses typically on two areas:

✦ **Independent verification** of whether your organization complies with its existing policies and procedures for computer security. This part is the nontechnical aspect of the security audit.

✦ **Independent testing** of how effective your security controls (any hardware and software mechanisms you use to secure the system) are. This part is the technical aspect of the security audit.

Why do you need security audits? For the same reason you need financial audits — mainly to verify that everything is being done the way it's supposed to be done. For public as well as private organizations, management may want independent security audits to assure themselves that their security is A-okay. Irrespective of your organization's size, you can always perform security audits on your own, either to prepare for independent security audits or simply to know that you're doing everything correctly.

No matter whether you have independent security audits or a self-assessment, here are some of the benefits you get from security audits:

+ Periodic risk assessments that consider internal and external threats to systems and data

+ Periodic testing of the effectiveness of security policies, security controls, and techniques

+ Identification of any significant deficiencies in your system's security (so you know what to fix)

+ In the case of self-assessments, preparation for any annual independent security testing that your organization might have to face

## Nontechnical aspects of security audits

The nontechnical side of computer security audits focuses on your organization-wide security framework. The audit examines how well the organization has set up and implemented the policies, plans, and procedures for computer security. Some of the items to be verified follow:

+ Evidence that risks are periodically assessed

+ The existence of an entity-wide security program plan

+ A security program-management structure is in place

+ Computer security responsibilities are clearly assigned

+ Effective security-related personnel policies are in place

+ The security program's effectiveness is monitored and changes are made when needed

As you may expect, the nontechnical aspects of the security audit involve reviewing documents and interviewing appropriate individuals to find out how the organization manages computer security. For a small organization or a home PC, expecting plans and procedures in documents is ridiculous. In those cases, simply make sure that you have some technical controls in place to secure your system and your network connection.

### Technical aspects of security audits

The technical side of computer security audits focuses on testing the technical controls that secure your hosts and network. The testing involves determining

+ **How well the host is secured.** Are all operating system patches applied? Are the file permissions set correctly? Are user accounts protected? Are file changes monitored? Are log files monitored? And so on.

+ **How well the network is secured.** Are unnecessary Internet services turned off? Is a firewall installed? Are remote logins secured with tools such as SSH? Are TCP wrapper access controls used? And so on.

Typically, security experts use automated tools to perform these two security reviews for both individual hosts and the entire network.

# Implementing a Security Test Methodology

A key element of a computer security audit is a security test that checks the technical mechanisms used to secure a host and the network. The security test methodology follows these high-level steps:

1. Take stock of the organization's networks, hosts, network devices (routers, switches, firewalls, and so on), and Internet connection.

2. If there are many hosts and network connections, determine what are the important hosts and network devices that need to be tested. The importance of a host depends on the kinds of applications it runs. For example, a host that runs the corporate database would be more important than the hosts that serve as desktop systems.

3. Test the hosts individually. Typically, this step involves logging in as a system administrator and checking various aspects of host security, from passwords to system log files.

4. Test the network. This step is usually performed by attempting to break through the network defenses from another system on the Internet. If there's a firewall, the testing checks that the firewall is indeed configured correctly.

5. Analyze the test results of both host and network tests to determine vulnerabilities and risks.

Each of the two types of testing — host and network — focuses on three areas of overall computer security:

+ **Prevention:** Includes the mechanisms (nontechnical and technical) that help prevent attacks on the system and the network

✦ **Detection:** Refers to techniques such as monitoring log files, checking file integrity, and using intrusion detection systems that can detect when someone is about to or has already broken into your system

✦ **Response:** Includes the steps for tasks such as reporting an incident to authorities and restoring important files from backup after a computer security incident occurs

For host and network security, each of these areas has some overlaps. For example, prevention mechanisms for host security (such as good passwords or file permissions) can also provide network security. Nevertheless, thinking in terms of the three areas — prevention, detection, and response — does help.

## Some common computer vulnerabilities

Before you can think of prevention, however, you have to know the types of problems you're trying to prevent. In other words, what are the common security vulnerabilities? The prevention and detection steps typically depend on the specific vulnerabilities. Basically, the idea is to check whether a host or a network has the vulnerabilities that crackers exploit.

### Online resources on computer vulnerabilities

Several online resources identify and categorize computer security vulnerabilities:

✦ **SANS Institute** publishes a list of the top 20 most critical Internet security vulnerabilities — the Top Cyber Security Risks index — at `www.sans.org/top20`.

✦ **CVE** (Common Vulnerabilities and Exposures) is a list of standardized names of vulnerabilities. For more information on CVE, see `http://cve.mitre.org`. Using the CVE name to describe vulnerabilities is common practice.

✦ **National Vulnerability Database (NVD)** is a searchable index of information on computer vulnerabilities, published by the National Institute of Standards and Technology (NIST), a United States government agency. NVD is online at `http://nvd.nist.gov`.

### Typical computer vulnerabilities

The SANS Internet security vulnerabilities list includes several types of vulnerabilities, such as Windows, cross-platform, and UNIX. Of these, UNIX and cross-platform vulnerabilities are relevant to Linux. Table 3-1 summarizes some common UNIX and cross-platform vulnerabilities that apply to Linux.

### Table 3-1    Some Common Vulnerabilities to UNIX Systems

| *Vulnerability Type* | *Description* |
| --- | --- |
| BIND DNS | Berkeley Internet Name Domain (BIND) is a package that implements Domain Name System (DNS), the Internet's name service that translates a name to an IP address. Some versions of BIND have vulnerabilities. |
| Apache Web server | Some Apache Web server modules (such as `mod_ssl`) have known vulnerabilities. Any vulnerability in Common Gateway Interface (CGI) programs used with Web servers to process interactive Web pages can provide attackers a way to gain access to a system. |
| Authentication | User accounts often have no passwords or have weak passwords that are easily cracked by password-cracking programs. |
| CVS, Subversion | Concurrent Versions System (CVS) is a popular source-code control system used in Linux systems. Subversion is another version control system for Linux that is becoming popular. These version control systems have vulnerabilities that can enable an attacker to execute arbitrary code on the system. |
| `sendmail` | `sendmail` is a complex program used to transport mail messages from one system to another, and some versions of `sendmail` have vulnerabilities. |
| SNMP | Simple Network Management Protocol (SNMP) is used to remotely monitor and administer various network-connected systems ranging from routers to computers. SNMP lacks good access control, so an attacker may be able to reconfigure or shut down your system if it is running SNMP. |
| Open Secure Sockets Layer (OpenSSL) | Many applications, such as Apache Web server, use OpenSSL to provide cryptographic security for a network connection. Unfortunately, some versions of OpenSSL have known vulnerabilities that could be exploited. |
| Network File System (NFS) and Network Information Service (NIS) | Both NFS and NIS have many security problems (for example, buffer overflow, potential for denial-of-service attacks, and weak authentication). Also, NFS and NIS are often misconfigured, which could allow local and remote users to exploit the security holes. |
| Databases | Databases such as MySQL and PostgreSQL are complex applications and can be difficult to correctly configure and secure. These databases have many features that can be misused or exploited to compromise the confidentiality, availability, and integrity of data. |
| Linux kernel | The Linux kernel is susceptible to many vulnerabilities, such as denial of service, execution of arbitrary code, and `root`-level access to the system. |

## Host-security review

When reviewing host security, focus on assessing the security mechanisms in each of the following areas:

+ **Prevention:** Install operating system updates, secure passwords, improve file permissions, set up a password for a boot loader, and use encryption

+ **Detection:** Capture log messages and check file integrity with Tripwire (a tool that can detect changes to system files)

+ **Response:** Make routine backups and develop incident response procedures

The following sections review a few of these host-security mechanisms.

### Operating system updates

Linux distributions release updates soon. When security vulnerabilities are found, Linux distributions release an update to fix the problem. Many distributions offer online updates that you can enable and use to keep your system up-to-date. The details of updating the operating system depend on the distribution. See Book V, Chapter 4 for information on how to update Linux online.

### File permissions

Protect important system files with appropriate file ownerships and file permissions. The key procedures in assigning file-system ownerships and permissions are as follows:

+ Figure out which files contain sensitive information and why. Some files may contain sensitive data related to your work or business, whereas many other files are sensitive because they control the Linux system configuration.

+ Maintain a current list of authorized users and what they are authorized to do on the system.

+ Set up passwords, groups, file ownerships, and file permissions to allow only authorized users to access the files.

Table 3-2 lists some important system files in Linux, showing the typical numeric permission setting for each file (this may differ slightly based on the distribution). See Chapter 2 of this minibook for more on numeric permission settings.

### Table 3-2     Important System Files and Their Permissions

| File Pathname | Permission | Description |
|---|---|---|
| /boot/grub/menu.lst | 600 | GRUB boot loader menu file |
| /etc/cron.allow | 400 | List of users permitted to use cron to submit periodic jobs |
| /etc/cron.deny | 400 | List of users who can't use cron to submit periodic jobs |
| /etc/crontab | 644 | System-wide periodic jobs |
| /etc/hosts.allow | 644 | List of hosts allowed to use Internet services that are started using TCP wrappers |
| /etc/hosts.deny | 644 | List of hosts denied access to Internet services that are started using TCP wrappers |
| /etc/logrotate.conf | 644 | File that controls how log files rotate |
| /etc/pam.d | 755 | Directory with configuration files for pluggable authentication modules (PAMs) |
| /etc/passwd | 644 | Old-style password file with user account information but not the passwords |
| /etc/rc.d | 755 | Directory with system-startup scripts |
| /etc/securetty | 600 | TTY interfaces (terminals) from which root can log in |
| /etc/security | 755 | Policy files that control system access |
| /etc/shadow | 400 | File with encrypted passwords and password expiration information |
| /etc/shutdown.allow | 400 | Users who can shut down or reboot by pressing Ctrl+Alt+Delete |
| /etc/ssh | 755 | Directory with configuration files for the Secure Shell (SSH) |
| /etc/sysconfig | 755 | System configuration files |
| /etc/sysctl.conf | 644 | Kernel configuration parameters |

*(continued)*

**Book VI Chapter 3**

**Performing Computer Security Audits**

## Table 3-2 *(continued)*

| File Pathname | Permission | Description |
| --- | --- | --- |
| /etc/syslog.conf | 644 | Configuration file for the syslogd server that logs messages |
| /etc/udev/udev.conf | 644 | Configuration file for udev — the program that provides the ability to dynamically name hot-pluggable devices and create the device files in the /dev directory |
| /etc/vsftpd | 600 | Configuration file for the Very Secure FTP server |
| /etc/vsftpd.ftpusers | 600 | List of users who can't use FTP to transfer files |
| /etc/xinetd.conf | 644 | Configuration file for the xinetd server |
| /etc/xinetd.d | 755 | Directory containing configuration files for specific services that the xinetd server can start |
| /var/log | 755 | Directory with all log files |
| /var/log/lastlog | 644 | Information about all previous logins |
| /var/log/messages | 644 | Main system message log file |
| /var/log/wtmp | 664 | Information about current logins |

Another important check is to look for executable program files that have the setuid permission. If a program has setuid permission and is owned by root, the program runs with root privileges, no matter who actually runs the program. You can find all setuid programs with the following find command:

```
find / -perm +4000 -print
```

You may want to save the output in a file (just append > *filename* to the command) and then examine the file for any unusual setuid programs. For example, a setuid program in a user's home directory is unusual.

### Password security

Verify that the password, group, and shadow password files are protected. In particular, the shadow password file has to be write-protected and readable only by `root`. The filenames and their recommended permissions are shown in Table 3-3.

**Table 3-3          Ownership and Permission of Password Files**

| File Pathname | Ownership | Permission |
|---|---|---|
| /etc/group | root.root | 644 |
| /etc/passwd | root.root | 644 |
| /etc/shadow | root.root | 400 |

### Incident response

*Incident response* is the policy that answers the question of what to do if something unusual does happen to the system. The policy tells you how to proceed if someone breaks into your system.

Your response to an incident depends on how you use your system and how important it is to you or your business. For a comprehensive incident response, remember these key points:

✦ Figure out how critical and important your computer and network are and identify who or what resources can help you protect your system

✦ Take steps to prevent and minimize potential damage and interruption

✦ Develop and document a comprehensive contingency plan

✦ Periodically test the contingency plan and revise the procedures as appropriate

## Network-security review

*Network security review* focuses on assessing the security mechanisms in each of the following areas:

✦ **Prevention:** Set up a firewall, enable packet filtering, disable unnecessary `inetd` or `xinetd` services, turn off unneeded Internet services, use TCP wrappers for access control, and use SSH for secure remote logins.

✦ **Detection:** Use network intrusion detection and capture system logs.

✦ **Response:** Develop incident response procedures.

Some key steps in assessing the network security are described in the following three subsections.

### Services started by inetd or xinetd

Depending on your distribution, the inetd or xinetd server may be configured to start some Internet services such as TELNET and FTP. The decision to turn on some of these services depends on factors such as how the system connects to the Internet and how the system is being used. You can usually turn off most inetd and xinetd services.

Debian, Ubuntu, and Xandros use inetd to start some services. Look at the /etc/inetd.conf file to see what services inetd is configured to start. You can turn off services by commenting out the line in /etc/inetd. conf — just place a pound sign (#) at the beginning of the line.

Fedora and SUSE use xinetd as the server that starts other Internet services on demand. To see which xinetd services are turned off, check the configuration files in the /etc/xinetd.d directory for all the configuration files that have a disable = yes line. (The line doesn't count if it's commented out by placing # at the beginning of the line.) You can add a disable = yes line to the configuration file of any service that you want to turn off.

Also check the following files for any access controls used with the inetd or xinetd services:

✦ /etc/hosts.allow lists hosts allowed to access specific services.

✦ /etc/hosts.deny lists hosts denied access to services.

### Standalone services

Many services, such as apache or httpd (Web server) and sendmail (mail server), start automatically at boot time, assuming they're configured to start that way.

In Fedora and SUSE, you can use the chkconfig command to check which of these standalone servers are set to start at various run levels. (See Book V, Chapter 1 for more about run levels.) Typically, your Fedora or SUSE system starts up at run level 3 (for text login) or 5 (for graphical login). Therefore, what matters is the setting for the servers in levels 3 and 5. To view the list of servers, type **chkconfig --list | more**. When you do a self-assessment of your network security and find that some servers shouldn't be running, you can turn them off for run levels 3 and 5 by typing **chkconfig --level 35 *servicename* off**, where *servicename* is the name of the service you want to turn off.

In some distributions, you can use a GUI tool to see which services are enabled and running at any run level. In Fedora, choose System⇨ Administration⇨Server Settings⇨Services. In SUSE, from the main menu choose System⇨YaST, then click System on the left side of the window, and then click Runlevel Editor on the right side of the window.

When you audit network security, make a note of all the servers that are turned on — and then try to determine whether they should really *be* on, according to what you know about the system. The decision to turn on a particular service depends on how your system is used (for example, as a Web server or as a desktop system) and how it's connected to the Internet (say, through a firewall or directly).

### Penetration test

A penetration test is the best way to tell what services are really running on a Linux system. *Penetration testing* involves trying to get access to your system from an attacker's perspective. Typically, you perform this test from a system on the Internet and try to see if you can break in or, at a minimum, get access to services running on your Linux system.

Knoppix running on a laptop is ideal for performing penetration tests because Knoppix is a Live CD distribution that comes bundled with scanning tools such as nmap and Nessus. All you have to do is boot from the Knoppix CD, and you're ready to do the penetration test.

One aspect of penetration testing is to see what ports are open on your Linux system. The *port number* is simply a number that identifies TCP/IP network connections to the system. The attempt to connect to a port succeeds only if a server is running, or "listening," on that port. A port is considered to be open if a server responds when a connection request for that port arrives.

The first step in penetration testing is to perform a port scan. The term *port scan* describes the automated process of trying to connect to each port number to see if a valid response comes back. Many available automated tools can perform port scanning — you can install and use a popular port-scanning tool called nmap (described later in this chapter).

After performing a port scan, you know which ports are open and could be exploited. Not all servers have security problems, but many servers have well-known vulnerabilities. An open port provides a cracker a way to attack your system through one of the servers. In fact, you can use automated tools called *vulnerability scanners* to identify vulnerabilities that exist in your system (some vulnerability scanners are described in the following sections). Whether your Linux system is connected to the Internet directly (through DSL or cable modem) or through a firewall, use the port-scanning and vulnerability-scanning tools to figure out if you have any holes in your defenses.

## Exploring Security Testing Tools

Many automated tools are available to perform security testing. Some of these tools are meant for finding the open ports on every system in a range of IP addresses. Others look for the vulnerabilities associated with open ports. Yet other tools can capture (or *sniff*) those weaknesses and help you analyze them so that you can glean useful information about what's going on in your network.

You can browse a list of the top 100 security tools (based on an informal poll of nmap users) at `http://sectools.org`. Table 3-4 lists a number of these tools by category. A few of the freely available vulnerability scanners are described in the next few sections.

**Table 3-4    Some Popular Computer Security Testing Tools**

| Type | Names of Tools |
|------|----------------|
| Port scanners | nmap, Strobe |
| Vulnerability scanners | Nessus Security Scanner, SAINT, SARA, Whisker (CGI scanner), ISS Internet Scanner, CyberCop Scanner, Vetescan, Retina Network Security Scanner |
| Network utilities | Netcat, hping2, Firewalk, Cheops, ntop, ping, ngrep, AirSnort (802.11 WEP encryption-cracking tool) |
| Host-security tools | Tripwire, lsof |
| Packet sniffers | tcpdump, Ethereal, dsniff, sniffit |
| Intrusion detection | Snort, Abacus portsentry, scanlogd, NFR, LIDSSystems (IDSs) |
| Password-checking tools | John the Ripper, LC4 |
| Log analysis and monitoring tools | logcolorise, tcpdstats, nlog, logcheck, LogWatch, Swatch |

## nmap

nmap (short for *network mapper*) is a port-scanning tool. It can rapidly scan large networks and determine what hosts are available on the network, what services they offer, what operating system (and the operating system version) they run, what type of packet filters or firewalls they use, and dozens of other characteristics. You can read more about nmap at `http://nmap.org`.

If nmap is not already installed, you can easily install it on your distribution. Fedora and Knoppix come with nmap. In Debian and Ubuntu, you can install it with the command `apt-get install nmap`. In SUSE, click Install and Remove Software from the Software category in YaST Control Center (from the main menu, choose System➪YaST), use the software search facility of YaST to find nmap, and then install it. In Xandros, you can use the `apt-get install nmap` command; after you run Xandros Networks, choose Edit⇨Set Application Sources and click the Debian Unsupported Site link as a source.

If you want to try out `nmap` to scan your local area network, type a command similar to the following (replace the IP address range with addresses appropriate for your network):

`nmap -O -sS 192.168.0.4-8`

Here's a typical output listing from that command:

```
Starting nmap 3.81 ( http://www.insecure.org/nmap/ ) at 2010-08-28 16:20 EDT
Interesting ports on 192.168.0.4:
(The 1659 ports scanned but not shown below are in state: closed)
PORT STATE SERVICE
21/tcp open ftp
22/tcp open ssh
111/tcp open rpcbind
631/tcp open ipp
MAC Address: 00:C0:49:63:78:3A (U.S. Robotics)
Device type: general purpose
Running: Linux 2.4.X|2.5.X|2.6.X
OS details: Linux 2.4.18 - 2.6.7
Uptime 9.919 days (since Thu Aug 18 18:18:15 2010)
. . . Lines deleted . . .
Nmap finished: 5 IP addresses (5 hosts up) scanned in 30.846 seconds
```

As you can see, `nmap` displays the names of the open ports and hazards a guess at the operating system name and version number.

## Nessus

The Nessus Security Scanner is a modular security auditing tool that uses plug-ins written in the Nessus scripting language to test for a wide variety of network vulnerabilities. Nessus uses a client/server software architecture with a server called `nessusd` and a client called `nessus`.

Knoppix already comes with Nessus, so you don't have to download or install anything. To start Nessus, from the main menu choose System⇨ Security⇨NESSUS Security Tool.

To install Nessus, first try your Linux distribution's usual method for installing new software packages. In Debian, Fedora, and Ubuntu, type **apt-get install nessus nessusd** to install the packages. In SUSE, click Install and Remove Software from the Software category in YaST Control Center (from the main menu, choose System⇨YaST) and then use YaST's search facility to find the Nessus packages. Select the packages and click Accept to install them. In Xandros, choose Edit⇨Set Application Sources and click the Debian Unsupported Site link as a source. Then type **apt-get install nessus nessusd.**

For some distributions, you have to download Nessus from `www.nessus.org/download` and install it. Before you try to install Nessus, you must install the `sharutils` RPM. That package includes the `uudecode` utility that the Nessus installation script needs.

To download and install Nessus, follow these steps. (These instructions work on all Linux distributions.)

1. **At `www.nessus.org/download`, select the version of Nessus you want to download.**

   For Linux systems, download the Nessus 2.2.5 installer.

2. **Type the following command to install Nessus. (You must have the development tools, including The GIMP Toolkit, installed.)**

   ```
   sh nessus-installer-2.2.5.sh
   ```

   Respond to the prompts from the installer script to finish the installation. You can usually press Enter to accept the default choices.

When the installation is finished, follow these steps to use Nessus. (In Knoppix, from the main menu choose System➪Security➪NESSUS Security Tool and then go to Step 8.)

1. **Log in as `root` and then type the following:**

   ```
   nessus-mkcert
   ```

   This command creates the Nessus SSL certificate used for secure communication between the Nessus client and the Nessus server.

2. **Provide the requested information to complete the certificate generation process.**

3. **Create a `nessusd` account with the following command:**

   ```
   nessus-adduser
   ```

4. **When prompted, enter your username, password, and any rules. (Press Ctrl+D if you don't know what rules to enter.) Then press the Y key.**

5. **(Optional) Configure `nessusd` by editing the configuration file `/usr/local/etc/nessus/nessusd.conf`.**

   If you want to try Nessus, you can proceed with the default configuration file.

6. **Start the Nessus server with this command:**

   ```
   nessusd -D
   ```

7. **Run the Nessus client by typing the following command in a terminal window:**

   ```
   nessus
   ```

The Nessus Setup window appears.

8. **Type a `nessusd` username and password and click the Log In button.**

9. **When Nessus displays the certificate used to establish the secure connection and asks if you accept it, click Yes.**

    After the client connects to the server, the Log In button changes to Log Out, and a Connected label appears at its left.

    `nessusd` gives you an option to enable plug-ins that can scan for specific vulnerabilities, but some of these may crash hosts and disrupt your network during the scan. If you want to try any of the plug-ins, select and enable them. If you want to be safe, click the Enable All but Dangerous Plugins link.

10. **Click the Target Selection tab and enter a range of IP addresses to scan all hosts in a network.**

    For example, to scan the first eight hosts in a private network 192.168.0.0, enter the address as

    ```
    192.168.0.0/29
    ```

    Don't use Nessus to scan any network that you don't own. Scanning other networks is usually against the law, and there could be serious consequences.

11. **Click Start the Scan.**

    Nessus starts scanning the IP addresses and checks for many different vulnerabilities. Progress bars show the status of the scan.

After Nessus completes the vulnerability scan of the hosts, it displays the result in a nice combination of graphical and text formats. The report is interactive — you can select a host address to view the report on that host, and you can drill down on a specific vulnerability to find details, such as the CVE number that identifies the vulnerability and a description of the vulnerability.

# Book VII

# Linux Servers

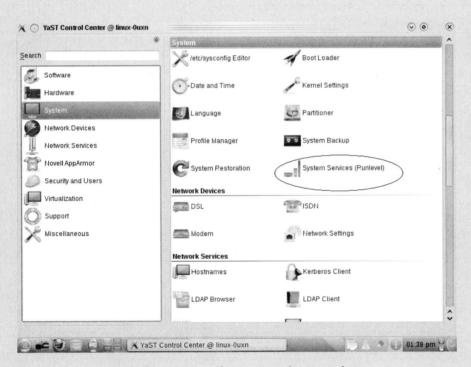

Specify services that start when you boot

# Contents at a Glance

## Chapter 1: Managing Internet Services . . . . . . . . . . . . . . . . . . . . . . . .455

Understanding Internet Services ............................................................... 455
Using the Internet Super Server................................................................. 461
Running Standalone Servers ...................................................................... 464

## Chapter 2: Managing Mail and News Servers . . . . . . . . . . . . . . . . . .473

Installing the Mail Server .......................................................................... 473
Installing the INN Server ............................................................................ 486
Configuring and Starting the INN Server .................................................. 486
Setting Up Local Newsgroups .................................................................... 493

## Chapter 3: Managing DNS . . . . . . . . . . . . . . . . . . . . . . . . . . . . . . . . . . .495

Understanding Domain Name System (DNS) ............................................ 495
Configuring DNS.......................................................................................... 501

## Chapter 4: Working with Samba and NFS . . . . . . . . . . . . . . . . . . . . . .515

Sharing Files with NFS................................................................................ 515
Setting Up a Windows Server Using Samba.............................................. 519

# Chapter 1: Managing Internet Services

## In This Chapter

✔ Finding out about Internet services

✔ Controlling servers through inetd or xinetd

✔ Using chkconfig or update-rc.d to manage servers

✔ Using GUI utilities to configure services to start at boot time

The Internet is a world of clients and servers. Clients make requests to servers, and servers respond to the requests. For example, your Web browser is a client that downloads information from Web servers and displays it to you. Of course, the clients and servers are computer programs that run on a wide variety of computers. A Linux system is an ideal system to run different types of servers — from a Web server to a Windows file and print server. This chapter provides an overview of a typical Internet service and its client/server architecture, and discusses how to manage the servers in Linux. You can use the information in this chapter to manage any server running on your Linux system.

## Understanding Internet Services

*Internet services* are network applications designed to deliver information from one system to another. By design, each Internet service is implemented in two parts — a *server* that provides information and one or more *clients* that request information.

Such a *client/server* architecture is the most common way to build distributed information systems. The clients and servers are computer programs that run on these computers and communicate through the network. The neat part is that you can run a client at your desktop computer and access information from a server running on a computer anywhere in the world (as long as it's on the Internet).

The Web itself, e-mail, and FTP (File Transfer Protocol) are examples of Internet services that use the client/server model. For example, when you use the Web, you use the Web browser client to download and view Web pages from the Web server.

Client/server architecture requires clients to communicate with the servers. That's where the *Transmission Control Protocol/Internet Protocol* — TCP/IP — comes in. TCP/IP provides a standard way for clients and servers to exchange packets of data. The next few sections explain how TCP/IP-based services communicate.

## TCP/IP and sockets

Client/server applications such as the Web and FTP use TCP/IP for data transfers between client and server. These Internet applications typically use TCP/IP communications utilizing the *Berkeley sockets interface* (so named because the socket interface was introduced in Berkeley UNIX around 1982). The sockets interface is nothing physical — it's simply some computer code that a computer programmer can use to create applications that can communicate with other applications on the Internet.

Even if you don't write network applications using sockets, you may have to use or set up many network applications. Knowledge of sockets can help you understand how network-based applications work, which in turn helps you find and correct any problems with these applications.

### Socket definition

Network applications use sockets to communicate over a TCP/IP network. A *socket* represents one end-point of a connection. Because a socket is bidirectional, data can be sent as well as received through it. A socket has three attributes:

+ The *network address* (the IP address) of the system

+ The *port number,* identifying the process (a *process* is a computer program running on a computer) that exchanges data through the socket

+ The *type of socket,* identifying the protocol for data exchange

Essentially, the IP address identifies a computer (host) on the network; the port number identifies a process (server) on the node; and the socket type determines the manner in which data is exchanged — through a connection-oriented (stream) or connectionless (datagram) protocol.

### Connection-oriented protocols

The socket type indicates the protocol being used to communicate through the socket. A connection-oriented protocol works like a normal phone conversation. When you want to talk to your friend, you have to dial your friend's phone number and establish a connection before you can have a conversation. In the same way, connection-oriented data exchange requires both the sending and receiving processes to establish a connection before data exchange can begin.

In the TCP/IP protocol suite, TCP — *Transmission Control Protocol* — supports a connection-oriented data transfer between two processes running on two computers on the Internet. TCP provides reliable two-way data exchange between processes.

As the name TCP/IP suggests, TCP relies on IP — *Internet Protocol* — for delivery of packets. IP does not guarantee delivery of packets; nor does it deliver packets in any particular sequence. IP does, however, efficiently move packets from one network to another. TCP is responsible for arranging the packets in the proper sequence, detecting whether errors have occurred, and requesting retransmission of packets in case of an error.

TCP is useful for applications intended to exchange large amounts of data at a time. In addition, applications that need reliable data exchange use TCP. (For example, FTP uses TCP to transfer files.)

In the sockets model, a socket that uses TCP is referred to as a *stream socket*.

### Connectionless protocols

A connectionless data-exchange protocol does not require the sender and receiver to explicitly establish a connection. It's like shouting to your friend in a crowded room — you can't be sure that your friend hears you.

In the TCP/IP protocol suite, the *User Datagram Protocol* (UDP) provides connectionless service for sending and receiving packets known as *datagrams*. Unlike TCP, UDP does not guarantee that datagrams ever reach their intended destinations. Nor does UDP ensure that datagrams are delivered in the order they're sent.

UDP is used by applications that exchange small amounts of data at a time or by applications that don't need the reliability and sequencing of data delivery. For example, SNMP (Simple Network Management Protocol) uses UDP to transfer data.

In the sockets model, a socket that uses UDP is referred to as a *datagram socket*.

### Sockets and the client/server model

Two sockets are needed to complete a communication path. When two processes communicate, they use the client/server model to establish the connection. Figure 1-1 illustrates the concept. The server application listens on a specific port on the system — the server is completely identified by the IP address of the system where it runs and the port number where it listens for connections. The client initiates a connection from any available port and tries to connect to the server (identified by the IP address and port number).

When the connection is established, the client and the server can exchange data according to their own protocol.

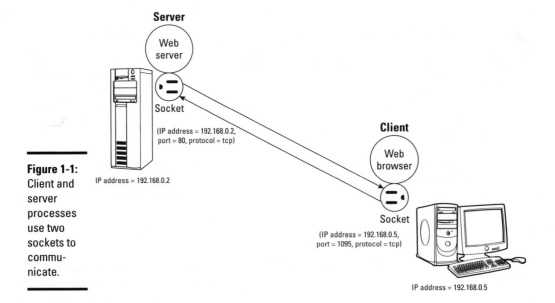

**Server**

Web server

Socket

(IP address = 192.168.0.2, port = 80, protocol = tcp)

IP address = 192.168.0.2

**Client**

Web browser

Socket

(IP address = 192.168.0.5, port = 1095, protocol = tcp)

IP address = 192.168.0.5

**Figure 1-1:**
Client and server processes use two sockets to communicate.

The sequence of events in socket-based data exchanges depends on whether the transfer is connection-oriented (TCP) or connectionless (UDP).

For a connection-oriented data transfer using sockets, the server listens on a specific port, waiting for clients to request connection. Data transfer begins only after a connection is established.

For connectionless data transfers, the server waits for a datagram to arrive at a specified port. The client does not wait to establish a connection; it simply sends a datagram to the server.

Regardless of whether it's a server or a client, each application first creates a socket. Then it *associates* (binds) the socket with the local computer's IP address and a port number. The IP address identifies the machine (where the application is running), and the port number identifies the application using the socket.

Servers typically listen to a well-known port number so that clients can connect to that port to access the server. For a client application, the process of binding a socket to the IP address and port is the same as that for a server, but the client can use 0 as the port number — the sockets library automatically uses an unused port number for the client.

For a connection-oriented stream socket, the communicating client and server applications have to establish a connection. The exact steps for establishing a connection depend on whether the application is a server or a client.

In the client/server model, the server has to be up and running before the client can run. After creating a socket and binding the socket to a port, the server application sets up a queue of connections, which determines how many clients can connect to the server. Typically, a server listens to anywhere from one to five connections. However, the size of the listen queue is one of the parameters you can adjust (especially for a Web server) to ensure that the server responds to as many clients as possible. After setting up the listen queue, the server waits for a connection from a client.

Establishing the connection from the client side is somewhat simpler. After creating a socket and binding the socket to an IP address, the client establishes a connection with the server. To make the connection, the client must know the host name or IP address of the server, as well as the port on which the server accepts connection. All Internet services have well-known standard port numbers.

After a client establishes a connection to a server via a connection-oriented stream socket, the client and server can exchange data by calling the appropriate sockets' API functions. Like a conversation between two persons, the server and client alternately send and receive data — the meaning of the data depends on the message protocol that the server and clients use. Usually, a server is designed for a specific task; inherent in that design is a message protocol that the server and clients use to exchange necessary data. For example, the Web server and the Web browser (client) communicate using HTTP (HyperText Transfer Protocol).

## Internet services and port numbers

The TCP/IP protocol suite is the lingua franca of the Internet because the Internet services *speak* TCP/IP. These services make the Internet tick by making possible the transfer of mail, news, and Web pages. Each Internet service has its own protocol that relies on TCP/IP for the actual transfer of the information. Each service also has one or more assigned port numbers that it uses to do whatever it's designed to do. Here are some well-known Internet services and their associated protocols:

✦ **DHCP (Dynamic Host Configuration Protocol):** Dynamically configures TCP/IP network parameters on a computer. DHCP is used, primarily, to assign dynamic IP addresses and other networking information such as name server, default gateway, and domain names that are needed to configure TCP/IP networks. The DHCP server listens on port 67.

✦ **FTP (File Transfer Protocol):** Transfers files between computers on the Internet. FTP uses two ports: Data is transferred on port 20, and control information is exchanged on port 21.

✦ **HTTP (HyperText Transfer Protocol):** Sends documents from one system to another. HTTP is the underlying protocol of the Web. By default, the Web server and client communicate on port 80.

✦ **SMTP (Simple Mail Transfer Protocol):** Exchanges e-mail messages between systems. SMTP uses port 25 for information exchange.

✦ **NNTP (Network News Transfer Protocol):** Distributes news articles in a store-and-forward fashion across the Internet. NNTP uses port 119.

✦ **SSH (Secure Shell):** Enables secure remote login and other secure network services over an insecure network. SSH uses port 22.

✦ **TELNET:** Enables a user on one system to log into another system on the Internet. (The user must provide a valid user ID and password to log into the remote system.) TELNET uses port 23 by default, but the TELNET client can connect to any specified port.

✦ **NFS (Network File System):** Shares files among computers. NFS uses Sun's Remote Procedure Call (RPC) facility, which exchanges information through port 111.

✦ **NTP (Network Time Protocol):** Synchronizes the system time on a client computer with that on a server with a more accurate clock. NTP uses port 123.

✦ **SNMP (Simple Network Management Protocol):** Manages all types of network devices on the Internet. Like FTP, SNMP uses two ports: 161 and 162.

✦ **TFTP (Trivial File Transfer Protocol):** Transfers files from one system to another. (It's typically used by X terminals and diskless workstations to download boot files from another host on the network.) TFTP data transfer takes place on port 69.

Each service is provided by a *server process* — a computer program that runs on a system awaiting client requests that arrive at the well-known port associated with its service. Thus, the Web server expects client requests at port 80, the standard port for HTTP service.

The /etc/services text file on your Linux system stores the association between a service name and a port number (as well as a protocol). Here is a small subset of entries in the /etc/services file from a Linux system:

```
ftp-data 20/tcp
ftp 21/tcp
fsp 21/udp fspd
ssh 22/tcp # SSH Remote Login Protocol
```

```
ssh 22/udp
telnet 23/tcp
smtp 25/tcp mail
time 37/tcp timserver
time 37/udp timserver
rlp 39/udp resource # resource location
nameserver 42/tcp name # IEN 116
whois 43/tcp nicname
tacacs 49/tcp # Login Host Protocol (TACACS)
```

A quick look through the entries in the `/etc/services` file shows the breadth of networking services available under TCP/IP.

Port number 80 is designated for Web services. In other words, if you set up a Web server on your system, that server listens to port 80. By the way, IANA — the Internet Assigned Numbers Authority (`www.iana.org`) — is the organization responsible for coordinating the assignment of port numbers below 1,024.

# Using the Internet Super Server

The client/server architecture of Internet services requires that the server be up and running before a client makes a request for service. It's probably a bad idea to run all the servers all the time — doing so is impractical because each server process uses up system resources in the form of memory and processor time. Besides, you don't really need *all* the services up and ready at all times. Instead, run a single server that listens to all the ports and then starts the appropriate server when a client request comes in. Such a server is known as the *Internet super server* because it starts various services on demand.

The two Internet super servers are `inetd` and `xinetd`. The `inetd` server is the older one and is still used in some Linux distributions such as Debian, Knoppix, Ubuntu, and Xandros. The `xinetd` server is a replacement for `inetd`, offering improved access control and logging. The name `xinetd` stands for *extended* `inetd`. Distributions such as Fedora and SUSE use `xinetd`.

## Using inetd

In Linux distributions that use `inetd`, the system starts `inetd` when the system boots. The `inetd` server reads a configuration file named `/etc/inetd.conf` at startup. This file tells `inetd` which ports to listen to and what server to start for each port. For example, the entry in the `/etc/inetd.conf` file that starts the IMAP (Internet Message Access Protocol) on one server looks like this:

```
imaps stream tcp nowait root /usr/sbin/tcpd /usr/sbin/imapd
```

The first item on this line, imaps, tells inetd the name of the service. inetd uses this name to look up the port number from the /etc/services file. If you type **grep imaps /etc/services**, you find that the port number of the IMAP service is 993. This tells inetd to listen to port 993 for FTP service requests.

The rest of the fields on the IMAP entry have the following meanings:

+ The second and third fields of the entry, stream and tcp, tell inetd that the FTP service uses a connection-oriented TCP socket to communicate with the client. For services that use the connectionless UDP sockets, these two fields are dgram and udp.

+ The fourth field, nowait, tells inetd to start a new server for each request. If this field is wait, inetd waits until the server exits before starting the server again.

+ The fifth field provides the user ID that inetd uses to run the server. In this case, the server runs the FTP server as root.

+ The sixth field specifies the program to run for this service and the last field is the argument that inetd passes to the server program. In this case, the /usr/sbin/tcpd program is provided /usr/sbin/imapd as an argument.

The /usr/sbin/tcpd program is an access control facility, or a *TCP wrapper,* for Internet services. Because unnecessary Internet services are often the sources of security vulnerabilities, you may want to turn off any unneeded services or at least control access to the services. The tcpd program can start other services, such as FTP and TELNET, but before starting the service, tcpd consults the /etc/hosts.allow file to see if the host requesting service is allowed that service. If nothing is in /etc/hosts.allow about that host, tcpd checks the /etc/hosts.deny file to see if the service should be denied. If both files are empty, tcpd allows the host access to the requested service. You can place the line ALL:ALL in the /etc/hosts.deny file to deny all hosts access to any Internet services.

Browse through the /etc/inetd.conf file on your system to find out the kinds of services that inetd is set up to start. Nowadays, most inetd services are turned off, and many others, such as FTP, are started by stand-alone servers. In any case, if you should see any services that you want to turn off, simply place a hash mark (#) at the beginning of the lines that start these services. When you make such a change to the /etc/inetd.conf file, type **/etc/init.d/inetd restart** to restart the inetd server.

## Using xinetd

Linux distributions that use xinetd start xinetd when the system boots. The xinetd server reads a configuration file named /etc/xinetd.conf at startup. This file tells `xinetd` which ports to listen to and what server to start for each port. The file can contain instructions that include other configuration files. In Linux, the `/etc/xinetd.conf` file looks like the following:

```
# Simple configuration file for xinetd
#
# Set some defaults and include /etc/xinetd.d/
defaults
{
instances = 30
log_type = FILE /var/log/xinetd.log
log_on_success = HOST EXIT DURATION
log_on_failure = HOST ATTEMPT
cps = 50 10
}
includedir /etc/xinetd.d
```

Comment lines begin with the hash mark (#). The defaults block of attributes, enclosed in curly braces ({ . . . }), specifies default values for some attributes. These default values apply to all other services in the configuration file. The `instances` attribute is set to `30`, which means that no more than 30 servers can be simultaneously active for any service.

The last line in the `/etc/xinetd.conf` file uses the `includedir` directive to include all files inside the `/etc/xinetd.d` directory, excluding files that begin with a period (.). The idea is that the `/etc/xinetd.d` directory contains all service-configuration files — one file for each type of service the `xinetd` server is expected to manage. Type **ls /etc/xinetd.d** to see the `xinetd` configuration files for your system. Each file in `/etc/xinetd.d` specifies attributes for one service that `xinetd` can start.

For example, SUSE Linux uses `xinetd` to start some services, including the `vsftpd` (Very Secure FTP daemon) server. (A *daemon* is a process that runs continuously and never dies.) Type **cat /etc/xinetd.d/vsftpd** to see the `xinetd` configuration for the `vsftpd` service. Here's a typical listing of that file on a SUSE system:

```
# default: off
# description:
# The vsftpd FTP server serves FTP connections. It uses
# normal, unencrypted usernames and passwords for authentication.
# vsftpd is designed to be secure.
service ftp
{
socket_type = stream
protocol = tcp
wait = no
user = root
server = /usr/sbin/vsftpd
}
```

The filename (in this case, `vsftpd`) can be anything; what matters is the service name that appears next to the `service` keyword in the file. In this case, the line `service ftp` tells `xinetd` the name of the service. `xinetd` uses this name to look up the port number from the `/etc/services` file.

The attributes in `/etc/xinetd.d/vsftpd`, enclosed in curly braces (`{ . . . }`), have the following meanings:

✦ The `socket_type` attribute is set to `stream`, which tells `xinetd` that the FTP service uses a connection-oriented TCP socket to communicate with the client. For services that use the connectionless UDP sockets, this attribute is set to `dgram`.

✦ The `wait` attribute is set to `no`, which tells `xinetd` to start a new server for each request. If this attribute is set to `yes`, `xinetd` waits until the server exits before starting the server again.

✦ The `user` attribute provides the user ID that `xinetd` uses to run the server. In this case, the server runs the TELNET server as `root`.

✦ The `server` attribute specifies the program to run for this service. In this case, `xinetd` runs the `/usr/sbin/vsftpd` program to provide the FTP service.

Browse through the files in the `/etc/xinetd.d` directory on your Linux system to find out the kinds of services `xinetd` is set up to start. If you want to turn off any service (many are already disabled), you can do so by editing the configuration file for that service and adding the following line inside the curly braces that enclose all attributes:

```
disable = yes
```

When you make such a change to the `xinetd` configuration files, you must restart the `xinetd` server by typing the following command:

```
/etc/init.d/xinetd restart
```

You can typically configure services to run under `xinetd` or as a standalone service. For example, SUSE starts the Very Secure FTP daemon (`vsftpd`) under the control of `xinetd`. Debian and Fedora, however, run `vsftpd` as a standalone server.

# Running Standalone Servers

Starting servers through `inetd` or `xinetd` is a smart approach but not always efficient. A Web server controlled by `inetd` or `xinetd`, would be started often because every time a user clicks a link on a Web page, a request arrives for the Web service. For such high-demand services, starting the server in a standalone manner is best. In standalone mode, the server can run as a daemon. That means the server listens on the assigned port, and whenever a request arrives, the server handles it by making a copy of itself. In this way, the server keeps running as long as the machine is running — in theory, forever. A more efficient strategy, used for Web servers, is to run multiple copies of the server and let each copy handle some of the incoming requests.

You can easily configure your Linux system to start various standalone servers automatically, as shown in this section.

## Starting and stopping servers manually

To start a service that's not running, use the server command. For example, if the Web server (called httpd in Fedora) isn't running, you can start it by issuing a special shell script with the following command:

```
/etc/init.d/httpd start
```

That command runs the /etc/init.d/httpd script with start as the argument. If the httpd server is already running and you want to stop it, run the same command with stop as the argument, like this:

```
/etc/init.d/httpd stop
```

To stop and start a server again, just use restart as the argument:

```
/etc/init.d/httpd restart
```

You can also check the status of any service by using status as the argument:

```
/etc/init.d/httpd status
```

In Debian, Ubuntu, and SUSE, where the Web server program is called apache2, type **/etc/init.d/apache2 start** to start the Web server. In Knoppix and Xandros, type **/etc/init.d/apache start**. Use that same command with arguments stop or restart to stop the Web server or restart it.

What are all the services that you can start and stop? Well, the answer is in the files in the /etc/init.d directory. To get a look at it, type the following command:

```
ls /etc/init.d
```

All the files you see listed in response to this command are the services installed on your Linux system — and you can start and stop them as needed. You typically find 65 to 70 services listed in the /etc/init.d directory.

## Starting servers automatically at boot time

You can start, stop, and restart servers manually by using the scripts in the /etc/init.d directory, but you want some of the services to start as soon as you boot the Linux system. You can configure servers to start automatically at boot time by using a graphical server-configuration utility or a command.

The command for configuring services to start automatically depends on the distribution. In Debian, Knoppix, Ubuntu, and Xandros, use the update-rc.d command. In Fedora and SUSE, use the chkconfig command. Both commands are explained in the following sections.

### Using the chkconfig command in Fedora and SUSE

The chkconfig program is a command-line utility in Fedora and SUSE for checking and updating the current setting of servers in Linux. Various combinations of servers are set up to start automatically at different run levels. Each *run level* represents a system configuration in which a selected set of processes runs. You're usually concerned about run levels 3 and 5 because run level 3 is for text mode login and run level 5 is for logging in through a graphical interface.

The chkconfig command is simple to use. For example, suppose that you want to automatically start the named server at run levels 3 and 5. All you have to do is log in as root and type the following command at the shell prompt:

```
chkconfig --level 35 named on
```

To see the status of the named server, type the following command:

```
chkconfig --list named
```

You see a line of output similar to the following:

```
named 0:off 1:off 2:off 3:on 4:off 5:on 6:off
```

The output shows you the status of the named server at run levels 0 through 6. As you can see, named is set to run at run levels 3 and 5.

If you want to turn off named, you can do so with this command:

```
chkconfig --level 35 named off
```

You can use chkconfig to see the status of all services, including the ones started through xinetd. For example, you can view the status of all services by typing the following command:

```
chkconfig --list | more
```

The output shows the status of each service for each of the run levels from 0 through 6. For each run level, the service is either on or off. At the very end of the listing, `chkconfig` displays a list of the services that `xinetd` controls. Each `xinetd`-based service is also marked `on` or `off`, depending on whether `xinetd` is configured to start the service.

### Using the update-rc.d command in Debian, Knoppix, Ubuntu, and Xandros

In Debian, Knoppix, Ubuntu, and Xandros, you can use the `update-rc.d` command to set up services that should start when the system boots at specific boot levels. The easiest way to set up is to use the `defaults` option in a command of this form:

```
update-rc.d service defaults
```

where *service* is the name of the script file in the `/etc/init.d` directory that starts and stops the service, among other things.

When you use the defaults option, `update-rc.d` sets up *symbolic links* — shortcuts, in other words — to start the service in run levels 2, 3, 4, and 5 and stop the service in run levels 0, 1, and 6. A sequence number controls the order in which each service is started. (Services with smaller sequence numbers start before those with larger sequence numbers, and the numbers typically range from 00 through 99.) If you do not specify a sequence number explicitly, `update-rc.d` uses a sequence number of 20 when you use the `defaults` option.

You can also start and stop a service at specific run levels as well as in a specific sequence. For example, to start a service at run levels 2 and 5 at a sequence number of 85 and stop it at run levels 0, 1, and 6 at a sequence of 90, use the following command:

```
update-rc.d service start 85 2 5 . stop 90 0 1 6 .
```

Remember that *service* must be the name of a script file in the `/etc/init.d` directory.

If you need to stop a service from starting at system startup, type **update-rc.d -f** *service* **remove** in a terminal window, where *service* is the name of the script file in `/etc/init.d` that starts or stops that service.

### Using a GUI service configuration utility

If you don't like typing commands, you may be able to use a GUI tool to configure the services. Fedora and SUSE include such tools to manage the services.

In Fedora, choose System⇨System Settings⇨Service Manager from the KDE desktop and enter the `root` password when prompted. You can then turn on or off services from the Service Configuration window, as shown in Figure 1-2.

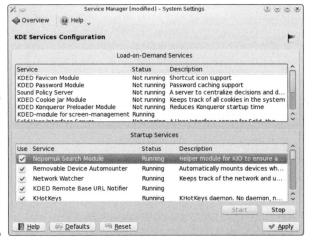

**Figure 1-2:** In Fedora, this is where you set services to start automatically at boot time.

The Service Configuration utility shows the names of services in a scrolling list. Each line in the list shows the name of a service with a check box in front of the name. A check mark in the box indicates that the service is selected to start at boot time for the current run level. When the dialog box first appears, many services are already selected.

You can scroll up and down the list and click the check box to select or deselect a service. If you click the check box, the check mark alternately turns on and off. Additionally, the utility also shows you whether the selected service is currently running.

After you select all the servers you want to start when the system boots, click the Apply button on the toolbar to save the changes.

By default, the service configuration utility configures the selected services for the current run level. That means if you're selecting services from the graphical desktop, the system is in run level 5 and the services you configure are set to start at run level 5. If you want to set up the services for a different level, select that run level from the Edit Runlevel menu.

In SUSE, you can configure the services from YaST Control Center by opening the main menu and choosing System⇨Control Center (YaST). Click System in the left window and then click System Services (Runlevel). YaST opens the System Services (Runlevel) window, as shown in Figure 1-3. To enable or disable services at specific run levels, click the Expert Mode button and edit the services in the new list that appears.

**Figure 1-3:**
In SUSE, use this YaST window to specify services that start at boot time.

**Book VII**
**Chapter 1**

**Managing Internet Services**

Table 1-1 shows a list of the services, along with a brief description of each one. The first column shows the name of the service, which is the same as the name of the program that has to run to provide the service. You may not see all these services listed when you run the GUI service configuration utility on your system because the exact list of services depends on what is installed on your Linux system.

| Table 1-1 | Some Common Services in Linux |
|---|---|
| *Service Name* | *Description* |
| acpid | Listens to Advanced Configuration and Power Interface (ACPI) events from the kernel and notifies other programs when such events occur. ACPI events can occur when the kernel puts the computer into a low-power state (for example, standby mode) to save energy. |
| apache, apache2, or httpd | Runs the Apache World Wide Web (WWW) server. |
| apmd | Monitors the Advanced Power Management (APM) BIOS and logs the status of electric power (AC or battery backup). |

*(continued)*

### Table 1-1 *(continued)*

| Service Name | Description |
|---|---|
| atd | Runs commands scheduled by the at and cron commands. |
| autofs | Automatically mounts file systems (for example, when you insert a CD-ROM in the CD-ROM drive). |
| cron or crond | Runs user-specified programs according to a periodic schedule set by the crontab command. |
| gpm | Enables the use of the mouse in text mode screens. |
| innd | The InterNetNews daemon — the Internet news server you can use to support local newsgroups on your system. |
| isdn | Starts and stops ISDN (Integrated Services Digital Network) services — a digital communication service over regular phone lines (enable only if you have ISDN service). |
| named | Translates host names into IP addresses. named is a server for the Domain Name System (DNS). You can run a copy on your system if you want. |
| network or networking | Enables you to activate or deactivate all network interfaces configured to start at system boot time. |
| nfs or nfsserver | Enables sharing of file systems specified in the /etc/ exports file using the Network File System (NFS) protocol. |
| nfslock | Provides file-locking capability for file systems exported using the Network File System (NFS) protocol, so other systems (running NFS) can share files from your system. |
| pcmcia | Provides support for PCMCIA devices. |
| portmap | Works with any software that relies on Remote Procedure Calls (RPC). For example, NFS requires the portmap service. |
| samba, smb, or smbfs | Starts and stops the Samba smbd and nmbd services, which support LAN Manager services on a Linux system. |
| sendmail | Moves mail messages from one machine to another. Start this service if you want to send mail from your Linux system. If you don't plan to use your Linux system as a mail server, don't start the sendmail server because it can slow down the booting process and consume unnecessary resources. |
| snmpd | Manages networks. snmpd stands for Simple Network Management Protocol daemon. |
| spamassassin | Runs spamd — the SpamAssassin mail filter program. |
| ssh or sshd | Runs the OpenSSH (Secure Shell) secure remote login facility. |

| Service Name | Description |
|---|---|
| syslog or syslogd | Logs various error and status messages in a log file (usually, the /var/log/messages file). This service is used by many other programs (including other services). Always run this service. |
| vsftpd | Transfers files using the File Transfer Protocol (FTP). vsftpd stands for Very Secure FTP daemon. |
| winbind | Starts and stops the Samba winbindd server, which provides a name-switch capability similar to that provided by the /etc/nsswitch.conf file. |
| xfs | Starts and stops the X font server. |
| xinetd | Starts other Internet services, such as TELNET and FTP, whenever they are needed. This server is the Internet super server, a replacement for the older inetd. |
| ypbind | Runs on Network Information System (NIS) clients and binds the clients to an NIS domain. You don't have to start ypbind unless you're using NIS. |

**Book VII
Chapter 1**

**Managing Internet
Services**

# Chapter 2: Managing Mail and News Servers

## In This Chapter

✔ Installing and using sendmail

✔ Testing mail delivery manually

✔ Configuring sendmail

✔ Installing the InterNetNews (INN) server

✔ Configuring and starting INN

✔ Setting up local newsgroups

*E*lectronic mail (e-mail) is one of the popular services available on Internet hosts. E-mail software comes in two parts: a mail transport agent (MTA), which physically sends and receives mail messages, and a mail user agent (MUA), which reads messages and prepares new messages. This chapter describes the e-mail service and shows you how to configure the `sendmail` server on a Linux PC.

Internet newsgroups provide another convenient way, besides e-mail, to discuss various topics and share your knowledge with others. Linux comes with the software you need to read newsgroups and set up your own system as a news server. This chapter also describes how to configure and run the popular InterNetNews server and shows how to set up local newsgroups for your corporate intranet (or even your home network).

## Installing the Mail Server

Depending on the choices you made during your Linux installation, you may have already installed the mail server software on your system. You can choose from several mail servers, such as `exim`, `postfix`, and `sendmail` — your `sendmail` is briefly covered in this chapter. If `sendmail` is not installed, you can easily install it.

In Debian, Ubuntu, and Xandros, type **dpkg -l sendmail\*** to see if `sendmail` is installed. In Fedora and SUSE, type **rpm -qa | grep sendmail** to see if the `sendmail` package is installed.

In Debian and Ubuntu, type **apt-get install sendmail** to install the `sendmail` server. In Fedora, log in as `root`, and type **rpm -ivh sendmail\***. In SUSE, click Software Management in the YaST Control Center's Software category. Then use YaST's search facility to find the `sendmail` package and install it.

## Using sendmail

To set up your system as a mail server, you must configure the `sendmail` mail transport agent properly. `sendmail` has the reputation of being a complex but complete mail-delivery system. Just one look at `sendmail`'s configuration file — `/etc/mail/sendmail.cf` in Fedora or `/etc/sendmail.cf` in SUSE — can convince you that `sendmail` is indeed complex. Luckily, you don't have to be an expert on the `sendmail` configuration file. All you need is one of the predefined configuration files — such as the one installed on your system — to use `sendmail`.

Your system already has a working `sendmail` configuration file — `/etc/mail/sendmail.cf`. The default file assumes you have an Internet connection and a name server. Provided that you have an Internet connection and that your system has an official domain name, you can send and receive e-mail from your Linux PC.

To ensure that mail delivery works correctly, your system's name must match the system name that your ISP has assigned to you. Although you can give your system any hostname you want, other systems can successfully deliver mail to your system only if your system's name is in the ISP's name server.

## A mail-delivery test

To try the `sendmail` mail transfer agent, you can use the `mail` command to compose and send a mail message to any user account on your Linux system. As a test, compose a message and send it to yourself. For example, here's how to send a message using the `mail` command. (Input appears in boldface.)

```
mail edulaney
Subject: Testing e-mail
This is from my Linux system.
.
```

The `mail` command is a simple mail user agent. In the preceding example, the addressee (`edulaney`) is specified in the command line. The `mail` program prompts for a subject line. Following the subject, enter the message and end it with a line that contains only a period. You will be prompted for a Cc:, but leave that blank. After ending the message, the mail user agent passes the message to sendmail (the mail transport agent) for delivery to the specified address. sendmail delivers the mail message immediately. To verify the delivery of mail, type **mail** to run the mail command again and read the message.

If any of your mail server software is not properly installed, you should be prompted during this test to install any needed components and resolve the problem.

Thus, the initial sendmail configuration file is adequate for sending and receiving e-mail, at least within your Linux system. External mail delivery also works, provided that your Linux system has an Internet connection and a registered domain name.

If you have an ISP account that provides your Linux system with a dynamic IP address, you have to use a mail client such as Evolution or Mozilla Mail, which contacts your ISP's mail server to deliver outbound e-mail.

## *The mail-delivery mechanism*

On an Internet host, the sendmail mail transport agent delivers mail using the Simple Mail Transfer Protocol (SMTP). SMTP-based mail transport agents listen to TCP port 25 and use a small set of text commands to exchange information with other mail transport agents. SMTP commands are simple enough that you can use them manually from a terminal to send a mail message. The telnet command opens a TELNET session to port 25 (the port on which sendmail expects SMTP commands). The sendmail process on the Linux system immediately replies with an announcement.

You can type **HELP** to view a list of SMTP commands. To get help on a specific command, type **HELP *commandname***. Type **HELO localhost** to initiate a session with the host. The sendmail process replies with a greeting. To send the mail message, start with the MAIL FROM: command, which specifies the sender of the message. Next, use the RCPT TO: command to specify the recipient of the message. If you want to send the message to several recipients, provide each recipient's address with the RCPT TO: command.

To enter the mail message, use the DATA command. In response to the DATA command, sendmail displays an instruction that you have to end the message with a period on a line by itself. After doing this, the sendmail process displays a message indicating that the message is accepted for delivery. You can then quit the sendmail session with the QUIT command.

## The sendmail configuration file

You don't have to understand everything in the sendmail configuration file, sendmail.cf, but you need to know how that file is created. That way, you can make minor changes if necessary and regenerate the sendmail.cf file.

In SUSE, you can configure sendmail through the YaST Control Center — choose System⊸Control Center (YaST) from the main menu. Click Network Services in the left side of the window, and then click Mail Transfer Agent in the right side of the window. YaST displays a window that you can use to configure sendmail. First you specify the general settings, then the settings for outgoing mail, and finally the settings for incoming mail. After you exit the mail configuration utility, YaST stores the mail settings in the files /etc/sysconfig/sendmail and /etc/sysconfig/mail and then runs SuSE config to update the sendmail configuration file (/etc/sendmail.cf).

You can also generate the sendmail.cf file from a number of *m4 macro files* (text files in which each line eventually expands to multiple lines that mean something to some program). These macro files are organized into a number of subdirectories in the /usr/share/sendmail-cf directory in Fedora or the /usr/share/sendmail directory in SUSE. You can read the README file in that directory to find out more about the creation of sendmail configuration files.

### The m4 macro processor

The m4 macro processor generates the sendmail.cf configuration file, which comes with the sendmail package in Linux. The main macro file, named sendmail.mc, generic_linux.mc, or linux.mc, is included with the sendmail package.

So what's a macro? A *macro* is basically a symbolic name for code that handles some action, usually in a shorthand form that substitutes for a long string of characters. A *macro processor* such as m4 usually reads its input file and copies it to the output, processing the macros along the way. The processing of a macro generally involves performing some action and generating some output. Because a macro generates a lot more text in the output than merely the macro's name, the processing of macros is referred to as *macro expansion.*

The m4 macro processor is *stream-based.* That means it copies the input characters to the output while it's busy expanding any macros. The m4 macro processor does not have any concept of lines, so it copies newline characters (that mark the end of a line) to the output. That's why in most m4 macro files you see `dnl`, an `m4` macro that stands for *delete through newline*. The `dnl` macro deletes all characters starting at the `dnl` up to and including the next newline character. The newline characters in the output don't cause any harm; they merely create unnecessary blank lines. The `sendmail` macro package uses `dnl` to avoid such blank lines in the output configuration file. Because `dnl` basically means delete everything up to the end of the line, m4 macro files also use `dnl` as the prefix for comment lines.

To see a simple use of `m4`, consider the following `m4` macro file, which defines two macros — `hello` and `bye` — and uses them in a form letter:

```
dnl #################################################
dnl # File: ex.m4
dnl # A simple example of m4 macros
dnl #################################################
define(`hello', `Dear Sir/Madam')dnl
define(`bye',
`Sincerely,
Customer Service')dnl
dnl Now type the letter and use the macros
hello,
This is to inform you that we received your recent inquiry.
We will respond to your question soon.
bye
```

Type this text (using your favorite text editor) and save it in a file named `ex.m4`. You can name a macro file anything you like, but using the `.m4` extension for `m4` macro files is customary.

Before you process the macro file by using `m4`, note the following key points about the example:

✦ Use the `dnl` macro to start all the comment lines, as in the first four lines in the example.

✦ End each macro definition with the `dnl` macro. Otherwise, when `m4` processes the macro file, it produces a blank line for each macro definition.

✦ Use the built-in `m4` command `define` to define a new macro. The macro name and the value are both enclosed between a pair of left and right single quotes (`'  .  .  .  '`). Note that you cannot use the plain single quote to enclose the macro name and definition.

Now process the macro file `ex.m4` by typing the following command:

```
m4 ex.m4
```

m4 processes the macros and displays the following output:

```
Dear Sir/Madam,
This is to inform you that we received your recent inquiry.
We will respond to your question soon.
Sincerely,
Customer Service
```

Sounds just like a typical customer service form letter, doesn't it?

If you compare the output with the ex.m4 file, you see that m4 prints the form letter on standard output, expanding the macros hello and bye into their defined values. If you want to save the form letter in a file called letter, use the shell's output redirection feature, like this:

```
m4 ex.m4 > letter
```

What if you want to use the word *hello* or *bye* in the letter without expanding them? You can do so by enclosing these words in a pair of single quotes (' . . . '). You have to do so for other predefined m4 macros, such as define. To use *define* as a plain word, not as a macro to expand, type **'define'**.

### The sendmail macro file

The simple example in the preceding section gives you an idea of how m4 macros are defined and used to create configuration files such as the sendmail.cf file. You find many complex macros stored in files in the /usr/share/sendmail-cf directory in Fedora or the /usr/share/sendmail directory in SUSE. A top-level macro file (called sendmail.mc in Fedora and linux.mc in SUSE), described later in this section, brings in these macro files with the include macro (used to copy a file into the input stream).

To avoid repeatedly mentioning different file and directory names for different distributions such as Fedora and SUSE, I use the file and directory names for Fedora in the following discussions. The general discussions apply to sendmail in all Linux distributions, but you have to replace the file and directory names with those for your specific distribution.

By defining its own set of high-level macros in files located in the /usr/share/sendmail-cf directory, sendmail essentially creates its own macro language. The sendmail macro files use the .mc extension. The primary sendmail macro file you configure is sendmail.mc, located in the /etc/mail directory.

Compared to the `/etc/mail/sendmail.cf` file, the `/etc/mail/send mail.mc` file is shorter and easier to work with. Here are some lines from the `/etc/mail/sendmail.mc` file that comes with Fedora:

```
divert(-1)dnl
dnl #
dnl # This is the sendmail macro config file for m4. If you make changes to
dnl # /etc/mail/sendmail.mc, you will need to regenerate the
dnl # /etc/mail/sendmail.cf file by confirming that the sendmail-cf package is
dnl # installed and then performing a
dnl #
dnl # /etc/mail/make
dnl #
include(`/usr/share/sendmail-cf/m4/cf.m4')dnl
VERSIONID(`setup for linux')dnl
OSTYPE(`linux')dnl
dnl #
dnl # Do not advertise sendmail version.
dnl #
dnl define(`confSMTP_LOGIN_MSG', `$j Sendmail; $b')dnl
dnl #
dnl # default logging level is 9, you might want to set it higher to
dnl # debug the configuration
dnl #
dnl define(`confLOG_LEVEL', `9')dnl
dnl #
dnl # Uncomment and edit the following line if your outgoing mail needs to
dnl # be sent out through an external mail server:
dnl #
dnl define(`SMART_HOST', `smtp.your.provider')dn
. . . lines deleted . . .
dnl #
dnl MASQUERADE_AS(`mydomain.com')dnl
dnl #
dnl # masquerade not just the headers, but the envelope as well
dnl #
dnl FEATURE(masquerade_envelope)dnl
dnl #
dnl # masquerade not just @mydomainalias.com, but @*.mydomainalias.com as well
dnl #
dnl FEATURE(masquerade_entire_domain)dnl
dnl #
dnl MASQUERADE_DOMAIN(localhost)dnl
dnl MASQUERADE_DOMAIN(localhost.localdomain)dnl
dnl MASQUERADE_DOMAIN(mydomainalias.com)dnl
dnl MASQUERADE_DOMAIN(mydomain.lan)dnl
MAILER(smtp)dnl
MAILER(procmail)dnl
dnl MAILER(cyrusv2)dnl
```

If you make changes to the `/etc/mail/sendmail.mc` file, you must generate the `/etc/mail/sendmail.cf` file by running the `sendmail.mc` file through the `m4` macro processor with the following command. (You have to log in as `root`.)

```
m4 /etc/mail/sendmail.mc > /etc/mail/sendmail.cf
```

The comments also tell you that you need the `sendmail-cf` package to process this file.

From the previous section's description of `m4` macros, you can see that the `sendmail.mc` file uses `define` to create new macros. You can also see the liberal use of `dnl` to avoid inserting too many blank lines into the output.

The other uppercase words (such as `OSTYPE`, `FEATURE`, and `MAILER`) are `sendmail` macros. These are defined in the `.m4` files located in the subdirectories of the `/usr/share/sendmail-cf` directory and are incorporated into the `sendmail.mc` file with the following `include` macro:

```
include(`usr/share/sendmail-cf/m4/cf.m4')dnl
```

The `/usr/share/sendmail-cf/m4/cf.m4` file, in turn, includes the `cfhead.m4` file, which includes other `m4` files, and so on. The net effect is as follows: As the `m4` macro processor processes the `sendmail.mc` file, the macro processor incorporates many `m4` files from various subdirectories of `/usr/share/sendmail-cf`.

Here are some key points to note about the `/etc/mail/sendmail.mc` file:

✦ `VERSIONID('setup for linux')` macro inserts the version information enclosed in quotes into the output.

✦ `OSTYPE('linux')` specifies Linux as the operating system. You have to specify this macro early to ensure proper configuration.

   Placing this macro right after the `VERSIONID` macro is customary.

✦ `MAILER(smtp)` describes the mailer. According to instructions in the `/usr/share/sendmail-cf/README` file, `MAILER` declarations are always placed at the end of the `sendmail.mc` file and `MAILER(smtp)` always precedes `MAILER(procmail)`. The mailer `smtp` refers to the SMTP mailer.

✦ `FEATURE` macros request various special features. For example, `FEATURE(`blacklist_recipients')` turns on the capability to block incoming mail for certain usernames, hosts, or addresses. The specification for what mail to allow or refuse is placed in the access database (stored in `/etc/mail/access.db` file). You also need the `FEATURE(`access_db')` macro to turn on the access database.

✦ `MASQUERADE_AS(`mydomain.com')` causes `sendmail` to label outgoing mail as having come from the host *mydomain*.`com` (replace *my domain* with your domain name). The idea is for a large organization to set up a single `sendmail` server that handles the mail for many subdomains and makes everything appear to come from a single domain. (For example, mail from many departments in a university appears to come from the university's main domain name.)

✦ `MASQUERADE_DOMAIN`(subdomain.mydomain.com) instructs `send mail` to send mail from an address such as `user@subdomain.my domain.com` as having originated from the same username at the domain specified by the `MASQUERADE_AS` macro.

The sendmail macros such as `FEATURE` and `MAILER` are described in the `/usr/share/sendmail-cf/README` file. Consult that file to find out more about the sendmail macros before you make changes to the `sendmail.mc` file.

## Syntax of the sendmail.cf file

The `sendmail.cf` file's syntax is designed to be easy to parse by the `send mail` program because `sendmail` reads this file whenever it starts. Human readability was not a primary consideration when the file's syntax was designed. Still, with a little explanation, you can understand the meaning of the control lines in `sendmail.cf`.

Each `sendmail` control line begins with a single-letter operator that defines the meaning of the rest of the line. A line that begins with a space or a tab is considered a continuation of the previous line. Blank lines and lines beginning with a pound sign (#) are comments.

Often, no space is between the single-letter operator and the arguments that follow the operator, which makes the lines even harder to understand. For example, `sendmail.cf` uses the concept of a *class* — essentially a collection of phrases. You can define a class named P and add the phrase `REDIRECT` to that class with the following control line:

```
CPREDIRECT
```

Because everything runs together, the command is hard to decipher. On the other hand, to define a class named `Accept` and set it to the values `OK` and `RELAY`, write the following:

```
C{Accept}OK RELAY
```

This command may be slightly easier to understand because the delimiters (such as the class name, `Accept`) are enclosed in curly braces.

Other, more recent control lines are even easier to understand. For example, the line

```
O HelpFile=/etc/mail/helpfile
```

defines the option `HelpFile` as the filename `/etc/mail/helpfile`. That file contains help information that `sendmail` uses when it receives a `HELP` command.

Table 2-1 summarizes the one-letter control operators used in `sendmail.cf`. Each entry also shows an example of that operator. This table helps you understand some of the lines in `sendmail.cf`.

| Table 2-1 | Control Operators Used in sendmail.cf |
|---|---|
| *Operator* | *Description* |
| C | Defines a class; a variable (think of it as a set) that can contain several values. For example, `Cwlocalhost` adds the name `localhost` to the class `w`. |
| D | Defines a macro, a name associated with a single value. For example, `DnMAILER-DAEMON` defines the macro n as MAILER-DAEMON. |
| F | Defines a class that's been read from a file. For example, `Fw/etc/mail/local-host-names` reads the names of hosts from the file `/etc/mail/local-host-names` and adds them to the class `w`. |
| H | Defines the format of header lines that `sendmail` inserts into a message. For example, `H?P?Return-Path: <$g>` defines the `Return-Path:` field of the header. |
| K | Defines a map (a key-value pair database). For example, `Karith arith` defines the map named `arith` as the compiled-in map of the same name. |
| M | Specifies a mailer. The following lines define the `procmail` mailer: `Mprocmail, P=/usr/bin/procmail, F=DFMSPh nu9, S=EnvFromSMTP/HdrFromSMTP, R=EnvToSMTP/HdrFromSMTP, T=DNS/RFC822/X-Unix, A=procmail -Y -m $h $f $u`. |
| O | Assigns a value to an option. For example, `O AliasFile=/etc/aliases` defines the `AliasFile` option to `/etc/aliases`, which is the name of the `sendmail` alias file. |
| P | Defines values for the precedence field. For example, `Pjunk=-100` sets to $-100$ the precedence of messages marked with the header field `Precedence: junk`. |

| Operator | Description |
|---|---|
| R | Defines a rule. (A rule has a left side and a right side; if input matches the left side, the right side replaces it. This rule is called *rewriting*.) For example, the rewriting rule R$* ; $1 strips trailing semicolons. |
| S | Labels a ruleset you can start defining with subsequent R control lines. For example, Scanonify=3 labels the next ruleset as canonify and ruleset 3. |
| T | Adds a username to the trusted class (class t). For example, Troot adds root to the class of trusted users. |
| V | Defines the major version number of the configuration file. For example, V10/Berkeley defines the version number as 10. |

## Other sendmail files

The /etc/mail directory contains other files that sendmail uses. These files are referenced in the sendmail configuration file, /etc/mail/sendmail.cf in Fedora and /etc/sendmail.cf in SUSE. For example, here's how you can search for the /etc/mail string in the /etc/mail/sendmail.cf file in Fedora:

```
grep "\/etc\/mail" /etc/mail/sendmail.cf
```

Here's what the grep command displays as a result of the search on a typical Fedora system:

```
Fw/etc/mail/local-host-names
FR-o /etc/mail/relay-domains
Kmailertable hash -o /etc/mail/mailertable.db
Kvirtuser hash -o /etc/mail/virtusertable.db
Kaccess hash -T<TMPF> -o /etc/mail/access.db
#O ErrorHeader=/etc/mail/error-header
O HelpFile=/etc/mail/helpfile
O UserDatabaseSpec=/etc/mail/userdb.db
#O ServiceSwitchFile=/etc/mail/service.switch
#O DefaultAuthInfo=/etc/mail/default-auth-info
Ft/etc/mail/trusted-users
```

You can ignore the lines that begin with a hash mark, or number sign (#) because sendmail treats those lines as comments. The other lines are sendmail control lines that refer to other files in the /etc/mail directory.

Here's what some of these sendmail files are supposed to contain. (Note that not all of these files have to be present in your /etc/mail directory, and even when present, some files may be empty.)

✦ `/etc/mail/access`: Names or IP addresses or both of hosts allowed to send mail (useful in stopping *spam* — unwanted e-mail).

✦ `/etc/mail/access.db`: Access database generated from the `/etc/mail/access` file.

✦ `/etc/mail/helpfile`: Help information for SMTP commands.

✦ `/etc/mail/local-host-names`: Names by which this host is known.

✦ `/etc/mail/mailertable`: Mailer table used to override how mail is routed. (For example, the entry `comcast.net smtp:smtp.comcast.net` tells `sendmail` that mail addressed to `comcast.net` has to be sent to `smtp.comcast.net`.)

✦ `/etc/mail/relay-domains`: Hosts that permit relaying.

✦ `/etc/mail/trusted-users`: List of users allowed to send mail using other user's names without a warning.

✦ `/etc/mail/userdb.db`: User database file containing information about each user's login name and real name.

✦ `/etc/mail/virtusertable`: Database of users with virtual-domain addresses hosted on this system.

The `/etc/mail` directory sometimes contains other files — `/etc/mail/certs` and the files with the `.pem` extension — that are meant for supporting Privacy Enhanced Mail (PEM) in `sendmail` by using the STARTTLS extension to SMTP. The STARTTLS extension uses TLS (more commonly known as SSL — Secure Sockets Layer) to authenticate the sender and encrypt mail. RFC 2487 describes STARTTLS. (This RFC is available online at `http://ietf.org/rfc/rfc2487.txt`.)

If you edit the `/etc/mail/mailertable` file, you have to type the following command before the changes take effect:

```
makemap hash /etc/mail/mailertable < /etc/mail/mailertable
```

Here is an easier way to make sure that you rebuild everything necessary after making any changes — just type the following commands while logged in as `root`:

```
cd /etc/mail
make
```

The first command changes the current directory to `/etc/mail`, and the second command runs the `make` command, which reads a file named `Makefile` in `/etc/mail` to perform the steps necessary to rebuild everything. (To find out more about `make` and `Makefile`, see Book VIII, Chapter 1.)

## The .forward file

Users can redirect their own mail by placing a `.forward` file in their home directory. The `.forward` file is a plain-text file with a comma-separated list of mail addresses. Any mail sent to the user is instead forwarded to these addresses. If the `.forward` file contains a single address, all e-mail for that user is redirected to that single e-mail address. For example, suppose a `.forward` file containing the following line is placed in the home directory of a user named `emily`:

```
ashley
```

This line causes `sendmail` to automatically send all e-mail addressed to `emily` to the username `ashley` on the same system. User `emily` does not receive mail at all.

You can also forward mail to a username on another system by listing a complete e-mail address. For example, you can add a `.forward` file with the following line to send messages addressed to username `wilbur` to the mail address `wilbur@somewhereelse.net`:

```
wilbur@somewhereelse.net
```

To keep a copy of the message on the original system, in addition to forwarding to the preceding specified address, add the following line to the `.forward` file:

```
wilbur@somewhereelse.net, wilbur\
```

Simply append the username and end the line with a backslash (\). The backslash at the end of the line stops `sendmail` from repeatedly forwarding the message.

## The sendmail alias file

In addition to the `sendmail.cf` file, `sendmail` also consults an alias file named `/etc/aliases` to convert a name into an address. The location of the alias file appears in the `sendmail` configuration file.

Each *alias* is typically a shorter name for an e-mail address. The system administrator uses the `sendmail` alias file to forward mail, to create a mailing list (a single alias that identifies several users), or to refer to a user by several different names. For example, here are some typical aliases:

```
brown: glbrown
all: jessica, isaac, alex, caleb, glbrown
```

After defining any new aliases in the /etc/aliases file, you must log in as root and make the new alias active by typing the following command:

```
sendmail -bi
```

# Installing the INN Server

This section describes how to configure InterNetNews (INN), a TCP/IP-based news server. First you have to install INN.

In Debian, Ubuntu, and Xandros, type **dpkg -l inn\*** to see if inn is installed. In Fedora and SUSE, type **rpm -q inn** and see if the inn package is installed.

In Debian and Ubuntu, type **apt-get install inn** to install the INN server. In Fedora, log in as root, mount the DVD, and type **cd /media/ cdrom/Fedora/RPMS** followed by **rpm -ivh inn\***. In SUSE, click Software Management in the YaST Control Center's Software category. Then use YaST's search feature to look for inn, select the relevant packages from the search results, and install them. In Xandros, first run Xandros Networks, choose Edit⇨Set Application Sources, and click the Debian Unsupported Site link as a source. Then type **apt-get install inn** to install the INN server.

# Configuring and Starting the INN Server

Much of the INN (InterNetNews) software is ready to go as soon as you install it. All you need to do is to brush up a bit on the various components of INN, edit the configuration files, and start innd — the INN server. The INN server is sometimes referred to as the *news server*.

If you want to run a news server that supports a selection of Internet news-groups, you also have to arrange for a *news feed* — the source from which your news server gets the newsgroup articles. Typically, you can get a news feed from an ISP, but the ISP charges an additional monthly fee to cover the cost of resources required to provide the feed. (Your normal ISP charges cover reading news from the ISP's server; you have to pay additional charges only if you want to run your own server and get a news feed.) You need the name of the upstream server that provides the news feed, and you have to provide that server with your server's name and the newsgroups you want to receive.

By the way, you don't need an external news feed if you're running a news server to support local newsgroups that are available only within your organization's network. How to set up local newsgroups is described in the "Setting Up Local Newsgroups" section of this chapter.

Depending on the newsgroups you want to receive and the number of days you want to retain articles, you have to set aside appropriate disk space to hold the articles. The newsgroups are stored in a directory hierarchy (based on the newsgroup names) in the /var/spool/news directory of your system. If you're setting up a news server, you may want to devote a large disk partition to the /var/spool/news directory.

In your news server's configuration files, enter the name of the server providing the news feed. At the same time, add to the configuration files the names of any downstream news servers (if any) that receive news feeds from your server. Then you can start the news server and wait for news to arrive. Monitor the log files to ensure that the news articles sort and store properly in the /var/spool/news directory on your system.

The following sections introduce you to INN setup, but you can find out more about INN from the Internet Systems Consortium (ISC), a nonprofit corporation dedicated to developing and maintaining open source Internet software, such as BIND (an implementation of Domain Name System), DHCP (Dynamic Host Configuration Protocol), and INN. Rich Salz originally wrote INN; ISC took over the development of INN in 1996. You can find out more about INN and can access other resources at ISC's INN Web page at www. isc.org/sw/inn/.

## *InterNetNews components*

INN includes several programs that deliver and manage newsgroups. It also includes a number of files that control how the INN programs work. The most important INN programs are the following:

✦ innd: Accepts connections from other feed sites, as well as from local newsreader clients, but it hands off local connections to the nnrpd. The news server. innd runs as a *daemon* (a background process that keeps itself running to provide a specific service) and listens on the NNTP port (TCP port 119).

✦ nnrpd: Handles requests from local newsreader clients. nnrpd is a special server invoked by innd.

✦ expire: Removes old articles based on the specifications in the text file /etc/news/expire.ctl.

✦ nntpsend: Invokes the innxmit program to send news articles to a remote site by using NNTP. The configuration file /etc/news/nntpsend.ctl controls the nntpsend program.

✦ ctlinnd: Enables you to control the innd server interactively. The ctlinnd program can send messages to the control channel of the innd server.

**Book VII
Chapter 2**

**Managing Mail and News Servers**

The other vital components of INN are the control files. Most of these files are in the /etc/news directory of your Linux system, although a few are in the /var/lib/news directory. Between those two directories, you have more than 30 INN control files. Some important files include the following:

+ /etc/news/inn.conf: Specifies configuration data for the innd server. (To view online help for this file, type **man inn.conf**.)

+ /etc/news/newsfeeds: Specifies what articles to feed downstream to other news servers. (The file is complicated, but you can get help by typing **man newsfeeds**.)

+ /etc/news/incoming.conf: Lists the names and addresses of hosts that provide news feeds to this server. (To view online help for this file, type **man incoming.conf**.)

+ /etc/news/storage.conf: Specifies the storage methods to be used when storing news articles. (To view online help for this file, type **man storage.conf**.)

+ /etc/news/expire.ctl: Controls expiration of articles, on a per-newsgroup level, if desired. (To view online help for this file, type **man expire.ctl**.)

+ /var/lib/news/active: Lists all active newsgroups, showing the oldest and newest article number for each, and each newsgroup's posting status. (To view online help for this file, type **man active**.)

+ /var/lib/news/newsgroups: Lists newsgroups and a brief description of each.

+ /etc/news/readers.conf: Specifies hosts and users who are permitted to read news from this news server and post news to newsgroups. The default file allows only the localhost to read news; you have to edit it if you want to allow other hosts in your local area network to read news. (To view online help for this file, type **man readers.conf**.)

The next few sections describe how to set up some of the important control files.

### The inn.conf file

The inn.conf file holds configuration data for all INN programs — which makes it the most important file. Each line of the file has the value of a parameter in the following format:

*parameter*: *value*

Depending on the *parameter*, the *value* is a string, a number, or true or false. As in many other configuration files, comment lines begin with a pound sign (#).

Most of the parameters in the default `inn.conf` file in the `/etc/news` directory do not require changes. You may want to edit one or more of the parameters shown in Table 2-2.

| Table 2-2 | Configuration Parameters in /etc/news/inn.conf |
|---|---|
| *Parameter Name* | *Set This To* |
| `mta` | The command used to start the mail transfer agent that is used by `innd` to transfer messages. The default is to use `sendmail`. |
| `organization` | The name of your organization in the way you want it to appear in the `Organization:` header of all news articles posted from your system. Users may override this parameter by defining the `ORGANIZATION` environment variable. |
| `ovmethod` | The type of overview storage method. (The *overview* is an index of news articles in the newsgroup.) The default method is `tradindexed`, which is fast for reading news but slow for storing news items. |
| `pathhost` | The name of your news server as you want it to appear in the Path header of all postings that go through your server. If `pathhost` isn't defined, the fully qualified domain name of your system is used. |
| `pathnews` | The full pathname of the directory that contains INN binaries and libraries. The default `pathnews` is set to `/usr/lib/news`. |
| `domain` | The domain name for your server. |
| `allownewnews` | True if you want INN to support the `NEWNEWS` command from newsreaders. In the past, this option was set to false because the `NEWNEWS` command used to reduce the server's performance, but now the default is set to true because modern servers can easily handle the `NEWNEWS` command. |
| `hiscachesize` | The size in kilobytes that you want INN to use for caching recently received message IDs that are kept in memory to speed history lookups. This cache is used only for incoming feeds, and a small cache can hold quite a few history file entries. The default setting of 0 disables history caching. If you have more than one incoming feed, you may want to set this parameter to a value of 256 (for 256KB). |
| `innflags` | Any flags you want to pass to the INN server process when it starts. |

### The newsfeeds file

The newsfeeds file (found at /etc/news/newsfeeds) specifies how incoming news articles are redistributed to other servers and to INN processes. If you provide news feeds to other servers, you have to list these news feeds in this file. (You also must have an entry labeled ME, which serves a special purpose explained later in this section.)

The newsfeeds file contains a series of entries, one for each feed. Each feed entry has the following format:

```
site[/exclude,exclude . . . ]\
:pattern,pattern . . . [/distrib,distrib . . . ]\
:flag,flag . . . \
:param
```

Each entry has four fields separated by a colon (:). Usually, the entries span multiple lines, and a backslash (\) at the end of the line continues a line to the next. Here's what the four fields mean:

✦ The first field, *site*, is the name of the feed. Each name must be unique, and for feeds to other news servers, the name is set to the hostname of the remote server. Following the name is an optional slash and an exclude list (/exclude,exclude . . . ) of names. If any of the names in this list appear in the Path line of an article, that article isn't forwarded to the feed. You can use an exclude list if you don't want to receive articles from a specific source.

✦ The second field is a comma-separated list of newsgroup *patterns,* such as *,@alt.binaries.warez.*,!control*,!local*, followed by an optional *distribution* list. The distribution list is a list of comma-separated keywords, with each keyword specifying a specific set of sites to which the articles are distributed. The newsgroup patterns essentially define a subscription list of sites that receive this news feed. An asterisk (*) matches all newsgroups. A pattern beginning with @ causes newsgroups matching that pattern to be dropped. A pattern that begins with an exclamation mark (!) means the matching newsgroups are not sent. The simple pattern-matching syntax used in INN configuration files is referred to as a *wildmat* pattern.

✦ The third field is a comma-separated list of *flags* — fields that determine the feed-entry type and set certain parameters for the entry. You see numerous flags; type **man newsfeeds** and read the man page for more information about the flags.

✦ The fourth field is for parameters whose values depend on the settings in the third field. Typically, this field contains names of files or external programs that the INN server uses. You can find more about this field from the newsfeeds man page.

Now that you know the layout of the /etc/news/newsfeeds file, you can study that file as an example. The default file contains many sample feed entries, but only two are commented out:

✦ ME is a special feed entry that's always required. It serves two purposes. First, the newsgroup patterns listed in this entry are used as a prefix for all newsgroup patterns in all other entries. Second, the ME entry's distribution list determines what distributions your server accepts from remote sites.

✦ The controlchan feed entry is used to set up INN so that an external program is used to handle control messages. (These messages are used to create new newsgroups and remove groups.) For example, the following controlchan entry specifies the external program /usr/lib/news/bin/controlchan to handle all control messages, except cancel messages (meant for canceling an article):

```
controlchan!\
:!*,control,control.*,!control.cancel\
:Tc,Wnsm:/usr/lib/news/bin/controlchan
```

In addition to these feed entries, you add entries for any actual sites to which your news server provides news feeds. Such entries have the format

```
feedme.domain.com\
:!junk,!control/!foo\
:Tm:innfeed!
```

where feedme.domain.com is the fully qualified domain name of the site to which your system sends news articles.

## The incoming.conf file

The incoming.conf file describes which hosts are allowed to connect to your host to feed articles. For a single feed, you can add an entry like

```
peer mybuddy {
hostname: a-feed-site.domain.com
}
```

where *mybuddy* is a label for the peer and a-feed-site.domain.com identifies the site that feeds your site.

Keep in mind that simply adding a site's name in the incoming.conf file does not cause that remote site to start feeding news to your site; it simply enables your server to accept news articles from the remote site. At the remote site, your buddy has to configure his or her server to send articles to your site.

## The readers.conf file

The `readers.conf` file specifies the host names or IP addresses from which newsreader clients (such as Mozilla) can retrieve newsgroups from your server. For example, the following `readers.conf` file allows *read access* and *post access* (meaning you can submit articles) from localhost and from any host in the network 192.168.0.0:

```
auth "localhost" {
hosts: "localhost, 127.0.0.1, stdin"
default: "<localhost>"
}
access "localhost" {
users: "<localhost>"
newsgroups: "*"
access: RPA
}
auth "localnet" {
hosts: 192.168.0.0/24
default: "<localnet>"
}
access "localnet" {
users: "<localnet>"
newsgroups: "*"
access: RPA
}
```

## InterNetNews startup

In addition to the configuration files, you also have to initiate `cron` jobs that perform periodic maintenance of the news server. In Fedora, these `cron` jobs are already set up. Therefore, you're now ready to start the INN server — innd.

Before you start `innd`, you must run `makehistory` and `makedbz` to initialize and rebuild the INN history database. Type **man makehistory** and **man makedbz** to find out more about these commands. To create an initial history database, associated indexes, and set the ownerships and permissions of some files, type the following commands:

```
/usr/lib/news/bin/makehistory -b -f history -O -l 30000 -I
cd /var/lib/news
/usr/lib/news/bin/makedbz -s `wc -l < history` -f history
chown news.news *
chown news.news /var/spool/news/overview/group.index
chmod 664 /var/spool/news/overview/group.index
```

To start `innd` in Fedora, log in as `root` and type **/etc/init.d/innd start**. (Alternatively, you can type **service innd start**.) In Debian, SUSE, Ubuntu, and Xandros, type **/etc/init.d/inn start**. To ensure that innd starts at boot time, type **chkconfig --level 35 innd on** in Fedora and `chkconfig --level 35 inn on` in SUSE. In Debian and Xandros, type `update-rc.d inn defaults`.

If you make any changes to the INN configuration files, remember to restart the server by invoking the `/etc/init.d` script with `restart` as the argument.

# Setting Up Local Newsgroups

If you want to use newsgroups as a way to share information within your company, you can set up a hierarchy of local newsgroups. Then you can use these newsgroups to create virtual communities within your company, where people with shared interests can informally discuss issues and exchange knowledge.

## Defining a newsgroup hierarchy

The first task is to define a hierarchy of newsgroups, deciding what each newsgroup discusses. For example, if your company name is XYZ Corporation, here's a partial hierarchy of newsgroups you might define:

✦ `xyz.general`: General items about XYZ Corporation

✦ `xyz.weekly.news`: Weekly news

✦ `xyz.weekly.menu`: The weekly cafeteria menu and any discussions about it

✦ `xyz.forsale`: A listing of items offered for sale by employees

✦ `xyz.jobs`: Job openings at XYZ Corporation

✦ `xyz.wanted`: Wanted (help, items to buy, and so on) postings by employees

✦ `xyz.technical.hardware`: Technical discussions about hardware

✦ `xyz.technical.software`: Technical discussions about software

## Updating configuration files

Following are the steps you follow to update the configuration files for your local newsgroups and restart the news server:

1. **Add descriptive entries for each newsgroup to the `/var/lib/news/newsgroups` file.**

   Add to this file a line for each local newsgroup — type its name followed by a brief description. For example, here's what you might add for the `xyz.general` newsgroup:

   ```
   xyz.general General items about XYZ Corporation
   ```

2. **Edit the ME entry in the `/etc/news/newsfeeds` file and add the phrase `,!xyz.*` to the comma-separated list of newsgroup patterns.**

   This step ensures that your local newsgroups are not distributed outside your site.

3. **Add a storage method to use for the local newsgroups.**

   For example, you can add the following lines in `/etc/news/storage.conf` to define the storage method for the new xyz hierarchy of newsgroups (change *xyz* to whatever you name your local newsgroups):

   ```
   method tradspool {
   class: 1
   newsgroups: xyz.*
   }
   ```

4. **To make these changes effective, restart the news server.**

   Type `service innd restart` in Fedora or `/etc/init.d/inn restart` in Debian, SUSE, Ubuntu, and Xandros.)

## Adding the newsgroups

The final step is to add the newsgroups. After you update the configuration files and run `innd`, adding a local newsgroup is easy. Log in as `root` and use `ctlinnd` to perform this task. For example, here's how you add a newsgroup named `xyz.general`:

```
/usr/lib/news/bin/ctlinnd newsgroup xyz.general
```

That's it! That command adds the `xyz.general` newsgroup to your site. If you use the traditional storage method, the `innd` server creates the directory `/var/spool/news/articles/xyz/general` the first time an article is posted and stores articles for that newsgroup in that directory.

After you create all the local newsgroups, users from your intranet can post news articles and read articles in the local newsgroups. If they have problems accessing the newsgroups, make sure that the `/etc/news/readers.conf` file contains the IP addresses or names of the hosts that have access to the innd server.

## Testing your newsgroups

For example, add a newsgroup named `local.news` on an INN server running on your Linux system by using the instructions explained in the previous sections. Then start a newsreader and set up a new news account with the news server set to the INN server. Then access the `local.news` newsgroup. Try it! You'll like it.

# Chapter 3: Managing DNS

## In This Chapter

✔ **Understanding DNS**

✔ **Exploring BIND**

✔ **Finding out how to configure DNS**

✔ **Setting up a caching name server**

✔ **Configuring a primary name server**

**D**omain Name System (DNS) is an Internet service that converts a fully qualified domain name, such as www.debian.org, into its corresponding IP address, such as 194.109.137.218. You can think of DNS as the directory of Internet hosts — DNS is the reason why you can use easy-to-remember hostnames even though TCP/IP requires numeric IP addresses for data transfers. DNS is basically a hierarchy of distributed DNS servers. This chapter provides an overview of DNS and shows you how to set up a caching DNS server on your Linux system.

# Understanding Domain Name System (DNS)

In TCP/IP networks, each network interface (for example, an Ethernet card or a dial-up modem connection) is identified by an IP address. Because IP addresses are hard to remember, an easy-to-remember name is assigned to the IP address — much like the way a name goes with a telephone number. For example, instead of having to remember that the IP address of Debian's Web server is 194.109.137.218, you can simply refer to that host by its name, www.debian.org. When you type **www.debian.org** as the URL in a Web browser, the name www.debian.org is translated into its corresponding IP address. This process is where the concept of DNS comes in.

## What is DNS?

Domain Name System is a distributed, hierarchical database that holds information about computers on the Internet. That information includes hostname, IP address, and mail-routing specifications. Because this information resides on many DNS hosts on the Internet, DNS is called a *distributed* database. The primary job of DNS is to associate hostnames to IP addresses and vice versa.

In ARPANET — the precursor to today's Internet — the list of hostnames and corresponding IP addresses was maintained in a text file named HOSTS. TXT, which was managed centrally and periodically distributed to every host on the network. As the number of hosts grew, this static host table quickly became unreasonable to maintain. DNS was proposed by Paul Mockapetris to alleviate the problems of a static host table. As formally documented in Requests for Comment (RFCs) 882 and 883 (published in November 1983, see www.faqs.org/rfcs/rfc882.html and www.faqs.org/rfcs/rfc883. html), the original DNS introduced two key concepts:

✦ The use of hierarchical domain names, such as www.ee.umd.edu and www.debian.org

✦ The use of DNS servers throughout the Internet — a form of *distributed responsibility* — as a means of managing the host database

Today, DNS is an Internet standard documented in RFCs 1034 and 1035. The standard has been updated and extended by many other RFCs — 1101, 1183, 1348, 1886, 1995, 1996, 2136, 2181, 2308, 2845, 2930, 2931, 3007, 3110, 3226, 3403, 3596, 3597, 3645, 3646, 4025, 4033, 4034, and 4035. The earlier updates define data encoding, whereas later ones focus on improving DNS security. To read these and other RFCs online, visit the RFC page at the Internet Engineering Task Force (IETF) Web site at www.ietf.org/rfc.html.

DNS defines the following:

✦ A hierarchical domain-naming system for hosts

✦ A distributed database that associates every domain name with an IP address

✦ Library routines (resolvers) that network applications can use to query the distributed DNS database (this library is called the *resolver library*)

✦ A protocol for DNS clients and servers to exchange information about names and IP addresses

Nowadays, all hosts on the Internet rely on DNS to access various Internet services on remote hosts. As you may know from experience, when you obtain Internet access from an Internet Service Provider (ISP), your ISP provides you with the IP addresses of *name servers* — the DNS servers your system accesses whenever hostnames are mapped to IP addresses.

If you have a small LAN, you may decide to run a DNS server on one of the hosts or use the name servers provided by the ISP. For medium-sized networks with several subnets, you can run a DNS server on each subnet to provide efficient DNS lookups. On a large corporate network, the corporate domain (such as www.microsoft.com) is further subdivided into a hierarchy of subdomains; several DNS servers may be used in each subdomain.

The following sections provide an overview of the hierarchical domain-naming convention and describe BIND — the DNS software used on most UNIX systems, including Linux.

## Discovering hierarchical domain names

DNS uses a hierarchical tree of domains to organize the *namespace* — the entire set of names. Each higher-level domain has authority over its lower-level subdomains. Each domain represents a distinct block of the namespace and is managed by a single administrative authority. Figure 3-1 illustrates the hierarchical organization of the DNS namespace.

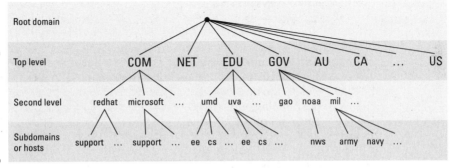

**Figure 3-1:**
The DNS namespace is organized as a hierarchy.

The root of the tree is called the *root domain* and is represented by a single dot (.). The top-level, or root-level, domains come next. The top-level domains are further divided into second-level domains, which, in turn, can be broken into further subdomains.

The top-level domains are relatively fixed and include well-known domains such as COM, NET, ORG, EDU, GOV, and MIL. These are the commonly used top-level domains in the United States. These top-level domains came about as the Internet came to widespread use in the early 1990s.

Another set of top-level domain names is for the countries. These domain names use the two-letter country codes assigned by the International Organization for Standardization (abbreviated as ISO, see www.iso.org). For example, the top-level country code domain for the United States is US. In the United States, many local governments and organizations use the US domain. For example, mcps.k12.md.us is the domain name of the Montgomery County Public Schools in the state of Maryland, in the United States.

The *fully qualified domain name* (FQDN) is constructed by stringing together the subdomain names, from lower level to higher level, using a period (.) as a separator. For example, REDHAT.COM is a fully qualified domain name;

so is EE.UMD.EDU. Note that each of these may also refer to a specific host computer. Figure 3-2 illustrates the components of a fully qualified domain name.

**Figure 3-2:**
A fully qualified domain name has a hierarchy of components.

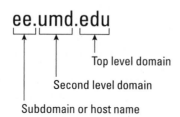

ee.umd.edu

Top level domain

Second level domain

Subdomain or host name

Domain names are case-insensitive. Therefore, as far as DNS is concerned, the domains UMD.EDU and umd.edu both represent University of Maryland's domain. The norm, however, is to type domain names in all lowercase.

## Exploring Berkeley Internet Name Domain (BIND)

Most UNIX systems, including Linux, come with the BIND system — a well-known implementation of DNS. The BIND software is installed during the Linux installation as long as you select the name server when selecting the packages for installation.

In Debian, Ubuntu, and Xandros, type **dpkg -l bind*** to see if BIND is installed. In Fedora and SUSE, type **rpm -q bind** and see if the BIND package is installed.

In Debian and Ubuntu, type **apt-get install bind9** to install BIND. In Fedora, log in as root, mount the DVD, and type **cd /media/cdrom/ Fedora/RPMS** followed by **rpm -ivh bind***. In SUSE, click Software Management in the YaST Control Center's Software category. Then use YaST's search facility to look for *bind,* select the relevant packages, and install them. In Xandros, first run Xandros Networks, choose Edit⇨Set Application Sources, and click the Debian Unsupported Site link as a source. Then type **apt-get install bind9** to install the BIND server.

BIND includes three major components:

✦ The named daemon (the name server), which responds to queries about hostnames and IP addresses

✦ A resolver library that applications can use to resolve hostnames into IP addresses (and vice versa)

✦ Command-line DNS utility programs (DNS clients), such as `dig` (Domain Internet Groper) and `host`, that users can use to query DNS

The next few sections describe these components of BIND. Later sections explain how to configure the resolver and the name server.

### named — the BIND name server

The `named` daemon is the name server that responds to queries about hostnames and IP addresses. Based on the configuration files and the local DNS database, `named` either provides answers to queries or asks other servers and caches their responses. The `named` server also performs a function referred to as *zone transfer,* which involves copying data among the name servers in a domain.

The name server operates in one of three modes:

✦ **Primary, or master:** In this case, the name server keeps the master copy of the domain's data on disk. One primary server is for each domain or subdomain.

✦ **Secondary, or slave:** A secondary name server copies its domain's data from the primary server using a zone transfer operation. You can have one or more secondary name servers for a domain.

✦ **Caching:** A caching name server loads the addresses of a few authoritative servers for the root domain and gets all domain data by caching responses to queries it has resolved by contacting other name servers. Primary and secondary servers also cache responses.

A *name server* can be authoritative or not, depending on what information it's providing. As the term implies, the response from an authoritative name server is supposed to be accurate. The primary and secondary name servers are authoritative for their own domains, but they are not authoritative for responses provided from cached information.

Caching name servers are never authoritative because all their responses come from cached information.

To run a name server on your Linux system, you have to run `named` with the appropriate configuration files. Later in this chapter, you'll find out about the configuration files and data files that control how the name server operates.

### Resolver library

Finding an IP address for a hostname is referred to as *resolving the hostname.* Network-aware applications, such as a Web browser or an FTP client, use a *resolver library* to perform the conversion from the name to an IP address.

Depending on the settings in the `/etc/host.conf` file, the resolver library consults the `/etc/hosts` file or makes a DNS query to resolve a hostname to its IP address. The resolver library queries the name servers listed in the `/etc/resolv.conf` file.

You don't have to know much about the resolver library unless you're writing network-aware applications. To run Internet services properly, all you have to know is how to configure the resolver. Later in this chapter, you will see how to configure the server and other aspects of DNS.

### DNS utility programs

You can use the DNS utility programs — `dig` and `host` — to try out DNS interactively from the shell prompt. These utility programs are DNS clients. You can use them to query the DNS database and debug any name server set up on your system. By default, these programs query the name server listed in your system's `/etc/resolv.conf` file.

You can use `dig`, the Domain Internet Groper program, to look up IP addresses for a domain name or vice versa. For example, to look up the IP address of `ftp.redhat.com`, type

```
dig ftp.redhat.com
```

`dig` prints the results of the DNS query in great detail. Look in the part of the output labeled ANSWER SECTION: for the result. For example, here's what that section looks like for this sample query:

```
;; ANSWER SECTION:
ftp.redhat.com. 300 IN A 209.132.183.61
```

This output means that the name `ftp.redhat.com` refers to the IP address `209.132.183.61`.

*Reverse lookups* (finding hostnames for IP addresses) are also easy with `dig`. For example, to find the hostname corresponding to the IP address `209.132.183.61`, type the following:

```
dig -x 209.132.183.61
```

Again, the answer appears in the ANSWER SECTION of the output, which, for this example, looks like this:

```
;; ANSWER SECTION:
61.132.183.209.in-addr.arpa. 600 IN PTR ftp.redhat.com.
```

In this case, the hostname corresponding to the IP address *209.132.183.61* is `ftp.redhat.com`.

You can also query DNS by using the host program, which produces output in a compact format. For example, here's a typical use of host to look up an IP address for a hostname:

```
host www.gao.gov
```

This command generates the following output:

```
www.gao.gov has address 161.203.16.77
www.gao.gov mail is handled by 5 listserv.gao.gov.
```

By default, host prints the IP address and any *MX record.* These records list the names of mail handlers for the host.

For a reverse lookup, use the -t ptr option along with the IP address as an argument, like this:

```
host -t ptr 161.203.16.2
```

Here's the relay from host:

```
2.16.203.161.in-addr.arpa domain name pointer www.gao.gov.
```

In this case, host prints the PTR record (from the DNS database) that shows the hostname corresponding to the IP address. (PTR refers to *pointer,* and the PTR record specifies the name corresponding to an address.)

You can also try other types of records, such as CNAME (for canonical name), as follows:

```
host -t cname www.ee.umd.edu
```

The response from host is

```
www.ee.umd.edu is an alias for ajclark.eng.umd.edu.
```

This output indicates that the *canonical name* (or alias) for www.ee.umd. edu is ajclark.eng.umd.edu.

# Configuring DNS

You configure DNS by using a number of configuration files. The exact set of files depends on whether you're running a name server and, if so, the type of name server — caching or primary. Some configuration files are needed whether you run a name server or not.

## *Configuring the resolver*

You don't need a name server running on your system to use the DNS clients (`dig` and `host`). You can use them to query your domain's name server. Typically, your ISP provides you with this information. You have to list the IP addresses of these name servers in the `/etc/resolv.conf` file — the resolver library reads this file to determine how to resolve hostnames. The format of this file is

```
domain your-domain.com
search your-domain.com
nameserver A.B.C.D
nameserver X.Y.Z.W
```

where `A.B.C.D` and `X.Y.Z.W` are the IP addresses (dot-separated numeric addresses, such as 192.168.0.1) of the primary and secondary name servers that your ISP provides you.

The `domain` line lists the local domain name. The `search` line specifies the domains on which a hostname is searched first (usually, you put your own domain in the `search` line). The domain listed on the `search` line is appended to any hostname before the resolver library tries to resolve it. For example, if you look for a host named `mailhost`, the resolver library first tries `mailhost.your-domain.com`; if that fails, it tries `mailhost`. The search line applies to any hostname that you try to access. For example, if you're trying to access `www.redhat.com`, the resolver first tries `www.redhat.com.your-domain.com` and then `www.redhat.com`.

Another important configuration file is `/etc/host.conf`. This file tells the resolver what to do when attempting to resolve a hostname. A typical `/etc/host/conf` file contains the following line:

```
order hosts,bind
```

This command tells the resolver to consult the `/etc/hosts` file first, and if the resolver does not find an entry there, query the name server listed in the `/etc/resolv.conf` file. The `/etc/hosts` file usually lists any local host-names and their IP addresses. Here's a typical line from the `/etc/hosts` file:

```
127.0.0.1 lnbp200 localhost.localdomain localhost
```

This line says that the IP address `127.0.0.1` is assigned to the hostnames `lnbp200`, `localhost.localdomain`, and `localhost`.

In the latest version of the Linux kernel — the one that uses GNU C Library version 2 (glibc 2) or later — the name service switch (NSS) file, `/etc/nsswitch.conf`, controls how services such as the resolver library, NIS, NIS+, and local files such as `/etc/hosts` and `/etc/shadow` interact. For example, the following hosts entry in the `/etc/nsswitch.conf` file specifies that the resolver library first try the `/etc/hosts` file, then try NIS+, and finally try DNS:

```
hosts: files nisplus dns
```

To find more about the `/etc/nsswitch.conf` file, type **man nsswitch.conf** in a terminal window.

## Configuring a caching name server

A simple but useful name server is one that finds answers to hostname queries (by using other name servers) and then remembers the answer (by saving it in a cache) for the next time you need it. This caching name server can shorten the time it takes to access hosts you have accessed recently because the answer is already in the cache.

When you install BIND, the configuration files for a caching name server are installed as well, so you can start running the caching name server without much work. This section describes the configuration files and what you have to do to start the caching name server.

### The /etc/named.conf file

The first configuration file you need is `/etc/named.conf`. (That's the name in Fedora and SUSE; in Debian, Ubuntu, and Xandros, the BIND configuration file is called `/etc/bind/named.conf`.) The `named` server reads this configuration file when it starts. You already have this file if you installed BIND. Here's an example `/etc/named.conf` file:

```
options {
directory "/var/named";
dump-file "/var/named/data/cache_dump.db";
statistics-file "/var/named/data/named_stats.txt";
/*
* If there is a firewall between you and nameservers you want
* to talk to, you might need to uncomment the query-source
* directive below. Previous versions of BIND always asked
* questions using port 53, but BIND 8.1 uses an unprivileged
* port by default.
*/
// query-source address * port 53;
};
//
// a caching only nameserver config
//
controls {
inet 127.0.0.1 allow { localhost; } keys { rndckey; };
};
zone "." IN {
type hint;
file "named.ca";
};
```

```
zone "localdomain" IN {
type master;
file "localdomain.zone";
allow-update { none; };
};
zone "localhost" IN {
type master;
file "localhost.zone";
allow-update { none; };
};
zone "0.0.127.in-addr.arpa" IN {
type master;
file "named.local";
allow-update { none; };
};
zone "0.0.0.0.0.0.0.0.0.0.0.0.0.0.0.0.0.0.0.0.0.0.0.0.0.0.0.0.0.0.0.0.ip6.arpa" IN
{
type master;
file "named.ip6.local";
allow-update { none; };
};
zone "255.in-addr.arpa" IN {
type master;
file "named.broadcast";
allow-update { none; };
};
zone "0.in-addr.arpa" IN {
type master;
file "named.zero";
allow-update { none; };
};
include "/etc/rndc.key";
```

Comments are C-style (`/* . . . */`) or C++-style (starts with `//`). The file contains block statements enclosed in curly braces (`{ . . . }`) and terminated by a semicolon (`;`). A block statement, in turn, contains other statements, each ending with a semicolon.

This `/etc/named.conf` file begins with an `options` block statement with a number of option statements. The `directory` option statement tells `named` where to look for all other files that appear on file lines in the configuration file. In this case, `named` looks for the files in the `/var/named` directory.

In SUSE, the `directory` option in `/etc/named.conf` refers to the `/var/lib/named` directory, which means that all other BIND configuration files are in `/var/lib/named`. In Debian and Xandros, the configuration files are explicitly specified to be in the `/etc/bind` directory.

The `controls` statement in `/etc/named.conf` contains security information so that the `rndc` command can connect to the `named` service at port 953 and interact with `named`. In this case, the `controls` statement contains the following line:

```
inet 127.0.0.1 allow { localhost; } keys { rndckey; };
```

This command says that `rndc` can connect from `localhost` with the key named `rndc`. (The file `/etc/rndc.key` defines the key and the encryption algorithm to be used.)

The `rndc` (remote name daemon control) utility is a successor to the older `ndc` (name daemon controller) utility used to control the `named` server by sending it messages over a special control channel, a TCP port where `named` listens for messages. The `rndc` utility uses a cryptographic key to authenticate itself to the `named` server. The `named` server has the same cryptographic key so that it can decode the authentication information sent by `rndc`.

After the `options` statement, the `/etc/named.conf` file contains several `zone` statements, each enclosed in curly braces and terminated by a semicolon. Each `zone` statement defines a zone. The first zone is named . (root zone); it's a hint zone that specifies the root name servers. (When the DNS server starts, it uses the hint zone to find a root name server and get the most recent list of root name servers.)

The next two zone statements in `/etc/named.conf` are master zones. (A *master zone* is simply the master copy of data for a domain.) The syntax for a *master zone statement* for an Internet class zone (indicated by the `IN` keyword) is as follows:

```
zone "zone-name" IN {
type master;
file "zone-file";
[ . . . other optional statements . . . ]
};
```

`zone-name` is the name of the zone, and `zone-file` is the zone file that contains the resource records (RR) — the database entries — for that zone. The next two sections describe zone file formats and resource record formats.

### Zone file formats

The zone file typically starts with a number of directives, each of which begins with a dollar sign ($) followed by a keyword. Two commonly used directives are `$TTL` and `$ORIGIN`.

For example, the line

```
$TTL 86400
```

uses the `$TTL` directive to set the default Time To Live (TTL) for subsequent records with undefined TTLs. The value is in seconds, and the valid TTLs are in the range 0 to 2147483647 seconds. In this case, the directive sets the default TTL as 86400 seconds (or one day).

The `$ORIGIN` directive sets the domain name that is appended to any unqualified records. For example, the following `$ORIGIN` directive sets the domain name to `localhost`:

```
$ORIGIN localhost.
```

If there is no `$ORIGIN` directive, the initial `$ORIGIN` is the same as the zone name that comes after the zone keyword in the `/etc/named.conf` file.

After the directives, the zone file contains one or more resource records. These records follow a specific format, which are outlined in the next section.

### Resource record (RR) formats

You have to understand the format of the resource records before you can understand and intelligently work with zone files. Each resource record (RR) has the following format. (Optional fields are shown in square brackets.)

```
[domain] [ttl] [class] type data [;comment]
```

The fields are separated by tabs or spaces and may contain some special characters, such as an @ for the domain and a semicolon (;) to indicate the start of a comment.

The first field, which must begin at the first character of the line, identifies the domain. You can use the @ to use the current `$ORIGIN` for the domain name for this record. If you have multiple records for the same domain name, leave the first field blank.

The optional `ttl` field specifies the Time To Live — the duration for which the data can be cached and considered valid. You can specify the duration in one of the following formats:

+ *N*, where *N* is the number of seconds
+ *N*W, where *N* is the number of weeks
+ *N*D, where *N* is the number of days
+ *N*H, where *N* is the number of hours
+ *N*M, where *N* is the number of minutes
+ *N*S, where *N* is the number of seconds

The letters W, D, H, M, and S can also be in lowercase. Thus, you can write `86400` or `1D` (or `1d`) to indicate a duration of one day. You can also combine these letters to specify more precise durations, such as 5w6d16h to indicate 5 weeks, 6 days, and 16 hours.

The *class* field specifies the network type. The most commonly used value for this field is IN for Internet.

Next in the resource record is the *type* field, which denotes the type of record (such as SOA, NS, A, or PTR). Table 3-1 lists the DNS resource record types. The *data* field comes next, and its content depends on the *type* field.

| Table 3-1 | | DNS Resource Record Types |
|---|---|---|
| *Type* | *Name* | *Description* |
| A | IPv4 to IPv6 Transition Address | Specifies the IPv6 address corresponding to a name using a format suitable for transition from IPv4 to IPv6 |
| AAAA | IPv6 Address | Specifies the IPv6 host address corresponding to a name |
| AS | Address | Specifies the IP address corresponding to a hostname |
| CERT | Digital Certificate | Holds a digital certificate |
| CNAME | Canonical Name | Defines the nickname or alias for a hostname |
| DNAME | Delegation Name | Replaces specified domain name with another name to be looked up |
| HINFO | Host Info | Identifies the hardware and operating system for a host |
| KEY | Public Key | Stores a public key associated with a DNS name |
| MX | Mail Exchanger | Identifies the host that accepts mail meant for a domain (used to route e-mail) |
| NS | Name Server | Identifies authoritative name servers for a zone |
| PTR | Pointer | Specifies the name corresponding to an address (used for *reverse mapping* — converting an IP address to a hostname) |
| RP | Responsible Person | Provides the name of a technical contact for a domain |
| SIG | Signature | Contains data authenticated in the secure DNS (see RFC 2535 for details) |

**Book VII Chapter 3**

**Managing DNS**

*(continued)*

**Table 3-1** *(continued)*

| Type | Name | Description |
|------|------|-------------|
| SOA | Start of Authority | Indicates that all subsequent records are authoritative for this zone |
| SRV | Services | Lists well-known network services provided by the domain |
| TXT | Text | Includes comments and other information in the DNS database |

Read the resource records in the zone files, at least the ones of type SOA, NS, A, PTR, and MX, which are some of the most commonly used. (You'll find the zone files in the /etc/bind directory in Debian and Xandros, the /var/named directory in Fedora, and the /var/lib/named directory in SUSE.) Next, there is a brief description of these records, illustrating each record type through an example.

A typical SOA record follows:

```
@ 1D IN SOA @ root (
42 ; serial
3H ; refresh -- 3 hours
15M ; retry -- 15 minutes
1W ; expiry -- 1 week
1D ) ; minimum -- 1 day
```

The first field specifies the domain as @, which means the current domain (by default, the zone name, as shown in the /etc/named.conf file). The next field specifies a TTL of one day for this record. The class field is set to IN, which means the record is for Internet. The type field specifies the record type as SOA. The rest of the fields constitute the data for the SOA record. The data includes the name of the primary name server (in this case, @, or the current domain), the e-mail address of the technical contact, and five times enclosed in parentheses.

The NS record specifies the authoritative name servers for a zone. A typical NS record looks like the following:

```
. 3600000 IN NS A.ROOT-SERVERS.NET.
```

In this case, the NS record lists the authoritative name server for the root zone. (Note that the name of the first field is a single period.) The Time To Live field specifies that the record is valid for 1,000 hours (3,600,000 seconds). The class is IN, for Internet; and the record type is NS. The final field lists the name of the name server (A.ROOT-SERVERS.NET.), which ends with a period.

An A record specifies the address corresponding to a name. For example, the following A record shows the address of A.ROOT-SERVERS.NET. as 198.41.0.4:

```
A.ROOT-SERVERS.NET. 3600000 A 198.41.0.4
```

In this case, the network class isn't specified because the field is optional, and the default is IN.

PTR records are used for reverse mapping — converting an address to a name. Consider the following example:

```
1 IN PTR localhost.
```

This record comes from a file for a zone named 0.0.127.in-addr.arpa. Therefore, this record says that the name associated with the address 127.0.0.1 is localhost.

An MX record specifies the name of a host that accepts mail on behalf of a specific domain. For example, here's a typical MX record:

```
Server7 IN MX 10 mailhub.lnbsoft.com.
```

This record says that mail addressed to the host named server7 in the current domain is sent to mailhub.lnbsoft.com. (This host is called a *mail exchanger*.) The number 10 is the preference value. For a list of multiple MX records with different preference values, the ones with lower preference values are tried first.

Armed with this bit of information about resource records, you can go through the zone files for the caching name server.

**Book VII
Chapter 3**

**Managing DNS**

### The root zone file

There are 13 root name servers for the Internet; most root servers are located in the United States. Information about the 13 root name servers is in the zone file referenced in the zone statement for the root zone in the /etc/named.conf file. (The root zone file is /var/named/named.ca in Fedora, /etc/bind/db.root in Debian, Ubuntu, and Xandros, and /var/lib/named/root.hint in SUSE.) The following listing shows the root zone file:

```
; This file holds the information on root name servers needed to
; initialize cache of Internet domain name servers
; (e.g. reference this file in the "cache . <file>"
; configuration file of BIND domain name servers).
;
; This file is made available by InterNIC
; under anonymous FTP as
; file /domain/named.cache
; on server FTP.INTERNIC.NET
```

```
; -OR- RS.INTERNIC.NET
;
; last update: Jan 29, 2004
; related version of root zone: 2004012900
;
;
; formerly NS.INTERNIC.NET
;
. 3600000 IN NS A.ROOT-SERVERS.NET.
A.ROOT-SERVERS.NET. 3600000 A 198.41.0.4
;
; formerly NS1.ISI.EDU
;
. 3600000 NS B.ROOT-SERVERS.NET.
B.ROOT-SERVERS.NET. 3600000 A 192.228.79.201
;
; formerly C.PSI.NET
;
. 3600000 NS C.ROOT-SERVERS.NET.
C.ROOT-SERVERS.NET. 3600000 A 192.33.4.12
;
; formerly TERP.UMD.EDU
;
. 3600000 NS D.ROOT-SERVERS.NET.
D.ROOT-SERVERS.NET. 3600000 A 128.8.10.90
;
; formerly NS.NASA.GOV
;
. 3600000 NS E.ROOT-SERVERS.NET.
E.ROOT-SERVERS.NET. 3600000 A 192.203.230.10
;
; formerly NS.ISC.ORG
;
. 3600000 NS F.ROOT-SERVERS.NET.
F.ROOT-SERVERS.NET. 3600000 A 192.5.5.241
;
; formerly NS.NIC.DDN.MIL
;
. 3600000 NS G.ROOT-SERVERS.NET.
G.ROOT-SERVERS.NET. 3600000 A 192.112.36.4
;
; formerly AOS.ARL.ARMY.MIL
;
. 3600000 NS H.ROOT-SERVERS.NET.
H.ROOT-SERVERS.NET. 3600000 A 128.63.2.53
;
; formerly NIC.NORDU.NET
;
. 3600000 NS I.ROOT-SERVERS.NET.
I.ROOT-SERVERS.NET. 3600000 A 192.36.148.17
;
; operated by VeriSign, Inc.
;
. 3600000 NS J.ROOT-SERVERS.NET.
J.ROOT-SERVERS.NET. 3600000 A 192.58.128.30
;
; operated by RIPE NCC
;
. 3600000 NS K.ROOT-SERVERS.NET.
K.ROOT-SERVERS.NET. 3600000 A 193.0.14.129
;
; operated by ICANN
```

```
;
. 3600000 NS L.ROOT-SERVERS.NET.
L.ROOT-SERVERS.NET. 3600000 A 198.32.64.12
;
; operated by WIDE
;
. 3600000 NS M.ROOT-SERVERS.NET.
M.ROOT-SERVERS.NET. 3600000 A 202.12.27.33
; End of File
```

This file contains NS and A resource records that specify the names of authoritative name servers and their addresses for the root zone (indicated by the . in the first field of each NS record).

The comment lines in the file begin with a semicolon. These comments give you hints about the location of the 13 root name servers. This file is a necessity for any name server because the name server has to be able to reach at least one root name server.

### The localhost.zone file

The /etc/named.conf file includes a zone statement for the localhost zone that specifies the zone file as localhost.zone. That file is located in the /var/named directory in Fedora, in the /var/local/named directory in SUSE, and in /etc/bind/db.local in Debian and Xandros. Here's a listing of what the localhost.zone file contains:

```
$TTL 86400
$ORIGIN localhost.
@ 1D IN SOA @ root (
42 ; serial (d. adams)
3H ; refresh
15M ; retry
1W ; expiry
1D ) ; minimum
1D IN NS @
1D IN A 127.0.0.1
```

This zone file starts with a $TTL directive that sets the default TTL (Time To Live) to one day (86400 seconds) for subsequent records with undefined TTLs. Next, the $ORIGIN directive sets the domain name to localhost.

After these two directives, the localhost.zone file contains three resource records (RRs): an SOA record, an NS record, and an A record. The SOA and NS records specify localhost as the primary authoritative name server for the zone. The A record specifies the address of localhost as 127.0.0.1.

### The zone file for reverse mapping 127.0.0.1

The third zone statement in the /etc/named.conf file specifies a reverse-mapping zone named 0.0.127.in-addr.arpa. For this zone, the zone file is `/var/named/named.localhost` in Fedora, `/var/lib/named/127.0.0.zone` in SUSE, and `/etc/bind/db.127` in Debian, Ubuntu, and Xandros. This zone file contains the following:

```
$TTL 86400
@ IN SOA localhost. root.localhost. (
1997022700 ; Serial
28800 ; Refresh
14400 ; Retry
3600000 ; Expire
86400 ) ; Minimum
IN NS localhost.
1 IN PTR localhost.
```

The SOA and NS records specify `localhost` as the primary name server. The PTR record specifies `localhost` as the name corresponding to the address `127.0.0.1`.

The SOA record also shows `root.localhost.` as the e-mail address of the technical contact for the domain. The DNS zone files use the format *user.host.* (note the ending period) format for the e-mail address. When sending any e-mail to the contact, you have to replace the first period with @ and remove the final period.

### Caching name server: Startup and test

After you've studied the configuration files for the caching name server, you can start the name server and see it in operation.

To start the name server, log in as `root` and type **/etc/init.d/named start** in Fedora and SUSE. To ensure that the named server starts every time you reboot the system, type **chkconfig --level 35 named on** in Fedora and SUSE. In Debian, Ubuntu, and Xandros, type **/etc/init.d/bind9 start** to start the named server.

The named server writes diagnostic log messages in the `/var/log/messages` file. After you start named, you can check the log messages by opening `/var/log/messages` in a text editor. If no error messages are from named, you can proceed to test the name server.

Before you try the caching name server, you have to specify that name server as your primary one. To do so, make sure that the first line in the `/etc/resolv.conf` file is the following:

```
nameserver 127.0.0.1
```

Now you can use host to test the name server. For example, to look up the IP address of www.gao.gov by using the caching name server on localhost, type the following command:

```
host www.gao.gov localhost
```

Here's the resulting output from the host command:

```
Using domain server:
Name: localhost
Address: 127.0.0.1#53
Aliases:
www.gao.gov. has address 161.203.16.77
```

As the output shows, the host command uses localhost as the DNS server and returns the IP address of www.gao.gov. If you get output similar to this, the caching name server is up and running.

## Configuring a primary name server

The best way to configure a primary name server is to start by configuring a caching name server (as explained in the previous sections). Then, add master zones for the domains for which you want this name server to be the primary name server. For example, suppose you want to define a primary name server for the server7.net domain. Here are the steps I go through to configure that primary name server on a Fedora system (after logging in as root):

*1.* **Add the following zone statements to the /etc/named.conf file:**

```
zone "server7.net" IN {
type master;
file "server7.zone";
};
zone "0.168.192.in-addr.arpa" IN {
type master;
file "0.168.192.zone";
};
```

*2.* **Create the zone file /var/named/server7.zone with the following lines in it:**

```
$TTL 86400
$ORIGIN server7.net.
@ 1D IN SOA @ root.server7.net (
100 ; serial
3H ; refresh
15M ; retry
1W ; expiry
1D ) ; minimum
1D IN NS @
1D IN A 192.168.0.7
wxp IN A 192.168.0.2
```

3. **Create the zone file /var/named/0.168.192.zone with the following lines in it:**

```
$TTL 86400
; Remember zone name is: 0.168.192.in-addr.arpa
@ IN SOA server7.net. root.server7.net (
1 ; Serial
28800 ; Refresh
14400 ; Retry
3600000 ; Expire
86400 ) ; Minimum
IN NS server7.net.
7 IN PTR server7.net.
2 IN PTR wxp.server7.net.
```

4. **To test the new configuration, restart the named server with the following command:**

```
/etc/init.d/named restart
```

5. **Use dig or host to query the DNS server.**

For example, here's how to use host to check the address of the host wxp.server7.net at the DNS server running on localhost:

```
host wxp.server7.net localhost
```

This command results in the following output:

```
Using domain server:
Name: localhost
Address: 127.0.0.1#53
Aliases:
wxp.server7.net has address 192.168.0.2
```

If you want to use dig to check the DNS server, type the following command:

```
dig @localhost wxp.server7.net
```

That @localhost part specifies the DNS server that dig contacts.

When you successfully use dig to contact a DNS server, you can get a bit fancier with what you ask that server to do. Here, for example, is the command to type to try a reverse lookup with the IP address 192.168.0.2:

```
host 192.168.0.2 localhost
```

This command displays the following output:

```
Using domain server:
Name: localhost
Address: 127.0.0.1#53
Aliases:
2.0.168.192.in-addr.arpa domain name pointer wxp.server7.net
```

# Chapter 4: Working with Samba and NFS

## In This Chapter

✔ **Sharing files with Network File System**

✔ **Installing and configuring Samba**

✔ **Setting up a Windows server using Samba**

*I*f your local area network is like many others, it needs the capability to share files between systems that run Linux and other systems that don't. Thus, Linux includes two prominent file-sharing services:

+ **Network File System (NFS):** For sharing files with other UNIX systems (or PCs with NFS client software)

+ **Samba:** For file sharing and print sharing with Windows systems

This chapter describes how to share files using both NFS and Samba.

## Sharing Files with NFS

Sharing files through NFS is simple and involves two basic steps:

+ On the Linux system that runs the NFS server, you export (share) one or more directories by listing them in the /etc/exports file and by running the exportfs command. In addition, you must start the NFS server.

+ On each client system, you use the mount command to mount the directories that your server has exported.

The only problem in using NFS is that each client system must support it. Microsoft Windows doesn't come with NFS, so you have to buy NFS software separately if you want to share files by using NFS. However, using NFS if all systems on your LAN run Linux (or other variants of UNIX with built-in NFS support) makes sense.

NFS has security vulnerabilities. Therefore, you should not set up NFS on systems directly connected to the Internet without using the RPCSEC_GSS security that comes with NFS version 4 (NFSv4).

The Linux 2.6 kernel includes support for NFSv4, which is built on earlier versions of NFS. But unlike earlier versions, NFSv4 has stronger security and was designed to operate in an Internet environment. (RFC 3510 describes NFSv4; see www.ietf.org/rfc/rfc3530.txt.) NFSv4 uses the RPCSEC_GSS (GSS stands for Generic Security Services) protocol for security. You can continue to use the older user ID and group ID based authentication with NFSv4, but if you want to use RPCSEC_GSS you have to run three additional services: rpcsvcgassd on the server, rpsgssd on the client, and rpcidmapd on both the client and the server. For more information about NFSv4 implementation in Linux, visit www.citi.umich.edu/projects/nfsv4/linux.

The next few sections walk you through NFS setup, using an example of two Linux PCs on a LAN.

## Exporting a file system with NFS

Start with the server system that *exports* — makes available to the client systems — the contents of a directory. On the server, you must run the NFS service and also designate one or more file systems to export.

To export a file system, you have to add an appropriate entry to the /etc/exports file. For example, suppose that you want to export the /home directory and you want to enable the host named LNBP75 to mount this file system for read and write operations. You can do so by adding the following entry to the /etc/exports file:

```
/home LNBP75(rw,sync)
```

If you want to give access to all hosts on a LAN such as 192.168.0.0, you could change this line to

```
/home 192.168.0.0/24(rw,sync)
```

Every line in the /etc/exports file has this general format:

```
directory host1(options) host2(options) . . .
```

The first field is the directory being shared via NFS, followed by one or more fields that specify which hosts can mount that directory remotely and a number of options in parentheses. You can specify the hosts with names or IP addresses, including ranges of addresses.

The options in parentheses denote the kind of access each host is granted and how user and group IDs from the server are mapped to ID the client. (For example, if a file is owned by root on the server, what owner is that on the client?) Within the parentheses, commas separate the options. For example, if a host is allowed both read and write access — and all IDs are to be mapped to the anonymous user (by default, the anonymous user is named nobody) — the options look like this:

```
(rw,all_squash)
```

Table 4-1 shows the options you can use in the /etc/exports file. You find two types of options: general options and user ID mapping options.

| Table 4-1 | Options in /etc/exports |
|---|---|
| *Option* | *Description* |
| **General Options** | |
| secure | Allows connections only from ports 1024 or lower (default) |
| insecure | Allows connections from ports 1024 or higher |
| ro | Allows read-only access (default) |
| rw | Allows both read and write access |
| sync | Performs write operations (writing information to the disk) when requested (by default) |
| async | Performs write operations when the server is ready |
| no_wdelay | Performs write operations immediately |
| wdelay | Waits a bit to see whether related write requests arrive and then performs them together (by default) |
| hide | Hides an exported directory that's a subdirectory of another exported directory (by default) |
| no_hide | Causes a directory to not be hidden (opposite of hide) |
| subtree_ check | Performs subtree checking, which involves checking parent directories of an exported subdirectory whenever a file is accessed (by default) |
| no_subtree_ check | Turns off subtree checking (opposite of subtree_check) |
| insecure_ locks | Allows insecure file locking |
| **User ID Mapping Options** | |
| all_squash | Maps all user IDs and group IDs to the anonymous user on the client |
| no_all_ squash | Maps remote user and group IDs to similar IDs on the client (by default) |
| root_squash | Maps remote root user to the anonymous user on the client (by default) |

*(continued)*

**Book VII
Chapter 4**

**Working with
Samba and NFS**

**Table 4-1** *(continued)*

| Option | Description |
| --- | --- |
| **User ID Mapping Options** | |
| `no_root_squash` | Maps remote root user to the local root user |
| `anonuid=UID` | Sets the user ID of anonymous user to be used for the `all_squash` and `root_squash` options |
| `anongid=GID` | Sets the group ID of anonymous user to be used for the `all_squash` and `root_squash` options |

After adding the entry in the `/etc/exports` file, manually export the file system by typing the following command in a terminal window:

```
exportfs -a
```

This command exports all file systems defined in the `/etc/exports` file.

Now you can start the NFS server processes.

In Debian, start the NFS server by logging in as `root` and typing **/etc/init.d/nfs-kernel-server start** in a terminal window. In Fedora, type **/etc/init.d/nfs start**. In SUSE, type **/etc/init.d/nfsserver start**. If you want the NFS server to start when the system boots, type **update-rc.d nfs-kernel-server defaults** in Debian. In Fedora, type **chkconfig - -level 35 nfs on**. In SUSE, type **chkconfig - -level 35 nfsserver on**. In Xandros, type **update-rc.d nfs-user-server defaults**.

When the NFS service is up, the server side of NFS is ready. Now you can try to mount the exported file system from a client system and then access the exported file system as needed.

If you ever make any changes to the exported file systems listed in the `/etc/exports` file, remember to restart the NFS service. To restart a service, invoke the script in the `/etc/init.d` directory with `restart` as the argument (instead of the `start` argument that you use to start the service).

## Mounting an NFS file system

To access an exported NFS file system on a client system, you have to mount that file system on a mount point. The *mount point* is nothing more than a local directory. For example, suppose that you want to access the `/home` directory exported from the server named LNBP200 at the local directory /mnt/lnbp200 on the client system. To do so, follow these steps:

*1.* **Log in as root and create the directory with this command:**

```
mkdir /mnt/lnbp200
```

*2.* **Type the following command to mount the directory from the remote system (LNBP200) on the local directory /mnt/lnbp200:**

```
mount lnbp200:/home /mnt/lnbp200
```

After completing these steps, you can then view and access exported files from the local directory /mnt/lnbp200.

To confirm that the NFS file system is indeed mounted, log in as root on the client system and type **mount** in a terminal window. You see a line similar to the following about the NFS file system:

```
lnbp200:/home/public on /mnt/lnbp200 type nfs (rw,addr=192.168.0.4)
```

NFS supports two types of mount operations — hard and soft. By default, a mount is hard, which means that if the NFS server does not respond, the client keeps trying to access the server indefinitely until the server responds. You can soft mount an NFS volume by adding the -o soft option to the mount command. For a soft mount, the client returns an error if the NFS server fails to respond.

# Setting Up a Windows Server Using Samba

If you rely on Windows for file sharing and print sharing, you probably use Windows in your servers and clients. If so, you can still move to a Linux PC as your server without losing Windows file-sharing and print-sharing capabilities; you can set up Linux as a Windows server. When you install Linux from this book's companion DVD-ROM, you also get a chance to install the Samba software package, which performs that setup. All you have to do is select the Windows File Server package group during installation.

After you install and configure Samba on your Linux PC, your client PCs — even if they're running an old Windows operating system or one of the more recent Windows versions — can access shared disks and printers on the Linux PC. To do so, they use the Common Internet File System (CIFS) protocol, the underlying protocol in Windows file and print sharing.

With the Samba package installed, you can make your Linux PC a Windows client, which means that the Linux PC can access the disks and printers that a Windows server manages. At the same time, your Linux PC can be a client to other Windows systems on the network.

The Samba software package has these major components:

✦ `/etc/samba/smb.conf`: The Samba configuration file that the SMB server uses.

✦ `/etc/samba/smbusers`: A Samba configuration file that shows the Samba usernames corresponding to usernames on the local Linux PC.

✦ `nmbd`: The NetBIOS name server, which clients use to look up servers. (NetBIOS stands for *Network Basic Input/Output System* — an interface that applications use to communicate with network transports, such as TCP/IP.)

✦ `nmblookup`: A command that returns the IP address of a Windows PC identified by its NetBIOS name.

✦ `smbadduser`: A program that adds users to the SMB (Server Message Block) password file.

✦ `smbcacls`: A program that manipulates Windows NT access control lists (ACLs) on shared files.

✦ `smbclient`: The Windows client, which runs on Linux and allows Linux to access the files and printer on any Windows server.

✦ `smbcontrol`: A program that sends messages to the `smbd`, `nmbd`, or `winbindd` processes.

✦ `smbd`: The SMB server, which accepts connections from Windows clients and provides file-sharing and print-sharing services.

✦ `smbmount`: A program that mounts a Samba share directory on a Linux PC.

✦ `smbpasswd`: A program that changes the password for an SMB user.

✦ `smbprint`: A script that enables printing on a printer on an SMB server.

✦ `smbstatus`: A command that lists the current SMB connections for the local host.

✦ `smbtar`: A program that backs up SMB shares directly to tape drives on the Linux system.

✦ `smbumount`: A program that unmounts a currently mounted Samba share directory.

✦ `testparm`: A program that ensures that the Samba configuration file is correct.

✦ `winbindd`: A server that resolves names from Windows NT servers.

The following sections describe how to configure and use Samba.

## Installing Samba

You may have already installed Samba when you installed Linux. You can check first, and if you don't find Samba on your system, you can easily install it.

To see if Samba is installed, type **dpkg -l samba\*** in Debian, Ubuntu, and Xandros or type **rpm -q samba** in Fedora and SUSE.

In Debian and Ubuntu, type **apt-get install samba** to install Samba. In Fedora, log in as root and type **yum install samba samba-swat**. This installs not only samba but also the Web configuration interface, SWAT (Samba Web Administration Tool). In SUSE, click Software Management in the YaST Control Center's Software category. Then use YaST's search facility to look for samba, select the relevant packages, and install them. As for Xandros, you get Samba when you install Xandros.

After installing the Samba software, you have to configure Samba before you can use it.

## Configuring Samba

To set up the Windows file-sharing and print-sharing services, you can either edit the configuration file manually or use a GUI tool. Using the GUI tool is much easier than editing a configuration file. Fedora and SUSE come with GUI tools for configuring the Samba server.

In Fedora, choose System Settings➪Advanced➪Samba from the KDE desktop to open the Samba Server Configuration window. Enter a valid username and password at the prompt, and the configuration interface shown in Figure 4-1 appears, where you can create and edit entries in the configuration file /etc/samba/smb.conf.

In SUSE, you can configure Samba through the YaST Control Center — choose System➪Control Center (YaST) from the main menu. Click Network Services on the left side of the window and then click Samba Server on the right side of the window. In the window that appears, select a workgroup name (YaST displays the name of any existing Windows workgroup on your LAN) and click Next. Then you can select the server type, enable the server, and select what you want to share. After you exit the Samba server configuration utility, YaST stores the Samba settings in configuration files in the /etc/samba directory.

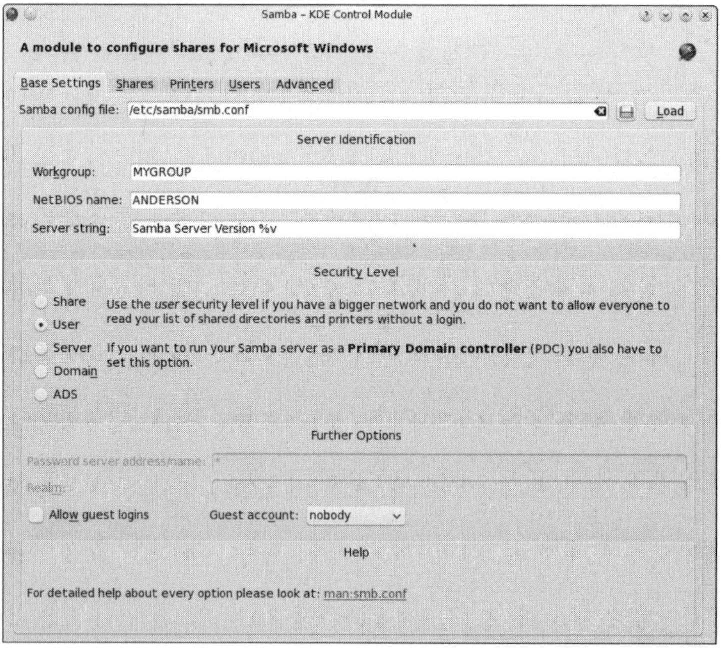

Samba – KDE Control Module

**A module to configure shares for Microsoft Windows**

Base Settings  Shares  Printers  Users  Advanced

Samba config file: /etc/samba/smb.conf                    Load

Server Identification

Workgroup:      MYGROUP

NetBIOS name:   ANDERSON

Server string:  Samba Server Version %v

Security Level

○ Share      Use the *user* security level if you have a bigger network and you do not want to allow everyone to
● User        read your list of shared directories and printers without a login.

○ Server     If you want to run your Samba server as a **Primary Domain controller** (PDC) you also have to
○ Domain      set this option.

○ ADS

Further Options

Password server address/name: *

Realm:

☐ Allow guest logins      Guest account: nobody ▾

Help

For detailed help about every option please look at: man:smb.conf

**Figure 4-1:**
Configure
Samba in
Fedora with
SWAT.

After configuring Samba, type the following command in a terminal window
to verify that the Samba configuration file is okay:

    testparm

If the command says that it loaded the files okay, you're all set to go. The
testparm command also displays the contents of the Samba configuration
file.

Samba uses the /etc/samba/smb.conf file as its configuration file. This is
a text file with a syntax similar to that of a Microsoft Windows 3.1 INI file.
You can edit that file in any text editor on your Linux system. Like the old
Windows INI files, the /etc/samba/smb.conf file consists of sections,
with a list of parameters in each section. Each section of the smb.conf file
begins with the name of the section in brackets. The section continues until
the next section begins or until the file ends. Each line uses the *name =
value* syntax to specify the value of a parameter. As in Windows INI files,
comment lines begin with a semicolon (;). In the /etc/samba/smb.conf
file, comments may also begin with a hash mark (#).

---

# Discovering more about Samba

This chapter is only an introduction to Samba. To find out more about Samba, you can consult the following resources:

✔ To view Samba documentation online, visit www.samba.org/samba/docs/man/Samba-HOWTO-Collection.

✔ *Using Samba,* 3rd Edition, by Jay Ts, Robert Eckstein, and David Collier-Brown (O'Reilly & Associates, 2007).

You should also visit www.samba.org to keep up with the latest news on Samba development. This site also has links to resources for learning Samba.

---

To start the Samba services automatically when the system reboots, type **update-rc.d samba defaults** in Debian, Ubuntu, and Xandros or type **chkconfig - -level 35 smb on** in Fedora and SUSE. To start Samba immediately, type **/etc/init.d/smb start** in Fedora and SUSE or type **/etc/init.d/samba start** in Debian, Ubuntu, and Xandros.

## Trying out Samba

You can now access the Samba server on the Linux system from one of the Windows systems on the LAN. Double-click the Network Neighborhood icon on the Windows 95/98/ME desktop. On Windows XP, choose Start⇨My Network Places and then click View Workgroup Computers. All the computers on the same workgroup are shown. In Vista and Windows 7, choose Start⇨Computer⇨Network.

When you see the Samba server, you can open it by double-clicking the icon. After you enter your Samba username and password, you can access the folders and printers (if any) on the Samba share.

You can use the smbclient program to access shared directories and printers on Windows systems on the LAN and to ensure that your Linux Samba server is working. One quick way to check is to type **smbclient -L** in a terminal window to view the list of services on the Linux Samba server itself.

# Book VIII

# Programming

"It's a wonderful idea, Ralph. But do you really think 'AnnoyPersonTP' and 'DumbMemoTP' will work as protocols on our TCP/IP suite?"

# Contents at a Glance

**Chapter 1: Programming in Linux** . . . . . . . . . . . . . . . . . . . . . . . . . . . . .527

An Overview of Programming................................................................527
Exploring the Software-Development Tools in Linux............................531
Understanding the Implications of GNU Licenses.................................550

**Chapter 2: Introductory Shell Scripting** . . . . . . . . . . . . . . . . . . . . . . .553

Trying Out Simple Shell Scripts.............................................................553
Exploring the Basics of Shell Scripting.................................................555

**Chapter 3: Working with Advanced Shell Scripting** . . . . . . . . . . . . .565

Trying Out sed .........................................................................................565
Working with awk and sed ......................................................................567
Final Notes on Shell Scripting ...............................................................571

# Chapter 1: Programming in Linux

## In This Chapter

✓ Figuring out programming

✓ Exploring the software-development tools in Linux

✓ Compiling and linking programs with GCC

✓ Using make

✓ Debugging programs with gdb

✓ Understanding the implications of GNU, GPL, and LGPL

*L*inux comes loaded with all the tools you need to develop software. (All you have to do is install them.) In particular, it has all the GNU software-development tools, such as GCC (C and C++ compiler), GNU make, and the GNU debugger. This chapter introduces you to programming, describes the software-development tools, and shows you how to use them. Although I provide examples in the C and C++ programming languages, the focus is not on showing you how to program in those languages but on showing you how to use various software-development tools (such as compilers, make, and debugger).

The chapter concludes with a brief explanation of how the Free Software Foundation's GNU General Public License (GPL) may affect any plans you might have to develop Linux software. You need to know about the GPL because you use GNU tools and GNU libraries to develop software in Linux.

## An Overview of Programming

If you've written computer programs in any programming language, you can start writing programs on your Linux system quickly. If you've never written a computer program, however, you need two basic resources before you begin to write code: a look at the basics of programming and a quick review of computers and their major parts. This section offers an overview of computer programming — just enough to get you going.

### A simplified view of a computer

Before you get a feel for computer programming, you need to understand where computer programs fit in with the overall scheme of computing.

Figure 1-1 shows a simplified view of a computer, highlighting the major parts that are important to a programmer.

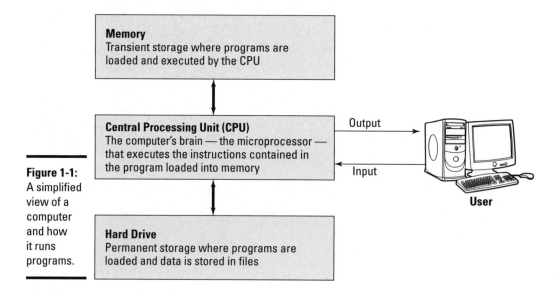

**Figure 1-1:**
A simplified view of a computer and how it runs programs.

At the heart of a computer is the *central processing unit* (CPU) that performs the instructions contained in a computer program. The specific piece of hardware that does the job (which its makers call a *microprocessor* and the rest of us call a *chip*) varies by system: In a Pentium PC, it's a Pentium; in a Sun SPARC workstation, it's a SPARC chip; in an HP UNIX workstation, it's a PA-RISC chip. These microprocessors have different capabilities but the same mission: Tell the computer what to do.

Random Access Memory (RAM), or just *memory,* serves as the storage for computer programs while the CPU executes them. If a program works on some data, that data is also stored in memory. The contents of memory aren't permanent; they go away (never to return) when the computer is shut down or when a program is no longer running.

The *hard drive* (also referred to as the *hard disk* or *disk*) serves as the permanent storage space for computer programs and data. The hard drive is organized into files, which are in turn organized in hierarchical directories and subdirectories (somewhat like organizing paper folders into the drawers in a file cabinet). Each file is essentially a block of storage capable of holding a variety of information. For example, a file may be a human-readable text file — or it may be a collection of computer instructions that makes sense only to the CPU. When you create computer programs, you work a lot with files.

For a programmer, the other two important items are the *input* and the *output* — the way a program gets input from the user and displays output to the user. The user provides input through the keyboard and mouse, and output appears on the monitor. However, a program may also accept input from a file and send output to a file.

## Role of the operating system

The *operating system* is a special collection of computer programs whose primary purpose is to load and run other programs. The operating system also acts as an interface between the software and the hardware. All operating systems include one or more command processors (called *shells* in Linux) that allow users to type commands and perform tasks, such as running a program or printing a file. Most operating systems also include a graphical user interface (such as GNOME and KDE in Linux) that allows the user to perform most tasks by clicking on-screen icons. Linux, Windows (whether the XP or Windows 7 version), and various versions of UNIX are examples of operating systems.

The operating system gives a computer its personality. For example, you can run Windows Vista or Windows XP on a PC. On that same PC, you can also install and run Linux. That means, depending on the operating system installed on it, the selfsame PC could be a Windows 7, Windows XP, or Linux system.

Computer programs are built *on top of* the operating system. That means a computer program must make use of the capabilities that the operating system includes. For example, computer programs read and write files by using the built-in capabilities of the operating system. (And if the operating system can't make coffee, no program can tell it to and still expect positive results.)

Although the details vary, most operating systems support a number of similar concepts. As a programmer, you need to be familiar with the following handful of concepts:

✦ A *process* is a computer program that is currently running in the computer. Most operating systems allow multiple processes to run simultaneously.

✦ A *command processor,* or *shell,* is a special program that allows the user to type commands and perform various tasks, such as run any program, look at a host of files, or print a file. In Windows Vista or Windows XP, you can type commands in a Command Prompt window.

✦ The term *command line* refers to the commands that a user types to the command processor. Usually a command line contains a command and one or more *options* — the command is the first word in the line and the rest are the *options* (specific behaviors for the computer).

✦ *Environment variables* are essentially text strings with names. For example, the PATH environment variable refers to a string that contains the names of directories. Operating systems use environment variables to provide useful information to processes. To see a list of environment variables in a Windows system, type **set** in the Command Prompt window. In Linux, you can type **printenv** to see the environment variables.

## *Basics of computer programming*

A *computer program* is a sequence of instructions for performing a specific task, such as adding two numbers or searching for some text in a file. Consequently, computer programming involves *creating* that list of instructions, telling the computer how to complete a specific task. The exact instructions depend on the programming language that you use. For most programming languages, you have to go through the following steps to create a computer program:

*1.* **Use a text editor to type the sequence of commands from the programming language.**

This sequence of commands accomplishes your task. This human-readable version of the program is called the *source file* or *source code*. You can create the source file with any application (such as a word processor) that can save a document in plain-text form.

Always save your source code as plain text. (The filename depends on the type of programming language.) Word processors can sometimes put extra instructions in their documents that tell the computer to display the text in a particular font or other format. Saving the file as plain text deletes any and all such extra instructions. Trust me, your program is much better off without such stuff.

*2.* **Use a *compiler* program to convert that text file — the source code — from human-readable form into machine-readable *object code*.**

Typically, this step also combines several object code files into a single machine-readable computer program, something that the computer can run.

*3.* **Use a special program called a *debugger* to track down any errors and find which lines in the source file might have caused the errors.**

*4.* **Go back to Step 1 and use the text editor to correct the errors, and repeat the rest of the steps.**

These steps are referred to as the *edit-compile-debug cycle* of programming because most programmers have to repeat this sequence several times before a program works correctly.

In addition to knowing the basic programming steps, you also need to be familiar with the following terms and concepts:

✦ *Variables* are used to store different types of data. You can think of each variable as being a placeholder for data — kind of like a mailbox, with a name and room to store data. The content of the variable is its value.

✦ *Expressions* combine variables by using operators. An expression may add several variables; another may extract a part of a string.

✦ *Statements* perform some action, such as assigning a value to a variable or printing a string.

✦ *Flow-control statements* allow statements to execute in various orders, depending on the value of some expression. Typically, flow-control statements include `for`, `do-while`, `while`, and `if-then-else` statements.

✦ *Functions* (also called *subroutines* or *routines*) allow you to group several statements and give the group a name. This feature allows you to execute the same set of statements by invoking the function that represents those statements. Typically, a programming language provides many predefined functions to perform tasks, such as opening (and reading from) a file.

# Exploring the Software-Development Tools in Linux

Linux includes the following traditional UNIX software-development tools:

✦ **Text editors** such as `vi` and `emacs` for editing the source code. (To find out more about `vi`, see Book II, Chapter 6.)

✦ A **C compiler** for compiling and linking programs written in C — the programming language of choice for writing UNIX applications (though nowadays, many programmers are turning to C++ and Java). Linux includes the GNU C and C++ compilers. Originally, the GNU C Compiler was known as GCC — which now stands for *GNU Compiler Collection*. (See a description at `http://gcc.gnu.org`.)

✦ The **GNU `make` utility** for automating the software *build process* — the process of combining object modules into an executable or a library. (The operating system can load and run an executable; a *library* is a collection of binary code that can be used by executables.)

✦ A **debugger** for debugging programs. Linux includes the GNU debugger gdb.

✦ A **version-control system** to keep track of various revisions of a source file. Linux comes with RCS (Revision Control System) and CVS (Concurrent Versions System). Nowadays, most open source projects use CVS as their version control system, but a recent version control system called Subversion is being developed as a replacement for CVS.

You can install these software-development tools in any Linux distribution:

✦ **Xandros:** Usually, the tools are installed by default.

✦ **Fedora:** Select the Development Tools package during installation.

✦ **Debian:** Type apt-get install gcc and then apt-get install libc6-dev in a terminal window.

✦ **SUSE:** Choose Main Menu⇨System⇨YaST, click Software on the left side of the window, and then click Install and Remove Software. Type gcc in the search field in YaST, select the relevant packages from the search results, and click Accept to install. If you find any missing packages, you can install them in a similar manner.

The next few sections briefly describe how to use these software-development tools to write applications for Linux.

## GNU C and C++ compilers

The most important software-development tool in Linux is GCC — the GNU C and C++ compiler. In fact, GCC can compile three languages: C, C++, and Objective-C (a language that adds object-oriented programming capabilities to C). You use the same gcc command to compile and link both C and C++ source files. The GCC compiler supports ANSI standard C, making it easy to port any ANSI C program to Linux. In addition, if you've ever used a C compiler on other UNIX systems, you should feel right at home with GCC.

### Using GCC

Use the gcc command to invoke GCC. By default, when you use the gcc command on a source file, GCC preprocesses, compiles, and links to create an executable file. However, you can use GCC options to stop this process at an intermediate stage. For example, you might invoke gcc by using the -c option to compile a source file and to generate an object file, but not to perform the link step.

Using GCC to compile and link a few C source files is easy. Suppose you want to compile and link a simple program made up of two source files. To accomplish this use the following program source; the task that is stored in the file `area.c` computes the area of a circle whose radius is specified at the command line:

```
#include <stdio.h>
#include <stdlib.h>
/* Function prototype */
double area_of_circle(double r);
int main(int argc, char **argv)
{
if(argc < 2)
{
printf("Usage: %s radius\n", argv[0]);
exit(1);
}
else
{
double radius = atof(argv[1]);
double area = area_of_circle(radius);
printf("Area of circle with radius %f = %f\n",
radius, area);
}
return 0;
}
```

You need another file that actually computes the area of a circle. Here's the listing for the `circle.c` file, which defines a function that computes the area of a circle:

```
#include <math.h>
#define SQUARE(x) ((x)*(x))
double area_of_circle(double r)
{
return 4.0 * M_PI * SQUARE(r);
}
```

For such a simple program, of course, we could place everything in a single file, but this example was contrived a bit to show you how to handle multiple files.

To compile these two files and to create an executable file named `area`, use this command:

```
gcc -o area area.c circle.c
```

This invocation of GCC uses the `-o` option to specify the name of the executable file. (If you don't specify the name of an output file with the `-o` option, GCC saves the executable code in a file named `a.out`.)

**Book VIII**
**Chapter 1**

**Programming in Linux**

If you have too many source files to compile and link, you can compile the files individually and generate *object files* (that have the .o extension). That way, when you change a source file, you need to compile only that file — you just link the compiled file to all the object files. The following commands show how to separate the compile and link steps for the sample program:

```
gcc -c area.c
gcc -c circle.c
gcc -o area area.o circle.o
```

The first two commands run gcc with the -c option compiling the source files. The third gcc command links the object files into an executable named area.

### Compiling C++ programs

GNU CC is a combined C and C++ compiler, so the gcc command also can compile C++ source files. GCC uses the file extension to determine whether a file is C or C++. C files have a lowercase .c extension whereas C++ files end with .C or .cpp.

Although the gcc command can compile a C++ file, that command doesn't automatically link with various class libraries that C++ programs typically require. Compiling and linking a C++ program by using the g++ command is easy because it runs gcc with appropriate options.

Suppose that you want to compile the following simple C++ program stored in a file named hello.C. (Using an uppercase C extension for C++ source files is customary.)

```
#include <iostream>
int main()
{
using namespace std;
cout << "Hello from Linux!" << endl;
}
```

To compile and link this program into an executable program named hello, use this command:

```
g++ -o hello hello.C
```

The command creates the hello executable, which you can run as follows:

```
./hello
```

The program displays the following output:

```
Hello from Linux!
```

A host of GCC options controls various aspects of compiling C and C++ programs.

### Exploring GCC options

Here's the basic syntax of the gcc command:

```
gcc options filenames
```

Each option starts with a hyphen (–) and usually has a long name, such as -funsigned-char or -finline-functions. Many commonly used options are short, however, such as –c, to compile only, and –g, to generate debugging information (needed to debug the program by using the GNU debugger, gdb).

You can view a summary of all GCC options by typing the following command in a terminal window:

```
man gcc
```

Then you can browse through the commonly used GCC options. Usually, you don't have to provide GCC options explicitly because the default settings are fine for most applications. Table 1-1 lists some of the GCC options you may use.

| Table 1-1 | Common GCC Options |
| --- | --- |
| *Option* | *Meaning* |
| -ansi | Supports only ANSI standard C syntax. (This option disables some GNU C-specific features, such as the __asm__ and __typeof__ keywords.) When used with g++, supports only ISO standard C++. |
| -c | Compiles and generates only the object file. |
| -DMACRO | Defines the macro with the string "1" as its value. |
| -DMACRO=DEFN | Defines the macro as DEFN, where DEFN is some text string. |
| -E | Runs only the C preprocessor. |
| -fallow-single-precision | Performs all math operations in single precision. |
| -fpcc-struct-return | Returns all struct and union values in memory, rather than in registers. (Returning values this way is less efficient, but at least it's compatible with other compilers.) |

*(continued)*

### Table 1-1 *(continued)*

| Option | Meaning |
|---|---|
| `-fPIC` | Generates position-independent code (PIC) suitable for use in a shared library. |
| `-freg-struct-return` | When possible, returns `struct` and `union` values registers. |
| `-g` | Generates debugging information. (The GNU debugger can use this information.) |
| `-I DIRECTORY` | Searches the specified directory for files that you include by using the `#include` preprocessor directive. |
| `-L DIRECTORY` | Searches the specified directory for libraries. |
| `-l LIBRARY` | Searches the specified library when linking. |
| `-mcpu=cputype` | Optimizes code for a specific processor. (`cputype` can take many different values — some common ones are `i386`, `i486`, `i586`, `i686`, `pentium`, `pentiumpro`, `pentium2`, `pentium3`, `pentium4`.) |
| `-o FILE` | Generates the specified output file (used to designate the name of an executable file). |
| `-O0` (two zeros) | Does not optimize. |
| `-O or -O1` (letter O) | Optimizes the generated code. |
| `-O2` (letter O) | Optimizes even more. |
| `-O3` (letter O) | Performs optimizations beyond those done for `-O2`. |
| `-Os` (letter O) | Optimizes for size (to reduce the total amount of code). |
| `-pedantic` | Generates errors if any non-ANSI standard extensions are used. |
| `-pg` | Adds extra code to the program so that, when run, this program generates information that the `gprof` program can use to display timing details for various parts of the program. |
| `-shared` | Generates a shared object file (typically used to create a shared library). |
| `-UMACRO` | Undefines the specified macros |
| `-v` | Displays the GCC version number. |
| `-w` | Doesn't generate warning messages. |
| `-Wl, OPTION` | Passes the `OPTION` string (containing multiple comma-separated options) to the linker. To create a shared library named `libXXX.so.1`, for example, use the following flag: `-Wl,-soname,libXXX.so.1`. |

## The GNU make utility

When an application is made up of more than a few source files, compiling and linking the files by manually typing the `gcc` command can get tiresome. Also, you don't want to compile every file whenever you change something in a single source file. These situations are where the GNU `make` utility comes to your rescue.

The `make` utility works by reading and interpreting a *makefile* — a text file that describes which files are required to build a particular program as well as how to compile and link the files to build the program. Whenever you change one or more files, `make` determines which files to recompile — and it issues the appropriate commands for compiling those files and rebuilding the program.

### Makefile names

By default, GNU `make` looks for a `makefile` that has one of the following names, in the order shown:

✦ `GNUmakefile`

✦ `makefile`

✦ `Makefile`

In UNIX systems, using `Makefile` as the name of the `makefile` is customary because it appears near the beginning of directory listings, where uppercase names appear before lowercase names.

When you download software from the Internet, you usually find a `Makefile`, together with the source files. To build the software, you only have to type `make` at the shell prompt and `make` takes care of all the steps necessary to build the software.

If your `makefile` doesn't have a standard name (such as `Makefile`), you have to use the `-f` option with `make` to specify the `makefile` name. If your `makefile` is called `myprogram.mak`, for example, you have to run `make` using the following command line:

```
make -f myprogram.mak
```

### The makefile

For a program made up of several source and header files, the `makefile` specifies the following:

✦ The items that `make` creates — usually the object files and the executable. Using the term *target* to refer to any item that `make` has to create is common.

✦ The files or other actions required to create the target.

✦ Which commands to execute to create each target.

Suppose that you have a C++ source file named form.C that contains the following preprocessor directive:

```
#include "form.h" // Include header file
```

The object file form.o clearly depends on the source file form.C and the header file form.h. In addition to these dependencies, you must specify how make converts the form.C file to the object file form.o. Suppose that you want make to invoke g++ (because the source file is in C++) with these options:

✦ -c (compile only)

✦ -g (generate debugging information)

✦ -O2 (optimize some)

In the makefile, you can express these options with the following rule:

```
# This a comment in the makefile
# The following lines indicate how form.o depends
# on form.C and form.h and how to create form.o.
form.o: form.C form.h
g++ -c -g -O2 form.C
```

In this example, the first noncomment line shows form.o as the target and form.C and form.h as the dependent files.

The line following the dependency indicates how to build the target from its dependents. This line must start with a tab. Otherwise, the make command exits with an error message, and you're left scratching your head because when you look at the makefile in a text editor, you can't tell the difference between a tab and a space. Now that you know the secret, the fix is to replace the spaces at the beginning of the offending line with a single tab.

The benefit of using make is that it prevents unnecessary compilations. After all, you can run g++ (or gcc) from a shell script to compile and link all the files that make up your application, but the shell script compiles everything, even if the compilations are unnecessary. GNU make, on the other hand, builds a target only if one or more of its dependents have changed since the last time the target was built. make verifies this change by examining the time of the last modification of the target and the dependents.

make treats the target as the name of a goal to be achieved; the target doesn't have to be a file. You can have a rule such as this one:

```
clean:
rm -f *.o
```

This rule specifies an abstract target named `clean` that doesn't depend on anything. This dependency statement says that to create the target `clean`, GNU `make` invokes the command `rm -f *.o`, which deletes all files that have the `.o` extension (namely, the object files). Thus, the effect of creating the target named `clean` is to delete the object files.

### Variables (or macros)

In addition to the basic capability of building targets from dependents, GNU `make` includes many features that make it easy for you to express the dependencies and rules for building a target from its dependents. If you need to compile a large number of C++ files by using GCC with the same options, for example, typing the options for each file is tedious. You can avoid this repetitive task by defining a variable or macro in `make` as follows:

```
# Define macros for name of compiler
CXX= g++
# Define a macro for the GCC flags
CXXFLAGS= -O2 -g -mcpu=i686
# A rule for building an object file
form.o: form.C form.h
$(CXX) -c $(CXXFLAGS) form.C
```

In this example, `CXX` and `CXXFLAGS` are `make` variables. (GNU `make` prefers to call them *variables,* but most UNIX `make` utilities call them *macros.*)

To use a variable anywhere in the `makefile`, start with a dollar sign (`$`) followed by the variable within parentheses. GNU `make` replaces all occurrences of a variable with its definition; thus, it replaces all occurrences of `$(CXXFLAGS)` with the string `-O2 -g -mcpu=i686`.

GNU `make` has several predefined variables that have special meanings. Table 1-2 lists these variables. In addition to the variables listed in Table 1-2, GNU `make` considers all environment variables (such as `PATH` and `HOME`) to be predefined variables as well.

| Table 1-2 | Some Predefined Variables in GNU make |
|---|---|
| *Variable* | *Meaning* |
| `$%` | Member name for targets that are archives. If the target is `libDisp.a(image.o)`, for example, `$%` is `image.o`. |
| `$*` | Name of the target file without the extension. |
| `$+` | Names of all dependent files with duplicate dependencies, listed in their order of occurrence. |
| `$<` | The name of the first dependent file. |

*(continued)*

### Table 1-2 *(continued)*

| Variable | Meaning |
|---|---|
| $? | Names of all dependent files (with spaces between the names) that are newer than the target. |
| $@ | Complete name of the target. If the target is libDisp.a image.o), for example, $@ is libDisp.a. |
| $^ | Names of all dependent files, with spaces between the names. Duplicates are removed from the dependent filenames. |
| AR | Name of the archive-maintaining program (default value: ar). |
| ARFLAGS | Flags for the archive-maintaining program (default value: rv). |
| AS | Name of the assembler program that converts the assembly language to object code (default value: as). |
| ASFLAGS | Flags for the assembler. |
| CC | Name of the C compiler (default value: cc). |
| CFLAGS | Flags that are passed to the C compiler. |
| CO | Name of the program that extracts a file from RCS (the default value is co). |
| COFLAGS | Flags for the RCS co program. |
| CPP | Name of the C preprocessor (default value: $(CC) -E). |
| CPPFLAGS | Flags for the C preprocessor. |
| CXX | Name of the C++ compiler (default value: g++). |
| CXXFLAGS | Flags that are passed to the C++ compiler. |
| FC | Name of the FORTRAN compiler (default value: f77). |
| FFLAGS | Flags for the FORTRAN compiler. |
| LDFLAGS | Flags for the compiler when it's supposed to invoke the linker ld. |
| RM | Name of the command to delete a file (Default value: rm -f). |

### A sample makefile

You can write a makefile easily if you use the predefined variables of GNU make and its built-in rules. Consider, for example, a makefile that creates the executable xdraw from three C source files (xdraw.c, xviewobj.c, and shapes.c) and two header files (xdraw.h and shapes.h). Assume that each source file includes one of the header files. Given these facts, here is what a sample makefile may look like:

```
############################################################
# Sample makefile
# Comments start with '#'
#
############################################################
# Use standard variables to define compile and link flags
CFLAGS= -g -O2
# Define the target "all"
all: xdraw
OBJS=xdraw.o xviewobj.o shapes.o
xdraw: $(OBJS)
# Object files
xdraw.o: Makefile xdraw.c xdraw.h
xviewobj.o: Makefile xviewobj.c xdraw.h
shapes.o: Makefile shapes.c shapes.h
```

This `makefile` relies on GNU `make`'s implicit rules. The conversion of `.c` files to `.o` files uses the built-in rule. Defining the variable `CFLAGS` passes the flags to the C compiler.

The target named `all` is defined as the first target for a reason — if you run GNU `make` without specifying any targets in the command line (see the `make` syntax described in the following section), the command builds the first target it finds in the `makefile`. By defining the first target `all` as `xdraw`, you can ensure that `make` builds this executable file, even if you don't explicitly specify it as a target. UNIX programmers traditionally use `all` as the name of the first target, but the target's name is immaterial; what matters is that it's the first target in the `makefile`.

### How to run make

Typically, you run `make` by simply typing the following command at the shell prompt:

```
make
```

When run this way, GNU `make` looks for a file named `GNUmakefile`, `makefile`, or `Makefile` — in that order. If `make` finds one of these makefiles, it builds the first target specified in that `makefile`. However, if `make` doesn't find an appropriate `makefile`, it displays the following error message and exits:

```
make: *** No targets specified and no makefile found. Stop.
```

If your `makefile` happens to have a different name from the default names, you have to use the `-f` option to specify the `makefile`. The syntax of the `make` command with this option is

```
make -f filename
```

where *filename* is the name of the `makefile`.

Even when you have a `makefile` with a default name such as `Makefile`, you may want to build a specific target out of several targets defined in the `makefile`. In that case, you have to use the following syntax when you run `make`:

```
make target
```

For example, if the `makefile` contains the target named `clean`, you can build that target with this command:

```
make clean
```

Another special syntax overrides the value of a `make` variable. For example, GNU `make` uses the `CFLAGS` variable to hold the flags used when compiling C files. You can override the value of this variable when you invoke `make`. Here's an example of how you can define `CFLAGS` as the option `-g -O2`:

```
make CFLAGS="-g -O2"
```

In addition to these options, GNU `make` accepts several other command-line options. Table 1-3 lists the GNU `make` options.

| Table 1-3 | Options for GNU make |
|---|---|
| *Option* | *Meaning* |
| `-b` | Ignores the variable given but accepts that variable for compatibility with other versions of `make`. |
| `-C DIR` | Changes to the specified directory before reading the `makefile`. |
| `-d` | Prints debugging information. |
| `-e` | Allows environment variables to override definitions of similarly named variables in the `makefile`. |
| `-f FILE` | Reads `FILE` as the `makefile`. |
| `-h` | Displays the list of `make` options. |
| `-i` | Ignores all errors in commands executed when building a target. |
| `-I DIR` | Searches the specified directory for included `makefiles`. (The capability to include a file in a `makefile` is unique to GNU `make`.) |
| `-j NUM` | Specifies the number of commands that the `make` command can run simultaneously. |
| `-k` | Continues to build unrelated targets, even if an error occurs when building one of the targets. |
| `-l LOAD` | Doesn't start a new job if load average is at least `LOAD` (a floating-point number). |

| Option | Meaning |
|--------|---------|
| -m | Ignores the variable given but accepts that variable for compatibility with other versions of make. |
| -n | Prints the commands to execute but does not execute them. |
| -o *FILE* | Does not rebuild the file named *FILE*, even if it is older than its dependents. |
| -p | Displays the make database of variables and implicit rules. |
| -q | Does not run anything, but returns 0 (zero) if all targets are up to date, 1 if anything needs updating, or 2 if an error occurs. |
| -r | Gets rid of all built-in rules. |
| -R | Gets rid of all built-in variables and rules. |
| -s | Works silently (without displaying the commands as they execute). |
| -t | Changes the timestamp of the files. |
| -v | Displays the version number of make and a copyright notice. |
| -w | Displays the name of the working directory before and after processing the makefile. |
| -W FILE | Assumes that the specified file has been modified (used with -n to see what happens if you modify that file). |

## The GNU debugger

Although make automates the process of building a program, that part of programming is the least of your worries when a program doesn't work correctly or when a program suddenly quits with an error message. You need a debugger to find the cause of program errors. Linux includes gdb — the versatile GNU debugger with a command-line interface.

Like any debugger, gdb lets you perform typical debugging tasks, such as the following:

✦ Set a breakpoint so that the program stops at a specified line

✦ Watch the values of variables in the program

✦ Step through the program one line at a time

✦ Change variables in an attempt to correct errors

The gdb debugger can debug C and C++ programs.

### Preparing to debug a program

If you want to debug a program by using gdb, you have to ensure that the compiler generates and places debugging information in the executable. The debugging information contains the names of variables in your program and the mapping of addresses in the executable file to lines of code in the source file. gdb needs this information to perform its functions, such as stopping after executing a specified line of source code.

To make sure that the executable is properly prepared for debugging, use the -g option with GCC. You can do this task by defining the variable CFLAGS in the makefile as

```
CFLAGS= -g
```

### Running gdb

The most common way to debug a program is to run gdb by using the following command:

```
gdb progname
```

progname is the name of the program's executable file. After progname runs, gdb displays the following message and prompts you for a command:

```
GNU gdb 6.3
Copyright 2004 Free Software Foundation, Inc.
GDB is free software, covered by the GNU General Public License, and you are
welcome to change it and/or distribute copies of it under certain conditions.
Type "show copying" to see the conditions.
There is absolutely no warranty for GDB. Type "show warranty" for details.
This GDB was configured as "i586-suse-linux".
(gdb)
```

You can type gdb commands at the (gdb) prompt. One useful command, help, displays a list of commands, as the next listing shows:

```
(gdb) help
List of classes of commands:
aliases -- Aliases of other commands
breakpoints -- Making program stop at certain points
data -- Examining data
files -- Specifying and examining files
internals -- Maintenance commands
obscure -- Obscure features
running -- Running the program
stack -- Examining the stack
status -- Status inquiries
support -- Support facilities
tracepoints -- Tracing of program execution without stopping the program
user-defined -- User-defined commands
Type "help" followed by a class name for a list of commands in that class.
Type "help" followed by command name for full documentation.
Command name abbreviations are allowed if unambiguous.
(gdb)
```

To quit gdb, type q and then press Enter.

gdb has a large number of commands, but you need only a few to find the cause of an error quickly. Table 1-4 lists the commonly used gdb commands.

| Table 1-4 | Common gdb Commands |
|---|---|
| *This Command* | *Does the Following* |
| break *NUM* | Sets a breakpoint at the specified line number, *NUM*. (The debugger stops at breakpoints.) |
| bt | Displays a trace of all stack frames. (This command shows you the sequence of function calls so far.) |
| clear *FILENAME: NUM* | Deletes the breakpoint at a specific line number, *NUM*, in the source file *FILENAME*. For example, clear xdraw.c:8 clears the breakpoint at line 8 of file xdraw.c. |
| continue | Continues running the program being debugged. (Use this command after the program stops due to a signal or breakpoint.) |
| display *EXPR* | Displays the value of an expression, *EXPR* (consisting of variables defined in the program) each time the program stops. |
| file *FILE* | Loads the specified executable file, *FILE*, for debugging. |
| help *NAME* | Displays help on the command named *NAME*. |
| info break | Displays a list of current breakpoints, including information on how many times each breakpoint is reached. |
| info files | Displays detailed information about the file being debugged. |
| info func | Displays all function names. |
| info local | Displays information about local variables of the current function. |
| info prog | Displays the execution status of the program being debugged. |

*(continued)*

**Table 1-4** *(continued)*

| | |
|---|---|
| info var | Displays all global and static variable names. |
| kill | Ends the program you're debugging. |
| list | Lists a section of the source code. |
| make | Runs the make utility to rebuild the executable without leaving gdb. |
| next | Advances one line of source code in the current function without stepping into other functions. |
| print EXPR | Shows the value of the expression EXPR. |
| quit | Quits gdb. |
| run | Starts running the executable that is currently running. |
| set variable VAR=VALUE | Sets the value of the variable VAR to VALUE. |
| shell CMD | Executes the UNIX command CMD, without leaving gdb. |
| step | Advances one line in the current function, stepping into other functions, if any. |
| watch VAR | Shows the value of the variable named VAR whenever the value changes. |
| where | Displays the call sequence. Use this command to locate where your program died. |
| x/F ADDR | Examines the contents of the memory location at address ADDR in the format specified by the letter F, which can be o (octal), x (hex), d (decimal), u (unsigned decimal), t (binary), f (float), a (address), i (instruction), c (char), or s (string). You can append a letter indicating the size of data type to the format letter. Size letters are b (byte), h (halfword, 2 bytes), w (word, 4 bytes), and g (giant, 8 bytes). Typically, ADDR is the name of a variable or pointer. |

## Finding bugs by using gdb

To understand how you can find bugs by using gdb, you need to see an example. The procedure is easiest to show with a simple example, so the following, dbgtst.c, is a contrived program that contains a typical bug.

```
#include <stdio.h>
static char buf[256];
void read_input(char *s);
int main(void)
{
char *input = NULL; /* Just a pointer, no storage for string */
read_input(input);
/* Process command. */
printf("You typed: %s\n", input);
/* . . . */
return 0;
}
void read_input(char *s)
{
printf("Command: ");
gets(s);
}
```

This program's main function calls the read_input function to get a line of input from the user. The read_input function expects a character array in which it returns what the user types. In this example, however, main calls read_input with an uninitialized pointer — that's the bug in this simple program.

Build the program by using gcc with the -g option:

```
gcc -g -o dbgtst dbgtst.c
```

Ignore the warning message about the gets function being dangerous; I'm trying to use the shortcoming of that function to show how you can use gdb to track down errors.

To see the problem with this program, run it and type test at the Command: prompt:

```
./dbgtst
Command: test
Segmentation fault
```

The program dies after displaying the Segmentation fault message. For such a small program as this one, you can probably find the cause by examining the source code. In a real-world application, however, you may not immediately know what causes the error. That's when you have to use gdb to find the cause of the problem.

To use gdb to locate a bug, follow these steps:

## *1.* Load the program under gdb.

For example, type gdb dbgtst to load a program named dbgtst in gdb.

**2. Start executing the program under gdb by typing the** run **command. When the program prompts for input, type some input text.**

The program fails as it did previously. Here's what happens with the dbgtst program:

```
(gdb) run
Starting program: /home/edulaney/swdev/dbgtst
Command: test
Program received signal SIGSEGV, Segmentation fault.
0x400802b6 in gets () from /lib/tls/libc.so.6
(gdb)
```

**3. Use the where command to determine where the program died.**

For the dbgtst program, this command yields this output:

```
(gdb) where
#0 0x400802b6 in gets () from /lib/tls/libc.so.6
#1 0x08048474 in read_input (s=0x0) at dbgtst.c:16
#2 0x08048436 in main () at dbgtst.c:7
(gdb)
```

The output shows the sequence of function calls. Function call #0 — the most recent one — is to the gets C library function. The gets call originates in the read_input function (at line 16 of the file dbgtst.c), which in turn is called from the main function at line 7 of the dbgtst.c file.

**4. Use the list command to inspect the lines of suspect source code.**

In dbgtst, you may start with line 16 of dbgtst.c file, as follows:

```
(gdb) list dbgtst.c:16
11 return 0;
12 }
13 void read_input(char *s)
14 {
15 printf("Command: ");
16 gets(s);
17 }
18
(gdb)
```

After looking at this listing, you can tell that the problem may be the way read_input is called. Then you list the lines around line 7 in dbgtst.c (where the read_input call originates):

```
(gdb) list dbgtst.c:7
2 static char buf[256];
3 void read_input(char *s);
4 int main(void)
5 {
6 char *input = NULL; /* Just a pointer, no storage for string */
7 read_input(input);
8 /* Process command. */
9 printf("You typed: %s\n", input);
10 /* . . . */
11 return 0;
(gdb)
```

At this point, you can narrow the problem to the variable named `input`. That variable is an array, not a `NULL` (which means zero) pointer.

### Fixing bugs in gdb

Sometimes you can fix a bug directly in `gdb`. For the example program in the preceding section, you can try this fix immediately after the program dies after displaying an error message. An extra buffer named `buf` is defined in the `dbgtst` program, as follows:

```
static char buf[256];
```

We can fix the problem of the uninitialized pointer by setting the variable input to `buf`. The following session with `gdb` corrects the problem of the uninitialized pointer. (This example picks up immediately after the program runs and dies, due to the segmentation fault.)

```
(gdb) file dbgtst
A program is being debugged already. Kill it? (y or n) y
Load new symbol table from "/home/edulaney/sw/dbgtst"? (y or n) y
Reading symbols from /home/edulaney/sw/dbgtst . . . done.
(gdb) list
1 #include <stdio.h>
2 static char buf[256];
3 void read_input(char *s);
4 int main(void)
5 {
6 char *input = NULL; /* Just a pointer, no storage for string */
7 read_input(input);
8 /* Process command. */
9 printf("You typed: %s\n", input);
10 /* . . . */
(gdb) break 7
Breakpoint 2 at 0x804842b: file dbgtst.c, line 7.
(gdb) run
Starting program: /home/edulaney/sw/dbgtst
Breakpoint 1, main () at dbgtst.c:7
7 read_input(input);
(gdb) set var input=buf
(gdb) cont
Continuing.
Command: test
You typed: test
Program exited normally.
(gdb)q
```

As the preceding listing shows, if the program is stopped just before read_ input is called and the variable named input is set to `buf` (which is a valid array of characters), the rest of the program runs fine.

After finding a fix that works in `gdb`, you can make the necessary changes to the source files and make the fix permanent.

**Book VIII Chapter 1**

**Programming in Linux**

# Understanding the Implications of GNU Licenses

You have to pay a price for the bounty of Linux. To protect its developers and users, Linux is distributed under the GNU GPL (General Public License), which stipulates the distribution of the source code.

The GPL doesn't mean, however, that you can't write commercial software for Linux that you want to distribute (either for free or for a price) in binary form only. You can follow all the rules and still sell your Linux applications in binary form.

When writing applications for Linux, be aware of two licenses:

+ The **GNU General Public License** (GPL), which governs many Linux programs, including the Linux kernel and GCC

+ The **GNU Library General Public License** (LGPL), which covers many Linux libraries

The following sections provide an overview of these licenses and some suggestions on how to meet their requirements. Don't take anything in this book as legal advice. Instead, you should read the full text for these licenses in the text files on your Linux system, and then show these licenses to your legal counsel for a full interpretation and an assessment of applicability to your business.

## The GNU General Public License

The text of the GNU General Public License (GPL) is in a file named COPYING in various directories in your Linux system. For example, type the following command to find a copy of that file in your Linux system:

```
find /usr -name "COPYING" -print
```

After you find the file, you can change to that directory and type more COPYING to read the GPL. If you can't find the COPYING file, turn to the back of this book to read the GPL.

The GPL has nothing to do with whether you charge for the software or distribute it for free; its thrust is to keep the software free for all users. GPL requires that the software is distributed in source-code form and by stipulating that any user can copy and distribute the software in source-code form to anyone else. In addition, everyone is reminded that the software comes with absolutely no warranty.

The software that the GPL covers isn't in the public domain. Software covered by GPL is always copyrighted, and the GPL spells out the restrictions on the software's copying and distribution. From a user's point of view, of course, GPL's restrictions aren't really restrictions; the restrictions are benefits because the user is guaranteed access to the source code.

If your application uses parts of any software the GPL covers, your application is considered a *derived work,* which means that your application is also covered by the GPL and you must distribute the source code to your application.

Although the GPL covers the Linux kernel, the GPL doesn't cover your applications that use the kernel services through system calls. Those applications are considered normal use of the kernel.

If you plan to distribute your application in binary form (as most commercial software is distributed), you must make sure that your application doesn't use any parts of any software the GPL covers. Your application may end up using parts of other software when it calls functions in a library. Most libraries, however, are covered by a different GNU license, which is described in the next section.

You have to watch out for only a few library and utility programs the GPL covers. The GNU dbm (gdbm) database library is one of the prominent libraries GPL covers. The GNU bison parser-generator tool is another utility the GPL covers. If you allow bison to generate code, the GPL covers that code.

Other alternatives for the GNU dbm and GNU bison aren't covered by GPL. For a database library, you can use the Berkeley database library db in place of gdbm. For a parser-generator, you may use yacc instead of bison.

## The GNU Lesser General Public License

The text of the GNU Lesser General Public License (LGPL) is in a file named COPYING.LIB. If you have the kernel source installed, a copy of COPYING.LIB file is in one of the source directories. To locate a copy of the COPYING.LIB file on your Linux system, type the following command in a terminal window:

```
find /usr -name "COPYING*" -print
```

This command lists all occurrences of COPYING and COPYING.LIB in your system. The COPYING file contains the GPL, whereas COPYING.LIB has the LGPL.

**Book VIII
Chapter 1**

**Programming
in Linux**

The LGPL is intended to allow use of libraries in your applications, even if you don't distribute source code for your application. The LGPL stipulates, however, that users must have access to the source code of the library you use and that users can make use of modified versions of those libraries.

The LGPL covers most Linux libraries, including the C library (`libc.a`). Thus, when you build your application on Linux by using the GCC compiler, your application links with code from one or more libraries that the LGPL covers. If you want to distribute your application in only binary form, you need to pay attention to LGPL.

One way to meet the intent of the LGPL is to provide the object code for your application and a `makefile` that relinks your object files with any updated Linux libraries the LGPL covers.

A better way to satisfy the LGPL is to use *dynamic linking,* in which your application and the library are separate entities, even though your application calls functions in the library when it runs. With dynamic linking, users immediately get the benefit of any updates to the libraries without ever having to relink the application.

# Chapter 2: Introductory Shell Scripting

## In This Chapter

✓ Trying some simple shell scripts

✓ Discovering the basics of shell scripting

✓ Exploring bash's built-in commands

Linux gives you many small and specialized commands, along with the plumbing necessary to connect these commands. Take *plumbing* to mean the way in which one command's output can be used as a second command's input. bash (short for Bourne-Again Shell) — the default shell in most Linux systems — provides this plumbing in the form of I/O redirection and pipes. bash also includes features such as the if statement that you can use to run commands only when a specific condition is true, and the for statement that repeats commands a specified number of times. You can use these features of bash when writing programs called *shell scripts* — task-oriented collections of shell commands stored in a file.

This chapter shows you how to write simple shell scripts, which are used to automate various tasks. For example, when your Linux system boots, many shell scripts stored in various subdirectories in the /etc directory (for example, /etc/init.d) perform many initialization tasks.

## Trying Out Simple Shell Scripts

If you're not a programmer, you may feel apprehensive about programming. But shell *scripting* (or programming) can be as simple as storing a few commands in a file. In fact, you can have a useful shell program that has a single command.

Shell scripts are popular among system administrators. If you are a system administrator, you can build a collection of custom shell scripts that help you automate tasks you perform often. If a hard drive seems to be getting full, for example, you may want to find all files that exceed some size (say, 1MB) and that have not been accessed in the past 30 days. In addition, you may want to send an e-mail message to all users who have large files, requesting that they archive and clean up those files. You can perform all these tasks with a shell script. You might start with the following find command to identify large files:

```
find / -type f -atime +30 -size +1000k -exec ls -l {} \; > /tmp/largefiles
```

This command creates a file named /tmp/largefiles, which contains detailed information about old files taking up too much space. After you get a list of the files, you can use a few other Linux commands — such as sort, cut, and sed — to prepare and send mail messages to users who have large files to clean up. Instead of typing all these commands manually, place them in a file and create a shell script. That, in a nutshell, is the essence of shell scripts — to gather shell commands in a file so that you can easily perform repetitive system administration tasks.

bash scripts, just like most Linux commands, accept command-line options. Inside the script, you can refer to the options as $1, $2, and so on. The special name $0 refers to the name of the script itself.

Here's a typical bash script that accepts arguments:

```
#!/bin/sh
echo "This script's name is: $0"
echo Argument 1: $1
echo Argument 2: $2
```

The first line runs the /bin/sh program, which subsequently processes the rest of the lines in the script. The name /bin/sh traditionally refers to the Bourne shell — the first UNIX shell. In most Linux systems, /bin/sh is a symbolic link to /bin/bash, which is the executable program for bash.

Save this simple script in a file named simple and make that file executable with the following command:

```
chmod +x simple
```

Now run the script as follows:

```
./simple
```

It displays the following output:

```
This script's name is: ./simple
Argument 1:
Argument 2:
```

The first line shows the script's name. Because you have run the script without arguments, the script displays no values for the arguments.

Now try running the script with a few arguments, like this:

```
./simple "This is one argument" second-argument third
```

This time the script displays more output:

```
This script's name is: ./simple
Argument 1: This is one argument
Argument 2: second-argument
```

As the output shows, the shell treats the entire string within the double quotation marks as a single argument. Otherwise, the shell uses spaces as separators between arguments on the command line.

This sample script ignores the third argument because the script is designed to print only the first two arguments.

# Exploring the Basics of Shell Scripting

Like any programming language, the bash shell supports the following features:

+ Variables that store values, including special built-in variables for accessing command-line arguments passed to a shell script and other special values.

+ The capability to evaluate expressions.

+ Control structures that enable you to loop over several shell commands or to execute some commands conditionally.

+ The capability to define functions that can be called in many places within a script. bash also includes many built-in commands that you can use in any script.

The next few sections illustrate some of these programming features through simple examples. (It is assumed that you're already running bash, in which case, you can try the examples by typing them at the shell prompt in a terminal window. Otherwise, all you have to do is open a terminal window, and bash runs and displays its prompt in that window.)

## Storing stuff

You define variables in bash just as you define environment variables. Thus, you may define a variable as follows:

```
count=12 # note no embedded spaces allowed
```

To use a variable's value, prefix the variable's name with a dollar sign ($). For example, $PATH is the value of the variable PATH. (This variable is the famous PATH environment variable that lists all the directories that bash searches when trying to locate an executable file.) To display the value of the variable count, use the following command:

```
echo $count
```

bash has some special variables for accessing command-line arguments. In a shell script, $0 refers to the name of the shell script. The variables $1, $2, and so on refer to the command-line arguments. The variable $* stores all the command-line arguments as a single variable, and $? contains the exit status of the last command the shell executes.

From a bash script, you can prompt the user for input and use the read command to read the input into a variable. Here is an example:

```
echo -n "Enter value: "
read value
echo "You entered: $value"
```

When this script runs, the read value command causes bash to read whatever you type at the keyboard and store your input in the variable called value.

*Note:* The -n option prevents the echo command from automatically adding a new line at the end of the string that it displays.

## Calling shell functions

You can group a number of shell commands that you use consistently into a *function* and assign it a name. Later, you can execute that group of commands by using the single name assigned to the function. Here is a simple script that illustrates the syntax of shell functions:

```
#!/bin/sh
hello() {
echo -n "Hello, "
echo $1 $2
}
hello Jane Doe
```

When you run this script, it displays the following output:

```
Hello, Jane Doe
```

This script defines a shell function named `hello`. The function expects two arguments. In the body of the function, these arguments are referenced by `$1` and `$2`. The function definition begins with `hello()` — the name of the function, followed by parentheses. The body of the function is enclosed in curly braces — `{ . . . }`. In this case, the body uses the `echo` command to display a line of text.

The last line of the example shows how a shell function is called with arguments. In this case, the `hello` function is called with two arguments: `Jane` and `Doe`. The `hello` function takes these two arguments and prints a line that says `Hello, Jane Doe.`

## Controlling the flow

In `bash` scripts, you can control the flow of execution — the order in which the commands are executed — by using special commands such as `if`, `case`, `for`, and `while`. These control statements use the exit status of a command to decide what to do next. When any command executes, it returns an exit status — a numeric value that indicates whether or not the command has succeeded. By convention, an exit status of zero means the command has succeeded. (Yes, you read it right: Zero indicates success!) A nonzero exit status indicates that something has gone wrong with the command.

For example, suppose that you want to make a backup copy of a file before editing it with the `vi` editor. More importantly, you want to avoid editing the file if a backup can't be made. Here's a `bash` script that takes care of this task:

```
#!/bin/sh
if cp "$1" "#$1"
then
vi "$1"
else
echo "Failed to create backup copy"
fi
```

This script illustrates the syntax of the `if-then-else` structure and shows how the exit status of the `cp` command is used by the `if` command to determine the next action. If `cp` returns zero, the script uses `vi` to edit the file; otherwise, the script displays an error message and exits. By the way, the script saves the backup in a file whose name is the same as that of the original, except for a hash mark (#) added at the beginning of the filename.

TIP

Don't forget the final `fi` that terminates the `if` command. Forgetting `fi` is a common source of errors in `bash` scripts.

You can use the `test` command to evaluate any expression and to use the expression's value as the exit status of the command. Suppose that you want a script that edits a file only if it already exists. Using `test`, you can write such a script as follows:

```
#!/bin/sh
if test -f "$1"
then
vi "$1"
else
echo "No such file"
fi
```

A shorter form of the `test` command is to place the expression in square brackets ([ . . . ]). Using this shorthand notation, you can rewrite the preceding script like this:

```
#!/bin/sh
if [ -f "$1" ]
then
vi "$1"
else
echo "No such file"
fi
```

*Note:* You must have spaces around the two square brackets.

Another common control structure is the `for` loop. The following script adds the numbers 1 through 10:

```
#!/bin/sh
sum=0
for i in 1 2 3 4 5 6 7 8 9 10
do
sum=`expr $sum + $i`
done
echo "Sum = $sum"
```

This example also illustrates the use of the `expr` command to evaluate an expression.

The `case` statement is used to execute a group of commands based on the value of a variable. For example, consider the following script:

```
#!/bin/sh
echo -n "What should I do -- (Y)es/(N)o/(C)ontinue? [Y] "
read answer
case $answer in
y|Y|"")
echo "YES"
;;
c|C)
echo "CONTINUE"
;;
n|N)
echo "NO"
;;
*)
echo "UNKNOWN"
;;
esac
```

Save this code in a file named `confirm` and type `chmod +x confirm` to make it executable. Then try it out like this:

```
./confirm
```

When the script prompts you, type one of the characters y, n, or c and press Enter. The script displays YES, NO, or CONTINUE, respectively. For example, here's what happens when you type **c** (and then press Enter):

```
What should I do -- (Y)es/(N)o/(C)ontinue? [Y] c
CONTINUE
```

The script displays a prompt and reads the input you type. Your input is stored in a variable named `answer`. Then the `case` statement executes a block of code based on the value of the `answer` variable. For example, when you type c, the following block of commands executes:

```
c|C)
echo "CONTINUE"
;;
```

The `echo` command causes the script to display CONTINUE.

From this example, you can see that the general syntax of the case command is as follows:

```
case $variable in
value1 | value2)
command1
command2
. . . other commands . . .
;;
value3)
command3
command4
. . . other commands . . .
;;
esac
```

Essentially, the case command begins with the word case and ends with esac. Separate blocks of code are enclosed between the values of the variable, followed by a closing parenthesis and terminated by a pair of semicolons (;;).

## Exploring bash's built-in commands

bash has more than 50 built-in commands, including common commands such as cd and pwd, as well as many others that are used infrequently. You can use these built-in commands in any bash script or at the shell prompt. Table 2-1 describes most of the bash built-in commands and their arguments. After looking through this information, type help *command* to read more about a specific built-in command. For example, to find out more about the built-in command test, type the following:

```
help test
```

Doing so displays the following information:

```
test: test [expr]
Exits with a status of 0 (true) or 1 (false) depending on
the evaluation of EXPR. Expressions may be unary or binary. Unary
expressions are often used to examine the status of a file. There
are string operators as well, and numeric comparison operators.
File operators:
-a FILE True if file exists.
-b FILE True if file is block special.
-c FILE True if file is character special.
-d FILE True if file is a directory.
-e FILE True if file exists.
-f FILE True if file exists and is a regular file.
-g FILE True if file is set-group-id.
-h FILE True if file is a symbolic link.
```

```
-L FILE True if file is a symbolic link.
-k FILE True if file has its 'sticky' bit set.
-p FILE True if file is a named pipe.
-r FILE True if file is readable by you.
-s FILE True if file exists and is not empty.
-S FILE True if file is a socket.
-t FD True if FD is opened on a terminal.
-u FILE True if the file is set-user-id.
-w FILE True if the file is writable by you.
-x FILE True if the file is executable by you.
-O FILE True if the file is effectively owned by you.
-G FILE True if the file is effectively owned by your group.
( . . . Lines deleted . . . )
```

Where necessary, the online help from the `help` command includes a considerable amount of detail.

### Table 2-1    Summary of Built-in Commands in bash Shell

| This Function | Does the Following |
|---|---|
| `. filename [arguments]` | Reads and executes commands from the specified `filename` using the optional `arguments`. (Works the same way as the `source` command.) |
| `: [arguments]` | Expands the `arguments` but does not process them. |
| `[ expr ]` | Evaluates the expression `expr` and returns zero status if `expr` is true. |
| `alias [name[=value] . . . ]` | Allows one `value` to equal another. For example, you could set `xyz` to run `bg`. |
| `bg [job]` | Puts the specified `job` in the background. If no `job` is specified, it puts the currently executing command in the background. |
| `break [n]` | Exits from a `for`, `while`, or `until` loop. If `n` is specified, the `n`th enclosing loop is exited. |
| `cd [dir]` | Changes the current directory to `dir`. |
| `command [-pVv] cmd [arg . . . ]` | Runs the command `cmd` with the specified arguments (ignoring any shell function named `cmd`). |

*(continued)*

**Table 2-1** *(continued)*

| *This Function* | *Does the Following* |
|---|---|
| `continue [n]` | Starts the next iteration of the `for`, `while`, or `until` loop. If *n* is specified, the next iteration of the *n*-th enclosing loop is started. |
| `declare [-frxi] [name[=value]]` | Declares a variable with the specified *name* and optionally, assigns it a *value*. |
| `dirs [-l] [+/-n]` | Displays the list of currently remembered directories. |
| `echo [-neE] [arg . . . ]` | Displays the arguments on standard output. |
| `enable [-n] [-all]` | Enables or disables the specified built-in commands. |
| `eval [arg . . . ]` | Concatenates the arguments and executes them as a command. |
| `exec [command [arguments]]` | Replaces the current instance of the shell with a new process that runs the specified *command.* with the given *arguments* |
| `exit [n]` | Exits the shell with the status code *n*. |
| `export [-nf] [name[=word]] . . .` | Defines a specified environment variable and exports it to future processes. |
| `fc -s [pat=rep] [cmd]` | Reexecutes the command after replacing the pattern *pat* with *rep*. |
| `fg [jobspec]` | Puts the specified job, *jobspec*, in the foreground. If no job is specified, it puts the most recent job in the foreground. |
| `hash [-r] [name]` | Remembers the full pathname of a specified command. |
| `help [cmd . . . ]` | Displays help information for specified built-in commands. |
| `history [n]` | Displays past commands or past n commands, if you specify a number n. |
| `jobs [-lnp] [ jobspec . . . ]` | Lists currently active jobs. |
| `kill [-s sigspec \| -sigspec] [pid \| jobspec] . . . let arg [arg . . . ]` | Evaluates each argument and returns 1 if the last *arg* is 0. |

| This Function | Does the Following |
|---|---|
| `local [name[=value] . . . ]` | Creates a local variable with the specified *name* and *value* (used in shell functions). |
| `logout` | Exits a login shell. |
| `popd [+/-n]` | Removes the specified number of entries from the directory stack. |
| `pushd [dir]` | Adds a specified directory, *dir*, to the top of the directory stack. |
| `pwd` | Prints the full pathname of the current working directory. |
| `read [-r] [name . . . ]` | Reads a line from standard input and parses it. |
| `readonly [-f] [name . . . ]` | Marks the specified variables as read-only so that the variables cannot be changed later. |
| `return [n]` | Exits the shell function with the return value *n*. |
| `set [--abefhkmnptuvxldCHP] [-o option] [arg . . . ]` | Sets various flags. |
| `shift [n]` | Makes the *n*+1 argument $1, the *n*+2 argument $2, and so on. |
| `times` | Prints the accumulated user and system times for processes run from the shell. |
| `trap [-l] [cmd] [sigspec]` | Executes *cmd* when the *sigspec* signal is received. |
| `type [-all] [-type |-path] name [name . . . ]` | Indicates how the shell interprets each *name*. |
| `ulimit [-SHacdfmstpnuv [limit]]` | Controls resources available to the shell. |
| `umask [-S] [mode]` | Sets the file creation mask — the default permission to the *mode* specified for the files. |
| `unalias [-a] [name . . . ]` | Undefines a specified alias. |
| `unset [-fv] [name . . . ]` | Removes the definition of specified variables. |
| `wait [n]` | Waits for a specified process (*n* represents its PID) to terminate. |

Some external programs may have the same name as bash built-in commands. If you want to run any such external program, you have to specify explicitly the full pathname of that program. Otherwise, bash executes the built-in command of the same name.

# Chapter 3: Working with Advanced Shell Scripting

## In This Chapter

✔ Trying out the sed command

✔ Working with the awk and sed commands

✔ Reading some final notes on shell scripting

The preceding chapter introduced you to some of the power available through shell scripting. All the scripts in that chapter were simple bash routines that allow you to run commands and repeat operations a number of times.

This chapter builds upon that knowledge by showing how to incorporate two powerful tools — sed and awk — into your scripts. These two utilities move your scripts to the place where the only limit to what you can do becomes your ability to figure out how to ask for the output you need. Although sed is the stream editor and awk is a quick programming language, they complement each other so well that it is not uncommon to use one with the other. The best way to show how these tools work is to walk through some examples.

## Trying Out sed

The following are sample lines of a colon-delimited employee database that has five fields: unique id number, name, department, phone number, and address.

```
1218:Kris Cottrell:Marketing:219.555.5555:123 Main Street
1219:Nate Eichhorn:Sales:219.555.5555:1219 Locust Avenue
1220:Joe Gunn:Payables:317.555.5555:21974 Unix Way
1221:Anne Heltzel:Finance:219.555.5555:652 Linux Road
1222:John Kuzmic:Human Resources:219.555.5555:984 Bash Lane
```

This database has been in existence since the beginning of the company and has grown to include everyone who now works, or has ever worked, for the company. A number of proprietary scripts read from the database, and the company cannot afford to be without it. The problem is that the telephone company has changed the 219 prefix to 260, so all entries in the database need to be changed.

This is precisely the task for which sed was created. As opposed to standard (interactive) editors, a *stream editor* works it way through a file and makes changes based on the rules it is given. The rule in this case is to change 219 to 260. It's not quite that simple, however, because if you use the command

```
sed 's/219/260/'
```

the result is not completely what you want (changes are in **bold**):

```
1218:Kris Cottrell:Marketing:260.555.5555:123 Main Street
1260:Nate Eichhorn:Sales:219.555.5555:1219 Locust Avenue
1220:Joe Gunn:Payables:317.555.5555:26074 Unix Way
1221:Anne Heltzel:Finance:260.555.5555:652 Linux Road
1222:John Kuzmic:Human Resources:260.555.5555:984 Bash Lane
```

The changes in the first, fourth, and fifth lines are correct. But in the second line, the first occurrence of 219 appears in the employee id number rather than in the phone number and was changed to 260. If you wanted to change more than the very first occurrence in a line, you could slap a g (for global) into the command:

```
sed 's/219/260/g'
```

That is *not* what you want to do in this case, however, because the employee id number should not change. Similarly, in the third line, a change was made to the address because it contains the value that is being searched for; no change should have been made because the employee does not have the 219 telephone prefix.

The first rule of using sed is to identify what makes the location of the string you are looking for unique. If the telephone prefix were encased in parentheses it would be much easier to isolate. In this database, though, that is not the case and the task becomes a bit more complicated.

If you said that the telephone prefix must appear at the beginning of the field (denoted by a colon), the result would be much closer to what you want:

```
sed 's/:219/:260/'
```

Again, bolding has been added to the changes:

```
1218:Kris Cottrell:Marketing:260.555.5555:123 Main Street
```

```
1219:Nate Eichhorn:Sales:260.555.5555:1219 Locust Avenue
1220:Joe Gunn:Payables:317.555.5555:26074 Unix Way
1221:Anne Heltzel:Finance:260.555.5555:652 Linux Road
1222:John Kuzmic:Human Resources:260.555.5555:984 Bash Lane
```

The accuracy has increased, but there is still the problem of the third line. Because the colon helped to identify the start of the string, it may be tempting to turn to the period to identify the end:

```
sed 's/:219./:260./'
```

But the result still isn't what was hoped for (note the third line):

```
1218:Kris Cottrell:Marketing:260.555.5555:123 Main Street
1219:Nate Eichhorn:Sales:260.555.5555:1219 Locust Avenue
1220:Joe Gunn:Payables:317.555.5555:260.4 Unix Way
1221:Anne Heltzel:Finance:260.555.5555:652 Linux Road
1222:John Kuzmic:Human Resources:260.555.5555:984 Bash Lane
```

Because the period has a special meaning of *any character,* a match is found whether the 219 is followed by a period, a 7, or any other single character. Whatever the character, it is replaced with a period. The replacement side of things isn't the problem; the search needs to be tweaked. By using the \ character, we can override the special meaning of the period and specify that you are indeed looking for a period and not any single character:

```
sed 's/:219\./:260./'
```

The result becomes:

```
1218:Kris Cottrell:Marketing:260.555.5555:123 Main Street
1219:Nate Eichhorn:Sales:260.555.5555:1219 Locust Avenue
1220:Joe Gunn:Payables:317.555.5555:21974 Unix Way
1221:Anne Heltzel:Finance:260.555.5555:652 Linux Road
1222:John Kuzmic:Human Resources:260.555.5555:984 Bash Lane
```

And the mission is accomplished.

# Working with awk and sed

The second example involves a database of books that includes the ISBN number of each title. Formerly, ISBN numbers were ten digits and included an identifier for the publisher and a unique number for each book. As of 2007, ISBN numbers are now thirteen digits for new books. Old books (those published before the first of 2007) have both the old 10-digit and a new 13-digit number that can be used to identify them. For this example, the existing 10-digit number will stay in the database and a new field will be added to the end of each entry holding the ISBN-13 number.

To come up with the ISBN-13 number for the existing entries in the database, you start with 978, then use the first 9 digits of the old ISBN number. The 13th digit is a mathematical calculation (a check digit) obtained by doing the following:

*1.* Add all odd-placed digits (the first, the third, the fifth, and so on).

*2.* Multiply all even-placed digits by 3 and add them.

*3.* Add the total of Step #2 to the total of Step #1.

*4.* Find out what you need to add to round the number up to the nearest 10. This value becomes the 13th digit.

For example, consider the 10-digit ISBN 0743477103. It first becomes 978074347710 then:

*1.* 9+8+7+3+7+1=35

*2.* 7*3=21 ; 0*3=0; 4*3=12; 4*3=12; 7*3=21; 0*3=0; 21+0+12+12+21+0=66

*3.* 66+35=101

*4.* 110-101=9. The ISBN-13 thus becomes: 9780743477109

The beginning database resembles:

```
0743477103:Macbeth:Shakespeare, William
1578518520:The Innovator's Solution:Christensen, Clayton M.
0321349946:(SCTS) Symantec Certified Technical Specialist:Alston, Nik
1587052415:Cisco Network Admission Control, Volume I:Helfrich, Denise
```

And you want the resulting database to change so each line resembles something like this:

```
0743477103:Macbeth:Shakespeare, William:9780743477109
```

The example that follows accomplishes this goal. It's not the prettiest thing ever written, but it walks through the process of tackling this problem illustrating the use of awk and sed. I have also included writing to temporary files so you can examine those files and see the contents at various stages. Clean programming would mitigate the use of temporary files everywhere possible, but that also makes it difficult to follow the action at times. That said, here is one solution out of dozens.

## Step one: Pull out the ISBN

Given the database as it now exists, the first order of business is to pull out the existing ISBN — only the first 9 digits because the tenth digit, which was just a checksum, no longer matters — and slap 978 to the beginning. The 9 digits we want are the first 9 characters of each line, so we can pull them out by using the cut utility:

```
cut -c1e-9 books
```

Because a mathematical operation will be performed on the numbers comprising this value that works with each digit, I'll add a space between each number in the new entry:

```
sed 's/[0-9]/& /g'
```

Now it's time to add the new code to the beginning of each entry (the start of every line):

```
sed 's/^/9 7 8 /'
```

And finally, I'll do an extra step of removing the white space at the end of the line just to make the entry a bit cleaner:

```
sed 's/ $//'
```

Then I'll write the results to a temporary file that can be examined to make sure all is working as it should. The full first step then becomes:

```
cut -c1-9 books | sed 's/[0-9]/& /g' | sed 's/^/9 7 8 /' | sed 's/ $//' > isbn2
```

***Note:*** the `sed` operations could be combined in a script file to increase speed and decrease cycles. However, I am walking through each operation step-by-step to show what is going on, and am not worried about creating script files for this one-time-only operation.

Examining the temporary file, the contents are as follows:

```
9 7 8 0 7 4 3 4 7 7 1 0
9 7 8 1 5 7 8 5 1 8 5 2
9 7 8 0 3 2 1 3 4 9 9 4
9 7 8 1 5 8 7 0 5 2 4 1
```

## Step two: Calculate the 13th digit

We've taken care of the first 12 digits of the ISBN number. Now we need to compute those 12 digits to figure out the 13th value. Because the numbers are separated by a space, `awk` can interpreted them as fields. The calculation will take several steps:

1. Add all the odd-placed digits: x=$1+$3+$5+$7+$9+$11.

2. Add all the even-placed digits and multiply by 3: y=($2+$4+$6+$8+$10+$12)*3.

3. Add the total of Step #2 to the total of Step #1: x=x+y.

**4.** Find out what you need to add to round the number up to the nearest 10 by computing the modulo when divided by 10, and then subtracting it from 10. The following awk command gets everything in place except the transformation:

```
awk '{ x=$1+$3+$5+$7+$9+$11 ; y=$2+$4+$6+$8+$10+$12 ; y=y*3 ; x=x+y ;
      y=x%10 ; print y }'
```

Everything is finished except subtracting the final result from 10. This is the hardest part. If the modulo is 7, for example, the check digit is 3. If the modulo is 0, however, the check digit does not become 10 (10 – 0), but stays 0. My solution is to use the transform function of sed:

```
sed 'y/12346789/98764321/'
```

Combining the two operations into one, the second step thus becomes:

```
awk '{ x=$1+$3+$5+$7+$9+$11 ; y=$2+$4+$6+$8+$10+$12 ; y=y*3 ; x=x+y ; y=x%10 ;
      print y }' | sed 'y/12346789/98764321/' > isbn3
```

Examining the temporary file, the contents are

```
9
4
1
5
```

## Step three: Add the 13th digit to the other 12

The two temporary files can now be combined to get the correct 13-digit ISBN number. Just as cut was used in the earlier step, paste can be used now to combine the files. The default delimiter for paste is a tab, but we can change that to anything with the –d option. I will use a space as the delimiter, and then use sed to strip the spaces (remember that the isbn2 file has spaces between the digits so that they can be read as fields):

```
paste -d" " isbn2 isbn3 | sed 's/ //g'
```

Finally, I want to add a colon as the first character of each entry to make it easier to append the newly computed ISBN to the existing file:

```
sed 's/^/:/'
```

And the entire command becomes:

```
paste -d" " isbn2 isbn3 | sed 's/ //g' | sed 's/^/:/' > isbn4
```

Examining the temporary file, the contents are

```
:9780743477109
:9781578518524
:9780321349941
:9781587052415
```

## Step four: Finish the process

The only operation remaining is to append the values in the temporary file to the current database. I'll use the default tab delimiter in the entry, and then strip it out. Technically, I could specify a colon as the delimiter and avoid the last part of the last steps. However, I would rather have my value complete there and be confident that I am stripping characters that don't belong (tabs) instead of running the risk of adding more than should be there. The final command is

```
paste books isbn4 | sed 's/\t//g' > newbooks
```

The final file looks like this:

```
0743477103:Macbeth:Shakespeare, William:9780743477109
1578518520:The Innovator's Solution:Christensen, Clayton M.:9781578518524
0321349946:(SCTS) Symantec Certified Technical Specialist:Alston,
    Nik:9780321349941
1587052415:Cisco Network Admission Control, Volume I:Helfrich,
    Denise:9781587052415
```

Again, this result can be accomplished in many ways. This solution is not the cleanest, but it does illustrate the down-and-dirty use of sed and awk.

# Final Notes on Shell Scripting

It takes a while to get used to shell scripting, like any other aspect of computing. After you become comfortable writing scripts, however, you'll find that you can automate any number of operations and make your task as an administrator simpler. The following tips can be helpful to keep in mind:

**Book VIII
Chapter 3**

+ After you create a script, you can run it automatically on a one-time basis by using at or on a regular basis by using cron.

+ You can use conditional expressions, such as if, while, and until, to look for events to occur (such as someone accessing a file they should not) or to let you know when something that should be there goes away (for example, a file is removed or a user terminates).

**Working with
Advanced Shell
Scripting**

✦ You can set permissions on shell scripts in the same way you set permissions for other files. For example, you can create scripts that are shared by all members of your administrative group (use `case` to create menus based upon `LOGNAME`).

# Appendix: About the DVD

## In This Appendix

✓ **Running live Linux directly from the DVD**

✓ **Permanently installing Linux**

✓ **What you'll find on the DVD**

✓ **Troubleshooting**

The *Linux All-in-One Desk Reference For Dummies* companion DVD includes live versions of popular Linux distributions. You can run these distributions on your Windows PC directly from the DVD:

✦ Ubuntu

✦ Fedora

✦ Mandriva

✦ openSUSE

✦ Linux Mint

In addition, you can permanently install several Linux distributions directly from the DVD.

This appendix briefly describes the DVD and tells you how to get started with the installation.

If you're considering a permanent installation of Linux, make sure you have backup copies of files from your PC before you begin installing Linux.

## System Requirements

Make sure that your computer meets the minimum system requirements shown in the following list. If your computer doesn't match up to most of these requirements, you may have problems using the software and files on the DVD:

✦ A PC with a processor running at 400 MHz or faster for graphical installation

✦ At least 512MB of total RAM installed on your computer for graphical installation

✦ At least 1GB free space on your hard drive for a minimal installation; 5GB of free space recommended if you plan to install most packages so that you can try out everything covered in this book

✦ A DVD-ROM drive

✦ A graphics card and a monitor capable of displaying at least 256 colors

✦ A sound card

## DVD Installation Instructions

To use a Linux distribution from the companion DVD, boot your PC with the companion DVD.

If your PC lets you insert a DVD with the power off, that's the easiest way to boot from the DVD. Insert the DVD, and then switch the power on. The *Linux All-in-One For Dummies* title screen appears, and you're ready to install Linux. The following sections show how to start or install the included distributions.

If you can't insert a DVD into your Windows PC with the power off, here's what you have to do while Windows is running:

*1.* **Insert the DVD into the drive.**

The Ubuntu Menu screen appears.

If you don't want to run Ubuntu now, don't worry. Although you see the Ubuntu Menu screen, you can use any of the included Linux distributions when the DVD reboots the computer.

*2.* **Click Demo and Full Installation.**

The menu asks whether you want to reboot.

*3.* **Click Reboot Now, and then click Finish.**

Your computer shuts down and then reboots with the DVD's startup screen. You're ready to try out or permanently install a live version of Linux.

The following sections show how to add Linux to your PC.

## Starting Linux

After you reboot your PC with the *Linux All-in-One For Dummies* DVD, you can use one of the following Linux distributions.

If you don't enter a command within 30 seconds after the DVD boots, the DVD automatically starts a live version of Ubuntu.

### Ubuntu

To run a live version of Ubuntu, enter **ubuntu** at the boot prompt after the DVD boots. Your PC grinds and sighs, and then displays the Ubuntu desktop.

To permanently install Ubuntu on your PC, start the live version of Ubuntu from the DVD and then click Install on the default desktop. Then follow the prompts to install Ubuntu on your PC.

### Fedora

To run a live version of Fedora, follow these steps after the DVD boots:

1. **At the boot prompt, enter the command** fedora.

   You see the Log In screen.

2. **At the Log In screen, enter the username** fedora.

   Your PC whirls and twirls, and then displays Fedora's default desktop.

To permanently install Fedora on your PC, start the live version of Fedora from the DVD and then click Install to Hard Drive on the default desktop. Follow the prompts to install Fedora on your PC.

### OpenSUSE

To run a live version of SUSE, enter **suse** at the boot prompt after the DVD boots. Your PC shimmies and shakes, and then displays the openSUSE desktop.

To permanently install SUSE on your PC, start the live version of SUSE from the DVD and then click Install on the default desktop. Follow the prompts to install SUSE on your PC.

### Linux Mint

To run a live version of Debian, enter **mint** at the boot prompt after the DVD boots. Your PC whistles and whirls, and then displays the Mint desktop.

### *Other options*

The *Linux All-in-One For Dummies* DVD includes other options and utilities at the boot prompt.

### *Check*

If you have difficulty booting your PC from the DVD, you can confirm that you have a good copy of the DVD. Enter **check** at the boot prompt. The DVD will start a self testing process. If the DVD passes the test, it will then attempt to boot Fedora from the DVD.

### *Memtest*

The DVD includes the utility memtest to check your computer's performance. To start the test process, enter **check** at the boot prompt. A full test may take half an hour or more. You can press Esc at any time to end the test.

### *Local*

You can bypass all features of the DVD. Just enter **local** at the boot prompt. Your PC will boot with its usual default operating system (Windows, probably).

Otherwise, by default, the DVD boots Ubuntu after 30 seconds.

## *What You'll Find on the DVD*

This section provides a summary of the software and other goodies on the DVD. If you need help with installing the items provided on the DVD, refer to the installation instructions in the preceding section.

*Shareware programs* are fully functional, free, trial versions of copyrighted programs. If you like a particular program, register with its author for a fee and receive licenses, enhanced versions, and technical support.

*Freeware programs* are free, copyrighted games, applications, and utilities. You can copy them to as many PCs as you like — for free — but they offer no tech support.

*Trial, demo,* or *evaluation* versions of software are usually limited by time or functionality (such as not letting you save a project after you create it).

*GNU software* is governed by its own license, which is included in the folder of the GNU software. There are no restrictions on distribution of GNU software. See the GNU license at the root of the DVD or the back of this book for details.

The detailed software list for each Linux distribution varies somewhat, but most distributions include the following (typical version numbers shown):

+ Linux kernel 2.6.x with driver modules for major PC hardware configurations, including IDE/EIDE and SCSI drives, PCMCIA devices, CD drives, and DVD drives

+ A complete set of installation and configuration tools for setting up devices and services

+ A graphical user interface based on the X Window System, with GNOME and KDE graphical desktops

+ Full TCP/IP networking for Internet, LANs, and intranets

+ Tools for connecting your PC to your Internet Service Provider (ISP) using PPP, DSL, or dial-up serial communications programs

+ A complete suite of Internet applications, including electronic mail (`sendmail`, `mail`), news (INN), TELNET, FTP, DNS, and NFS

+ Evolution or an equivalent e-mail and calendar application

+ OpenOffice.org office suite with word processor, spreadsheet, presentation software, and more

+ Apache Web server (to turn your PC into a Web server) and Mozilla Firefox Web browser (to surf the Net)

+ Samba LAN Manager software for Microsoft Windows connectivity

+ Several text editors (for example, GNU `emacs`; `vim`)

+ Graphics and image manipulation software, such as The GIMP, Xfig, Gnuplot, Ghostscript, Ghostview, and ImageMagick

+ Programming languages (GNU C and C++, Perl, Tcl/Tk, Python, Ruby, and GNU AWK) and software development tools (GNU Debugger, CVS, RCS, GNU Bison, flex, TIFF, and JPEG libraries)

+ Support for industry standard Executable and Linking Format (ELF) and Intel Binary Compatibility Specification (iBCS)

+ A complete suite of standard UNIX utilities from the GNU project

+ Tools to access and use DOS files and applications (`mtools`)

+ Text formatting and typesetting software (`groff`, TeX, and LaTeX)

# Troubleshooting

If you have difficulty installing or using the materials on the companion DVD, consult the detailed installation and troubleshooting instructions in Book I.

If you still have trouble with the DVD-ROM, please call the Wiley Product Technical Support phone number: (800) 762-2974. Outside the United States, call 1(317) 572-3994. You can also contact Wiley Product Technical Support through the Internet at www.wiley.com/techsupport. Wiley Publishing will provide technical support only for installation and other general quality control items; for technical support on the applications themselves, consult the program's vendor or author.

To place additional orders or to request information about other Wiley products, please call (800) 225-5945.

# Wiley Publishing, Inc.
# End-User License Agreement

**READ THIS.** You should carefully read these terms and conditions before opening the software packet(s) included with this book "Book". This is a license agreement "Agreement" between you and Wiley Publishing, Inc. "WPI". By opening the accompanying software packet(s), you acknowledge that you have read and accept the following terms and conditions. If you do not agree and do not want to be bound by such terms and conditions, promptly return the Book and the unopened software packet(s) to the place you obtained them for a full refund.

1. **License Grant.** WPI grants to you (either an individual or entity) a nonexclusive license to use one copy of the enclosed software program(s) (collectively, the "Software") solely for your own personal or business purposes on a single computer (whether a standard computer or a workstation component of a multi-user network). The Software is in use on a computer when it is loaded into temporary memory (RAM) or installed into permanent memory (hard disk, CD-ROM, or other storage device). WPI reserves all rights not expressly granted herein.

2. **Ownership.** WPI is the owner of all right, title, and interest, including copyright, in and to the compilation of the Software recorded on the physical packet included with this Book "Software Media". Copyright to the individual programs recorded on the Software Media is owned by the author or other authorized copyright owner of each program. Ownership of the Software and all proprietary rights relating thereto remain with WPI and its licensers.

3. **Restrictions on Use and Transfer.**

   **(a)** You may only (i) make one copy of the Software for backup or archival purposes, or (ii) transfer the Software to a single hard disk, provided that you keep the original for backup or archival purposes. You may not (i) rent or lease the Software, (ii) copy or reproduce the Software through a LAN or other network system or through any computer subscriber system or bulletin-board system, or (iii) modify, adapt, or create derivative works based on the Software.

   **(b)** You may not reverse engineer, decompile, or disassemble the Software. You may transfer the Software and user documentation on a permanent basis, provided that the transferee agrees to accept the terms and conditions of this Agreement and you retain no copies. If the Software is an update or has been updated, any transfer must include the most recent update and all prior versions.

4. **Restrictions on Use of Individual Programs.** You must follow the individual requirements and restrictions detailed for each individual program in the "About the CD" appendix of this Book or on the Software Media. These limitations are also contained in the individual license agreements recorded on the Software Media. These limitations may include a requirement that after using the program for a specified period of time, the user must pay a registration fee or discontinue use. By opening the Software packet(s), you agree to abide by the licenses and restrictions for these individual programs that are detailed in the "About the CD" appendix and/or on the Software Media. None of the material on this Software Media or listed in this Book may ever be redistributed, in original or modified form, for commercial purposes.

5. **Limited Warranty.**

   **(a)** WPI warrants that the Software and Software Media are free from defects in materials and workmanship under normal use for a period of sixty (60) days from the date of purchase of this Book. If WPI receives notification within the warranty period of defects in materials or workmanship, WPI will replace the defective Software Media.

   **(b)** WPI AND THE AUTHOR(S) OF THE BOOK DISCLAIM ALL OTHER WARRANTIES, EXPRESS OR IMPLIED, INCLUDING WITHOUT LIMITATION IMPLIED WARRANTIES OF MERCHANTABILITY AND FITNESS FOR A PARTICULAR PURPOSE, WITH RESPECT TO THE SOFTWARE, THE PROGRAMS, THE SOURCE CODE CONTAINED THEREIN, AND/OR THE TECHNIQUES DESCRIBED IN THIS BOOK. WPI DOES NOT WARRANT THAT THE FUNCTIONS CONTAINED IN THE SOFTWARE WILL MEET YOUR REQUIREMENTS OR THAT THE OPERATION OF THE SOFTWARE WILL BE ERROR FREE.

   **(c)** This limited warranty gives you specific legal rights, and you may have other rights that vary from jurisdiction to jurisdiction.

6. **Remedies.**

   **(a)** WPI's entire liability and your exclusive remedy for defects in materials and workmanship shall be limited to replacement of the Software Media, which may be returned to WPI with a copy of your receipt at the following address: Software Media Fulfillment Department, Attn.: *Linux All-in-One For Dummies,* 4th Edition, Wiley Publishing, Inc., 10475 Crosspoint Blvd., Indianapolis, IN 46256, or call 1-800-762-2974. Please allow four to six weeks for delivery. This Limited Warranty is void if failure of the Software Media has resulted from accident, abuse, or misapplication. Any replacement Software Media will be warranted for the remainder of the original warranty period or thirty (30) days, whichever is longer.

   **(b)** In no event shall WPI or the author be liable for any damages whatsoever (including without limitation damages for loss of business profits, business interruption, loss of business information, or any other pecuniary loss) arising from the use of or inability to use the Book or the Software, even if WPI has been advised of the possibility of such damages.

   **(c)** Because some jurisdictions do not allow the exclusion or limitation of liability for consequential or incidental damages, the above limitation or exclusion may not apply to you.

7. **U.S. Government Restricted Rights.** Use, duplication, or disclosure of the Software for or on behalf of the United States of America, its agencies and/or instrumentalities "U.S. Government" is subject to restrictions as stated in paragraph (c)(1)(ii) of the Rights in Technical Data and Computer Software clause of DFARS 252.227-7013, or subparagraphs (c) (1) and (2) of the Commercial Computer Software - Restricted Rights clause at FAR 52.227-19, and in similar clauses in the NASA FAR supplement, as applicable.

8. **General.** This Agreement constitutes the entire understanding of the parties and revokes and supersedes all prior agreements, oral or written, between them and may not be modified or amended except in a writing signed by both parties hereto that specifically refers to this Agreement. This Agreement shall take precedence over any other documents that may be in conflict herewith. If any one or more provisions contained in this Agreement are held by any court or tribunal to be invalid, illegal, or otherwise unenforceable, each and every other provision shall remain in full force and effect.

# GNU General Public License

Version 3, 29 June 2007

Copyright © 2007 Free Software Foundation, Inc. <http://fsf.org/>

Everyone is permitted to copy and distribute verbatim copies of this license document, but changing it is not allowed.

## Preamble

The GNU General Public License is a free, copyleft license for software and other kinds of works.

The licenses for most software and other practical works are designed to take away your freedom to share and change the works. By contrast, the GNU General Public License is intended to guarantee your freedom to share and change all versions of a program–to make sure it remains free software for all its users. We, the Free Software Foundation, use the GNU General Public License for most of our software; it applies also to any other work released this way by its authors. You can apply it to your programs, too.

When we speak of free software, we are referring to freedom, not price. Our General Public Licenses are designed to make sure that you have the freedom to distribute copies of free software (and charge for them if you wish), that you receive source code or can get it if you want it, that you can change the software or use pieces of it in new free programs, and that you know you can do these things.

To protect your rights, we need to prevent others from denying you these rights or asking you to surrender the rights. Therefore, you have certain responsibilities if you distribute copies of the software, or if you modify it: responsibilities to respect the freedom of others.

For example, if you distribute copies of such a program, whether gratis or for a fee, you must pass on to the recipients the same freedoms that you received. You must make sure that they, too, receive or can get the source code. And you must show them these terms so they know their rights.

Developers that use the GNU GPL protect your rights with two steps: (1) assert copyright on the software, and (2) offer you this License giving you legal permission to copy, distribute and/or modify it.

For the developers' and authors' protection, the GPL clearly explains that there is no warranty for this free software. For both users' and authors' sake, the GPL requires that modified versions be marked as changed, so that their problems will not be attributed erroneously to authors of previous versions.

Some devices are designed to deny users access to install or run modified versions of the software inside them, although the manufacturer can do so. This is fundamentally incompatible with the aim of protecting users' freedom to change the software. The systematic pattern of such abuse occurs in the area of products for individuals to use, which is precisely where it is most unacceptable. Therefore, we have designed this version of the GPL to prohibit the practice for those products. If such problems arise substantially in other domains, we stand ready to extend this provision to those domains in future versions of the GPL, as needed to protect the freedom of users.

Finally, every program is threatened constantly by software patents. States should not allow patents to restrict development and use of software on general-purpose computers, but in those that do, we wish to avoid the special danger that patents applied to a free program could make it effectively proprietary. To prevent this, the GPL assures that patents cannot be used to render the program non-free.

The precise terms and conditions for copying, distribution and modification follow.

# Terms and Conditions

0.  **Definitions.** "This License" refers to version 3 of the GNU General Public License. "Copyright" also means copyright-like laws that apply to other kinds of works, such as semiconductor masks. "The Program" refers to any copyrightable work licensed under this License. Each licensee is addressed as "you". "Licensees" and "recipients" may be individuals or organizations. To "modify" a work means to copy from or adapt all or part of the work in a fashion requiring copyright permission, other than the making of an exact copy. The resulting work is called a "modified version" of the earlier work or a work "based on" the earlier work. A "covered work" means either the unmodified Program or a work based on the Program.

    To "propagate" a work means to do anything with it that, without permission, would make you directly or secondarily liable for infringement under applicable copyright law, except executing it on a computer or modifying a private copy. Propagation includes copying, distribution (with or without modification), making available to the public, and in some countries other activities as well.

    To "convey" a work means any kind of propagation that enables other parties to make or receive copies. Mere interaction with a user through a computer network, with no transfer of a copy, is not conveying.

    An interactive user interface displays "Appropriate Legal Notices" to the extent that it includes a convenient and prominently visible feature that (1) displays an appropriate copyright notice, and (2) tells the user that there is no warranty for the work (except to the extent that warranties are provided), that licensees may convey the work under this License, and how to view a copy of this License. If the interface presents a list of user commands or options, such as a menu, a prominent item in the list meets this criterion.

1.  **Source Code.** The "source code" for a work means the preferred form of the work for making modifications to it. "Object code" means any non-source form of a work. A "Standard Interface" means an interface that either is an official standard defined by a recognized standards body, or, in the case of interfaces specified for a particular programming language, one that is widely used among developers working in that language.

    The "System Libraries" of an executable work include anything, other than the work as a whole, that (a) is included in the normal form of packaging a Major Component, but which is not part of that Major Component, and (b) serves only to enable use of the work with that Major Component, or to implement a Standard Interface for which an implementation is available to the public in source code form. A "Major Component", in this context, means a major essential component (kernel, window system, and so on) of the specific operating system (if any) on which the executable work runs, or a compiler used to produce the work, or an object code interpreter used to run it.

    The "Corresponding Source" for a work in object code form means all the source code needed to generate, install, and (for an executable work) run the object code and to modify the work, including scripts to control those activities. However, it does not include the work's System Libraries, or general-purpose tools or generally available free programs which are used unmodified in performing those activities but which are not part of the work. For example, Corresponding Source includes interface definition files associated with source files for the work, and the source code for shared libraries and dynamically linked subprograms that the work is specifically designed to require, such as by intimate data communication or control flow between those subprograms and other parts of the work.

    The Corresponding Source need not include anything that users can regenerate automatically from other parts of the Corresponding Source.

The Corresponding Source for a work in source code form is that same work.

2. **Basic Permissions.** All rights granted under this License are granted for the term of copyright on the Program, and are irrevocable provided the stated conditions are met. This License explicitly affirms your unlimited permission to run the unmodified Program. The output from running a covered work is covered by this License only if the output, given its content, constitutes a covered work. This License acknowledges your rights of fair use or other equivalent, as provided by copyright law.

You may make, run and propagate covered works that you do not convey, without conditions so long as your license otherwise remains in force. You may convey covered works to others for the sole purpose of having them make modifications exclusively for you, or provide you with facilities for running those works, provided that you comply with the terms of this License in conveying all material for which you do not control copyright. Those thus making or running the covered works for you must do so exclusively on your behalf, under your direction and control, on terms that prohibit them from making any copies of your copyrighted material outside their relationship with you.

Conveying under any other circumstances is permitted solely under the conditions stated below. Sublicensing is not allowed; section 10 makes it unnecessary.

3. **Protecting Users' Legal Rights From Anti-Circumvention Law.** No covered work shall be deemed part of an effective technological measure under any applicable law fulfilling obligations under article 11 of the WIPO copyright treaty adopted on 20 December 1996, or similar laws prohibiting or restricting circumvention of such measures.

When you convey a covered work, you waive any legal power to forbid circumvention of technological measures to the extent such circumvention is effected by exercising rights under this License with respect to the covered work, and you disclaim any intention to limit operation or modification of the work as a means of enforcing, against the work's users, your or third parties' legal rights to forbid circumvention of technological measures.

4. **Conveying Verbatim Copies.** You may convey verbatim copies of the Program's source code as you receive it, in any medium, provided that you conspicuously and appropriately publish on each copy an appropriate copyright notice; keep intact all notices stating that this License and any non-permissive terms added in accord with section 7 apply to the code; keep intact all notices of the absence of any warranty; and give all recipients a copy of this License along with the Program.

You may charge any price or no price for each copy that you convey, and you may offer support or warranty protection for a fee.

5. **Conveying Modified Source Versions.** You may convey a work based on the Program, or the modifications to produce it from the Program, in the form of source code under the terms of section 4, provided that you also meet all of these conditions:

a) The work must carry prominent notices stating that you modified it, and giving a relevant date.

b) The work must carry prominent notices stating that it is released under this License and any conditions added under section 7. This requirement modifies the requirement in section 4 to "keep intact all notices".

c) You must license the entire work, as a whole, under this License to anyone who comes into possession of a copy. This License will therefore apply, along with any applicable section 7 additional terms, to the whole of the work, and all its parts, regardless of how they are packaged. This License gives no permission to license the work in any other way, but it does not invalidate such permission if you have separately received it.

d) If the work has interactive user interfaces, each must display Appropriate Legal Notices; however, if the Program has interactive interfaces that do not display Appropriate Legal Notices, your work need not make them do so.

A compilation of a covered work with other separate and independent works, which are not by their nature extensions of the covered work, and which are not combined with it such as to form a larger program, in or on a volume of a storage or distribution medium, is called an "aggregate" if the compilation and its resulting copyright are not used to limit the access or legal rights of the compilation's users beyond what the individual works permit. Inclusion of a covered work in an aggregate does not cause this License to apply to the other parts of the aggregate.

6. **Conveying Non-Source Forms.** You may convey a covered work in object code form under the terms of sections 4 and 5, provided that you also convey the machine-readable Corresponding Source under the terms of this License, in one of these ways:

a) Convey the object code in, or embodied in, a physical product (including a physical distribution medium), accompanied by the Corresponding Source fixed on a durable physical medium customarily used for software interchange.

b) Convey the object code in, or embodied in, a physical product (including a physical distribution medium), accompanied by a written offer, valid for at least three years and valid for as long as you offer spare parts or customer support for that product model, to give anyone who possesses the object code either (1) a copy of the Corresponding Source for all the software in the product that is covered by this License, on a durable physical medium customarily used for software interchange, for a price no more than your reasonable cost of physically performing this conveying of source, or (2) access to copy the Corresponding Source from a network server at no charge.

c) Convey individual copies of the object code with a copy of the written offer to provide the Corresponding Source. This alternative is allowed only occasionally and noncommercially, and only if you received the object code with such an offer, in accord with subsection 6b.

d) Convey the object code by offering access from a designated place (gratis or for a charge), and offer equivalent access to the Corresponding Source in the same way through the same place at no further charge. You need not require recipients to copy the Corresponding Source along with the object code. If the place to copy the object code is a network server, the Corresponding Source may be on a different server (operated by you or a third party) that supports equivalent copying facilities, provided you maintain clear directions next to the object code saying where to find the Corresponding Source. Regardless of what server hosts the Corresponding Source, you remain obligated to ensure that it is available for as long as needed to satisfy these requir e) Convey the object code using peer-to-peer transmission, provided you inform other peers where the object code and Corresponding Source of the work are being offered to the general public at no charge under subsection 6d.

A separable portion of the object code, whose source code is excluded from the Corresponding Source as a System Library, need not be included in conveying the object code work.

A "User Product" is either (1) a "consumer product", which means any tangible personal property which is normally used for personal, family, or household purposes, or (2) anything designed or sold for incorporation into a dwelling. In determining whether a product is a consumer product, doubtful cases shall be resolved in favor of coverage. For a particular product received by a particular user, "normally used" refers to a typical or common use of that class of product, regardless of the status of the particular user or of the way in which the particular user actually uses, or expects or is expected to use, the product. A product is a consumer product regardless of whether the product has substantial commercial, industrial or non-consumer uses, unless such uses represent the only significant mode of use of the product.

"Installation Information" for a User Product means any methods, procedures, authorization keys, or other information required to install and execute modified versions of a covered work in that User Product from a modified version of its Corresponding Source. The information must suffice to ensure that the continued functioning of the modified object code is in no case prevented or interfered with solely because modification has been made.

If you convey an object code work under this section in, or with, or specifically for use in, a User Product, and the conveying occurs as part of a transaction in which the right of possession and use of the User Product is transferred to the recipient in perpetuity or for a fixed term (regardless of how the transaction is characterized), the Corresponding Source conveyed under this section must be accompanied by the Installation Information. But this requirement does not apply if neither you nor any third party retains the ability to install modified object code on the User Product (for example, the work has been installed in ROM).

The requirement to provide Installation Information does not include a requirement to continue to provide support service, warranty, or updates for a work that has been modified or installed by the recipient, or for the User Product in which it has been modified or installed. Access to a network may be denied when the modification itself materially and adversely affects the operation of the network or violates the rules and protocols for communication across the network.

Corresponding Source conveyed, and Installation Information provided, in accord with this section must be in a format that is publicly documented (and with an implementation available to the public in source code form), and must require no special password or key for unpacking, reading or copying.

7. **Additional Terms.** "Additional permissions" are terms that supplement the terms of this License by making exceptions from one or more of its conditions. Additional permissions that are applicable to the entire Program shall be treated as though they were included in this License, to the extent that they are valid under applicable law. If additional permissions apply only to part of the Program, that part may be used separately under those permissions, but the entire Program remains governed by this License without regard to the additional permissions.

When you convey a copy of a covered work, you may at your option remove any additional permissions from that copy, or from any part of it. (Additional permissions may be written to require their own removal in certain cases when you modify the work.) You may place additional permissions on material, added by you to a covered work, for which you have or can give appropriate copyright permission.

Notwithstanding any other provision of this License, for material you add to a covered work, you may (if authorized by the copyright holders of that material) supplement the terms of this License with terms:

a) Disclaiming warranty or limiting liability differently from the terms of sections 15 and 16 of this License; or

b) Requiring preservation of specified reasonable legal notices or author attributions in that material or in the Appropriate Legal Notices displayed by works containing it; or

c) Prohibiting misrepresentation of the origin of that material, or requiring that modified versions of such material be marked in reasonable ways as different from the original version; or

d) Limiting the use for publicity purposes of names of licensors or authors of the material; or

e) Declining to grant rights under trademark law for use of some trade names, trademarks, or service marks; or

f) Requiring indemnification of licensors and authors of that material by anyone who conveys the material (or modified versions of it) with contractual assumptions of liability to the recipient, for any liability that these contractual assumptions directly impose on those licensors and authors.

All other non-permissive additional terms are considered "further restrictions" within the meaning of section 10. If the Program as you received it, or any part of it, contains a notice stating that it is governed by this License along with a term that is a further restriction, you may remove that term. If a license document contains a further restriction but permits relicensing or conveying under this License, you may add to a covered work material governed by the terms of that license document, provided that the further restriction does not survive such relicensing or conveying.

If you add terms to a covered work in accord with this section, you must place, in the relevant source files, a statement of the additional terms that apply to those files, or a notice indicating where to find the applicable terms.

Additional terms, permissive or non-permissive, may be stated in the form of a separately written license, or stated as exceptions; the above requirements apply either way.

8. **Termination.** You may not propagate or modify a covered work except as expressly provided under this License. Any attempt otherwise to propagate or modify it is void, and will automatically terminate your rights under this License (including any patent licenses granted under the third paragraph of section 11).

However, if you cease all violation of this License, then your license from a particular copyright holder is reinstated (a) provisionally, unless and until the copyright holder explicitly and finally terminates your license, and (b) permanently, if the copyright holder fails to notify you of the violation by some reasonable means prior to 60 days after the cessation.

Moreover, your license from a particular copyright holder is reinstated permanently if the copyright holder notifies you of the violation by some reasonable means, this is the first time you have received notice of violation of this License (for any work) from that copyright holder, and you cure the violation prior to 30 days after your receipt of the notice.

Termination of your rights under this section does not terminate the licenses of parties who have received copies or rights from you under this License. If your rights have been terminated and not permanently reinstated, you do not qualify to receive new licenses for the same material under section 10.

9. **Acceptance Not Required for Having Copies.** You are not required to accept this License in order to receive or run a copy of the Program. Ancillary propagation of a covered work occurring solely as a consequence of using peer-to-peer transmission to receive a copy likewise does not require acceptance. However, nothing other than this License grants you permission to propagate or modify any covered work. These actions infringe copyright if you do not accept this License. Therefore, by modifying or propagating a covered work, you indicate your acceptance of this License to do so.

10. **Automatic Licensing of Downstream Recipients.** Each time you convey a covered work, the recipient automatically receives a license from the original licensors, to run, modify and propagate that work, subject to this License. You are not responsible for enforcing compliance by third parties with this License.

An "entity transaction" is a transaction transferring control of an organization, or substantially all assets of one, or subdividing an organization, or merging organizations. If propagation of a covered work results from an entity transaction, each party to that transaction who receives a copy of the work also receives whatever licenses to the work the party's predecessor in interest had or could give under the previous paragraph, plus a right to possession of the Corresponding Source of the work from the predecessor in interest, if the predecessor has it or can get it with reasonable efforts.

You may not impose any further restrictions on the exercise of the rights granted or affirmed under this License. For example, you may not impose a license fee, royalty, or other charge for exercise of rights granted under this License, and you may not initiate litigation (including a cross-claim or counterclaim in a lawsuit) alleging that any patent claim is infringed by making, using, selling, offering for sale, or importing the Program or any portion of it.

11. **Patents.** A "contributor" is a copyright holder who authorizes use under this License of the Program or a work on which the Program is based. The work thus licensed is called the contributor's "contributor version".

A contributor's "essential patent claims" are all patent claims owned or controlled by the contributor, whether already acquired or hereafter acquired, that would be infringed by some manner, permitted by this License, of making, using, or selling its contributor version, but do not include claims that would be infringed only as a consequence of further modification of the contributor version. For purposes of this definition, "control" includes the right to grant patent sublicenses in a manner consistent with the requirements of this License.

Each contributor grants you a non-exclusive, worldwide, royalty-free patent license under the contributor's essential patent claims, to make, use, sell, offer for sale, import and otherwise run, modify and propagate the contents of its contributor version.

In the following three paragraphs, a "patent license" is any express agreement or commitment, however denominated, not to enforce a patent (such as an express permission to practice a patent or covenant not to sue for patent infringement). To "grant" such a patent license to a party means to make such an agreement or commitment not to enforce a patent against the party.

If you convey a covered work, knowingly relying on a patent license, and the Corresponding Source of the work is not available for anyone to copy, free of charge and under the terms of this License, through a publicly available network server or other readily accessible means, then you must either (1) cause the Corresponding Source to be so available, or (2) arrange to deprive yourself of the benefit of the patent license for this particular work, or (3) arrange, in a manner consistent with the requirements of this License, to extend the patent license to downstream recipients. "Knowingly relying" means you have actual knowledge that, but for the patent license, your conveying the covered work in a country, or your recipient's use of the covered work in a country, would infringe one or more identifiable patents in that country that you have reason to believe are valid.

If, pursuant to or in connection with a single transaction or arrangement, you convey, or propagate by procuring conveyance of, a covered work, and grant a patent license to some of the parties receiving the covered work authorizing them to use, propagate, modify or convey a specific copy of the covered work, then the patent license you grant is automatically extended to all recipients of the covered work and works based on it.

A patent license is "discriminatory" if it does not include within the scope of its coverage, prohibits the exercise of, or is conditioned on the non-exercise of one or more of the rights that are specifically granted under this License. You may not convey a covered work if you are a party to an arrangement with a third party that is in the business of distributing software, under which you make payment to the third party based on the extent of your activity of conveying the work, and under which the third party grants, to any of the parties who would receive the covered work from you, a discriminatory patent license (a) in connection with copies of the covered work conveyed by you (or copies made from those copies), or (b) primarily for and in connection with specific products or compilations that contain the covered work, unless you entered into that arrangement, or that patent license was granted, prior to 28 March 2007.

Nothing in this License shall be construed as excluding or limiting any implied license or other defenses to infringement that may otherwise be available to you under applicable patent law.

12. **No Surrender of Others' Freedom.** If conditions are imposed on you (whether by court order, agreement or otherwise) that contradict the conditions of this License, they do not excuse you

from the conditions of this License. If you cannot convey a covered work so as to satisfy simultaneously your obligations under this License and any other pertinent obligations, then as a consequence you may not convey it at all. For example, if you agree to terms that obligate you to collect a royalty for further conveying from those to whom you convey the Program, the only way you could satisfy both those terms and this License would be to refrain entirely from conveying the Program.

13. **Use with the GNU Affero General Public License.** Notwithstanding any other provision of this License, you have permission to link or combine any covered work with a work licensed under version 3 of the GNU Affero General Public License into a single combined work, and to convey the resulting work. The terms of this License will continue to apply to the part which is the covered work, but the special requirements of the GNU Affero General Public License, section 13, concerning interaction through a network will apply to the combination as such.

14. **Revised Versions of this License.** The Free Software Foundation may publish revised and/or new versions of the GNU General Public License from time to time. Such new versions will be similar in spirit to the present version, but may differ in detail to address new problems or concerns.

Each version is given a distinguishing version number. If the Program specifies that a certain numbered version of the GNU General Public License "or any later version" applies to it, you have the option of following the terms and conditions either of that numbered version or of any later version published by the Free Software Foundation. If the Program does not specify a version number of the GNU General Public License, you may choose any version ever published by the Free Software Foundation.

If the Program specifies that a proxy can decide which future versions of the GNU General Public License can be used, that proxy's public statement of acceptance of a version permanently authorizes you to choose that version for the Program.

Later license versions may give you additional or different permissions. However, no additional obligations are imposed on any author or copyright holder as a result of your choosing to follow a later version.

15. **Disclaimer of Warranty.** THERE IS NO WARRANTY FOR THE PROGRAM, TO THE EXTENT PERMITTED BY APPLICABLE LAW. EXCEPT WHEN OTHERWISE STATED IN WRITING THE COPYRIGHT HOLDERS AND/OR OTHER PARTIES PROVIDE THE PROGRAM "AS IS" WITHOUT WARRANTY OF ANY KIND, EITHER EXPRESSED OR IMPLIED, INCLUDING, BUT NOT LIMITED TO, THE IMPLIED WARRANTIES OF MERCHANTABILITY AND FITNESS FOR A PARTICULAR PURPOSE. THE ENTIRE RISK AS TO THE QUALITY AND PERFORMANCE OF THE PROGRAM IS WITH YOU. SHOULD THE PROGRAM PROVE DEFECTIVE, YOU ASSUME THE COST OF ALL NECESSARY SERVICING, REPAIR OR CORRECTION.

16. **Limitation of Liability.** IN NO EVENT UNLESS REQUIRED BY APPLICABLE LAW OR AGREED TO IN WRITING WILL ANY COPYRIGHT HOLDER, OR ANY OTHER PARTY WHO MODIFIES AND/OR CONVEYS THE PROGRAM AS PERMITTED ABOVE, BE LIABLE TO YOU FOR DAMAGES, INCLUDING ANY GENERAL, SPECIAL, INCIDENTAL OR CONSEQUENTIAL DAMAGES ARISING OUT OF THE USE OR INABILITY TO USE THE PROGRAM (INCLUDING BUT NOT LIMITED TO LOSS OF DATA OR DATA BEING RENDERED INACCURATE OR LOSSES SUSTAINED BY YOU OR THIRD PARTIES OR A FAILURE OF THE PROGRAM TO OPERATE WITH ANY OTHER PROGRAMS), EVEN IF SUCH HOLDER OR OTHER PARTY HAS BEEN ADVISED OF THE POSSIBILITY OF SUCH DAMAGES.

17. **Interpretation of Sections 15 and 16.** If the disclaimer of warranty and limitation of liability provided above cannot be given local legal effect according to their terms, reviewing courts shall apply local law that most closely approximates an absolute waiver of all civil liability in connection with the Program, unless a warranty or assumption of liability accompanies a copy of the Program in return for a fee.

**END OF TERMS AND CONDITIONS**

# Index

## Numbers & Symbols

10Base2, Ethernet cables, 201

10Base5, Ethernet cables, 201

10BaseT Ethernet ports, 182–183, 188, 201

100BaseT Ethernet ports, 182–183, 187, 189, 201

100BaseT2, Ethernet cables, 201

100BaseT4, Ethernet cables, 201

100BaseTX, Ethernet cables, 201

802.11a, wireless Ethernet network standard, 207–208

802.11b, wireless Ethernet network standard, 207–208

802.11g, wireless Ethernet network standard, 207–208

802.11n, wireless Ethernet network standard, 207

80x86 processors, Linux support, 10

* (asterisk),104–106

@ (at sign), 126, 234

\ (backslash), 101

$ (dollar sign), 505–506

.. (dot-dot) characters, 125

>> (double greater than) characters, 104

?? (double question marks), 117

!! (exclamation points), 107

/ (forward slash), 119–121, 344–345

> (greater than) character, 103–104

- (hyphen), 112

. (period), 262

| (pipe) character, 102

# (pound sign), 253

? (question mark), 105, 253

" (quotation marks), 70, 101

; (semicolon), 102

. (single dot), 125

[ and ] square brackets, 105, 558

~ (tilde) character, 125

## A

A drive, /dev/fd0 device name, 361

absolute pathnames, 125

Accessories, main menu category, 82

ACPI setting, BIOS configuration, 51

Active window, 86, 94

ad hoc mode, 208–209

Administration menu subcategory, 91–92

administrative tasks, GNOME System Menu, 84–85

Advanced Encryption Standard (AES), WPA2, 210

Advanced Packaging Tool (APT)
DEB files, 374, 377–378
online updates, 383
software installation, 58–60

Advanced Research Projects Agency (ARPA), 197

aggregators, RSS feed readers, 275–276

alerts, security, 404–405

aliases, sendmail mail server, 485–486

Alpha AXP processors, 10

AMD processors, LSB standards, 16

AMD64 processors, 10

anonymous FTP
downloading/unpacking tar files, 378–379
Web browser downloads, 281–282

AOL Instant Messenger (AIM), 233

Apache httpd, 22

Application Starter, KDE Desktop, 90

application, TCP/IP layer, 196

application-proxy gateway firewall, 429

applications. See also software
Applixware, 21
audio CDs, 150–151
building from source files, 378–382
calculators, 148
calendars, 147–148
CD burners, 151–152
CrossOver Office, 21
DEB files, 374–378
digital cameras, 149–150
distribution component, 11, 20–21
file associations, 79, 89
file managers, 154–160
frequently used access in KDE Desktop, 90
graphics editing, 152–154
multimedia, 149–152
online updates, 382–388
opening in KDE Desktop, 91
OpenOffice.org office suite, 21, 143–147
recently used access in KDE Desktop, 92

applications *(continued)*
  RPM files, 367–374
  sample listings, 138–143
  sound files, 151
  source RPMs (SRPMs), 382
  Windows CD burners, 37
Applications menu
  category, 91
Applixware, productivity
  software, 21
`apt-cache` command,
  377–378
`apt-get` command
  DEB files, 374, 377–378
  online updates, 383
  software, 58–60
architecture, 369, 374
archives, 26. *See also*
  backups
arguments, 70, 100–101, 105
Arkeia, backup utility, 354
articles, newsgroup
  postings, 270–271
asterisk (*), 104–106
Asymmetric DSL (ASDL), 180
`at` command, 325–327
AT Attachment (ATA), 35
AT modem cables, 192
at sign (@), 126, 234
`atd` daemon, 325–327
attachments, e-mail, 235
audio CDs, 150–151
audits. *See* security audits
authentication
  dial-up networking,
    193–194
  Open Secure Shell
    (OpenSSH), 424–426
  security policy, 396
authorization, 396
automated backups,
  358–359
automated tasks, 292
`awk` command, 567–571

# B

B drive, `/dev/Fd1` device
  name, 361
Back button, navigation, 257
backbones, 176
backgrounds, Desktop, 79
backslash (\), 101
backups. *See also* archives
  automated, 358–359
  incremental+, 358
  multivolume archive,
    356–357
  prior to installation, 32, 38
  single-volume archive,
    355–356
  strategies, 353–354
  system administration
    tasks, 292
  tapes, 357–358
  `tar` command, 26,
    354–359
  utilities, 354
Balsa, mail user agent
  (MUA), 234–235
base station, 209
baseband, cables, 201
`bash` shell. *See also* shells;
    shell scripts; scripts
  automatic command
    completion, 105
  Bourne-Again SHell, 69
  built-in commands,
    560–563
  combining commands, 102
  command history, 107
  command listing, 108–111
  command syntax, 100–102
  control structures, 555,
    557–560
  counting text file words/
    lines, 115
  date/time display, 113–114
  expressions, 555
  file processing commands,
    114–117

filename wildcards,
    104–106
  functions, 555–557
  I/O redirection
    commands, 102–104
  killing running
    processes, 113
  process list display,
    112–113, 115
  process management
    commands, 112–113
  repeating previously
    typed commands, 107
  saving error messages to
    a file, 104
  script support, 69
  sorting text files, 115–116
  splitting large files,
    116–117
  substituting/deleting file
    characters, 116
  variables, 555, 556
Berkley Internet Name
  Domain (BIND),
  498–501
Berkley sockets
  interface, 456
`binary` command, 287
BIOS configuration
  ACPI setting, 51
  CPU cache, 51
  USB device boot order, 43
bit bucket, 104
block devices, 321
blogs, RSS feeds, 274
BogoMIPS, 66, 67
Bookmark button, 257
Bookmarks toolbar, 256–257
boot commands, 48–51
boot loader, 65, 227–228
Boot Manager, 229
boot messages, startup, 66
bootable flash drive, 41–43
booting, 65, 306–307
bottom panel, 85–86, 94–95
Bourne-Again SHell.
    *See* shells

broadband over power lines (BPL), 178
browsers. *See* Web browsers
BRU, backup utility, 354
bulletin board systems (BBSs), 261
burning
  CDs/DVDs, 32, 37, 151–152
  Nautilus File Manager, 155–156
businesses, security, 393–394

## C

C compiler, 531–536
c shell, switch shells, 100
C programming language, LSB standards, 15
C++ compiler, 531–536
C++ programming language, 15
CA ARCserve Backup for Linux, 354
Cable Modem Termination System (CMTS), 185–186
cable modems, 177–178, 184–189
cable/DSL routers, 188
cables, 201–203
caching name server, 503–513
cal command, 114
Calc, spreadsheet application, 145–146
calculators, 148
calendars
  applications, 147–148
  KDE Desktop display, 94
  printing current month, 114

Carrier-Sense Multiple Access/Collision Detection (CSMA/CD), 200
case statement, 559–560
cat command, 101, 104
CD burner application, 37
cd command, 102, 125
CD-ROMs
  burning, 32, 37, 151–152
  desktop icon display, 58
  file backups, 26
  mounting/unmounting drives, 25, 132–133
central processing unit (CPU), 528. *See also* processors
CERT Coordination Center, 404
chains, iptables command, 432
Challenge Handshake Authentication Protocol (CHAP), 193
chap-secrets file, 193–194
character devices, 320–321
characters, 116
chgrp command, 340–341, 411
chip. *See* central processing unit; processors
chkconfig command, 306–307, 446–447
chmod command, 128–129, 341, 411–412
chsh command, 100
client/server model, 457–459
colon command mode, 168
command history, 107
command interpreter. *See* shells
command line, 70, 529–530
command-line client, 283–287

command mode, 164
command processors, 529
command shortcuts, 78
commands
  arguments, 100–101
  automatic completion, 105
  bash shell built-in, 560–563
  combining shell, 102
  concatenating, 102
  directory listings, 126–128
  directory navigation, 124–125
  directory permissions, 126–129
  disk-space usage, 133–135
  ed text editor, 166–167
  file ownership, 128–129
  file processing, 114–117
  file search, 131–132
  File Transfer Protocol (FTP), 284–286
  I/O redirection, 102–104
  kernel module management, 322
  Linux command listing, 108–111
  mounting/unmounting drives, 132–133
  mtools utility, 365
  process management, 112–113
  repeating previously typed, 107
  saving error messages to a file, 104
  shell command format, 70
  shell command syntax, 100–102
  shell scripts, 117–118
  vi text editor, 169–171
  Yum, 385–387
Common Vulnerabilities and Exposures (CVE), 440
compilers, 17, 24, 530, 532–536

compressed tarball, 378–379
Computer menu category, 91
Concurrent Version System
  (CVS), 532
conditional expressions, 571
configuration files, 47–48
connectionless protocols, 457
connection-oriented
  protocols, 456–457
consoles, 99
context menus, 78–79,
  88–89
Control Center, 229
control structures, 555–560
COPYING file, 550–551
COPYING.LIB file, 551–552
cp command, 129–130
CPU cache, 51
CPU processes, 310–315
crackers, 391–392, 408
cron jobs, 327–330
crontab command,
  327–330, 358–359
CrossOver Office, 21
ctlinnd program, 487
current directory, 124–126

## D

Data Over Cable Service
  Interface (DOCSIS), 186
data protection, 396
date command, 113–114
date and time, 85
dates, display, 94, 113–114
DEB files, 374–378
Debian
  Advanced Packaging Tool
    (APT), 58–59, 374,
    377–378
  anonymous FTP
    downloads, 282
  automatic Samba
    startup, 523

automatic server
  startup, 307
automatic standalone
  server startup, 466–469
Berkley Internet Name
  Domain (BIND),
  498–501
command-line FTP
  client, 283
/etc/inittab file, 305
Evolution e-mail reader,
  237–240
gFTP client, 278–279
inetd server, 446,
  461–462
installation information
  gathering, 32
Internet super server
  configuration, 423
InterNetNews (INN)
  server, 486–493
KFTPGrabber, 280–281
KNode newsreader, 266,
  271–272
Kopete IM client, 247
manual standalone
  server, 465
mounting/unmounting
  devices, 349
name server startup, 512
Nessus Security Scanner,
  449–451
network startup on
  system boot, 227–228
NFS server startup,
  350, 518
nmap (network mapper),
  448–449
online updates, 383
OpenSSH configuration,
  425–426
PPP connection setup, 193
release versions, 15
Rhythmbox, 151
Samba installation, 521

security updates, 405
sendmail mail server,
  473–486
software development
  tools, 531–532
software installation,
  58–60
standalone servers, 422
Synaptic Package
  Manager, 59–60
system administration
  tools, 293
Thunderbird e-mail
  reader, 241–244
debuggers. *See also* GNU
  debugger
  programming errors, 530
  software development
    tools, 532
decimal notation, 197–198
Denial of Service (DoS)
  attack, 391, 394
deselect command,
  376–377
Desktop Activity Settings
  command, 88–89
Desktop Pager, 93
detection
  host security review, 442
  network security, 445
  security audit test, 440
  security mitigation, 397
/dev directory, 319–321
device files, 319–321
devices
  /etc/fstab
    configuration file,
    349–350
  backup media, 353–354
  block devices, 320
  character devices,
    320–321
  floppy drives, 360–362
  major device numbers, 320
  minor device numbers, 320

mounting/unmounting, 132–133, 347–350
network devices, 321
peripherals, 24, 26
`udev` program, 321
`df` command, 133–135, 314
dial-up networking, 177–178, 189–194
`dig` program, 500
digiKam, 149–150
digital cameras, 149–150
Digital Equipment Corporation (DEC, 200
digital signatures, GNU Privacy Guard (GnuPG), 415–417
Digital Subscriber Line (DSL), 176–184
directories. *See also* folders
  absolute pathname, 125
  copying files between, 129–130
  creating, 130–131
  current directory display, 124
  deleting, 131, 157, 160
  hierarchical structure, 344–347
  Linux structure, 119–124
  listing commands, 126–128
  moving files between, 130
  navigation commands, 124–125
  permission commands, 126–128
  `/proc` file system listing, 317–318
  relative names, 125
  renaming, 157, 160
  switching between, 102, 125
directory paths, 253
Directory Services, 398

DIRECWAY, Internet connection, 178
disk partitions, 31–34, 38–39
disk performance, 314–315
disk usage, 314–315
disks. *See also* hard drives
  disk-space usage commands, 133–135
  types, 25
display adapters. *See* video cards
distributions
  applications, 20–21
  Debian release types, 15
  distribution-specific version numbers, 15
  `dists` folder, 37
  Filesystem Hierarchy Standard (FHS), 345
  Firefox installation, 255
  GNU General Public License (GLP), 14
  GNU software, 17–20
  GUIs, 20–21
  hardware compatibility checking, 35–36
  Internet servers, 22
  Linux Standard Base (LSB), 15–16
  Live CD/DVD, 14
  versus Live CDs, 31
  log in process, 66
  network protocols, 21
  NFS server startup, 350
  online documentation, 23
  online help, 23
  online updates, 382–388
  opening a CD/DVD, 58
  package descriptions, 11–14
  QTParted partition tool, 33–34
  security updates, 405

software development tools, 22–23
software installation, 58–63
text mode installation, 46
X Window System, 20–21
`dists` folder, 37
DIX standard, 200–201
`dmesg` command, 66, 203
documentation, online, 23
documents
  e-mail attachments, 235
  frequently used access in KDE Desktop, 90
  GNOME creation, 79
  GnuPG encryption/decryption, 420–421
  recently used access in KDE Desktop, 92
  World Wide Web formats, 249–250
dollar sign ($) character, 505–506
Dolphin
  copying files/folders, 160
  deleting files/directories, 160
  folder creation, 160
  renaming files/directories, 160
  viewing files/folders, 158
  viewing text files, 160
Domain Name System (DNS)
  Berkley Internet Name Domain (BIND), 498–501
  caching name server, 503–513
  country codes, 497
  dial-up networking, 190
  distributed hierarchical database, 495
  distributed responsibility, 496

Domain Name System
(DNS) *(continued)*
/etc/named.conf file,
503–505
fully qualified domain
name (FQDN), 497–498
hierarchical domain
names, 496–498
Internet service, 495
localhost.zone file, 511
master zones, 505
namespaces, 497–498
primary name server,
513–514
resolver configuration,
502–503
resource record (RR)
formats, 506–509
reverse lookups, 500–501
reverse mapping, 511–512
root domain, 497
root zone file, 509–511
standards, 496
subdomains, 496–498
top-level domains, 497
utility programs, 500–501
zone file formats, 505–506
domain names, 253
DOS partition, 359–360,
362–366
dot-dot (..) characters, 125
dotted-decimal notation, 197
dotted-quad notation, 197
double greater than (>>)
characters, 104
double question marks (??)
characters, 117
downstream data, 184–186
dpkg command, 374–376
driver modules, 322–324
drivers
loadable driver modules,
322–324
printer setup, 56
software-based modems,
35, 191

drives, mounting/
unmounting, 132–133
DSL/cable modem NAT
router, 204–206
du command, 133–135, 314
DVD drive, 32, 35
DVD-ROMs
burning, 32, 37
desktop icon display, 58
file backups, 26
mounting/unmounting
drives, 25, 132–133
Dynamic Host Configuration
Protocol (DHCP), port
67, 198, 459

## E

ed, text editor, 163–167
edit-compile-debug cycle,
programming, 530–531
Electronic Industries
Association/
Telecommunications
Industries Association
(EIA/TIA), 201–202
e-mail
at (@) sign address
conventions, 234
attachments, 235
GNOME top panel icon, 85
HTML messages, 235–236
Internet service, 22, 175
Internet Service Provider
(ISP) setup, 236
Linux supported mail
readers, 236
mail transport agent
(MTA), 234–235
mail user agent (MUA),
234–235
security alerts, 404–405
encryption
GNU Privacy Guard
(GnuPG), 398, 414–421
public key, 414–415

env command, 338–340
environment variables
displaying, 530
operating system
concept, 530
viewing the current
environment, 338–340
Epiphany, browser, 255
error messages, 104
/etc/fstab file, 349–350
/etc/group file, 337–338
/etc/host.conf file, 219
/etc/hosts file, 218
/etc/hosts.allow
file, 220
/etc/hosts.deny file,
220–221
/etc/inittab file,
302–304
/etc/modprobe.conf file,
323–324
/etc/mtools.conf file,
363–364
/etc/named.conf file,
503–505
/etc/network/
interfaces file,
227–228
/etc/networks file, 219
/etc/nsswitch.conf, 221
/etc/passwd file
password storage,
407–408
user accounts, 335–336
/etc/resolv.conf file,
219–220
/etc/samba/smb.conf
file, 520
/etc/samba/smbusers,
520
/etc/shadow file, 408–409
Ethernet cards
cable modem, 186–187
Digital Subscriber Line
(DSL), 27, 179, 181–182

Ethernet hubs, 182–183
Ethernet LANs, 199–203
Evolution Mail
  e-mail reader, 237–240
  GNOME top panel icon, 85
  mail user agent (MUA),
    234–235
Examples folder, Ubuntu
  Live CD, 36–37
exclamation points (!!), 107
executable files, set user ID
  permissions, 413–414
expire program,
  InterNetNews (INN), 487
expressions
  bash shell support, 555
  evaluating, 558
  programming, 531
eXtensible Markup
  Language (XML), 274
external drives, 353–354

# F

Favorites menu category,
  KDE Desktop, 90
Fedora
  anonymous FTP
    downloads, 282
  automatic Samba
    startup, 523
  automatic server
    startup, 306–307
  automatic standalone
    server startup, 466–469
  Berkley Internet Name
    Domain (BIND),
    498–501
  /etc/fstab file, 350
  Evolution e-mail reader,
    237–240
  gFTP client, 278–279
  GNOME Ghostview
    application, 154

Internet super server
  configuration, 423
InterNetNews (INN)
  server, 486–493
KDE Akregator RSS reader,
  275–275
KFTPGrabber, 280–281
Login Manager, 229
name server startup, 512
Nessus Security Scanner,
  449–451
network startup on
  system boot, 228
NFS server startup,
  350, 518
nmap (network mapper),
  448–449
online updates, 383–387
opening a CD/DVD, 58
OpenSSH configuration,
  425–426
Pidgin IM client, 246–247
Red Hat Package Manager
  (RPM) files, 61–62
Rhythmbox, 151
RPM commands, 368
Samba configuration, 521
Samba installation, 521
security level
  configuration tool,
  431–432
security updates, 405
sendmail mail server,
  473–486
Service Configuration
  utility, 467–468
software development
  tools, 531–532
software installation,
  61–62
Software Update, 383–384
source RPMs (SRPMs),
  382
standalone servers,
  422, 446

system administration
  tools, 293–294
wireless network
  configuration, 213–216
X Multimedia System
  (XMMS), 378–379
xinetd server, 446,
  461–464
Yum updater, 385–387
Fedora Live USB Creator,
  bootable flash drives,
  42–43
fiber-to-the-home
  (FTTH), 178
file managers, 154–160
file sharing
  Network File System
    (NFS), 350–352,
    515–519
  Samba, 519–523
file systems
  backing up/restoring files,
    352–359
  copying files between
    directories, 129–130
  creating directories,
    130–131
  deleting a directory, 131
  deleting files, 130
  device mounting/
    unmounting, 347–350
  directory listing
    commands, 126–127
  directory navigation
    commands, 124–125
  directory structure,
    119–124
  disk-space usage
    commands, 133–135
  /etc/fstab
    configuration file,
    349–350
  file ownership commands,
    128–129

file systems *(continued)*
  file permission
    commands, 127–129
  file searches, 131–132
  Filesystem Hierarchy
    Standard (FHS), 345
  floppy disk, 360–362
  hierarchy, 344–347
  information organization,
    343–344
  mounting a DOS partition,
    359–360
  mounting a Windows
    partition, 359–360
  mounting/unmounting
    commands, 132–133
  moving files between
    directories, 130
  mtools command,
    362–366
  Network File System
    (NFS), 350–352, 515–519
  NTFS partition mount, 362
  pathnames, 120–121, 345
  root directory, 119–121
  Samba, 519–523
  standard directories
    listing, 346
  supported types, 26–27
  sysfs, 321
  system administration
    tasks, 292
  top-level directories,
    121–122
  /usr directory listing, 346
  usr subdirectories, 123
  /var directory listing, 346
  var subdirectories,
    123–124
File Transfer Protocol (FTP)
  anonymous FTP
    downloads, 281–282
  binary command, 287
  command-line client,
    283–287
  disabling prompting, 287

gFTP, 277–279
  KFTPGrabber, 280–281
  port 21, 199, 460
  supported Linux
    clients, 277
  TCP/IP application layer
    protocol, 196
  vsftpd server, 22
  Web browser as FTP
    client, 281–282
file transfer utilities, 22, 399
file:// protocol, 252
filenames
  asterisk (*) wildcard, 104,
    105–106
  case-sensitive, 120
  character limitations, 120
  DEB file conventions, 374
  Red Hat Package Manager
    (RPM) conventions, 369
  URL conventions, 253
files. *See also* text files
  application associations,
    79, 89
  backup devices, 26
  backup strategies,
    353–354
  changing ownership,
    340–341
  character deletions, 116
  character substitutions,
    116
  content display, 102
  copying between
    directories, 129–130
  copying in Dolphin, 160
  default permissions,
    412–413
  deleting, 130, 157, 160
  devices, 319–321
  /dev/null, 104
  e-mail attachments, 235
  GNOME search, 83–84
  hierarchical structure,
    344–347

moving between
    directories, 130
  Nautilus File Manager
    navigation, 157
  ownership, 410–411
  permissions, 127–129,
    410–414
  processing commands,
    114–117
  /proc file system listing,
    317–318
  renaming, 157, 160
  RSS feed, 274–275
  saving error messages, 104
  search commands,
    131–132
  set user ID permissions,
    413–414
  splitting, 116–117
  standard input, 103
  standard output, 103–104
  system configuration
    listing, 307–310
  viewing, 155, 158–159
Filesystem Hierarchy
  Standard (FHS)
  LSB standards, 15
  UNIX-like operating
    systems, 345
find command, 131–132
Firefox
  anonymous FTP
    downloads, 281–282
  GNOME top panel icon, 85
  home page display,
    258–259
  menus, 258
  startup process, 255–256
  status bar, 257
  tabbed browsing, 256
  Thunderbird e-mail
    reader, 241–244
  toolbars, 256–257
  Web browser, 255–260
  Web surfing, 259–260

`firestarter` package, Ubuntu, 187
firewalls
  application-proxy gateway, 429
  controlled internal network access point, 392
  data processing, 426–427
  desirable characteristics, 427–428
  `firestarter` package, 187
  Internet connections, 27
  `iptables` command, 432–435
  Network Address Translation (NAT), 430
  packet filters, 428
  stateful inspection, 428–429
fixed wireless broadband (FWB or WiMAX), 178
flash drive
  backup media, 353–354
  BIOS configuration boot order, 43
  Linux installation process, 41–43
floppy disks
  backup media, 353–354
  mounting/unmounting, 360–362
  splitting large files, 116–117
  `tar` program archives, 26
flow-control statements, 531
FOCUS-LINUX, 404
folders. *See also* directories
  Dolphin, 158–160
  GNOME, 78–79
  KDE Desktop, 89
  Nautilus File Manager, 155, 157
`for` loop, `bash` shell, 558

forums, newsgroup similarities, 261
Forward button, 257
`FORWARD` chain, 432–435
`.forward` file, 485
forward slash (/)
  file system hierarchy, 344–345
  `root` directory, 119–121
frames, Ethernet LANs, 201
Free Lossless Audio Codec (FLAC) format, 151
Free Software Foundation (FSF), 16
`ftp` command, 283
`ftp://` protocol, 252
full distributions, versus Live CDs, 31
fully qualified domain name (FQDN) 497–498
functions
  `bash` shell support, 555
  calling, 556–557
  programming, 531
FVWM, graphical user interface (GUI), 77

## G

Gadu-Gadu, IM protocol, 233
Games, main menu category, 82
Games menu subcategory, KDE Desktop, 91
gateways, LAN to Internet connections, 204–206
`gcc` command, 532–536
`gdb` command, GNU debugger, 544–549
gFTP, FTP client, 277–279
gigahertz (GHz), processor speed, 35
GNOME Ghostview, 152, 154
GNOME Straw, 275

GNU C compiler (gcc), ANSI-standard C programs, 24
GNU C++ compiler (g++), ANSI-standard C++ programs, 24
GNU compiler for Java (gcj), 24
GNU debugger. *See also* debuggers
  `gdb` command, 544–549
  program preparations, 544
  task types, 543
  troubleshooting programs, 24
GNU `emacs` editor, source files, 24
GNU General Public License (GPL)
  distributions, 14
  programming, 550–551
GNU Image Manipulation Program (GIMP), 21, 152–154
GNU Lesser General Public License (LGPL), programming, 551–552
GNU `make` utility
  large programs, 24
  `makefile` file elements, 537–539
  makefile names, 537
  `running a makefile`, 541–543
  `sample makefile`, 540–541
  software development tools, 531
  variables, 539–540
GNU `makefile` file, 537
GNU Object Model Environment (GNOME)
  aligning icons, 79
  audio CD playback, 150–151
  bottom panel, 85–86

GNU Object Model
Environment (GNOME)
*(continued)*
calculator application, 148
command shortcuts, 78
context menus, 78–79
desktop backgrounds, 79
desktop cleanup, 79
document creation, 79
Evolution e-mail reader,
237–240
file/application
associations, 79
folder creation, 78
gFTP client, 277–279
graphical user interface
(GUI), 20–21
help viewers, 23
icon context menus, 79–80
icon property display, 80
log out versus shut
down, 73
Login Manager, 229
Main Menu button, 81–83
menu hierarchy, 81–82
Nautilus File Manager,
154–157
network startup on
system boot, 229
opening folders, 79
panels, 80–86
Pidgin IM client, 246–247
Places Menu button, 83–84
renaming icons, 80
searches, 83–84
system administration
tools, 293, 296–297
System Menu button,
84–85
System Monitor, 226–227
Text Editor startup,
161–162
Thunderbird e-mail
reader, 241–244
top panel, 81, 85

Trash icon, 80
trashing icons, 80
virtual consoles, 100
GNU Privacy Guard
(GnuPG)
digital signatures, 415–417
document encryption/
decryption, 420–421
host security issues, 398
key exchange, 418–419
key pairs, 417–418
public key encryption,
414–415
signing a file, 419–420
GNU profiling utility
(gprof), 24
GNU software, 17–20
GNU's Not UNIX, GNU
Project, 16
Google Groups, 48, 273
Google Search button, 257
GParted, partition editor,
38–39
GRand Unified Bootloader
(GRUB), installation
troubleshooting, 47
graphical desktops
distribution package, 11
graphical user interface
(GUI), 20–21
help viewers, 23
graphical user interfaces
(GUIs), distribution
component, 20–21
graphics editors,
applications, 152–154
Graphics, main menu
category, 82
Graphics menu
subcategory, 91
greater than (>), file
redirection, 103–104
grep command, file text
search, 101
group IDs, user accounts,
337–338

groupadd command,
337–338
groupdel command, 338
groups
changing file ownership,
340–341
deleting, 338
host security issues, 398
new groups, 337–338
user accounts, 334
GRUB boot loader
Linux startup, 65–66
recovering from forgotten
root password, 300
gzip program, 378–379

## H

hard drives. *See also* disks
accessing in KDE
Desktop, 91
backup prior to Linux
installation, 32, 38
defined, 25
GParted partitions, 38–39
hardware component, 35
partitions, 31–34, 38–39
performance monitoring,
314–315
programming
concepts, 528
hardware
DVD drive, 35
hard drives, 35
installation compatibility
checking, 35–36
installation information
gathering, 32
keyboards, 35
memory, 36
modems, 35
monitors, 35
mouse, 35
network cards, 35
printers, 36

processors, 35
programming concepts, 527–529
SCSI controller, 36
sound cards, 36
system administration tasks, 292
video cards, 36
hardware abstraction layer (HAL), mounting/unmounting devices, 350
`hdparm` program, performance monitoring, 315–315
head end. *See* Cable Modem Termination System (CMTS)
Help, GNOME top panel icon, 85
help system, 23
`history` command, repeating previously type commands, 107
Home button, Firefox navigation, 257
home directory, tilde (~) character, 125
home page, Firefox display, 256, 258–259
host address, TCP/IP networking, 197
host connectivity, configuration viewing, 223
`host` program, Domain Name System (DNS), 500, 501
host security, system administration tasks, 292
hosts
    security audits, 442–445
    security issues, 397–398
hot plugs, USB devices, 26

`hotplug` program, 321
HP PA-RISC processors, 10
HTML anchors, URL conventions, 253
`http://` protocol, 251–252
`https://` protocol, 252
hubs
    cable modem connections, 187–189
    DSL connections, 182–183
    Ethernet LANs, 202
    LAN to Internet connections, 204–206
hypertext links. *See* links
HyperText Markup Language (HTML)
    e-mail attachments, 235–236
    Web document format, 250
HyperText Transfer Protocol (HTTP)
    Apache `httpd` server, 22
    port 80, 199, 460
    TCP/IP application layer protocol, 196
    Web document transfers, 250
`hyphen (-) character`, creation, 112

## 1

I/O redirection, shell commands, 102–104
i386 processors, 10
IA32 architecture processors, 10
IBM mainframes, 10
IBM zSeries processors, LSB standards, 16
icon context menus
    GNOME Desktop element, 79–80
    KDE Desktop, 89

icons
    GNOME, 80
    KDE Desktop, 89
    property display in GNOME, 80
    property display in KDE Desktop, 89
    trashing, 80, 89
ICQ, IM protocol, 233
IEEE, Wi-Fi standards, 207–208
`if-then-else` structure, `bash` shell, 557–558
image editors, GNU Image Manipulation program (GIMP), 21
images, e-mail attachments, 235
impact, risk analysis, 394–395
Impress, presentation application, 146–147
`in.telnetd`, TELNET protocol, 22
incident handling, security policy element, 396
incident response, host security review, 445
`incoming.conf` file, InterNetNews (INN), 488, 491
incremental backups, `tar` command, 358
independent testing, 437
independent verification, security audits, 437
`inetd` server
    Internet super server, 461–462
    network security review, 446
    standalone services, 422–423
information sharing, Internet service, 176

infrastructure mode, wireless Ethernet networks, 208–209
init process
  changing run levels, 304–305
  Linux startup, 301–303
  startup scripts, 305–306
init 0 command, shut down, 72
initialization vector (IV), WEP, 210
inn.conf file, InterNetNews (INN), 488–489
innd program
  InterNetNews (INN), 487
  news server, 22
INPUT chain, iptables command, 432–435
input/output (I/O), programming, 529
installation
  bootable flash drive, 41–43
  booting from the DVD drive, 32
  burning CDs/DVDs, 32
  Debian applications, 58–60
  Firefox, 255
  full distributions versus Live CDs, 31
  hard drive backup prior to Linux installation, 32, 38
  hard drive partitions, 31–34
  hardware compatibility checking, 35–36
  hardware information gathering, 32
  InterNetNews (INN), 486
  Nessus Security Scanner, 450
  reboot process, 34

Red Hat Package Manager (RPM) files, 371–372
software development tools, 531–532
source RPMs (SRPMs), 382
system administration tasks, 292
text mode, 46
troubleshooting, 45–54
Ubuntu, 39–40
Ubuntu applications, 58–60
instant messaging (IM)
  Linux supported clients, 236
  one-to-one chat, 233
Institute of Electrical and Electronics Engineers (IEEE), 802-series, 201
Integrated Drive Electronics (IDE), device connection type, 35
Integrated Services Digital Network (ISDN), 180
integrity check (IC) field, WEP, 210
Intel 32-bit (IA32) processors, LSB standards, 15–16
Intel 64-bit (IA64) processors, LSB standards, 16
Intel, Ethernet development, 200
Intel processors, 10
International Organization for Standardization (ISO), country codes, 497
Internet. *See also* World Wide Web
  backbones, 176
  broadband over power lines (BPL), 178
  cable modem, 177, 184–189

dial-up networking, 177, 189–194
Digital Subscriber Line (DSL), 176–184
DIRECWAY, 178
e-mail service, 175
fiber-to-the-home (FTTH), 178
fixed wireless broadband (FWB or WiMAX), 178
information sharing, 176
local area network (LAN) connections, 204–206
main menu category, 82
network of networks, 176
network security issues, 399
newsgroups, 176
remote access, 176
satellite Internet access, 178
security concerns, 391–392
security policy, 396
StarBand, 178
TCP/IP protocol, 197
World Wide Web service, 175
Internet Control Message Protocol (ICMP), host connectivity check, 223
Internet Engineering Task Force (IETF)
  DNS standards, 496
  IPv6, 198
Internet menu subcategory, KDE Desktop, 91
Internet Message Access Protocol version 4 (IMAP4), e-mail, 234–235
Internet Protocol (IP)
  connection-oriented protocol, 457
  dial-up networking, 190

network connections, 176
TCP/IP network layer
protocol, 196
Internet Relay Chat (IRC),
IM protocol, 233
Internet servers, 22
Internet Service Provider
(ISP)
e-mail setup, 236
Internet connection
methods, 176–177
news servers, 261, 266
Internet services
Berkley sockets
interface, 456
client/server architecture,
455–456
connectionless
protocols, 457
connection-oriented
protocols, 456–457
disabling standalone
services, 422
network applications, 455
network security, 399
network security
review, 446
penetration test, 447
port numbers, 198–199,
459–460
security policy, 396
server process, 460–461
super server
configuration, 422–423
TCP wrapper
configuration, 423–424
TCP/IP, 456
Internet super server,
461–464
Internet Systems
Consortium (ISC), 487
InterNetNews (INN)
configuration, 486–493
control files, 488
`ctlinnd` program, 487

`expire` program, 487
`incoming.conf` file,
488, 491
`inn.conf` file, 488–489
`innd` program, 487
installation, 486
`newsfeeds` file, 488,
490–491
`nnrpd` program, 487
`nntpsend` program, 487
`readers.conf` file,
488, 492
startup, 492–493
internetworking,
interconnection of
networks, 176
IP addresses, TCP/IP
networking, 197–198
IP routing tables,
configuration viewing,
222–223
IP version 6 (IPv6), IP
addresses, 198
`iptables` command
firewall configuration, 27
packet filtering, 187,
432–435
ISO images, burning CDs/
DVDs, 37
ISOLINUX boot loader, Live
CDs, 65–66
items, cutting/copying in
KDE Desktop, 89
`iwconfig` command, 216

# *J*

Jabber, IM protocol, 233
jiffy, time measurement, 67
job scheduling, system
administration tasks,
324–330
jobs, current status in KDE
Desktop, 94

# *K*

K Desktop Environment
(KDE)
Administration menu
subcategory, 91–92
Application Starter, 90
Applications menu
category, 91
bottom panel, 94–95
calculator application, 148
CD player application,
150–151
Computer menu
category, 91
configuration settings,
95–98
context menus, 88–89
current date display, 94
currently open window
display, 93
cutting/copying items, 89
Dolphin application, 154,
157–160
Evolution e-mail reader,
237–240
Favorites menu
category, 90
file associations, 89
frequently used
applications/
documents, 90
Games menu
subcategory, 91
graphical user interface
(GUI), 20–21, 87
Graphics menu
subcategory, 91
hard drive access, 91
help viewers, 23
icon context menus, 89
icon property display, 89
Internet menu
subcategory, 91
K3b application, 152

K Desktop Environment (KDE) *(continued)*
KFTPGrabber client, 277, 280–281
KMail e-mail reader, 244–246
KNode newsreader, 266, 271–272
Kontact application, 147–148
KWrite text editor, 161–162
Leave menu category, 91
log out, 73, 91
Login Manager, 229
Main Menu button, 90–93
menu hierarchy, 90–93
Multimedia menu subcategory, 92
network connection information display, 94
network startup on system boot, 229
Office menu subcategory, 92
opening a folder, 89
opening applications, 91
panel, 87–88, 90–94
panel configuration settings, 94–95
recently used applications/documents, 92
Recently Used menu category, 91
removable memory device access, 91
renaming icons, 89
Samba configuration, 521
Settings menu subcategory, 92
switching between applications, 94
System menu subcategory, 93

System Settings, 97–98
system time display, 94
trashing icons, 89
Utilities menu subcategory, 93
virtual consoles, 100
workspace navigation, 93
K3b, CD/DVD burner, 152
KDE Akregator, RSS feed reader, 275–276
kernel. *See* Linux
key exchange, GNU Privacy Guard (GnuPG), 418–419
key pairs, 417–418
keyboards, peripheral device, 26, 35
KFTPGrabber, FTP client, 280–281
`kill` command, killing running processes, 113
Klipper Clipboard, KDE Desktop panel icon, 94
KMail
e-mail reader, 244–246
mail user agent (MUA), 234–235
KNode, newsgroup reader, 266, 271–272
Knoppix
automatic standalone server startup, 466–469
boot commands, 48–51
CD/DVD desktop icon display, 58
`inetd` server 461–462
K3b application, 152
manual standalone server, 465
Nessus Security Scanner, 449–451
`nmap` (network mapper), 448–449
penetration tests, 447
QTParted partition tool, 33–34

`root` user, 299
system administration tools, 294–295
Konqueror, Web browser, 255
Konsole command, KDE Desktop terminal window access, 88–89
Kontact, calendar application, 147–148
Kopete, IM client, 247
KWrite, KDE Desktop text editor, 161–162

## L

Leave command, KDE Desktop, 88–89
Leave menu category, KDE Desktop, 91
less than (<), file redirection, 103
letter codes, file permissions, 128–129
LILO boot loader
Linux startup, 65–66
recovering from forgotten `root` password, 300
links
at (@) sign character, 126
World Wide Web, 251–253
Linux
boot options listing, 51–54
command listing, 108–111
configuration file listing, 307–310
distribution contents, 16–23
distribution packages, 11–14
distribution-specific version numbers, 15
enabling packet filtering, 430–435
environment variables listing, 340

Filesystem Hierarchy Standard (FHS), 345
FTP clients, 277
GUI sysadmin tools, 293–298
Linux Standard Base (LSB), 15–16
mail readers, 236
multiuser/multitasking operating system, 11
network protocols, 21
network setup tools, 27
newsreaders, 266
online updates, 382–388
open source project, 11
OpenOffice.org applications, 21
operating system processes, 9–11
platforms, 10
/proc file systm listing, 317–318
shell settings, 68–72
shutting down, 72–73
standalone services listing, 469–471
startup process, 65–68
Web browsers, 255
version numbers, 14–15
Linux Assigned Names And Numbers Authority (LANANA), 320
Linux Standard Base (LSB)
  binary standards, 15–16
  Filesystem Hierarchy Standard (FHS), 345
Live CDs
  versus bootable flash drive, 41, 44
  distribution packages, 14
  versus full distributions, 31
  ISOLINUX boot loader, 65–66
  PC boot process, 32
  Ubuntu, 36–37

liveusb-creator program, bootable flash drives, 42–43
loadable driver modules, 322–324
loadable kernel modules. *See* loadable driver modules
local area networks (LANs). *See also* networks
  Ethernet LAN setup, 199–203
  Internet connections, 204–206
local loop, Digital Subscriber Line (DSL), 178
local newsgroups. *See also* newsgroups
  configuration file updates, 493–494
  hierarchy, 493
  newsgroup addition, 494
  testing, 494
local printers, configuration settings, 55–57
localhost.zone file, Domain Name System (DNS), 511
locate command, file searches, 132
Location text box, Firefox navigation, 257
Lock Screen command, KDE Desktop, 88–89
log files
  host security issues, 398
  system security monitoring, 421
log ins, root, 111–112
log out
  KDE Desktop, 91
  versus shut down, 73
Log Out dialog box, shutting down properly, 72–73

Login Manager, network startup on system boot, 229
logins, root, 66, 68
Logout, GNOME top panel icon, 85
LONE-TAR, backup utility, 354
loop length, Digital Subscriber Line (DSL), 181
loops per jiffy (LPJ), time measurement, 67
ls command, directory listing, 126–127

## M

macro file, sendmail mail server, 478–481
macros, GNU make utility, 539–540
mail command, mail-delivery test, 474–475
mail readers
  Evolution, 237–240
  KMail, 244–246
  mail user agent (MUA), 234–235
  supported types, 236
  Thunderbird, 241–244
mail servers, 234–235
mail transport agent (MTA), e-mail server, 234–235
mail user agent (MUA), e-mail reader, 234–235
mailing lists, security alerts, 404–405
mailto: protocol, URL conventions, 252
Main Menu button
  GNOME Desktop, 81–83
  KDE Desktop, 90–93
major device numbers, 320
Makefile file, 537

makefile file, 537–539
man command, online
    documentation, 23
managed mode, wireless
    Ethernet networks, 209
Mandriva Enterprise
    Server 5, LSB 4.0
    certification, 16
master zones, Domain Name
    System (DNS), 505
MD5 message-digest
    algorithm, password
    encryption, 409
media, backups, 353–354
megahertz (MHz),
    processor speed, 35
memory
  256MB minimum
    requirement, 35
  hardware component, 36
  performance monitoring,
    313–314
  programming
    concepts, 528
  signal 11 (SIGSEV) error, 51
  system information
    display, 315–318
menus
  Firefox, 258
  GNOME hierarchy, 81–82
  KDE Desktop hierarchy,
    90–93
m4 macro processor,
    476–478
mget command, FTP
    transfers, 287
microfilters, Digital
    Subscriber Line (DSL),
    181–182
microprocessor. *See*
    processors; central
    processing unit
million-bits-per-second
    (Mbps), 176
minor device numbers,
    device files, 320

MIPS R4x00 processors, 10
MIPS R5x00 processors, 10
misc.test newsgroup,
    news postings, 271
mitigation, risk analysis,
    394, 396–397
mkdir command, creating
    a directory, 130–131
modems
  dial-up networking
    connections, 191
  Digital Subscriber Line
    (DSL), 179
  GUI Internet dial-up
    tools, 27
  hardware component, 35
  Internet connection
    methods, 176–177
  LAN to Internet
    connections, 204–206
moderated newsgroup,
    spam reduction, 264
modprobe command,
    loadable driver
    modules, 323–324
monitors, hardware
    component, 35
monolithic program, 322
more command, file
    content display, 71
Motorola 6800
    processors, 10
mount command
  devices, 347–350
  DOS partition, 359–360
  drives, 132–133
  Windows partition,
    359–360
mount points, Network File
    System (NFS), 518
mounting
  devices, 347–350
  disks, 25
  DOS partition, 359–360
  floppy disks, 360–362

Network File System
    (NFS), 518–519
  Windows partition,
    359–360
mouse, peripheral device,
    26, 35
Mozilla Firefox. *See* Firefox
Mozilla Mail. *See*
    Thunderbird
Mozilla Navigator, Web
    browser, 255
MP3 files, sound file
    playback, 151
MS-DOS file system, mtools
    command, 362–366
MSN Messenger, IM
    protocol, 233
mtools command, MS-DOS
    file system access,
    362–366
multimedia, applications,
    149–152
Multimedia menu
    subcategory, KDE
    Desktop, 92
multivolume archive, tar
    command, 356–357
mv command, moving files
    between directories, 130

## N

named daemon, BIND
    component, 498–499
namespaces, Domain Name
    System (DNS), 497–498
National Vulnerability
    Database (NVD), 440
Nautilus File Manager
  burning CDs, 151–152
  burning CDs/DVDs,
    155–156
  copying files, 157
  deleting files/directories,
    157

folder creation, 157
graphical shell
    application, 154–157
moving files between
    folders, 157
renaming files/directories,
    157
switching views, 156–157
viewing files/folders, 155
Navigation toolbar, 256–257
Nero, burning CDs/DVDs, 37
Nessus Security Scanner,
    security auditing tool,
    449–451
`netfilter`, packet
    filtering software,
    430–431
Netscape, RSS versions, 274
`netstat` command,
    network status check,
    224–225
Network Address
    Translation (NAT)
    routers
cable modems, 187–189
DSL connections, 182–183
firewalls, 430
network address
    socket attribute, 456
    TCP/IP networking, 197
network cards, 35
Network connection, KDE
    Desktop panel icon, 94
network devices, 321
Network File System (NFS)
file sharing, 350–352,
    515–519
file system export, 351,
    516–518
Linux support, 26
mount points, 518
mounting, 352, 518–519
NSVv4 standard, 516
port 111, 199, 460
RPCSEC_GSS protocol, 516
security vulnerabilities,
    351

network interfaces, 222
Network News Transfer
    Protocol (NNTP)
    `innd` server, 22
    newsgroups, 262
    port 119, 199, 460
network printers, 55–57
network security, system
    administration tasks,
    292
network status, system
    administration tasks,
    292
Network Time Protocol
    (NTP), port 123, 460
Network
GNOME top panel icon, 85
TCP/IP layer, 196
networks. *See also* local
    area networks (LANs);
    wireless Ethernet
    networks
connection information
    display in KDE
    Desktop, 94
distribution component, 21
internetworking, 176
IP addresses, 197–198
Network File System
    (NFS), 26
protocols, 21
security issues, 397–399
setup tools, 27
TCP/IP layers, 195–197
news postings, newsgroup
    conventions, 270–271
`news://` protocol, URL
    conventions, 252–253
news servers
InterNetNews (INN),
    486–493
newsgroup, 261
news services, Internet
    service, 22
`newsfeeds` file,
    InterNetNews (INN),
    488, 490–491

newsgroups. *See also* local
    newsgroups
hierarchy, 262–264
Internet service, 176
InterNetNews (INN),
    486–493
Linux-related listing,
    264–265
`misc.test`, 271
moderated
    newsgroups, 264
naming conventions,
    262–263
newsreaders, 266–272
postings, 270–271
reading/researching from
    Web sites, 272–273
security alerts, 404
spam concerns, 264
subscriptions, 269–270
supported
    newsreaders, 266
top-level categories,
    263–264
Usenet origination,
    261–262
NewsMonster, RSS feed
    reader, 275
newsreaders
KNode, 266, 271–272
newsgroup
    requirement, 261
Pan, 266
Thunderbird, 266–271
NFS servers, startup
    methods, 350
`nmap` (network mapper),
    port-scanning tool,
    448–449
`nmbd` name server,
    Samba, 520
`nmblookup` command,
    Samba, 520
`nnrpd` program,
    InterNetNews (INN),
    487

nntpsend program,
InterNetNews (INN), 487
Notifications and Jobs, KDE
Desktop panel icon, 94
NT File System (NTFS)
GParted partitions, 38–39
partition mounting, 362

## O

object code, programming
element, 530
Office menu subcategory,
KDE Desktop, 92
Office, main menu
category, 82
Ogg Vorbis files, XMMS
playback, 151
one-time jobs, scheduling,
325–327
online documentation,
distribution
component, 23
online updates
Debian, 383
Fedora, 383–387
SUSE, 387
Ubuntu, 383
Xandros Networks,
387–388
Open Office, productivity
software, 21
Open Secure Shell
(OpenSSH), remote
login security, 424–426
open source, Linux
distributions, 11
Open windows
GNOME bottom panel
icon, 86
KDE Desktop panel
icon, 93
OpenOffice.org office suite,
applications, 143–147

openSUSE. *See also* SUSE
Evolution e-mail reader,
237–240
hard drive partitions,
33–34
LSB 3.1 certification, 16
rebooting after installing
Linux, 34
operating systems
Filesystem Hierarchy
Standard (FHS), 345
host security review
element, 442
Linux processes, 9–11
programming role,
529–530
system administration
tasks, 292
orthogonal frequency-
division multiplexing
(ODFM), Wi-Fi
standards, 208
OS indicator, GNOME top
panel icon, 85
OUTPUT chain, iptables
command, 432–435
ownership
changing users,
340–341, 411
file commands, 128–129
files, 410–411
host security, 398, 445
viewing, 410

## P

package name
DEB file conventions, 374
RPM filename
conventions, 369
packet filter firewall,
characteristics, 428
packet filtering
enabling, 430–435
firewall characteristics, 428

iptables command,
432–435
security level
configuration tool,
431–432
packet sniffing, wireless
Ethernet networks,
225–226
packets, Ethernet LANs, 201
Pan, newsreader, 266
panel icons, KDE Desktop,
93–94
Panel toolbox, KDE Desktop
panel icon, 94
panels
GNOME Desktop, 80–86
KDE Desktop, 87–88, 90–94
pap-secrets file, dial-up
networking, 193–194
parent directory, dot-dot
(..) characters, 125
partitions
GParted partition editor,
38–39
Linux installation on a
Windows PC, 31–34,
38–39
mounting, 359–360
NT File System (NTFS), 362
passwd command,
recovering from
forgotten root
password, 300
Password Authentication
Protocol (PAP), dial-up
networking, 193–194
passwords
dial-up networking,
193–194
/etc/passwd file,
407–408
host security issues, 398
host security review
element, 444–445
password-cracking
programs, 408

pluggable authentication modules (PAMs), 409–410
  recovering from forgotten, 299–301
  root account, 66, 112, 299–301
  shadow passwords, 408–409
  system administration tasks, 291
pathnames, file system hierarchy, 120–121, 345
penetration test, network security review, 447
Pentium processors, 10
Pentium II processors, 400 MHz minimum requirement, 35
performance monitoring
  disk performance, 314–315
  disk usage, 314–315
  top utility, 310–312
  uptime command, 312–313
  vmstat utility, 313–314
period (.) character, newsgroup hierarchy, 262
peripheral
  defined, 24
  installation information gathering, 32
Perl, scripting language, 24
permissions
  changing, 411–412
  changing file ownership, 340–341
  default, 412–413
  directory commands, 126–129
  host security issues, 398
  host security review, 442–445

set user ID, 413–414
shell scripts, 572
viewing, 410
physical, TCP/IP layer, 196
Pidgin, IM client, 246–247
ping command, host connectivity check, 223
pipe (|) character, shell commands, 102
pixels, screen resolution, 35
Places Menu button, GNOME Desktop, 83–84
Playstation 3, 10
pluggable authentication modules (PAMs), password security, 408–409
Point-to-Point Protocol (PPP), dial-up networking, 190, 192–193
policies, security framework, 392, 395–396
port numbers
  application layer protocols, 196
  Internet services, 198–199, 459–460
  penetration tests, 447
  socket attribute, 456
  URL conventions, 253
port scans, penetration tests, 447
Portable Operating System Interface (POSIX), LSB standards, 15
Post Office Protocol (POP), TCP/IP application layer protocol, 196
Post Office Protocol version 3 (POP3), e-mail, 234–235
pound sign (#), HTML anchor, 253

PowerPC processors, 10
PowerPC 32-bit (PPC32) processors, LSB standards, 15–16
PowerPC64 processors, 10
PPP over Ethernet (PPPoE) protocol, Digital Subscriber Line (DSL), 184
presentations, Impress, 146–147
prevention
  host security review, 442
  network security review, 445
  security audit test, 439
primary name server, Domain Name System (DNS), 513–514
printenv command, viewing environment variables, 530
printer configuration tool, 55–57
printers
  adding new, 55–56
  configuration settings, 55–57
  descriptive names, 57
  peripheral device, 26, 36
  system administration tasks, 291
printing, 57, 114
probability, risk analysis, 394–395
/proc file system, 315–318
process file system, 315–318
process ID (PID)
  list display, 113
  viewing currently running processes, 301
processes
  list display, 112–113, 115
  operating system concept, 529

processes *(continued)*
performance monitoring, 310–315
System Monitor, 226–227
viewing currently running, 301
processors. *See also* central processing unit (CPU)
BogoMIPS measurement, 66, 67
hardware component, 35
LSB standards, 15–16
performance monitoring, 310–315
supported types, 10
programming
C compiler, 531–536
C++ compiler, 531–536
edit-compile-debug cycle, 530–531
GNU debugger, 543–549
GNU licenses, 550–552
GNU `make` utility, 531, 537–543
hardware concepts, 527–529
operating system concepts, 529–530
process steps, 530–531
terms, 531
text editors, 531
`prompt` command, 287
protections, security mitigation, 397
protocols
network, 21
URL conventions, 251–253
`ps ax` command, process list display, 112–113, 115
`ps` command, currently running programs display, 71

public key encryption
GNU Privacy Guard (GnuPG), 414–415
Open Secure Shell (OpenSSH), 424–426
`pwd` command, current directory display, 124
Python, programming language, 24

**Q**

QTParted, hard drive partitions, 33–34
queries
Domain Name System (DNS), 500–501
`rpm` command, 369–371
question mark (?) character
file wildcards, 105
HTML anchor, 253
quotation marks (") shell command format, 70, 101

**R**

random access memory (RAM), 24–25
RC4 encryption algorithm, WEP, 209–210
reaction, security mitigation, 397
`readers.conf` file, InterNetNews (INN), 488, 492
Really Simple Syndication (RSS) feeds
aggregators, 275–276
file elements, 274–275

versions, 274
XML 1.0 specification, 274
Recent Pages button, 257
Recently Used menu category, KDE Desktop, 91
recurring jobs, scheduling, 327–330
Red Hat Enterprise Linux Version 5, LSB 3.1 certification, 16
Red Hat Package Manager (RPM) files
filename conventions, 369
installation, 371–372
package information display, 371
package search, 370
queries, 369–371
removing, 372
software installation, 61–62
uninstalled package information, 370
upgrading, 372–373
verification reports, 373–374
version number display, 369
viewing installed, 370
relative names, directories, 125
release numbers, RPM filename conventions, 369
Reload button, Firefox navigation, 257
remote access, Internet service, 176
Remote Authentication Dial-In User Service (RADIUS), WAP2, 210

remote login
  Internet service, 22
  Secure Shell (SSH),
    424–426
Remote Procedure Call
    (RPC), port 111, 199
removable memory
    devices, accessing in
    KDE Desktop, 91
resolutions, monitors, 35
resolver, Domain Name
    System (DNS)
    configuration, 502–503
resolver library, BIND
    component, 498–500
Resource Description
    Format (RDF), RSS
    versions, 274
resource record (RR)
    formats, Domain Name
    System (DNS), 506–509
response
  host security review, 442
  network security
    review, 445
  security audit test, 440
  security mitigation, 397
responsibilities, security
    policy element, 396
restart command,
    manual standalone
    server start/stop, 465
reverse lookups, Domain
    Name System (DNS),
    500–501
reverse mapping, 511–512
Revision Control
    System (RCS)
  software development
    tools, 532
  source file access, 24

revision numbers, DEB file
    conventions, 374
Rhythmbox, sound file
    playback, 151
risk analysis, security
    framework, 393–394
rm command,
    deleting files, 130
rmdir command, deleting
    a directory, 131
root account
  creating, 298–301
  logins, 66, 68
  passwords, 66, 299–301
  su - command, 112, 299
  sudo command, 112
  superuser creation,
    111–112
root directory, file system
    structure, 119–121
root domain, 497
root zone file, Domain
    Name System (DNS),
    509–511
routers
  LAN to Internet
    connections, 204–206
  Network Address
    Translation (NAT),
    182–183, 187–189
routines, programming
    elements, 531
RPCSEC-GSS protocol,
    Network File System
    (NFS), 516
rpm command, Red Hat
    Package Manager
    (RPM) files, 368–374
Run command, KDE
    Desktop, 88–89

run levels
  changing, 304–305
  init process, 301–303
  runlevel command,
    302–303

**S**

Samba
  components, 520
  configuration, 521–523
  file sharing package, 27
  installation, 521
  running, 523
  Samba Web
    Administration Tool
    (SWAT), 521–522
  Windows file sharing,
    519–523
Samba Web Administration
    Tool (SWAT), Samba
    configuration, 521–522
SANS Institute, computer
    vulnerabilities, 440
satellite Internet access, 178
/sbin/ifconfig
    command, network
    interface, 222
/sbin/ifup command,
    network startup on
    system boot, 227–228
/sbin/route command,
    IP routing table,
    222–223
scientific calculators,
    applications, 148
script directories, cron
    jobs, 330
scripts, *See also* bash
    shell; shell scripts
  bash shell support, 69
  shell script, 117–118
  startup, 305–306

SCSI controller, hardware
component, 36
searches
  find command, 131–132
  Google Groups, 273
  grep command, 101
  Places Menu, 83–84
  Red Hat Package Manager
    (RPM) files, 370
  sendmail mail server,
    483–484
Secure Shell (SSH) protocol
  network security, 399
  port 22, 199, 460
  remote login security,
    424–426
  sshd command, 22
security
  alerts, 404–405
  business requirements,
    393–394
  default file permissions,
    412–413
  Denial of Service (DoS)
    attacks, 391, 394
  digital signatures, 415–417
  directories, 410–414
  Directory Services, 398
  files, 410–414
  firewalls, 426–435
  framework elements,
    392–393
  GNU Privacy Guard
    (GnuPG), 398, 414–421
  host issues, 397–398
  implementing solutions,
    396–397
  Internet connection
    concerns, 391–392
  Internet services, 421–424
  iptables command,
    432–435
  Nessus Security Scanner,
    449–451

Network Address
  Translation (NAT), 430
network issues, 397–399
NFS file system
  vulnerabilities, 351
nmap (network mapper),
  448–449
ownerships, 410–411
packet filtering, 430–435
passwords, 407–410
permissions, 410–414
pluggable authentication
  modules (PAMs),
  409–410
policy development, 392,
  395–396
public key encryption,
  414–415
recovering from forgotten
  root password, 301
remote logins, 424–426
risk analysis, 394
Secure Shell (SSH),
  424–426
shadow passwords,
  408–409
system administration
  tasks, 292
system monitoring, 421
TCP wrapper, 423–424
terms, 400–404
unauthorized access, 394
unauthorized information
  disclosure, 394
updates, 404–405
user ID permissions,
  413–414
security audits
  benefits, 438
  host-security reviews,
    442–445
  independent testing, 437

independent
  verification, 437
network-security reviews,
  445–447
nontechnical aspects, 438
reasons for, 438
security policy, 396
standalone services,
  446–447
technical aspects, 439
test implementation,
  439–447
vulnerabilities, 440–441
Security Enhanced Linux
  (SELinux), host
  security, 398
security updates, 398
sed command, shell
  scripts, 565–571
Segment Violation
  Signal (SIGSEGV)
  error, installation
  troubleshooting, 51
semicolon (;) character,
  concatenating
  commands, 102
sendmail mail server
  aliases, 485–486
  configuration, 474–481
  described, 22
  .forward file, 485
  macro file, 478–481
  mail-delivery test, 474–475
  mail transport agent
    (MTA), 234–235
  m4 macro processor,
    476–478
  searches, 483–484
  sendmail.cf file,
    481–483
Simple Mail Transfer
  Protocol (SMTP), 475
sendmail.cf file, control
  operators, 481–483

`server` command, manual standalone server start/stop, 465

server process, Internet services, 199, 460–461

servers. *See also* Web servers
  automatic startup on system boot, 306–307
  `inetd`, 461–462
  Internet super server, 422–423, 461–464
  InterNetNews (INN), 486–493
  mail transport agent (MTA), 234–235
  manual start/stop, 306
  standalone, 422, 464–471
  World Wide Web structure, 250–251
  `xinetd`, 461, 462–464

Service Configuration utility, automatic standalone server, 467–468

Session Manager, network startup on system boot, 229

`set` command, viewing environment variables, 530

Settings menu subcategory, 92

`setuid` programs, permissions, 413–414

Setup, booting from the DVD drive, 32

Setup. *See* BIOS configuration

shadow passwords, security, 408–409

shared libraries, dynamically linked libraries, 24

shell scripts. *See also* `bash` shell; scripts
  accepting arguments, 554–555
  administrator uses, 553–554
  `awk` command, 567–571
  backing up a file before editing, 557–558
  command execution based on variable value, 559–560
  conditional expressions, 571
  editing only an existing file, 558
  `init` process element, 302
  number addition, 558
  one-time run, 571
  permissions, 572
  reading input into a variable, 556
  recurring run, 571
  `sed` command, 565–567
  shell function syntax, 556–557
  task automation benefits, 553–554
  writing, 117–118

shells. *See also* `bash` shell
  command format, 70
  command interpreter application, 17
  command listing, 108–111
  Nautilus File Manager, 154–157
  startup, 69
  switching between, 100
  terminal windows, 99–100
  virtual consoles, 99–100

Short Message Service (SMS), IM protocol, 233

shortcuts, GNOME commands, 78

Show Desktop: Hide, GNOME bottom panel icon, 86

shutdown, system administration tasks, 292

Simple Mail Transfer Protocol (SMTP)
  port 25, 199, 460
  mail transport agent (MTA), 234–235
  `sendmail` server, 22, 475
  TCP/IP application layer protocol, 196

Simple Network Management Protocol (SNMP), ports 161, 162, 199, 460

single dot (.) character, current directory, 125

single-volume archive, `tar` command, 355–356

Small Computer System Interface (SCSI), device connection type, 35

`smbadduser` program, 520

`smbcacls` program, 520

`smbclient` program, 520

`smbcontrol` program, 520

`smbd` server, 520

`smbount` program, 520

`smbpasswd` program, 520

`smbprint` script, 520

`smbstatus` command, 520

`smbtar` program, 520

`smbumount` program, 520

sniffing, network packets, 225–226

socket type, socket attribute, 456

sockets
    Internet services, 456
    TCP/IP networking,
        457–459
softmodems, software-
    based modems, 35, 191
software. *See also*
    applications
    building from source files,
        378–382
    Debian installation, 58–60
    downloading, 378–379
    Fedora installation, 61–62
    host security issues, 398
    SUSE installation, 62
    system administration
        tasks, 292
    Ubuntu installation, 58–60
    unpacking, 378–379
    Xandros Desktop
        installation, 62–63
software development
    tools, distribution
        component, 22–23
Software Update, Fedora
    online updates, 383–384
sort command, file
    sorting, 103, 115–116
sorts, text files, 115–116
Sound & Video, main menu
    category, 82
sound cards, peripheral
    device, 26, 36
sounds, volume control in
    KDE Desktop, 94
source code
    distribution package, 11
    programming, 530
    saving as plain text, 530
source files
    GNU emacs editor, 24
    programming element, 530
    Revision Control System
        (RCS), 24
    software building, 378–382

source RPMs (SRPMs),
    installation, 382
spaces, shell command
    format, 70, 101
spam, newsgroup, 264
split command, splitting
    large files, 116–117
splitters, cable modem
    connections, 186–187
spreadsheets, Calc, 145–146
square brackets [ and ]
    file wildcards, 105
    scripts, 558
sshd, remote logins, 22
stable release, Debian
    distributions, 15
Stallman, Richard, GNU
    Project, 16
standalone servers
    automatic boot time
        startup, 466–469
    listing, 469–471
    manual start/stop, 465
standalone services
    disabling, 422
    network security review
        element, 446–447
StarBand, Internet
    connection, 178
startup scripts, viewing,
    305–306
startup, system
    administration
        tasks, 292
stateful inspection firewall,
    characteristics,
        428–429
statements, programming
    element, 531
statistical attacks, WEP
    defenses, 210
status bar, Firefox, 257
status command,
    standalone servers, 465

stderr (standard
    error) device, shell
        commands, 102
stdin (standard
    input) device, shell
        commands, 102
stdout (standard
    output) device, shell
        commands, 102–103
Stop button, Firefox
    navigation, 257
su - command, root
    account creation,
        112, 299
subroutines, programming
    elements, 531
subscriptions, newsgroups,
    269–270
Subversion, Concurrent
    Versions System (CVS),
        version information, 24
sudo command, root
    account, 112
Sun SPARC processors, 10
Sun, Remote Procedure Call
    (RPC), 199
SUSE. *See also* openSUSE
    adding user accounts,
        333–334
    automatic Samba
        startup, 523
    automatic server startup,
        306–307
    automatic standalone
        server startup, 466–469
    Berkley Internet Name
        Domain (BIND),
            498–501
    commercial distribution, 14
    digiKam application,
        149–150
    /etc/fstab file, 349
    firewall configuration, 432
    Internet super server
        configuration, 423

InterNetNews (INN) server, 486–493

K3b application, 152

KDE Akregator RSS reader, 275–276

KDE calculator application, 148

KNode newsreader, 266, 271–272

Kopete IM client, 247

manual standalone server, 465

name server startup, 512

Nessus Security Scanner, 449–451

network startup on system boot, 228

NFS server startup, 350, 518

nmap (network mapper), 448–449

online updates, 387

opening a CD/DVD, 58

OpenSSH configuration, 425–426

recovering from forgotten root password, 300

Samba configuration, 521

Samba installation, 521

security updates, 405

sendmail mail server, 473–486

software development tools installation, 531–532

software installation, 62

standalone servers, 422, 446

system administration tools, 295–296

wireless network configuration, 216

xinetd server, 446, 461–464

YaST Control Center, 62

YaST Online Update (YOU), 387

SUSE Linux Enterprise 11, LSB 4.0 certification, 16

swap files, 313–314

switches
 cable modem connections, 189
 DSL connections, 182–183

Symmetric DSL (SDSL), DSL variant, 180

Synaptic Package Manager, GUI package installer, 59–60

sysfs file system, device naming, 321

system administration
 automatic server startup on system boot, 306–307
 changing file ownership, 340–341
 changing run levels, 304–305
 configuration files, 307–310
 defined, 25
 device files, 319–321
 /etc/inittab file, 302–304
 GUI tools, 293–298
 init process, 301–303
 job scheduling, 324–330
 loadable driver modules, 322–324
 manual server start/stop, 306
 one-time jobs, 325–327
 performance monitoring, 310–315
 /proc file system, 315–318

recovering from forgotten root password, 299–300

recurring jobs, 327–330

root account creation, 298–301

shell script uses, 553–554

startup scripts, 305–306

task types, 291–293

udev program, 321

system information, /proc file system, 315–318

System Menu button, GNOME Desktop element, 84–85

System menu subcategory, KDE Desktop, 93

System Monitor, wireless Ethernet network status, 226–227

system performance, system administration tasks, 292

System Settings, KDE Desktop control center, 97–98

system shutdown, 292

system startup, 292

## T

Tab key, 105

tabbed browsing, Firefox, 256

tabs, shell command format, 70, 101

Talk, GNOME top panel icon, 85

tape drives
 backup media, 353–354
 file backups, 26
 tar command backups, 357–358

tar command
  automated backups, 358–359
  downloading/unpacking software, 378–379
  file backups, 26
  incremental backups, 358
  multivolume archive, 356–357
  single-volume archive, 355–356
  syntax, 354–355
  tapes, 357–358
task automation, 292
TCP wrapper, 423–424
TCP/IP networking
  client/server model, 457–459
  configuration, 203–204, 217–221
  connectionless protocols, 457
  connection-oriented protocols, 456–457
  /etc/host.conf file, 219
  /etc/hosts file, 218
  /etc/hosts.allow file, 220
  /etc/hosts.deny file, 220–221
  /etc/networks file, 219
  /etc/nsswitch.conf file, 221
  /etc/resolv.conf file, 219–220
  Internet services, 198–199, 456
  IP addresses, 197–198
  mail transport agents (MTAs), 234–235
  port numbers, 198–199
  sockets, 457–459
tcpdump command, 225–226

televisions, cable modem connections, 187
telinit command, 305
TELNET protocol
  in.telnetd, 22
  port 23, 199, 460
Temporal Key Integrity Protocol (TKIP), 210
terminal windows
  Konsole command, 88–89
  opening, 99–100
terms, 400–404, 531
test command, 558
test page, printing, 57
testing release, Debian distributions, 15
testparm program, Samba, 520, 522
text editors
  ed, 163–167
  GNOME, 161–162
  GNU emacs, 24
  KDE Desktop, 161–162
  software development tools, 531
  source code creation, 530
  vi, 167–171
text files. See also files
  counting words/lines, 115
  grep command search, 101
  RSS feeds, 274–275
  shell scripts, 117–118
  sorting, 115–116
  viewing in Dolphin, 160
text input mode, 164, 168
text mode, 46
text terminal, 17
thick Ethernet, 201
thicknet, 201
thickwire, 201
thinwire, 201
thousand-bits-per-second (Kbps), 176
threats, risk analysis, 394

Thunderbird
  e-mail reader, 241–244
  mail user agent (MUA), 234–235
  newsgroup reader, 266–271
tilde (~) character, 125
time
  current date/time display, 113–114
  KDE Desktop panel icon, 94
  system time display in KDE Desktop, 94
time of execution, 326, 328–329
Tool Command Language (Tcl/Tk), 24
toolbars, Firefox, 256–257
top utility, 310–312
top panel, GNOME Desktop, 81, 85
top-level directories, 121–122
top-level domains, 497
tr command, 116
Transmission Control Protocol (TCP), 196, 457
Transmission Control Protocol/Internet Protocol (TCP/IP), 21, 189–190, 195–197
transport, TCP/IP layer, 196
Trash icon, GNOME, 80, 86
Tripware, 398, 421
Trivial File Transfer Protocol (TFTP), port 69, 199, 460
troubleshooting
  installation, 45–54
  Knoppix boot commands, 48–51
  Linux kernel boot options, 51–54
  PC reboot problems, 51

signal 11 (SIGSEV) error, 51
USB device boot order, 43
X Window System, 46–48
two-way splitter, 186–187

# U

Ubuntu
adding user accounts, 332–334
Advanced Packaging Tool (APT), 58–59
automatic Samba startup, 523
automatic standalone server startup, 307, 466–469
Berkley Internet Name Domain (BIND), 498–501
burning CDs/DVDs, 37
dial-up modems, 193
Examples folder, 36–37
firestarter package, 187
GParted partition editor, 38–39
help window display, 23
inetd servers, 446
installation process, 39–40
Internet super server configuration, 423
InterNetNews (INN) server, 486–493
Live CD boot process, 36–37
manual standalone server, 465
name server startup, 512
Nessus Security Scanner, 449–451
network startup on system boot, 227–228

nmap (network mapper), 448–449
online updates, 383
opening a CD/DVD, 58
PPPoE DSL connection setup, 184
root user privileges, 299
Samba, 521
security updates, 405
sendmail mail server, 473–486
software, 58–60
standalone servers, 422
sudo command, 112
Synaptic Package Manager, 59–60
system administration tools, 296–297
TCP/IP networking configuration, 203–204
Ubuntu 9.04, 16
udev program, 321
UltraSPARC processors, 10
uname command, 70–71
unauthorized access, 394
unauthorized information disclosure, 394
Uniform Resource Locator (URL), 251–253
United States Computer Emergency Readiness Team (US-CERT), 404
UNIX, Linux, 9
UNIX-to-UNIX Copy Protocol (UCCP), 262
unmask command, 412–413
unmount command, 133, 348
unshielded twisted-pair cable (UTP), 201
unstable release, 15
update-rc.d command, 307, 467
updates, 404–405, 442

upstream data, 184–186
uptime command, 70, 312–313
USB drives, 353–354
USB ports
device boot order, 43
device connection point, 35
digital camera access point, 150
peripheral device connection point, 26
US-CERT National Cyber Alert System, 404–405
Usenet, 261–262
user access, 399
user accounts
adding/removing, 291, 331–335
changing file ownership, 340–341
deleting groups, 338
deleting with userdel command, 335
/etc/group file, 337–338
/etc/passwd file, 335–336
group addition, 334
group IDs, 337–338
host security issues, 398
modifying with usermod command, 335
new group, 337–338
set user ID permissions, 413–414
useradd command, 334–335
User Datagram Protocol (UDP), 196, 457
user environment, 338–340
user file-creation mask, 412–413
useradd command, 334–335

userdel command, 335
UserLand Software, 274
usermod command, 335
usr subdirectories, 123
Utilities menu
    subcategory, 93
utilities, system
    administration
    tasks, 292

# V

var subdirectories,
    123–124
variables
    bash shell, 555
    defining, 556
    GNU make utility, 539–540
    programming, 531
    reading input, 556
verification reports, Red
    Hat Package Manager
    (RPM) files, 373–374
version numbers
    DEB file, 374
    distribution-specific, 15
    Linux kernel, 14
    RPM filename, 369
    Subversion, 24
version-control system, 532
vi, text editor, 167–171
video cards, 20, 36
virtual consoles, 99–100
virtual memory, 313–314
viruses, 235
visual command mode 168
vmstat utility, 313–314
VMWare, init 0
    command, 72
Volume
    GNOME top panel icon, 85
    KDE Desktop panel icon, 94

vsftpd, file transfer
    server, 22
vulnerabilities, 394–395,
    440–441
vulnerability scanners, 447

# W

wc command, 115
Web browsers
    anonymous FTP
        downloads, 281–282
    data transfer process,
        253–254
    downloading/unpacking
        tar files, 378–379
    Epiphany, 255
    Firefox, 255–260
    FTP client use, 281–282
    HTML document client
        software, 250
    Konqueror, 255
    Mozilla Navigator, 255
Web pages. *See also* World
    Wide Web; Web sites
    HTML messages, 235–236
    Uniform Resource Locator
        (URL), 251–253
Web servers. *See also*
    servers
    data transfer process,
        253–254
    HTML document software,
        250
Web sites. *See also* Web
    pages; World Wide Web
Applixware, 21
Arkeia, 354
BRU, 354
CA ARCserve Backup for
    Linux, 354

cable modem transfer
    speed check, 186
CERT Coordination
    Center, 404
CodeWeavers, 21
Common Vulnerabilities
    and Exposures (CVE),
    440
CrossOver Office, 21
DistroWatch.com, 11
DSL availability, 181
DSL provider distance
    limits, 177
Epiphany, 255
Fedora Live USB Creator, 42
Filesystem Hierarchy
    Standard (FHS), 345
Firefox, 255
FOCUS-LINUX, 404
gFTP, 277
GNOME Straw, 275
GNU Compiler
    Collection, 531
GNU Image Manipulation
    Program (GIMP), 154
GNU Project, 16
Google Groups,
    48, 264, 273
International Organization
    for Standardization
    (ISO), 497
Internet Engineering Task
    Force (IETF), 496
Internet Systems
    Consortium (ISC), 487
KDE Akregator, 275
KFTPGrabber, 277
Linux Assigned Names
    And Numbers Authority
    (LANANA), 320
Linux-compatible
    hardware, 36

Linux downloads, 28
Linux IPv6 HOWTO, 198
Linux kernel version
    numbers, 14
Linux Standard Base
    (LSB), 16
LONE-TAR, 354
National Vulnerability
    Database (NVD), 440
Nessus Security
    Scanner, 450
netfilter
    documentation, 431
NewsMonster, 275
nmap (network mapper),
    448
NSVv4 standard, 516
Open Office, 21
Open Source Initiative, 11
OppenOffice.org, 143
Oracle, 21
Pan, 266
reading/researching
    newsgroups, 272–273
Resource Description
    Format (RDF), 274
RFC 1321, 409
Samba documentation, 523
SANS Institute, 440
signal 11 (SIGSEV) error, 51
software-based modems,
    35, 191
Thunderbird, 267
top 100 security tools, 448
Tripware, 398, 421
United States Computer
    Emergency Readiness
    Team (US-CERT), 404
US-CERT National Cyber
    Alert System, 404
vistasource.com, 21

Wi-Fi Alliance, 208
X desktops, 77
X Multimedia System
    (XMMS), 379
X.Org Foundation, 20
XFree86 Project, 20
Yum, 385
Web surfing, Firefox,
    259–260
weblog. *See* blogs, RSS
    feeds
Wi-Fi Alliance
    Wi-Fi Protected Access
        (WPA), 210
    Wi-Fi Protected Access 2
        (WPA2), 210
    Wi-Fi Protected Access
        (WPA), WEP, 210
    Wi-Fi Protected Access 2
        (WPA2), WEP, 210
wildcards, 104–106
winbindd server, 520
windows
    icons, mouse, and pointer
        (WIMPS), 68
    open window display in
        KDE Desktop, 93
    switching between in KDE
        Desktop, 94
Windows PC
    bootable flash drive,
        41–43
    booting from the DVD
        drive, 32
    CD burner application, 37
    hard drive partitioning,
        38–39
    Linux partitions, 31,
        32–34, 38–39
    partition mounting,
        359–360

rebooting after installing
    Linux, 34
Samba file sharing,
    519–523
Windows WAV format, 151
Winmodems, 35, 191
Wired Equivalent Privacy
    (WEP), 209–210
wireless access point
    (WAP), 212
wireless Ethernet networks.
    *See also* networks
ad hoc mode, 208–209
base station, 209
boot time configuration,
    227–228
configuration settings,
    213–216
hardware setup, 211–212
host connectivity
    check, 223
IEEE standards, 207–208
infrastructure mode,
    208–209
interface checks, 222
IP routing table check,
    222–223
managed mode, 209
packet sniffing, 225–226
status check, 224–225
System Monitor, 226–227
Wired Equivalent Privacy
    (WEP), 209–210
wireless access point
    (WAP), 212
Wireless Fidelity (Wi-Fi), 207
word processors, Writer,
    143–145
workspace, 93
Workspace Switcher, 86
workstations, 43

World Wide Web. *See also*
    Internet; Web pages;
    Web sites
  document formats,
    249–250
  HyperText Markup
    Language (HTML), 250
  HyperText Transfer
    Protocol (HTTP), 250
  Internet service, 22, 175
  links, 251–253
  server structure, 250–251
  Web browsers, 253–254
  Web servers, 253–254
worms, e-mail attachments,
  235
Writer, word processor,
  143–145
wvdialconf program, 190

## *X*

X Multimedia System
  (XMMS), 378–379
X Window System
  configuration file, 47–48
  distributions, 20
  graphical user interface
    (GUI), 11, 20–21
  installation trouble, 46–48
  keyboard/mouse, 35
  LSB standards, 15
  memory requirements, 36
  video card compatibility, 36
X.Org X11, X Window
  System distribution, 20
X86_64 processors, LSB
  standards, 16
Xandros
  automatic Samba
    startup, 523
  automatic server startup,
    307, 466–469
  Berkley Internet Name
    Domain (BIND),
    498–501

digiKam application,
  149–150
inetd server, 446,
  461–462
Internet super server
  configuration, 423
InterNetNews (INN)
  server, 486–493
Kopete IM client, 247
manual standalone
  server, 465
name server startup, 512
network startup on
  system boot, 227–228
NFS server startup,
  350, 518
OpenSSH configuration,
  425–426
Samba installation, 521
sendmail mail server,
  473–486
software development
  tools, 531–532
standalone servers, 422
system administration
  tools, 297–298
Thunderbird newsreader,
  266–271
Xandros Desktop
  burning CDs, 151–152
  commercial distribution, 14
  hard drive partitions, 33
  opening a CD/DVD, 58
  software installation,
    62–63
Xandros File Manager, 58
Xandros Networks, 62–63
Xandros File Manager
  burning CDs, 151–152
  Xandros Desktop, 58
Xandros Networks
  nmap (network mapper),
    448–449
  online updates, 387–388
  security updates, 405
  software, 62–63
Xandros Server 1.0, 16

Xerox, Ethernet, 200
Xerox Palo Alto Research
  Center (PARC), Ethernet
  development, 200
Xfce, graphical user
  interface (GUI), 77
XFree86, X Window System
  distribution, 20
xinetd server
  Internet super server,
    461–464
  network security
    review, 446
  standalone services,
    422–423
XMMS, sound file
  playback, 151

## *Y*

Yahoo!, IM protocol, 233
YaST
  adding user accounts,
    333–334
  automatic standalone
    server startup, 458–469
  Berkley Internet Name
    Domain (BIND),
    498–501
  firewall configuration, 432
  Nessus Security Scanner,
    449–451
  NFS server startup, 350
  nmap (network mapper),
    448–449
  Samba installation, 521
  security updates, 405
  software development
    tools, 531–532
  standalone servers, 446
  SUSE application, 62
  system administration
    tools, 295–296
  wireless network
    configuration, 216
YOU (YaST Online
  Update), 387

YaST Online Update (YOU),
SUSE online updates,
387
Yum (Yellow dog Updater,
Modified), 385–387

# Z

ZIP disks, backup media,
353–354
Zip drives, tar program
archives, 26
zone file formats, Domain
Name System (DNS),
505–506

## Business/Accounting & Bookkeeping

Bookkeeping For Dummies
978-0-7645-9848-7

eBay Business
All-in-One For Dummies,
2nd Edition
978-0-470-38536-4

Job Interviews
For Dummies,
3rd Edition
978-0-470-17748-8

Resumes For Dummies,
5th Edition
978-0-470-08037-5

Stock Investing
For Dummies,
3rd Edition
978-0-470-40114-9

Successful Time
Management
For Dummies
978-0-470-29034-7

## Computer Hardware

BlackBerry For Dummies,
3rd Edition
978-0-470-45762-7

Computers For Seniors
For Dummies
978-0-470-24055-7

iPhone For Dummies,
2nd Edition
978-0-470-42342-4

Laptops For Dummies,
3rd Edition
978-0-470-27759-1

Macs For Dummies,
10th Edition
978-0-470-27817-8

## Cooking & Entertaining

Cooking Basics
For Dummies,
3rd Edition
978-0-7645-7206-7

Wine For Dummies,
4th Edition
978-0-470-04579-4

## Diet & Nutrition

Dieting For Dummies,
2nd Edition
978-0-7645-4149-0

Nutrition For Dummies,
4th Edition
978-0-471-79868-2

Weight Training
For Dummies,
3rd Edition
978-0-471-76845-6

## Digital Photography

Digital Photography
For Dummies,
6th Edition
978-0-470-25074-7

Photoshop Elements 7
For Dummies
978-0-470-39700-8

## Gardening

Gardening Basics
For Dummies
978-0-470-03749-2

Organic Gardening
For Dummies,
2nd Edition
978-0-470-43067-5

## Green/Sustainable

Green Building
& Remodeling
For Dummies
978-0-470-17559-0

Green Cleaning
For Dummies
978-0-470-39106-8

Green IT For Dummies
978-0-470-38688-0

## Health

Diabetes For Dummies,
3rd Edition
978-0-470-27086-8

Food Allergies
For Dummies
978-0-470-09584-3

Living Gluten-Free
For Dummies
978-0-471-77383-2

## Hobbies/General

Chess For Dummies,
2nd Edition
978-0-7645-8404-6

Drawing For Dummies
978-0-7645-5476-6

Knitting For Dummies,
2nd Edition
978-0-470-28747-7

Organizing For Dummies
978-0-7645-5300-4

SuDoku For Dummies
978-0-470-01892-7

## Home Improvement

Energy Efficient Homes
For Dummies
978-0-470-37602-7

Home Theater
For Dummies,
3rd Edition
978-0-470-41189-6

Living the Country Lifestyle
All-in-One For Dummies
978-0-470-43061-3

Solar Power Your Home
For Dummies
978-0-470-17569-9

Available wherever books are sold. For more information or to order direct: U.S. customers visit www.dummies.com or call 1-877-762-2974.
U.K. customers visit www.wileyeurope.com or call (0) 1243 843291. Canadian customers visit www.wiley.ca or call 1-800-567-4797.

## Internet

Blogging For Dummies,
2nd Edition
978-0-470-23017-6

eBay For Dummies,
6th Edition
978-0-470-49741-8

Facebook For Dummies
978-0-470-26273-3

Google Blogger
For Dummies
978-0-470-40742-4

Web Marketing
For Dummies,
2nd Edition
978-0-470-37181-7

WordPress For Dummies,
2nd Edition
978-0-470-40296-2

## Language & Foreign Language

French For Dummies
978-0-7645-5193-2

Italian Phrases
For Dummies
978-0-7645-7203-6

Spanish For Dummies
978-0-7645-5194-9

Spanish For Dummies,
Audio Set
978-0-470-09585-0

## Macintosh

Mac OS X Snow Leopard
For Dummies
978-0-470-43543-4

## Math & Science

Algebra I For Dummies,
2nd Edition
978-0-470-55964-2

Biology For Dummies
978-0-7645-5326-4

Calculus For Dummies
978-0-7645-2498-1

Chemistry For Dummies
978-0-7645-5430-8

## Microsoft Office

Excel 2007 For Dummies
978-0-470-03737-9

Office 2007 All-in-One
Desk Reference
For Dummies
978-0-471-78279-7

## Music

Guitar For Dummies,
2nd Edition
978-0-7645-9904-0

iPod & iTunes
For Dummies,
6th Edition
978-0-470-39062-7

Piano Exercises
For Dummies
978-0-470-38765-8

## Parenting & Education

Parenting For Dummies,
2nd Edition
978-0-7645-5418-6

Type 1 Diabetes
For Dummies
978-0-470-17811-9

## Pets

Cats For Dummies,
2nd Edition
978-0-7645-5275-5

Dog Training For Dummies,
2nd Edition
978-0-7645-8418-3

Puppies For Dummies,
2nd Edition
978-0-470-03717-1

## Religion & Inspiration

The Bible For Dummies
978-0-7645-5296-0

Catholicism For Dummies
978-0-7645-5391-2

Women in the Bible
For Dummies
978-0-7645-8475-6

## Self-Help & Relationship

Anger Management
For Dummies
978-0-470-03715-7

Overcoming Anxiety
For Dummies
978-0-7645-5447-6

## Sports

Baseball For Dummies,
3rd Edition
978-0-7645-7537-2

Basketball For Dummies,
2nd Edition
978-0-7645-5248-9

Golf For Dummies,
3rd Edition
978-0-471-76871-5

## Web Development

Web Design All-in-One
For Dummies
978-0-470-41796-6

## Windows Vista

Windows Vista
For Dummies
978-0-471-75421-3

# How-to?
# How Easy.

From hooking up a modem to cooking up a casserole, knitting a scarf to navigating an iPod, you can trust Dummies.com to show you how to get things done the easy way.

Visit us at Dummies.com

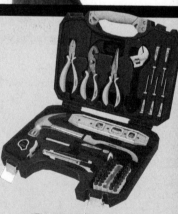